T0191517

Lecture Notes in Computer Science 670

Edited by G. Goos and J. Hartmanis

Advisory Board: W. Brauer   D. Gries   J. Stoer

J.C.P. Woodcock P.G. Larsen (Eds.)

FME '93:
Industrial-Strength
Formal Methods

First International Symposium
of Formal Methods Europe
Odense, Denmark, April 19-23, 1993
Proceedings

Springer-Verlag

Berlin Heidelberg NewYork
London Paris Tokyo
Hong Kong Barcelona
Budapest

Series Editors

Gerhard Goos
Universität Karlsruhe
Postfach 69 80
Vincenz-Priessnitz-Straße 1
W-7500 Karlsruhe, FRG

Juris Hartmanis
Cornell University
Department of Computer Science
4130 Upson Hall
Ithaca, NY 14853, USA

Volume Editors

James C. P. Woodcock
Oxford University Computing Laboratory, Programming Research Group
11 Keble Road, Oxford OX1 3QD, U.K.

Peter G. Larsen
The Institute of Applied Computer Science (IFAD)
Forskerparken 10, 5230 Odense M, Denmark

CR Subject Classification (1991): D.1-2, F.3.1, J.1

ISBN 3-540-56662-7 Springer-Verlag Berlin Heidelberg New York
ISBN 0-387-56662-7 Springer-Verlag New York Berlin Heidelberg

© Springer-Verlag Berlin Heidelberg 1993
Printed in Germany

Typesetting: Camera ready by author/editor
Printing and binding: Druckhaus Beltz, Hemsbach/Bergstr.
45/3140-543210 - Printed on acid-free paper

Preface

In September 1988 I attended the second *VDM Symposium* in Dublin, and suggested, first to Cliff Jones, and then to Dines Bjørner, that we should widen the scope of the Symposium to include the Z notation. I was pushing at an open door, and the next symposium, held in Kiel in April 1990, was devoted to VDM and Z. This process of widening the scope of the symposium continued with the next in the series: it was held in Noordwijkerhout in October 1991, and covered Formal Software Development Methods.

This trend towards a broader range of methods also reflects a change that has been made in the organisation that lies behind the series. All four VDM symposia were organised by VDM Europe, an advisory board sponsored by the Commission of the European Communities. The board's working group was made up from academia and industry, and met several times each year to discuss the industrial usage of model-oriented formal methods, most usually those connected with VDM (including RAISE and MetaSoft). This board has evolved into Formal Methods Europe, and this volume contains the proceedings of its first symposium.

The last few years have borne witness to the remarkable diversity of formal methods, with applications to sequential and concurrent software, to real-time and reactive systems, and to hardware design. In that time, many theoretical problems have been tackled and solved, and many continue to be worked upon. Yet it is by the suitability of their industrial application and the extent of their usage that formal methods will ultimately be judged. This symposium will focus on *The Application of Industrial-Strength Formal Methods.* We have encouraged papers to address the difficulties of scaling their techniques up to industrial-sized problems, and of their suitability in the work-place, and to discuss techniques that are formal (that is, they have a mathematical basis), and that are industrially applicable. Papers tackling theoretical issues were much encouraged, providing that they contained a justification of the practical advantages that follow. We received over 140 submissions of various kinds, with a strong representation from outside Europe, in particular Australia and the United States. We invited three speakers to address the symposium, and accepted seven industrial usage reports and 32 papers, complemented by eight tutorials on various formal methods, and an exhibition of over 20 formal methods tools.

This volume has four parts to it: the contributions of invited speakers; industrial reports; papers; and descriptions of the tools exhibited. We have three distinguished invited speakers: Professor Cliff Jones, Professor Willem-Paul de Roever, and Peter Lupton (whose talk is not recorded in the proceedings). The industrial usage reports describe practical experiences from the applications of formal methods in challenging industrial environments. The papers cover a wide variety of methods and notations. We have modal logic, the refinement calculus, RAISE, CCS, Petri Nets, VDM, Z, LOTOS, OBJ, Sprint, and B, and deal with the combination of formal and informal techniques, object-orientation, applications to high-assurance systems involving both safety and security, and papers on theory and its relevance to practice.

J.C.P.Woodcock
Oxford, February 1993

Acknowledgments

Many people have contributed to the planning, organisation and success of FME'93.

Programme Committee	**Organising Committee**
Jim Woodcock (PC Chairman)	Peter Gorm Larsen (OC Chairman)
Peter Gorm Larsen (OC Liaison)	Poul Bøgh Lassen (Tools Exhibition)
J.-R. Abrial	Michael Andersen
Tim Denvir	Kees de Bruin
Eugene Dürr	René Elmstrøm
Ian Hayes	Søren Larsen
Steve King	Erik Toubro Nielsen
Hans Langmaack	Henrik Aagaard Pedersen
Mícheál Mac an Airchinnigh	
Kees Middelburg	
Søren Prehn	
Hans Toetenel	

Local Organisers
Kirsten Johansen
Bitten Filstrup
Lone Weidemann
Susanne Rasmussen
} KongresBureau Fyn

In addition, the invaluable contributions of the following should be acknowledged: Alejandro Moya, CEC, for his continued support to Formal Methods Europe; Alfred Hofmann of Springer-Verlag for their continued interest in publishing these proceedings; Miss Frances Page for her expert assistance in helping to organise submitted papers and referees' reviews; Steve King for his assistance in solving (almost all) the LaTeX and postscript problems with the proceedings.

The final addition to the conference programme were the presentations by a number of European projects on formal specification and design. We wish to thank all these projects for their interest in FME'93.

We would also like to thank Odense Teknikum for being so flexible that it has been possible to host the FME'93 symposium there.

External Referees

All submitted papers—whether accepted or rejected—were refereed by the programme committee members and a number of external referees. This symposium would not have been possible without their voluntary and dedicated work.

Michael Andersen	Derek Andrews	Rob Arthan
Rudolf Berghammer	Wiet Bouma	Jonathan Bowen
Stephen Brien	Manfred Broy	David Carrington
Flemming Damm	Werner Damm	Tony Darlison
Roger Duke	Hans Dieter Ehrich	René Elmstrøm
John Fitzgerald	Catriona Fox	Jacob Frost
Martin Fränzle	Jean Goubault	Christian Gram
Jan Friso Groote	Lindsay Groves	Anthony Hall
Bo Stig Hansen	Friedrich Wilhelm von Henke	Mike Hinchey
Ronald Huijsman	Kees Huizin	Dave Jackson
Roger Jones	Jan van Katwijk	Peter Kearney
Trevor King	Hans Kloosterman	Peter Kluit
Hans Jörg Kreowski	Bernd Krieg-Brückner	Kevin Lano
Ole Bjerg Larsen	Søren Larsen	Poul Bøgh Lassen
George Leih	Peter Lindsay	Hans Henrik Løvengreen
Wayne Luk	Brendan Mahony	Derek Mannering
Andrew Martin	Swapan Mitra	Carroll Morgan
Maurice Naftalin	Manfred Nagl	John Nicholls
Ernst Rüdiger Olderog	Jens Palsberg	Peter Pepper
Nico Plat	Ben Potter	Kees Pronk
Anders P. Ravn	Joy Reed	Wolfgang Reisig
Hans Rischel	Gordon Rose	Jeff Sanders
Steve Schneider	Danny de Schreye	Karen Seidel
Robin Sharp	Jane Sinclair	Jens Ulrik Skakkebæk
Arne Skou	Gregor Snelting	Ruud Sommerhalder
Jan Springintveld	John Staples	Jørgen Staunstrup
Werner Stephan	Andrew Stevens	Werner Struckmann
Mario Südholt	Paul Taylor	Hans Tonino
Mark Utting	Hugo Velthuijsen	Friedrich Vogt
Nigel Ward	Jim Welsh	Han Zuidweg

We apologise if, inadvertently, we have omitted a referee from the above list. To the best of our knowledge the list is accurate.

Symposium Sponsors

The symposium would not have been possible without the kind support and financial assistance of the associations and corporations listed below:

Scandinavian Airlines System (SAS)
Odense Steel Shipyard Ltd.
Deutsche System Technik
Fyns Telefon
Praxis
Lloyd's Register
DDC International
Space Software Italia
Computer Resources International (CRI)
ICL Data A/S (SUN Division)

Oxford University and The Institute of Applied Computer Science (IFAD) have both been most generous in their support of the symposium.

Tutorial Programme

Copies of this material will be handed out to all participants in the tutorial part of the symposium.

The tutorials of FME'93 present a comprehensive account of the current state of the art. The chosen tutorials have been particularly selected to fit the subtitle of the symposium: *Industrial-strength Formal Methods*. We would like to thank all tutors for their kind willingness to give these tutorials.

The tutorials are:

Functional Programming	*Phil Wadler*
Coloured Petri Nets	*Kurt Jensen*
Data Refinement	*Tim Clement*
CCS with Tool Support	*Kim G. Larsen*
Proof in Z with Tool Support	*Roger Jones*
LOTOS with Tool Support	*Jeroen Schot*
Prototype Verification System (PVS)	*John Rushby*
Provably Correct Systems (ProCoS)	*Anders P. Ravn*

Table of Contents

Invited Lectures

Industrial Usage Reports

Papers

XI

Reasoning about Interference in an Object-Based Design Method

C. B. Jones

Department of Computer Science
Manchester University, M13 9PL, UK
cbj@cs.man.ac.uk

Abstract. The property of a (formal) development method which gives the development process the potential for productivity is *compositionality*; compositional development methods for concurrent systems are elusive because of *interference*. A companion paper shows how object-based concepts can be used to provide a designer with control over interference and proposes a transformational style of development in which concurrency is introduced only in the final stages of design. That approach relies on restrictions to the object graphs which can arise and works for systems which involve limited interference. The current paper discusses the problems of interference and shows how a suitable logic can be used to reason – during design – about those systems where interference plays an essential role. Here again, concepts are used in the design notation which are taken from object-oriented languages since they offer control of granularity and ways of pinpointing interference. A further paper is in preparation which discusses the semantics of the object-based design notation.

1 Introduction

Development of any large computer system is difficult but formal methods like VDM have been shown to help control the development process – and provide useful documentation – of sequential systems. A method which permits one step of design to be justified before proceeding to the next stage of design is said to be compositional: compositional formal methods can contribute to the productivity of the design task by reducing the 'scrap and rework' inherent in approaches which fail to detect mistakes until long after they are made.

Clearly, an attack on the problem of developing concurrent systems should preserve what is usable from methods aimed at sequential systems; a companion paper [Jon93a] shows how some classes of concurrent programs can be designed by adding a transformational step to development using sequential methods like data reification and operation decomposition (see also Section 3 below). Where the methods themselves are not adequate, at least the lessons from sequential development should be taken over. Paramount among these is the need for compositionality. But years of research (cf. [dR85, HdR86]) has shown that finding compositional development methods for concurrent systems has proved extremely difficult. In the case of shared-variable programs interference manifests itself by processes reading and changing a collection of variables (state) which they have in common. Such interference makes the conventional view of extensional denotations give way to more complex spaces such as resumptions. Interference also invalidates conventional pre/post-condition reasoning. Section 2 reviews some earlier attempts to accommodate interference. But this is not the only problem. Interference forces a discussion of granularity which is often handled in an *ad hoc* way by declaring, for example, that assignment statements should be atomic. Related to this is the difficulty that – in the presence of interference – it is even necessary to be careful about what is meant by an assertion. These are all problems to which the current paper attempts to contribute solutions. Other difficulties of concurrency such as deadlocks and fairness remain to be tackled.

The approach taken in this – and the related papers – is to employ concepts from object-oriented programming. The general idea to obtain more tractable concurrent programs by making judicious language restrictions has a long pedigree: the development from semaphores, through conditional critical sections and monitors to languages like CSP can be seen in this light. At first sight, it is tempting to hope that notations like CSP and CCS finesse the problem of interference by abolishing states; on closer examination, it becomes clear that interfering communication can be equally troublesome. Not only are shared variables not the root of the problem, it could even be argued that process algebras are too draconian in completely abolishing states. It would appear that object-based concepts can provide a middle way (not unlike monitors [Hoa74]) where the degree of isolation (or the amount of interference permitted) can be controlled by the designer. Even the specific idea to make tractable the development of concurrent programs by using object-oriented concepts is not new and the current line owes much to the work on POOL [AR89]. The first paper in the current series [Jon93a] shows how object-based techniques limit interference; it also discusses the design notation ($\pi o \beta \lambda$) in more detail than in this paper. But a general development method for concurrent systems has to be able to cope with interference; the current paper shows how object-based concepts can be used to pinpoint and reason about interference in a way which limits the proof obligations which arise. Object-oriented languages are not a complete solution to the problems of concurrency. Indeed, this author remains unconvinced that inheritance – one of the key object-oriented concepts – is well-enough thought out to be used in any program development method. The references of object-based techniques are also open to the same abuses as more general pointers and the realization that invariants were essential to reason about the object graphs which evolve was one of the key steps in the current author's research.

Section 3 shows the sort of transformational development – usable on simple object graphs – which is discussed in more detail in [Jon93a]; Section 5 tackles the problem of interference when such simple object graphs do not suffice; Section 4 discusses the logic used. Several comments have been made about the earlier paper in this series; [Jon93b] attempts to fix the semantics of the $\pi o \beta \lambda$ design notation.

2 Background

There are many aspects of concurrent programs and many different problems in their development; this paper focuses on interference. It is argued above that methods of reasoning about concurrent programs must accommodate interference. To provide

3

useful compositionality, development methods must offer help at the earliest stages of design: proofs at lower levels of detail are of less value than those in early design phases because it is early design mistakes which cause most 'scrap and rework'. The main idea is to structure the design (record) so as to be provable; much of the motivation of the ideas presented here has been to offer ways of formalizing steps of development which are intuitively acceptable.

It might appear that interference completely rules out the possibility of compositional development but a number of authors have attempted to tame this dragon by recording facts about interference in specifications. An early attempt is presented in [FP78] but this does not offer compositionality. The interference approach in [Jon81, Jon83a, Jon83b] suggested a compositional approach related to the Owicki/Gries method [Owi75, OG76]: rely and guarantee conditions were used to record acceptable – and limits on – interference; proof obligations were given for operation decomposition including parallel statements. The original rely/guarantee method did not cope with liveness issues but there has recently been a flurry of activity and both Stølen [Stø90, Stø91a, Stø91b] and Xu [XH91, Xu92] have proposed extensions to cover liveness. It was always clear that [Jon81] presented only an existence proof of ways of recording and reasoning about interference and that more research was required to make the ideas useful in practice (but [WD88, GR89], for example, show the method has been used in industry). The attempt to find compositional development methods for parallel programs has influenced others – including some work on temporal logic (see [BKP84, dR85]) and the VVSL specification language [Mid90]; related references include [BK84, Sta85, Sti86, Sti88, Sta88, BM88, Ded89, Bro89, SW91, Col92]. But by the time the ideas were being recognised, it had become clear that it was possible to improve on the rather heavy proof rules for rely/guarantee conditions and to replace them by a logic with a more pleasing algebra [Jon91b, Jon91a]. Unfortunately, experiments on larger examples showed that there were still too many proof obligations to discharge: this problem has been tackled by bringing selected ideas from object-oriented programming languages into the specification and development method.

3 Limiting interference

This section presents the development of a program in which interference plays no essential part. The purpose of the example is to illustrate how the object-based concepts can be used to constrain interference and how those constraints are recorded.

Where interference is limited, it is often a good development strategy to design first a sequential program and to introduce concurrency only in the final steps of the design process. This strategy is illustrated in this section. The transformation from sequential to concurrent program preserves observational equivalence but is only valid because the object graph which can be generated (in this case a linear linked list) prevents interference. Section 5 presents an alternative development where a DAG-like object graph allows interference; that development is also shown to satisfy the specification below.

The 'Sieve of Eratosthenes' can be used to test primality up to some stated maximum. Its justification has been used in the literature to illustrate several ways of reasoning about concurrency. The implementation developed in this section is in the spirit of various programs shown in the POOL literature (versions exist in different dialects in [Ame86, AdB90]) but a *test* function has been added here since without some 'observer' it was difficult to discuss behaviour and the POOL specifications were forced to talk about internal states.

Specification

It is easy to write a specification for a prime number tester; what follows already embodies the use of a sieve since starting at a user-oriented view shows nothing extra. The specification could be written in a specification notation like that used in VDM.[1] Here, the operations are described as methods of a class called *Primes*. (Using the structure of the implementation language to fix the specification is reminiscent of the way interface languages are used for Larch [GHW85, GH93].) It is obvious that a *test* method is required; here the *new* method is also given explicitly since it has a parameter. In $\pi o\beta\lambda$, explicit *new* methods are allowed and make it possible to define non-trivial initialization; where no explicit *new* method is given, any initialization values on the instance variables are applied to each new object instance created. The specifications of the methods are[2]

$Primes$ class
vars max: $\mathbb{N}$; $sieve$: $\mathbb{N}$-set
$new(n$: $\mathbb{N})$ method r: ref($Primes$)
  post $r = $ self $\land max = n \land sieve = \{2 \le i \le max \mid is\text{-}prime(i)\}$
$test(n$: $\mathbb{N})$ method r: $\mathbb{B}$
  rd $max, sieve$
  pre $2 \le n \le max$
  post $r \Leftrightarrow (n \in sieve)$

Instances of *Primes* are created by new $Primes(n)$ which returns a reference, say p. Providing the pre-condition is respected, any process to which p is disclosed can then use $p!test(i)$ to obtain a Boolean value which indicates whether i is prime or composite. Although there may be many concurrent threads, only one method can be active at one time in each instance of *Primes* (of course, there can be many instances). It is up to the developer of *Primes* to avoid unwanted interference by keeping control of any internal references.

Reification involving class instances

Concurrency is introduced in this design; this preliminary step creates one process (here, instances of *Sift*) per prime. These instances form a linked-list object graph in which the variable l of one instance contains the reference of the next instance (with a nil value of l marking the end of the list). The constraint that ensures that

---

[1] Throughout this paper, VDM notation [Jon90] is used for sequences, maps etc.
[2] In VDM each operation has a list of rd/wr state component names; here the local states make it more convenient to have write access as the default and to mark read access as a restriction.

the object graph stays simple is to mark the *l* pointers as private. Such pointers cannot be copied. Other than the last, each instance of *Sift* also has an *m* value. In order to ensure that all such values are primes, an initialization phase sifts out any composites by passing to the next instance any potential prime which its *m* does not divide (*m* div *n* is a predicate). At the end of the list of instances, an uninitialized process receives a number which must be a prime, stores it and creates a new instance of *Sift*. Testing for primality is similar. Thus the instance variables of *Sift* are

Sift class
vars *m*: [ℕ] ← nil; *l*: private ref(*Sift*) ← nil

The initial specification of *Primes* is given in terms of local assertions on each method. In contrast, the invariant which plays a part in this design step concerns the multiple instances of *Sift* which are created. The use of such references requires that assertions are couched in terms of a global state ($\sigma \in \Sigma$) which is viewed as a map from references to instances

$$\Sigma = Ref \xrightarrow{m} Inst$$

Variable names are treated as selectors to objects of *Inst* (thus, if *p* is a reference to an instance of *Sift*, $m(\sigma(p))$ selects the natural number in *m*). The state is a Curried argument to functions which depend on Σ. The predicate *is-linked-list*: $Ref \times Name \to \Sigma \to \mathbb{B}$ and the function *extract-seq*: $Ref \times Name \times Name \to \Sigma \to X^*$ should be obvious.[3] In terms of these, it is straightforward to define an invariant which limits the object graph of *Sift* instances to a linear list and, furthermore, requires that the *m* values are in ascending order (*is-ascending*: $\mathbb{N}^* \to Bool$ is assumed to be obvious).

$inv : Ref \to \Sigma \to \mathbb{B}$

$inv(sr)(\sigma) \quad \triangle$
$\quad$ *is-linked-list*$(sr, l)(\sigma) \wedge$ *is-ascending*(*extract-seq*$(sr, l, m)(\sigma))$

The intuitive idea that the *m* values in this linear list represent the *sieve* value in the specification of *Primes* can be formalized by a retrieve function

---

[3] See [Jon93a] for a fuller discussion; the definitions are

is-linked-list$(p, l)(\sigma) \quad \triangle$
$\quad \exists pl \in Ref^* \cdot$
$\quad\quad pl(1) = p \wedge l(\sigma(pl(\text{len } pl))) = $ nil $\wedge$
$\quad\quad \forall i \in \{1, \ldots, \text{len } pl - 1\} \cdot pl(i + 1) = l(\sigma(pl(i)))$

extract-seq$(p, l, n)(\sigma) \quad \triangle$
$\quad$ if $p = $ nil then []
$\quad$ elif $n(\sigma(p)) = $ nil then *extract-seq*$(l(\sigma(p)), l, n)(\sigma)$
$\quad$ else $[n(\sigma(p))] \frown$ *extract-seq*$(l(\sigma(p)), l, n)(\sigma)$
$\quad$ fi

pre *is-linked-list*$(p, l)(\sigma)$

$$retr : Ref \rightarrow \Sigma \rightarrow \mathbb{N}\text{-set}$$

$$retr(p)(\sigma) \quad \underline{\triangle} \quad \text{elems } extract\text{-}seq(p, l, m)(\sigma)$$

Now, still following the general pattern of development steps by data reification in [Jon90], the methods of *Primes* can be specified on this representation as follows.

> *Primes* class
> vars max: $\mathbb{N}$; sr: private ref($Sift$) ← nil
> $new(n: \mathbb{N})$ method r: ref($Primes$)
>   post $r = $ self $\wedge$ $max = n \wedge retr(sr)(\acute{\sigma}) = \{2 \leq i \leq max \mid is\text{-}prime(i)\}$
> $test(n: \mathbb{N})$ method r: $\mathbb{B}$
>   rd $max, sieve$
>   pre $2 \leq n \leq max$
>   post $r \Leftrightarrow (n \in retr(sr)(\sigma))$

Notice that clauses of the invariant such as *is-linked-list* do not have to be stated explicitly in, for example, the post-condition of *new*.

Decomposition

It is a straightforward task to write sequential object-oriented programs which satisfy the method specifications of *Primes* which has resulted from the reification and which also preserve the invariant. In a fully formal operation decomposition one would need inference rules about the specifically object-oriented statements which supplement those (e.g. in [Jon90]) for iterative statements etc. In the code which follows, an outline proof is adumbrated by assertions.

> *Primes* class
> vars max: $\mathbb{N}$; sr: private ref($Sift$) ← nil
> $new(n: \mathbb{N})$ method r: ref($Primes$)
> ctr: $\mathbb{N}$
> $max \leftarrow n$
> $sr \leftarrow$ new $Sift$
> $\left\{ retr(sr)(\sigma) = \{\,\} \right\}$
> $ctr \leftarrow 2$
>   while $ctr \leq max$ do
> $sr!setup(ctr)$
> $\left\{ retr(sr)(\sigma) = \{i \in \{2, \ldots, ctr\} \mid is\text{-}prime(i)\} \right\}$
> $ctr \leftarrow ctr + 1$
>   od
> $\left\{ retr(sr)(\sigma) = \{i \in \{2, \ldots, max\} \mid is\text{-}prime(i)\} \right\}$
>   return self
> $test(n: \mathbb{N})$ method r: $\mathbb{B}$
>   return $sr!test(n)$

Sift class
vars m: $[\mathbb{N}] \leftarrow$ nil; l: private ref($Sift$) $\leftarrow$ nil
$setup(n\colon \mathbb{N})$ method
  if $m =$ nil then $(m \leftarrow n;\ l \leftarrow$ new $Sift)$
  elif $\neg\ m$ div n then $l!setup(n)$
  else skip
  fi
  return
$test(n\colon \mathbb{N})$ method r: $\mathbb{B}$
  if $m =$ nil $\vee\ n < m$ then return false
  elif $m = n$ then return true
  else return $l!test(n)$
  fi

The formal argument would use structural induction over the linked-list structure to promote results about one instance to properties of the whole network.

Equivalent code

The real interest is how to move from the sequential solution to one which realizes the potential for concurrency which is inherent in the many instances of *Sift*. As the code above stands, any invocation of *setup* of *Sift* will not release its invoker until the effect has travelled all the way along the linked list and the returns have come all of the way back. One might suspect that this delay is unnecessary; it can be proved to be so because there is a transformation rule

$$S; \text{return } e \quad \leadsto \quad \text{return } e; S \tag{1}$$

providing e is not affected by S and S only changes (other than its own state) states reachable by private references. This justifies moving the return statement to the first position in *setup*. The method now releases its invoker as soon as possible and generates activity further along the list; once the method in one instance terminates, it is open to have further methods invoked even though the activity from the first call is still going on. The point of the rule in Equation 1 is that it preserves observational equivalence. The same transformation can be applied to *new* of *Primes*.

In essence, a similar transformation is required for *test* of *Sift* but there is an additional problem. Although the work of returning the required Boolean value can be delegated along the list, concurrency cannot be achieved unless the *test* method has completed. This means that the normal return path cannot be used. The semantics of yield e works like return e for the method in which it is written but passes the identification of the process which invoked the call (and is awaiting an answer) to the expression e. The equivalence used is

$$\text{return } l!m(x) \quad \leadsto \quad \text{yield } l!m(x) \tag{2}$$

providing l is a private reference and only refers via private references. Thus the final code is as follows.

```
Primes class
vars max: ℕ; sr: private ref(Sift) ← nil
new(n: ℕ) method r: ref(Primes)
  ctr: ℕ
  max ← n
  return self
  sr ← new Sift
  ctr ← 2
  while ctr ≤ max do sr!setup(ctr); ctr ← ctr + 1 od
test(n: ℕ) method r: 𝔹
  return sr!test(n)

Sift class
vars m: [ℕ] ← nil; l: private ref(Sift) ← nil
setup(n: ℕ) method
  return
  if m = nil then (m ← n; l ← new Sift)
  else if ¬ m div n  then l!setup(n)  fi
  fi
test(n: ℕ) method r: 𝔹
  if m = nil ∨ n < m then return false
  elif m = n then return true
  else yield l!test(n)
  fi
```

The development route adopted in this section is to employ data reification and operation decomposition for sequential programs until the final step of development; concurrency is introduced by transformations which preserve observational equivalence. The validity of the transformations relies on restrictions to the object graphs. Where, as in Section 5, sharing of references occurs this is not an appropriate development method.

4 Global safety assertions

The arguments employed in Section 5 use global assertions about the evolution of computations. Assertions about the environment of computations mirror what were rely conditions in [Jon81, Stø90]. Thus

$$p_1(e) \Rightarrow p_2(S \backslash e)$$

states that S will satisfy p_2 if run in an environment (e) which satisfies p_1. The separation of environment assumptions mirrors the way that pre-conditions invite a developer to make assumptions about the starting conditions in which a program will be executed.

Both predicates of one state $p: \Sigma \to \mathbb{B}$ and relations on states $r: \Sigma \times \Sigma \to \mathbb{B}$ are allowed. Terms in the expressions will typically need to refer to the values of variables within objects. Where there is a danger of ambiguity, terms like

$$b(\sigma(p)) \text{ or } b(\overleftarrow{\sigma}(p))$$

will be written but in most cases it is safe to write

$$p!b \text{ or } \overleftarrow{p!b}$$

In either case it is assumed that the values are accessed between methods. It is sometimes necessary to ensure that whole terms are evaluated at the same time and to mark this it is possible to write, for some expression e, $p!(e)$.

The assertions are written in a logic which is a development of that presented in [Jon91a]. The basic operator for safety reasoning is

$$S \text{ links } r$$

meaning that any method execution of S makes state transitions which satisfy the relation r. Some arguments can be documented more concisely using derived operators – for example

$$\boxed{\text{confirms-}\textit{defn}} \quad \frac{S \text{ links } (\overleftarrow{p} \Rightarrow p)}{S \text{ confirms } p}$$

$$\boxed{\text{maintains-}\textit{defn}} \quad \frac{S \text{ links } (\overleftarrow{p} \Leftrightarrow p)}{S \text{ maintains } p}$$

An operator which asserts that S does terminate – and that the final state satisfies p is $S \text{ fin } p$.

The following two inference rules are used below

$$\boxed{\parallel\text{-links}} \quad \frac{\bigwedge_i (S_i \text{ links } r)}{\parallel_i S_i \text{ links } r}$$

$$\boxed{\parallel\text{-}I} \quad \frac{\bigwedge_i (S_i \text{ links } r)}{\bigwedge_i (e \text{ links } r \Rightarrow S_i \backslash e \text{ fin } p_i)}{e \text{ links } r \Rightarrow (\parallel_i S_i) \backslash e \text{ fin } \bigwedge_i p_i}$$

5 Reasoning about interference

This section shows how to cope with interference; both specifications and development steps must be considered. A program is developed which employs concurrency in much the same way as [Jon83a] implements the prime sieve – here, of course, the program is built from multiple instances of classes. The development in this section is based on the initial specification of Section 3. The final program uses an acyclic directed graph (DAG) of objects: references which are shared by several objects bring with them many of the problems of shared variables but the fact that the interface of an object is constrained by the available methods simplifies reasoning about interference. But there is a price to pay for the interference: the DAG object graph can no longer support the form of induction proof outlined in Section 3.

Reification

A straightforward step of data reification could represent *sieve* of Section 3 as an array of Booleans (giving its characteristic function). A general array is however too flexible in that its elements could be changed by assignment in either direction between the two Boolean values; furthermore, such an array offers no scope for distribution. Given that *sieve* is initialized to a large set and then elements are only ever removed, it is a better design decision to place each Boolean in a separate instance of a class *El* which only has a method which deletes its element; these separate instances provide potential parallelism. The instances are located via a map

$$\mathbb{N} \xrightarrow{m} Ref(El) \tag{3}$$

The *El* class is simple enough that it is easier to document the design decisions directly in its code than to interpose a specification.

```
El class
vars b: 𝔹 ⟵ true
test() method r: 𝔹
    rd b
    return b
del() method
    b ⟵ false
    return
```

Instances of *El* are initialized (to true) when created by a new statement. Notice that there is (after creation) only a *del* method available thus restricting interference. This intuitive idea can be formalised by

$$p \in Ref(El) \;\Rightarrow\; p!test() \text{ links } (p!b \;\Leftrightarrow\; \overleftarrow{p!b})$$

Which (by maintains-*defn*) can be re-written

$$p \in Ref(El) \;\Rightarrow\; p!test() \text{ maintains } p!b$$

and similarly

$$p \in Ref(El) \;\Rightarrow\; p!del() \text{ confirms } \neg(p!b) \tag{4}$$

Since there are only these two methods, any designer can rely on *El*'s contribution to an environment *e* satisfying

$$e \text{ confirms } \neg(p!b) \tag{5}$$

Furthermore

$$p \in Ref(El) \;\Rightarrow\; p!del() \text{ fin } (\neg\, p!b) \tag{6}$$

The map of Equation 3 is stored in a variable *v* of (an instance of) class *Vector* which provides via its method *lu* a way of looking up the reference to *El* for an index.[4] Since the references to *El* are to be returned as results they must be marked as shared. In contrast to those marked private, pointers which are tagged shared can be copied. Thus

Vector class
vars max: $\mathbb{N}$; v: $\mathbb{N} \xrightarrow{m}$ shared ref(El)
$new(n$: $\mathbb{N})$ method r: ref($Vector$)
  post $r = $ self $\wedge$ $max = n \wedge$ *is-oneone*$(v) \wedge \forall i \in \{2, \ldots, max\} \cdot b(\sigma(v(i)))$
$lu(n$: $\mathbb{N})$ method r: ref(El)
  rd max, v
  pre $2 \leq n \leq max$
  return $v(n)$

The requirement that v be a one:one mapping (*is-oneone*) ensures that there is one instance of *El* per index. Attentive readers might be concerned about undefinedness in the post-condition of *new*; the LPF logic (cf. [CJ91]) ensures that there is no difficulty.

Getting back to the task of re-specifying the methods of *Primes* on this representation, it is necessary to relate the representation to the abstraction (i.e. *sieve*) in the normal way: the function which retrieves *sieve* of the specification is

$$retr : Ref(Vector) \rightarrow \Sigma \rightarrow \mathbb{N}\text{-set}$$

$$retr(sr)(\sigma) \triangleq \text{let } m = rmap(v(\sigma(sr)))(\sigma) \text{ in } \{i \in \text{dom } m \mid m(i)\}$$

$$rmap : (\mathbb{N} \xrightarrow{m} Ref(El)) \rightarrow \Sigma \rightarrow (\mathbb{N} \xrightarrow{m} \mathbb{B})$$

$$rmap(rm)(\sigma) \triangleq \{i \mapsto b(\sigma(rm(i))) \mid i \in \text{dom } rm\}$$

Adequacy etc. can be proved.

The specification of the main part of *Primes* (its *new* method) is

Primes class
vars max: $\mathbb{N}$; sr: shared ref($Vector$)
$new(n$: $\mathbb{N})$ method r: ref($Primes$)
  post $r = $ self$\wedge max = n \wedge retr(sr)(\sigma) = \{i \mapsto$ *is-prime*$(i) \mid i \in \{2, \ldots, max\}\}$
$test(n$: $\mathbb{N})$ method r: $\mathbb{B}$
  return $(sr!lu(n))!test()$

Completing the proof that this is a reification of *Primes* at the beginning of Section 3 is not difficult. The interesting part of the design task is the use of parallelism which now follows.

---

[4] In the $\pi o\beta\lambda$ design notation, as it stands, some of the potential for concurrency is squandered because the mapping v introduces an addressing bottleneck. It would be possible to use multiple copies of *Vector* after its initialization and Pierre America (private communication) has ideas about *pragmas* which would request 'one copy per processor' (justification of this split would be trivial). If it were possible to use the natural numbers themselves as references, the program and its development would be shorter and more parallelism would be available (such a 'program' is given in Appendix A) but the fact that a separate mapping from natural numbers to references is required here makes no difference to the sort of interference proof required.

Decomposition of *Vector* and *Primes*

Developing code to satisfy the specification of the *new* method of *Vector* is an easier job than for *Primes*. Since this is the first exposure to the parallel statement of $\pi o\beta\lambda$, the easier task is tackled first. The post-condition of *new* (of *Vector*) can be satisfied if new *El* is invoked to set up each $v(i)$. This could be achieved by a while statement but here it is possible to use a parallel statement which creates independent threads. Since each $v(i)$ is independent, no interference can arise. Thus the code is

```
Vector class
vars max: ℕ; v: ℕ ⟶ᵐ shared ref(El)
new(n: ℕ) method r: ref(Vector)
    max ← n

        ‖        v(i) ← new El
    i∈{2,...,max}

    return self
lu(n: ℕ) method r: ref(El)
    pre 2 ≤ n ≤ max
    return v(n)
```

Transformation rule 1 can be used to justify placing the return after the first assignment in *new*.

It is now time to turn to the interesting task of designing *Primes* so as to satisfy the specification above. The *new* method has to create an instance of *Vector* (which sets the b in each *El* to true) and then arrange that the b of each composite number is 'deleted' (set to false). This deletion could be implemented by nested loops and such a sequential approach would pose no interference problems. Here the design decision is to use parallel instances of a *Rem* process: each $Rem(i, sr)$ is responsible for sieving out those composites of which i is a factor; sr gives access to the instance of *Vector*. Given that sr is shared by the parallel instances of *Rem*, the object graph is a DAG. It is easy to see from the types of the variables containing references that no cycles can be present.

It is now essential to face the problem of interference. The designer of *Primes* might choose to make a step in which the *new* method is designed and justified in terms of a specification for *Rem* (postponing its implementation). In order to obtain an understanding of the specification for (the *new* method of) *Rem*, the simplification where it is assumed to run in the absence of interference is considered first. An initial stab at a post-condition might be[5]

$$retr(sr)(\overleftarrow{\sigma}) - retr(sr)(\sigma) = mults(i)$$

But, even for isolated instances of *Rem*, this is wrong because (other than the first instance executed) some composite $c \in mults(i)$ – which the ith instance of *Rem* would have deleted – might be absent from its initial state because it was removed

---

[5] Where $mults: ℕ → ℕ$-set yields the set of multiples of i which are not greater than max.

by some earlier invocation of Rem (with an index which is another factor of c). The correct post-condition for an isolated version of Rem is

$$retr(sr)(\overleftarrow{\sigma}) - retr(sr)(\sigma) = mults(i) \cap retr(sr)(\overleftarrow{\sigma}) \tag{7}$$

If instances of Rem are run in parallel, interference can occur and it is possible that this can delete elements which are not multiples of i in Equation 7. This suggests focusing on the actions of $Rem(i, sr)$ by writing a dynamic constraint

$$\text{new } Rem(i, sr) \text{ links } (retr(sr)(\overleftarrow{\sigma}) - retr(sr)(\sigma) \subseteq mults(i)) \tag{8}$$

Use of $\|$-links of Section 4 makes it possible to conclude from Equation 8 that

$$\| \text{ new } Rem(i, sr) \text{ links } (retr(sr)(\overleftarrow{\sigma}) - retr(sr)(\sigma) \subseteq \bigcup_i mults(i)) \tag{9}$$

So far so good – but this is not enough for the designer of $Primes$ since it is necessary to show that enough elements are removed (Equation 8 is satisfied by skip). Referring back to Equation 7, what is missing is a constraint that

$$\text{new } Rem(i, sr) \backslash e \text{ fin } (retr(sr)(\sigma) \cap mults(i) = \{\,\})$$

But the designer of Rem will be unable to construct an implementation which achieves this requirement unless permission is given to rely on

$$e \text{ links } (retr(sr)(\sigma) \subseteq retr(sr)(\overleftarrow{\sigma}))$$

So the specification of the new method for Rem includes

$$\begin{aligned} e \text{ links } (retr(sr)(\sigma) \subseteq retr(sr)(\overleftarrow{\sigma})) \Rightarrow \\ \text{new } Rem(i, sr) \backslash e \text{ fin } (retr(sr)(\sigma) \cap mults(i) = \{\,\}) \end{aligned} \tag{10}$$

Since the environment of $Primes$ cannot reference sr, it is possible to use $\|$-I of Section 4 to conclude

$$\text{new } Primes \text{ fin } retr(sr)(\sigma) \cap \bigcup_i mults(i) = \{\,\}$$

So the class $Primes$ (with annotations) is

$Primes$ class
vars max: $\mathbb{N}$; sr: shared ref($Vector$)
$new(n: \mathbb{N})$ method r: ref($Primes$)
$\quad max \leftarrow n$
$\quad sr \leftarrow \text{new } Vector(max)$
$\quad \left\{ \text{let } m = rmap(v(\sigma(sr)))(\sigma)) \text{ in rng } m = \{true\} \right\}$

$$\underset{i \in \{2,\dots,\lceil \sqrt{max} \rceil\}}{\|} \quad \text{new } Rem(i, sr)$$

$\quad \Big\{ \text{let } m = rmap(v(\sigma(sr)))(\sigma)) \text{ in}$

$$\forall i \in \{2, \dots, max\} \cdot m(i) \Leftrightarrow is\text{-}prime(i) \Big\}$$

$\quad$ return self
$test(n: \mathbb{N})$ method r: $\mathbb{B}$
$\quad$ return $(sr!lu(n))!test()$

Decomposition of *Rem*

The remaining task is to develop code which satisfies the requirements on *Rem* (cf. Equations 8 and 10). It follows by ∥-links from Equation 4 that

$$\|_{m \in \{2,\ldots,\lfloor max/i \rfloor\}} (sr!lu(i * m))!del()$$
$$\text{links } (retr(sr)(\overleftarrow{\sigma}) - retr(sr)(\sigma) \subseteq mults(i)) \tag{11}$$

from which Equation 8 is a consequence. The post-condition in Equation 10 requires ∥-*I* again so *Rem* satisfies the annotations shown in the following.

Rem class
$new(i: \mathbb{N}, sr: \text{ref})$ method

$$\|_{m \in \{2,\ldots,\lfloor max/i \rfloor\}} (sr!lu(i*m))!del()$$

$$\left\{ \text{let } m = rmap(v(\sigma(sr))(\sigma)) \text{ in } \forall c \in mults(i) \cdot \neg m(c) \right\}$$
return

Final code transformation

The class *El* can be transformed (using transformation rule 1) to place the return statement at the beginning of the *del* method.

El class
vars $b: \mathbb{B} \leftarrow$ true
$test()$ method $r: \mathbb{B}$
 return b
$del()$ method
 return
 $b \leftarrow$ false

6 Further work

The main area of current work on $\pi o \beta \lambda$ is to define its semantics in a way which makes the justification of proof rules as straightforward as possible. Attempts at defining operational or denotational semantics of $\pi o \beta \lambda$ appear to be forced to define a low level of granularity in order to show that this can be avoided! The current semantics is given by a mapping to Milner's π-calculus [MPW92]. A full account of this is planned for [Jon93b]. The logic being used here has similarities with Lamport's TLA [Lam91] and it might be worth defining $\pi o \beta \lambda$ by relating it to TLA. At a minimum, TLA and UNITY [CM88] should influence the choice of logical operators in $\pi o \beta \lambda$'s logic; [Col93] and recent developments reported by Misra on UNITY are close in spirit to what is being sought for $\pi o \beta \lambda$'s logic.

 The above examples have not illustrated reasoning about liveness (other than termination); a further paper will be written which demonstrates the use of progresses of [Jon91a].

Acknowledgements

The author is grateful to Mario Wolczko, Carlos Figueiredo, Trevor Hopkins, John Sargeant, Michael Fisher and John Gurd for stimulating discussions on topics related to the implementation of object-based languages and machine architectures. Manfred Broy indicated the usefulness of constant channel names during an enjoyable visit to Munich. Anders Ravn made useful comments on a draft of this paper; both Ian Hayes and Pierre Collette provided detailed technical comments on [Jon92]. The stimulating discussions of IFIP's WG2.3 are acknowledged. The support of a Senior Fellowship from the SERC is gratefully acknowledged.

References

[AdB90]   P. America and F. de Boer. A proof system for process creation. In *[BJ90]*, pages 303–332, 1990.

[Ame86]   Pierre America. A proof theory for a sequential version of POOL. Technical Report 0188, Philips Research Laboratories, Philips Research Laboratories, Nederlandse Philips Bedrijven, B.V., September 1986.

[AR89]   Pierre America and Jan Rutten. *A Parallel Object-Oriented Language: Design and Semantic Foundations*. PhD thesis, Free University of Amsterdam, 1989.

[BG91]   J. C. M. Baeten and J. F. Groote, editors. *CONCUR'91 – Proceedings of the 2nd International Conference on Concurrency Theory*, volume 527 of *Lecture Notes in Computer Science*. Springer-Verlag, 1991.

[BJ90]   M. Broy and C. B. Jones, editors. *Programming Concepts and Methods*. North-Holland, 1990.

[BJM88]   R. Bloomfield, R. B. Jones, and L. S. Marshall, editors. *VDM'88: VDM – The Way Ahead*, volume 328 of *Lecture Notes in Computer Science*. Springer-Verlag, 1988.

[BK84]   H. Barringer and R. Kuiper. Hierachical development of concurrent systems in a temporal logic framework. In *Proceedings of NSF/SERC Seminar on Concurrency*, CMU, Pittsburgh, 1984.

[BKP84]   H. Barringer, R. Kuiper, and A. Pnueli. Now you can compose temporal logic specification. In *Proceedings of 16th ACM STOC*, Washington, May 1984.

[BM88]   J. Bruijning and C.A. Middelburg. Esprit project 1283: VIP VDM extensions: Final report. Technical Report 2.0, PTT Research, Neher Laboratories, The Netherlands, 1988.

[Bro89]   Manfred Broy. On bounded buffers: Modularity, robustness, and reliability in reactive systems. Technical Report MIP-8920, Universitat Passau, Fakultat fur mathematik und Informatik, June 1989.

[CJ91]   J. H. Cheng and C. B. Jones. On the usability of logics which handle partial functions. In C. Morgan and J. C. P. Woodcock, editors, *3rd Refinement Workshop*, pages 51–69. Springer-Verlag, 1991.

[CM88]   K. M. Chandy and J. Misra. *Parallel Program Design: A Foundation*. Addison-Wesley, 1988.

[Col92]   Pierre Collette. Semantic rules to compose rely-guarantee specifications. Technical Report RR 92-25, Universit'e de Louvain, 1992.

[Col93]   Pierre Collette. Application of the composition principle to unity-like specifications. In *TAPSOFT'93*, Lecture Notes in Computer Science. Springer-Verlag, 1993.

[Ded89]   Frank Dederichs.   Zur strukturierung von spezifikationen verteilter systeme, March 1989.

[dR85]   W. P. de Roever. The quest for compositionality: A survey of assertion-based proof systems for concurrent programs: Part I: Concurrency based on shared variables. In E. J. Neuhold and G. Chroust, editors, *Formal Models in Programming*. North-Holland, 1985.

[FP78]   N. Francez and A. Pnueli. A proof method for cyclic programs. *Acta Informatica*, 9:133–157, 1978.

[GH93]   J. V. Guttag and J. J. Horning. *Larch: Languages and Tools for Formal Specification*. Springer-Verlag, 1993.

[GHW85]   J. V. Guttag, J. J. Horning, and J. M. Wing. Larch in five easy pieces. Technical Report 5, DEC, SRC, July 1985.

[GR89]   David Grosvenor and Andy Robinson. An evaluation of rely-guarantee, March 1989. Submitted to Formal Aspects of Computer Science.

[HdR86]   J. Hooman and W. P. de Roever. The quest goes on: a survey of proof systems for partial correctness of CSP. In J.W. de Bakker, W. P. de Roever, and G. Rozenberg, editors, *Current Trends in Concurrency*, pages 343–395. Springer-Verlag, 1986. LNCS 224.

[Hoa74]   C. A. R. Hoare. Monitors: An operating system structuring concept. *Communications of the ACM*, 17(10):549–557, October 1974.

[Jon81]   C. B. Jones. *Development Methods for Computer Programs including a Notion of Interference*. PhD thesis, Oxford University, June 1981. Printed as: Programming Research Group Technical Monograph 25.

[Jon83a] C. B. Jones. Specification and design of (parallel) programs. In *Proceedings of IFIP'83*, pages 321–332. North-Holland, 1983.

[Jon83b] C. B. Jones. Tentative steps toward a development method for interfering programs. *ACM Transactions on Programming Languages and Systems*, 5(4):596–619, 1983.

[Jon90]   C. B. Jones. *Systematic Software Development using VDM*. Prentice Hall International, second edition, 1990.

[Jon91a] C. B. Jones. Interference resumed. In P. Bailes, editor, *Engineering Safe Software*, pages 31–56. Australian Computer Society, 1991.

[Jon91b] C. B. Jones. Interference revisited. In J. E. Nicholls, editor, *Z User Workshop*, pages 58–73. Springer-Verlag, 1991.

[Jon92]   C. B. Jones. An object-based design method for concurrent programs. Technical Report UMCS-92-12-1, Manchester University, 1992.

[Jon93a] C. B. Jones. Constraining interference in an object-based design method. In *TAPSOFT'93*, Lecture Notes in Computer Science. Springer-Verlag, 1993.

[Jon93b] C. B. Jones. Giving semantics to an object-based design notation. In *CONCUR'93*, Lecture Notes in Computer Science. Springer-Verlag, 1993.

[Lam91]   L. Lamport. The temporal logic of actions. Technical Report 79, Digital, SRC, 1991.

[Mid90]   C. A. Middelburg. *Syntax and Semantics of VVSL A Language for Structured VDM Specifications*. PhD thesis, PTT Research, Department of Applied Computer Science, September 1990.

[MPW92]   R. Milner, J. Parrow, and D. Walker. A calculus of mobile processes. *Information and Computation*, 100:1–77, 1992.

[OG76]   S. S. Owicki and D. Gries. An axiomatic proof technique for parallel programs I. *Acta Informatica*, 6:319–340, 1976.

[Owi75]   S. Owicki. *Axiomatic Proof Techniques for Parallel Programs*. PhD thesis, Department of Computer Science, Cornell University, 1975. 75-251.

[PT91]   S. Prehn and W. J. Toetenel, editors. *VDM'91 – Formal Software Development Methods. Proceedings of the 4th International Symposium of VDM Europe, Noordwijkerhout, The Netherlands, October 1991. Vol.1: Conference Contributions*, volume 551 of *Lecture Notes in Computer Science*. Springer-Verlag, 1991.

[Sta85]   Eugene W Stark. A proof technique for rely/guarantee properties, August 1985.

[Sta88]   Eugene W Stark. Proving entailment between conceptual state specifications. *Theoretical Computer Science*, 56:135–154, 1988.

[Sti86]   C. Stirling. A compositional reformulation of Owicki-Gries' partial correctness logic for a concurrent while language. In *ICALP'86*. Springer-Verlag, 1986. LNCS 226.

[Sti88]   C. Stirling. A generalisation of Owicki-Gries's Hoare logic for a concurrent while language. *TCS*, 58:347–359, 1988.

[Stø90]   K. Stølen. *Development of Parallel Programs on Shared Data-Structures*. PhD thesis, Manchester University, 1990. available as UMCS-91-1-1.

[Stø91a]   K. Stølen. A Method for the Development of Totally Correct Shared-State Parallel Programs. In *[BG91]*, pages 510–525, 1991.

[Stø91b]   K. Stølen. An Attempt to Reason About Shared-State Concurrency in the Style of VDM. In *[PT91]*, pages 324–342, 1991.

[SW91]   J. Sa and B. C. Warboys. Specifying concurrent object-based systems using combined specification notations. Technical Report UMCS-91-7-2, Manchester University, 1991.

[WD88]   J. C. P. Woodcock and B. Dickinson. Using VDM with rely and guarantee-conditions: Experiences of a real project. In *[BJM88]*, pages 434–458, 1988.

[XH91]   Qiwen Xu and Jifeng He. A theory of state-based parallel programming by refinement: Part I. In J. Morris, editor, *Proceedings of The Fourth BCS-FACS Refinement Workshop*. Springer-Verlag, 1991.

[Xu92]   Qiwen Xu. *A Theory of State-based Parallel Programming*. PhD thesis, Oxford University, 1992.

A   Using constant references

This appendix indicates how constants (in this case natural numbers) could be used as channel names: writing el_i for $i \in \mathbb{N}$

    Primes class
    vars max: $\mathbb{N}$
    $new(n: \mathbb{N})$ method r: ref(*Primes*)
      $max \leftarrow n$

$$\mathop{\|}_{i \in \{2,\ldots,max\}} \text{new } El(i)$$

$$\mathop{\|}_{i \in \{2,\ldots,\lceil \sqrt{max} \rceil\}} Rem(i)$$

      return self
    $test(n: \mathbb{N})$ method r: $\mathbb{B}$
      return $el_n!test()$

    Rem: class
    $new(i: \mathbb{N})$ method

$$\mathop{\|}_{m \in \{2,\ldots,\lfloor max/i \rfloor\}} (el_{i*m})!del();$$

      return

    El class
    vars b: $\mathbb{B}$
    $new(i)$ method
      $b \leftarrow$ true
    $test()$ method r: $\mathbb{B}$
      return b
    $del()$ method
      return
      $b \leftarrow$ false

Using Relative Refinement for Fault Tolerance *

Antonio Cau** and Willem-Paul de Roever***

Institut für Informatik und Praktische Mathematik II
Preußerstr. 1-9
Christian-Albrechts-Universität zu Kiel
D-2300 Kiel 1, Germany

Abstract. A general refinement methodology is presented based on ideas of Stark, and it is explained how these can be used for the systematic development of fault-tolerant systems. Highlights are: (1) A detailed and comprehensive exposition of Stark's temporal logic and development methodology. (2) A formalization of a general systematic approach to the development of fault-tolerant systems, accomplishing increasing degrees of coverage with each successive refinement stage. That is, faults are already identified and modeled at the first implementation level, which is shown to be a relative refinement, i.e., correct for all computations in which faults do not occur. The second implementation is a fail-stop implementation, i.e., an implementation that stops on the first detected occurrence of a fault. This implementation is also a relative refinement, i.e., correct in all computations in which the program never stops. The final implementation is correct in all computations, except those that display severe faults that violate the fault-tolerance assumptions, such as all n components failing in an n-way redundant way in case of stable storage. (3) A detailed example of a multi-disk system providing stable storage, illustrating this general methodology.

1 Introduction

Current formal methods are far from solving the problems in software development. The simplest view of the formal paradigm is that one starts with a formal specification and subsequently decomposes this specification in subspecifications which composed together form a correct refinement. These subspecifications are decomposed into "finer" subspecifications. This refinement process is continued until one gets subspecifications for which an implementation can easily be given. This view is too idealistic in a number of respects. First of all, most specifications of software are wrong (certainly most informal ones unless they have been formally analyzed) and contain inconsistencies [9]. Secondly, even if a formal specification is produced, this is only after a number of iteration steps because writing a correct specification is a process whose difficulty is comparable with that of producing a correct implementation, and should therefore be structured, resulting in a number of increasingly less abstract layers with specifications which tend to increase in detail (and therefore become less readable [8]). Thirdly, even an incorrect refinement step may be

---

* Partially supported by ESPRIT/BRA project 6021 (REACT)
** E-mail: ac@informatik.uni-kiel.dbp.de
*** E-mail: wpr@informatik.uni-kiel.dbp.de

useful in the sense that from this incorrect refinement step one can easier derive the correct refinement step. This is especially the case with intricate algorithms such as those concerning specific strategies for solving the mutual exclusion problem. An interesting illustration of this third view is provided by E.W. Dijkstra's "Tutorial on the split binary semaphore" [5] in which he solves the readers/writers problem by subsequently improving incorrect refinement steps till they are correct. If this master of style prefers to approximate and finally arrive at his correct solution using formally incorrect intermediate stages, one certainly expects that a formally correct development process for that paradigm is difficult to find! The strategy described in [5] is necessarily informal, reflecting the state of the art in 1979. We have formalized this strategy in [3].

In the present paper we present a formal development strategy for deriving a correct refinement step using relative correct intermediate stages, and its application to fault tolerant systems. The formal strategy is as follows: one starts with an implementation for a specified fault tolerant system. This implementation contains some faults, i.e., the refinement step is incorrect because of these faults. It is however relative correct because when these faults don't occur it is a correct implementation. In the next step we try to detect these faults, i.e., we construct a detection layer upon the previous implementation that stops that implementation when it detects an error caused by these faults. This is called a fail-stop implementation [7] and it is better than the previous one because now at least the implementation stops on the occurrence of a fault. The second implementation is also relative correct because when no faults occur and the detection layer doesn't detect any error it is correct. In the third approximation we recover these faults, i.e., we don't stop anymore upon the detection of an error but merely recover the fault by executing some special program that neutralizes that fault. This third approximated refinement step is correct under the assumption that certain conditions are fulfilled, which exclude the occurrence of faults different from the ones neutralized, i.e., it is relative correct. We use Stark's formalism in order to describe this process of approximation. In this formalism a specification is separated into a safety (machine) part and a liveness (validity) part. The machine part is used by us for describing the faulty implementation and the validity part for restricting the machine part to the correct behavior of that implementation. It is this separation that enables us to handle incorrect approximations: although the machine part of the implementation doesn't refine the specification, the intersection of the machine part and the validity part of the implementation does refine the specification, indeed.

The structure of the paper is as follows: In sect. 2 we introduce Stark's formalism and give some simplifications/improvements based on [4]. We present in sect. 3 the formal development of a fault tolerant system for stable storage, using the proto-formalization of [10]. Section 4 contains a conclusion.

2 Stark's Formalism

2.1 Introduction

In this section we present Stark's Dense time Temporal Logic (DTL) formalism for describing correct refinement steps ([11, 12] are not easily accessible) and our use of it to describe incorrect refinement steps. Our simplification of this logic is based on that of [4]. In sect. 2.2 the semantic notions of module and machine are defined. The idea is that modules are a kind of black box notion. Machines are introduced to relate them to actual computations. Stark's machine notion is a handy normal form reminiscent of Lamport's notion of "machine closure" [1], and makes it easy to define liveness properties as global restrictions on the machine's behavior. Stark makes a distinction between local -safety- properties and global properties, such as liveness. Here is where we depart from Stark's formalism: instead of using the global condition for defining liveness, by excluding computations which do not satisfy certain fairness assumptions, we use it for describing the allowed behavior of a machine by removing behavior which is undesirable in other respects. Another important reason for using Stark's formalism is that Stark's dense time temporal logic deals with the stuttering problem in an elegant abstract way, with the added advantage that one can express *within this logic* what a correct development step is (also Lamport's notion of correct refinement step can be expressed within that logic). We adopt in sect. 2.3 a slightly simplified/improved version of the logic as defined in [4]. Figure 1 illustrates the underlying model. A salient feature of Stark's DTL is the "immediately after" operator $'$.

In sect. 2.4 the semantic notion of a correct refinement step of modules is defined. The idea is that a module can play a certain role in a refinement step. This role can be an abstract one, a composite one, or a concrete one. During a refinement step an abstract module is implemented by a collection of concrete modules. A third kind of module, the composite module, relates these abstract and concrete modules with each other. It first defines how the concrete modules are composed and secondly describes how internal behavior, arising from internal events, is abstracted away from within this composed module. So the composite module defines actually the refinement relation between the abstract and concrete modules.

In sect. 2.5 machines and their allowed computations are related to correct refinement steps, expressed by verification conditions. These verification conditions are expressed in DTL. This section also explains how Stark's formalism can be used to describe relative refinement steps.

2.2 Modules and Machines

In [11] a method for specifying reactive systems is introduced. Such systems are assumed to be composed of one or more *modules*. A module is specified by the pair $\langle E, B \rangle$ where E is syntactic and denotes a finite set of possible events, called *interface*, and B is semantic and denotes its *allowed (visible) behavior*.

An *event* is an observable instantaneous occurrence during the operation of a module, that can be generated by that module or its environment and that is of interest at the given level of abstraction. E always contains a λ_E-event which represents all, at that level, uninteresting events. We model faults also with events because

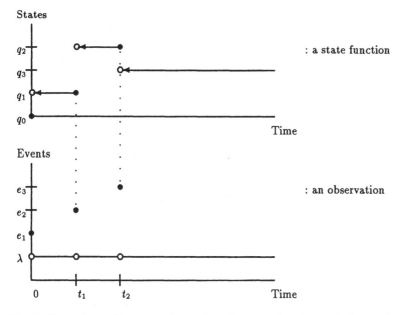

Fig. 1. This picture illustrates the notion of a state function and observation, which together characterise the notion of computation of a machine. It illustrates the following computation: the initial state is q_0, on the occurrence of event e_1 the state changes in q_1. Between time 0 and time t_1 there are no interesting event occurrences, only of the uninteresting stuttering event λ, so the state doesn't change until the next interesting event e_2 occurs resulting in state q_2, and so on.

a fault is an observable instantaneous occurrence during the operation of a module. It is generated by the environment of the module and is of interest at our level of abstraction.

The B-part of specification $\langle E, B \rangle$ characterizes the allowed behavior of the module. An *observation* x over interface E is a function from $[0, \infty)$ -representing the time domain- to E, such that $x(t) \neq \lambda$ for at most finitely many $t \in [0, \infty)$ in each bounded interval; this means that in any bounded interval only a finite number of interesting events can occur (the so called finite variability condition). Figure 1 illustrates the notion of observation. At time 0 the event e_1 occurs, at time t_1 event e_2, and at time t_2 event e_3; at all other moments the event λ occurs.

Let $Obs(E)$ denote the set of all observations over E. Then the *allowed behavior* B is a subset of $Obs(E)$. $Beh(E)$ denotes the set of all behaviors at interface E, i.e., the set of all subsets $Obs(E)$..

Until now we have specified the allowed behavior of a module by a set of observations. We now introduce a state-transition formalism to generate this set. In this state-transition formalism, at any instant of time a module can be thought of as being in a *state*. In each state an event may cause a transition to another state. With a state-transition relation one specifies which event can occur in a particular state and what the state will be after the occurrence of that event. Thus a state-transition specification describes the desired functioning of a module in terms of computations of an idealized machine, i.e., an observation now corresponds with a computation of that machine.

One can divide the properties that can be specified by the state-transition technique in two classes. The first class consists of the so called *local (safety) properties*, which describe how an event causes a state transformation to the next state. The second class consists of the so called *global properties*; these describe the global relationship between events and states that cannot be directly described in terms of state successor relations.

The local properties are specified by the above mentioned machine and the global properties are specified by defining a set of *validity conditions* to be satisfied by computations of that machine. The set of computations that satisfy the validity conditions is called the *set of valid computations*. The intersection of this set with the set of computations that are generated by the machine describes the allowed behavior of the corresponding module.

The machine M that specifies the local properties of a module is defined as follows: $M = (E_M, Q_M, IQ_M, TR_M)$ where:

- E_M : is the interface of M; events labeled with a$\downarrow$ are input events, events labeled with a$\uparrow$ are output events, and events without an arrow are internal events,
- Q_M : is the countably infinite set of states of M; a state is a function from the set of observable variables Var and freeze variables F ($Var \cap F =$) to the set of values Val, i.e., $Q_M : (Var \cup F) \rightarrow Val$. Note: the "normal" variables will be bold faced in order to distinguish them from freeze variables.
- IQ_M : a non-empty subset of Q_M, the set of initial states,
- TR_M : the state-transition relation (finite), $TR_M \subseteq Q_M \times E_M \times Q_M$, such that for all q the stuttering step $\langle q, \lambda_{E_M}, q \rangle \in TR_M$ and that for all $q, r \in Q_M$ $\langle q, \lambda_{E_M}, r \rangle \in TR_M$ iff $r = q$. This latter condition expresses the requirement that λ-events can not change a state. Furthermore M is input-cooperative, i.e., in every state of M any input event can be received; therefore the state-transition relation for an input event ist defined for all states of M.

A *state function* over a set of states Q is a function $f : [0, \infty) \rightarrow Q$ such that for all $t \in [0, \infty)$, there exists $\varepsilon_t > 0$ such that f is constant on intervals of type $(t - \varepsilon_t, t] \cap [0, \infty)$ and $(t, t + \varepsilon_t]$. We write $f(t^{\rightarrow})$ for the value of the state just before and at time t (the first type of interval) and write $f(t^{\circ\rightarrow})$ for the value of f just after time t (the second type of interval). Figure 1 illustrates the notion of state function. At time 0 the machine is in state q_0, in interval $(0, t_1]$ the machine is in state q_1, and so on.

A *history* over an interface E and a state set Q is a pair $X = \langle Obs_X, State_X \rangle$, where Obs_X is an observation over E (a function from $[0, \infty)$ to E), and $State_X$ is a state function over Q. These two concepts are related by the notion of *computation* of a machine M. A computation of M intuitively expresses that an observation and a state function fit together in that at any moment of time t any triple consisting of (1) the state just before and including t, (2) the observation at t, and (3) the state just after t, belongs to the state transition relation of M (see fig. 1). For a formal definition we need the notion of *step at t* in history X.

Let $Hist(E,Q)$ denote the set of all histories over interface E and state set Q. If $X \in Hist(E,Q)$ and $t \in [0,\infty)$, then define the *step* occurring at time t in X by: $Step_X(t) = \langle State_X(t^{\rightarrow}), Obs_X(t), State_X(t^{\circ\rightarrow}) \rangle$.

A *computation of a machine* M is a history $X \in Hist(E_M, Q_M)$ such that: $State_X(0) \in IQ_M$ and $Step_X(t) \in TR_M$ for all $t \in [0,\infty)$.

$Comp(M)$ denotes the set of all computations of M, and $Reachable_M$ the set of reachable states of M.

2.3 Stark's dense linear time logic DTL

As mentioned above, the global properties are described by a set of validity conditions. Stark uses a dense time temporal logic to describe these validity conditions. Our modified temporal logic DTL looks like the one of Stark and is defined as follows:

Syntax

variables are elements of Var
values of variables are elements of Val
freeze variables are elements of F; $F \cap Var = \emptyset$
events are elements of E_M
special symbol e
event term e $= f$ where f denotes an element of E_M
state terms x and x' where x is an element of Var, denoting the current state, and x' is the "immediately after" state (' denotes the "immediately after" temporal operator)
terms can be event terms, state terms, freeze variables or function symbols
quantification over freeze variables using $\forall, \exists$
formulae are built from terms, and relation symbols using boolean connectives, quantification and
temporal operators $\square$, $\diamond$ and '

Examples of DTL formulae

$(\mathbf{x} = 0 \wedge e = d_0) \rightarrow \mathbf{x}' = 1$ (a state-transition), $\square \mathbf{x} > 0$ (a safety property), and $\square(\mathbf{x} = 0 \rightarrow \diamond \mathbf{x} > 0)$ (a liveness property).

Semantics

We take as semantic model histories (a history is a pair $\langle Obs_h, State_h \rangle$). Let $h^{(\tau)}$ denote the history $\lambda t.h(t + \tau)$.
For all freeze variables $v \in F$, $v(h) = State_h(0)(v)$. Note: because v is a freeze variable the value doesn't change in a history, at time 0 it is initialized.
For all variables $v \in Var$, $v(h) = State_h(0^{\rightarrow})(v) = State_h(0)(v)$.
For all variables $v \in Var$, $v'(h) = State_h(0^{\circ\rightarrow})(v)$.
For e , $e(h) = Obs_h(0)$.
For f with interpretation $\overline{f}$, and $t_1, \ldots, t_n$ are terms, $f(t_1, \ldots, t_n)(h) =$

$\overline{f}(t_1(h), \ldots, t_n(h))$.

$h \models R(t_1, \ldots, t_n)$ if $\overline{R}$ is the interpretation of R, and $t_1, \ldots, t_n$ are terms, and $\overline{R}(t_1(h), \ldots, t_n(h))$ holds;

$h \models \neg \varphi$ if $h \not\models \varphi$;

$h \models \varphi \rightarrow \psi$ if $h \models \neg \varphi$ or $h \models \psi$;

$h \models \exists x.\varphi$ if there exists an assignment $State_{h'}(0)$ differing from $State_h(0)$ only in the value assigned to freeze variable x such that $h' \models \varphi$;

$h \models \Diamond \varphi$; if there exists an $t \in [0, \infty)$ such that $h^{(t)} \models \varphi$;

$h \models \Box \varphi$; if for all $t \in [0, \infty)$ $h^{(t)} \models \varphi$;

The initial states and the transition relation of a machine, can and will be, from now on be expressed as DTL formulae. The *enabling condition* of an event in a machine M, denoted by $Enabled_M(e)$ is the precondition for the transition that corresponds with that event. The local properties of a module Z can now be expressed by formula $IQ_Z \wedge \Box TR_Z$. Thus $\text{Comp}(M_Z) \overset{\text{def}}{=} \{X \in Hist(E_Z, Q_Z) \mid X \models IQ_Z \wedge \Box TR_Z\}$. The liveness properties can now be added, expressed by some extra DTL formula V_Z, the *validity condition*. The complete behavior of module Z is the following set of histories: $\{X \in \text{Comp}(M_Z) \mid X \models V_Z\}$, and is described by DTL formula $IQ_Z \wedge \Box TR_Z \wedge V_Z$.

2.4 Modules and correct refinement steps

In Stark's view there are three kinds of roles a module can play during a refinement step. The first one is that of an *abstract* module -then it serves as a high level specification of a system. The second one is that of a *concrete* one, serving as a lower level specification of a system component. A concrete module may become an abstract module in the next refinement step. The third one is that of a *composite* one, defined as the Cartesian product of the abstract module and the concrete modules, and used as a device for defining a refinement mapping between the abstract module and the parallel composition of the concrete modules for that development step. The interface of the composite module is the Cartesian product of the interfaces of the abstract module and the concrete modules.

To specify a refinement step of a system one therefore needs an abstract module, a composite module, and one or more concrete modules. An *interconnection* relates these modules with each other, i.e., it relates the interface of the composite module with both the interface of the abstract module and the interface of the concrete modules. Hence it characterizes a refinement relation between an abstract module and a set of concrete modules. It defines how an event on the abstract level is implemented by events on the concrete level.

An interconnection $\mathcal{I}$ is a pair $\langle \alpha, \langle \delta_j \rangle_{j \in J} \rangle$ where:

- α denotes a function from the interface $E = A \times \prod_{j=1}^{N} F_j$ of the composite module, with $\lambda_E = \langle \lambda_A, \lambda_{F_1}, \ldots, \lambda_{F_N} \rangle$, to the interface A of the abstract module such that $\alpha(\lambda_E) = \lambda_A$ holds; α is called an *abstraction* function,

- δ_j denotes a function from interface $E = A \times \prod_{j=1}^{N} F_j$ of the composite module, with $\lambda_E = \langle \lambda_A, \lambda_{F_1}, \ldots, \lambda_{F_N} \rangle$, to interface F_j of the j-th concrete module such that $\delta_j(\lambda_E) = \lambda_{F_j}$ holds; δ_j is called a *decomposition* function.

So intuitively the requirement upon both α and the δ_j's is that uninteresting events of the composite module are not turned into interesting events of the abstract or concrete modules.

The definition of interconnection can easily be extended to (hold between the) behaviors of the mentioned modules. When $\mathcal{I}$ is an interconnection between the interfaces of the modules, $\mathcal{I}^*$ denotes the corresponding interconnection between the behaviors of the modules. We shall omit the * from now on when we use the interconnection between behaviors of modules. Although this is not mathematically correct, we hope it is clearer for the reader.

With the above defined interconnection the allowed behavior of the composite module can be defined as $\alpha^{-1}(B_A) \cap \bigcap_{j=1}^{N} \delta_j^{-1}(B_j)$ where B_A denotes the allowed behavior of the abstract module A and B_j that of module j. A *refinement step* is defined as a triple $\langle \mathcal{I}, S_A, \langle S_j \rangle_{j \in J} \rangle$ where $\mathcal{I}$ is the interconnection (between behaviors), S_A the specification $\langle A, B_A \rangle$ ($B_A \in Beh(A)$ denotes the set of allowed behaviors of the abstract module) of the abstract module, and S_i the specification $\langle F_i, B_i \rangle$ ($B_i \in Beh(F_i)$) denotes the set of allowed behaviors of concrete module i) of concrete module i.

A refinement step is *correct* if the following, hopefully now intuitively obvious, inclusion holds: $\bigcap_{j=1}^{N} \delta_j^{-1}(B_j) \subseteq \alpha^{-1}(B_A)$.

2.5 Describing (relative) correct refinement steps in DTL

With every kind of module we can associate a machine -whether abstract, concrete or composite. For concrete and abstract modules this is obvious, but how is this done for a composite module? First we assume that the sets of states of the abstract and the concrete machines are disjoint. So every machine has its own set of states. If we have an abstract machine M_A, described by temporal formula $IQ_A \wedge \Box TR_A$, concrete machines M_j, described by temporal formula $IQ_j \wedge \Box TR_j$, and if we have furthermore an interconnection $\mathcal{I} = \langle \alpha, \langle \delta_j \rangle_{j \in J} \rangle$ that links both kinds of machines, then we can construct the composite machine M_c as follows:

- The interface $E_c \overset{\text{def}}{=} E_A \times \prod_{j=1}^{N} F_j$ as in the definition of the composite module.
- The set of states $Q_c \overset{\text{def}}{=} Q_A \times \prod_{j \in J} Q_j$, i.e, the product of (1) the set of states of the abstract machine, and (2) the product of the sets of states of all the concrete machines.
- The set of initial states IQ_c of M_c is defined by: $IQ_c \overset{\text{def}}{=} IQ_A \wedge \bigwedge_{j \in J} IQ_j$.
- In order to express the state-transition relation TR_c of the composite machine, we use the definitions of α and the δ_j's to transform event terms in TR_A and TR_j into event terms of TR_c. Event term e $= d$ in TR_A is transformed into e $= \alpha^{-1}(d)$ and event term e $= f$ in TR_j into e $= \delta_j^{-1}(f)$ (Note: α^{-1} and δ_j^{-1} are not functions (in general), so $\alpha^{-1}(d)$ and $\delta^{-1}(f)$ are sets. But these sets are finite because the interfaces are finite. Thus e $= \alpha^{-1}(d)$ and e $= \delta_j^{-1}(f)$ are not proper defined expressions but can be translated into $\bigvee_{g \in \alpha^{-1}(d)}(\text{e} = g)$ and $\bigvee_{h \in \delta_j^{-1}(J)}(\text{e} = h)$. But nevertheless we will use e $= \alpha^{-1}(d)$ and e $= \delta_j^{-1}(f)$ for clarity although it is mathematically wrong.) We introduce the following notation:

$[f]_\alpha \overset{\text{def}}{=} f[\alpha^{-1}(d)/d]$ for $d \in E_A$ and $[f]_{\delta_j} \overset{\text{def}}{=} f[\delta_j^{-1}(f)/f]$ for $f \in F_j$.

Then the state-transition relation TR_c of M_c is defined as follows:

$TR_c \overset{\text{def}}{=} \Box([TR_A]_\alpha \wedge \bigwedge_{j \in J}[TR_j]_{\delta_j})$,

with $[TR]_\beta$ for abstraction/decomposition function β defined by replacing any occurrence $e = f$ in TR by $e = [f]_\beta$.

The correctness condition of the refinement step, as seen above, is as follows:

$\bigcap_{j=1}^{N} \delta_j^{-1}(B_j) \subseteq \alpha^{-1}(B_A)$.

In the present formalism, this translates into

$\bigcap_{j=1}^{N} \delta_j^{-1}(\{X \in Comp(M_j) : X \models V_j\}) \subseteq \alpha^{-1}(\{X \in Comp(M_A) : X \models V_A\})$.

The following temporal formula expresses this condition:

$\bigwedge_{j \in J}[IQ_j \wedge \Box TR_j \wedge V_j]_{\delta_j} \rightarrow [IQ_A \wedge \Box TR_A \wedge V_A]_\alpha$

Due to the separation of the allowed behavior into a machine part (a pure safety DTL formula) and a validity part (a pure liveness DTL formula) -see [2] for an explanation of pure safety and pure liveness- we can split this verification condition into two verification conditions, one for machines and one for validity:

- *maximality* : any event that can be generated by the system of concrete machines can also be performed by the abstract machine, i.e.,
  $\forall e \in E_c.(Reachable_c \wedge \bigwedge_{j \in J} Enabled(\delta_j(e))) \rightarrow Enabled(\alpha(e))$
  where $Reachable_c$ is a condition that checks if a state of the composite machine is reachable, $Enabled(\delta_j(e))$ is the enabling condition of event $\delta_j(e)$ of machine j, and $Enabled(\alpha(e))$ is the enabling condition of event $\alpha(e)$ of the abstract machine.
- *validity* : any allowed computation of each concrete machine corresponds with an allowed computation of the abstract machine, i.e.,
  $Comp(M_c) \models (\bigwedge_{j \in J}[V_j]_{\delta_j}) \rightarrow [V_A]_\alpha$
  where V_j is the validity condition of module j, and V_A is the validity condition of the abstract module.

Next we explain how to describe *relative correct* refinement steps in the development of a program, as promised in sect. 1. Well, as said before, instead of using the validity condition for expressing a liveness condition, we use it for characterizing the correct computations of a machine. Now in general that latter condition is not a pure liveness condition. Furthermore, since the machine part describes the implementation as developed until now, it contains in general also the unallowed computations. But since the total specification is the intersection of the machine part and the validity part, the total specification is still *relatively correct*. More formally:

Let the abstract specification be denoted by $IQ_A \wedge \Box TR_A \wedge V_A$, where V_A is a pure liveness condition, i.e., the machine part of the abstract specification doesn't characterize unallowed computations.

Each concrete specification is denoted by $IQ_j \wedge \Box TR_j \wedge P_j \wedge L_j$ where P_j is the part that characterizes the allowed computations of the machine part and L_j is the pure liveness part, i.e., the validity condition has been split up into P_j and L_j. In the stable storage example of the next section the P_j part is always a safety condition that *disallows certain transition of TR_j from being taken*. This allows us to express the *relative* correctness of a refinement step as follows:

For correctness we have to prove, as seen above,

$\bigwedge_{j \in J} [IQ_j \wedge \square TR_j \wedge P_j \wedge L_j]_{\delta_j} \rightarrow [IQ_A \wedge \square TR_A \wedge V_A]_\alpha.$

Because (1) both P_j and TR_j are safety conditions, (2) the conjunction of two safety conditions is again a safety condition, and (3) P_j disallows certain transitions of TR_j from being taken, $\square TR_j \wedge P_j$ can be transformed into $\square TRnew_j$, which is also expressed as a safety condition. Note: $TRnew_j$ is a new transition relation. So we get the following:

$\bigwedge_{j \in J} [IQ_j \wedge \square TRnew_j \wedge L_j]_{\delta_j} \rightarrow [IQ_A \wedge \square TR_A \wedge V_A]_\alpha.$

This form allows one to use Stark's two verification conditions, because $TRnew_j$ is a pure safety condition and L_j a pure liveness condition.

3 Relative Refinement of Fault Tolerant Systems

3.1 Introduction

In this chapter we first introduce in sect. 3.2 a *general methodology* for proving fault tolerant systems correct. This general methodology uses the relative refinement concept of sect. 2.5. The remaining sections of this chapter give an illustration of this general methodology by applying it to a fault tolerant system consisting of a number of disks implementing stable storage. Section 3.3 introduces this application. In sections 3.4, 3.5, 3.6 and 3.7 the four steps of this general methodology are applied to the stable storage example.

3.2 The General Methodology

The general methodology consists of four steps. In the first step we give the abstract specification A (a DTL formula) of the fault tolerant system. In this specification no faults are visible, hence don't occur as observables. The designer's task is to give an implementation of this system under the assumption that only faults from certain classes can occur. These faults are called *anticipated faults*. These are faults which may affect the implementation in that they may give rise to errors in the state of the implementation, resulting subsequently in failures of that implementation. But the implementation must be such that these errors and faults -this is why they are called *anticipated* faults- are not leading to failures. This justifies the very term fault tolerance, and explains the very task to be carried out by fault tolerant systems. This task will be described in step 2,3 and 4 of the general methodology.

The second step of the general methodology, *identifies* the anticipated faults which can affect an implementation I. This implementation serves as first approximation to the final implementation of A. It should be clear that I is not a refinement of A because of the possible occurrences of anticipated faults. I is only a refinement when these faults do not occur, i.e., I is a *relative refinement* of A. We have seen in sect. 2.5 that this relative refinement step can expressed using ordinary refinement, i.e., $I \wedge NFO$ is a refinement of A where NFO expresses that the anticipated faults never occur. So in step 2 the proof obligation is:

$$I \wedge NFO \rightarrow A. \tag{1}$$

Note: we have omitted the abstraction and decomposition functions that were needed to describe a refinement step in DTL because these would complicate the explanation of the general methodology.

In the third step of our development one specifies *how these anticipated faults are detected,* i.e., one has to specify a detection layer DL_{fs} for these faults. This layer is added in bottom-up fashion to the implementation I of the second step and stops upon detection of the first error, i.e., DL_{fs} is a *fail-stop* implementation. So the second approximation to the final implementation consists of the parallel composition of I and DL_{fs}. Is this approximation a refinement of A? No, because when in I a fault occurs, and DL_{fs} detects the corresponding error, the whole approximation stops. One would like to have (eventually) an approximation that doesn't stop. This means that one must consider $I \wedge NFO$ instead of I. But then DL_{fs} should detect no error because if it detects an error and the fact that no corresponding fault has occurred the detection layer is not "correct". So $I \parallel DL_{fs}$ is a relative refinement of A can be described by the following ordinary refinement:
$$[(I \wedge NFO) \parallel (DL_{fs} \wedge NED)]_{DL_{fs}} \rightarrow A \qquad (2).$$
(Note: $\parallel$ can be expressed in DTL using certain abstraction and decomposition functions.) Here NED expresses that no errors are detected, and $[\ldots]_{DL_{fs}}$ the hiding of the detection layer. Proof obligation (2) is proved using the result of (1): under the assumption that $\neg NED \rightarrow \neg NFO$ (error detected implies corresponding fault occurred) the following holds
$$[(I \wedge NFO) \parallel (DL_{fs} \wedge NED)]_{DL_{fs}} \rightarrow (I \wedge NFO)$$
Using (1) one infers (2).

In the fourth step of our development one specifies the course of action after detection of an anticipated fault, i.e., *one specifies the corrective action to be undertaken after detection of such a fault.* This means in general that one needs *redundancy,* i.e., several copies of I and DL components, because when a detection layer DL detects an error, the state before that error has to be recovered and that can only be done by accessing another copy of I through its corresponding detection layer DL. Note that the DL component doesn't stop anymore on the detection of an error but merely waits for the corrective action to be undertaken. Say, we need N copies of I and DL. These will be abbreviated by respectively $\overline{I}$ and $\overline{DL}$. Thus the final implementation consists of $\overline{I} \parallel \overline{DL} \parallel ER$ where ER is the error recovery layer. This implementation is correct if following holds:
$$[\overline{I} \parallel \overline{DL} \parallel ER \wedge REC]_{DL,ER} \rightarrow A \qquad (3).$$
Here REC is global restriction on the the kind of faults that can occur. One can prove the correctness of (3) using (2) (and therefore also (1)). First one proves the case when no faults occur:
$$[(\overline{I} \wedge NFO) \parallel \overline{DL} \parallel (ER \wedge REC)]_{DL,ER} \rightarrow A.$$
Under the assumption that $NFO \rightarrow NED$ holds one can infer
$$(\overline{I} \wedge NFO) \parallel \overline{DL} \parallel (ER \wedge REC) \rightarrow (\overline{I} \wedge NFO) \parallel (\overline{DL} \wedge NED) \parallel (ER \wedge REC).$$
And under the assumption that $REC \rightarrow \neg NED$ holds one can infer
$$[(\overline{I} \wedge NFO) \parallel \overline{DL} \parallel (ER \wedge REC)]_{ER} \rightarrow (I \wedge NFO) \parallel (DL_{fs} \wedge NED).$$
Using (2) one now can infer
$$[\overline{I} \wedge NFO) \parallel \overline{DL} \parallel (ER \wedge REC)]_{DL,ER} \rightarrow A.$$
The second case to be considered is when faults do occur
$$[(\overline{I} \wedge \neg NFO) \parallel \overline{DL} \parallel (ER \wedge REC)]_{DL,ER} \rightarrow A.$$
Under the assumption that $NED \rightarrow NFO$ holds one can infer
$$(\overline{I} \wedge \neg NFO) \parallel \overline{DL} \parallel (ER \wedge REC) \rightarrow (\overline{I} \wedge \neg NFO) \parallel (\overline{DL} \wedge \neg NED) \parallel (ER \wedge REC).$$
And under the assumption that $\neg NED \rightarrow REC$ holds (i.e., the detected error is

recovered -this is actually a programming problem), one can infer

$$[(\overline{I} \wedge \neg NFO) \parallel \overline{DL} \parallel (ER \wedge REC)]_{ER} \to (I \wedge NFO) \parallel (DL_{FS} \wedge NED)$$

Using step (2) one now can infer

$$[(\overline{I} \wedge \neg NFO) \parallel \overline{DL} \parallel (ER \wedge REC)]_{DL,ER} \to A.$$

Combining the two cases together one gets

$$[\overline{I} \parallel \overline{DL} \parallel (ER \wedge REC)]_{DL,ER} \to A.$$

Recapitulating: in the proof above the following assumptions have been made:
$(NFO \leftrightarrow NED$: perfect detection,
$(\neg NED \leftrightarrow REC)$: perfect recovery and
step (1): implementation I is a relative refinement of A.

This ends our description of a general methodolology for proving fault-tolerant systems (qualitatively) correct.

3.3 Application: Introduction

Stable storage is defined as follows. A disk is used to store and retrieve data. During these operations some faults can occur in the underlying hardware. To make the disk more reliable one introduces layers for the detection and correction of errors, due to these faults. The system with these detection and correction layers is called "stable storage". This stable storage is a fault tolerant system because it stores and retrieves data in a reliable way under the assumption that faults from a certain class are recovered (corrected). This class consists of two kinds of faults. The first one consists of faults that damage the disk surface -the contents of the disk are said to be corrupted by these faults. The second one consists of faults that affect the disk control system, and results into the contents of the disk being read from or written to the wrong location. Notice that other kinds of faults, such as power failure or physical destruction of the whole stable storage system, are not taken into account. I.e., stable storage should function correctly provided such latter faults do not occur.

3.4 Application: First Step

Introduction In step 1, as seen in sect. 3.2, the abstract specification A of a stable storage system is given, i.e., the system as we ideally would like it to look like: no faults are observed. If they occur internally, they should be repaired by the system without leaving any observable trace. For that is the meaning of 'stable' here!

Specification The abstract specification of stable storage specifies the following: The user signals with an request event that he wants to read the contents of some location of a medium for stable storage. This medium then responds by sending the requested contents. The user can also signal with a write event that some data have to be written on some location of the medium. Note: we have a very simple stable storage medium that can handle only one request at a time. If the user requests the contents of location before the stable storage medium has responded to a previous request then our stable storage medium will get into the error state and will not respond anymore to any request from the user.

We specify this medium by a machine M (and V-set V) which is in this case rather simple because this is an idealized machine with no faults. It only ensures that the user and the stable storage medium communicate with each other correctly. The specification $A \stackrel{\text{def}}{=} M \wedge V$ where M and V are specified below:

1. **Events:**

   The events act as signals between the user and stable storage.

   $E : \{r(sn)\downarrow, s(c)\uparrow, w(sn,d)\downarrow : sn \in SN \wedge c, d \in INF\}$

   where SN is the set of sector numbers: $[1,.., SNMAX]$ and INF is the set of information items that could be stored and retrieved by stable storage; it will not be further specified.

   $r(sn)$: a request to read sector sn; $s(c)$: the response to the previous request where c are the contents of sector sn; $w(sn,d)$: write information item d onto sector sn.

2. **States:**

   $Q : (\{SS[i] : i \in SN\} \rightarrow INF) \times (s : \{idle, retr, error\}) \times (bf : SN)$

   $SS[i] = v_i$: sector i contains information item v_i; s stands for stable storage state, i.e., describes the current state of stable storage as follows: s = $idle$: stable storage is waiting for an event to occur, s = $retr$: the user has requested some contents of stable storage and stable storage is $retrieving$ them, s = $error$: the user has requested the contents of a location before stable storage has responded to a previous request. Variable **bf** is used to store the current sector from which the user has requested the contents.

3. **Initial States:**

   $IQ \stackrel{\text{def}}{=} \forall i \in SN.SS[i] = dflt \wedge s = idle$

   Where $dflt \in INF$ is some default information item.

   Stable storage is waiting for an event to occur and each location (sector) of stable storage contains some default information item.

4. **Transitions:**

   Figure 2 illustrates the transitions of stable storage, in a notion reminiscent of Harel's Statecharts [6]. Note: in this figure transitions of the form e/a occur, where e is an event and a an action. For example $r(sn)\downarrow$ /**bf**' $= sn$. The meaning of this transition is that when event $r(sn)$ occurs variable **bf** gets as new value sn. The ' is the "immediately after" temporal operator of DTL. So in state s = $retr$ the value of **bf** equals sn.

5. **Validity conditions:**

   As said before, the validity must express the fact that the user and the stable storage medium must communicate correctly; for instance, it is not allowed that the user generates an $r(sn)$ event or $w(sn,d)$ before the stable storage medium has replied with an $s(c)$ event to a previous $r(sn)$ event. This is because our version of stable storage can only handle one request at a time.

   $V \stackrel{\text{def}}{=} R \rightarrow G$

   $R \stackrel{\text{def}}{=} \Box(s = retr \rightarrow (e \neq r(sn) \wedge e \neq w(sn,d)))$

   This expresses that the user will never generate the request and write events when the stable storage medium is busy retrieving the contents of some sector. So R expresses that the user should live with the fact that the stable storage medium can only handle one request at a time.

   $G \stackrel{\text{def}}{=} \Box(e = r(sn) \rightarrow \Diamond e = s(SS[sn]))$

   When the user requests the contents from some sector, the stable storage medium

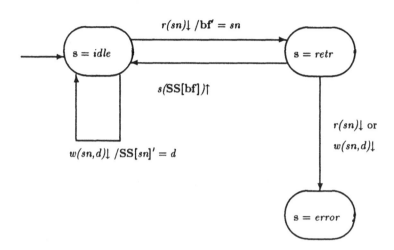

Fig. 2. Transitions of Stable Storage

should guarantee that the user eventually gets these contents. Thus, the validity condition expresses the property that the stable storage never enters into the *error* state.

3.5 Application: Second step

Introduction In this step, which is the first stage in our task to develop a fault tolerant system, we give the specification of a physical disk. This specification is a first approximation to our fault tolerant system, i.e., it acts as the undecorated basic layer of our desired implementation. In this specification we must specify which are the anticipated faults of our system, i.e., we have to specify which faults are the focus of our interest that could affect a physical disk. These faults are represented in our formalism as events.

Specification We must specify a physical disk, the anticipated faults and their impact on the physical disk. We take as anticipated faults the following ones (cf. [10]):

- Damages of the disk surface causing corruption of the contents of a physical sector.
- Disk control faults causing the contents of a particular physical sector to be read from or written to a wrong location.

These faults are described using two events: the *dam* event, standing for the fault expressing damage to the disk surface and the *csf* event standing for a fault in the disk control system.

In analogy to the specification of stable storage, the user signals with an *rP(psn)* event that it wants to read the contents of physical sector *psn*. The physical disk then signals with an $sP(c)$ event that it has retrieved the contents from this location. With an $wP(psn, d)$ event the user signals that the physical disk has to store information item d onto sector psn. Because stable storage can handle only one request at a time, we take a physical disk with the same feature. The formal specification $I \stackrel{\text{def}}{=} M_{PD} \wedge V_{PD}$ where M_{PD} and V_{PD} are defined below:

1. **Events:**
   $$E_{PD} = \{rP(psn)\downarrow, sP(c)\uparrow, wP(psn,d)\downarrow, csf(psn)\downarrow, dam(psn)\downarrow : psn \in PSN \wedge c, d \in PHY\}$$
   where PSN is the set of Physical Sector Numbers : $[1, \ldots, PSNMAX]$ and PHY the set of information items that can be stored and retrieved by the PHYsical disk.
   $rP(psn)$: the request to read the contents of physical sector psn; $sP(c)$: the response to the previous request where c are the contents from phy. sector psn; $wP(psn, d)$: write information item d onto physical sector psn.

2. **States:**
   We must somehow model how the anticipated faults can affect the disk. Therefore we introduce array **C** to model the effect of an csf event. **C** is a mapping from sector numbers to sector numbers. The initial value of **C** is the identity mapping. When a csf event occurs a sector number will be remapped to another sector number. So the physical disk will retrieve the contents from the location mapped into by **C**. To describe the effect of an dam event we introduce array **P** which is a mapping from sector numbers to set of information items that can be stored on a sector plus a special information item cd indicating that the sector contains corrupted data. As in the specification of stable storage we also need a variable **pds** indicating the current state of the physical disk and a variable **pbf** for storing the current physical sector number. More formally:
   $$Q_{PD} : (\{\mathbf{P}[i] : i \in PSN\} \rightarrow PHY \cup \{cd\}) \times (\{\mathbf{C}[i] : i \in PSN\} \rightarrow PSN)$$
   $$\times(\mathbf{pds} : \{idle, retr, error\}) \times (\mathbf{pbf} : PSN)$$
   $\mathbf{C}[i] = j$: the control system maps sector i to sector j. $\mathbf{P}[i] = v_i$: physical sector i contains information item v_i. $\mathbf{pds} = idle$: the physical disk is waiting for an event to occur. $\mathbf{pds} = retr$: the user has requested some contents of the physical disk and the physical disk is currently $retr$ieving them. $\mathbf{pds} = error$: the user has requested the contents of a location before the physical disk has responded to a previous request.

3. **Initial States:**
   $$IQ_{PD} \stackrel{\text{def}}{=} \forall i \in PSN.(\mathbf{P}[i] = dflt \wedge \mathbf{C}[i] = i) \wedge \mathbf{pds} = idle$$
   All sectors contain the default data item $dflt$ and the control system has not been affected by control system fault.

4. **Transitions:**
   Figure 3 illustrates the transitions of the physical disk.

5. **Validity conditions:**
   $$V_{PD} \stackrel{\text{def}}{=} R_{PD} \rightarrow G_{PD}$$
   $$R_{PD} \stackrel{\text{def}}{=} \Box(pds = retr \rightarrow (e \neq rP(psn) \wedge e \neq wP(psn,d)))$$
   The rely condition R_{PD} expresses that the user never generates the request and write events before the physical disk has responded to a previous request.

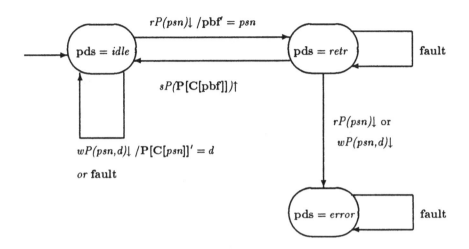

Fig. 3. Transitions of the physical disk, where
  fault stands for $(csf(psn)\downarrow /C'[psn] = j)$ or $(dam(psn)\downarrow /P'[psn] = cd)$, for some $j \in PSN$.

$G_{PD} \overset{\text{def}}{=} \Box(e = rP(psn) \rightarrow \Diamond e = sP(\mathbf{P}[\mathbf{C}[psn]]))$
The physical disk then guarantees that the user will get eventually a response to a request.

Correctness As seen in sect. 3.2 one must define the condition NFO that expresses that the anticipated faults never occur. NFO is defined as follow:
$NFO \overset{\text{def}}{=} \Box(e \neq dam(psn) \wedge e \neq csf(psn))$
For correctness of relative refinement one has to prove $[I \wedge NFO]_\delta \rightarrow [A]_\alpha$ where $\alpha : E \times E_{PD} \rightarrow E$ and $\delta : E \times E_{PD} \rightarrow E_{PD}$. The proof of this is given in the full paper and goes intuitively as indicated in section 2.5, i.e., NFO and $\Box TR_{PD}$ (the DTL formula corresponding to fig. 3) are taken together resulting in a new state-transition relation which is the same as fig. 3 except that the **fault** transitions are removed. Comparing this new state-transition relation with that of TR (the DTL formula corresponding to fig. 2) shows that these are the same except that states and events have another name.

3.6 Application: Third Step

Introduction In this step, the second stage in our development of the fault tolerant system, we specify the layer that detects the faults that we assumed could affect the physical disk (the anticipated faults); this layer is added in bottom-up fashion to the physical disk specified in section 3.5. The detection layer acts as a sort of "interface" between the user and the physical disk. It stops the machine when an anticipated fault is detected by the detection mechanism, i.e., the whole system (detection layer plus physical disk) stops when such a fault occurs. This is called a *fail-stop imple-mentation* [7]. It also informs the user which kind of anticipated fault has occurred. As seen above, there are two classes of anticipated faults. Consequently there are two kinds of detection mechanisms. The first one checks whether the contents read from the physical disk are corrupted, i.e., detects errors due to damage of the disk surface. This is done with a cyclic redundancy mechanism [7]. The second one checks whether the contents read from the physical disk originate from the right location. This is done using an address checking mechanism [7] which encodes the location of the contents of the physical disk inside these contents.

Specification The detection layer consists of three parts: the first part checks whether the data retrieved from the physical disk is affected by a corrupt data fault (the fault that damages the disk surface), using a cyclic redundancy check (CRC) mechanism [7]. The second part checks whether the data retrieved from the physical disk is from the correct physical location, i.e., whether it is affected by a disk control system fault, using an address checking (ADR) mechanism [7]. The third part prevents further access by the user of the physical disk when one of these two mechanisms detects a fault by having the detection layer act as "interface" between the user and the physical disk; the detection layer refuses to communicate with the user and the physical disk when such faults occur. Furthermore this part gives a message to inform the user which anticipated fault has occurred.

The protocol of this interface between user and physical disk is as follows. If the user wants to read the contents of some physical sector it generates an rD event for the detection disk layer (the interface). This layer generates after receipt of this event an rP event. That event is received by the physical disk. The physical disk then signals with an sP event to the detection layer that it has retrieved the contents of that physical sector, upon which the detection layer signals with an sL event to the user that the contents are retrieved. The same holds mut. mut. for the writing of data onto the physical disk. The events will be explained below. We also introduce logical sector numbers; these logical sector numbers will be needed in the fourth step, but we give them already here. In the fourth step, when the detection layer detects that data from a physical sector number is affected by a disk surface damage fault, the correct data will be written to another physical sector number. In order to retrieve these contents from this new location *logical* sector numbers are introduced. When contents are stored at a new physical sector the logical sector number will be pointing to this new sector. So actually the data are retrieved from their logical sector (number). In this section however, the mapping between the logical sector numbers and the physical sector numbers will be the identity mapping because they are not needed here. The specification of detection layer is $DL_{fs} \overset{\text{def}}{=} M_{DL} \wedge V_{DL}$ where M_{DL} and V_{DL} are defined below:

1. **Events:**
   $$E_{DL} \overset{\text{def}}{=} \{rD(lsn)\!\downarrow, sD(dc)\!\uparrow, wD(lsn,d_1)\!\downarrow, rP(psn)\!\uparrow, sP(c)\!\downarrow, wP(psn,d)\!\downarrow$$
   $$: lsn \in LSN \wedge psn \in PSN \wedge dc, d_1 \in LOG \wedge c, d \in PHY\}$$
   where LSN is the set of logical sector numbers: $([1, ..., LSNMAX])$, LOG the set of data items that the user wants to store on, or retrieve from, the physical disk and PHY the set information items that can be stored on or retrieved from the

physical disk. (Note: an item from *PHY* is an crc-encoded and address-encoded item of *LOG*.)

rD(lsn): the request from the user to read logical sector *lsn*. *sD(c)*: the response of the detection layer to the previous request where *c* are the crc-decoded and address-decoded contents of logical sector *lsn*. *wD(lsn,d)*: (user signal) write information item *d* onto logical sector *lsn*. *rP(psn)*: the request from the detection layer to read physical sector *psn*. *sP(c)*: the response of the physical disk to the previous request where *c* is the crc-encoded and address-encoded contents of physical sector *psn*. *wP(psn,d)*: (detection layer signal) write information item *d* onto physical sector *psn*.

2. **States:**

$Q_{DL} : (\mathbf{dls} \rightarrow \{idle, retrD, retrP, sent, stop1, stop, error, write\})$
$\times (\mathbf{pbf} \rightarrow PHY) \times (\mathbf{msg} \rightarrow \{DSDF, DCSF\} \bigcup LOG)$
$\times (\mathbf{lbf} \rightarrow LSN) \times (\mathbf{LS} : LSN \rightarrow PSN)$

dls stands for detection layer state, i.e., the current state of the detection layer. **dls** = *idle*: the detection layer is waiting for an event from the user to occur. **dls** = *retrD*: the user has requested some contents and the *D*etection layer is *retr*ieving them. **dls** = *retrP*: the detection layer has requested some contents and the *P*hysical disk is retrieving them. **dls** = *sent*: the physical disk has *sent* the requested contents and these contents are correct according to the detection layer, i.e., not corrupted by the anticipated faults. **dls** = *stop1*: the physical disk has sent the requested contents and these contents are not correct according to the detection layer, i.e., at least one fault has affected the contents. **dls** = *stop*: the detection layer will not repond to any request from the user or physical disk, i.e., it *stops*. **dls** = *error*: the user has requested the contents of a location before the detection layer has responded to a previous request, or the physical disk has responded to a request not given by the detection layer. **dls** = *write*: the user has signaled that some data has to be *writ*ten onto the physical disk and the detection layer is taking care of that. **msg** is a variable indicating the contents which the user has requested, or, if the contents are not correct, which anticipated fault has occurred, i.e., *DSDF* upon a *D*isk *S*urface *D*amage *F*ault and *DCSF* upon a *D*isk *C*ontrol *S*ystem *F*ault. **pbf** is a variable to store the crc-encoded and address encoded contents of a physical sector. **lbf** is a variable to store the logical sector number from which the user has requested the contents. **LS** is a mapping from logical sector numbers to physical sector numbers.

3. **Initial states:**

In the initial state the detection layer is ready to receive events from the user and the mapping between the logical sector numbers and the physical sector numbers is the identity mapping.

$IQ_{DL} \stackrel{\text{def}}{=} \mathbf{lds} = idle \wedge \bigwedge_{i \in PSN} \mathbf{LS}[i] = i$

4. **Transitions:** Are described in fig. 4. In this figure transitions of the form $e[c]/a$ occur. The meaning of this transition is that when event e occurs and condition c holds then action a will be performed. The intuitive meaning of **ok** is that contents just retrieved from the physical disk are not affected by the two kinds of fault, of **error** is that contents are affected. The **uwrite** transition is the signal of the user towards the detection layer that data has to be written. The **dwrite**

transition is the signal from the detection layer towards the physical disk that data has to be written.

To describe the two detecting mechanisms as transitions, the set $ADR \stackrel{\text{def}}{=} LOG \times PSN$ and the following functions are needed (see [7] for more information about this CRC-coding):

$CC : PHY \rightarrow Bool$ (CrcCheck): used to check whether data from the physical disk is damaged by a disk surface fault. $CD : PHY \rightarrow ADR$ (CrcDecode): used to decode the CRC-coded physical data into ADR format. $CE : ADR \rightarrow PHY$ (CrcEncode): used to encode data in ADR format into physical CRC format. $AC : ADR \times PSN \rightarrow Bool$ (AdrCheck): used to check whether data is read from the correct physical location. $AD : ADR \rightarrow LOG$ (AdrDecode): used to decode data in ADR format into LOG format. $AE : LSN \times LOG \rightarrow ADR$ (AdrEncode): used to encode a physical sector number and a information item given by the user into ADR format.

5. **Validity conditions:**

$V_{DL} \stackrel{\text{def}}{=} R_{DL} \rightarrow G_{DL}$

$R_{DL} \stackrel{\text{def}}{=} \Box(e = rP(psn) \rightarrow \Diamond e = sP(\mathbf{P}[psn]))$

The rely condition R_{DL} expresses the fact that when the detection layer requests the contents of a physical disk sector it eventually gets these contents.

$G_{DL} \stackrel{\text{def}}{=} \Box(e = rD(lsn) \rightarrow \Diamond(e = sD(AD(CD(\mathbf{P}[\mathbf{LS}[lsn]])))))$

The guarantee condition G_{DL} expresses the fact that, when the user requests the contents from a logical sector, the detection layer eventually sends the contents of the physical sector to which this logical sector number is mapped.

Correctness As seen in sect. 3.2 one needs the condition NED that expresses that no errors are detected. This condition is defined as follows:

$NED \stackrel{\text{def}}{=} \Box(\bigwedge_{i \in PSN}(CC(\mathbf{P}[i]) \leftrightarrow \mathbf{P}[i] \neq cd) \wedge (AC(CD(\mathbf{P}[i]), i)) \leftrightarrow \mathbf{C}[i] = i)$.

For correctness one only have to prove that $NFO \rightarrow NED$ holds.

3.7 Fourth Step: Error Recovery Layer

Introduction In this step we specify the error recovery layer. This is the layer that tries to correct the errors detected by the detection layer. The technique we use for error recovery is that of the *mirrored disk concept* [7]. This mirrored disk concept is as follows: instead of one physical disk and corresponding detection layer, we maintain N physical disks with identical contents and N corresponding detection layers ($N > 1$). In case some information can no longer be retrieved from one disk, the information is still available on another one. The user requests some contents from the error recovery layer. The error recovery layer selects a disk from which it can retrieve these contents. Then it requests these contents from the corresponding detection layer of that disk. The detection layer requests the contents from the physical disk and checks whether the contents are correct. The detection layer signals if the contents are correct and, if not, it will signal which error it has detected. If the contents are correct the error recovery layer will send them to the user and is then ready for new requests from the user. As seen before the detection layer can detect two kinds of errors. The error recovery layer will react as follows on these errors:

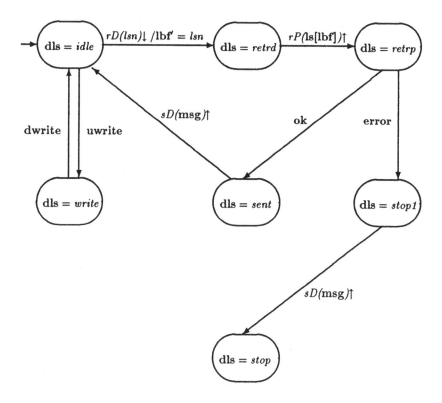

Fig. 4. Transitions of the detection layer where
 ok stands for $sP(c) \downarrow [CC(c) \wedge \neg AC(CD(c), \mathbf{LS[lbf]}))]/\mathbf{msg}' = AD(CD(c)))$,
 error stands for $sP(c) \downarrow [CC(c) \wedge AC(CD(c), \mathbf{LS[lbf]}))]/\mathbf{msg}' = DCSF$ or
  $sP(c) \downarrow [\neg CC(c)]/\mathbf{msg}' = DSDF$,
 uwrite stands for $wD(lsn, d1) \downarrow /\mathbf{pbf}', \mathbf{lbf} = CE(AE(lsn, d1)), lsn$ and
 dwrite stands for $wP(\mathbf{LS[lbf]}, \mathbf{pbf}) \uparrow$

ad (1) First, the error recovery layer selects another disk from which it can retrieve
the requested contents and, when the corresponding detection layer signals that
the contents are correct, the error recovery layer writes these contents to another
location of the affected disk. In order to retrieve these contents from this new
location *logical* locations are introduced. When contents are stored at a new
physical location the logical location will be pointing to this new location. So
actually the data are retrieved from their logical location. Subsequently, the error
recovery layer sends the contents to the user and is ready to receive new requests
from the user. When the detection-layer of the second disk also reports an error,
the error recovery layer will react as described in *ad(1)* and *ad(2)* depending on
the kind of error detected.

ad (2) First, the error recovery layer disables the faulty disk and next it selects
another disk from which it can retrieve the requested contents; when the corre-

sponding detection layer signals that the contents are correct, the error recovery layer will pass them on to the user. When the detection-layer of the second disk also reports an error the error recovery layer reacts as described in *ad(1)* and *ad(2)* depending on the kind of error detected.

This error recovery process only works if we make the following assumptions:
(I) In order to store the contents on a new physical location enough spare locations should be available on an affected disk.
(II) Furthermore, the following must always hold in order to recover the *ad(1)*-type of error on a disk or to retrieve the contents from a logical location: for all logical locations there exists at least one non-disabled physical disk that has correct data stored on that logical location. This condition guarantees that, each logical location contains correct data (on which disk we don't know, but it is a non-disabled one and it is not a disk whose type 1 error has to be repaired).

Specification The error recovery layer acts as interface between the user and the N detection layers of the N physical disks. The user requests with an *rR* event the contents of some logical sector. Upon receipt of this event, the error recovery layer requests these contents with an *rD* event from one of the non-disabled detection layers. This detection layer responds with an *sD* event. As seen in the third step there are three possibilities:

1. If this *sD* event is a message saying that the (to this detection layer correspond- ing) physical disk has been affected by a disk control system fault then this detection layer will be disabled and the error-recovery layer will send an *rD* event to another non-disabled detection layer.
2. If the *rD* event is a message that the (to this detection layer corresponding) physical disk has been affected by a disk surface damage fault then the error recovery layer requests the contents with an *rD* to another non-disabled detection layer until it finds a detection layer that responds with the correct contents. Then the error recovery layer can "repair" the physical disk that has been affected by a disk surface damage fault by generating an *wR* write event with the correct data to the same logical sector number of the corresponding detection layer of that physical disk. The design decision we make is that the detection layer has to find the spare physical sector to which these contents can be written. After that, the error recovery layer responds with an *sE* event to the request of the user.
3. If *rD* event contains normal data the error recovery layer will respond with an *sE* event that it has retrieved the requested contents.

The user signals with an *wE* event to the error recovery layer that some data have to be written into a logical sector. The error recovery layer generates an *wD* write event with these contents to all non-disabled detection layers to ensure that the corresponding physical disks have identical contents. These physical disks have of course stored these contents not on the same physical sector but on the same logical sector.

The error recovery layer will not be specified in detail because it is rather lengthy. Only the validity condition will be given.

Validity Conditions:

$V_{ER} \stackrel{\text{def}}{=} R_{ER} \rightarrow G_{ER}$

$R_{ER} \stackrel{\text{def}}{=} \Box(\text{e} = rD_i\,(lsn) \rightarrow \Diamond\text{e} = sD_i\,(c))$

The rely condition R_{ER} expresses that when the error recovery layer requests some contents from a detection layer then the detection layer eventually responds to that request.

$G_{ER} \stackrel{\text{def}}{=} \Box(\text{e} = rE(lsn) \rightarrow \Diamond\text{e} = sE(\mathbf{P}[\mathbf{LS}_i[lsn]])))$

In that case the error recovery layer can guarantee that the user will get the requested contents.

Correctness As seen above the error recovery process is only correct under certain restriction on the occurrence of faults. Computations in which the error recovery process doesn't work are: computations in which a physical disk has an error of type 1 and has no spare locations to store the correct contents, or in which a disk has an type 1 error and all the other disks are disabled. Thus condition REC is as follows

$REC \stackrel{\text{def}}{=} \Box(\forall lsn \in LSN.\exists i \in \mathbf{Ena}.CC_i(\mathbf{P}[\mathbf{LS}[lsn]]) \wedge AC(CD(\mathbf{P}[\mathbf{LS}[lsn]]), lsn)$

This expresses that for all logical sector numbers there exists a non-disabled disk that has correct data stored on that logical sector.

The condition that there are enough spare locations will be included in the condition NED of the detection layers because we have made the design decision that the detection layer is responsible for finding the spare sectors.

For correctness of the final implementation one must prove, as seen in sect. 3.2, the following assumptions:

$(NFO \leftrightarrow NED$: perfect detection,

$(\neg NED \leftrightarrow REC)$: perfect recovery and

step (1): implementation I is a relative refinement of A.

4   Conclusion

In this paper we have shown that it is possible to formally specify the development of a fault tolerant system. We have used Stark's formalism in a special way in order to achieve this. The part originally intended to specify liveness properties is used for deletion of faulty and undesirable computations. This also enables us to prove correctness of an implementation that couldn't be proven correct otherwise using standard techniques, because it is impossible to prove that an implementation with faulty and undesirable computations can implement in some sense a specification that specifies only good and desirable computations.

Acknowledgements

I would like to thank Henk Schepers and Ruurd Kuiper; Amir Pnueli and all other anonymous referees for their comments.

References

1. M. Abadi and L. Lamport. The existence of refinement mappings. In *Third annual symposium on Logic in Computer Science*, pages 165–175, July 1988.
2. B. Alpern and F.B. Schneider. Defining liveness. *Information Processing Letters*, 21(4):181–185, 1985.
3. A. Cau, R. Kuiper, and W.-P. de Roever. Formalising Dijkstra's development strategy within Stark's formalism. In R. C. Shaw C. B. Jones and Tim Denvir, editors, *Proc. 5th. BCS-FACS Refinement Workshop*, 1992.
4. E. Diepstraten and R. Kuiper. Abadi & Lamport and Stark: towards a proof theory for stuttering, dense domains and refinements mappings. In *LNCS 430:Proc. of the REX Workshop on Stepwise Refinement of Distributed Systems, Models, Formalisms, Correctness*, pages 208–238. Springer-Verlag, 1990.
5. E.W. Dijkstra. A tutorial on the split binary semaphore, 1979. EWD 703.
6. D. Harel. Statecharts: A visual formalism for complex systems. *Science of Computer Programming*, 8(3):231–274, 1987.
7. P.A. Lee and T. Anderson. *Fault Tolerance Principles and Practice*, volume 3 of *Dependable Computing and Fault-Tolerant Systems*. Springer-Verlag, second, revised edition, 1990.
8. S. Lee, S. Gerhart, and W.-P. de Roever. The evolution of list-copying algorithms and the need for structured program verification. In *Proc. of 6th POPL*, 1979.
9. P.R.H. Place, W.G. Wood, and M. Tudball. Survey of formal specification techniques for reactive systems. Technical Report, 1990.
10. H. Schepers. Terminology and Paradigms for Fault Tolerance. Computing Science Notes 91/08 of the Department of Mathematics and Computing Science Eindhoven University of Technology, 1991.
11. E.W. Stark. *Foundations of a Theory of Specification for Distributed Systems*. PhD thesis, Massachusetts Inst. of Technology, 1984. Available as Report No. MIT/LCS/TR-342.
12. E.W. Stark. A Proof Technique for Rely/Guarantee Properties. In *LNCS 206: Fifth Conference on Foundations of Software Technology and Theoretical Computer Science*, pages 369–391. Springer-Verlag, 1985.

Specification and Validation of a Security Policy Model

Tony Boswell

Logica Cambridge Limited, Betjeman House, 104 Hills Road, Cambridge, CB2 1LQ.

Abstract. This paper describes the development of a formal security policy model, in Z, for the NATO Air Command and Control System (ACCS): a large, distributed, multi-level-secure system. The model was subject to manual validation, and some of the issues and lessons in both writing and validating the model are discussed.

1 Introduction

One of the most common applications of formal methods is in the development of secure systems (29% of UK projects using Z according to [1]), where a formal security policy model is one requirement for certification at some higher levels of assurance. With the increasing emphasis on appropriate use of formal methods for safety-critical systems, the development of such systems is likely to require similar approaches and face similar issues to those encountered in the security field. The security policy model forms part of the specification of the a system, and was therefore written as a high level representation, to be applied, in this case, to components of ACCS as well as to the system as a whole. The Formaliser tool (see [4]) was used to provide syntax and type-checking facilities, but the remaining validation was performed manually.

The formal validation of a formal security policy model would ideally be part of the system development. However given the lack of suitable mature, 'industrial-strength' tools and the cost of a formal validation activity, informal validation generally represents a suitable compromise. The aim in this case was not to provide formal proof of theorems, or even to discharge proof obligations formally, but to produce rigorous arguments which could convey a suitable level of confidence without incurring the time and effort overheads which would have been required to construct formal arguments. Knowing that validation would be manual, attention was focussed on relevant issues during the initial production and amendment of the model, and attempts were made to ease the validation process by making the model as modular as possible.

2 Background to the System

A security policy model formalises some of the computer security (compusec) requirements from a System Electronic Information Security Policy (which also includes other security aspects such as communications security (encryption, protocols, etc.) and emanations security (TEMPEST)). In this case the model was primarily concerned with describing and integrating the rules for access control. The aim was to cover both mandatory and discretionary access controls (MAC and DAC), based on the Bell & LaPadula model [2]; integrity controls based on the Clark & Wilson model [3]; and the use of two-person rule for some operations. As a brief summary of the 'input' models, the Bell & LaPadula model describes the well-known 'no read up' and 'no write down' rules (or simple security and '*'- properties) for preserving mandatory security. 'No read up' indicates that no subject is allowed to read from an object with a classification higher than the subject's clearance, and is the usual rule we think of in connection with classified information. 'No write down' requires that information at some classification cannot be written to an object at a lower classification. Bell & LaPadula also add discretionary access controls which govern the modes of access by subjects to objects (e.g. read, write, modify and execute).

The Clark & Wilson model is concerned with maintaining the integrity of a system, and separation of duties and responsibilities. This involves identifying particular 'controlled data items', which are only accessible through particular 'transformation procedures', thus controlling the ways in which the items may be modified and hence controlling integrity.

A number of other security requirements also had to be included: some were lower-level than would be ideal (e.g. modelling of access groups for terminals), but others were more general (such as a need for trusted subjects). Separation of responsibility also needed to be taken further to cover the full range of requirements for two-person rule.

Since the security policy model forms part of the system specification, developed in parallel with the functional requirements, it was neither possible nor desirable to identify the detailed components which comprise the objects and subjects of the system, nor to address controls on particular functions. It was therefore necessary to produce an abstract data structure, and to use primitive operations, which could be mapped onto more concrete elements when interpreting the specification and producing a design. Having done this, the two input models had to be integrated and expressed in terms of the target structure, then further integrated with the additional requirements for two-person rule and other system-specific security requirements. Complexity was thus a significant issue, and a further aim was therefore to use formality to provide a simplified exposition of the integrated rules, without allowing the formal notation to add to the complexity.

The Z version of Formaliser, Logica's interactive formal notation editor, was used to support the development of the model. Formaliser uses a syntax-directed approach to editing, ensuring that only legal syntax is entered, and provides additional type checking facilities which can be applied at the schema level or below (e.g. for individual predicates). The advantages of using such a tool are well known, and confirmed by the experience on this project.

3 Technical Approach

Development of the model was primarily a practical activity: the aim was to produce the finished product, rather than to research different approaches, and the time available was correspondingly limited. This dictated that a comparatively simple approach should be taken, to minimise the risk of problems arising from the method itself. In addition, it was known that validation would be done manually, producing an informal argument; and it seemed that this stage would benefit from simplification of the expressions used, with an emphasis on using modularity to achieve self-contained units (in the form of schemas or function definitions, for example) wherever possible.

The first step was to distil some fundamental, abstract constraints into a natural language description, and from these to derive suitable, loosely object-based data structures which would also steer a natural validation strategy. This activity provided a rapid vehicle for experimenting with concepts, and also provided basic documentation in the early stages of the model, enabling other members of the team to gain a high-level understanding of the approach and its intended direction. In parallel with the initial description, basic Z schemas were produced to define types and their relations, and to sketch the form of a state and its security properties. The security requirements were also loosely ordered for implementation, with the idea of adding them in layers.

The initial description took objects as the basic entities in the system (the fundamental class), and considered subjects as a subclass of objects. This makes sense because in certain instances subjects can be operated upon by other subjects (e.g. when their clearance is changed), in which case they are treated as objects for the purposes of security checks. Further subclasses of objects were distinguished (e.g. commands), and subjects were further split into processes and users. Processes were the natural active agents in the system, and inherited properties from users on whose behalf they act.

At this point the structure could be represented diagrammatically, which was a benefit in understanding a rather complex system of inheritance relationships between the entities. Although the visual information was deducible from formal properties, pictures give an additional viewpoint, which is useful in itself, and emphasise the very structural properties which are important for much of the validation. Diagrams were used purely for visualising the model in its early stages, and were not included in the final documentation. A more complete and systematic means of representation[1], showing more of the system context, and suitable for inclusion in the natural language description of the model, would have been even more useful. In the author's opinion, the use of diagrams as explanatory material (helping to bridge semantic gaps[2]) is an important topic, and worthy of further exploration as an aid to integrating formal methods into an industrial process design. The particular difficulty seems to be in identifying useful and meaningful diagrams (or diagraming methods) which have a suitably clear interpretation in Z terms such that, for example, changes to either representation imply the changes necessary in the other.

Having established the basic data structure for the active entities, the remainder of the system state was defined (comprising tables of subject-object accesses, permissions of subjects to objects, and so forth). A number of functions were also defined to act as 'syntactic sugar', making predicates more readable, and providing an additional benefit as 'interface definitions' for accessing properties of entities.

The fundamental approach was then to identify the static security properties (e.g.

---

[1] For further discussion of this area see for example [5], [6] and [7].

[2] For a more detailed discussion of semantic gaps and where they arise, see [8].

those in the Bell & LaPadula model), and the dynamic security properties (e.g. that an object usually remains at the same classification during a state transition) and to express these from two different points of view: the state based and the operation based. Thus operations would be carried out within dynamic security constraints, and the resulting state should differ (in security-significant ways) from the start state only by the changes due to the operation. Describing two overlapping perspectives means that a certain amount of duplication can arise, but also gives two natural approaches to validation. When wholly manual argument is the aim, it is easier to be able to cross-check two such views than to work with a single complex view.

The properties of a secure state were identified, and a state transition schema defined. As an example, the simple security property (no read up) must hold in any secure state, and is represented statically as:

$$
\begin{array}{|l}
\hline
\_SSP \_\!\!\_\!\!\_\!\!\_\!\!\_\!\!\_ \\
\quad SystemElements \\
\hline
\quad \forall\, proc : ProcessId;\ obj : ObjectId;\ mode : AccessMode\ | \\
\qquad (proc, obj, mode) \in cat \wedge mode \in ReadControlModes\ \bullet \\
\qquad (clearanceOf\ proc)\ dominates\ (secLevelOf\ obj)\ \vee \\
\qquad (proc, obj, mode) \in activeTwoPersonRuleOps \\
\hline
\end{array}
$$

('cat' is the current access table which records all currently active accesses by subjects to objects in particular modes. The two-person rule complication is discussed below.)

Hence the system state was defined as the combination of static security rules applied to elements of the system: *SystemState* $\hat{=}$ *SSP* $\wedge$ *STARP* $\wedge$ ...

To control complexity, the checks necessary for mandatory and discretionary access controls during operations were then defined separately for privileged and unprivileged subjects. Generally speaking, checks for each type of access were defined separately and an appropriate combination taken to define an overall check for each operation. Parcelling up constraints into checking functions in this way helped to separate different aspects of the model (such as the security constraints on individual operations, state security constraints and invariants), which provides another aspect of modularity to help with validation. In addition, the use of these standard checking functions means that a checklist based on intrinsic properties (such as the correct domain of a function) can be applied whenever the checking function is used, thus helping to make manual validation systematic.

The dynamic checks for each type of operation were then of the form:

$$
\begin{array}{|l}
\hline
\_MACChecks \_\!\!\_\!\!\_\!\!\_\!\!\_ \\
\quad \Delta SystemState \\
\quad \_MACCanRead\_ : ProcessId \leftrightarrow ObjectId \\
\hline
\quad \forall\, proc : dom\ processNamed;\ obj : dom\ objectNamed\ \bullet \\
\qquad (proc\ MACcanRead\ obj) \Leftrightarrow \\
\qquad\quad (clearanceOf\ proc)\ dominates\ (secLevelOf\ obj)\ \wedge \\
\qquad\quad (writeLevelOf'\ proc)\ dominates\ (secLevelOf\ obj) \\
\hline
\end{array}
$$

Since there are a number of aspects (e.g. MAC and DAC) in the checks related to an operation, a further level of 'bundling' was added, so that a set of top-level checking functions was defined, with the structure:

```
┌─ Checks ──────────────────────────────────────────────
│ ΔSystemState
│ _ canRead _ : ProcessId ↔ ObjectId
├────────────────────────────────────────────────────────
│ ∀ proc : dom processNamed; obj : dom objectNamed •
│     (proc canRead obj) ⇔
│         (proc MACCanRead obj) ∧
│         ((instigatorOf proc, obj) DACOkayForMode Read)
└────────────────────────────────────────────────────────
```

Each operation was then defined by two schemas: the first specifying the invariants for the operation, and the second stating the (security-relevant) effects. Thus, for reading, the invariants ensure that properties of the system elements involved do not change:

```
┌─ ReadInvariants ──────────────────────────────────────
│ ΔSystemState
│ Checks
├────────────────────────────────────────────────────────
│ objectNamed' = objectNamed
│ apt' = apt
│ currentSubjects' = currentSubjects
│ ...
└────────────────────────────────────────────────────────
```

Schemas defining individual operations then identified the state components involved (subject, object, access mode, etc), and applied the appropriate checks, requiring that operation invariants also hold. Although in many cases the predicates describing an operation are basically simple, given that the checking functions have already been defined, incorporating two-person rule adds a number of complications. This format enabled the two aspects to be separated, which was important because of the incremental way in which the model was produced.

The operations were then combined with a collection of general state-change invariants to produce a schema defining a secure state transition. Security-significant changes in state components (e.g. a change to the contents of an object) were identified and interpreted as the result of one of the available operations. The constraints for this operation (along with the general invariants) were then required to be satisfied for the change to be acceptable.

Having completed the basic Bell & LaPadula requirements, the addition of integrity rules was relatively straightforward. Extra attributes were added to system entities, a static integrity requirement defined (like *SSP* above), dynamic checks written (like *MACCanRead* in *MACChecks* above), and the top-level checks (such as *canRead* in *Checks* above) redefined to include the dynamic check. A similar process was required to add privileges, which enable trusted subjects to break some of the standard security rules in controlled and limited ways. Thus the top-level checks changed in a comparatively simple way from the form:

$$(proc\ canOperateOn\ obj) \Leftrightarrow (proc\ MACCanOperateOn\ obj)\ \wedge$$
$$((instigatorOf\ proc,\ obj)\ DACOkayForMode\ mode)$$

to:

$$(proc\ canOperateOn\ obj) \Leftrightarrow ((proc\ MACCanOperateOn\ obj)\ \vee$$
$$(procMACCanPrivOperateOn\ obj))\ \wedge$$
$$((instigatorOf\ proc,\ obj)\ DACOkayForMode\ mode)\ \wedge$$
$$(proc\ integrityOkayFor\ mode)$$

Adding two-person rule was not quite as straightforward. The basic notion behind two-person rule is that some operations require the collusion of two different operators (probably from particular defined roles). The other security checks are concerned only with single operations and single users, and the model of state transitions was set up with this in mind. Two-person rule checks, however, have to co-ordinate the actions of two separate users, and the solution adopted was to introduce two extra commands: one to request an operation under two-person rule, the other to grant or deny permission. Having made this step, the two-person rule constraints could be contained within a single checking function, and applied as an alternative way of satisfying an operation schema. Thus the template for an operation schema had the final form:

$$< change\ in\ system > \Rightarrow$$
$$(< request\ for\ change > \wedge < two\text{-}person\ rule\ not\ required > \wedge$$
$$< security\ okay >)$$
$$\vee$$
$$(< request\ is\ approval\ for\ two\text{-}person\ rule\ operation > \wedge$$
$$< subject\ is\ an\ appropriate\ approver >)$$

Although the incremental approach was useful in allowing foundations to be laid in the form of the more well understood rules, before moving on to the more exploratory areas, it did have some disadvantages. As the later rules were clarified, the roles of entities in the model tended to change in certain (usually slight) ways. This meant that the number of 'special case' predicates increased, and at times required fundamental changes to simplify the model. Indeed, it would have been useful to have the time to rewrite the model after the final rules had been established. This is, of course, a well-known and oft-heard cry from software developers, and the same sort of 'smoothing principles', which help avoid escalating complexity due to enhancements, can be applied to formal models (e.g. ensuring modularity with low coupling and high cohesion). However when dealing with items such as formal models, which appear early in the lifecycle, the question of whether time should be set aside for a final rewrite is perhaps worthy of careful attention.

4 Validation

Syntax and type-checking having been performed by Formaliser as the model was developed, the validation consisted of two parts: the definition of an initial state, and an informal argument that each operation could produce a valid, secure final state when applied to a valid, secure start state. Definition of an initial state was straightforward for a trivial example and, because of the difference between trivial and realistic states, the argument was oriented towards making explicit the rules for forming suitable (trivial or non-trivial) initial states.

The operation validation was mainly based on an informal extraction of pre-conditions for each operation, and a demonstration that a suitable final state could be deduced from the start state by applying a minimal set of modifications, as suggested by the predicates in the operation definition. An element of redundancy was present in both state and operation definitions, and this made the operation validation easier by allowing separate views of the model to be considered. The presence of a predicate in an operation schema indicated a suitable modification to the state and allowed a suitably self-contained view of the operation (also useful when validating changes to the model); the static constraints were made similarly self-contained.

A number of additional checking techniques were used, in either systematic or ad hoc manner, and included the following (not too surprising) checklist points:

1. Type subsetting should be appropriate (e.g. looking for functions applied to arguments drawn from a superset of their domain, or for domains which should be constrained to a suitable subset).
2. Tables and functions must have their members well defined (e.g. all processes making current accesses must be in the domain of the function representing known processes).
3. Invariants on entities must be initially established by the operations which create the entities.
4. In state change schemas, dashed and undashed items should be correct (especially where dashed and undashed items are mixed in the same predicate).
5. Where quantification is made over a subset of a domain set, elements from outside the subset should be correctly dealt with (excluded or handled elsewhere).
6. Where properties of an object are changed by an operation, the other properties should be explicitly constrained, or irrelevant to security.

It seems almost unnecessary to say that the validation process revealed many errors and inconsistencies in the original form of the model, leading to approximately 30 itemised changes. Most of these were comparatively minor, such as constraining the domain of a quantified variable, or removing unnecessary predicates. A few had more far-reaching consequences however, and led to additional invariants, and hence the need for further work in checking the implications of these constraints on other functions.

5 Other Issues and Reflections

There were a number of peripheral issues which the project touched upon to varying degrees, and which seem worthy of mention here, along with some retrospective views and lessons.

Schema Size: Although there was a deliberate effort to keep individual schemas small and cohesive, the size inevitably grew as the model progressed. [1] includes the results of a survey of the 'proportions' of Z models which indicated that most schemas were between 6 and 10 lines long, with none over 20 lines. Most ACCS schemas were between 11 and 20 lines long, with several over 20 lines. Since conventional wisdom favours the smaller schema, it is perhaps of interest to briefly consider the reasons why several 'giant' schemas (>20 lines) were included. These schemas comprised:

1. Those which defined checking and 'syntactic sugar' functions: these were simply collections of similar functions consisting of a large number of separate definitions. They could have been separated into a number of individual schemas, but whether this would be beneficial is unclear.
2. The state transition schema: this also included a large number of separate definitions to identify security-significant changes. With hindsight, this could perhaps have been split into a number of smaller schemas.
3. The schema describing the basic system elements: this was large due to the constraints on membership of tables such as the current access table. The schema could have been split up, but (since it was in fact 21 lines long) there seems no compelling reason to do so.

The author's general conclusion is that large schemas are acceptable where they consist of separate definitions of entities which are genuinely connected by the theme of the schema, and where the entire content of the schema does not have to be absorbed at one time in order to understand the model.

High and Low-Level Requirements: A security policy model can play at least three different roles. It can model the subject area, defining what it is to be secure; it can specify required properties of the system; and it can specify functionality. This 'overloading' is a reflection of the fact that practical security measures do involve mixed levels of abstraction (from access control rules to blocking covert channels in an implementation).

Not surprisingly, the different potential roles result in a tension between abstraction and 'completeness' (i.e. lower-level details) in the model. Although a security policy model generally does not address all areas of security for a system, it is intended to act as a baseline for the areas it does cover, and a pressure towards detail is thus generated. Another cause of added detail can be questions of interpretation. For example: if the model represents processes in some particular way, then the question arises as to how these should be mapped onto the processes supported by an operating system. In clarifying the interpretation questions (e.g. are processes reusable in the system?), or catering for a range of possible mappings, additional low-level detail tends to build up. There is a further pressure for detail which can arise from the detailed requirements of individual application areas within a system: these are frequently very closely tied to functional requirements, and the pressure should be resisted.

In each case, a compromise position needs to be reached, and the question is thus how best to achieve it. For the ACCS model, the defence of abstraction was generally to show that the particular detailed behaviour was allowed, or that undesirable behaviour was implicitly prevented. The concern of those who argue for inclusion of detail is primarily that requirements may otherwise be forgotten. This suggests that the way in which the model is documented could again be important: a method is needed of recording detailed requirements in the context of an abstract model. The same problem affects many requirements specifications, and one possible remedy is the use of modelling tools which support annotations attached to model elements, and links between the elements. The use of such features has been investigated as part of the ASAM project[3], which is concerned with methods and tools for safety argumentation, using both formal and informal arguments.

More generally however, a way is still needed of integrating formal methods (including both modelling and specification) into a satisfactory process design. The needs of the development process are intrinsically linked to the ways in which formal methods should be used on a project (for example, a sequence of increasingly detailed models might be produced, or an abstract model with 'modules' which could be instantiated with a separately specified lower-level mechanism[4]). In the case of low-level details, the best approach would seem to be to combine an informal technique for recording and managing detailed requirements as well as the more abstract requirements in a model.

General Scaling Issues: The model comprised just over 65 schemas in total, and the feasibility of manual validation relied very much on the structure. It was advantageous to have the form of the model reflect both the fundamental data structures, and the structure of checks during operations. It seems likely that a more fully object-oriented notation could provide better support for this. The ability to break up the validation process for an operation into chunks was of considerable importance in making it manageable, particularly within the time constraints. The way in which top-level security checks were built from more basic constituents was found to be useful in splitting up the problem into suitable steps, as was the high-level division of an operation schema into ordinary and two-person rule cases.

Having said this, the size of the model was, in the author's opinion, about as large as could be managed by a manual approach, even when validation is informal. Some thought was therefore given as to how both the resulting confidence in the model, and the feasible model size might be increased, without having to move to formal, machine-based proof activities. The key to this seems to be in the systematic documentation of final and intermediate results, so that conclusions drawn en route to a goal are reusable, and the structure of the argument (and hence its relation to the properties of the model) is clearer. It is possible that the results of the ASAM project mentioned above could be usefully applied to this sort of validation. In particular, the tools developed by ASAM use a specific form in which arguments are presented to make their structure apparent, and this could help both in setting out arguments, and in identifying reusable components.

---

[3] A research project with York University and the Civil Aviation Authority under the DTI Advanced Technology Software Engineering programme (IED/1751).

[4] For discussion of an approach to reuse through the use of frameworks and architectural templates, see [9].

6 Conclusions

The ACCS project demonstrated the use of Z in producing a formal security policy model, and succeeded in completing an informal validation by manual methods. Two principal conclusions emerged regarding the implications for building the model and limits on the size of models susceptible to this approach. Firstly: the needs of manual validation can used to guide the development of the model, directing it towards a structure which views to be separated, and in which constraints are collected into cohesive units (whether schemas, functions, or type structure). Secondly: the size of the model was important and, although modularity assists the validation, the 65 schemas examined appear to represent close to the maximum feasible size.

Other lessons which emerged emphasised the usefulness of diagrams, and suggested that it could be fruitful to explore the use of more systematic methods of diagraming, to help bridge gaps between informal views of a system and a Z model, and to assist informal reasoning and reviewing in the early stages of model development. The tension between high and low-level requirements was also noted, and the need for integration of formal methods into a practical industrial process design identified as an important requirement for producing suitable compromise positions.

References

1. Barden, R., Stepney, S., Cooper D.: The Use of Z. Z User Workshop York 1991. Ed. J Nicholls. Springer-Verlag (1992).
2. Bell, D.E., LaPadula, L.J.: Secure Computer System: Unified Exposition and Multics Interpretation. MTR-2997 Revision 1. (March 1976).
3. Clark, D.D., Wilson, D.R.: A Comparison of Commercial and Military Computer Security Policies. Proceedings of the IEEE Symposium on Security and Privacy (1987).
4. Flynn, M., Hoverd, T., Brazier, D.: Formaliser - An Interactive Support Tool for Z. Z User Workshop Oxford 1989. Ed. J Nicholls. Springer-Verlag (1989).
5. Semmens, L., Allen, P.: Using Yourdon and Z: an Approach to Formal Specification Z User Workshop Oxford 1990. Ed. JE Nicholls. Springer-Verlag (1991).
6. Polack, F., Whiston, M., Hitchcock, P.: Structured Analysis - A Draft Method for Writing Z Specifications. Z User Workshop York 1991. Ed. J Nicholls. Springer-Verlag (1992).
7. Stepney, S.: Entity Relationship Diagrams and Z - The Best of Both Worlds. Logica Advanced Software Engineering Division Technical Report 3 (1991).
8. Penny, D.A., Holt, R.C., Godfrey, M.W.: Formal Specification in Metamorphic Programming. VDM '91 - 4th International Symposium of VDM Europe Proceedings. Springer-Verlag (1991).
9. Garlan, D., Delisle, N.: Formal Specifications as Reusable Frameworks VDM '90 - 3rd International Symposium of VDM Europe Proceedings. Springer-Verlag (1990).

Experiences from Applications of RAISE

Bent Dandanell[1], Jesper Gørtz[2], Jan Storbank Pedersen[1], Eld Zierau[2]

[1] Computer Resources International A/S, Bregnerødvej 144, DK-3460 Birkerød,
Denmark, e-mail: raise@csd.cri.dk
[2] CAP GEMINI TECHNO LOGIC A/S, Produktionsvej 2, DK-2600 Glostrup, Denmark,
e-mail: ez@sypro.dk

Abstract. The formal method RAISE and its associated specification language, RSL, are assessed by a number of consumers in the LaCoS project. The consumers apply the technology to their industrial applications and document their experience in a number of assessment reports. This report is based on the consumers' response to using RAISE and RSL and covers the first 1 1/2 year of the LaCoS project.

1 Introduction

The LaCoS[3] project is an ESPRIT[4] II project aimed at demonstrating the feasibility of using formal methods for industrial development of software. The basis of LaCoS is the RAISE[5] method, language and associated tools produced as part of an ESPRIT I project. The partners in the LaCoS project are divided into *consumers* who are applying RAISE and *producers* who are further evolving RAISE based on the industrial experience gained by the consumers.

The consumers and their current applications are:

- Bull SA (Concurrent data server)
- Inisel Espacio SA (Image exploitation)
- Lloyd's Register of Shipping (Condition/performance monitoring predictive system and Safe monitoring and control systems)
- MATRA Transport SA (Automated train protection)
- Space Software Italia SpA (Tethered satellite system)
- Technisystems Ltd. (International shipping transaction system)

The RAISE producers are:

- CRI A/S
- BNR Europe Ltd.
- CAP GEMINI TECHNO LOGIC A/S

During the LaCoS project a number of applications of RAISE are conducted by the consumer partners within different industrial areas. The objective of these

---

[3] Large-scale Correct Systems using formal methods
[4] European Strategic Programme for Research and Development in Information Technology
[5] Rigorous Approach to Industrial Software Engineering

applications is to assess the utility of RAISE in real applications[6]. Each application has an associated consultant who helps the consumer in using RAISE and gathers information on the use of RAISE. The consumers document their experiences in a series of assessment reports. Additional information is provided in the form of course evaluation schemes and monthly management reports and from work packages that involve both consumers and producers. The collective experiences of the consumers and the consultants are presented in a series of experience reports. This paper is based on the second experience report, [DGP92], which covered the period from the beginning of the LaCoS project in July 1990 to January 1992[7].

The consumers' objectives for participating in the project are briefly described in section 2. Section 3 discusses key issues that are relevant for technical managers who are considering introducing formal methods. Section 4 describes experiences with the RAISE technology in more detail. Finally section 5 describes further development of RAISE within LaCoS.

2 Application Objectives

All the consumer partners aim to evaluate RAISE — discover its strengths and weaknesses, assess its utility for their products in their particular application domains. At the same time, their continual feedback helps the producers improve the technology. More detailed aims are to evaluate

- the use of the RAISE specification language (RSL[8]) in requirements analysis and capture, including the discovery of errors, omissions and contradictions, the production of better natural language requirements from specifications, and the use of specifications to assist in effective communication between client and developer
- the applicability of the RAISE method to the consumer's particular domain, including generating domain specific methodological guidelines, producing generic, reusable specifications and developments of these, and assessing appropriate and practical degrees of rigour
- the adequacy of the RAISE method and tools to produce good low level designs and target code, where typical quality attributes are maintainability, speed, reconfigurability, reliability, correctness and having good associated documentation
- the ease with which the RAISE language, method and tools can be learned by staff and assimilated into companies. This involves the relation of RAISE to existing standards, methods and tools
- the effect of RAISE on their productivity.

These items are not listed in order of importance — different partners have different priorities.

---

[6] An overview of RAISE can be found in [HPS92] and a more complete description of the LaCoS project can be found in [DaG91].

[7] Preliminary experiences from the initial part of the project are documented in [CDG91], of which [CDG91a] is a shorter version.

[8] A complete tutorial and reference manual may be found in [Rlg92].

The people involved in the LaCoS applications have varying levels of education and training. The average engineer has a masters degree in a mathematics-related field (Physics, Computer Science or Mathematics itself). The prior knowledge of formal methods varies from several years of academic experience to no knowledge at all.

A somewhat fuller description of the applications may be found in [DaG91]. Readers interested in more detail should contact the authors.

3 Key Issues

'Has the time come to introduce formal methods in our company? Should we use formal methods in this specific project?' To support these vital decisions this paper attempts to answer a set of technical key questions about the usefulness of RAISE.

Not all of them can be answered satisfactorily at this stage in the LaCoS project, but at least some indication of likely answers may be given.

3.1 How does RAISE fit into the software lifecycle?

The RAISE method as described in the "RAISE Method Manual" [BrG90] follows the waterfall model, with its strengths and weaknesses. In particular, it encourages a clear formal specification of requirements before development is started. It is also necessary to specify the general structure and the complete interfaces before separate development of parts can be undertaken. This means that in practice a great deal of time is spent apparently in the "initial specification" phase although in practice much design investigation is being done at the same time. In fact the method as applied seems to be very strongly iterative.

The method manual deals mainly with development but is weak on how to formalise requirements[9] and has little to say about testing or maintenance. The strong points are on separate development and refinement techniques, which must be supplemented or adapted for proper managerial control.

On the other hand RAISE is a very flexible method for specific tasks such as requirements elicitation and analysis, specifying and reasoning about a design or developing a complete subsystem. Used that way RAISE should fit in with most other techniques and methods.

RAISE does not attempt to provide a complete CASE environment — obvious shortcomings in this respect are e.g. an encyclopedia and graphical tools. As a notation and technique in the developer's personal toolbox some poor man's tools are desirable, e.g. portable programs for formatting and syntax check of simple RSL ASCII text files.

3.2 Does RAISE conform to standards and recommendations?

RAISE is not yet recommended by any existing international standards, but it seems consistent with prominent standards such as ISO 9001, IEC65A (secretariat) 96,

---

[9] Unfortunately it is much easier to say what characterises a good specification than it is to describe how to produce one!

IEEE 1012-1986, ESA PSS-05 [ESA91] (see [Man92]). With respect to the demanding interim UK MoD DefStan 00-55 ([MoD91]) RAISE appears to come closer to conformance than other methods (see [Gra92]). Work has now started on obtaining BSI and ISO standards for RSL.

3.3 Which types of developments is it good for?

RSL is a extensive language where several previously more or less unrelated approaches have been successfully unified. This gives a coherent language that can be used in many styles but still remaining within the same framework.

RSL is a wide-spectrum formal language that fully integrates functional and concurrent features and support for modularity. The method and the supporting tools provide the opportunity to refine abstract specifications into concrete programs.

The target appears to be high-quality — not cost-sensitive — software that lends itself to mathematical modelling and reasoning, e.g. embedded systems with mainly functional or synchronisation requirements.

Specifications can be prototyped by means of translators or developed into low-level designs by modelling target language features. The first actual translations have now been made and justification of properties and refinements has started.

3.4 How much does it cost initially?

To use RAISE a high investment in training and skilled personnel is necessary.

A RAISE team displays various competence profiles and includes the roles of project manager, systems analyst, developer, target language expert, RAISE expert, QA reviewer — all of whom should be experienced in their field, possibly excepting a minority of developers working under guidance. Some of these roles are well suited for external consultancy.

Depending on whether basic or full knowledge of RSL is required, three to twelve months of practical experience is needed before a team member becomes completely effective.

Prerequisites for learning and using RSL are a good understanding of software engineering, basic knowledge of mathematical logic, an open mind and motivation for abstract work.

3.5 What is the effect on productivity?

Use of formal methods means more time spent on specification and design which implies early discovery of design errors and ambiguities in requirements.

Adherence to the RAISE method means that requirements or design changes are documented in their proper place, so the inevitable backtracking becomes visible.

Testing cannot be avoided and must be done in the same scale as usual, but fewer errors should be found and accordingly less error correction will be necessary.

There are no consolidated findings on productivity yet.

3.6 What is the effect on the quality of the end product?

It is yet too early to evaluate the quality of the produced systems since work is still being done on all the applications.

Formal specification of the system has increased the quality of the system documentation and requirement documents by defining a consistent terminology for the domain.

3.7 How efficient are the tools?

The tools provide a useful environment for entering, editing and browsing specifications. The consumers have rated the RAISE toolset well beyond a prototype version for most of its components.

The tools are, except for a few specialized tools, based on SG [ReT88] and hence use syntax directed editing. One such tool, the module editor, has been found particularly useful in learning RSL, whereas some users later found syntax directed editing constraining.

Building the RAISE library on top of Oracle was found to result in too much overhead compared to the facilities gained compared to basing it directly on Unix files.

The syntactic and semantic checks performed by the module editor have increased the quality of the specifications produced. The checks are similar to those performed on a program by a compiler front end.

3.8 Is it suited for requirements specification?

When establishing and documenting the requirements to a system, writing a formal RSL specification has helped in clarifying the requirements, even in cases where the requirements are ultimately defined in informal natural language. In particular, attempting to formalize requirements often leads to an early identification of difficult areas in the application.

When discussing requirements with an end-user, one cannot expect to be able to use an RSL specification directly, except in rare cases. However, a formal requirement specification can be used as the basis for writing a natural language one, often including graphical representations of the system, that can be discussed with the end-user.

RSL specifications may be used for prototyping, but in order for the construction of the prototype not to be too time consuming, it requires that only certain parts of RSL are used. This is the case both if the prototype is obtained by use of one of the automatic translators that are part of the RAISE tools and if it is hand-coded in a high-level language like ML.

3.9 Is it suited for special investigation and QA?

An RSL specification can express the functional aspects of a system that is to be developed. Such a specification can hence be used for analysing the functional requirements for consistency and other properties. Non-functional requirements, such as performance requirements, cannot be described in RSL and hence an analysis of these cannot be based on the RSL specification alone.

The verification and validation activities described by the RAISE method help with the fault detection aspects of quality assurance. Also, experience has shown that RSL specifications are well suited for walk-throughs and inspections due to the formality (non-ambiguity) and abstraction of the specifications. However, only people who know RSL can perform such walk-throughs and inspections.

Even when conducting verification and validation on specifications, logical errors or failure to meet a requirement may occur. Such errors may not be detected before the implementation and test of the system, leading to costly error corrections. This problem may be partly solved if executable code is produced earlier in the life-cycle for parts of an RSL specification.

Some work has been done on basing test specifications on an RSL specification, [Fox91]. Several of the test cases were derived from proof obligations. The work is still ongoing.

3.10   Does RAISE help project management?

The decomposition of a system into manageable parts that can be subjected to separate development helps project management. The development of individual parts can be better tracked due to separate development. The method advises a decomposition into a set of separately developed components, but the distinction between the development stages for components is not as clear as was originally anticipated, particularly because development is iterative in nature.

No application has reported difficulties in using RAISE within their existing standards and procedures.

There are no existing metrics that support the estimation of time to be spent in the various stages. There are primarily two reasons for this. Firstly, training in the use of RSL has been an intrinsic part of all applications and hence it is not possible to isolate the pure application work. Secondly, all the applications are still being developed and hence an evaluation of the effort spent cannot be produced yet.

Formal methods are expected to move a great amount of the development away from coding and debugging. Formal methods focus more on the conceptual work. A consequence is that software engineers and managers involved one way or another in formal specification and development must be keen on conceptual work as opposed to trial and error development. The fruit of the work will not be immediately available if it is felt to be the code. The benefits of formality are therefore often not sensed for newcomers in the field before the first executable program emerges.

Formal methods are not a good remedy for poor management. Like any other methods the use of formal methods requires proper procedures and general awareness from management to obtain maximal utilisation.

4   Detailed Experiences

This section addresses detailed experiences with core elements of RAISE. Section 4.1 is about experiences made with the RAISE method and section 4.2 contains detailed experiences made with RSL.

4.1   Experiences with the RAISE Method

The experiences gained using the RAISE method have been quite dependent on the focus of the applications. For safety critical systems there is of course a focus on verification and proofs of critical parts. Other applications focus on possibilities for making prototypes and having clear and precise documentation of complex systems that will help in maintenance and enhancement aspects.

Phase-approach and Waterfall Model The RAISE method has fitted well within most companies' overall company methodologies. This will probably always be the case for most phase oriented methodologies following a waterfall approach.

At the detailed level, however, the method was found too strict. It was found that borders between steps within the phases in practice got blurred, because development was essentially iterative.

The method manual is focused on the intermediate phases concentrating on the technical aspects rather than the pragmatic ones. It is weak on how to create an initial specification from user requirements and how to get from a concrete formal specification to effective executable code.

The method has not covered all ways that RAISE can be applied in a project life cycle. In particular, reverse engineering has been used to good effect in one application. From existing code a series of abstractions were created, and at each level of abstraction appropriate properties were formulated and justified (by hand). This led to the discovery of a potentially critical fault in the code. This had remained undiscovered in a year of testing (and, it turned out, was prevented from being found by testing because of the design of the scheduler). Concurrency shows even more sharply the limitations of testing for finding faults.

Separation of Work Tasks Decomposition of a specification was not found easy — more guidelines would be helpful. As for other aspects these are expected to come when more experience has been gained. In some of the applications decomposition techniques from other methods have been used.

Requirements and Initial Specification For all formal methods a big task is to create the initial specification. The hard part is to achieve the right abstraction level and make a model that describes the system. It requires good knowledge about systems engineering in general as well as knowledge of formal methods and of the application in hand. Therefore it is not surprising that production of the initial specification has been found a hard task, and more guidelines for how to create the initial specification, how to choose style and how to be abstract have been requested. Producing good guidelines is, of course difficult. Generally it is something that can only be taught by examples (of which our stock is steadily increasing) and learnt with experience.

One of the strengths of RSL is that it offers a lot of different styles, but this can also create confusion when doing a specification for the first time. However, several noticed that they would expect to use less time the next time on the basis of knowing RSL better.

In several of the applications there was rewriting of the specification and changing of its style. This was either because the first specification was not appropriate, or as part of an abstraction process. It was in some cases found that it was easier to start out with a concrete model oriented approach for the first specification and then produce a more abstract specification from it. The first specification is used to explore the requirements, test their feasibility by constructing a model, construct a prototype, etc. The more abstract specification is used as a basis for further development.

There have been variations in the form of the initial specifications produced. Some chose to keep at an abstract level where not all functional requirements could be incorporated. Others chose to let the specification have modules with different levels of abstraction in order to capture all functional requirements from the outset.

As expected it was found that RSL was not necessarily useful for communication with users. RSL was mainly used internally for the development team, beginning from the requirements analysis. However, in one case the client was an engineer and in this case it was found quite useful to use an axiomatic specification in discussions of the properties of the system. In the other cases graphical representation or derived natural language was used as communication aid.

For some of the applications the requirements have been changing through the process of specifying the system — for others it has been a matter of extension to already existing systems.

As for other formal methods, most users have found that doing the initial specification has helped to make precise formulations, where ambiguities and inconsistencies in requirements were uncovered.

Development Steps and Design Good design requires different qualities:

- It has to be readable and understandable.
- Its decomposition needs to meet demands for separate development.
- Its structure needs to meet demands regarding translation possibilities.

It is not easy to say whether a design meets the above requirements.

Using RSL in design was found good as documentation of the design. Sometimes the design decisions concerning implementation of abstract data types and invariants can be forgotten during the development process. In such cases the RSL specification is a reminder of the original ideas of the design.

Backtracking is a normal phenomenon in all engineering processes. Adding new requirements can mean that backtracking is necessary. One finding was that in specifications that had been broken into a lot of small components the backtracking was found very costly.

The implementation relation between specifications has been checked to varying degrees. The tools did not yet support justifications, so the justifications done had to be done by hand. Most consumers used inspection and reviews as validation for development steps.

According to the type of application in hand, there are different views on the appropriate rigour for justifications. For applications where the main issue is to create documentation and rapid prototypes, the implementation relation is not very important, while for applications with safety critical aspects, a precise definition and justification of the steps is important.

Though the refinements done have been informal and the justifications have not been formal, it was noted that it was of great help doing them. It has helped to find out what the specification actually meant and to find specification errors.

Translation Not all translation can be done by the translators. There are at the moment only translators for C++ and Ada. There are aspects of RSL that provably cannot be mapped into any programming language, e.g. quantification in general. Depending on the target language there can be problems of mapping into constructs with the same semantics as in the specification, e.g. concurrency constructs. Another problem may be that the produced code does not meet performance and resource requirements.

It was stressed from several of the consumers that prototyping is a very important issue. Prototypes are important in communication with clients and users as well as in the final validation of the specification. This feedback has resulted in the translators now being much more effective for this purpose.

It is also important to notice that translation is not only a question of pushing a button. Knowledge of the target language is necessary in order to develop a translatable RSL specification with appropriate interface functions.

A problem that may arise later is how translated code conforms with coding standards. It may turn out to be hard to enforce such standards if translators are used. An example could be that naming conventions cannot be followed.

Testing Currently the RAISE method has few guidelines for testing, beyond pointing out that testing is by no means unnecessary when using formal methods. In all cases the final system has to be tested against the reality. The errors found will probably be of different character than normally. In the application where a full translation has been made, the interesting errors were the specification errors rather than coding errors in translator generated code. Expectedly, the final findings will also be that less errors are found than normally.

Supporting Toolbox A range of different supporting tools or methodologies have been used. One example is Yourdon structure charts for decomposition. Other examples are flow-chart diagrams and finite automata for analysis of the system. Especially for communication with clients or customers different graphical approaches have been used.

4.2 Experiences with the RAISE Specification Language (RSL)

This section addresses three aspects of RSL: its adequacy for specifying system properties, how easy it is to learn, and how easy it is to use.

Adequacy of RSL All consumers have been able to express their system specifications in RSL. This is mainly due to the wide-spectrum nature of RSL. Particular strong points emphasized were the structuring mechanisms and concurrency parts of RSL. However, some aspects of their requirements have caused difficulties:

- Attempts have been made in RSL at specifying object-oriented features like those of HyperLisp, i.e. polymorphism and dynamic creation of objects. The result was that they were very hard to express and that the RSL specifications constructed could best be characterized as work-arounds.
- A number of the expected target programming languages for a RAISE development have special constructs for handling 'exceptions'. RSL has no such construct, which may make it difficult for the developed program to fully utilize those constructs offered by the target language.
- RSL does not address real-time aspects, which makes an RSL specification incapable of expressing time constraints in a way that can be formally related to the remaining parts of the RSL specification.

Ease of Learning Since RSL is a large language it takes longer to learn than most other specification languages. But as RSL is also more wide-spectrum than those other languages, a longer learning curve was to be expected.

Seeing RSL as a very high level programming language has turned out to be helpful for some in the beginning of the training period.

The fact that RSL typically offers several alternative ways of specifying something is generally a strength, but when learning the language this richness sometimes makes it difficult to choose which constructs to use.

The underlying formal semantics of RSL has been hard to comprehend for those who tried, mainly because the existing documentation [Mil90a] was not adequate. It is not necessary to read the formal semantics to get an intuition of the language, but it is needed in order to get a deep understanding of the language and to answer hard questions. The justification handbook [GeP91] is one aid in this, and other work is proceeding with the aim of providing a more accessible semantic description.

Ease of Use Users of RSL have been satisfied with its ability to express specifications at the desired level of abstraction. The process of abstraction itself may, however, be difficult.

The integration between the concurrency constructs of RSL and the rest of the language was found to be successful, in that people could use the concurrency features as a natural part of their specification. However, certain technicalities, such as the use of 'test' functions in connection with interlocking, were found tricky to use.

Comments in RSL specifications seem to have been the main means of tracing requirements. The current rules governing placement of comments have, however, been found far too restrictive.

The RAISE Tools The core tool, 'eden' is a structure-oriented editor supporting writing and continous type checking of RAISE entities. This editor has been useful as a learning aid for the RSL syntax. Moreover, the checks performed by the module editor have helped remove errors in specifications.

Translation is not comparable to compilation. Even though there are translators for Ada and C++, developers need to have a deep knowledge of the target language.

5 Further Development of RAISE

The future development of RAISE method, language and tools is based on feedback from the applications. In addition two specific issues are being dealt with: systems engineering and integration, and reuse of components.

5.1 Systems Engineering

Current concerns are metrics (for measuring the effectiveness of RAISE in the applications and for project planning) and the relation of RAISE to standards. Future work will look at requirements tracking and specialised methods (for example, for safety critical systems).

5.2 Reusable Components

Work has now started on assembling a library of reusable components. Three main areas have been identified:

- standard data types
- abstractions of particular target language constructs (such as arrays)
- environmental interfaces

Note that a reusable component is typically not just a specification but also a development with target code (or even a range of these).

References

[BrG90]   Brock, S., George, C., RAISE Method Manual, LACOS/CRI/DOC/3, 1990

[CDG91]   Chalmers, D.L., Dandanell, B., Gørtz, J., Storbank Pedersen, J., Zierau, E., Experiences from Applications of RAISE — Report 1, LACOS/CRI/CONS/-13, 1991

[CDG91a]   Chalmers, D.L., Dandanell, B., Gørtz, J., Storbank Pedersen, J., Zierau, E., Using RAISE — First Impressions from the LaCoS Applications, in "VDM'91: Formal Software Development Methods", LNCS 551, Springer-Verlag, 1991

[DGP92]   Dandanell, B., Gørtz, J., Storbank Pedersen, J., Zierau, E., Experiences from Applications of RAISE — Report 2, LACOS/SYPRO/CONS/20, 1992

[DaG91]   Dandanell, B., George, C., The LaCoS Project, LACOS/CRI/BDH/8, 1991

[ESA91]   ESA Board for Software Standardisation and Control (BSSC), ESA Software Engineering Standards, ESA PSS-05-0 Issue 2, 1991

[Fox91]   Fox, C., SCP — Testing Working Paper, LACOS/LLOYD'S/CJF/8, 1991

[GeP91]   George, C., Prehn, S., The RAISE Justification Handbook, LACOS/CRI/-DOC/7, 1992

[Gra92]   Granville, R, Assessment of RAISE against UK MoD DefStan 00-55, LACOS/-
           LLOYD'S/RJG/29, 1992
[HPS92]   Haxthausen, A., Prehn, S., Storbank Pedersen, J., RAISE Overview, RAISE/-
           CRI/DOC/9, 1992
[Man92]   Manero, E., RAISE and ESA Software Engineering Lifecycles, Proceedings of
           the Second Symposium 'Ada in AEROSPACE', pp. 411-437, 1992
[Mil90a]   Milne, R., Semantic Foundations of RSL, RAISE/CRI/DOC/4, 1990
[MoD91]   UK Ministry of Defence, Interim Defence Standard, MoD 00-55, UK Ministry
           of Defence, 1991
[ReT88]   Reps, T.W., Teitelbaum, T., The Synthesizer Generator, Springer Verlag, New
           York, 1988
[Rlg92]   The RAISE Language Group, The RAISE Specification Language, Prentice
           Hall, 1992

Role of VDM(++) in the Development of a Real-Time Tracking and Tracing System

ir. E.H. Dürr * and drs. E.M. Dusink

Cap Gemini Innovation, Rijswijk, The Netherlands
E-mail: durr@fys.ruu.nl

Abstract. This article describes our experience with the use of the formal specification languages VDM and VDM++, in the evolutionary development of a real-time distributed system for the tracing and tracking of load-units in combined road-rail traffic.

1 Introduction

At the Dutch research department of the Cap Gemini Sogeti Group, Innovation Rijswijk, we used VDM [Jones90] and VDM++ [Dürr91, Dürr92a, Dürr92b] for the specification and development in a medium sized project (44 man years) to support the necessary evolutionary development of a tracing and tracking system.

VDM++ is an object oriented extension of VDM especially designed to support parallel and real-time specifications. The risk management principles of the Spiral Method approach [Boehm89] were the basis for our software engineering approach. The project described here is called *CombiCom*, an abbreviation of *Combined Transport Communication System*. The CombiCom project is part of the EC DGXIII Drive II programme for Advanced Transport Telematics (project nr. V2003) [Combi92].

Cap Gemini Innovation is coordinator for this project - a consortium of 7 companies, mainly out of the transport world - and is responsible for the hardware/software implementation.

2 Description of the Problem Domain

The use of the railways for long distance ($\geq 200\ km$) freight transport in Europe has a number of advantages over the road traffic alternative. Especially in environmentally sensitive areas like the Alps, rail is the preferred traffic mode, also in view of increasing traffic demands within the growing European Market. The combination of a long distance rail corridor and local road transport from the terminals on both ends of the corridor (thus a combined traffic mode), could provide an attractive transport offer. There is however one serious problem involved here. Because the load itself, is not accompanied by a driver, there is a "black hole" of information during the rail part of the journey. Nowadays one can only wait at a receiving terminal for the arrival of a train. There is no way available to get early warnings about a possible

---

* and Utrecht University, Department for Computers and Physics

delay. Statistics show that approximately 20% of the freight trains have a delay of more than 15 minutes.

This lack of information compared with road transport, where a driver can give his client a telephone call, immediately after the cause of a delay, makes the use of the combined traffic alternative unattractive for Just In Time logistic applications as e.g. for the transport of fruits, for hazardous goods or the use in tightly coupled production schemes.

The introduction of a real-time information system, together with automatic identification, which monitors the movements of load-units (containers, swap-bodies, semi-trailers etc.) could provide the signalling of deviations from a schedule and inform the traffic agents and their clients at an early moment in time.

The CombiCom project aims at the introduction of such an information system on the corridor Rotterdam-Köln-Verona.

Because the world of combined traffic agents consists of separate companies in each country - affiliated to the railways - there is no central authority available and political reasons exclude a centralised solution all over Europe. We therefore decided to design a distributed system in which each terminal would have a workstation, providing access to commonly shared data. The workstations are linked to each other by a fast X.25 network. Entry and exit of a workstation in the system had to be realised without interuption of the functions of the other nodes. To each terminal a number of so-called Automatic Identification Equipment (AIE) installations is coupled.

The identification is realised in the AIE's by sending a high frequency beam (2-5 GHz) from an antenna to a tag, an electronic device which is attached to the load unit and the wagon. The reflected beam is modulated by the contents of the tag. A concentrator takes care of the translation into the ASCII pattern representing the contents of the tag. There are 128 bytes available in the programmable tag for an (unique) identification number and for some additional information like owner, size, max. payload etc. The reading equipment alongside the railway track is able to provide this information with train speeds upto 280 km/h with a fault rate of less then 1 per million readings.

The CombiCom information architecture provides the terminal agent through a graphical interface, the possibility to enter a so called transport transaction into the system before a load-unit enters the corridor. A transport transaction contains apart from some static identifying information also a planned time table: a combination of locations and times and an allowed time-window. This information is distributed to all locations on this route.

Later the sensor installations provide the system, when the train is on its way, with the real-time observations on the movements of the load-units. Deviations from the planned schedule cause an alarm to be raised. An alarm is an internal event in the system, raised at one of the many nodes of the system. This alarm message is then transferred to the terminal agent responsible for this transport transaction.

A query mechanism is available to obtain information about what transport transactions are planned from other terminals to arrive in the near future and to enquire about the precise position of a certain load-unit.

The system also provides clients of the terminal agents with the possibility to send in bookings and status report requests by EDI messages. Ultimately the system is capable to relay an internal alarm message as an EDI message directly to a client. The various processes involved in the system and their communication links for three nodes are shown in the next figure. (User stands for User-Interface)

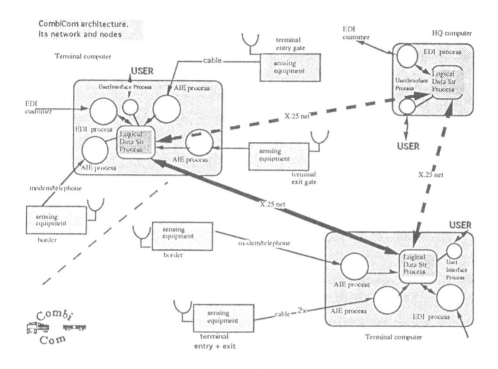

Fig. 1. Important architectural components of CombiCom

3 Role of the Formal Specification in the Design

At an early stage, we became aware of the fact that this system, which operates between several cooperating combined traffic agents in Europe, had a distributed real-time character and the consequences of a failure of the architecture would cause considerable - economic - damage. These requirements led to the decision to use formal specifications for the design and the use of Ada for the implementation. The last choice was also motivated by the fact, that the use of a wide range of different (UNIX) workstations was required. The real-time requirements were concentrated on two items:

1. an incoming stream of data from the readers at any moment.
2. alarms had to be raised within 1 minute on every relevant node.

On the other hand our transport partners had no clear idea at the beginning of the consequences of the introduction of such a system and were unable to describe their requirements. We therefore decided to start with a functional specification of a non-distributed version in VDM. In the course of this activity the logic of the system became clear and we were able to ask the right questions to our transport partners. One could describe this analysis activity as an efficient way of requirement elicitation and formalisation. The next risk-reducing step was to transform this one functional specification into an object oriented distributed specification. With this step the (formal) description of the message passing through the network and the added data structures for the fault-tolerant behaviour (concurrency protocols) also came in. We divided the introduction of the system in three phases (subsystems):

Phase 1: The Wagon Monitoring
Phase 2: The Monitoring of Load Units
Phase 3: The Clients EDI interface.

The phased introduction will enable the transport partners to get accustomed gradually to the full system and provide us with early reactions on the daily behaviour of the system. Each of these phases will consist again of three steps:

1. The description of a protocol for the use of the functions of this phase.
2. The collection of the reactions on this protocol and the derivation of the formal specification of this subsystem.
3. The implementation of this subsystem and the User-Interface.

Because all subsystems are derived out of one global functional formal specification, all the future interactions are already included.

4 Role of the Formal Specification for the Other Partners

From the commencement of the project, it was clear that our transport partners were not able to read a formal specification and didn't want to learn to read it. We therefore invested extra energy in making for them readable representations. These representations were:

- pictorial representations of the system components
- descriptions in internal articles of how the system would behave at the user-interface
- a set of protocol descriptions in which we indicated the input actions the system expects and which reactions it will issue.
- A fairly complete demo, based on the first prototype with which they could 'play' just 5 months from project start.
- Two informal architecture descriptions in the form of reports.

In the reactions it became clear that they appreciated these representations very much. Someone even indicated, that he liked these things much more then other representation like data flow diagrams, ER diagrams and structure charts.

The fact that there was a formal specification was considered very reassuring by the other partners. It was accepted that all questions were answered by our team on the basis of these documents. It gave us the possibility to react on all issues raised long before there was one line of software really running.

In the end an analogous situation as in construction engineering was established. There was a maquette like representation for the users and the construction drawings were only used by the specialists. The formal specification was just our internal "construction" drawing and the users accepted that we needed it for our work. The division of these two target groups for the communication had only advantages: it forced us to make our ideas clear to the transport partners, and prevented us from using all kind of computer jargon and concepts in those presentations.

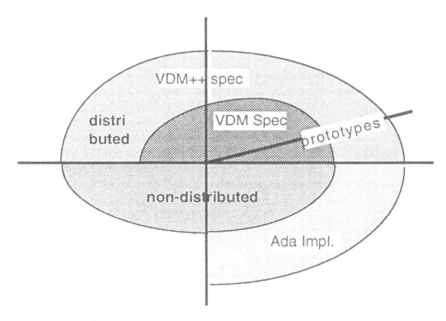

Fig. 2. Our Spiral Approach with Formal Specifications

5 The VDM Specification

Especially in this project it was important to provide early results, to ensure real involvement of the other partners and to get concrete reactions as soon as possible. We therefore aimed at a prototype with a rather complete user-interface and a functionally complete logical structure. We derived this first prototype out of the VDM specification and implemented this in Ada. A graphical user-interface was added - realised with Hypercard[2] - and the communication with the Ada kernel was implemented.

This complete demonstration gave rise to a large number of reactions and enabled our partners to start thinking about the consequences of such a system in their

---

[2] Hypercard is a trademark of Apple Computer Inc, Cupertino CA, USA.

daily work. The EDI messages were agreed upon in their first version and internally these messages were parsed by software generated by Aflex and Ayacc, the Ada counterparts of Lex and Yacc. All the comments and changes were recorded as changes in the formal specification. The formal specification was also the basis for all the answers on questions like: what if...? This formal specification functioned as a description of the logical behaviour of the system in the future. These changes could much more easily be carried out at the smaller specification level, than ever would have been possible on the program level.

The prototype implementation made use of the file-sharing capability of our Local Network, thus creating the illusion of a distributed system. The prototype itself was a collection of Ada tasks running on one machine. Together however they realised the entire functionality of the VDM specification. There was on the other hand no notion of distribution in this software prototype.

The VDM specification contained a number of type declarations, the abstract storage types and the state of the system, together with the essential operations. All operations were specified implicitly and most of types and the state had (rather large) invariants. The size of this functional specification was about 20 pages VDM with some annotations. In principle all the user functionality (and thus the interface functions), could be expressed in a combination of these basic operations.

It appeared to be easy to specify and to alter the system at this level. Annotations were used in the VDM specification to explain the semantics of some of the types. E.g. the type Time: although the name gives a clear indication of what is meant, the system covers more than one time zone thus a more precise choice is necessary. We left the formal specification of the user interface out. This part was documented by a series of screen dumps and underlying Hypercard scripts. The size of the first prototype implementation was approximately 5 Kloc. of Ada code, split over 20 packages.

6 The VDM++ Specification

The Object Oriented Analysis/Design concepts proved to be very useful for this kind of a distributed system. In VDM++ Objects can be stand-alone active virtual machines, so a mapping of the real-world components of the system on to VDM++ classes was carried out quite naturally. After this identification of the Classes we had to distribute the functionality of our first one node functional specification over the already defined set of system entities. E.g. the 'big' map in the state of the one node had to be spread over a number of sub-maps in all the individual nodes of the distributed version. The same holds for the combination of local operations: together they had to ensure the same pre and post conditions as the high level one node specification. This "Splitting" operation was carried out along the principles indicated in the "Irish School of the VDM" [Air91].

At the level of this VDM++ specification the real network behaviour with the queues, the addressing scheme, the internal messages, the sensor protocols and the BNF EDI grammars came in. Because we also made the step towards a concurrent design, we had to ensure correctness of the operations for creation and updating over the collection of local states in the nodes. We made a choice for the use of the

Hierarchical Time Stamp Ordering Algorithms, because we wanted to avoid locking [Cell88]. The invariants included in the Algorithmic descriptions in this book were used in the specification. VDM++ also enables the inclusion of real-time requirements. We used these to derive from the higher level descriptions the upper bounds for the execution time of the set of local operations and the speed of the network.

Although the VDM++ specification did experience quite a number of versions, the initial steps were made quite naturally and it really supported the iterative process. Because we aimed at an Ada implementation in the end there was somewhere in the middle of the version line a shift from the pure OO concepts of VDM++ towards the more limited language constructs of Ada (8x). When Ada 9x appears on the market (with its protected records), this move will not be necessary anymore. The move was only syntactical in those cases were an active object was implemented by a (static) task. For the more passive objects, packages were used, and we had to imitate the Class and instantiation principles in package declarations with private types. We consequently avoided the use of pointers in our Ada implementation of the cooperating kernels, because we couldn't find a secure solution for a restart after a local failure [Holz89].

We made a VDM++ specification for each of subsystems and were able to reuse a large number of class definitions in the subsequent phases. The total number of Classes was about 40.

7 The Ada Implementation

Because we already anticipated in the VDM++ specification the more limited Ada environment, the mapping of Classes onto Tasks and Packages involved in most cases a syntactical translation. The VDM++ workspace (in our case a hierarchy of workspaces) specified the main program structure and the declaration and startup of the tasks on the different nodes was derived from this part of the specification. The usefulness of inheritance was limited in our system. In the cases it appeared we simply copied the super state components also in the package representing the subclass and did the same with the operations as far as they were used in the subclass. In some cases in which the inheritance contained much overriding a variant record structure with discriminants offered an elegant implementation.

The ultimate size of the Ada code will be approximately 40 Kloc of Ada code excluding the user-interface software. The translation process went rather smoothly. Each team member took one or more Classes as his/her responsibility and started writing the Ada Specification. Then this Ada specification was reviewed by the entire team and compared with the VDM++ specification. Suggestions were implemented in a new version and a new review followed. After some iterations the specification was accepted by the team and put formally under version control. Then the coding of the body was carried out along the same lines. All pre and post conditions out of the VDM++ specification appeared also in the Ada code. If possible the precondition was programmed in an expression which was the parameter in our own Assert function. The second parameter was the name of the package together with the operation name. A failure in an assert raised an exception during the production phase of the code. At the end this Assert function will be redefined as one of the logging facilities. Our experience is that this approach prevented lots of small mistakes especially in signalling unexpected input values.

8 Role of Proof Obligations

VDM is a method which asks for proofs, not only for refinement steps but also on one level of specification. Satisfyability, for example has to be shown [Jones90, Jones91], and is defined as:

- for each valid input a valid output has to be defined;
- invariants have to be maintained under operations.

The operations in the functional specification were analysed with respect to implementability and satisfyability, and during reviews the questions about them were kept in mind.

Especially, the fact that invariants had to stay invariant under an operation uncovered a lot of oversights, which, if no formal specification was done, no programmer would have seen. The post conditions of the operations could be easily related to the invariants.

The design step to a distributed system delivered the proof obligation of the retrieve and abstract function. Here, no formal proof was given, but an informal discussion about correctness was part of the reviews. The derivation from one global specification into a number of individual classes was done by using the calculus of the Irish VDM school for the crucial data structures.

The concurrent version added a number of proof obligations for the deadlock freedom and liveliness of the operations under arbitrary interleaving. By reusing the proofs of the timestamp ordering algorithms we managed to prove these properties for our system. VDM++ also adds a number of its own proof obligations, especially those related with inheritance and concurrency.

The proofs for the class state invariants versus the set of operations was only in details different from the VDM satisfyability proof.

It was the obligation of each programmer to show that the proposed Ada implementation of a procedure satisfies the method post condition and if applicable the invariants of a modified data structure. In many cases this was so obvious that no formal proof was given. These would have been only a citation of the post conditions of some assignments. In more difficult cases the proof was really carried out during the team reviews and this approach prevented many mistakes.

9 Conclusions

We have concluded from this project, which is still going on, that the combination of a Spiral approach, the Chief Designers Team structure and the use of VDM and especially VDM++ towards an Ada implementation enabled us to produce this complicated system in a short time (1 year).

The difficulties normally involved in clarifying the user requirements were substantially reduced. The fact that in an early phase of the project the logic of the architecture were described was very helpful in many discussions with the transport partners.

The number of errors found in the reviewed software modules was very low; a further test period for the next year will provide some statistics in the near future.

Although it will be difficult to prove, we have the feeling that the formal specification with OO concepts helped us enormously in the choice of the right abstractions and generalisations during the design period. This resulted in a much smaller system (less code) than we would have been able to achieve in the classical way.

As a last conclusion: *Formal specifications are a really useful Software Engineering tool, but beware of providing a playground for mathematicians.*

References

[Air91]   Micheàl Mac an Airchinnigh, *Tutorial Lecture Notes on the Irish School of the VDM*, VVDM'91 Formal Software Development Methods vol 2, Lecture Notes in Computer Science nr. 552, Springer Verlag Berlin, Germany.

[Boehm89] Barry W. Boehm, *Software Risk Management*, IEEE Computer Society Press nr. 1906, Washington, USA .

[Cell88]   W. Cellary, E. Gelenbe, T. Morzy, *Concurrency Control in Distributed Database Systems* , Studies in Computer Science and AI nr. 3, North-Holland, Elseviers Science Publishers, Amsterdam, 1988.

[Combi92] CombiCom Internal Deliverable S.1.X, Formal specification of the CombiCom architecture, CombiCom Consortium.

[Dürr91]   E.H. Dürr, *VDM++, Language Reference manual*, Utrecht University, Faculty of Physics and Astronomy, Internal Report RUU-FI-91-6.

[Dürr92a] E.H. Dürr and J. van Katwijk, *VDM++, A Formal Specification Language for Object Oriented Designs*, Conference Proceedings Tools Euro '92 in Technology of Object-Oriented Languages and Systems,Tools 7, Prentice Hall International,1992.

[Dürr92b] E.H. Dürr and J. van Katwijk, *VDM++, A Formal Specification Language for Object Oriented Designs*, IEEE Conference Proceedings CompEuro '92 in Computer Systems ans Software Engineering, IEEE Computer Society Press nr 2760, California,1992.

[Holz89]   R. Holzapfel, G. Winterstein, *Ada in safety critical applications*, Ada in Industry, proceedings of the Ada-Europe Conference 1988, Cambridge University Press, Great Britain.

[Jones90] C.B. Jones, *Systematic Software Development using VDM*, Prentice Hall International second edition, 1990.

[Jones91] C.B. Jones, K.D. Jones, P.A. Lindsay, R. Moore, *Mural, A Formal Development Support System*, Springer Verlag, London, 1991.

The Integration of LOTOS with an Object Oriented Development Method

Mikael Hedlund

Ascom Tech AG
Freiburgstrasse 370
3018 Berne, Switzerland
hedlund@tech.ascom.ch

Abstract. This paper describes the first step in an attempt of transferring the formal description technique (FDT) LOTOS from a research department to a development department within the Ascom Group. The existing development methods used within the department had to be taken into consideration. It was found that LOTOS would fit best as a complement to the Object Oriented (OO) development method used - Objectory[1]. Methodical and representational aspects of integrating LOTOS with this method were studied and are presented in the paper.

1 Introduction

The Informatics division of Ascom Tech AG - a member of the Ascom Group - participated in the ESPRIT project Lotosphere, with the aim of developing and promoting the formal description technique LOTOS (see [1]). Within this project, methods and tools were developed together with trial applications. As an internal continuation of this work, a project, in which a first attempt of transferring the LOTOS technology to a development department at Ascom Hasler - a telecommunications company within the group - has been carried out. The department is engaged in the development of products in the network management area. The objective of the project was to investigate if and how LOTOS could be used in the development process at the department, with the overall aim of increasing quality of software specifications.

The project was divided in two phases, to allow management on the development side to assess the progress and to decide on continuation. The first part consisted of analysis of existing methods, and finding ways of using LOTOS within these; it was a necessary prerequisite that LOTOS could be used in conjunction with the development methods that are currently used within the department. The results of the analysis showed that LOTOS could potentially be used as a complement to the object oriented method *Objectory*. This meant that a possible integration of LOTOS and Objectory had to be studied. This integrational problem can be viewed from two perspectives: a methodical - where and how can LOTOS be used within the Objectory method? and a representational - how can we best represent those OO constructs that are used in Objectory models? The work in the first part resulted

---

[1] Objective Systems SF AB, Sweden

in a suggestion on how these problems could be solved. In the second part of the project, a modeling task was carried out, with the aim of improving and verifying the ideas presented in the first part. The result of the whole project, provided a basis for the management of the development department to decide whether or not to incorporate LOTOS in the development process.

In this paper we will describe the work on integrating LOTOS with Objectory seen from the two perspectives mentioned above. We will not describe the LOTOS language, design method and tools, but refer to [2] as an introduction to the language, [3] as an introduction to the design method and [4] for a description of the tools.

2 Integrational Aspects

2.1 A Methodical Perspective

It was clear at an early stage of the project that the current development environment should be taken as an input; it would not be feasible to use LOTOS as a stand-alone method. A preliminary analysis showed that LOTOS may be used as a formal component in the OO method Objectory. Objectory divides the development trajectory into three main phases (see [5]):

1. Analysis
   - Requirement analysis
   - Robustness analysis
2. Construction
   - Design
   - Implementation
3. Testing

The analysis phase is divided in two parts, the first resulting in a requirement model and the second in an analysis model. The input document to the analysis phase is a requirement specification, normally written in natural language. This forms the basis in the creation of the requirement model which consists of a *Use Case model*, a *Problem Domain Model* and a *User Interface Description*. The construction phase is divided in design and implementation, resulting in a design model and an implementation model respectively. In the last phase, the testing of the implementation results in a test model. The most important concept of the method is that of a *use case*, which is a part of the use model. A *use case* describes a sequence of events, caused by a user utilizing one specific part the systems functionality - the description consists of informal text. The full set of use cases completely describes the functionality of the modeled system. These use cases are mapped onto objects both in the analysis and the design models.

Each of the phases were investigated systematically, to find out exactly how and where LOTOS could be used, taking the characteristics as input. In the analysis phase of Objectory, it is stated that object descriptions should be non-formal, so the usage of LOTOS is excluded from this phase. In the design sub-phase, though, it is allowed to use formal descriptions. However, in Objectory, no formal description techniques are used. Instead, object behaviour is described through a combination of *informal text, interaction diagrams* and *state-diagrams*. Interaction diagrams are used for describing the sequencing of messages or stimuli being sent between objects, a state diagram describes the possible state changes of an object due to external or internal stimuli and informal text is used for describing the functionality of operations (methods). The idea, was to combine all these semi-formal descriptions in the design phase into one formal description in LOTOS. We presented two alternative ways of doing this. The first alternative is to completely replace the diagrams and text by LOTOS; hence using LOTOS as a *design* tool. The second alternative is to use LOTOS as a *verification tool*; a LOTOS specification would be derived from the diagram descriptions and tested in a simulator. Feed-back on the test results would then be given to the Objectory designer. The use cases, represented in LOTOS, would be used as test cases for the complete specification. That is, by running a test case against the specification, we can show that it implements the use case corresponding to the test case. Hence, the major strength of using LOTOS in this context, is that it makes specifications less ambiguous and it adds testability.

There was concern at the development department that LOTOS would be too difficult to use for the average designer and implementer. The approach of using LOTOS as a verification tool, means that the designer would still work with the usual diagram techniques, and only one or a few LOTOS experts would be working on the verification part. Hence, this approach is the most likely one in a continuation of the project. An interesting possibility with this approach is to have parts of the LOTOS code automatically generated through the support of a tool. This possibility may be explored within the existing supporting tool for Objectory - *OrySE*.

3 The Representational Perspective

Object oriented description techniques are in general characterized by the concepts of *objects, classes* and *inheritance*; where an object represents some modularization of specification, classes a collection of objects and inheritance a relation for promoting successive modification of specifications. Objects have a state that is hidden from its environment (*encapsulation* or data hiding). The behaviour of an object is observed and affected through an interface (of operations). LOTOS is a language based on constructs describing processes and process communication. Unfortunately, LOTOS was designed before the ideas of OO techniques were established, which means that there is no support for modeling OO constructs in LOTOS. In order to use LOTOS within the framework of Objectory, we had to investigate ways of representing these constructs in LOTOS. There exists no precise description of the semantics of Objectory constructs, so we had to rely on intuitive interpretations of these. Furthermore, not all OO constructs may be fully represented in LOTOS. As a consequence of this, testing of a LOTOS specification, representing an Objectory model, may not lead to the discovery of all types of errors that may appear in the original OO model. There may also be errors in the LOTOS specification that do not have corresponding errors in the Objectory specification. However, a sub-set of errors found in the testing of the LOTOS specification, will have a correspondence in the Objectory model. Finding this sub-set of errors, should lead to an improvement of quality in Objectory models, and this is the justification for using LOTOS.

3.1 Representation of Object Classes

Even though LOTOS is not OO, there are features of the language that makes it suitable for writing specifications in an OO style. The behaviour of a process is observed and affected through a well defined interface (of gates), which makes it suitable for modeling object behaviour. Communication between objects can be modeled by process communication through synchronization. To enable the modeling of Objectory constructs in LOTOS, we presented a set of *mapping rules* from OO constructs to LOTOS and a set of *usage rules* defining how these constructs may be used. Some of the previous work on OO LOTOS, can be found in [6], [7], [8] and [9]. The examples presented below, give a simplified description of the representation used (partly based on work described in [10] and [11]).

The following is a simple example of the representation of a class template in pseudo-LOTOS. The class represents a set of displays, with attributes for position on screen and size, and operations for moving and re-sizing the display.

```
process Display1 [rec, send] (ownId) :=
create !ownId ?objId;
Display2 [rec,send] (objId, X-init, Y-init, Size-init) |||
Display1 [rec,send] (ownId)
endproc

process Display2 [rec, send] (ownId, X ,Y ,Size) : noexit :=
Display3 [rec, send] (ownId, X, Y, Size)
>> accept X, Y, Size in
Display2 [rec, send] (ownId, X, Y, Size)
endproc

process Display3 [rec,send] (ownId, X, Y, Size)
                    exit(Coordinate, Coordinate, Integer) :=
rec
        !Resize              (* Operation Name *)
        ?param:PARAMETER     (* Parameter *)
        ?sendId:OBJECTID     (* Sending object id *)
        !ownId;              (* Own Id *)
(* Place for operation definition *)

exit (X ,Y, Size)

[]
rec
        !Move                (* Operation Name *)
        ?param:PARAMETER     (* Parameter *)
        ?sendId:OBJECTID     (* Sending object id *)
        !ownId;              (* Own Id *)
(* Place for operation definition *)
```

```
exit (X ,Y, Size)
endproc
```

An object class template is represented as a triple of LOTOS processes: $< P_1, P_2, P_3 >$, where P_1 serves as an abstraction to achieve encapsulation and is used when instantiating the class, P_3 is the re-usable part and is used when creating sub-classes. P_2 is an auxiliary process which is used to handle a problem that occurs in sub-classing, due to the recursive nature of the template definition (see below). In the first process, we find that the *Display2* process is spawned using the LOTOS interleaving operator $|||$. In parallel with the spawned process, *Display1* calls itself recursively to allow further instantiations of the process. The operations of the object is defined in the third process *Display3*.

The attributes of the class is represented as formal parameters of the second and third processes of the process triple. An additional formal parameter is the unique identifier of the object instance (*ownId*). Communication between objects take place over the gates *rec* and *send* using special channel processes (see next section). The set of operations belonging to an object is modeled as a choice expression in which each individual clause represents the behaviour for one particular operation - modeled as an action prefix expression: *header; Body*. The definition of the operations have been left out in this example. These would otherwise consist of operation calls to other objects and possibly return of results. An operation is completed by an exit statement in which the state is passed back to the second process and caught in the accept statement. An object class is instantiated by synchronization on the gate *create* in which a unique identifier for the instance is passed as a parameter.

As an example of inheritance, a sub-class *colourDisplay* can now be defined using the third process definition of *Display* as follows:

```
process colourDisplay1 [rec,send] (ownId) : noexit :=
  create !ownId ?objId;
  colourDisplay2 [rec,send] (objId, xInit, yInit, sizeInit, colourInit) |||
  colourDisplay1 [rec,send] (ownId)
endproc

process colourDisplay2 [rec,send]
  (ownId, X,Y ,Size ,Colour) : noexit :=
colourDisplay3 [rec,send] (ownId, X,Y,Size,Colour)
  >> accept X, Y:Coordinate, Size:Size, colour:Colour in
     colourDisplay2 [rec,send] (ownId, X,Y,Size,Colour)
endproc

process colourDisplay3 [rec,send]
      (ownId, X,Y ,Size ,Colour)
      :exit(Coordinate, Coordinate, Size, Colour, ownId) :=

(Display3 [rec,send] (ownId, X,Y,Size) (* Inherit Display *)
  >>
(* Accept attributes of display, add Colour attribute in exit *)
accept X, Y:Coordinate, Size:Size in exit (X,Y,Size,Colour))
```

```
[]
rec (* Extended behaviour *)
        !changeColour
        ?col:PARAMETER
        ?sendId
        !ownId ;
(* Place for operation definition *)

exit(X,Y,Size,Colour)
endproc
```

The new class extends the *Display* class with one attribute (*Colour*) and one operation (*changeColour*). Note that the attributes of the display process is caught in the accept statement and extended by the attribute *Colour* in the exit statement. It is now possible to see why we are using an additional process to hold the operations of *Display*. Should we only have had one process, then, after calling either of the operations defined in *Display* (*Resize* or *Move*) in an instance of *colourDisplay*, the available operations would only be those of *Display*, not including the extensions in *colourDisplay*.

3.2 Object Communication and Composition

There is a problem in LOTOS when we try to compose objects (or processes) in a behaviour expression so that objects can communicate in an arbitrary manner. It should be possible for all objects to communicate with all other object in the most general case. This is not possible to realize in a composition of objects using only the LOTOS parallel operators (see also [12] and [13]). In Objectory, all communication takes place over channels. By modeling channels as LOTOS processes, we can solve this configuration problem:

```
process channel [rec,send] (sendId:OBJECTID,recId:OBJECTID): noexit :=
    send                        (* Receive op on the send gate *)
        ?opn:OPERATION          (* Operation name *)
        ?param:PARAMETER        (* Parameter *)
        !sendId                 (* Id of Calling Object *)
        !recId;                 (* Id of Called Object *)
    rec                         (* Pass to receiving object *)
        !opn
        !param
        !sendId ;
        !recId

    channel [rec,send] (sendId, recId)
endproc
```

Operation calls are received on the gate *send* and passed on to the receiving object on gate *rec*. There will be one instance of the channel process for each channel relation in the Objectory model. The channel processes are finally composed with the object processes in a behaviour expression *B* using the LOTOS parallel operators as follows:

```
(object1 [rec,send] (id1)         |||
     . . .
  objectn [rec,send] (idn))

   ||

(channel [rec,send] (id1, id4)  |||
     . . .
  channel [rec,send] (id3, idn))
```

A test case t representing a sequence of events in a use case, is put in parallel with the behaviour expression: $B \, |[rec, send, success]| \, t$ where an event on gate *success* represents a successful test execution.

4 Trial Application

The methodical and representational ideas were tested in a modeling work that concluded the project. The work was carried out within the framework of an existing development project at the department. The LOTOS model was built by taking the Objectory model as input, and manually translating it into LOTOS. The majority of the errors (eg. missing formal parameters, operations and relations) were found in this process of translation, as a consequence of formalizing the description. The LOTOS model (approx. 3000 lines including comments) was finally tested and simulated in the tool environment LITE. The test cases consisted of sequences of LOTOS events corresponding to the events in the use cases. An incompleteness or inconsistency in the specification will, with the right test case, lead to a dead-lock in the simulation. The following example is a part of a larger test case:

```
(* Set Network Elements *)
send !setNetworkElements ?param:Parameter ?sendId:ObjectId ?targId:ObjectI
rec  !setNetworkElements !param !sendId !targId;

send !quit ?param:Parameter ?sendId:ObjectId ?targId:ObjectId;
rec  !quit !param !sendId !targId;

  . . .

success;

stop
```

In this test case there is no restriction on the data passed between the objects. The correctness of data can be checked by adding concrete values to the events in the test case. A test case checks both the sending and the receiving of operation calls.

5 Problems Encountered

We did experience some problems in modeling OO constructs in LOTOS. It is possible to distinguish between two types of problems. One type of problem depends on weaknesses in the mapping rules; it is not possible to find constructs or structures in LOTOS that will model a particular OO construct well. The other type of problem relates to the application of the mapping rules; there exists a rule for an OO construct, but it does not map onto a straight-forward representation in LOTOS, which means that care has to be taken when applying the rule. An example of the former type of problem, is the mapping of the *inheritance* relation. One can distinguish between two types of usage of inheritance, namely specialization and sub-typing. Sub-typing implies that an instance of a super class could be replaced by an instance of the sub-class. Hence, the sub-class extends the behaviour of the super class. Specialization on the other hand, possibly means modification of behaviour (see for example [9] for a discussion on inheritance). In LOTOS we can only easily model sub-typing. One example of the latter type of problem is the preservation of *encapsulation*. Since we are simulating an object by a structure built on top of LOTOS, it is only through the obedience of the usage rule that encapsulation can be preserved (see for example [11] for a presentation on how encapsulation can be handled).

The LOTOS modeling work took a relatively long time to carry out. However, this is partly explained by the fact that we were spending a large part of the time revising the LOTOS modeling concepts and making documentation of the process. It may be tempting for a decision maker to compare the time it takes to make a formal model with the time it takes to make a corresponding non-formal model using another method. However, it is not possible to make such a comparison at a stage when integration issues are being worked out; the process of using the formal description technique is not defined, rather it is being defined as the work progresses.

Normally, when any new technology is introduced in development, it is because there exists an identified need to do so. Hence, the source of the driving force is the needs. These needs are crystallized into a set of requirements, which form the basis when deciding what technology, or what particular product, to use. In our case the situation was different. We started off with a solution; ie. LOTOS language, method and tools. Our task was to analyze the development process, and to find out if there existed any needs that our solution LOTOS could fulfil. Hence, the order in which the work was carried out, was reversed to the order one would normally expect. However, this is a consequence of the situation at the company, where the knowledge about formal methods among management in general is not so good, and the driving force, initially, has to come from the research department. The research department in turn has a good knowledge about LOTOS, and less knowledge about other FDTs. This meant that the result may not be optimal, but it is a starting point of a process in which better solutions may be sought.

6 Conclusion

In investigating the potential use of LOTOS within a development department at Ascom Hasler AG, it was found that LOTOS could be used as a complement to an object oriented development method (Objectory). Various aspects of integrating LOTOS within this method were studied.

Formal methods do not always cover the whole development trajectory in a way that they can be used on their own in industrial software development. However, in many cases they may complement already existing development methods used in industry. In Objectory we found that LOTOS could be used for describing object behaviour. The strength of using LOTOS in this context, is that specifications become less ambiguous and testability is added. Before formal methods become commonplace and integrated in commercially available methods, there seems to be a transitional period in which the users have to handle the integration issues themselves. There are two different perspectives that need to be considered in this context. On the one hand, there is the methodical perspective; we must find out where and how the formal description technique could be used and, indeed, if it needs to be used. On the other hand, we must handle the representational aspects; how can we merge the different description techniques that two different methods normally imply? The Objectory method were systematically analyzed, and a proposal to where LOTOS could be used within the method were presented. Furthermore, a suggestion as to how OO constructs used within Objectory can be represented in LOTOS were given, out of which a simplified sub-set is presented in this paper.

The ideas presented on the methodical and representational issues were tested in a larger modeling task carried out within the framework of an existing development project. Several errors in the original Objectory model were found when this model were formalized in LOTOS, indicating that the use of LOTOS could lead to a better quality of Objectory specifications. Hence, even though LOTOS is not an object oriented language, and the use of it is dependent on a set of mapping rules, there seems to be a potential for quality improvements using LOTOS in an object oriented context.

References

1. Vissers C.A. et al.: Lotosphere, an attempt towards a Design Culture, Proceedings 3rd Lotosphere Workshop and Seminar, Pisa '92
2. Logrippo L., Haj-Hussein M.: An Introduction to Lotos: learning by examples Computer Networks & ISDN Systems 23 (5) 1992
3. Gomez S. P.: The Lotos Design Methodology: Guidelines, Lotopshere report Lo/WP3/T1.1/N0044/V04, March 1992.
4. Lite User Manual Editor Caneve, Salvatori, Lotosphere 1992
5. Jacobsson I.: Object-Oriented Software Engineering, ACM Press Book/Addison-Wesley, 1992
6. Cusack E. et al: An object oriented interpretation of LOTOS, Proceed. FORTE '90, Vancouver, Canada
7. Mayr T.: Specification of Object-Oriented Systems in Lotos, Proceed. FORTE '88, Stirling, Scotland
8. Black S.: Objects and Lotos, Proceed. FORTE '89, Vancouver, Canada
9. Rudkin S.: Inheritance in Lotos, Proceed. FORTE '91, Sydney, Australia
10. Dijkerman E. M.: Object Oriented Specification Style in Lotos, PTT Research Report 917 RNL/1989
11. Clarc B.: Use of the Object-Based Style in Implementation-Oriented Lotos Specifications, Presentation at the 2nd Lotosphere Workshop, Berlin 1991

12. Fredlund L-A, Orava F.: Modeling Dynamic Communication Structures in LOTOS, FORTE '91 Sydney
13. Buhr R.J.A., Vidger M.: Using LOTOS in a Design Environment, FORTE '91, Sydney
14. Information Processing Systems - Open Systems Interconnection - Structure of Management Information - Part 1 - 4 ISO/IEC 10165-(1-4), CCITT X.720
15. Information Processing Systems - Open Systems Interconnection - LOTOS - A formal description technique based on the temporal ordering of observational behaviour, ISO 8807, 1989-02-15

An Industrial Experience on LOTOS-Based Prototyping for Switching Systems Design*

Gonzalo León[1], Juan C. Yelmo[1], Carlos Sánchez[1], F. Javier Carrasco[2] and Juan J. Gil[2]

[1] Telematic Engineering Department, Technical University of Madrid, Spain
[2] Software Technology Division, Telefónica I+D, Madrid, Spain

Abstract. This paper summarizes the experience obtained in the definition of a LOTOS based development methodology and its pragmatic introduction in common industrial practice.

The work has been done within a technology transfer model where the development of medium-to-large size case studies plays a predominant role. A case study, development of a gateway between DSS1 and SS7 ISDN signalling systems, was chosen as a representative example of industrial product in the switching application domain. The case study was developed by automatic code generation from a LOTOS specification. Later, its functionality was enhanced to provide *demo* facilities in order to evaluate the development approach.

From this experience a practical methodology to combine LOTOS with conventional techniques has been defined.

1 Introduction

Standardization of FDTs occurred several years ago and, since then, many efforts have been promoted to complete a first generation of tools, to understand the best methods to generate a large specification and to test their adequacy in different application domains [1]. However, less effort has been devoted to incorporate them in the industrial common practice.

Early trials have not been completely successful. The reasons range from a poor background in designers and managers to use the new technology or problems to understand its side effects, to the lack of experience with a restricted set of available tools, very far from the performance, friendliness or reliability offered by their counterparts in more conventional techniques. Afterwards, strong difficulties to introduce them while keeping the experience and organizational methods preexistent in the company have slowed its use.

Today, there is a broad recognition that the use of FDTs in a large company to design and implement critical large systems is not only dependent on the benefits expected from the FDT in an isolated way. It will be the result of a carefully planned strategy where many aspects should be concurrently addressed. Before incorporating a new FDT, industries need to ensure that:

---

* This work has been partly sponsored by the Spanish CDTI (Technological and Industrial Development Center) within the MEDAS (Advanced Methodology for Communication Systems Development) research project.

1. The FDT under evaluation perfectly covers the characteristics of the systems designed in that industry.
2. It is possible to use preexistent tools and methods in those parts of the life cycle not covered by the FDT.
3. Progressive and smooth technology transfer to allow designers acquire hands-on experience on tools, methods, reasoning framework and methodological guidelines before a final decision is taken.

To satisfy the above requirements and to accelerate the use of LOTOS [2] technology in a specific industrial context, pilot projects thinking in technological transfer goals instead of the products themselves seem the most promising approach. This is the realm of the effort summarized in this paper.

2 The MEDAS Project and the Technology Transfer of FDTs

This work has been carried out in the framework of the MEDAS (Advanced Methodology for Communication Systems Development) research project. Its main goal was the definition of methodological guidelines and a set of tools to support the design of communication and switching systems by using FDT and particularly LOTOS, and to validate the proposed methodology within an industrial environment. Project partners came from both academic and industrial world: the Telematic Engineering Department of the Technical University of Madrid (DIT-UPM) and Telefónica I+D (from the Spanish PTT industrial group and covering R & D activities).

In order to assess the validity of the proposed life cycle model and the tools designed, two medium size case studies, quite similar to the products usually developed by the institutions participating in the project, were defined. That is, two real size systems on which software engineering techniques can be applied and that deserve the industrial world interest.

The role of the industrial partner in the project was considered to be a driving factor. Firstly, it would contribute to define the design methodology based on FDTs, having in mind its introduction within their current practices. Secondly, it would select a final case study for the validation process, with the intention of converting it in a product, and industrialize the methodology. The role of the academic partner is to provide the LOTOS tools and experience, and to lead the technology transfer process. Cooperation in the detailed specification, implementation and methodological guidelines were addressed through mixed working teams.

The MEDAS project as a whole could be considered as a technology transfer project. To do that, the project defined a technology transfer model [3] where the FDT is introduced progressively in several cycles.

The first cycle is more related with academic activities intended to motivate and to select the FDTs to be used (initially, LOTOS and SDL). Identification of the development context in the industry was also analyzed. As a result, a decision on proceeding with the second phase was taken.

The second one, already finished, covered the methodological aspects of the LOTOS based development by designing a first case study. In parallel, transference of

LOTOS tools and identification of the life cycle combining the Tesys-B methodology [3] and LOTOS methods were planned. The results were encouraging by demonstrating the feasibility of the use of LOTOS in the industry. Demonstrations were prepared to convince managers on the capability of the proposed technique in comparison with conventional methods.

The third one, started in early 1992, is aimed at generating a complete product by using the proposed life cycle, tools and documentation as it is usually done in conventional product development. In this case, maintenance aspects will be also considered.

3 LOTOS Introduction in a Software Development Process

LOTOS and its associated mathematical theory can be used to formally support a stepwise refinement design process, following the approach proposed in the LOTO-SPHERE ESPRIT project [5]. In such a design process, the system is constructed incrementally in a sequence of design steps in order to produce some product which fulfills a given user requirement document.

In each design step a LOTOS model of the system is produced which is a formalization of the functional requirements of the system being designed at a given level of abstraction. The formal design must be complemented by a conceptual design which will be done according to conventional software engineering techniques.

The use of LOTOS allows that conformance against the reference specification and verification in design steps be verified analytically. In practice, it appears that verification of complex designs is beyond the scope of pragmatic methods. The testing approach is considered mature enough to be applied today in industrial development. In this sense, the *testing equivalence* [6] is used by selecting a set of tests having sufficient coverage to obtain enough confidence about the preservation of the equivalence.

The method described above is incomplete and ideal. It is just a design method and not a complete life cycle model. It does not cover indispensable software engineering issues (e.g. requirements capture, project management, configuration control, etc.). That is why the LOTOSPHERE methodology must be complemented with production methods that cover the whole software development process. In this sense, we are working on a development method combining LOTOS and conventional techniques inspired on the spiral software development model [7].

The spiral (meta)model proposed by Boehm [8] is a development process model in which requirements are generated and validated in a risk driven cyclic fashion.

The risk driven nature of the spiral model guides developers to postpone detailed elaboration of low-risk software elements and to avoid going too deep in their design until high-risk elements of the design are stabilized. Risk management [9] requires appropriate attention to early resolution techniques such as early prototyping and simulation. The spiral model may incorporate prototyping as a risk resolution strategy at any stage of development. Actually, an evolutionary process model can be seen as an instantiation of the spiral metamodel.

---

[3] Development methodology used in the X.25-based Spanish public data network IBER-PAC [4]

LOTOS permits to construct an initial and non-ambiguous description of a system and, by the stepwise refinement design process, to obtain formal descriptions of the system at different abstraction levels. We can go further and use LOTOS to support a software development methodology that, starting from a formal specification of a system, allows to obtain a chain of *animatable* prototypes that evolve (in an assisted and semiautomatic manner) towards the final system. Fig. 1 shows the instantiation of our integrated model used in the development of the case studies.

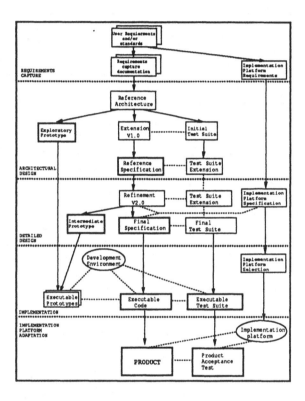

Fig. 1. Life cycle model application

Some advantages of implementing a risk resolution strategy as a LOTOS-based evolutionary process model are

1. Verify the feasibility of design alternatives.
2. Validate the system behavior against user's requirements.
3. Product simulation and quality/performance metrics measurement (in this case you have to complement the LOTOS model with time, probabilities, priorities, etc.) [10].
4. Semiautomatic prototype/product generation from the LOTOS specification.

4 Industrial Experience

In this section we consider some of the experiences obtained in the LOTOS-based design and implementation of a first case study: an interworking gateway between the ISDN signalling access interface and the Signalling System No. 7 [11].

4.1 Groups and Working Method

The development activity associated with each case study started with a rigorous scheduling identifying concurrent activities, phases, milestones and working groups. Our main concern was to establish a proper intertwining between activities and a good interaction between working groups.

A good level of cooperation is not only a question of management but also a technical issue that depends on the working method and, in our case, on the capabilities of the formal technique and tools to support teamwork. In this sense, we have emphasized the use of graphical aids during the phases devoted to architectural and high level design by using a tool based on the PTD architectural graphical language [12] and enclosing this kind of graphic designs with every specification exchanged between team members. In this way, we have tried to overcome some difficulties encountered in LOTOS readability, difficulties not satisfactorily resolved by the standard for G-LOTOS.

Once the overall architecture was decided, it was decomposed into design units which were distributed between several subteams. Automatic construction of the whole system has to be done regarding maintenability and coherence between different versions. For this purpose we have used a version management tool. Design units are made independently and dependency information is maintained. The composite system specification is built automatically from the individual design units under the control of a configuration management system [4].

At each design step (level of abstraction), the system is validated in order to ensure compliance with the user requirements by either executing a test suite with the transformational tool *LOLA* [13] to partially prove testing equivalence [6] w.r.t. the reference specification or, with detailed designs, by generating an executable prototype with the *TOPO* [14] LOTOS to C/ADA compiler. Test sequences are written in LOTOS and composed automatically by the configuration management tool. Then, the specification is expanded with *LOLA* or compiled with *TOPO* and executed as an ordinary process.

When a new design step is accomplished, all changes are applied through the individual design units and then rebuilt automatically. Previous design steps and alternative refinements are maintained in order to keep track of the design history and to permit prior stages to be revisited.

4.2 First Case Study: An Interworking Gateway between DSS1 and SS7

Gateway Context. The first case study, intended to assess the validity of the proposed life cycle model and the tools designed, was aimed at specifying a gateway between the call control protocol of the Digital Subscriber Signalling System No. 1

(DSS1) and the ISDN user part (ISUP) of Signalling System No. 7 (SS7), as stated in the Q.699 CCITT Recommendation [11]. This Recommendation defines (not always in detail, or even completely) the relationship between signalling information conveyed via the DSS1 protocol and similar signalling information conveyed via the SS7 ISUP. The above relationship is described within the context of supporting the provision of basic bearer service for a call within an ISDN or mixed ISDN/non ISDN environment. As an illustrative example of supplementary services a user-user signalling functionality was also included.

Fig. 2 shows the interworking gateway context within the Integrated Services Digital Network. In this figure *resources* means all the exchange functionalities that do not matter to our case study. We place our gateway functionality inside the box labeled *call control*.

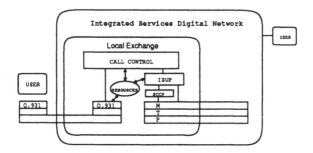

Fig. 2. DSS1-SS7 interworking context

The context depicted in Fig. 2 represents the starting point for the architectural design of our case study and its further development will be detailed in the following sections.

The Specification. Interworking between ISDN common channel signalling protocols is not straightforward in spite of being both elaborated by CCITT. The lack of one-to-one correspondence between primitives and differences in its structure and contents, are the main difficulties.

The gateway has to order the interchange of primitives between both protocols (behaviour) and map the information elements/parameters (data structures) carried by these primitives. Recommendation Q.699 [11] deals mostly with the first task but the second one is the most cumbersome.

In order to cope with the previous tasks our reference specification has been written using a *constraint-oriented* LOTOS style. This style supports extensional description with modularity and parallel composition. A high level gateway PTD [12] representation is shown in Fig. 3

Process Call_manager is the interface with the system resources and keeps track of call identifiers in order to be able to manage simultaneous *One-gateway* instantiations. Fig. 3 shows also a refinement of *One-gateway* and the code automatically generated by the tool.

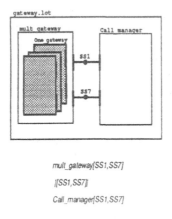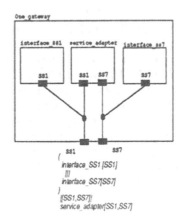

mult_gateway[SS1,SS7]

|[SS1,SS7]|

Call_manager[SS1,SS7]

(
interface_SS1 [SS1]
|||
interface_SS7[SS7]
)
|[SS1,SS7]|
service_adapter[SS1,SS7]

Fig. 3. High Level Specification

Prototyping. An exploratory implementation prototype was developed aimed at enhancing visibility, introducing non-functional requirements and simulating functionality in an environment close to the implementation platform.

The gateway prototype is composed of C code automatically generated from the LOTOS specification with C language *annotations*[4], and hand written routines to implement user and environment interface. Automatically generated code represents 90% of the whole number of C lines code. Fig. 4 depicts the prototype environment.

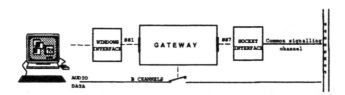

Fig. 4. The prototype and its environment

The demonstrator consists of gateway instantiations in different hosts over an Ethernet network. The SS7 common signalling channel is simulated with a socket connection between both instantiations. The gateway also controls a pair of simulated information channels (B channels); one simulates a data communication with the "talk" $UNIX^{TM}$ utility and the other one makes use of the audio facilities of a SUN *SparcStation*^{TM}.

The user interface is based on X-WINDOWS, where we have one window for each B channel and another one for a menu driven interactive subscriber access (D

---

[4] Annotations [14] are additional implementation information provided to the compiler in a procedural language.

channel). Fig. 5 is a snapshot of the user interface of the prototype.

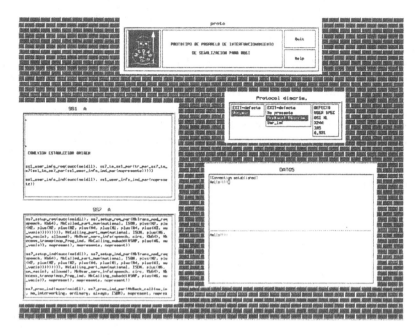

Fig. 5. Prototype interface

Results. The next table summarizes the most important data about the prototype development:

Table 1. Prototype development

Parameter	SPECIFICATION LOTOS		PROTOTYPE			
	behav.	data	automated code behav.	data	Annota-tions	hand code
No. lines	1700	3000	4436	27599	119	3220
Tests						
- acceptance		70	interactive validation			
- reject		40				
Efforts (m/m)		30	3			3

TOPO implements abstract data types by a rewrite system machinery which results in very inefficient code. The ratio of C lines to ACT ONE (LOTOS) lines is 10 to 1, while in the behaviour part the ratio is only 2.6 to 1. It would be necessary to use hand written implementations of abstract data types to improve efficiency. Notice that the effort is shifted from implementation to specification code w.r.t. conventional approaches.

We have used the prototype like a project demonstrator to help in the technology transfer process. This perspective increases the amount of hand written code for improving the user interface.

The LOTOS specifications can be a good start point to construct prototypes in which their codes are automatically generated by tools as TOPO. The main difficulties are caused by the high abstraction level of the language and the lack of I/O concept. Therefore, user and environment interface must be made by hand. Nevertheless, a library of C routines generated in this case study could be reused to speed up the generation of more demonstrators in new case studies.

5 Conclusions and Future Work

The experiences carried out in the MEDAS project, summarized in this paper, has globally demonstrated the validity of LOTOS for large switching product development. As a basis for the introduction of LOTOS, the development of well chosen case studies, relevant to the application domain of the industry, plays a major role.

During the development process different prototypes were designed: an abstract specification to validate the functional description and others to validate the implementation. Both types are necessary and they cover different aspects. From the organizational standpoint, it was clear that working groups and associated roles need to be integrated in the internal industrial organization. Support for life cycle management is also required.

A second case study, the development of an interworking unit between traditional X.25-based Packet Switched Data Networks and the rapidly emerging high speed data networks with SMDS service [15], was started to cover efficiency aspects in code generation and to define an industrial methodology to be used as a reference framework for further projects. This new case study is also being developed in SDL (a well known FDT in the industry) with automatic code generation. Both products will be confronted in a real scenario for comparative evaluation analysis.

References

1. **IEEE-Software** Special Issue on Formal Methods, September 1990.
2. **ISO/EC** : *Information Processing Systems - Open Systems Interconnection - LOTOS - A Formal Description Technique Based on the Temporal Ordering of Observational Behaviour.* ISO/IEC 1988.
3. **G. León**. *On the Technology Transfer of Formal Methods: An Experience on LOTOS.* In FORTE'90, Madrid.
4. **A. Cazorla, J.C. Moreno**. *Manual de metodología del proyecto TESYS-B* (in Spanish). Telefónica I+D, TESYS_B_0000_0055_MOP, internal report, April 1990.
5. **The Lotosphere Consortium** *The Lotosphere Integrated Tool Environment Lite.* In FORTE'91, Sydney.

6. **E. Brinksma, G. Scollo, and C. Steenbergen.** *LOTOS Specifications, Their Implementations and Their Test.* In sixth International Workshop on Protocol Specification, Testing and Verification. Montreal, June 1986.

7. **G. León, J.C. Yelmo.** *On the intertwining of FDTs and conventional software development processes for communication systems: an incremental approach.* Proceedings of the V International Conference on Software Engineering and its Applications, Toulouse, December 1992.

8. **Barry W. Boehm.** *A Spiral Model of Software Development and Enhancement.* IEEE Computer, May 1988.

9. **Barry W. Boehm.** *Software risk management: principles and practice.* IEEE software, January 1991.

10. **C. Miguel, A. Fernández, J.M. Ortuño and L. Vidaller.** *A LOTOS based Performance Evaluation Tool.* To be published in the Forthcoming Special Issue of "Computer Networks and ISDN Systems" on TOOLS FOR FDTs, 1992.

11. **CCITT Q.699** : *Interworking between digital subscriber signalling system layer 3 protocol and the signalling system no. 7 ISDN user part.* Blue book 1988.

12. **J. Sánchez, G. León.** *PTD: Architectural System Description Support Based on Visual Specification Languages.* The EUROMICRO Journal, Sept 1992.

13. **J. Quemada, S. Pavon and A. Fernández.** *Transforming LOTOS specifications with LOLA- The Parameterized Expansion.* In FORTE'88, Stirling.

14. **J. Mañas and T. de Miguel.** *From LOTOS to C.* In FORTE'88, Stirling.

15. **Bellcore TR-TSV-000772.** *Generic System Requirements in support of Switched Multi-Megabit Data Service.* Issue 1, May 1991.

Towards an Implementation-oriented Specification of TP Protocol in LOTOS*

Ing Widya[1] and Gert-Jan van der Heijden[2]

[1] University of Twente, P.O. Box 217, 7500 AE Enschede, The Netherlands
[2] Océ Nederland B.V., P.O. Box 101, 5900 MA Venlo, The Netherlands

Abstract. This paper presents an exercise in the specification and implementation design of a realistic OSI Application-layer protocol in accordance with the LotoSphere methodology. It also reports some of the experiences acquired during the design process. The main motivation of the work presented is the need to have a genuine assessment of the design methodology for its industrial applicability.
The OSI Transaction Processing protocol is selected as a design example due to its distributed nature and its entangled compositional structure, comprising of OSI common application service elements, i.e. AC-SE and CCR-SE, and TP specific elements. This paper focusses on the design trajectory of the TP specific parts.
The design process starts with an informal protocol description and after several design steps ends with an implementation specified in LOTOS. This process is globally constrained by realizability and open-endedness requirements. The derived implementation is expressed in a state(-machine) oriented way and is in a design sense close to a realization. UNIX workstations with a running ISODE are selected as realization environment. An alternative design approach which suitably fits ISODE is exposed but not elaborated. A second design cycle has been undertaken to enable some evaluation of the open-endedness of the specification.

1 Introduction

In ESPRIT II project 2304 LotoSphere [1] an integrated design methodology for distributed (communication) systems is developed. The methodology has to satisfy industrial needs for design such as the availability of design guidelines, methods, correctness preserving transformation techniques, and design support tools which are robust, easy to use and well-documented.

Several tasks within the project assess the industrial applicability of the methodology by applying it to design examples, see for instance [2, 3, 4]. They form a testbed of the methodology. One of the examples is a protocol based on the first OSI/DIS Transaction Processing (TP) [5]. This protocol is selected as an example because of its distributed nature and its entangled compositional structure which comprises several OSI common application service elements, such as Association Control Service Element (AC-SE) [6] and Commitment, Concurrency and Recovery (CCR-SE) [7], and TP specific elements. This structure enables a modular design approach

---

* This work has been supported by the CEC under the ESPRIT II program in project 2304.

where elements of the protocol may be designed by different groups in a relatively independent way.

This paper reports the design activity undertaken by the task-group that specifies and implements[3] the TP specific components of OSI-TP. Due to the limitation in manpower, the design trajectory does not include the realization of the protocol, though some realization aspects are considered during the design process to enable a tailored implementation strategy. Also because of the limitation only a subset of the TP-protocol functionality will be considered; only a profile of OSI-TP is selected as design example. This restriction is not in conflict with the task-group objective to assess the design methodology. On the contrary, this approach focusses on the main design issues instead of being entangled in complicated but irrelevant design details.

TP design activity deals with the complexity of an OSI Application-layer protocol and applies an implementation strategy which is adapted to the target realization environment. Other testbed examples of the project, i.e. AC-SE, CCR-SE, ISDN Layer 3 and Mini-Mail, complement the design activity presented here, for instance, by including design phases concerning protocol design and by realizing specifications in C.

This paper emphasizes the specification - implementation rationale and reports on some experiences acquired during the design process. The applied design process aims at the derivation of a qualitative specification which is suitable for realization. The process starts with formalizing a subset of the informal description of OSI-TP Protocol. This specification in LOTOS is then transformed in several design steps to an implementation, also expressed in LOTOS. The design process is constrained by the overall design objectives, i.e. the realizability and open-endedness[4] quality requirements.

The realizability of the specifications is tested along with the refinements of the specifications ultimately yielding a product which is in a design sense close to a realization. Though the realization phase is not planned to be elaborated, the realization environment is investigated to provide sufficient "bottom-up" information for a suitable implementation-realization strategy. The realization environment is UNIX workstations with a running ISO Development Environment (ISODE) [8]. The latter is a realization of the OSI stack. The open-endedness of the specification, on the other hand, is evaluated by means of a second design cycle that incorporates an extension of the first-cycle functionality. Because the results of this part of the work were quite obvious, not much attention is given to this subject in this paper.

This paper has the following structure. The next section gives a short introduction to OSI Transaction Processing. The section thereafter briefly exposes the Design Methodology. Section 4 explains the TP design trajectory. Section 5 describes the design process of the first design cycle. The status of the specifications is described in Sect. 6. Section 7 reports some experiences. The last section gives finally the conclusions of the work.

---

[3] In this paper, an implementation denotes a specification in LOTOS which reflects realization aspects; see also Sect. 3.

[4] Open-ended refers to openness to new service/protocol functionalities.

2 Transaction Processing

A *transaction* may be defined as a set of interrelated, distributed, and on-line operations that fulfils certain properties, see e.g. [9]. The main characterizing property is the all or nothing effect of the distributed operations of a transaction, called *atomicity*. Other properties are for example the consistency of the operations and the non-interfering property of concurrent transactions, i.e. the isolation of partial results.

Application transactions are for instance travel agent transactions, banking transactions, and transactions in design systems. The following example of a travel agent transaction shows the distributed nature of a transaction.

A client of a travel agency may wish to book a holiday. This client requires a return flight from A to C, which includes an intercontinental flight from A to B and a domestic flight from B to C. It is not necessary, however, to fly with the same company for both flights. Besides this the client needs a car and hotel accommodation. These booking operations typically require an on-line multiparty communication between the travel agency, the hotel-, car lease-, and plane reservation systems. If one of the operations involved cannot be satisfied, the client may wish to cancel all reservations (Atomicity). It is furthermore unacceptable for the travel agent to make a mistake, i.e. to introduce inconsistencies, or that another transaction interferes by reserving the same seat.

OSI-TP concerns with the *interoperability* of distributed processing of application transactions. It provides the users with communication and coordination facilities which can be used to enforce the required transaction properties. Coordinating services for concurrency, e.g. commitment and rollback service elements, play a major role in TP.

As shown in the previous example, the distributed operations of a transaction are clustered in application subsystems. These subsystems may be distributed over several system sites. In OSI-TP, clusters are interrelated in a *tree structure*. Thus, a tree models the multiparty relationship between the local activities of the TP service users involved in a transaction. In such a tree structure one can distinguish three types of nodes: the root-node, leaf-nodes and intermediate-nodes. These nodes are connected to one another by branches, which in this case are called transaction branches. In TP, the root-node is the protocol entity whose service-user is initiating the transaction. During processing of a transaction a user may expand the transaction tree dynamically. Each expansion implies the addition of a new transaction branch to the transaction tree. The protocol entity attached to the initiating user becomes the superior of the new transaction branch. The remote entity becomes the subordinate. Entities which do not have subordinates are *leaves*. The other entities, except the root, are called the *intermediates*.

The relationship between two TP service users is expressed in the concept of a *dialogue*. A dialogue may be viewed as a virtual connection between two TP service users. When a dialogue has been established, it is possible for the TP service users to exchange data in preparation of a transaction, followed by the initiation of the transaction.

3 The Design Methodology

This section briefly exposes the applied design methodology, a detailed description may be found in [10]. The methodology is based on the use of the formal description technique LOTOS [11] and consists of design methods, guidelines, transformation techniques and design support tools. The methods are basically top-down with the option to iterate a design towards a qualitative product. It also encourages a cyclic design approach to enable a gradual design evolution leading to an ultimate product with the desired functionality.

The methodology identifies three design phases: the architectural, the implementation, and the realization phase. The architectural phase includes requirements engineering to capture the essential properties of the design. These are then refined and formalized in LOTOS yielding the so-called *architecture*. The architecture expresses the functionality of the design at the appropriate level of abstraction, thus avoiding details for instance of realization aspects. The architecture is then transformed into an *implementation*, which is also specified in LOTOS and which reflects realization constructs. Finally, in the realization phase, the implementation is converted into code which is executable in the target realization environment.

4 TP Design Trajectory

As mentioned before, the design activity presented in this paper starts with the informal OSI-TP protocol specification and yields an implementation which is expressed in LOTOS and is close to a realization. In accordance with the design method, TP design process comprises design cycles. The first cycle incorporates an OSI-TP subset which supports serial and interleaving but non-interfering transactions in an error-free communication environment. This subset enables the validation of the derived specifications by simulating them in an environment where service users are configured in a realistic transaction tree. It also preserves many of the essential characteristics of a TP system, such as facilities for distributed atomic commitment. The corresponding protocol is also sufficiently complex to function as a genuine design example.

The first formalized specification, i.e. the architecture, is to be viewed as a specification which describes observable behaviour of the protocol and reveals the external appearance of the protocol structure as viewed by a system designer. This specification has the appropriate level of abstraction and is expressed in a certain style of construction, called *resource-constraint* oriented style [12]. This is because the revealed structure comprises the functional resources. The specification does not show realization aspects. Realization constructs are reflected in refined specifications, e.g. in the implementation.

The architectural specification is then iteratively updated and refined yielding a "linear" chain of versions, which is well maintainable in the design environment where designers are remotely located. Specifications are updated to correct design decisions or design errors which are for example found during testing. In the refinement steps, placeholders in earlier versions to contain behaviour expressions of unspecified parts are elaborated in the target versions with preservation of the specified behaviour of the early versions. The architectural specifications are denoted as

A i, with i = 1,..,4, in Fig. 1. These specifications are all expressed in the resource-constraint oriented style, which is suitable for expressing communication protocols. The structure of the specifications matches with the structure of the informal specification in the ISO standard. This makes matters simpler for the designers, and yields specifications which are better comprehensible to readers already familiar with OSI-TP standard.

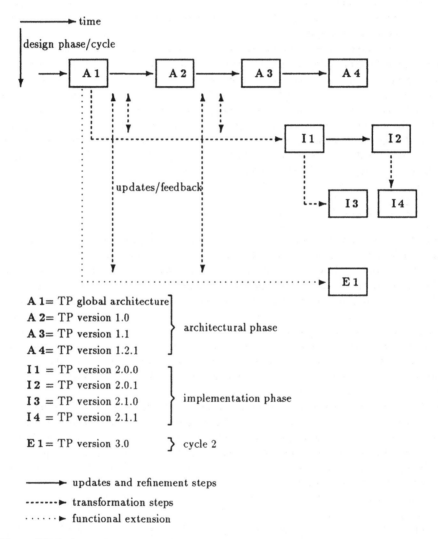

Fig. 1. TP design trajectory.

Due to the design-time limitation, the implementation phase is started along with the refinements of the architectural specifications instead of waiting for a stable version. The implementation phase consists of two stages. The first stage comprises transformation steps, which are performed manually, and yields intermediate specifications with simpler LOTOS constructs and structures. These specifications are denoted by I 1 and I 2 in Fig. 1. The second stage comprises a combination of a tool-aided and some manually performed transformations and yields *state(-machine)* oriented specifications, denoted by I 3 and I 4 in the figure mentioned previously.

In the next section, the design process is described in more details and an alternative implementation strategy which leads to designs which closely match the ISODE realization environment is discussed. This strategy is not well supported by the LotoSphere methodology, which emphasize on solutions where knowledge of past events is basically captured in the behaviour part of the LOTOS specifications in several processes. The alternative strategy, on the other hand, requires protocol knowledge of the past basically being captured in the abstract data type (ADT) part.

The second design cycle extends the functionality of the first-cycle specifications by including some OSI-TP rollback features. The extended system supports transactions which either will commit or rollback. Collisions of commit and rollback requests within a transaction tree are not supported in the extended system. This cycle only elaborates the architectural phase, because it is meant to have some evaluation on the open-endedness of the first-cycle specifications.

5 TP Design Process

5.1 Architectural Phase

The chosen subset of OSI-TP functionality mentioned in the previous section comprises TP functional units which contain service elements related to dialogue control, data transfer, error reporting, and transaction commitment procedures. For simplicity of the design, all protocol options, e.g. rollback, recovery and, consequently, error- and calamity-reporting services are not supported.

The following design steps have been applied in the construction of the first resource-constraint oriented specification.

Step 1:
At the highest hierarchical level of the specification, the structure of the specification has been determined by applying commonly used OSI protocol constructs ([13]). This yields a decomposition of the skeleton TP protocol into a TP protocol-layer and an underlying Presentation service. The protocol-layer consists of many protocol entities which are parameterized by an address identifier. Each entity, in turn, consists of invocations of reusable TP nodes. Thus,

```
process TP_protocol[...](ads:SetOfAEAds):noexit:=
  hide ... in  (TP_P_layer[...](ads) |[...]| P_Service[...](...) )
  where

  process TP_P_layer[...](ads:SetOfAEAds):noexit:=
    choice ad:AEAd []
    [ad IsIn ads] ->
      (TP_P_Entity[...](ad) ||| TP_P_layer[...](Remove(ad,ads)))
  endproc
```

```
process TP_P_Entity[...](ad:AEAd):noexit:=
  (* free_invs models the limitation of resources *)
  let free_invs:SetOfAEInvs = <Any set of Invocation Identifiers> in
  TP_PE_invocations[...](ad,free_invs)
endproc

process TP_PE_invocations[...](ad:AEAd,free_invs:SetOfAEInvs):noexit:=
  choice inv:AEInv [] [(inv IsIn free_invs)] -> i;
    ( TP_PE_invocation[...](ad,inv)
      |||
      i; TP_PE_invocations[...](ad,Remove(inv,free_invs)) )
endproc

process TP_PE_invocation[...](ad:AEAd,inv:AEInv):noexit:=
  let free_brs:SetOfBrs=<Any set of Transaction Branch Identifiers> in
  TP_Node[...](ad,inv,free_brs) >> TP_PE_invocation[...](ad,inv)
endproc
  ...
  ...
endproc
```

Step 2:

This step analyzes the protocol entities in its environment. It comprises matters like the investigation on TP service primitives and the classification of these service primitives. This step refines the skeleton specification by defining the external gates and the corresponding event-structures. It also gives better insight on what functionality should be implemented in the first cycle and the global consequences to the design. This step for instance yields the definition of the external gate **tp** and the hidden gate **p**.

Step 3:

This step identifies the functional resources inside the protocol entity in accordance with the OSI Application Layer Structure [14]. This yields a resource composition of TP protocol entity, consisting of several TP Single Association Objects (TP-SAOs), which are sub-entities that manage and control the interworking with the peer protocol entities, and a Multiple Association Control Function (MACF), see also Fig. 2. This function MACF provides the interface to the TP service user and controls the TP-SAOs. The TP-SAOs on their turn are the users of the Presentation service. In this architecture, each TP-SAO would consist of 4 application service elements: AC-SE, CCR-SE, TP-ASE and a User-definable ASE (U-ASE), controlled by the Single Association Control Function (SACF).

Step 4:

This iterative step adjusts and refines the decomposition of TP protocol layer into a TP specific layer on top and a Common Application (CA) layer at the bottom, see also [15]. The common application service elements AC-SE and CCR-SE which were originally located inside TP-SAO are now moved to the CA-layer and the updated TP-SAO only consists of TP-ASE and U-ASE. An analysis of the primitive exchanges between these protocol resources leads to the definitions of the gate **nn**

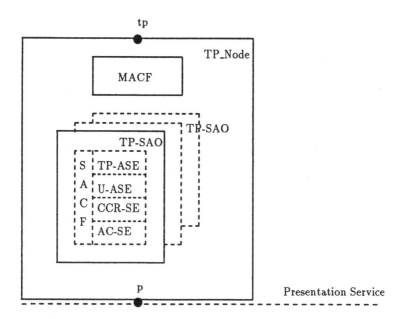

Fig. 2. Structure of a TP_Node.

for interactions between TP-ASE and MACF, the gate **uu** for interactions between U-ASE and MACF, and the gate **ca** for the interactions between the TP specific components and the common application service elements in the CA-layer.

The advantages of the sublayering are the possibility to reuse the CA-layer for other Application-layer protocols and the separation of functionalities by a well defined service boundary which forms a better basis for testing and the division of design tasks. A disadvantage is for instance the splitting of the coordination function SACF in a part residing in the TP specific layer and a part residing in the CA layer. Incorporation of protocol mechanisms to improve efficiency, e.g. concatenations of protocol data units (PDUs), are therefore difficult or impossible to realize. If these mechanisms will be needed in a later phase, the protocol entities of these sublayers could be merged together in another design iteration or a new design cycle.

As was mentioned earlier, this paper describes the TP specific parts only. For convenience, we drop the word "specific" and denote the depleted layer as "TP protocol layer" in the sequel.

This design step yields the process **TP_Node** depicted in Fig. 3. A node is either a root-node or an intermediate- (/leaf-) node. The MACF part of an intermediate- or leaf-node comprises entities, i.e. **M_Branch** and **M_SubBranch** in the figure, that control the transaction branches and an entity, i.e. **M_Manage- Branches**, that manages these controlling entities. A root-node is a special case of an intermediate-node because it does not have a superior. Thus, its specification does not contain the process **M_SubBranch**, which represents the controlling part of a transaction branch at the subordinate side.

Step 5:

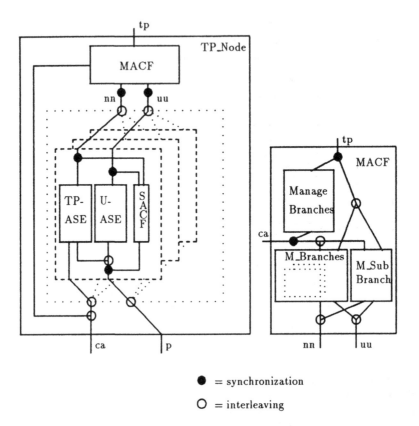

● = synchronization

○ = interleaving

Fig. 3. Refined structure of a TP_Node.

The protocol resources are then specified using mainly the constraint-oriented style, which expresses externally observable behaviour of processes as conjunction of constraints [12]. Some components, typically the simple ones, are specified using the state-oriented style or the monolithic style.

Step 6:
Finally, design support tools are used to check the specification for syntax- and static semantics correctness and to simulate the dynamic properties.

Design step 6 has led to some revisions of the specification. Refinement steps have also been performed yielding new versions with additional behaviour for example behaviour concerning late dialogue rejections. These refinements are also checked and simulated by tools.

5.2 Implementation Phase

The objective of the chosen implementation trajectory is to transform a resource-constraint oriented TP Protocol specification to an implementation comprising of several processes which are specified in the state-oriented style and whose interaction structure is restricted to two-way synchronizations. This implementation will then be realizable, because states explosion will be prevented and interactions between the extended finite state machines (EFSMs) will be realizable in standard C/UNIX.

First, the applied implementation trajectory is discussed. Then, an alternative implementation strategy, i.e. a function-call oriented approach, is explained briefly.

5.2.1 TP Implementation Trajectory.

The implementation phase is divided into two subphases. The first yields an intermediate specification where multi-way synchronizations between certain processes are transformed to two-way synchronizations. The remaining multi-way synchronizations are harmless, because they will be eliminated during the transformation of these processes into EFSM representations in the second subphase. The transformations discussed in the first subphase are inspired by some of the transformations discussed in the guidelines of the design methods [16] but are adapted to TP specific needs and all are performed manually. This enables correct and relatively easy replacements of the multi-way synchronizations. The following design steps are performed.

Adjustment of the protocol structure to ISODE capabilities.

In this design step, the CCR-SE component is moved from the CA layer to the TP (specific) protocol layer. The incorporated CCR-SE component is a simplified version of the CCR-SE component specified within the project [17]. It is tailored to match the chosen profile. Since the target realization environment ISODE 6.0 contains a realization of AC-SE, this component remains in the CA layer. Thus, the adjusted CA service can now be directly provided by ISODE.

This restructuring causes the split of gate ca into gates c and a. The c gate will be used for interactions with CCR. It is a hidden gate in the process TP_Node and associated with it is an adapted event structure. The a gate is defined at the CA service boundary and is used to access AC-SE.

Multi-way to two-way synchronizations transformations.

As was mentioned earlier, these transformations are performed manually, because specific knowledge of TP is necessary. Many multi- to two-way synchronization transformations yield a kind of handshake procedure, for instance a procedure comprising a vote phase followed either by a commit or a cancel phase. The transformations used here yield a one phase procedure. They induce additional hidden gates that are needed to realize multi-way synchronizations by means of two-way synchronization mechanisms.

Firstly, the behaviour of the control function SACF, i.e. the component which typically causes multi-way synchronizations, is partitioned and migrated into the components which are usually controlled by SACF. It is not clear, however, whether this partitioning step will also succeed in general cases.

Identification of EFSM components:
A design substep is the identification of protocol resources which will be converted into the state-oriented style. The following criteria are applied to identify EFSM

candidates:

- The architecture of the resource-constraint-oriented protocol version should be preserved as much as possible.
- The interactions between the identified resources should be minimal (*orthogonality*). This condition is fulfilled when the architecture of the resource-constraint-oriented version is preserved.
- The number of identified resources and the number of their states should be manageable.
- The multi-way synchronizations between the identified resources should be transformable to two-way synchronizations.

The application service elements, i.e. the processes TP_ASE, U_ASE, and CCR_SE, are well-defined and self-contained communication functions. They are in a certain sense orthogonal modules of TP Protocol, and therefore suitable EFSM candidates. The process MACF manages all transaction branches, which in some applications could be large in number. MACF is therefore liable to state explosion and hence not suited as an EFSM candidate. Its component processes, i.e. M_Branch, M_SubBranch, and ManageBranches, are however suitable candidates. Thus the following six EFSM candidates are selected: TP_ASE, U_ASE, CCR_SE, M_Branch, M_SubBranch and ManageBranches.

Elimination of multi-way synchronizations:
In the resource-constraint oriented specification several *absorption* processes are defined. They are only required to fulfil LOTOS synchronization conditions. They do not contribute to any TP specific constraints. Therefore, these processes are not regarded as genuinely participating processes in a multi-way synchronization. They will become useless after the elimination of multi-way synchronizations, and thus discarded in this step.

After analysing the specification, three cases of three-way synchronizations are identified. These three-way synchronizations were resolved by introducing new hidden gates. This implied that one three-way synchronization had to be replaced by two subsequent two-way synchronizations, one of which occurs at the hidden gate. *Example:* The old specification

```
process MACFRoot[tp,nn,c,a,uu]:=
  ManageBranches[tp,c,a] |[tp,c,a]| M_Branches[tp,nn,c,a,uu]
endproc
```

becomes

```
process MACFRoot[tp,nn,c,a,uu]:=
  hide as in
    ManageBranches[tp,c,as] (* synchr. at gate "a" replaced *)
    |[tp,c,as]| M_Branches[tp,nn,c,a,uu,as]
endproc
```

Resolving non-deterministic behaviour.
This design step reduces non-deterministic behaviour of the specification. In the architectural specification, some distributions of service primitives are not imposed by a specific order. This design step restricts this behaviour by explicitly prescribing an order.

Transformations to the state-oriented style.
This design step yields the implementation of the protocol, i.e. the version which consists of processes that are expressed in the state-oriented style. Multi-way synchronizations between these processes are removed in a previous design step. This transformation step is performed in two substeps: tool aided transformations of processes to EFSMs and the compression of the generated state machines.

SMILE Aided Transformations:
The derivation of the EFSMs is performed with the help of the LITE tool SMILE [18]. Selection predicates which put constraints only on variables that are not declared in the experiment offers are automatically transformed to guards by SMILE. These guards are realizable in C, e.g. by "if-then-else" or "switch – case" structures.

Compression of SMILE output:
The state-oriented processes derived by SMILE are voluminous and unreadable. They are improved by hand to yield a concise and readable specification. The following redundancies produced by SMILE are removed: the extended identifiers, the internal exits, duplicate and superfluous parameters, superfluous gates, superfluous predicates, superfluous states. Furthermore, the lay-out of the specification is manually polished, e.g. by removing superfluous square brackets.

5.2.2 Function-call Oriented Approach.

The approach described in the previous subsection works well if the target environment offers some facilities w.r.t. multi-tasking and inter-process communication. Else it is more laborious to implement a protocol machine as a set of communicating EFSMs on a single processor. A protocol realization in ISODE consists of a group of function-calls. Most of these functions correspond to outgoing service primitives and calling such a function can be explained as an issue of the corresponding service primitive. There are several ways to detect incoming service primitives. First they can be passed via one of the return parameters of a function-call for an outgoing service primitive. Secondly it is possible to call a *ReadRequest* function. This function looks for incoming service primitives and if one has arrived it is passed through by means of the return parameters.

When applying the function-call oriented approach, each function should still be aware of the state of the protocol. This may be done using **static** or global data structures. The data inside these structures can be manipulated by the functions and will not be lost upon return of the function-call. In the implementation, this requires refined ADT specifications instead of refinements on the behaviour part. This way of implementing a protocol seems a very good approach to the TP designers, because it is considered that using this "ISODE" style, it will be more easy to build a realization that can communicate well with ISODE. A predefined implementation construct approach [21] may be used here. TP application designers should be supported with these predefined constructs at TP service users level. In turn, these constructs should be specified by ISODE predefined implementation constructs.

5.3 Realization Phase

Some of the realization issues which were used to guide the earlier described implementation phase are discussed in this section. The implementation phase yields protocol entities, each of which is specified as cooperating EFSMs. The realization of these entities in ISODE may be achieved by converting these EFSMs to C-ex tasks and linking them to a C-ex version of ISODE [19]. Other alternatives that are suitable to realize the state-oriented protocol realize the interaction concept by inter-process communications such as UNIX sockets and pipes, or by communication via shared memory such as in SUN-OS light-weight processes, see e.g. COLOS [20].

In addition, predefined ISODE constructs [21] could also be applied. This will require an intermediate design where some of the EFSMs identified earlier have to be internally reconfigured such that state transitions representing an ISODE construct are obtained. A preliminary study of the protocol gives the impression that this regrouping of primitives will not cause structural changes *among* the EFSMs due to the orthogonality of the components.

Another design step which must be performed in the realization phase concerns the error-handling procedures. As was mentioned earlier, the selection predicates which put constraints on only values of variables that are not declared at the experiment offers are transformed to guards by SMILE. The transformation of the remaining selection predicates is only useful if *unanticipated environment behaviour*, i.e. the error handling, is included in the specification. This will yield a realizable structure because all events offered at the external gates will be accepted by the protocol entity. The incorporation of error handling was not planned in the implementation phase. It may be included in the realization phase if necessary.

6 Status of the Specifications

The specifications discussed in this paper have been syntactically and semantically checked by the LITE tools [23]. Some testing by means of dynamic simulations using SMILE have been performed. The interworking between several protocol entities configured in a realistic transaction tree has been validated by simulations in a user environment. This transaction tree consists of a root-, two child-, and a grandchild-node. The TOPO compiler has been used to produce the prototype executables for the simulations.

Furthermore a second-design cycle to extend the specified functionality has been undertaken. The main reason for doing this, was to check the open-endedness of the specification. The global architectural structure of this extended specification is identical to the global structure of the first-cycle specification. Only some LOTOS processes at the bottom of the hierarchy of the extended specification have adapted structures. Details of this extended specification may be found in [22]. This second cycle has indeed shown that the first-cycle specification is open-ended in this respect.

The implementation has been subjected to the same tests as the architectural specification. During these tests several erroneous primitive orderings were found and most of them have been corrected. However the implementation accepts some unpermitted service primitive sequences during a short period in certain two-way synchronization interactions. Unfortunately these unpermitted sequences are caused by the elimination process of multi-way synchronizations. These unpermitted sequences are now difficult to remove, because of the semantics of LOTOS. In LOTOS it is not possible to specify priorities for event-offerings. Now when several events are offered, each of them is allowed to happen. With the help of priority-levels one can specify which of the events should occur first. With the help of such mechanism the unpermitted sequences mentioned previously are easily removed. In a realization in C (or in COLOS), these erroneous primitive orderings can be eliminated when certain internal interactions are scheduled prior to external interactions.

7 Experiences

LotoSphere design methodology enabled unexperienced designers to specify and implement a profile of a complex protocol in an effectively short time.

Difficulties were however encountered when applying the formal technique in the early steps of a design stage, especially when applying the constraint-oriented style. In practice, the process of designing goes along with the process of understanding the design. Accordingly, engineers have the habit to make non-detailed skeletons of specifications in their first design trials to experiment with different compositional structures. The design technique, however, required sufficiently detailed and precise notations before design supporting tools could be used. Without the help of tools, unexperienced designers remain unaware of the correctness and the implications of a chosen architectural structure. The ability to make first trails in an informal way with the help of tools was felt missing in the design environment.

On the other hand, in the late design phases the preciseness of LOTOS, i.e. the unambiguous interpretation of the behaviour of a LOTOS process, helped the designers in efficiently transform their architectural specification to specifications that are closer to realizations. The availability of design guidelines, including generic correctness preserving transformations, considerably improved the effectiveness of the design process. This impression is supported by the fact that the implementation phase used only one-third of the manpower used in the architectural phase.

In many distributed systems, only a few of the interworking processes need to interact at a certain moment, the others are not involved in this interaction. The set of interacting processes changes dynamically. As usual, the interworking between the LOTOS processes in the specifications discussed here were specified in a static and conjunctive way. The static structure implied that interworking processes which were not involved in a particular interaction had to offer "don't-care" events to fulfill LOTOS synchronization requirement. These events were specified in the so-called *absorbing* processes. These processes easily induce design errors such as unpermitted event orderings, they slow-down dynamic simulations, and not to mention that specification of these processes took time. These processes were undesirable because they actually did not contribute to the semantics, but they were necessary. In the implementation phase, these absorbing processes became obsolete due to the interactions that were limited to two-way synchronizations.

Transformations of TP protocol specific architectural structures and behaviour were sufficient with simplified forms of the previously mentioned generic transformation techniques. Most transformations were therefore performed manually and thus prone to human mistakes. Use of design supporting tools was found essential in these cases, especially the use of the dynamic simulator and the compiler. The tools were also useful to test the composition of the components which were designed by different partners. The compiler was often used to test the observable behaviour of a TP protocol entity or of cooperating protocol entities. The simulator was used to evaluate external as well as internal behaviour of protocol components. It was also used to pinpoint errors after detecting observable errors during tests on compiled prototype executables. The reason to use the compiler was that the compiled code ran faster then a dynamic simulation session.

In the implementation phase, the design activity was mainly focussed on the behaviour part of the protocol. The realization of this part is not expected to be difficult. This will not be the case for the realization of the ADT part. This is due to the verboseness of the ADT part and the complexity of ISODE data structures. An approach which may (partly) solve the problem is the use of ASN.1 as a intermediate abstract syntax for the data structures where from ACT-ONE as well as ISODE-C structures can be derived by available data-compilers.

The implementation strategy proposed by the LotoSphere methodology is suitable for a target environments that facilitate multi-tasking or inter-process communication. These facilities are often slow in performance. The realization environment ISODE, on the other hand, provides a set of C-functions such that a desired service may be offered by scheduling appropriate function-calls. Realization structures supported by ISODE suit todays common practice. It will be very useful if the design methods support this type of implementation structure. In fact, specific types of predefined implementation constructs can be used for this purpose.

It was not possible to assess thoroughly the LotoSphere design methodology, mainly due to limitation of resources. Generation of test suites with a large or a full coverage and application of correctness preserving transformations using tools, except the derivations of the finite state machines, were not investigated. The other testbed tasks within the project have for example used refined test suites. The assessment performed with this work concentrated on the qualitative aspects, i.e. the realizability and open-endedness of specifications. It also tried the previously mentioned tools out on medium size specifications.

8 Conclusions

This paper describes the specification and implementation of a subset of OSI-TP Protocol in LOTOS. This activity was meant to assess the LotoSphere design methods and design support tools on their industrial applicability.

The identification of the distinct design phases, the step-wise and cyclic design approach with the possibility to iterate, enabled unexperienced designers to specify and transform specifications towards implementations in an effectively short time. This was also possible due to the availability of design guidelines and the appropriate use of specification styles. The design methods, moreover, support the achievement of approved quality in the designs. The functionality extension of the resource-constraint-oriented specification within a short period shows the open-endedness of the specification, for example. The derivation of the state-oriented specification is an example which shows the realizability of the specifications. Due to the carefully chosen architectural structure of the specification and the use of the resource-constraint-oriented specification style, design steps in the implementation phase, and also in some parts of the realization phase, were relatively easy to perform.

The preciseness of LOTOS expressions and the necessity to specify them in a sufficiently complete and accurate way may hamper unexperienced designers in the early design phase for example when these designers have not acquired good insight on the design. In the late design phases, on the other hand, these preciseness helps these designers in transforming the specifications in a more realizable form.

The use of some LITE tools during the design process has proven to be essential in order to achieve the required quality of specifications. The tools helped the designer in locating design errors effectively. The simulator tool was also used to generate the state-oriented specification though some polishing of the generated finite state machines were necessary.

Acknowledgement

The authors would like to thank Edwin van der Burg, François Juillot, Ron Greve, Frances Riddoch, and Franck Sadoun for their contributions in the reported TP design activity. They also like to thank Marcel Baveco and Marten van Sinderen for their support and advice.

References

1. C. A. Vissers, J. v.d. Lagemaat "Report on LotoSphere" *Proc. ESPRIT Technical Week*, Brussels, Nov. 1989

2. J. Navarro and P. San Martin, "Experience in the Development of an ISDN Layer 3 Service in LOTOS", in J. Quemada et.al. (eds), *Formal Description Techniques III*, North Holland, 1991 pages 327 – 336.

3. R. E. Booth, V. M. Jones, R. J. Clark, F. Juillot, G-J. van der Heijden, and I. Widya, "A formal development trajectory for OSI application layer protocols", *Proc. of the 5th International Conference on Putting into Practice Methods and Tools for Information System Design*, Nantes, Sept. 1992.

4. "LOTOS Industrial Application: Mini-Mail", E. Wiedmer, LotoSphere Project ESPRIT II 2304, Final Deliverable, Lo/WP3/T3.2/N0068, 1992

5. ISO/DIS 10026-3 Information Processing Systems – Open Systems Interconnection – Distributed Transaction Processing – Part 3: Protocol Specification, 1990.

6. ISO, "Protocol Specification for the Association Control Service Element", ISO/IS 8650, 1988.

7. ISO, "Protocol Specification for the Commitment, Concurrency and Recovery Service Element" ISO/IS 9805.3,

8. M. T. Rose, "The ISO Development Environment: User's Manual", ISODE 6.0, Performance Systems Int. Inc., Jan. 1990.

9. A. M. Fletcher, "An Overview of the OSI Transaction Processing Standard", *Proc. Int. Open Systems '89*, Online Publ., 1989, page 153 – 162.

10. L. F. Pires and C. A. Vissers, "Overview of the LotoSphere Design Methodology", *ESPRIT Conf. 1990*, Brussels Nov. 12 – 15, 1990.

11. ISO, "LOTOS – a Formal Description Technique Based on the Temporal Ordering of Observational Behaviour", ISO/IS 8807, 1988.

12. C. A. Vissers, G. Scollo and M. van Sinderen, "Architecture and Specification Style in Formal Descriptions of Distributed Systems", *Proc. IFIP WG6.1, PSTV VIII*, North Holland, 1989, page 189 – 204.

13. ISO, "Guidelines for the Application Estelle, LOTOS and SDS, ISO-IEC/TR 10167, 1990.

14. ISO, "Application Layer Structure", ISO/IS 9545, 1989.

15. M. van Sinderen and I. Widya, "On the Design and Formal Specification of a Transaction Processing Protocol", In J. Quemada et.al. (eds), *Formal Description Technique III*, North Holland, 1991, pages 411 – 426.

16. "The Lotosphere Design Methodology: Guidelines", LotoSphere Project ESPRIT II 2304, Lo/WP1/T1.1/N0044/V04, March 1992.

17. "LOTOS Specification of the OSI CCR Protocol: Architecture", Val. Jones and Robert Clark, LotoSphere Project ESPRIT II 2304, Lo/WP3/T3.1/UST/N0003.

18. H. Eertink and D. Wolz, "Symbolic Execution of LOTOS Specification", *Proceeding of the 5th International Conference on Formal Description Techniques*, ed. M. Diaz and R. Groz, Lannion, France, Oct. 1992, pp. 289 – 304.

19. "Implementation of the OSI Association Control Service Element Using C-ex", R. Levy, Computer Networks Laboratory, EPF-Lausanne, Switzerland, 1991

20. "Detailed Design Document: COLOS", E. Dubuis and K. Warkentyne, LotoSphere Project ESPRIT II 2304, Lo/WP2/T2.2/ASCOM/N0024, 1992.

21. "On the Use of Pre-Defined Implementation Constructs in Distributed Systems Design", L. F. Pires, M. van Sinderen and C. A. Vissers, *Third Workshop on Future Trends of Distributed Computing Systems in the 1990's*, Taipei, April 1992

22. "TP Protocol Version 3.0: a cycle 2 version", E. van der Burg, and I. Widya, LotoSphere Project ESPRIT II 2304, Lo/WP3/T3.1/UT/N0020/V2, 1992.

23. M. Caneve and E. Salvatori (eds), "Lite User Manual", ESPRIT II 2304 internal report Lo/WP2/N0034, April, 1991.

A Metalanguage for the Formal Requirement Specification of Reactive Systems *

Egidio Astesiano – Gianna Reggio

Università di Genova – Dipartimento di Informatica e Scienze dell'Informazione
Viale Benedetto XV,3 16132, Genova, Italy
astes, reggio cisi.unige.it

1 Introduction

Various formalisms have been proposed for the specification of software / hardware systems characterized by the possibility of performing some dynamic activities interacting with an external world, called reactive systems; however in the literature sometimes also terms as: concurrent, parallel, distributed, ... systems have been used for pointing out to some particualr features of the systems; here we simply use the term *reactive systems*. Some of these formalisms deal with properties at what we may call design level, when already architectural decisions have been taken and a specification determines essentially one structure, though still at a rather abstract level (we say abstract specifications). Among these, some, like CCS, CSP and variations, are more languages for describing elegant models than specification formalisms; others are instead suitable for expressing, with more or less generality, abstract properties about the static data, like PSF [12], LOTOS [10] and algebraic Petri nets [20] or about both the static data and the concurrent architecture, like SMoLCS [1, 2, 5]. The interested reader may wish to look at [3] for a survey dealing mainly with abstract specifications at the design level.

At the requirement level, the proposed formalisms are dealing with the abstract dynamic properties, i.e. those related to the possible events in a system life, usually classified in safety and liveness properties. There is a literature on formalisms based on temporal, deontic, event logic and others (see e.g. [15, 9, 17], also for references). Now the experience shows that also the structural properties of a system (including the static data) and their relationships with dynamic features of a system are fundamental also at the requirement level; however the specification mechanism should be able to avoid overspecification, not confusing requirements and design.

We intend in this paper to propose an approach, supported by a metalanguage (schema), for dealing, at the requirement level, with both static and dynamic properties.

The approach is based on a specification formalism which, according to the institution paradigm (see [6]), consists in models (semantic structures), sentences or formulae (syntax) and validity (semantics of sentences). A specification is a set of formulae determining a class of models, all those satisfying the formulae. The new and

* This work has been supported by "Progetto Finalizzato Sistemi Informatici e Calcolo Parallelo" of C.N.R. (Italy), Esprit-BRA W.G. COMPASS n. 6112 and by a grant ENEL-SPA/CRA (Milano Italy).

central idea of this paper is the proposed models, that we call entity algebras. Those models can support statements about the structure of reactive systems, dealing with the subcomponents of a system, without referring to detailed structuring combinators, which are essential at the design level, but here would spoil the generality of requirements.

In the first section we give a rather informal presentation of entity algebras, illustrated by a small example. In the second we present the syntax of a specification language and in the third section the notion of validity of a formula and the semantic of a specification; some examples concerning also the application to an industrial test case are reported in the fourth section. The used algebraic notions and notations are reported in Appendix A.

Two important comments are in order. First our metalanguage is rather schematic, in the sense that we can choose various formalisms for expressing the dynamic properties. Here, we give just a set of combinators, taken from the branching time logic, sufficient for expressing some common interesting requirements on reactive systems; for other choices, see e.g. [8] which uses a richer choice of branching time combinators and [17], which presents an event logic, where the properties on the activity of the elements are expressed in terms of relationships among occurrences of non-instantaneosus events. In general, depending on the specific application field (e.g., industrial plants handled by automatisms, software / hardware architectures and so on) one can choose a minimal set of combinators getting a formalism powerful enough but rather simple. The important point is that now the dynamic formulae are "anchored" to a term representing a dynamic element and so we have a formalism where it is possible to express requirements involving properties on the activity either of different systems or of a system and some of its components; for example we can express properties of the form "a new component which can eventually reach a certain situation cannot be added to a system satisfying some condition".

Second, though we do not insist on the more formal aspects, it can be shown formally (not a trivial task) that indeed we get an institution; the interested reader may look at [16, 4, 7] for a more formal presentation of entity algebras and specifications.

2 The Models

2.1 Entity Algebras

Here we introduce our models for reactive systems called *entity algebras* (*entity* is the word that we use for possibly structured dynamic elements).

The models should allow to represent the dynamic activity of the entities. We adopt the well-known and accepted technique which consists in viewing entities as labelled transition trees defined by a labelled transition system (see [13, 14]).

A *labelled transition system* (shortly *lts*) is a triple $(STATE, LAB, \rightarrow)$, where $STATE$ and LAB are sets, whose elements represent respectively the *states* and the *labels* of the system and $\rightarrow \subseteq STATE \times LAB \times STATE$ is the *transition relation*; $(s, l, s') \in \rightarrow$ is said a *transition* and is usually denoted by $s \xrightarrow{l} s'$.

An entity E can be represented by an lts LTS and an initial state $s_0 \in STATE$; then the states of LTS reachable by a sequence of transitions from s_0 represent the intermediate (interesting) situations of the activity of E and the transition relation of LTS the possibilities of E of passing from one situation to another. Note that here a transition $s \xrightarrow{l} s'$ has the following meaning: E in the state (situation) s has the *capability* of passing into the state (situation) s' by performing a transition whose interaction with the external (to E) world is represented by the label l; thus l contains both information on the conditions on the external world for the capability to become effective, and on the transformation of the external world induced by the execution of the transition.

The models should allow to represent the structure of the entities. Usually most of the reactive systems of interest are structured, i.e. are systems where dynamic subcomponents interact among them for determining the activity of the whole system (in general the dynamic subcomponents may be in turn structured systems). Think for example of the Ada programs (whose subcomponents are the tasks, while tasks have no subcomponents, they are simple) or a net of workstations on which UNIX is running (the subcomponents of the nets are the workstations, while the subcomponents of the workstations are the UNIX processes, which may be simple or have as subcomponents other processes). So in general in a system there are different "sorts" (types) of entities, all of them modelled by lts's. In the Ada case there are entities of sort "program" and "task", while in the workstation case of sort "net", "workstation" and "process". Thus the first component of our model is

$$\{LTS_{es}\}_{es \in ES},$$

where ES is the set of the various sorts of entities and for each $es \in ES$

$$LTS_{es} = (STATE_{es}, LAB_{es}, \rightarrow_{es}) \quad \text{is an lts.}$$

Then the models should allow to know which are the subcomponents of an entity (possibly none) with their sorts and how they are organized to get the whole entity; to this end we have *entity composers*, i.e. partial functions taking as arguments entities, also of different sorts, and returning an entity of a certain sort; precisely an entity composer of arity "$es_1 \times \ldots \times es_n \rightarrow es$", for $n \geq 0$ is:

- when $n > 0$, a partial function

$$Ec: STATE_{es_1} \times \ldots \times STATE_{es_n} \rightarrow STATE_{es};$$

- when $n = 0$, a constant
$$Ec \in STATE_{es}.$$

If $e = Ec(e_1, \ldots, e_n)$, then $e_1, \ldots, e_n$ are the *(immediate) subcomponents* of e.

By giving a set of entity composers, we get the complete views of the structure of the entities.

For example, assume $e = Ec(e_1, \ldots, e_n)$, $e_1 = Ec'(e_1', \ldots, e_k')$ and that $e_1', \ldots, e_k', e_2, \ldots, e_n$ have no subcomponents, i.e. for $i = 1, \ldots, k$ $e_i' = Ec_i'$ and for $j = 2$,

..., n $e_j = Ec_j$ with $Ec'_1, \ldots, Ec'_k$, $Ec_2, \ldots, Ec_n$ zero-ary entity composers; thus *a view of the structure* of e is given by the following graph

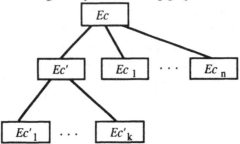

Notice that we have spoken of *a* view of the structure of e and not of *the* view of the structure, since there may be different views of the structure of an entity; think for example of a system where the subcomponents which reach an error situation do not affect any more the activity of the system, thus we can have, e.g.,

$$e = Ec(e_1, \ldots, e_n) = Ec''(e_1, \ldots, e_n, e_{n+1})$$

where e_{n+1} corresponds to an error situation and so there are two different views of the structure of e.

Clearly, in general, the activity of a structured entity is determined by the activity of its subcomponents, see the examples in the following subsection.

Since we are interested in having an algebraic framework, for getting a specification formalism integrating the specifications of abstract data types, we precisely define the models, whose main features have been introduced above, as algebras; see the Appendix A for a summary of algebraic definitions and notations.

Entity signatures should provide syntactic elements for representing all parts of the models, so they are particular signatures with predicates having:

- sorts for the various types of entities (*entity sorts*),
- predicate symbols corresponding to the transition relations of the entities and sorts for the associated labels,
- operation symbols corresponding to the entity composers;

obviously also sorts, operation and predicate symbols for representing and manipulating the data handled by the entities. Entity algebras will be partial algebras with predicates on entity signatures s.t. we can find at least a view of the structure of each element of entity sort. Entity signatures and algebras are formally given below.

- An *entity signature* $E\Sigma$ is a pair (Σ, ES), where $\Sigma = (S, OP, PR)$ is a signature with predicates, $ES \subseteq S$ (the set of the entity sorts) s.t. for each $es \in ES$ there exists a sort $l\text{-}es \in S$ (labels of the transitions of entities of sort es) and a predicate symbol $\_ \overset{\_}{\longrightarrow} \_ : es \times l\text{-}es \times es \in PR$ (representing the transitions of entities of sort es) .

For a given $E\Sigma$, the family of the *entity composers* is

$$EC(E\Sigma) = \{EC_{w,es}\}_{w \in ES^*, es \in ES},$$

where for all w, es $EC_{w,es} = OP_{w,es}$.

- An *entity algebra* EA on $E\Sigma = (\Sigma, ES)$ is just a Σ-many-sorted partial algebra with predicates s.t. each $e \in EA_{es}$, with $es \in ES$, is representable by a composition of interpretations of entity composer (more precisely, it is the interpretation of a term built using only the entity composer operations).

- The *structure views* on EA are the ordered trees with the nodes labelled by entity composers s.t. a node labelled by $Ec: s_1 \times \ldots \times s_n \to s$, has exactly n sons whose roots are labelled by composers with result sorts $s_1, \ldots, s_n$ respectively. Now we define by induction when one of such trees is a *view of the structure* of an entity:

  * Ec is a view of the structure of e iff $e = Ec$.

  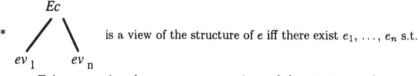

  * is a view of the structure of e iff there exist $e_1, \ldots, e_n$ s.t.

    $e = Ec(e_1, \ldots, e_n)$ and $ev_1, \ldots, ev_n$ are views of the structures of $e_1, \ldots, e_n$ respectively.

- We say that e is a *(proper) subentity* of a view ev iff there exists a (proper) subtree of ev which is a view for e.

2.2 A Small Example

For illustrating the models introduced before we give an entity algebra representing the reactive system modelling the executions of the programs of a very simple concurrent language *CL*.

In *CL* programs whatever number of sequential processes perform commands, whose syntax is given below, and evolve in an interleaving way interacting among them by exchanging signals in a synchronous way (handshaking communication).

$$com ::= \underline{skip} \mid com_1; com_2 \mid \underline{send\text{-}signal}(sig) \mid \underline{rec\text{-}signal}(sig) \mid com_1 + com_2 \mid seq$$

$\underline{skip}$ is the null command, $\underline{send\text{-}signal}$ and $\underline{rec\text{-}signal}$ are the commands for the signal exchange and "+" is the nondeterministic choice, where sig and seq are the nonterminals for signals and sequential commands not further detailed.

Let $C\Sigma$ be the entity signature given below, where "−" precedes comments, the key word "**esorts**" the list of the entity sorts, "**sorts**" the list of the remaining sorts and "**opns**", "**preds**" the list of the operations and predicate symbols respectively with their functionalities. Moreover for some of the operation and predicate symbols, we use a mixfix notation; for instance,

$$\_ \mid\mid \_: proc \times proc \to proc$$

means that we shall write $p_1 \mid\mid p_2$ instead of $\mid\mid(p_1, p_2)$; i.e. terms of appropriate sorts replace underscores.

sig $C\Sigma =$
    esorts $prog, proc$
       −   in this case there are two kinds of entities:
       −   CL programs and processes and so two entity sorts

sorts $l\text{-}prog, l\text{-}proc, sig$

opns

$\qquad C: \to proc \qquad$ for all commands C defined by the above BNF

$-\quad$ entity composers for entities of sort $proc$

$-\quad$ (they are simple entities, i.e. without dynamic subcomponents)

$\qquad TAU: \to l\text{-}proc \qquad - \quad$ process internal activity

$\qquad SEND, REC: sig \to l\text{-}proc$

$-\quad$ for labelling the process transitions corresponding to sending and

$-\quad$ receiving signals

$\qquad \alpha, \beta, \ldots: \to sig \qquad - \quad$ the signals are just Greek letters

$\qquad \underbrace{\_ \parallel \_ \ldots \_ \parallel \_}_{n \text{ times}} \_: \underbrace{proc \times \ldots \times proc}_{n \text{ times}} \to prog \qquad n \geq 1$

$-\quad$ entity composers for programs

$\qquad \tau: \to l\text{-}prog \qquad - \quad$ program internal activity

preds

$\qquad \_ \xrightarrow{} \_: proc \times l\text{-}proc \times proc \qquad - \quad$ transition predicate for processes

$\qquad \_ \Longrightarrow \_: prog \times l\text{-}prog \times prog \qquad - \quad$ transition predicate for programs

Let CL be the term-generated $C\Sigma$-algebra s.t.:

- the carriers of sorts sig, $l\text{-}proc$ and $l\text{-}prog$ are the sets of the ground terms of the corresponding sorts on $C\Sigma$; the carrier of $proc$ is the set of the quotient of the ground terms of sort $proc$ w.r.t. the identifications requiring that ";" is associative, "+" is associative, commutative and both have "skip" as identity; while CL_{prog} is the set of the finite non-empty parts of CL_{proc}.

  Here for simplicity the interpretation in CL of $Symb$, either a predicate or an operation symbol, will be simply written $Symb$ and analogously for ground terms, thus t^{CL} will be written t.

- $p_1 \parallel \ldots \parallel p_n = \{p_1, \ldots, p_n\}$ for all $n \geq 1$, while the interpretations of the other operations are defined in the obvious way;

- the interpretations of the transition predicates are defined by the following inductive rules.

$$\frac{}{sq \xrightarrow{TAU} p'} \quad sq \text{ sequential command}$$

$$\frac{}{\text{send-signal}(s) \xrightarrow{SEND(s)} \text{skip}} \qquad \frac{}{\text{rec-signal}(s) \xrightarrow{REC(s)} \text{skip}}$$

$$\frac{p_1 \xrightarrow{l} p_1'}{p_1; p_2 \xrightarrow{l} p_1'; p_2} \qquad \frac{p_1 \xrightarrow{l} p_1'}{p_1 + p_2 \xrightarrow{l} p_1'}$$

$$\frac{p_1 \xrightarrow{TAU} p_1'}{p_1 \parallel p_2 \parallel \ldots \parallel p_n \xrightarrow{\tau} p_1' \parallel p_2 \parallel \ldots \parallel p_n}$$

$$\frac{p_1 \xrightarrow{SEND(s)} p_1' \quad p_2 \xrightarrow{REC(s)} p_2'}{p_1 \parallel p_2 \parallel p_3 \parallel \ldots \parallel p_n \xrightarrow{\tau} p_1' \parallel p_2' \parallel p_3 \parallel \ldots \parallel p_n} \quad n \geq 2$$

Notice that since the interpretations of + and || are commutative, the above rules fully describe the activity of the *CL* programs.

The following examples show that our definition of entity algebras allows to formally describe several interesting situations occurring in reactive systems.

Different ways of composing some entities may be equivalent.

$$pg = \underline{\text{send-signal}}(\alpha) \mid\mid \underline{\text{rec-signal}}(\beta) \in \text{CL}_{prog}$$

is an entity whose structure may be seen in two different ways; indeed *pg* is also equal to

$$\underline{\text{rec-signal}}(\beta) \mid\mid \underline{\text{send-signal}}(\alpha);$$

that means that in *CL* programs the order of the processes in parallel is not relevant.
The two views of the structure of *pg* are graphically represented by

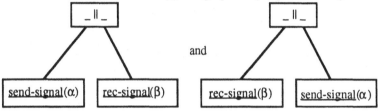

and

Compositions of different groups of entities may be equivalent. It is possible that an entity has some views of its structure with different number of subentities; indeed, for example,

$$pg' = \underline{\text{send-signal}}(\alpha) = \underline{\text{send-signal}}(\alpha) \mid\mid \underline{\text{skip}} = \underline{\text{send-signal}}(\alpha) \mid\mid \underline{\text{skip}} \mid\mid \underline{\text{skip}} = \ldots$$

Thus in the *CL* programs the processes which cannot perform any action (<u>skip</u>) do not matter.
Various views of the structure of *pg'* are graphically represented by:

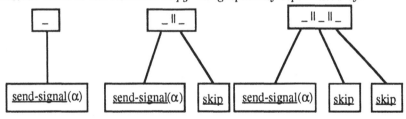

Sharing of subentities. Consider a language CL_1 differing from *CL* only for having a multilevel parallelism instead of a flat one; we just take a new signature $C\Sigma_1$ obtained from $C\Sigma$ by replacing the various operations "||" (entity composers for programs) with

$$\_: proc \to prog \qquad \_\mid\mid\mid\_: prog \times prog \to prog,$$

and give a $C\Sigma_1$-entity algebra CL_1 in the same way of CL. In this case an entity of sort *prog* has either one subentity of sort *proc* or two subentities of the same sort *prog*.

$$pg'' = (p_1 \mid\mid\mid p_2) \mid\mid\mid (p_1 \mid\mid\mid p_3),$$

is an entity where the subentity represented by p_1 is shared between the subentities "$p_1 \ ||| \ p_2$" and "$p_1 \ ||| \ p_3$"; a view of its structure is graphically represented by

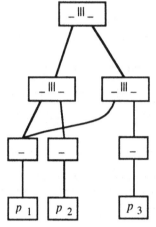

Entities may terminate and new entities may be created. Consider a language CL_2 differing from CL only for having commands corresponding to creation and termination of processes (terminate, create(p)). We take a new signature $C\Sigma_2$ obtained by adding to $C\Sigma$ operations corresponding to the new commands and

$$TERM: \to l\text{-}proc \qquad CREATE: proc \to l\text{-}proc;$$

and give the algebra CL_2 in the same way as CL; where the transitions due to the new commands are given by

$$\underline{\text{terminate}} \xrightarrow{TERM} \underline{\text{skip}} \qquad \underline{\text{create}(p)} \xrightarrow{CREATE(p)} \underline{\text{skip}}$$

$$\frac{p_1 \xrightarrow{TERM} p_1'}{p_1 \ || \ p_2 \ || \ \dots \ || \ p_n \overset{\tau}{\Longrightarrow} p_2 \ || \ \dots \ || \ p_n}$$

$$\frac{p_1 \xrightarrow{CREATE(p)} p_1'}{p_1 \ || \ p_2 \ || \ \dots \ || \ p_n \overset{\tau}{\Longrightarrow} p \ || \ p_1' \ || \ p_2 \ || \ \dots \ || \ p_n}$$

Graphically an example of a creation and of a termination of a process are shown by the transitions:

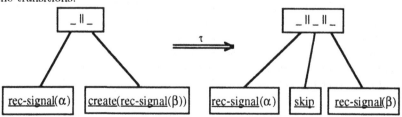

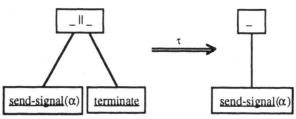

These last examples show also that an entity can modify its structure during a transition.

3 The Syntax of the Metalanguage

Now we look for an appropriate language for expressing abstract requirements on reactive systems formally described by entity algebras.

As a first attempt we could use first-order formulae on entity signatures (see Appendix A); with this language we can express some interesting properties. Consider the signature $C\Sigma$ introduced in Section 2.2; the axiom

$$\neg(\alpha = \beta)$$

requires that the signals (static elements) represented by α and β should be different; while

$$p_1 \parallel p_2 = p_2 \parallel p_1$$

requires that the order of the process components of a CL program does not matter; and

$$\not\exists p', p'', s, s' . tp \xrightarrow{SEND(s)} p' \wedge tp \xrightarrow{REC(s')} p''$$

requires that the process represented by the term tp cannot both receive and send signals.

However first-order logic on entity algebras has several limits:

1. concerning static properties: it cannot express properties about the structure of the entities without introducing some entity composers (as for the parallel composer $\_ \parallel \_$ before);
2. concerning dynamic properties: it can only express properties about the local activity (immediate future/past) of entities, but not e.g. liveness properties.

For overcoming these limits we extend first-order logic with:

1. Special predicates "*AllSub*" for checking which are the subentities of an entity. $\_ AllSub \_: es \times ent\text{-}set$, given a set of entities *eset* and an entity *e* of sort *es*, returns true iff *eset* is the set of all subentities (proper and not) of *e* w.r.t. some view of its structure. (Obviously we have also to introduce operations and predicates for handling set of entities.) We have found that such predicates are enough for expressing all properties of interest on the structure of entities (e.g. an entity is simple [has no subcomponents], there is an upper bound to the number of subcomponents, the activity of an entity is completely determined by the activity of its subcomponents and so on).

2. Classical temporal logic combinators similar to those of the branching time logic CTL (see [21]); briefly introduced below.

Given an entity e in an entity algebra EA, a global view of its activity is given by the set of all its *execution paths*, i.e. maximal sequences of labelled transitions of the form:

$$e \xrightarrow{\ l_1\ } \text{EA}\, e_1 \xrightarrow{\ l_2\ } \text{EA}\, e_2 \ldots$$

(clearly such sequences may be either finite or infinite); a sequence as above represents a possible behaviour of e. Thus a branching time-style property on the activity of e may be given saying either that all paths (there exists a path) for e satisfies some condition or there exists a path for e satisfying some condition. In our metalanguage we have the following combinators, where we assume that et is a term of entity sort:

- $\triangle$ (for all paths) s.t. $\triangle(et, \pi)$ holds iff "for every execution path σ starting from the entity represented by et the path formula π holds on σ";
- $\triangledown$ (exists a path) s.t. $\triangledown(et, \pi)$ holds iff "exists an execution path σ starting from the entity represented by et on which the path formula π holds".

We have borrowed $\triangle$ and $\triangledown$ from [21].

For the path formulae we have the combinators

- $\square$ (always), $\lozenge$ (eventually), for safety and liveness properties;
- $[\lambda x . \phi]$ which holds on a path σ whenever ϕ holds of the first state of σ;
- $<\lambda x . \phi>$ which holds on σ whenever ϕ holds of the first label of σ (if it exits)
- and the usual first-order combinators.

Notice that, due to the combinator $< \ldots >$ our logic includes also the so called "edge formulae" see [11].

Here, for lack of room we consider only such simple combinators; see [8] and [17] for other combinators, [8] presents also some examples motivating the introduction of $[\ldots]$ and $< \ldots >$. Notice that the choice of the metalanguage combinators for dynamic properties is in some sense orthogonal w.r.t. those for the structural properties.

Our metalanguage is then defined by putting together first-order logic with the formulae briefly introduced in 1. and 2. Formally, let $E\Sigma$ be an entity signature $((S, OP, PR), ES)$; then the axioms on $E\Sigma$ are a subclass of the dynamic formulas of [8] on a new signature $E\Sigma^{\text{ST}}$, obtained by enriching $E\Sigma$ with:

- the predicates $\_ AllSub \_: ent\text{-}set \times es$ for all $es \in ES$,
- the sort $ent\text{-}set$, whose elements are the finite sets of elements of any entity sort,
- the usual operations and predicates on finite sets of entities: $\emptyset$, $\_ \cup \_$, $\{\_\}$, $\_ \subseteq \_$.

Given a sort assignment X on $E\Sigma^{\text{ST}}$ the sets $DF_{E\Sigma}(X)$ of *dynamic formulae* and $P_{E\Sigma}(X, es)$ of *path formulae* of sort $es \in ES$ are inductively defined as follows (where $t, t_1, \ldots, t_n$ denote terms of appropriate sort on $E\Sigma^{\text{ST}}$, X and we assume that sorts are respected).

dynamic formulae

$Pr(t_1, \ldots, t_n) \in DF_{E\Sigma}(X)$ if Pr is a predicate of $E\Sigma^{\text{ST}}$

$t_1 = t_2 \in DF_{E\Sigma}(X)$

$\neg\phi_1, \ \phi_1 => \phi_2 \in DF_{E\Sigma}(X)$ if $\phi_1, \phi_2 \in DF_{E\Sigma}(X)$

$\forall x . \phi \in DF_{E\Sigma}(X)$ if $\phi \in DF_{E\Sigma}(X)$, $x \in X$

$\triangle(t, \pi) \in DF_{E\Sigma}(X)$ if t has sort es, $\pi \in P_{E\Sigma}(X, es)$, with $es \in ES$

path formulae

$[\lambda x . \phi] \in P_{E\Sigma}(X, es)$ if $x \in X_{es}$, $\phi \in DF_{E\Sigma}(X)$

$<\lambda x . \phi> \in P_{E\Sigma}(X, es)$ if $x \in X_{l\text{-}es}$, $\phi \in DF_{E\Sigma}(X)$

$\neg\pi_1, \pi_1 => \pi_2 \in P_{E\Sigma}(X, es)$ if $\pi_1, \pi_2 \in P_{E\Sigma}(X, es)$

$\forall x . \pi \in P_{E\Sigma}(X, es)$ if $\pi \in P_{E\Sigma}(X, es)$, $x \in X$

$\Box\pi \in P_{E\Sigma}(X, es)$ if $\pi \in P_{E\Sigma}(X, es)$

Moreover we consider the following derived combinators: $\exists$, $\vee$, $\equiv$ defined as usual; $\Diamond\pi =_{\text{def}} \neg\Box\neg\pi$ and $\bigtriangledown(t, \pi) =_{\text{def}} \neg \triangle (t, \neg\pi)$.

4 Validity of Formulae and Semantics of a Specification

Since $\phi \in DF_{E\Sigma}(X)$ is built on the richer signature $E\Sigma^{ST}$, first of all the validity of ϕ in an $E\Sigma$-entity algebra EA is the validity of ϕ in EA^{ST}, an appropriate extension of EA to an $E\Sigma^{ST}$-algebra, where the added sorts, operations and predicates are interpreted in the obvious way (e.g.: $eset\ AllSub^{EA^{ST}}\ e$ holds iff there exists ev a view of the structure of e s.t. $eset$ is the set of all subentities of ev), see [4] for a complete definition of EA^{ST}.

Moreover we need some preliminary definitions. We denote by $PATH(\text{EA}, es)$ the set of the execution paths for the entities of sort es, i.e. the set of all sequences having either of the two forms below:

(1) $e_0\ l_0\ e_1\ l_1\ e_2\ l_2 \ldots e_n\ l_n \ldots$ (infinite path)

(2) $e_0\ l_0\ e_1\ l_1\ e_2\ l_2 \ldots e_n\ l_n \ldots e_k\ k \geq 0$ (finite path)
     where for all $n \in \mathbb{N}$: $e_n \in \text{EA}_{es}$, $l_n \in \text{EA}_{l\text{-}es}$ and $(e_n, l_n, e_{n+1}) \in\to^{\text{EA}}$; moreover, in (2) for no e, l: $(e_k, l, e) \in\to^{\text{EA}}$ (there are no transitions starting from the final element of a finite path).

If σ is either (1) or (2) above, then

- $S(\sigma)$ denotes the first element of σ: e_0;
- $L(\sigma)$ denotes the second element of σ: l_0 (if it exists);
- $\sigma|_n$ denotes the path $e_n\ l_n\ e_{n+1}\ l_{n+1}\ e_{n+2}\ l_{n+2} \ldots$ (if it exists).

Let EA be an $E\Sigma$-entity algebra and $V: X \to$ EA be a variable evaluation; we define by multiple induction when a dynamic formula $\phi \in DF_{E\Sigma}(X)$ *holds in* EA *under* V (written EA, $V \models \phi$) and when a path formula $\pi \in P_{E\Sigma}(X, es)$ *holds on a path* $\sigma \in PATH(\text{EA}, es)$ *under* V (written EA, $\sigma, V \models \phi$).

dynamic formulae

EA, $V \models Pr(t_1, \ldots, t_n)$ iff $(t_1^{EA^{ST}, V}, \ldots, t_n^{EA^{ST}, V}) \in Pr^{EA^{ST}}$

EA, $V \models t_1 = t_2$ iff $t_1^{EA^{ST}, V} = t_2^{EA^{ST}, V}$
                            (both sides must be defined and equal)

EA, $V \models \neg\phi$ iff   EA, $V \not\models \phi$

EA, $V \models \phi_1 => \phi_2$ iff   either EA, $V \not\models \phi_1$ or EA, $V \models \phi_2$

$$EA, V \models \forall x . \phi \qquad \text{iff} \qquad \text{for all } v \in EA_s^{ST}, \text{ with } s \text{ sort of } x,$$
$$EA, V[v/x] \models \phi$$

$$EA, V \models \Delta(et, \pi) \qquad \text{iff} \qquad et^{EA^{ST}, V} \text{ is defined and for all}$$
$$\sigma \in PATH(EA, es), \text{ with } es \text{ sort of } et,$$
$$\text{s.t. } S(\sigma) = et^{EA^{ST}, V}, EA, \sigma, V \models \pi$$

path formulae

$$EA, \sigma, V \models [\lambda x . \phi] \qquad \text{iff} \qquad EA, V[S(\sigma)/x] \models \phi$$
$$EA, \sigma, V \models <\lambda x . \phi> \qquad \text{iff} \qquad \text{either } EA, V[L(\sigma)/x] \models \phi \text{ or}$$
$$L(\sigma) \text{ is not defined}$$

$$EA, \sigma, V \models \neg \pi \qquad \text{iff} \qquad EA, \sigma, V \not\models \pi$$
$$EA, \sigma, V \models \pi_1 => \pi_2 \qquad \text{iff} \qquad \text{either } EA, \sigma, V \models \pi_1 \text{ or } EA, \sigma, V \models \pi_2$$
$$EA, \sigma, V \models \forall x . \pi \qquad \text{iff} \qquad \text{for all } v \in EA_s, \text{ with } s \text{ sort of } x,$$
$$EA, \sigma, V[v/x] \models \pi$$

$$EA, \sigma, V \models \square \pi \qquad \text{iff} \qquad \text{for all } j \geq 0 \text{ s.t. } \sigma|_j \text{ is defined},$$
$$EA, \sigma|j, V \models \pi.$$

A formula $\phi \in DF_{E\Sigma}(X)$ is *valid* in EA (written $EA \models \phi$) iff $EA, V \models \phi$ for all variable evaluations V.

A specification is a pair $(E\Sigma, Ax)$, where $Ax \subseteq DF_{E\Sigma}(X)$, and usually its semantics is the class of its models, i.e. of the $E\Sigma$-algebras satisfying all formulae in Ax. But, consider the specification

$$TWO\_SIMPLE = (S\Sigma, \{\theta\})$$

where $S\Sigma$ is the entity signature:

sig $S\Sigma =$
    esorts *syst, proc*
    –   there are entities of two kinds: systems and processes
    sorts *l-syst, l-proc*
    preds
        $\_ \overset{-}{\longrightarrow} \_: proc \times l\text{-}proc \times proc$
        $\_ \Longrightarrow \_: syst \times l\text{-}syst \times syst$

and θ the following formula of our metalanguage

$$eset \; AllSub \; e => \exists p_1, p_2 : proc . p_1 \neq p_2 \land p_1 \neq e \land p_2 \neq e \land eset = \{p_1, p_2, e\}$$

which formalizes the requirement "the entities of sort *syst* are the parallel composition of two simple (i.e., without internal parallelism) entities of sort *proc*" (recall that an entity is always a subentity of itself). The models of *TWO_SIMPLE* are the $S\Sigma$-entity algebras EA s.t. θ holds in EA; but no such algebras exist. Indeed, since there are no operations of sort *syst* in $S\Sigma$, there are no entity composers and so, for each $S\Sigma$-entity algebra EA

$$EA \models eset \; AllSub \; e \qquad \text{iff} \qquad eset = \{e\}.$$

Thus the specification *TWO_SIMPLE* has no models. However it is easy to exhibit various entity algebras describing concurrent systems with two and only two simple process subcomponents; but they are entity algebras on signatures richer than $S\Sigma$. For example, all $P\Sigma$-entity algebras, where $P\Sigma$ is the entity signature $S\Sigma$ enriched by the operations

$Nil: \rightarrow proc$

$\_ \cdot \_ : l\text{-}proc \times proc \rightarrow proc$

$\_ + \_ : proc \times proc \rightarrow proc$

$\tau: \rightarrow l\text{-}proc$

$\_\|\_ : proc \times proc \rightarrow system$

seem sensible models of TWO_SIMPLE.

Our solution is to take as models of a specification $(E\Sigma, Ax)$ the entity algebras on a signature $E\Sigma'$, extending $E\Sigma$, satisfying the axioms in Ax; the extra syntactic elements in $E\Sigma' - E\Sigma$ (entity composers) allow us to describe the structure of the entities. Then the class of the models of an entity specification $(E\Sigma, Ax)$ is

{EA|EA is an $E\Sigma'$-entity algebra, where $E\Sigma \subseteq E\Sigma'$ and for all $\phi \in Ax$ EA $\models \phi$ }.

5 Examples and Applications

5.1 Requirements Specification of a Net of Workstations

Assume that we need to specify the initial requirements for a net of workstations; for simplicity we list only some of them, choosing the more interesting.

The net consists of several workstations and on each workstation several processes may run in parallel; moreover processes may be moved from a workstation to another. Some relevant properties of the net are informally listed below.

P1) Each workstation is deadlock free, i.e. if it is unable to perform any activity, then also each process component is so.

P2) Each workstation has only simple subcomponents (i.e., without internal parallelism).

P3) If a workstation receives a process from some other one, then such process should never reach some error situation, never create other processes and cannot go on forever to perform some activity.

P4) The net includes either a workstation with a cartridge reader or a workstation with a CD player but not both.

P5) The processes on a workstation perform their activity in an interleaving way (i.e. it cannot happen that two processes perform some activity simultaneously).

Now we formalize the above requirements in a very abstract way using our metalanguage, i.e. formalizing exactly only the above properties and thus without any kind of overspecification; e.g., we do not fix the topology of the net, nor the architecture of the workstations, nor the policy followed by the process scheduler, nor the commands executed by processes and so on, since these features are not a consequence of the informal requirements.

Note that in several usual specification formalisms, properties about the dynamic activity of the workstations, as P1) and P3), cannot be expressed also making some overspecification, since it is not possible to speak of the dynamic components of a systems and of their dynamic properties

Below the lines preceded by $-$ are line-by-line comments of the axioms, where the word in boldface directly corresponds to some logical combinators, and we use the following abbreviation for the formula checking whether e' is a proper subcomponent of e.

$$e' \; Is\_Sub \; e =_{\text{def}} \exists eset \, . \, eset \; AllSub \; e \; \wedge \; e' \in eset \; \wedge \; e' \neq e$$

spec A_NET =

    esorts $net, workstat, proc$ –   there are three kinds of entities

    sorts $l\text{-}net, l\text{-}workstat, l\text{-}proc$

    opns

        $CREATE: proc \rightarrow l\text{-}proc$

  –   labels for the transitions corresponding to create new processes

        $REC: proc \rightarrow l\text{-}workstat$

  –   labels for the transitions corresponding to receive a process from another

  –   workstation

    preds

        $Error: proc$ –   determines the process error situations

        $Has\_Cartridge, Has\_CD: workstat$

  –   determines the workstations having a cartridge reader and a CD player

  –   respectively

        $\_\xrightarrow{\quad} \_: proc \times l\text{-}proc \times proc$

        $\_\Rightarrow\_: workstat \times l\text{-}workstat \times workstat$

        $\_\rightsquigarrow\_: net \times l\text{-}net \times net$

    axioms

  –   P1)

        $\nexists w', l \,.\, w \xrightarrow{l} w' \;\wedge$

  –   **if** w is unable to perform any activity **and**

        $p \; Is\_Sub \; w \Longrightarrow$

  – p is one of its proper subcomponents **then**

        $\nexists p', l_1 \,.\, p \xrightarrow{l_1} p'$

  – p is unable to perform any activity

  –

  –   P2)

        $p \; Is\_Sub \; w \Longrightarrow \nexists e \,.\, e \; Is\_Sub \; p$

  –   **if** p is a proper subcomponent of w **then** p has not proper subcomponents

  –

  –   P3)

        $w \xRightarrow{REC(p)} w' \Longrightarrow$

  –   **if** p is received by w, **then**

        $\triangle(p, \square[\lambda x \,.\, \neg Error(x)]) \;\wedge$

  –   **in each case** p will never reach an error situation **and**

        $\triangle(p, \square < \lambda l \,.\, \nexists p' \,.\, l = CREATE(p') >) \;\wedge$

  –   **in each case** p will never create a new process **and**

        $\triangle(p, \Diamond[\lambda x \,.\, \nexists x', l \,.\, x \xrightarrow{l} x'])$

  –   **in each case** p cannot go on for ever to act (i.e., eventually it will

  –   reach a state where it cannot perform any activity)

  –

  –   P4)

        $\exists w \,.\, w \; Is\_Sub \; n \;\wedge\; (Has\_Cartridge(w) \vee Has\_CD(w)) \;\wedge$

  –   a net n has a proper subcomponent w having either a cartridge reader or

  –   a CD player **and**

        $\neg \exists w_1, w_2 \,.$

  –   has not both

        $w_1 \; Is\_Sub \; n \;\wedge\; Has\_Cartridge(w_1) \;\wedge\; w_2 \; Is\_Sub \; n \;\wedge\; Has\_CD(w_2))$

        –   a subcomponent having a cartridge and one having a CD player

- P5)
  $$w \overset{l}{\Rightarrow} w' =>$$
- **if** w perform some activity **then**

  $\exists eset, p, p', l' . (eset AllSub w \wedge p \in eset \wedge p \neq w \wedge p \overset{l'}{\longrightarrow} p' \wedge$
  - it has a proper subcomponent p performing some local activity **and**
    $(es - \{p\}) \cup p' \ AllSub \ w')$
  - such subcomponents is the only one which has modified its state
  - during the transition (i.e. such activity consists of some activity of only
  - one of its subcomponents)

We have experimented the above line-by-line natural language comments in some industrial applications ([18, 19]) and fairly believe that this device is an essential ingredient for making formal specifications acceptable to a wide community of users.

5.2 An Industrial Case Study

Our metalanguage for expressing the requirements of reactive system has been used in two industrial case studies in a project in cooperation with ENEL - SPA (the Italian national board for electric power). The two cases concern respectively the specification of a hydro-electric central for the production of electricity and a high-voltage substation for the distribution of electricity handled by automatisms (see [18, 19]). Here we briefly try to sketch the specification of the first case enlightening the role of the metalanguage.

The high-voltage substation has been specified at three different levels of abstraction.

Level 1: It formalizes the most relevant properties of the substation; this specification could be used e.g. in a contract with a firm realizing the plant. The substation is made by "functional units" of several kinds (Ae, Dd and Fa) and of two metallic bars, Ae's are put on one bar, while Dd's and Fa's are conneted to both bars; below there is a graphical representation of the structure of a substation having 6 functional units.

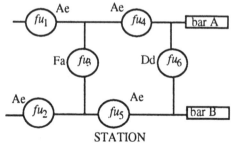

STATION

In this case the dynamic subcomponents are the functional units and using our framework we can describe how they are organized in a substation; the possibility of describing sharing of subcomponents (see section 2.2) allows to formalize the fact that Dd's and Fa's are connected to both bars.

The substation can receive orders of performing operations on the component functional units from an operator and informs such operator about the result of the required operations.

The abstract requirements specify what should happen when an order is received, but do not completely describe the execution of such orders. A sample property is:

$$st \xrightarrow{\quad Order(Close,id) \quad} st' \wedge$$

- **if** the substation receives the order of closing id **and**
  $(Is\_Ae(st, id) \vee Is\_Dd(st, id)) \wedge Is\_Open(st, id) =>$
- id is either an Ae or a Dd that is open, **then**
  $\triangle(st',$
- **in each case**
  $\Diamond(([\lambda x . Is\_Closed(x, id)] \wedge$
  - **eventually** the functional unit id will become closed **and**
    $\Diamond <\lambda l . l = Performed\_Operation>) \vee$
    - **eventually** it will inform the operator that the operation has
    - been performed **or**
    $\Diamond[\lambda x . Failure\_In\_Station(x)]]))$
  - **eventually** there will be a failure in the substation

Level 2: Here the design of the substation is refined by introducing an automatism for handling the operation received from the operator. Here the abstract requirements are only about the dynamic activity of the automatism while there are no requirements on its structure; instead the structure of the plant is fully specified by completely describing an appropriate realization of the functional units using standard devices and also the interactions of the automatism with the devices are completely defined.

Clearly this specification is an implementation of the first one: i.e. all of its models are models of the first.

Level 3: Here the design of the substation is completed by defining a particular automatism. This is not a requirement specification, but instead a design specification, i.e. a formal definition of one very specific reactive system, so we do not need to use all metalanguage; it is sufficient to use a small subset, precisley only the conditional axioms (i.e., formulae of the form $\wedge_{1 \geq i \geq nI} \phi_1 => \phi_{n+1}$, where for $i = 1, \ldots, n + 1$ ϕ_i is either an equation or an atom of the form $Pr(t_1, \ldots, t_m)$) and to take as models of a specifications the initial ones, see e.g. [1, 2, 3, 5]. Thus we have a uniform framework where to give specifications of reactive systems at different levels of abstraction.

6 Conclusion

The essential novelty of what we have presented lies in the possibility of specifying within the same formalism requirements about the static structure and the dynamic activity of a system.

Compared to the many formalisms using various forms of temporal logics, we have two distinguished features: the possibility of dealing both with different entities (of different sorts) and with the subcomponents of an entity, without lowering the abstraction level of a specification; moreover our formalism includes the usual specifications of abstract data types and it allows also to give integrate specifications of the dynamic and of the static features of a system.

The formalism has a clean mathematical support in the definition of an appropriate institution; to this end a key role is played by the definition of the class of models, which are entity algebras over extended signatures.

There is no room here for illustrating the possibility of relating such abstract requirement specifications to the design level specifications (e.g. the SMoLCS specifications of [2]); this can be done following an algebraic approach based on a notion of implementation, due to Sannella-Wirsing [22] (see [8, 4] for some examples).

Finally it may be of interest to mention the fact that the approach presented here is currently being used in some industrial case studies for relating requirements to more concrete design specifications, which have been already given (see Section 5.2).

A Algebras with Predicates

A *signature with predicates* is a triple $\Sigma = (S, OP, PR)$, where

- S is a set (the set of the *sorts*);
- OP is a family of sets: $\{OP_{w,s}\}_{w \in S^*, s \in S}{}^2$; $Op \in OP_{w,s}$ is an *operation symbol* (of arity w and result s);
- PR is a family of sets: $\{PR_w\}_{w \in S^*}$; $Pr \in PR_w$ is a *predicate symbol* (of arity w).

We write $Op: s_1 \times \ldots \times s_n \to s$ for $Op \in OP_{s_1 \ldots s_n, s}$ and $Pr: s_1 \times \ldots \times s_n$ for $Pr \in PR_{s_1 \ldots s_n}$. A *partial Σ-algebra with predicates* (shortly a Σ-algebra) is a triple

$$A = (\{A_s\}_{s \in S}, \{Op^A\})_{Op \in OP}, \{Pr^A\}_{Pr \in PR})$$

consisting of the carriers associated with the sorts, the interpretations of the operation symbols and the interpretations of the predicate symbols; i.e.:

- if $s \in S$, then A_s is a set;
- if $Op: s_1 \times \ldots \times s_n \to s$, then $Op^A: A_{s_1} \times \ldots \times A_{s_n} \to A_s$ is a partial function;
- if $Pr: s_1 \times \ldots \times s_n$, then $Pr^A \subseteq A_{s_1} \times \ldots \times A_{s_n}$.

Usually we write $Pr^A(a_1, \ldots, a_n)$ instead of $(a_1, \ldots, a_n) \in Pr^A$.

Given an S-indexed family of sets of variables X, the *term algebra* $T_\Sigma(X)$ is the Σ-algebra defined as follows:

- $x \in X_s$ implies $x \in T_\Sigma(X)_s$;
- $Op \in OP_{\Lambda,s}$ implies $Op \in T_\Sigma(X)_s$;
- $t_i \in T_\Sigma(X)_{s_i}$ for $i = 1, \ldots, n$ and $Op \in OP_{s_1 \ldots s_n, s}$ imply $Op(t_1, \ldots, t_n) \in T_\Sigma(X)_s$;
- $Op^{T_\Sigma(X)}(t_1, \ldots, t_n) = Op(t_1, \ldots, t_n)$ for all $Op \in OP$;
- $Pr^{T_\Sigma(X)} = \emptyset$ for all $Pr \in PR$.

If $X_s = \emptyset$ for all $s \in S$, then $T_\Sigma(X)$ is simply written T_Σ and its elements are called *ground terms*. If A is a Σ-algebra, $t \in T_\Sigma(X)$ and $V: X \to A$ is a *variable evaluation*, i.e. a sort-respecting assignment of values in A to all variables in X, then the *interpretation of t in A w.r.t. V*, denoted by $t^{A,V}$, is defined by induction as follows:

- $x^{A,V} = V(x)$;
- $Op^{A,V} = Op^A$;
- $Op(t_1, \ldots, t_n)^{A,V} = Op^A(t_1^{A,V}, \ldots, t_n^{A,V})$.

if t is a ground term, then we use the notation t^A. A Σ-algebra A is *term-generated* iff for all $s \in S$, for all $a \in A_s$ there exists $t \in (T_\Sigma)_s$ s.t. $a = t^A$.

The sets $F_\Sigma(X)$ of *first-order formulae* on Σ and X are inductively defined as follows (where $t_1, \ldots, t_n$ denote terms of appropriate sort and we assume that sorts are respected):

- $Pr(t_1, \ldots, t_n) \in F_\Sigma(X)$ if $Pr \in PR$
- $t_1 = t_2 \in F_\Sigma(X)$
- $\neg\phi_1, \phi_1 \Rightarrow \phi_2 \in F_\Sigma(X)$ if $\phi_1, \phi_2 \in F_\Sigma(X)$
- $\forall x . \phi \in F_\Sigma(X)$ if $\phi \in F_\Sigma(X)$, $x \in X$

Let A be a Σ-algebra and $V: X \to A$ be a variable evaluation we define by induction when a formula $\phi \in F_\Sigma(X)$ *holds in A under V* (written $A, V \models \phi$)

---

^{2} Given a set X, X^* denotes the set of the strings (finite sequences) over X.

- $A, V \models Pr(t_1, \ldots, t_n)$ iff $(t_1^{A,V}, \ldots, t_n^{A,V}) \in Pr^A$
- $A, V \models t_1 = t_2$ iff $t_1^{A,V} = t_2^{A,V}$ (both sides must be defined and equal)
- $A, V \models \neg\phi$ iff $A, V \not\models \phi$
- $A, V \models \phi_1 => \phi_2$ iff   either $A, V \not\models \phi_1$ or $A, V \models \phi_2$
- $A, V \models \forall x . \phi$ iff   for all $v \in A_s$, with s sort of x, $A, V[v/x] \models \phi$

A formula $\phi \in F_\Sigma(X)$ is *valid* in A (written $A \models \phi$) iff $A, V \models \phi$ for all evaluations V.

References

1. E. Astesiano, G.F. Mascari, G. Reggio, and M. Wirsing. On the parameterized algebraic specification of concurrent systems. In H. Ehrig, C. Floyd, M. Nivat, and J. Thatcher, editors, *Proc. TAPSOFT'85, Vol. 1*, number 185 in Lecture Notes in Computer Science, pages 342–358. Springer Verlag, Berlin, 1985.
2. E. Astesiano and G. Reggio. SMoLCS-driven concurrent calculi. In H. Ehrig, R. Kowalski, G. Levi, and U. Montanari, editors, *Proc. TAPSOFT'87, Vol. 1*, number 249 in Lecture Notes in Computer Science, pages 169–201. Springer Verlag, Berlin, 1987.
3. E. Astesiano and G. Reggio. Algebraic specification of concurrency (invited lecture). In *Recent Trends in Data Type Specification*, number 655 in Lecture Notes in Computer Science. Springer Verlag, Berlin, 1992.
4. E. Astesiano and G. Reggio. Entity institutions: Frameworks for dynamic systems, 1992. in preparation.
5. E. Astesiano and G. Reggio. A structural approach to the formal modelization and specification of concurrent systems. Technical Report PDISI-92-01, Dipartimento di Informatica e Scienze dell'Informazione, Università di Genova, Italy, 1992.
6. R.M. Burstall and J.A. Goguen. Introducing institutions. In E. Clarke and D. Kozen, editors, *Logics of Programming Workshop*, number 164 in Lecture Notes in Computer Science, pages 221–255. Springer Verlag, Berlin, 1984.
7. M. Cerioli and G. Reggio. Institutions for very abstract specifications. Technical Report PDISI-92-14, Dipartimento di Informatica e Scienze dell'informazione - Università di Genova, Italy, 1992.
8. G. Costa and G. Reggio. Abstract dynamic data-types: a temporal logic approach. In A. Tarlecki, editor, *Proc. MFCS'91*, number 520 in Lecture Notes in Computer Science, pages 103–112. Springer Verlag, Berlin, 1991.
9. J. Fiadeiro and T. Maibaum. Describing, structuring and implementing objects. In J.W. de Bakker, W. P. de Roever, and G. Rozemberg, editors, *Foundations of Object-Oriented Languages, Proc. REX School/Workshoop*, number 489 in Lecture Notes in Computer Science, pages 274–310. Springer Verlag, Berlin, 1991.
10. I.S.O. LOTOS – A formal description technique based on the temporal ordering of observational behaviour. IS 8807, International Organization for Standardization, 1989.
11. L. Lamport. Specifying concurrent program modules. *ACM TOPLAS*, (5), 1983.
12. S. Mauw and G.J. Veltink. An introduction to PSF_d. In J. Diaz and F. Orejas, editors, *Proc. TAPSOFT'89, Vol. 2*, number 352 in Lecture Notes in Computer Science, pages 272 – 285. Springer Verlag, Berlin, 1989.
13. R. Milner. *A Calculus of Communicating Systems*. Number 92 in Lecture Notes in Computer Science. Springer Verlag, Berlin, 1980.
14. G. Plotkin. An operational semantics for CSP. In D. Bjorner, editor, *Proc. IFIP TC 2-Working conference: Formal description of programming concepts*, pages 199–223. North-Holland, Amsterdam, 1983.

15. A. Pnueli. Applications of temporal logic to the specification and verification of reactive systems: a survey of current trends. In *Current Trends in Concurrency*, number 224 in Lecture Notes in Computer Science, pages 510–584. Springer Verlag, Berlin, 1986.
16. G. Reggio. Entities: an istitution for dynamic systems. In H. Ehrig, K.P. Jantke, F. Orejas, and H. Reichel, editors, *Recent Trends in Data Type Specification*, number 534 in Lecture Notes in Computer Science, pages 244–265. Springer Verlag, Berlin, 1991.
17. G. Reggio. Event logic for specifying abstract dynamic data types. In *Recent Trends in Data Type Specification*, number 655 in Lecture Notes in Computer Science. Springer Verlag, Berlin, 1992.
18. G. Reggio, D. Bertello, and E. Crivelli. Specification of a hydro-electric central. Technical Report PDISI-92-13, Dipartimento di Informatica e Scienze dell'Informazione – Università di Genova, Italy, 1992.
19. G. Reggio, A. Morgavi, and V. Filippi. Specification of a high-voltage substation. Technical Report PDISI-92-12, Dipartimento di Informatica e Scienze dell'Informazione – Università di Genova, Italy, 1992.
20. W. Reisig. *Petri nets: an introduction*. Number 4 in EATCS Monographs on Theoretical Computer Science. Springer Verlag, Berlin, 1985.
21. C. Stirling. Comparing linear and branching time temporal logics. In *Temporal logics of Specification*, number 398 in Lecture Notes in Computer Science. Springer Verlag, Berlin, 1989.
22. M. Wirsing. Algebraic specifications. In van Leeuwen Jan, editor, *Handbook of Theoret. Comput. Sci.*, volume B, pages 675–788. Elsevier, 1990.

Model Checking in Practice
The T9000 Virtual Channel Processor

Geoff Barrett

INMOS Limited, 1000 Aztec West, Almondsbury, Bristol, BS12 4SQ, UK

Abstract. One of the major obstacles to the integration of formal methods in the design of industrial products is the height and gradient of the learning curve. Anything which can alleviate this problem is of enormous benefit. Automatic model checking and visual specification styles provide a gentle introduction to the concept of refinement. This paper presents a case study of the design of the T9000 virtual channel processor as an illustration of the use of some non-standard CSP operators and a visual specification style. The development which is shown here has been implemented in a single model checking tool which is currently being integrated into the INMOS CAD system.

1 Introduction: Integrating Formal Methods in the Design

In 1989, INMOS embarked on the design of a new transputer, now launched as the T9000. The T9000 was to be a completely new design, retaining instruction-set compatibility with the T800, but with a complete re-implementation of the processor, and with a new virtual channel processor. The virtual channel processor would allow any number of logical channels to be multiplexed onto the four physical communication links. The T9000 would be implemented on a new manufacturing process, and the combined result of extra interconnect layers and finer geometries was to allow about five times as many transistors as the T800.

Although INMOS had already successfully used formal design methods in the T800 work (see [1, 6]), it was not easy to introduce them into the T9000 design. Many engineers are accustomed to verifying designs by simulation, and have little experience in the use of formal methods. In addition, many of the notations and tools produced by mathematicians for formal design work are unfamiliar to engineers, with the result that engineers will avoid using them until the complexity of the design makes it essential. Bringing together engineers and mathematicians was a continuing challenge throughout the T9000 work. Some of the problems encountered during the T9000 design are described in [4].

One of the problems to arise was that of designing and verifying the virtual channel processor. The design of the relatively simple communications hardware of the T800 had given rise to several problems, including a design fault which took over a month to locate. This is not surprising, as the communications hardware of the T800 consists of a collection of concurrent state machines, and has complex interactions with the processor and with the environment.

Any component as complex as the T9000 contains a number of different subcomponents such as the processor, floating point unit and communications processor.

Each of these has an associated set of design techniques and representations. There are many different representations in common use and these operate at varying levels of abstraction. Examples are an English specification, a timing diagram, a Z specification, an **occam** functional simulation, a VHDL description, the silicon layout, a circuit diagram. It is inevitable that a design will be expressed in several of these notations.

In our experience, it is *essential* that the descriptions of a design in different notations can be checked against each other. Many of the descriptions are large, so that it is desirable to use notations suitable for computer-assisted manipulation to simplify the construction of checkers and simulators; in this context informal pictures and natural language text are not suitable. The available techniques for checking the equivalence of two descriptions are:

- Visual inspection. This widely used technique is inconsistent with the scale of current designs. It is extremely error-prone and time-consuming, and is not consistent with the need for fast design iteration.
- Simulation of the design in two notations and comparison of the results (for example, the comparison of an **occam** functional description with an HDL implementation). This technique has its uses, but requires the construction of a test-suite of data to be run on the two simulations. It is easy to forget that the construction of the test-suite can often take more time than the design itself, and also that the speed of simulation can be a major problem.
- Automatic compilation (synthesis) of one description from another. This is likely to be reliable and fast, but depends on the correctness of the compiler.
- Automatic comparison of the two descriptions. This is likely to be reliable and fast, but again depends on the correctness of the comparison tool.
- Proof by hand that one description (the implementation) satisfies another (the specification). This technique is only possible where current theory is well enough developed. Also, it is not consistent with the need for fast design iteration (but there are cases where re-working a proof by hand can be much faster than simulation).
- Computer assisted/computer-checked proof. This technique is only applicable where current theory and tools are adequate.

The scale of current designs makes it important to design the design process itself. In particular, it is important to plan the notations to be used to represent each part of the design at each of the various levels of abstraction, and to identify the techniques to be used to establish equivalence between the representations. This makes it possible to expose weaknesses in the design process, especially those which are likely to cause delays as a result of time-consuming (and unanticipated) verification processes. At an early stage, it is often possible to develop new tools to assist in the process.

New capabilities are needed in CAD systems to support the use of verification tools. Any design will involve a number of standard tools, together with the need for specialised tools to be constructed as the design progresses. There is therefore a need for design databases in which the method for comparing two representations of a design is held as a program which takes as its parameters the two representations together with other information specific to the comparison being made.

2 VCP Specification

The T9000 virtual channel processor (VCP) is a device which allows any number of logical connections between two processors to be implemented by a single physical connection. Whereas the specification of a single logical connection is straightforward, the protocols which are needed in the hardware implementation are sufficiently complicated that some degree of automatic verification is essential.

The T9000 VCP can be specified as the interleaving of a number of channels:

$$VCP \cong \underset{i=0}{\overset{2^{17}-1}{\big|\big|\big|}} \; i : CHAN$$

This expression specifies that each of the channels should behave independently. We will not devote much attention to the specification of the VCP as a whole but rather, we will study the behaviour and implementation of individual channels.

A channel provides a point-to-point link between two processes. A single processor may execute any number of processes, but at most one may use any particular channel for input or output. When a process outputs a value to a channel, it is descheduled until a corresponding input process has received the value. Conversely, when a process inputs a value from a channel, it is descheduled until a corresponding output process has sent a value along the channel. While a process is descheduled, it may not engage in any actions. In particular, a descheduled process may not input or output from a channel.

2.1 Safety

Safety condition is a term used for a specification which states that something bad cannot happen. The specifications which are given in this section are typical of many safety specifications. For instance, the first specification given in this section is that an input is not terminated before it has begun.

In the specification of the channel, we consider a number of variables which describe, for instance, the number of inputs which have been started but not yet completed. The inequalities which govern the channel behaviour are given below. The expressions $\#in$ and $\#out$ stand for the number of inputs or outputs which have begun and $\#run(in)$ and $\#run(out)$ stand for the number of inputs or outputs which have terminated:

- no input terminates before it has begun:

$$0 \le INRI \cong \#in - \#run(in)$$

- an input cannot terminate before it has been matched by an output:

$$0 \le OUTRI \cong \#out - \#run(in)$$

- an output cannot terminate before it has been matched by an input:

$$0 \le INRO \cong \#in - \#run(out)$$

– no output terminates before it has begun:

$$0 \leq OUTRO \mathrel{\hat{=}} \#out - \#run(out)$$

Part of the specification formalises the assumptions which are made about the way processes behave and how channels are joined up:

– there is never more than one active input:

$$INRI \leq 1$$

– there is never more than one active output:

$$OUTRO \leq 1$$

In order to be able to define a finite state machine using these variables, we must be able to prove that each variable may only take on a finite range of values. This is clearly true of the variables $INRI$ and $OUTRO$, but we must prove that the other variables are also bounded. The proof proceeds as follows:

– the combined number of active inputs and outputs is given by both $OUTRI + INRO$ and $INRI + OUTRO$. Therefore:

$$OUTRI + INRO = INRI + OUTRO$$

– the following inequalities can be summed to give a bound of 2 on the combined number of active outputs and inputs:

$$0 \leq INRI \leq 1 \qquad 0 \leq OUTRO \leq 1$$
$$0 \leq INRI + OUTRO \leq 2$$

– using the equality and the inequality from above gives bounds on the number of inputs and outputs which have not caused a scheduling action:

$$0 \leq OUTRI \leq 2$$
$$0 \leq INRO \leq 2$$

The fact that there may be two output commands before an input is scheduled arises from the sequence of events: in, out, $run(out)$, out. At this stage, the only action which is possible is to reschedule the input.

The state transition diagrams which correspond to each of the variables are shown in Fig. 1. Each of the diagrams corresponds to one of the specification variables. The commands and responses of the VCP have the effect of changing the values of the variables (for instance, in increases the variable $INRO$) and this is noted on the diagrams by an arrow labelled with the action. Each of the diagrams may be interpreted as a predicate which restricts the overall behaviour of the channel. All of the restrictions are conjoined to give the safety specification of a channel[1]:

$$SAFE \mathrel{\hat{=}} INRI \wedge OUTRI \wedge INRO \wedge OUTRO$$

---

[1] Note that this is a specification in the traces model only.

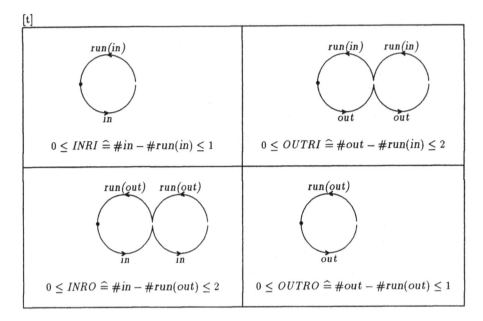

Fig. 1. State machines corresponding to the channel specification

2.2 Reliance

Rely condition is the term used for the specification which states the operating conditions of a process. In other words, the rely condition expresses restrictions on the way in which a process can be used. If an attempt is made to use a process outside its specified operating conditions, then the process may behave in any way it pleases; in particular, the process may break.

The specification of a channel relies on its environment to use the channel as a point to point connection between two processes, and therefore it relies on there being up to one active input and one active output at any one time. The rely condition, therefore, is the specification that the traces of its environment are composed of alternating sequences of in-$run(in)$ and out-$run(out)$ events:

$$RELY \cong INRI \wedge OUTRO$$

2.3 Liveness

Liveness condition is the term used for a specification which states that something good must happen. When specifying the interactions of a process with its environment, liveness conditions often take the form "the process must accept some action from the set A when condition p holds", or "the process must accept some action from the set A eventually". For instance, for many processes, certain events can be classed as commands and we might specify that the process can never refuse to accept a command.

The liveness specification of the VCP is particularly simple because the events in its alphabet can be partitioned into two sets. One of these sets contains the events which are the "commands" which the VCP must always be ready to obey, subject to the assumption that the channel is being used properly. The other set of events are the reactions to those commands and should be treated like commands by its environment. The VCP is free to schedule its reactions in any order and is therefore able to refuse all except one of them. The set of commands is $C \triangleq \{in, out\}$. The set of reactions is $R \triangleq \{run(in), run(out)\}$.

We will deal with the set of commands first. The specification which states that the process may never refuse any of its commands is RUN_C. However, this is too strong because the VCP assumes that only one input or output may be active simultaneously for any channel. The specification of liveness for commands can therefore be expressed as follows[2]:

$$COM \triangleq \lceil RELY \rceil \vee RUN_C \vee CHAOS_R$$

The specification $RUN_C \vee CHAOS_R$ allows any trace of commands and reactions. The specification $CHAOS_R$ allows any set of reactions to be refused, and the specification $\lceil RELY \rceil$ ensures that commands are only refused if they are not expected.

The specification for the reactions of the process can be expressed as follows:

$$RCT \triangleq \lceil SAFE \rceil \vee REACT_R \vee CHAOS_C$$

In this specification, $REACT_R \vee CHAOS_C$ allows any trace of commands and reactions. The specification $CHAOS_C$ allows any set of commands to be refused. The specification $\lceil SAFE \rceil \vee REACT_R$ only allows all reactions to be refused when it is unsafe to do any of them, but allows all except one to be refused under any other conditions.

Putting all the parts together gives the complete specification of a channel[3]:

$$CHAN \triangleq \lceil RELY \rceil_\perp \vee (\lfloor SAFE \rfloor \wedge COM \wedge RCT)$$

The first part of this specification allows the process to behave however it pleases if its environment should violate its operating restrictions. The second part only allows safe traces but makes no requirement about which events a process must accept. The third part is the liveness requirement for commands and the fourth part is the liveness requirement for reactions.

This sort of construction is so common that we define an abbreviation for it as follows[4]:

$$\begin{aligned} reactive(SAFE, RELY, C, R) \triangleq \\ \lceil RELY \rceil_\perp \vee (\lfloor SAFE \rfloor \wedge (\lceil RELY \rceil \vee RUN_C \vee CHAOS_R) \\ \wedge (\lceil SAFE \rceil \vee REACT_R \vee CHAOS_C)) \end{aligned}$$

---

[2] The specification $\lceil P \rceil$ allows only traces of P and insists that any possible event is accepted.

[3] The specification $\lceil P \rceil_\perp$ allows divergence outside the traces of P but insists that no possible action of P may be refused. The specification $\lfloor P \rfloor$ is the least deterministic, non-divergent process with the traces of P.

[4] Note that this specification will be inconsistent if the rely condition is not strong enough and that it is refined by weakening the rely condition.

where *SAFE* is the safety specification, *RELY* is the rely condition, C is the set of commands and R is the set of reactions.

3 The Transputer Link Protocol

A channel must be implemented in a distributed way between two processors. One processor *IN* is at the input end of the channel and has responsibility for rescheduling input processes. The other processor *OUT* is at the output end and has responsibility for rescheduling output processes. The processors are connected by a link, *LINK*. Each message along the channel is broken up and transmitted through the link as a sequence of packets.

The output side processor transmits a packet which is terminated with a symbol which indicates whether more packets are to come. The input side acknowledges each packet.

The events which the machines recognise are as follows:

run(in)	reschedule input
run(out)	reschedule output
in	receive input command
out	receive output command
sp	send/receive start of packet
eop	send/receive end of packet token
eom	send/receive end of message token
ack	send/receive packet acknowledgment

The inner part of the VCP implementation can now be described by the parallel composition of the three parts:

$$ILO \mathrel{\widehat{=}} IN \parallel LINK \parallel OUT$$

The packet actions are hidden:

$$IMP \mathrel{\widehat{=}} ILO \backslash \{sp(out), eop(out), eom(out), ack(out),$$
$$sp(in), eop(in), eom(in), ack(in)\}$$

The correctness of the implementation is established automatically:

$$CHAN \sqsubseteq IMP$$

3.1 The Output Machine

The diagrams which correspond to the output machine are shown in Fig. 2. The output machine specification introduces the technique of adding loops to the diagrams to specify that actions are only safe under certain conditions. The diagrams are interpreted as follows:

– no output terminates before it has begun and we rely on there only being one active output:

$$0 \leq OUT.OUTRO \mathrel{\widehat{=}} \#out - \#run(out) \leq 1$$

[t]

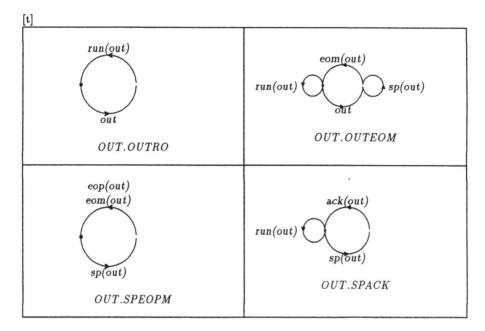

Fig. 2. Specification of the output machine

- only one message is completed for each output and the previous rely condition, along with the restriction that outputs may not be rescheduled when there is an incomplete message, suffice to show that there can be at most one more output than complete message:

$$0 \leq OUT.OUTEOM \ \hat{=} \ \#out - \#eom(out) \leq 1$$

packets may only be sent when there is an incomplete message; outputs may only be rescheduled when all messages are complete;
- packets are terminated with an end of packet or end of message token and only one packet can be sent at once:

$$0 \leq OUT.SPEOPM \ \hat{=} \ \#sp(out) - (\#eop(out) + \#eom(out)) \leq 1$$

- there can be at most one packet which has not been acknowledged and we rely on acknowledgements only coming when a packet has been sent:

$$0 \leq OUT.SPACK \ \hat{=} \ \#sp(out) - \#ack(out) \leq 1$$

an output may only be rescheduled when all packets have been acknowledged.

The safety condition for the output machine can be written as follows:

$$OUT.SAFE \ \hat{=} \ OUT.OUTRO \wedge OUT.OUTEOM \wedge$$
$$OUT.SPEOPM \wedge OUT.SPACK$$

The rely condition is:

$$OUT.RELY \cong OUT.OUTRO \wedge OUT.SPACK$$

(Note that the inclusion of the event run(out) does not affect this condition as it is not a command.) The set of commands is:

$$OUT.C \cong \{out, ack(out)\}$$

The set of reactions is:

$$OUT.R \cong \{run(out), sp(out), eop(out), eom(out)\}$$

The liveness specification of the output machine is, therefore:

$$OUT.LIVE \cong reactive(OUT.SAFE, OUT.RELY, OUT.C, OUT.R)$$

Finally, we must ensure that the output machine does not output an infinite number of packets in any one message. This can be specified as follows:

$$OUT \cong OUT.LIVE \wedge FAIR_{\{eop(out)\},\{eom(out),eop(out)\}}$$

The inclusion of the fairness condition ensures that the output machine will always eventually choose to send an end of message token instead of a simple end of packet token. Therefore, when the packet level events are hidden, there will be no divergence.

3.2 The Input Machine

The diagrams which correspond to the input machine are shown in Fig. 3. The specification illustrates the technique of creating different events to describe a single event which happens under different conditions and renaming these events to the single event. In this case, a distinction is made between commands which happen under three different conditions:

– whether there have been more inputs than terminated messages (*IN*);
– whether there have been more terminated messages than inputs (*EOM*);
– whether there have been more messages started than inputs (*PKT*).

An input event which happens, for example, when there have been more messages started than inputs is denoted *PKT1.in*. The diagrams are interpreted as follows:

– The first two diagrams represent the following predicates, repectively:

$$IN \cong \#in > \#eom(in)$$
$$EOM \cong \#in < \#eom(in)$$

In the first diagram, the events *IN0.sp(in)* and *IN1.sp(in)* are there in order to differentiate the condition under which a packet arrives – this is used in the last diagram. Otherwise, the first diagram states that the predicate *IN* becomes true when an input arrives and *EOM* is false. The predicate *IN* becomes false whenever a message is terminated. The fact that there is no event *EOM0.in* possible when *IN* is true means that we are relying on $\#in - \#eom(in) \leq 1$. The second diagram defines *EOM* similarly.

[t]

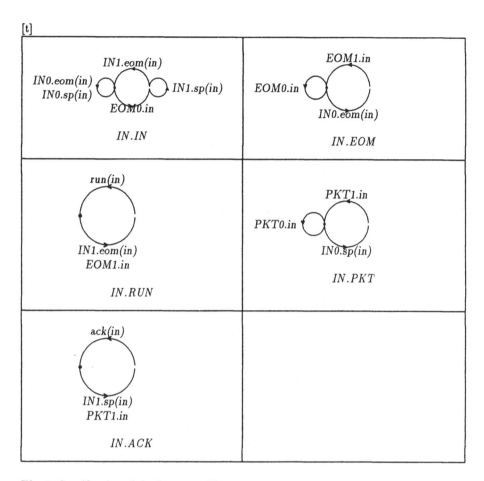

Fig. 3. Specification of the input machine

- The third diagram illustrates the conditions under which a run request is issued. There are two conditions: a complete message has arrived when an input happens, or else an input has happened when a message is terminated.
- The fourth diagram illustrates the predicate *PKT*. This determines whether there have been more started messages than inputs. We assume that the number of started messages can exceed inputs by no more than one.
- The fifth diagram illustrates the conditions under which an acknowledgement is issued: either an input happens when a message has begun, or else a packet arrives when there is an active input.

The safety specification is made up of the conjunction of these specifications after some renaming. Because the predicate *PKT* is only used in the last two specifications, and the predicate *EOM* is only used in the first three, it is possible to to strip off the decorations as the specifications are composed as follows:

$$IN.SAFE \;\hat{=}\; [strip_{IN}]\,([strip_{EOM}]\,(IN.IN \wedge IN.EOM \wedge IN.RUN)\wedge$$
$$[strip_{PKT}]\,(IN.PKT \wedge IN.ACK))$$

where the function $strip_P$ maps events $P0.a$ and $P1.a$ to a.

The rely condition is made up of two parts:

$$IN.RELY \;\hat{=}\; INRI \wedge IN.SPACK$$

This formalises the conditions that there may be no more than one active input and no more than one unacknowledged packet. The specification $INRI$ has been illustrated previously. The specification $IN.SPACK$ corresponds to the following predicate:

$$0 \leq \#sp(in) - \#ack(in) \leq 1$$

The commands of the input machine are as follows:

$$IN.C \;\hat{=}\; \{in, sp(in), eop(in), eom(in)\}$$

Its reactions are:

$$IN.R \;\hat{=}\; \{run(in), ack(in)\}$$

The complete specification of the input machine is:

$$IN \;\hat{=}\; reactive(IN.SAFE, IN.RELY, IN.C, IN.R)$$

As the astute reader may have noticed, this seemingly sensible specification is inconsistent and the checker will automatically signal that the specification states both that $eom(in)$ is unsafe and that it must be accepted after the trace: $eom(in), eom(in)$. The assumption which was made for the diagram $IN.EOMRI$ is invalid because we have omitted part of the rely condition. This part of the rely condition states that packets start and end in bracketed pairs:

$$0 \leq IN.SPEOPM \;\hat{=}\; \#sp(in) - (\#eop(in) + eom(in)) \leq 1$$

By including this as a conjunct of the rely condition, it is easily seen that the trace which revealed the inconsistency is not one which the input machine expects. The specification will now be accepted as consistent.

3.3 The Link

The final element in the implementation is the link which joins the input machine to the output machine. The function of the link is to pass packets from the output side to the input side and to pass acknowledgments in the other direction. A formal investigation of the link specification will not give any further insights and so is omitted from this description.

4 Summary of Notation

This paper has used a mixture of standard CSP operators, some new operators and diagrams of finite state machines. We chose models of CSP which are parameterised by the alphabet of the process, partly because this fits more comfortably with modern practices of strong typing, partly because it produces a more succinct notation and partly because it is less error-prone. The symbol $\mathcal{M}_\Sigma$ will be used to denote a model of CSP with alphabet Σ, and, in particular, the traces model will be denoted $\mathcal{T}_\Sigma$ and the infinite traces model as $\mathcal{I}_\Sigma$. For more detailed descriptions of the standard CSP operators see [3]. For a description of the infinite traces model see [2, 5].

A process, P, can be viewed as a finite state machine whenever the equivalence relation, $\equiv$, on traces, given below, partitions the traces of P into a finite number of classes.

$$s \equiv t \quad \Longleftrightarrow \quad P \text{ after } s = P \text{ after } t$$

The operators of CSP which are used in this paper are chosen so that whenever all of the operands are finite state machines, then the result of the operation is also a finite state machine. This is also true of the new operators. The consequence of this is that all of our specifications are viable as the input to a fully automated model checking program.

4.1 State Machine Diagrams

The dominant method of specification which we used was state machine diagrams. Typically, these are used to illustrate integer-valued functions. For instance, the function $\#in - \#run(in)$ is illustrated by the first state machine in Fig. 1. All functions can be illustrated by an infinite state diagram with arrows labelled by events to show how the state changes. A combination of specifications and assumptions about the environment combine to bound the values which the function can achieve. All of the functions which we require can be illustrated by a state machine with at most three states. More complicated functions are formed by conjoining the basic functions.

Once a function has been illustrated, arrows are added to the diagram to show how certain actions are only permitted under certain conditions. This amounts, in essence, to a restriction on the sequences of events which a process may perform and so the diagram is interpreted in the traces model as a process with the set of traces obtained by starting at the initial state and following the arrows.

4.2 CSP

We used the following standard CSP operators:

$CHAOS_{\Sigma}{:}\mathcal{M}_{\Sigma}$ may do anything except diverge

$RUN_{\Sigma}{:}\mathcal{M}_{\Sigma}$ may do anything except diverge or refuse an event

$\|{:}\mathcal{M}_{\Sigma_1} \times \mathcal{M}_{\Sigma_2} \to \mathcal{M}_{\Sigma_1 \cup \Sigma_2}$ parallel composition with co-operation on events in the intersection of the alphabets

$\interleave{:}\mathcal{M}_{\Sigma} \times \mathcal{M}_{\Sigma} \to \mathcal{M}_{\Sigma}$ independent parallel composition with no co-operation on events

$[f]{:}\mathcal{M}_{\Sigma_1} \to \mathcal{M}_{\Sigma_2}$ forward renaming of events

$\backslash X{:}\mathcal{M}_{\Sigma} \to \mathcal{M}_{\Sigma - X}$ hiding

4.3 New Specification-oriented Operators

The new operators which we introduced are as follows:

$\wedge{:}\mathcal{M}_{\Sigma_1} \times \mathcal{M}_{\Sigma_2} \to \mathcal{M}_{\Sigma_1 \cup \Sigma_2}$ logical conjunction of specifications

$\vee{:}\mathcal{M}_{\Sigma_1} \times \mathcal{M}_{\Sigma_2} \to \mathcal{M}_{\Sigma_1 \cup \Sigma_2}$ logical disjunction of specifications

$\lceil \cdot \rceil_{\perp}{:}\mathcal{T}_{\Sigma} \to \mathcal{I}_{\Sigma}$ the pre-deterministic process which has all traces but diverges on all traces except those given

$\lceil \cdot \rceil{:}\mathcal{T}_{\Sigma} \to \mathcal{I}_{\Sigma}$ the deterministic process with the given set of traces

$\lfloor \cdot \rfloor{:}\mathcal{T}_{\Sigma} \to \mathcal{I}_{\Sigma}$ the most non-deterministic non-divergent process with the given set of traces

$REACT_{\Sigma}{:}\mathcal{M}_{\Sigma}$ may do anything except diverge or deadlock

$FAIR_{B,\Sigma}{:}\mathcal{M}_{\Sigma}$ may do anything except diverge or an infinite trace which does not include infinitely many events not in B

The logical operators behave in a similar way to least upper bound and greatest lower bound, respectively, and they are, indeed, equal to those operators when the alphabets of the processes are equal. Consequently, the operator $\wedge$ is not defined between inconsistent specifications. This means that consistency should be checked each time the operator is used; we will be able to see the ways in which inconsistencies can arise from the definitions. Needless to say, the consistency of specifications can be checked automatically for finite state machines. In the traces model, the operator $\wedge$ is identical to parallel composition, $\|$.

The benefit of the logical operators is that they allow us to concentrate our attention on subsets of the alphabet of a process and then to combine the specifications in a sensible way. The formal definition of the operators is given below. The symbol s is used to stand for a finite sequence of events in $\Sigma_1 \cup \Sigma_2$, X is a subset of $\Sigma_1 \cup \Sigma_2$ and u is an infinite sequence of events in $\Sigma_1 \cup \Sigma_2$. The finite traces, divergences, failures and infinite traces of $P_1 \vee P_2$ are denoted by T, D, F and I, respectively, and those of P_i by T_i, D_i, F_i and I_i.

$$T \triangleq \left\{ s \mid s \upharpoonright \Sigma_1 \in T_1 \vee s \upharpoonright \Sigma_2 \in T_2 \right\}$$

$$D \triangleq \left\{ s \mid s \upharpoonright \Sigma_1 \in D_1 \vee s \upharpoonright \Sigma_2 \in D_2 \right\}$$

$$F \triangleq \left\{ (s, X) \mid (s \upharpoonright \Sigma_1, X \cap \Sigma_1) \in F_1 \vee (s \upharpoonright \Sigma_2, X \cap \Sigma_2) \in F_2 \right\}$$

$$I \triangleq \left\{ u \mid u \upharpoonright \Sigma_1 \in (I_1 \cup T_1) \vee u \upharpoonright \Sigma_2 \in (I_2 \cup T_2) \right\}$$

The definition of $P_1 \vee P_2$ satisfies the axioms of all the models of CSP.

Giving a direct definition of conjunction in terms of traces, failures and divergences is somewhat tricky, and therefore we give a definition in terms of an auxiliary operator $\upharpoonright$ defines the projection of a process onto a subset of its alphabet:

$$P_1 \wedge P_2 \triangleq \bigcap \{ Q \mid P_1 \sqsubseteq Q \upharpoonright \Sigma_1 \wedge P_2 \sqsubseteq Q \upharpoonright \Sigma_2 \}$$

The specifications are inconsistent just when this set is empty. We will return to this once we have defined the auxiliary operator. The finite traces, divergences, failures and infinite traces of $P \upharpoonright A$ are denoted by T, D, F and I, respectively, and those of P are denoted by T', D', F' and I'. The auxiliary operator is defined as follows:

$$T \triangleq \left\{ s \upharpoonright A \mid s \in T' \right\} \qquad D \triangleq \left\{ s \upharpoonright A \mid s \in D' \right\}$$

$$F \triangleq \left\{ (s \upharpoonright A, X \cap A) \mid (s, X) \in F' \right\} \qquad I \triangleq \left\{ u \upharpoonright A \mid u \in I' \right\}$$

This rather round about definition of conjunction is, perhaps, rather more strict than it might at first appear. For instance, it is not always the case that if $s \upharpoonright \Sigma_1$ is a trace of P_1 and $s \upharpoonright \Sigma_2$ is a trace of P_2, then s is a trace of $P_1 \wedge P_2$. For instance, consider a counter which can non-deterministically move up or right across a board which has a barrier to prevent any further movement from square $(2, 2)$. This restriction might be expressed as:

$$(u \rightarrow ((u \rightarrow \perp) \sqcap (r \rightarrow STOP)) \sqcap (r \rightarrow ((u \rightarrow STOP) \sqcap (r \rightarrow \perp))$$

The specification of deadlock freedom is:

$$DF \triangleq \mu X.((u \rightarrow X) \sqcap (r \rightarrow X))$$

Although both of these specifications allow all traces, they make inconsistent speci-fications about the states $\langle u, r \rangle$ and $\langle r, u \rangle$. Namely, in the first, that they are dead-locked and, in the second, that they may not deadlock. Therefore, these traces cannot be in the conjunction, which is:

$$(u \to u \to DF) \sqcap (r \to r \to DF)$$

Had we insisted on an external choice between the up and right movements, then there would have been no way of avoiding the inconsistency and the set of processes which implement both specifications would be empty.

The specification $\lceil P \rceil_\perp$ is used in the specification of rely conditions. The specifi-cation allows a process to diverge outside the traces of P but it must be deterministic until it diverges:

$$T \mathrel{\hat=} \Sigma^\star$$
$$D \mathrel{\hat=} \Sigma^\star - P$$
$$F \mathrel{\hat=} D \times \mathbb{P}(\Sigma) \cup \{(s, X) \mid s \in P \wedge X \subseteq \{a \in \Sigma \mid s\langle a \rangle \notin P\}\}$$
$$I \mathrel{\hat=} \Sigma^\omega$$

The specifications $\lceil P \rceil$ and $\lfloor P \rfloor$ are used in the specification of refusals. The specification $\lceil P \rceil$ only permits the traces of P but insists that any event which P can perform must be accepted. This also means that any infinite sequence of events which can be partially performed by P is possible. The formal definition is:

$$T \mathrel{\hat=} P$$
$$D \mathrel{\hat=} \emptyset$$
$$F \mathrel{\hat=} \{(s, X) \mid s \in P \wedge X \subseteq \{a \in \Sigma \mid s\langle a \rangle \notin P\}\}$$
$$I \mathrel{\hat=} \{u \in \Sigma^\omega \mid \forall s < u.s \in P\}$$

The specification $\lfloor P \rfloor$ only permits the traces of P but makes no statement about refusals. We also choose for it to state as little about the infinite behaviour as possible and so the infinite traces are those which can be partially performed by P. The formal definition is:

$$T \mathrel{\hat=} P \qquad\qquad D \mathrel{\hat=} \emptyset$$
$$F \mathrel{\hat=} \{(s, X) \mid s \in P, X \subseteq \Sigma\} \qquad I \mathrel{\hat=} \{u \in \Sigma^\omega \mid \forall s < u.s \in P\}$$

The specification $REACT_\Sigma$ is used in the specification of refusals. It makes no statement about traces but insists that there is no deadlock. Its formal definition is:

$$T \mathrel{\hat=} \Sigma^\star \qquad\qquad D \mathrel{\hat=} \emptyset$$
$$F \mathrel{\hat=} \{(s, X) \mid s \in \Sigma^\star, X \subset_{\neq} \Sigma\} \qquad I \mathrel{\hat=} \Sigma^\omega$$

The specification $FAIR_{B,\Sigma}$ makes no statement about traces or refusals but in-sists that any infinite trace must contain an infinite subsequence of events not from the set B. Its formal definition is:

$$T \mathrel{\hat=} \Sigma^\star \qquad\qquad D \mathrel{\hat=} \emptyset$$
$$F \mathrel{\hat=} \Sigma^\star \times \mathbb{P}(\Sigma) \qquad I \mathrel{\hat=} \{u \in \Sigma^\omega \mid u \setminus B \in \Sigma^\omega\}$$

5 The Model Checker

There are two model checking tools which are currently in use at INMOS. The first is a prototype tool which is completely written in SML, uses crude and inefficient algorithms and has only an SML interface. This tool implements the standard CSP operators used in this paper along with a direct implementation of the *reactive* operator and a "fair" hiding operator which calculates an approximation to $(P \wedge FAIR_{X,\alpha P}) \setminus X$. It is an approximation because, instead of signalling inconsistencies between P and $FAIR_{X,\alpha P}$, these turn up as divergent traces in the result. Furthermore, the operator is not monotonic and could lead to unsound implementations if a hierarchical development approach is used.

The main point of interest of the SML tool is its debugging interface. The result of checking a specification against its refinement is a list of bugs. From each bug, it is possible to form the weakest specification which will show up the bug. The exact location of a bug in an implementation can be pinpointed by forming weakest prespecifications. For instance, if the bug is an unsafe transition a after trace s and the implementation is $P \setminus X$, then it is possible to form the least deterministic process $Q_{s,a,X}$ such that $Q \not\sqsubseteq P$ implies that $P \setminus X$ has the trace $s \langle a \rangle$. Checking P against Q now reveals the causes of the error. Similar mechanisms exist for debugging parallel compositions. However, this mechanism is not powerful enough to provide a general prespecification of divergences before hiding, although the implementation of fairness specifications should provide a uniform solution to this problem.

Further plans for the SML tool involve providing different interfaces for it. For instance, it would be useful to be able to provide the source of this LaTeX document as input and to be able to manipulate state machine diagrams through a graphical interface.

The other tool which is used within INMOS is an early version of the FDR refinement checker from Formal Systems which is based on the prototype SML tool and which shares the SML interface. The algorithms used within the FDR tool are more sophisticated and can handle problems with larger numbers of states. Further details of this tool are available from Formal Systems.

6 Conclusion

Mathematical techniques have already been applied to the design of parts of VLSI chips. Most of this work is experimental, and requires an unusual combination of engineering, mathematical and programming skills. Sometimes new theoretical work is needed, and specialised tools may have to be constructed. Despite these difficulties, mathematical techniques are playing an important rôle in the design of microprocessors at INMOS, and techniques suitable for incorporation in standard computer-aided design systems are emerging.

The example presented in this paper is a subset of work which has been carried out on the VCP. An abstract description of the main components in the VLSI design of the VCP has been successfully checked against the full specification of the VCP. Work is still in progress to provide a tool to extract suitable state machine descriptions of VHDL designs in order to complete the connection between high level CSP descriptions and the lower levels of the design.

6.1 Experience

Two of the questions which have plagued the author for some time are: "How can an electronic engineer benefit from the theory of CSP without having to learn about it?" and "How can an electronic engineer be tricked into learning about the theory of CSP involuntarily?" Automatic model checking is the answer in both cases. First of all, a correct design can be verified without any pre-requisite knowledge of CSP. Secondly, the automatic discovery of errors in a design provides a gentle introduction to the basic concepts of CSP – after all, you can't remove an unwanted divergence if you don't understand what a divergence is. As the engineer's understanding of the errors deepens, better insights into how to avoid them are obtained. In this way, the learning curve is made shallower by providing useful results for minimal investment of effort.

Nevertheless, there has typically been great resistance to the sort of automatic and semi-automatic tools which have been introduced by proponents of formal methods. Much of this has been a problem with the interface. The mathematical notation which is required by many tools is completely alien to engineers who have been taught to use state machine diagrams and imperative programming languages. In order to succeed with the integration of formal methods in the design process, we must base our tools on familiar notations and understand the obstacles which first-time users have to overcome in order to gain benefit from them. This means that visual specifications have to be employed as far as possible; useful theorems have to be harnessed into techniques which can be applied automatically or semi-automatically; common idioms must be captured by easy-to-use primitives.

Another common mistake is to assume too much about the design process. No real design is either top-down or bottom-up[5]; rather it is a mixture of these. Any successful strategy for integrating formal methods into the design process must take this into account. This means that refinement should not be seen so much as a process of deriving an implementation from a specification (although such techniques can certainly be useful) but rather we should allow the design engineer to use raw intuition in creating the descriptions which are required for the various aspects of the design. The challenge for formal methods is to be able to match these descriptions against one another.

A complex and large design must contain a strategy for managing its own complexity. One mechanism to achieve this is to structure the design according to its core functionality. For instance, the complete virtual channel processor of the T9000 is a far more complicated device than we have indicated here: it contains features which allow selection between channels which are ready to communicate, ways in which to recover a channel from a software error (for instance, a violation of the rely conditions), and ways in which to recover from a hardware error (perhaps a packet lost in transmission). However, the core functionality is a mechanism which implements a channel. Bearing in mind that the main purpose of a specification is for the communication of designs between engineers, it is vital that the structure of the specification can reveal the most important or most used features of a design first. In particular, it is highly desirable for a specification to be structured in such a

---

[5] Although it has been known for certain circuit layouts to start at the top left and work across and down into the bottom right. This could be called top-down, left-right design.

way that features can be understood in isolation wherever possible. We believe that the specification calculus explained here goes a long way towards achieving this.

6.2 Future Directions

In the last ten years, VLSI designs have moved from 10^5 to 10^6 transistors. This has been achieved not only by advances in manufacturing, but also by advances in design techniques. Automated checking of silicon design rules and circuit connectivity have emerged and become a standard part of commercial CAD systems. In the next ten years, designs will move to over 10^8 transistors, and this will require a further advance in design techniques. Designs of this size must be constructed from independent modules, and the behaviour of these modules and their interfaces must be specified. Automated checking that the composition of such modules corresponds to an overall specification will become an essential part of future CAD systems.

An important development is the increasing use of synthesis tools. Much of the control logic in the T9000 is produced by synthesis from VHDL descriptions. Synthesisers will, in future, also support the construction of structures such as microcoded data paths. The result will be that the rôle of the engineer in VLSI design will change. The design of the basic cells used by the synthesiser is clearly an electronic design task, with the cells being verified by simulation. The design of the input to the synthesiser will not require skills in electronic design, but will require extensive use of behavioral descriptions and programs, with associated specification, transformation and proof tools.

6.3 Further Research

The specification of safety conditions is still far easier than that of liveness conditions, even with the introduction of the new operators described above. More attention must be paid to the development of CSP combinators which correspond to the specification styles and structures which are used naturally, particularly styles which can support a middle out development.

In the process of checking that one description refines another, we must not always assume that, when an error occurs, it is the implementation which is wrong! We often find that the necessity of considering a problem in more detail has led the designer to implement the right thing regardless of the specification. While it is possible and obvious how to track a mismatch through an implementation to the individual components of an implementation, this is not so easy with a specification. For instance, if an implementation is the parallel composition of two processes and the implementation is found to diverge erroneously, then it is clear that the divergence must have come from one or both of the processes and that the divergent process(es) must be fixed in order to meet the specification. Furthermore, the divergence can be traced through the structure of the rest of implementation until the precise cause has been pinpointed. On the other hand, what can we do if it is the specification which is at fault? Perhaps it is quite reasonable for the implementation to have diverged and the specification has failed to model it. The problem of finding how a behaviour arises is rather more tractable than the problem of finding out why a behaviour does not arise. However, the problem is not completely intractable:

when the specification is too strict about a safety condition, we can deduce that there is a refusal of the specification which is erroneous and pinpoint the cause of that refusal. But what is to be done about refusals and divergences? Is it possible to define a set of combinators for specifications which simplifies the problem?

Finally, although there are only countably many finite state machines with a given finite alphabet in the failures-divergence model of CSP, it can be shown that there are uncountably many in the infinite traces model. This means that it is not possible to define a language in which all possible infinite traces specifications can be made. On the other hand, there are only countably many fairness specifications which can be made for any given finite alphabet. Is this a sensible subset of infinite trace specifications?

Acknowledgements

I would like to thank Bill Roscoe for pointing out that the least upper bound operator could be used as a logical conjunction. Also, David May for his comments on an early draft of the paper and Victoria Griffiths for testing the methods and tools explained in this paper on some rather more substantial examples.

References

1. Barrett, G. *Formal Methods Applied to a Floating-Point Number System*, IEEE Trans Soft Eng, May 1989, pp. 611–621
2. Barrett, G. *The fixed point theory of unbounded nondeterminism*, Formal Aspects of Computing (1991) 3: 110–128
3. Hoare, CAR. *Communicating sequential processes*, Prentice-Hall International, London, 1985
4. May, MD, Barrett, G & Shepherd, DE. *Designing chips that work*, pp 3–19, *Mechanized reasoning and hardware design*, ed C.A.R. Hoare and M.J.C. Gordon, Prentice Hall International, 1992
5. Roscoe, AW & Barrett, G. *Unbounded Nondeterminism in CSP*, Proceedings of 5th International Conference on Mathematical Foundations of Programming Semantics, (29 March–1 April 1989, New Orleans, USA), LNCS 442, pp. 160–193
6. Shepherd, DE & Wilson, G. *Making chips that work*, New Scientist, vol 122, no 1664, 13 May 1989, pp 61–64

Algorithm Refinement
with Read and Write Frames

Juan Bicarregui

Systems Engineering Division
SERC Rutherford Appleton Laboratory
Oxon OX11 0QZ, UK

Abstract. The read and write frames of reference variables used in the VDM style of operation decomposition serve two purposes. Syntactically, they bind the variables that occur in the predicates of the operation specification; and semantically, they record what access to the state an implementation can be allowed to make. This paper examines the use of frames in these two roles, in particular considering the case when there is an invariant on the state. It argues that the two roles can be usefully distinguished.

A model for operation specification and refinement is developed where full account is taken of both syntactic and semantic roles of the frames. Consideration of their syntactic role gives rise to the idea that a part of the state can be independent of the rest with respect to the invariant that is in force: a definition of independence is given together with a syntactic sufficient-condition for it. The semantic role of the frames is examined in connection with notions of satisfiability and satisfaction. Satisfiability is modified to capture the restricted possible interdependencies between read and write variables and the rules for satisfaction are given that restrict the usual relation in order to respect the constraints on implementations imposed by the frames.

1 Introduction

There is little doubt that if we are to manage successfully the building of ever more complex software systems, the ability to break down the task in hand, separately tackle each sub-task, and then bring these separate solutions together with confidence that the whole will perform successfully, is crucial. Thus when developing a formalism of software specification and refinement the issue of compositionality must be central.

Following the process of top-down design, at any stage we have a specification of a system component and the design task is to develop a component that satisfies that specification. Typically the design will be the composition of several smaller components that, at this stage, will only be specified and which will later be developed independently themselves.

The problem can be described as follows. If we require that a specification S is to be refined by a design D, written

$$S \sqsubseteq D$$

then we can build a high level design which states that D should be some composition, C, of components $S_1 \ldots S_n$ which are themselves only specified at this stage,

$$D = C[S_1, \ldots, S_n]$$

such that, if each component is itself refined by a design,

$$S_i \sqsubseteq D_i$$

then the original specification must be satisfied by the composition of those designs.

$$S \sqsubseteq C[D_1, \ldots, D_n]$$

Compositionality states that the development of each S_i should be able to proceed independently of the others.

This paper considers two issues that arise when we examine compositionality in the process of algorithm refinement, taking as a starting point the VDM style of operation decomposition given, for example, in [Jones90]. The first consideration is that each sub-development, $S_i \sqsubseteq D_i$, should be truly independent of the rest. That is, that sufficient information should be contained in each S_i to characterise its valid implementations. In particular, attention is paid to the case where there is an invariant relating possible values of components of the state. The second issue is the matter of state access: the so called *frame problem* addressed by the "externals" clauses in the operation definition. Typically, each of the smaller components, S_i, involves just part of the state available to S, so that in the development of that S_i we want only to concern ourselves with that part of the state and should not have to look outside for contextual information. In VDM, the frame of reference of an operation is given explicitly by the read and write access conditions.

Of course the two issues are related since what is a sensible frame for an operation depends crucially on any invariant that may be in force on the state. The interaction of frames and invariants motivates us to distinguish the syntactic and semantic roles played by the read and write frames. The separation of these two roles yields a more expressive notation where read and write frames are freed from their use as syntactic binders for the variables in the specification and can instead play their intended role as indications of the constraints on the accesses that should be made by an implementation. The ramifications of this interpretation are examined and lead to a modified notion of satisfiability, that captures the restricted possible interdependencies between read and write variables, and a restricted satisfaction relation that respects the constraints on implementations imposed by the frames. This extra expressive power comes at the expense of some prolixity – a third frame is introduced into the definition of an operation – however the model proposed is envisaged as the basis for machine based support and it is anticipated that the extra complexity could be handled automatically and only come to the fore when explicitly relevant.

The rest of this section outlines the background to the work presented and gives two motivating examples which expose some ambiguities that can arise from the interaction of the read and write frames with the invariant. Section 2 develops a model for state-based operations with read and write frames and invariants. It gives a definition of when a part of the state is independent with respect to the invariant which is then used in an examination of the role that the read and write frames play in satisfiability and refinement. The usual satisfaction relation is restricted in order to respect the constraints on implementations imposed by the frames. The third section briefly discusses the present work in a broader perspective.

1.1 Background

Operation Decomposition in VDM. The starting point for the work given here is the treatment of operation decomposition in VDM given in [Jones87, Jones90]. In these works a clear exposition of the underlying principles is given through examples and a set of proof rules for verification of refinements. These rules are proved correct with respect to a denotational semantics. We take on board the arguments given there advocating the convenience of having postconditions relating before and after states and do not reiterate those arguments here. The rules do not, however, explicitly handle the frame of reference variables. An extension of the model is given in [Milne88], however, the rules there are rather cumbersome and no attempt to justify them is made.

[AhKee89] is perhaps the most detailed treatment of operation decomposition in the VDM style. A denotational semantics is given for a language that extends that of [Jones90] with arrays and procedures. A proof theory for this language is given and is shown to be sound and relatively complete with respect to the denotational semantics. In order to cater for blocks and procedures with static scoping, the usual Hoare triple is augmented by a syntactic environment with static and dynamic components. The static part of the environment may be compared with our set of read variables, and the work does indeed consider extending and contracting this frame. However, it does not distinguish the read-only from the read-write variables.

Other Approaches to Operation Decomposition. There is a large body of work stemming from [Dijkstra76] that considers verification of programs in the framework of a weakest precondition semantics. Mostly, this work only considers postconditions of one state which leads to some very elegant mathematics.

Some more recent works add specifications to the language bringing them closer to present concerns. [Morris87] gives an elegant treatment with "prescriptions" which makes use of higher ordinals to handle unbounded non-determinism. [Morgan86] includes a similar "specification statement" and explicitly handles the write variables and also postconditions of two states. Many previous works are brought together in [Morgan88] and the central ideas are presented in textbook form in [Morgan90] which gives a formalism for algorithm refinement via a set of proof rules defining valid refinements. In this treatment, all state variables are global with respect to read access, and a single "frame" is given that denotes those variables that are able to be written.

[Back88] and [BW90] do consider the frame of free variables available for use in expressions and also cater for specification statements through non-deterministic assignment statements. However, this work does not distinguish the read-only from the read-write variables. There, the frame cannot contract during development. This has the effect that x:=x is not refined by skip, since skip has a smaller read frame. Thus this frame is somewhat different from the read frame considered in this paper.

In the "B" method [Abrial90, ALNS91], a great deal of attention is paid to issues of framing and to the incremental construction of specifications and their refinements through the use of structured "abstract machines". Several forms of hierarchical composition of machines are provided embodying both full-hiding, where variables of the included machine are accessible only through the operations of that machine, and semi-hiding, where state variables can be read directly but written only through the operations. Thus, the frames for possible read and write access of operations are given through the structuring of a machine, whereas the actual read and write accesses made are given implicitly through the definition of operations as generalised substitutions.

1.2 Motivation

Two example operations are given that motivate the usefulness of a third frame. They both act on the same state, which although very simple, is already complex enough to expose the issues with which we wish to deal:

$State$ :: a : $\mathbf{N}$
$\quad\quad\quad b$: $\mathbf{N}$
$\quad\quad\quad c$: $\mathbf{N}$

$inv\text{-}State(a, b, c) \quad \triangleq$
$\quad a \in \{0, 1\} \wedge$
$\quad b \leq a \wedge$
$\quad c \in \{1, 2\}$

A quick syntactic inspection of the clauses in the invariant shows us that the components a and b are in some way "linked" whereas c is independent of a and b.

Example 1, choose_b. Let us consider the specification of an operation that writes b, say $choose\_b$.

$choose\_b$
ext rd b : $\mathbf{N}$
$\quad$ wr b : $\mathbf{N}$
post true

Clearly, because of the invariant, the operation is not free to choose any $b:\mathbf{N}$, rather it needs to ensure that the invariant is maintained, i.e. $b \leq a$. So one might be led to believe that such an operation specification should be meaningful only if it also has read access to a. On the other hand, it is possible to construct a correct implementation of the operation which does not require read access to a, for example both $b := 0$ and $b := b$ ensure that the invariant is maintained. Which of the possible implementations are valid depends on how we interpret the read frame when an invariant is in force.

Let us consider the first of these alternatives: we will restrict what we consider to be a well-formed operation so that state access is always "sensible" with respect to the invariant.

As a first cut, let us say that an operation specification must have read access to (at least) all the fields which appear in the same conjunct of the invariant that a write field appears in. Thus the operation reads sufficient of the state to ensure that all the relevant clauses in the invariant are maintained. (There is no need to consider those clauses not mentioning any writes since they will not be affected by the operation.)

This resolves the problems with the example *choose₋b* above which becomes:

choose₋b'
ext rd a, b : $\mathbb{N}$
   wr b : $\mathbb{N}$
post true

This is interpreted as if the relevant clauses, $b \leq a$ and $a \in \{0,1\}$, were added to the pre and post conditions so, for example, the satisfiability criterion would then quantify over the read frame and include the appropriate clauses of the invariant:

$$\forall a: N, \overleftarrow{b} : N \cdot a \in \{0,1\} \wedge \overleftarrow{b} \leq a \;\Rightarrow\; \exists b: N \cdot a \in \{0,1\} \wedge b \leq a \wedge \mathsf{true}$$

However, by restricting well-formedness in this way, we have lost some of the expressive power in the language. Perhaps we really did intend to specify that the operation should maintain the invariant while not reading a. That is, we did mean that the only valid implementations should be variants on $b := 0$ and $b := b$.

Example 2, set₋c. Now consider the operation specification:

set₋c
ext rd b
   wr c
post $c \in \{b, b+1\}$

This is a well-formed operation by the above criterion and does indeed specify a bona-fide operation with two obvious implementations $c := b$ and $c := b + 1$. But in order to know that it is satisfiable (ie. that $c \in \{1,2\}$) we need the information relating to a that is given in the first clause of the invariant. Furthermore, apart from the two obvious implementations, if we consider the extra information about a given in the first clause of invariant, then $c := 1$ is also a valid implementation.

Thus the "available information" for determining valid implementations must include all the clauses that could give us any information about fields that appear in clauses with fields that could be written. That is, we must take the transitive closure of the "appears in a clause with" relation. This closure partitions the state into parts which we will later call *independent* and in order to characterise the possible implementations of the specified operation we may need all the information from the invariant concerning fields that are "connected" to any field in the frame. So for an operation specification to have a well-defined meaning it must be considered in the context of all the parts of the state connected to variables appearing in its definition.

However, there is still good reason to keep the smaller read frame since it can give information as to what implementations are intended to be valid. In this case, for example, although we require access to a in order to ascertain what the valid implementations are, it is not intended that $c := a$ should itself be a valid implementation, which would in fact be the case if the read frame were extended to include a. Thus expanding the read frame to include all connected fields would change the meaning of the operation specification.

The approach investigated in this paper will be to give a third frame for each operation. This frame plays the "syntactic" role of carrying the declarations of all fields related to the fields in the read and write frames. The read and write frames are thus freed to play their "semantic" role: to give information about the access permitted of valid implementations.

2 A Model of Operations with Frames

2.1 Operation Definitions

We have motivated the need for a third frame which will simply be called *the frame*, as opposed to *the reads* and *the writes*. This frame must be an *independent part* of the state in a sense which is defined below. In order to make the operation definition independent of the state, it will also carry those clauses of the invariant that pertain to it.

Thus an operation definition is composed of six parts: the *frame* which carries the declaration of all the variables that are in scope and binds all the free variables that appear in the rest of the operation definition, the *invariant* which contains all the contextual information about these variables[1], the *reads* and *writes* which give information about access to the reference variables that must be maintained by any implementation and the *pre* and *post* which have their usual VDM interpretation, that is as if the invariant were conjoined to them[2].

$$OpDef :: \quad frame : \text{map } Id \text{ to } Type$$
$$invariant : Exp$$
$$reads : Id\text{-set}$$
$$writes : Id\text{-set}$$
$$pre : Exp$$
$$post : Exp$$

where

$$inv\text{-}OpDef(mk\text{-}OpDef(F, I, R, W, P, Q)) \triangleq$$
$$R \subseteq dom(F) \wedge$$
$$W \subseteq dom(F) \wedge$$
$$I : Exp(dom(F)) \wedge$$
$$P : Exp(dom(F)) \wedge$$
$$Q : Exp(dom(F) \cup \overline{dom(F)})$$

---

[1] The typing information could be put here instead of in the frame and the whole treatment carried out in an untyped logic

[2] The exposition in this paper does not deal with operations with parameters and results. Their treatment can be considered independently of issues covered here.

The notation in the last three clauses of the invariant is explained in the next section.

Note that we do not insist that the free variables of P and Q are restricted to R and W in the usual way, nor do we require that $R \supseteq W$ although the usefulness of write-only variables is uncertain.

It is also a requirement that a valid frame of an operation definition be an "independent part" of the frame of any operation that it refines. This requirement will later form part of the definition of the satisfaction relation but before we consider it in more detail we introduce some notation.

2.2 Notation

Hooking. If S is any set of identifiers, say

$$S = \{x_a \mid a \in \alpha\}$$

then $\overleftarrow{S}$ is the set with each identifier in S distinguished in some way, with a "$\overleftarrow{}$" say. That is,

$$\overleftarrow{S} = \{\overleftarrow{x_a} \mid x_a \in S\}$$

More generally if we want to distinguish just some of the members of S, those in $S_1 \subseteq S$ say, then we write:

$$\overleftarrow{S}^{S_1} \triangleq \{\overleftarrow{x_a} \mid x_a \in S_1\} \cup \{x_a \mid x_a \in S - S_1\}$$

Similarly, if E is an expression with free variables in S, written

$$E \colon Exp(S)$$

and $S_1 \subseteq S$, then

$$\overleftarrow{E}^{S_1} \triangleq E[\overleftarrow{\sigma_i}/\sigma_i]_{\sigma_i \in S_1}$$

Thus:

$$\overleftarrow{E}^{S_1} \colon Exp(\overleftarrow{S}^{S_1})$$

Identity. We define a shorthand notation for saying that the variables in a set are unchanged. Id_S is simply the conjunction of clauses each stating that a variable in S is unchanged.

$$Id_S \triangleq \bigwedge_{x_i \in S} x_i = \overleftarrow{x_i}$$

Quantification. Let F be a composite type

$$F :: f_1 : T_1$$
$$\vdots$$
$$f_n : T_n$$

and let S be a subset of the fields of F

$$S = \{f_{S_1}, \ldots, f_{S_k}\} \subseteq \{f_1, \ldots, f_n\}$$

Let E be an expression with free variables in S

$$E: Exp(f_{S_1}, \ldots, f_{S_k})$$

then we use the notations

$$\forall S \cdot E \;,\; \exists S \cdot E$$

to stand for the quantifications over the free variables from S. For example:

$$\forall S \cdot E \;\triangleq\; \forall v_1 : T_{S_1}, \ldots, v_k : T_{S_k} \cdot E[v_i/f_{S_i}]_{i=1,\ldots,k}$$

Similarly

$$\forall \overleftarrow{S} \cdot \overleftarrow{E}$$

is a shorthand for the corresponding hooked formula.

Invariants. Since we will be analysing the role of invariants on composite types it will be convenient to write them explicitly, $F \dagger I$, when we mean the type restricted by the invariant and we leave the undecorated type name, F, to denote the "free" type. Thus, for example:

$$\forall F \dagger I \cdot E \;\triangleq\; \forall F \cdot I \Rightarrow E$$

2.3 Independence of a Part of the State

We will first give a "semantic" definition of when a part of the state is independent with respect to the invariant, before reverting to a syntactic condition.

Definition. Let $S \subseteq F$ be a subset of the fields of a composite type with invariant, $F \dagger I$, and let T be the rest of the fields, $T = F - S$.

The part S of F is said to be an *independent part*, written $S \overset{\text{ind}}{\subseteq} F$, if and only if, swapping the S parts of two states that each satisfy the invariant maintains the invariant. That is if:

$$\forall F, \overleftarrow{F} \cdot I \wedge \overleftarrow{I} \;\Leftrightarrow\; \overleftarrow{I}^S \wedge \overleftarrow{I}^T$$

This can be shown to follow from the following, more succinct, definition which does not require one to show $\overleftarrow{I}^T$:

$$S \overset{\text{ind}}{\subseteq} F \;\triangleq\; \forall F \dagger I, \overleftarrow{F \dagger I} \cdot \overleftarrow{I}^S$$

The following theorem states that a part is independent exactly when it is possible to write the invariant in such a way that the independence of that part is syntactically obvious.

Theorem. A part S of composite type $F\dagger I$ is an independent part of F if and only if there are predicates $I_S: Exp(S)$ and $I_T: Exp(F - S)$ such that

$$F \dagger I = F\dagger(I_S \wedge I_T)$$

Proof. The proof proceeds by construction of the two required predicates. The key definition, the *restriction* of the invariant to a part of the state, is given below. The proof then follows easily by showing that the required predicates are the obvious restrictions of the invariant. For brevity, details are not given here.

Definition. For a part S of composite type $F\dagger I$, define I_S, the invariant *restricted to S* by

$$I_S \triangleq \exists \mathsf{F}-\mathsf{S} \cdot I$$

With this definition the following corollary gives a criterion for independence.

Corollary.

$$S \overset{\text{ind}}{\subseteq} F \quad \textit{iff} \quad \forall \mathsf{F} \cdot I_S \wedge I_{F-S} \Leftrightarrow I$$

It is easy to show that the syntactic condition for independence described in example 2, that is, the closure of the relation "appears in the same clause as", is a sufficient condition for independence. In practical cases, it is likely that this syntactic condition will yield a sufficiently fine partition of the state for refinement. Naturally, it would be simple for a support tool for specification to use this condition to infer a default frame and local invariant for an operation from the reads and writes and the state invariant.

This definition of independence is, of course, simply a statement that the state space should be the cartesian product of the spaces spanned by the independent part and by the rest. As such, independence may not be respected by a change of variables. That is, an independent part of the state need not be independent should a different, but equivalent, data model be chosen. As stated earlier, it is only sensible to "frame" an operation over an independent part of the state and thus greater independence between state components may be a sign of a cleaner data model. Within the frame, the reads and writes give extra constraints on what constitutes a valid implementation and thus restrict the usual satisfaction relation. Clearly however, it is only sensible to give such extra information once the final data variables for that frame are established.

2.4 Satisfiability

Given that we have an operation specification with a frame that is an independent part of the overall state and with the restricted invariant also given as part of the specification, it is possible to consider satisfiability (and refinement) using only local information.

The standard satisfiability condition, roughly stated, says that for any initial state satisfying the precondition, there must be a final state that satisfies the postcondition. For state F with invariant I and an operation with precondition P and postcondition Q, satisfiability can be stated formally as follows:

$$\forall \overleftarrow{F} \cdot \exists F \cdot \overleftarrow{P} \wedge \overleftarrow{I} \Rightarrow Q \wedge I$$

However, this tells us nothing about the fact that the implementation must respect the access conditions given by the read and write frames. How should the condition be generalised to accommodate this information?

A first attempt to rectify this might be simply to quantify over the read and write frames only, with a statement such as "for all values of the reads there must exist possible values of the writes such that . . .". Perhaps, for the above operation with the reads R and writes W, we would consider[3]:

$$\forall \overleftarrow{R} \cdot \exists W \cdot \overleftarrow{P} \wedge \overleftarrow{I} \Rightarrow \overleftarrow{Q}^{R-W} \wedge \overleftarrow{I}^{R-W}$$

However this is also inadequate since the invariant might mention variables outside the read and write frames which would then be free in the formula.

Neither would it be sufficient simply to expand the "frame" of universal quantification to encompass a wider set of variables: this would lose the intention that the choice of writes should be made without recourse to the value of variables outside the read frame.

The correct formulation is a condition that is "scoped over" the whole frame of the operation, but in which the quantifiers for the parts inside and outside the reads and writes have been interspersed to reflect the fact that values assigned to the writes can only depend on the part inside the reads and that these values should be valid irrespective of the values of fields outside the reads. This idea can be captured formally by rearranging the order of the quantifiers in the formula:

$$\forall \overleftarrow{R} \cdot \exists W \cdot \forall \overleftarrow{F-R} \cdot \overleftarrow{P} \wedge \overleftarrow{I} \Rightarrow \overleftarrow{Q}^{F-W} \wedge \overleftarrow{I}^{F-W}$$

The position in this formula of the existential quantification over W captures the fact that the values given to the writes can depend only on the reads, but not on those fields outside the reads. It brings to light the fact that the write frame is more than just a syntactic sugaring for an addition of the appropriate clauses, $x_i = \overleftarrow{x_i}$, to the postcondition.

2.5 Algorithm Refinement

As stated earlier, independence is not respected by a change of variables and in any case, read and write frames are of little relevance in the presence of data refinement. Thus, this paper concerns itself only with algorithm refinement; data refinement and operation modelling are considered in [BR91] and [BFLMR93].

---

[3] For variables outside the writes, where we know hooked and unhooked values are equal, we have the freedom to use hooked or unhooked variables as we like. Unlike the standard usage, in this section we choose to use the hooked names, so hooked variables appear for all the reads whereas unhooked variables only appear for the writes.

In order to generalise the definition of refinement to respect the access constraints given by the reads and writes, it is necessary to restrict the usual satisfaction relation. Rather than attempt to give a comprehensive proof theory for refinement here, a flavour of the treatment is given by stating a few rules that justify some valid refinements, primarily focusing on those aspects that relate to the frame.

For notational brevity, in this section we will write (F, I, R, W, P, Q) for $mk\text{-}OpDef(F, I, R, W, P, Q)$.

Weaken Pre and Strengthen Post. The rules for weakening the precondition and strengthening the postcondition contain no surprises. They are the obvious extensions of the usual rules.

$$\frac{P_A \wedge I \ \Rightarrow\ P_C}{(F, I, R, W, P_A, Q) \sqsubseteq (F, I, R, W, P_C, Q)}$$

$$\frac{\overleftarrow{P} \wedge \overleftarrow{I} \wedge Q_C \wedge I \wedge Id_{F-W} \ \Rightarrow\ Q_A}{(F, I, R, W, P, Q_A) \sqsubseteq (F, I, R, W, P, Q_C)}$$

Contract Reads and Writes. An implementation that achieves a specification whilst reading or writing fewer variables than the specification permits is obviously correct. Because the frame is unchanged, we can shrink the reads and writes without worrying about variables becoming unquantified.

$$\frac{R_A \supseteq R_C}{(F, I, R_A, W, P, Q) \sqsubseteq (F, I, R_C, W, P, Q)}$$

$$\frac{W_A \supseteq W_C}{(F, I, R, W_A, P, Q) \sqsubseteq (F, I, R, W_C, P, Q)}$$

Contract Frame. We can shrink the frame provided that the new frame is an independent part of the old, that no variable mentioned falls out of scope, and that the invariant is restricted to the new frame.

$$\frac{F_A \overset{\text{ind}}{\supseteq} F_C, \ (F_C, I_{F_C}, R, W, P, Q) \colon OpDef}{(F_A, I, R, W, P, Q) \sqsubseteq (F_C, I_{F_C}, R, W, P, Q)}$$

Note that the second condition described above is captured in the second hypothesis by insisting that the new $OpDef$ is well-formed, whilst the third is ensured by the fact that I_{F_C} in the conclusion is the invariant restricted to the concrete frame F_C.

Expand Frame. We can expand the overall frame, that is, declare new local variables. The new variables will not appear in the abstract specification though they can later appear in the implementation. Naturally, since they are to be used as local variables, they are available for reading and writing.

$$\frac{F \cap S = \phi}{(F, I, R, W, P, Q) \sqsubseteq \textsf{var } S \textsf{ in } (F \cup S, I, R \cup S, W \cup S, P, Q) \textsf{ end}}$$

The notation $\textsf{var } S$ is a shorthand similar to that given earlier for quantifiers. Say S is a set of type names, then $\textsf{var } S$ stands for the sequence of declarations $\textsf{var } v_1 \colon f_{S_1}, \ldots, v_k \colon f_{S_k}$.

Expanding Writes. Having permitted expansion of the reads and writes when we expand the frame, we have a choice as to whether to allow expansion of the writes within the frame provided we ensure $x = \overleftarrow{x}$ for the new write variables. This choice corresponds to whether the intention is that variables not in the writes should not be changed at any time during execution of the program section under development, or whether they just have to be reset to their original value by the end of the execution[4].

As we already have the possibility of expanding the reads and writes when the frame is expanded, we will insist that access conditions given by writes are "hard and fast". Thus, we do not permit expansion of the writes by variables that are already in the frame.

Guards. The usual rules for guarded commands, as in the definition of conditionals and loops, apply with the extra constraint that variables in the tests respect the read frame.

Assignments. It is in the rule for assignments that the read and write frames are ultimately employed: assignments can only be made to the write variables and the expression evaluated can only refer to read variables. Assuming it is is well-typed[5], the assignment, $x := e$, precisely satisfies the postcondition,

$$x = \overleftarrow{e}^{x} \wedge Id_{F-\{x\}}$$

thus we get the refinement rule

$$\frac{x \in W, e\colon Exp(R), Id_{F-\{x\}} \wedge I \wedge P \;\Rightarrow\; (Q \wedge I)\left[e/x, x/\overleftarrow{x}\right]}{(F, I, R, W, P, Q) \sqsubseteq x := e}$$

3 Discussion

The motivation for the present work came from an intention to develop interactive tools support for operation decomposition in the VDM style. There is much to be gained from mechanical support for this process. Indeed when developing a formalism, as well as considerations of soundness and completeness, there would seem to be good reason to keep the possibilities arising from mechanical support specifically in mind, since potential difficulties for pencil and paper methods may become unimportant when such support is provided.

Compositionality is of central importance to a design methodology and the extra complexity of explicitly carrying around the necessary contextual information is a small price to pay in the definition of an *abstract* model of the development process. How such information is stored and exhibited in practice is a separate concern. Indeed, to show all the context at each stage would introduce unnecessary clutter to

---

[4] The choice has repercussions on the possibilities for shared-state concurrency by using the frames to give conditions for non-interference in the parallel combination of operations. However, such issues are outside the scope of this paper.

[5] We also assume the definedness of e

the exposition and detract attention from the pertinent issues. Thus, it is important to know at each point in the development precisely which parts of the context have any bearing on the sub-specification under development and to be able to collect these together, if required, so that the development of that sub-specification can be considered independently.

As pointed out earlier, the interspersing of the universal and existential quantifiers over read and write frames in the satisfiability obligation reflects the fact that the read and write frames play more than a purely syntactic role in the decomposition process. The separation of the syntactic and semantic roles of the two traditional frames can lead to some "interesting" specifications. Why should a specification be constrained to deal with the same variables as the implementation? Although there is a danger of introducing some "surprise" refinements in this way, the specifier is always at liberty to coalesce the two frames if so desired.

Judicious use of read and write frames can add considerable expressiveness to the specification of an algorithm. As well as the obvious implications in the treatment of shared-state concurrency, there may also be the possibility of specifying some forms of "security" requirements in this way. By restricting the usual satisfaction relation, frames give greater control over the removal of non-determinism during refinement.

The overall frame "scopes" the semantics of the operation specification and gives rise to a degree of freedom in the interpretation of the operation outside this frame. [Lamport91] points out that an important decision in the design of his Temporal Logic of Actions, was that the semantics should be that "all can change" unless otherwise stated, as this permits more elegant laws concerning the concurrency combinators (p54). For the sake of modularity, for instance, it may be useful to have a frame outside of which we assume nothing. In [AL90] he also says

"A practical language must allow one to write a formula F so that y is a free variable of F even though it does not appear in the text." (pg 46)

In the context of this paper, it is a similar idea that has motivated the separation of the 'scoping' role of the syntactic frame from the its 'binding' role for the reads and writes.

Acknowledgements. I would like to acknowledge the considerable contribution of my colleagues to this work: I am grateful to Professor Cliff Jones for providing the framework upon which this is all based and to my colleagues at RAL, in particular the two Brians, Ritchie and Matthews, Chris Reade and Mike Spivey who, together and separately, have helped to clarify these ideas as they are represented both in my mind and on the page.

References

[AL90]   *Composing Specifications.* M. Abadi and L. Lamport. DEC Technical Report 66, October 1990.

[Abrial90] *Abstract Machines, Parts I, II and III.* J. R. Abrial. Unpublished, 1990.

[ALNS91]   *The B Method.* J. R. Abrial, M. K. O. Lee, D. S. Neilson and P. N. Scharbach. VDM '91, Formal Software Development Methods, LNCS 552, Springer-Verlag (1991).

[AhKee89]   *Operation Decomposition Proof Obligations for Blocks and Procedures.*
              J. A. Ah-Kee. Ph.D. Thesis. University of Manchester. 1989.

[Back88]   *A Calculus of Refinements for Program Derivations.* R.J.R. Back. Acta Infor-
              matica (1988).

[BW90]   *Duality in Specification Languages: A Lattice-theoretical Approach.*
              R.J.R. Back and J. von Wright. Acta Informatica 27, 1990, pp 583-625.

[BR91]   *Reasoning about VDM developments using the VDM support tool in Mural.*
              J.C. Bicarregui and B. Ritchie, in VDM '91 Formal Software Development
              Methods. LNCS 552, Springer-Verlag (1991).

[BFLMR93]   *Proof in VDM – A Practitioner's Guide.* J.C.Bicarregui, J.F. Fitzgerald,
              P.A. Lindsay, R. Moore and B. Ritchie, To appear Springer-Verlag (1993).

[Dijkstra76] *A Discipline of Programming.* E.W.Dijkstra, Prentice-Hall (1976).

[Jones87]   *VDM Proof Obligations and their Justification.* C.B.Jones, Proceedings of the
              VDM '87 Symposium, LNCS 252, Springer-Verlag(1987).

[Jones90]   C.B.Jones, *Systematic Software Development using VDM.* (second edition)
              Prentice Hall, 1990.

[Lamport91]   *The Temporal Logic of Actions.* L. Lamport, DEC Technical Report 79. De-
              cember 25, 1991.

[Milne88]   *Proof Rules for VDM Statements.* R. Milne, Proceedings of the VDM '88
              Symposium, LNCS 328, Springer-Verlag(1988).

[Morgan86]   *The Specification Statement.* C. Morgan. TOPLAS 10, 3 (July 1988).

[Morgan88]   *On the Refinement Calculus.* C. Morgan, K. Robinson and P. Gardiner. Ox-
              ford University Technical Monograph, PRG-70, 1988.

[Morgan90]   *Programming from Specifications.* C. Morgan, Prentice Hall, 1990.

[Morris87]   *A theoretical basis for stepwise refinement and the programming calculus.* J.
              Morris, Sci.Comput. Programming, 9 287-306 (1987).

Invariants, Frames and Postconditions: a Comparison of the VDM and B Notations

Juan Bicarregui and Brian Ritchie

Systems Engineering Division
SERC Rutherford Appleton Laboratory
Oxon OX11 0QZ, UK

Abstract. VDM and B are two "model-oriented" formal methods. Each gives a notation for the specification of systems as state machines in terms of a set of states with operations defined as relations on that set. Each has a notion of refinement of data and operations based on the principles of reduction of non-determinism and increase in definedness.

This paper makes a comparison of the two notations through an example of a communications protocol previously formalised in [BA91]. Two abstractions and two reifications of the original specification are given. Particular attention is paid to three areas where the notations differ: the use of postconditions that assume the invariant as opposed to postconditions that enforce it; the explicit "framing" of operations as opposed to the "minimal frame" approach; and the use of relational postconditions as opposed to generalised substitutions.

1   Introduction

In [BA92], Bruns and Anderson describe a communications protocol in CCS with value-passing. A data model for the values is given which is, in effect, a model of the state of the device. This model is defined in terms of the usual data constructors of model-oriented specification, but without the use of invariants.

The part of the protocol described is a mechanism for manipulating a series of flags that indicate the status of some shared-memory buffers. These flags are used to ensure that there is no "data-tearing" as multiple processors simultaneously read and write to the buffers. For the operations that update these flags, semaphores are used to ensure that each operation has uninterrupted access to the flags. Thus this part of the behaviour can be described as a purely sequential system.

This paper considers some alternative data-models for the specification (and reification) of these status flags. In particular, attention is paid to the use of invariants in the data model and frames of reference in the operation definitions, neither of which are available in the data modelling language of [BA92]. It is argued that these features can play a key role in describing the system in a "natural" fashion and can thus help to deepen our understanding of the model.

VDM [Jones90] and B [Abrial92b] are used for the analysis, and particular attention is paid to some areas where the notations differ: the use of postconditions that assume the invariant as opposed to postconditions that enforce it; the explicit "framing" of operations as opposed to the "minimal frame" approach; and the use of relational postconditions as opposed to generalised substitutions. In this small example, there is little scope for the effective use of structuring of specifications that is one of the major features of the B method. Familiarity with the basic concepts and notation of VDM and B is assumed.

The remainder of this first section is an informal description of the application and desired protocol. The second through fifth sections present the development in VDM. Section two presents a formal specification of the system at a level of abstraction similar to the "abstract" description of [BA92]. Motivated by an analysis of the invariant of that specification, section three describes two further abstractions that can be made. Section four provides an alternative model of the system that makes it possible to write more useful framing information about the operations, the fifth section extends this model to the "improved" protocol of [BA92]. The sixth section considers the development again using B, presenting those elements of the development that highlight the differences in the notations. The last section is a discussion of some of the points arising from the example and their treatment in the two notations.

1.1 The Multiprocessor Shared-Memory Information Exchange

The Multiprocessor Shared-Memory Information Exchange (MSMIE), is a protocol that addresses intra-subsystem communications with "several features which make it ideally suited to inter-processor communications in distributed, microprocessor based nuclear safety systems" [Santoline89]. It has been used in the embedded software of Westinghouse nuclear systems designs.

The protocol uses multiple buffering to ensure that no "data-tearing" occurs, that is, it ensures that data is never overwritten by one process whilst it is being read by another. One important requirement is that neither writing nor reading processes should have to wait for a buffer to become available; another is that "recent" information should be passed, via the buffers, from writers to readers. In the simplification considered in [BA92] it is assumed that information is being passed from a single writing "slave" processor, to several reading "master" processors.

The information exchange is realised by a system with three buffers. Very roughly, at any time, one buffer is available for writing, one for reading and the third is either in between a write and a read and hence contains the most recently written information, or between a read and a write and so is idle.

The status of each buffer is recorded by a flag which can take one of four values:

s - "assigned to slave." This buffer is reserved for writing, it may actually be being written at the moment or just marked as available for writing.

n - "newest." This buffer has just been written and contains the latest information. It is not being read at the moment.

m - "assigned to master." This buffer is being read by one or more processors.

i - "idle." This buffer is idle, not being read or written and not containing the latest data.

The names of the master processors that are currently reading are also stored in the state.

As mentioned earlier, neither the slave and master processors that access the buffers in parallel nor the actual transference of data are modelled here. This analysis concerns only the operations that modify the buffer status flags. These operations are protected by a system of semaphores which allow each operation uninterrupted access to the state and thus their behaviour is purely sequential.

There are three of these operations:

slave This operation is executed when a write finishes. *slave* sets the status of the buffer that was being written to "newest" thus replacing any other buffer with this status.

acquire This is executed when a read begins. The new reader name (passed as a parameter) is added to the set of readers and status flags are updated as appropriate.

release Executed when a read ends, this removes a reader from the set and updates flags as appropriate.

The details of the behaviour of these operations are quite intricate and their precise description is left to the formal specification in the following section.

It should be noted however that, as it stands, the protocol could have the undesirable property that information flow from slave to master can be held up indefinitely. This possibility is ruled out in the original system [Santoline89] via timing constraints whereas [BA92] suggests an improvement to the protocol (using a fourth buffer) that eliminates the possibility without recourse to timing arguments. This improved protocol is also examined in later sections.

2   A VDM Specification of MSMIE

The state in [BA92] is defined as

"a set of three pairs (a, l) where a is the buffer status, drawn from $\{i, s, n, m\}$, and l is the buffer identification, drawn from $\{1, 2, 3\}$. The buffers are given as a set rather than a tuple to enable pattern matching rules in the description of the protocol."

The pattern matching rules do indeed give a concise description of the transitions of the system, in particular, the associative and commutative properties of sets are used to good effect in order to avoid much repetitive case analysis. However, the present authors found that considerable effort was required to check that the patterns given were exhaustive and that the effects of overlaps between patterns were sensible. This difficulty is exacerbated by the fact that many of the states in the model are unreachable but no invariant on the state type is given to exclude them.

The specification given here makes the choice of a sequence of three buffers for the state description. In addition, an invariant is used to exclude unwanted values from the state type.

2.1 The State

Possible values of the status flags are given via an enumerated type; the type of the names of master (reading) processors is deferred.

types

$Status = \{s, m, n, i\}$

$MName = $ token

The state is composed of three buffer status flags and a set of the names of the currently reading masters. The invariant captures the fact that only certain states are reachable by the operations. It gives restrictions as to the possible combinations of status flags, namely that there is always exactly one buffer assigned to the writing slave; there is at most one currently being read and at most one with newest data that is not being read; and the set of reader names is empty precisely when there is no buffer being read. The initial state assigns one buffer to the slave and records that the other two buffers are idle.

state Σ of
    b : $Status^*$
    ms : $MName$-set
inv $mk\text{-}\Sigma(b, ms)$ $\triangleq$ len $b = 3 \wedge$
                       $count(s, b) = 1 \wedge$
                       $count(m, b) \in \{0, 1\} \wedge$
                       $count(n, b) \in \{0, 1\} \wedge$
                       $(count(m, b) = 0 \iff ms = \{\})$
init $mk\text{-}\Sigma(b, ms)$ $\triangleq$ $b = [s, i, i] \wedge ms = \{\}$
end
where[1]

   $count : Status \times Status^* \to \mathbb{N}$

   $count(status, l)$ $\triangleq$ len$(l \rhd status)$

A validation condition on the state. We observe that only four combinations of buffers are allowed by the invariant:

$\forall mk\text{-}\Sigma(b, ms): \Sigma \cdot \{b(1), b(2), b(3)\}_m \in \{\{s,i,i\}_m, \{s,i,n\}_m, \{s,i,m\}_m, \{s,n,m\}_m\}$

---

[1] Here, range restriction is used on sequences, viewing them as maps from natural numbers to elements.

where we have used $\{\dots\}_m$ as a notation for bags (multisets), for example $\{s,i,i\}_m$ is the bag containing one 's' and two 'i's.

Thus the invariant has captured, and brought to the fore, properties that would otherwise have to be deduced by looking in detail at the definitions of the operations. It makes it possible to build quickly our intuition of the workings of the specified machine. We know immediately that there is always one buffer reserved for writing, at most one being read, and at most one with newest data not being read.

2.2 The Operations

Slave. The first operation, *slave*, is executed when a write completes. It re-assigns the status of the buffer just written, previously s, to n, thus replacing any other n buffer. It also non-deterministically chooses another available buffer which is to be the new buffer reserved for writing and assigns to it status s.

> *slave* ()
>
> ext wr b : $Status^*$
>
> pre true
>
> post $\forall i \in \{1,2,3\}\cdot$
> $$(\overleftarrow{b}(i) = s \Rightarrow b(i) = n)\ \wedge$$
> $$(\overleftarrow{b}(i) = m \Rightarrow b(i) = m)$$

The postcondition may, at first sight, seem to be to liberal: what should happen to any buffer that had status n or i? However, in conjunction with the invariant and the frame, it ensures that no other n buffer remains, that exactly one new s buffer is chosen, and that no new m buffers are added. Thus for example we can write the following validation property for *slave* which can be proved in order to increase confidence in the correctness of the postcondition:

$$\overleftarrow{b}(i) \in \{n,i\}\ \Rightarrow\ b(i) \in \{i,s\}$$

Note that all three implications could have been equivalences without changing the operation.

Acquire. The second operation, acquire, is executed when a read is about to start. It adds the new reader's name, passed as a parameter, to the record of active readers and reassigns status flags as necessary.

If there is a buffer currently being read then the new read also begins to read that same buffer and no status change is required. Otherwise the new read starts on the buffer with newest data, status n, and reassigns the status of that buffer to m.

The operation can only be executed in these two situations and this information is recorded in the precondition which requires that there is either a status m or status n buffer. The precondition also records the fact that the operation is only required to function when the new reader is not already in the set of readers.

Note that, in selecting which buffer is to be read, it is not always possible to choose the buffer with newest data. This situation occurs when there are currently buffers with both status m and n, which arises when the data in the n buffer has become available since the start of an ongoing read, that is, when there has been a *slave* since an *acquire* for which there has not yet been a corresponding *release*. In this situation, were the new master to begin reading the n buffer, there would then be two buffers reserved for reading. Consequently, should another *slave* now occur, attempting to preserve this new data would leave no buffer being available for another write to start, thus contradicting one of the fundamental requirements of the protocol: that processors should never have to wait to gain access to buffers. The invariant is designed to prevent this possibility, by insisting that there is always one (and precisely one) buffer with status s.

acq $(l\!:\! MName)$

ext wr b : $Status^*$

    wr ms : $MName$-set

pre $l \notin ms \land$

    $\exists i \in \{1,2,3\} \cdot b(i) = n \lor b(i) = m$

post $ms = \overleftarrow{ms} \cup \{l\} \land$

    $\forall i \in \{1,2,3\} \cdot$

        if $\overleftarrow{b}(i) = n \land \overleftarrow{ms} = \{\}$ then $b(i) = m$ else $b(i) = \overleftarrow{b}(i)$

It is worth observing that the last line of the postcondition could have been written as

$$\text{if } \overleftarrow{b}(i) = n \text{ then } b(i) \in \{n, m\} \text{ else } b(i) = \overleftarrow{b}(i)$$

or simply as

$$\overleftarrow{b}(i) \neq n \land ms \neq \{\} \;\Rightarrow\; b(i) = \overleftarrow{b}(i).$$

The apparent non-determinism in the alternatives is illusory as the invariant will ensure that there is no real choice as to what status to assign to any buffer that previously had status n. However, the longer and apparently stronger postcondition is preferred as the shorter versions seem to be more cryptic.

Release. The release operation is executed when a reading, master processor finishes its read. The name of the processor is removed from the set of readers and again, status flags reassigned as required.

If this master is not the last one currently reading, then no change is required to the status flags. However, if this is the last master currently reading the m buffer, then this buffer must have its flag reassigned. There are two possibilities. On the one hand, should there be another buffer with status n available at this time, that is if a write has been completed since the current "chain of reads" began on this buffer, then the m buffer no longer contains the most recent data and so should now be set to i. On the other hand, if there has been no write since the chain of reads began, and hence there is no n buffer available, the m buffer contains the most recent data and its status should be reset to n.

$rel\ (l\colon MName)$

ext wr b : $Status^*$
    wr ms : $MName$-set

pre $l \in ms$

post $ms = \overleftarrow{ms} - \{l\} \land$
    $\forall i \in \{1, 2, 3\} \cdot$
        if $ms = \{\} \land \overleftarrow{b}\,(i) = \mathsf{m}$
        then $b(i) \in \{\mathsf{n}, \mathsf{i}\} \land count(\mathsf{n}, b) = 1$
        else $b(i) = \overleftarrow{b}\,(i)$

Again there is some choice as to how much of the information that is deducible from the invariant should be made explicit in the postcondition. For example the first conjunct of the 'then' clause $b(i) \in \{\mathsf{n}, \mathsf{i}\}$ could have been omitted as no other possibilities are permitted by the invariant, or alternatively, the whole 'then' clause could be replaced by a more explicit form

$$\text{if } \exists j \in \{1, 2, 3\} \cdot \overleftarrow{b}\,(j) = \mathsf{n} \text{ then } b(i) = \mathsf{i} \text{ else } b(i) = \mathsf{n}$$

It is debatable which gives the clearer specification.

This specification has given a fairly algorithmic description of which buffers are assigned to what status by each operation. This is a good level of abstraction at which to reason about whole system safety properties such as the freshness of the data transferred from slave to masters which is the focus of [BA92]. Much of the detail of this specification, however, is undesirable clutter for other purposes and it is interesting to give more "external" views of the system, as is done in the next section.

3   Two More-Abstract Specifications

In this section we give two formal abstractions of the above specification. The new specifications maintain the same external behaviour, however the abstract states are progressively simpler than the one just given. The abstractions arise by ignoring detail in the state model that is unnecessary to capture the external behaviour. Retrieve functions from concrete to abstract states are also given which are many-to-one thus demonstrating "implementation bias" in the concrete specification.

As it is usual to give more concrete specifications successively higher numbers, from now on we will use Σ_2 to refer to the state of the specification given earlier.

3.1 A First Abstraction: Ignoring the Identity of Buffers

Taking inspiration from the validation condition on the state of the above specification, we can give a more abstract specification where, rather than explicitly giving the status of each individual buffer, the state only records which of the four possible *combinations* of buffer the machine is in.

types

$$Status_1 = \{\text{sii}, \text{sin}, \text{sim}, \text{snm}\}$$

state Σ_1 of
    bs : $Status_1$
    ms : $MName$-set
inv $mk\text{-}\Sigma_1(bs, ms) \;\; \triangleq \;\; ms = \{\,\} \;\Leftrightarrow\; bs \in \{\text{sii}, \text{sin}\}$
init $mk\text{-}\Sigma_1(bs, ms) \;\; \triangleq \;\; bs = \text{sii} \wedge ms = \{\,\}$
end

operations

$slave$ ()

ext wr bs : $Status_1$

pre true

post $(\overleftarrow{bs} \in \{\text{sii}, \text{sin}\} \;\Rightarrow\; bs = \text{sin}) \;\;\wedge$
      $(\overleftarrow{bs} \in \{\text{sim}, \text{snm}\} \;\Rightarrow\; bs = \text{snm})$

As in the earlier specification of *slave*, there is no change to the readers of the m buffer, thus there is no need to access *ms*.

acq (l: $MName$)

ext wr bs : $Status_1$
    wr ms : $MName$-set

pre $l \notin ms \wedge bs \neq \text{sii}$

post $ms = \overleftarrow{ms} \cup \{l\} \wedge$
    if $\overleftarrow{ms} = \{\,\}$ then $bs = \text{sim}$ else $bs = \overleftarrow{bs}$

The definition of *rel* is similar to *acq* and for reasons of brevity has been omitted from this and all subsequent specifications. The complete specifications can be found in [BR93].

The retrieve function from the first, more concrete, specification to this one is simple to define by cases.

$retr_{2-1} : \Sigma_2 \to \Sigma_1$

$retr_{2-1}(mk\text{-}\Sigma(b_1, b_2, b_3, ms))$ $\triangleq$
 cases $(count(\text{n}, [b_1, b_2, b_3]), count(\text{m}, [b_1, b_2, b_3]))$ of
 $(0, 0) \to mk\text{-}\Sigma_1(\text{sii}, ms)$
 $(1, 0) \to mk\text{-}\Sigma_1(\text{sin}, ms)$
 $(0, 1) \to mk\text{-}\Sigma_1(\text{sim}, ms)$
 $(1, 1) \to mk\text{-}\Sigma_1(\text{snm}, ms)$
 end

This specification abstracts away from the behaviour of the individual buffers and so it does not help us to reason about the algorithm for updating them. However, it does exhibit a useful congruence on the original state space and makes the property of not returning to the sii states very clear. This observation motivates the following further abstraction.

3.2 A Further Abstraction

In this specification we abstract away from the buffers entirely: their place being taken by a single boolean flag that records whether a write has ever occurred. Although this specification is consequently extremely simple, it still exhibits the same external behaviour as the original.

state Σ_0 of
 b : **B**
 ms : $MName$-set
inv $mk\text{-}\Sigma_0(b, ms)$ $\triangleq$ $b = \text{false} \Rightarrow ms = \{\}$
init $mk\text{-}\Sigma_0(b, ms)$ $\triangleq$ $b = \text{false} \land ms = \{\}$
end

The operations specifications are now very simple:

operations

 $slave$ ()
 ext wr b : **B**
 pre true
 post $b = \text{true}$

 acq $(l : MName)$
 ext rd b : **B**
  wr ms : $MName$-set
 pre $b = \text{true} \land l \notin ms$
 post $ms = \overleftarrow{ms} \cup \{l\}$

The retrieve function is straightforward.

$$retr_{1\text{-}0} : \Sigma_1 \rightarrow \Sigma_0$$

$$retr_{1\text{-}0}(mk\text{-}\Sigma_1(bs, ms)) \quad \triangleq \quad mk\text{-}\Sigma_0(bs \neq \text{sii}, ms)$$

4 An Alternative View of MSMIE

The above specifications are based on the state recording the status of each buffer. Effectively, the state is a map from each buffer to its status. Returning to the original specification, we observe that there is always exactly one buffer with status s and at most one with status m or n. This makes it possible to invert the map and think of the state as mapping each status to a buffer.

This leads to a specification that is equivalent to the first one, but might yield a more efficient basis for an implementation. This change also makes it possible to specify the access constraints more closely.

4.1 The State

types

$$BName = \{1, 2, 3\}$$

$$MName = \text{token}$$

state Σ_3 **of**
$$\begin{aligned} s &: BName \\ n &: [BName] \\ m &: [BName] \\ ms &: MName\text{-set} \end{aligned}$$
inv $mk\text{-}\Sigma_3(s, n, m, ms) \quad \triangleq \quad (m = nil \Leftrightarrow ms = \{\}) \wedge$
$$nil\text{-}or\text{-}different([s, m, n])$$
init $mk\text{-}\Sigma_3(s, n, m, ms) \quad \triangleq \quad mk\text{-}\Sigma(1, nil, nil, \{\})$
end
where $nil\text{-}or\text{-}different([s, n, m])$ is true if and only if each of s, n and m are each mapped to distinct $BNAME$s or nil:

$$nil\text{-}or\text{-}different : [BNAME]^* \rightarrow \mathbf{B}$$

$$nil\text{-}or\text{-}different(l) \quad \triangleq \quad \forall i \in \text{inds } l \cdot l(i) = nil \vee l(i) \notin \text{elems}(i \triangleleft l)$$

It is perhaps worth noting that an alternative data model would consist of a single map from $Status$ to $BNAME$. However, we have chosen the above because this allows us to narrow the read and write frames of some of the operations.

The Retrieve Function. In this case we give the retrieve function implicitly, noting however that it is fully determined (and implementable):

$retr_{3\text{-}2}\ (mk\text{-}\Sigma_3(s, n, m, ms)\colon \Sigma_3)\ \sigma_2\colon \Sigma_2$

pre true

post let $mk\text{-}\Sigma_2(bs, ms_2) = \Sigma_2$ in
$\quad$ len $bs = 3\ \wedge$
$\quad \forall i \in \{1, 2, 3\}\cdot(s = i \ \Rightarrow\ b_i = s)\ \wedge$
$\qquad\qquad\qquad (n = i \ \Rightarrow\ b_i = n)\ \wedge$
$\qquad\qquad\qquad (m = i \ \Rightarrow\ b_i = m)\ \wedge$
$\qquad\qquad\qquad (i \notin \{s, n, m\} \ \Rightarrow\ b_i = i)$
$\quad \wedge\ ms_2 = ms$

4.2 The Operations

Slave.

$slave\ ()$

ext rd m : $[BName]$
$\quad$ wr n : $[BName]$
$\quad$ wr s : $BName$

pre true

post $n = \overleftarrow{s}$

The interaction between invariant and externals is interesting. Here, read access to m is required although m is not referred to in the specification. This is because m is linked to s via the invariant and the value of s which is not fully determined by the post-condition: any implementation will need to read m in order to ascertain what value it is valid to assign to s.

Thus rather than think of the externals clauses as giving information about the variables mentioned in the *specification*, we see them as giving details of what access to state variables an *implementation* of that operation can be allowed to make. This distinction separates their semantic role giving information about access to state variables from the syntactic role they play in binding the free variables of the pre- and post-condition.

Acquire.

$acq\ (l\colon MName)$

ext wr ms : $MName$-set
$\quad$ wr n, m : $[BName]$

pre $l \notin ms \wedge \neg\,(n = \mathsf{nil} \wedge m = \mathsf{nil})$

post $ms = \overleftarrow{ms} \cup \{l\}\ \wedge$
$\quad (\overleftarrow{ms} \neq \{\} \ \Rightarrow\ m = \overleftarrow{m} \wedge n = \overleftarrow{n})\ \wedge$
$\quad (\overleftarrow{ms} = \{\} \ \Rightarrow\ m = \overleftarrow{n} \wedge n = \mathsf{nil})$

Interestingly, the last conjunct of this postcondition could be considered to be redundant. When $\overline{ms} = \{\}$ and thus $\overline{m}$ is nil, then $ms = \{l\}$ and so m must be assigned a non nil value. Now, as read access to s is prohibited, the only buffer that we can be sure is not already in use is that previously assigned to n. So any implementation that respects the frames of reference must assign this buffer to m. Then the only remaining possible value for n is nil. However, to hide so much information in the externals clause seems to be counter-productive.

5   The Improved MSMIE

As mentioned earlier, Bruns and Anderson observe that, as it stands, the three buffer MSMIE can exhibit an undesirable behaviour. That is, it is possible for a series of overlapping reads, each beginning before the last ends, to lock-out indefinitely the latest data. They suggest an improved protocol that uses a fourth buffer to eliminate this possibility.

Surprisingly, although this new protocol exhibits the same external behaviour as the earlier one, there is no formal refinement relationship between them. To understand why this is, we recall that the part of the system modelled only concerns itself with the assignment of processors to buffers and so does not model the actual transfer of information from slave to masters. Thus, the values assigned to the status flags have no externally visible effect and all the machinations of the state can be seen as purely an implementation bias in the model.

However, the four-buffer version is a refinement of the most abstract specification given earlier, which gives another important reason for considering those abstractions. In particular, validations of the abstract model will carry over to both the three and four buffer versions.

Of course, in this case, it is the internal properties of the model itself that are of interest, as it is these properties that influence the "freshness" of the data read by the masters. In this respect, the four buffer protocol is indeed better behaved as it would lead to a system where the delay in information transfer is at worst equal to that of the three buffer version.

In the four buffer version of MSMIE, there is also an extra status possible for buffers. o is used to denote a buffer that is still being read but no longer contains most up-to-date information. Thus:

s as before, is a buffer that is reserved for writing
n as before, is a buffer that contains the latest data but is not being read (waiting for read)
m is a buffer being read, (and the newest such)
o is a buffer being read (but there is also a newer one being read)
ms is the set of masters reading m
os is the set of masters reading o.

New masters are always assigned to the n or the m buffer. m buffers are "demoted" to o status in a way that ensures that the o buffer will periodically become idle. In this way the protocol avoids the "refresh" problems of the three-buffer version. Again detailed descriptions of the mechanisms used to achieve this is given accompanying the formal text.

It might help to think of the status transitions $i \to s \to n$ as the write phase of a buffer and the transitions $n \to m \to o \to i$ as the read phase. We will see that this variant of MSMIE always has two buffers in write phase and two buffers in read phase.

5.1 The State

types

$$BName = \{1, 2, 3, 4\}$$

state Σ_4 **of**

$\quad s \; : \; BName$

$\quad n \; : \; [BName]$

$\quad m \; : \; [BName]$

$\quad o \; : \; [BName]$

$\quad ms \; : \; MName\text{-set}$

$\quad os \; : \; MName\text{-set}$

inv $mk\text{-}\Sigma_4(s, n, m, o, ms, os) \quad \triangleq$

$\quad\quad (m = nil \iff ms = \{\}) \wedge$

$\quad\quad (o = nil \iff os = \{\}) \wedge$

$\quad\quad (ms \cap os = \{\}) \wedge$

$\quad\quad (nil\text{-}or\text{-}different([s, n, m, o])) \wedge$

$\quad\quad (m = nil \wedge n = nil \Rightarrow o = nil)$

init $\sigma_4 \quad \triangleq \quad \sigma_4 = mk\text{-}\Sigma_4(1, nil, nil, nil, \{\}, \{\})$

end

The last conjunct in the invariant, which rules out the states corresponding to $\{s,o,i,i\}_m$, is the result of the way that readers of m are released which, as in the earlier specifications, ensures that there is always an m or an n buffer remaining.

A Validation Property for the State. The invariant only allows the following states corresponding to the following 7 combinations of buffer status:

$$\{s,i,i,i\}_m, \{s,i,i,n\}_m, \{s,i,i,m\}_m, \{s,i,m,n\}_m, \{s,i,m,o\}_m, \{s,i,n,o\}_m, \{s,m,n,o\}_m$$

Retrieve Function. As stated earlier this version is a data refinement of the most abstract model. The retrieve function is straightforward:

$$retr_{4\text{-}0} : \Sigma_4 \to \Sigma_0$$

$$retr_{4\text{-}0}(mk\text{-}\Sigma_4(s, n, m, o, ms, os)) \quad \triangleq$$

$$\quad mk\text{-}\Sigma_0(n = nil \wedge m = nil \wedge o = nil, ms \cup os)$$

5.2 The Operations

Slave.

$slave$ ()
ext rd m, o : $[BName]$
  wr n : $[BName]$
  wr s : $BName$
pre true
post $n = \overleftarrow{s}$

As before the implementation will require access to m and o in order to be able to set a valid s. That is:

$$s \in BName - \{n, m, o\}$$

This access requirement is recorded in the externals even though the predicates do not mention m and o.

Acquire. The descriptions of *acquire* and *release*, given via case analysis, are rather unwieldy. As different variables change in the different cases, the operations have to have wide write access and hence require clauses saying which variables do not change in that case. Thus we introduce a notational shorthand used in postconditions to say that certain state components are unchanged[2]:

$$Id : A^* \rightarrow \mathbf{B}$$

$$Id(l) \;\;\triangleq\;\; \forall i \in \text{inds}\, l \cdot l(i) = \overleftarrow{l(i)}$$

acq (l: $MName$)
ext wr ms, os : $MName$-set
  wr n, m, o : $[BName]$
pre $l \notin ms \cup os \wedge \neg\,(n = \text{nil} \wedge m = \text{nil})$
post $(ms \cup os = \overleftarrow{ms} \cup \overleftarrow{os} \cup \{l\}) \wedge$
  $(\overleftarrow{m} = \text{nil} \Rightarrow m = \overleftarrow{n} \wedge n = \text{nil} \wedge Id([o, os])) \wedge$
  $(\overleftarrow{m} \neq \text{nil} \wedge (\overleftarrow{o} \neq \text{nil} \vee n = \text{nil}) \Rightarrow Id([m, n, o, os])) \wedge$
  $(\overleftarrow{m} \neq \text{nil} \wedge \overleftarrow{o} = \text{nil} \wedge n \neq \text{nil}$
    $\Rightarrow o = \overleftarrow{m} \wedge m = \overleftarrow{n} \wedge n = \text{nil} \wedge os = \overleftarrow{ms} \wedge ms = \{l\})$

Acquire behaves in a manner similar to before: a reader is assigned to the n or the m buffer as appropriate. The only extra consideration is in the case where there is an n buffer waiting, and an m buffer being read, but no o buffer. In this case, where previously the new reader would have been assigned to the m buffer, it is now possible to begin the read on the n buffer, hence the improvement to

---

[2] This should be seen as a syntactic "macro", rather than an auxiliary function.

the freshness of the data exchanged. The buffer that was already being read is marked as o, and correspondingly the record of processors reading that buffer, ms, is moved to os; and the new read begins on the buffer that was n, thus making it into a new m and the new reader is recorded in ms. No more masters will be assigned to the o buffer until it has been through the write cycle again.

We have seen five specifications which exhibit the same external behaviour. All except for the most abstract incorporate some degree of implementation bias. However, it is this very bias that is the subject under investigation. In [BA92] validation conditions describing some desirable global properties of the protocol are expressed in the modal μ-calculus. For the purposes of comparison of the two notations considered in this paper it is sufficient to note that neither provides a formalism to express such conditions.

6 The Specification Using B

A similar series of specifications and refinements was constructed in B. In preference to presenting this material in full, we present only those parts that highlight the notational and stylistic differences between VDM and B which arose in this example.

This development was carried out using the current alpha-release of the B Toolkit [Abrial92a]. Although this has meant that the specifications have been required to conform exactly to the language supported by the machine[3], it has given us the advantages of automatic consistency checking that the toolkit provides. In this paper, we present the B machines as they were entered in the toolkit, though in some places syntactic sugaring may have made them more readily digestible.

6.1 The Two 'More-Abstract' Specifications

Figure 1 gives the B text for the two abstract specifications.

The first specification gives the most abstract specification of MSMIE as a machine $b0$. This corresponds to the VDM specification with state Σ_0. The machine is parameterised by a set $MNAME$ of master names which is assumed to be non-empty. The state consists of two variables $b0$ and ms. Unlike VDM, the typing information for the state variables is given in the invariant. Here, the first two clauses of the invariant give "static" (decidable) typing, and the third clause gives subtyping information. The initialisation and operations are given as generalised substitutions. At this level, the operations are very similar to the VDM ones presented earlier.

The major syntactic differences from VDM are that the types of the arguments are given explicitly as predicates. Also, the read and write frames of the

---

[3] In the VDM specifications, we have tried to follow the draft BSI standard as far as possible, but have allowed at least one notational extension in the Id function in the previous section.

MACHINE

  $b0(MNAME)$

VARIABLES

  $b0,$
  ms

INVARIANT

  $b0 \in BOOL$ $\wedge$
  $ms \in \mathbf{P}(MNAME)$ $\wedge$
  $b0 = FALSE \Rightarrow ms = \varnothing$

INITIALISATION

  $b0 := FALSE$ $||$
  $ms := \varnothing$

OPERATIONS

  $slave$ $\widehat{=}$
    $b0 := TRUE;$

  $acq(l1)$ $\widehat{=}$
    pre
      $l1 \in MNAME$ $\wedge$
      $b0 = TRUE$ $\wedge$
      $l1 \notin ms$
    then
      $ms := ms \cup \{l1\}$
    end;

  $rel(l1)$ $\widehat{=}$ $\ldots$

END

REFINEMENT
  $b1(MNAME)$

REFINES
  $b0$

SETS
  $STATUS = \{SII, SIN, SIM, SNM\}$

VARIABLES
  $b1,$
  ms

INVARIANT
  $b1 \in STATUS$ $\wedge$
  $ms = \varnothing \Leftrightarrow (b1 \in \{SII, SIN\})$ $\wedge$
  $b0 = FALSE \Leftrightarrow (b1 = SII)$

INITIALISATION
  $b1 := SII$ $||$
  $ms := \varnothing$

OPERATIONS
  $slave$ $\widehat{=}$
    $b1 \in \{SII, SIN\} \Longrightarrow b1 := SIN$
    $[]$
    $b1 \in \{SIM, SNM\} \Longrightarrow b1 := SNM;$

  $acq(l1)$ $\widehat{=}$
    pre
      $l1 \in MNAME$ $\wedge$
      $b1 \neq SII$ $\wedge$
      $l1 \notin ms$
    then
      $ms := ms \cup \{l1\}$
      $||$
      if $ms = \varnothing$ **then**
        $b1 := SIM$
      end
    end;

$\ldots$

Fig. 1. The B machine $b0$ and refinement $b1$

machine operations are implicit. The read frames are the full state of the machine and the variables written are determined by the generalised substitution, for example, those that appear on the left side of a simple substitution. Thus, the operation *slave* writes $b0$, and *acquire* writes *ms*. Framing is addressed further in the closing discussion.

The first reification $b1$ of $b0$ is presented in the right hand column of Figure 1 as a B refinement. It corresponds to the VDM specification with state Σ_1. Note that the B method makes a notational distinction between refinements and other specifications.

The concrete state also has two variables. By repeating the *ms* variable name, we are saying that this variable is the same as the one in the abstract specification. Technically, the new state variables include those of the abstract state as well any added here, however, the variables from the abstract state are subject to full hiding and cannot appear in the definition of operations. The relationship between abstract and concrete variables is given as part of the invariant – a coupling relation, as for example in [Morgan91]. In this example, the coupling relation appears as the last conjunct of the invariant. As in $b0$, the operation definitions are similar to those of the corresponding VDM specification.

6.2 Three Buffer Status

Now we proceed with a refinement $b2$ of $b1$ (Figure 2). This corresponds to the first VDM specification with state Σ_2. The data model (including the invariant) is similar to that of the VDM specification, and the coupling relation is similar to the retrieve function $retr_{2\text{-}1}$. Some informal comments have been added to the formal text.

Non-deterministic choice in a substitution is given by the notation "@$(v).S$", where v is a variable and S a generalised substitution. Here it is used in conjunction with guarded substitutions, in the form "@$(v).(P(v) \implies S)$" which can be read operationally as, "if there is any v such that $P(v)$, then apply the substitution S for one such v".

In this specification, we see a significant difference from the VDM in the presentation of the *slave* operation. Here, we have given a definition of *slave* which provides more explicit algorithmic information than its VDM counterpart. In particular, it breaks down the operation into seperate substitutions executed sequentially and could take one buffer through two changes of status. This style was found to be convenient here as the one "choice" that might be available, namely whether to choose the new slave to be the old newest or an old idle buffer, affects the outcome of two buffers. There is also a syntactic restriction prohibiting parallel substitutions to the same variable. The resulting operation definition has a far more programatic feel.

A similar change in style is reflected in the definitions of *acquire* and *release*, which for brevity are not included here.

REFINEMENT
  $b2(MNAME)$

REFINES
  $b1$

SETS
  $STATUSII = \{S2, I2, N2, M2\};$

VARIABLES
  $b2,$
  ms

INVARIANT
  /* typing */
  $b2 \in \mathsf{seq}(STATUSII)$ $\wedge$
  $ms \in \mathbf{P}(MNAME)$ $\wedge$
  /* subtyping */
  $size(b2) = 3$ $\wedge$
  $card(b2 \rhd \{S2\}) = 1$ $\wedge$
  $card(b2 \rhd \{M2\}) \in \{0, 1\}$ $\wedge$
  $card(b2 \rhd \{N2\}) \in \{0, 1\}$ $\wedge$
  $card(b2 \rhd \{M2\}) = 0 \Leftrightarrow (ms = \varnothing)$ $\wedge$
  /* coupling */
  $(card(b2 \rhd \{N2\}) = 0 \wedge card(b2 \rhd \{M2\}) = 0) \Leftrightarrow (b1 = SII)$ $\wedge$
  $(card(b2 \rhd \{N2\}) = 1 \wedge card(b2 \rhd \{M2\}) = 0) \Leftrightarrow (b1 = SIN)$ $\wedge$
  $(card(b2 \rhd \{N2\}) = 0 \wedge card(b2 \rhd \{M2\}) = 1) \Leftrightarrow (b1 = SIM)$ $\wedge$
  $(card(b2 \rhd \{N2\}) = 1 \wedge card(b2 \rhd \{M2\}) = 1) \Leftrightarrow (b1 = SNM)$

INITIALISATION
  $b2 := [S2, I2, I2]$ $\|$
  $ms := \varnothing$

OPERATIONS
  $slave \;\widehat{=}$
    (/* If there's a buffer that's set to N, find it and set it to I */
    $\exists z1.(z1 \in \{1,2,3\} \wedge b2(z1) = N2) \Longrightarrow$
      $@(z1).(z1 \in \{1,2,3\} \wedge b2(z1) = N2 \Longrightarrow b2 := (b2 \lhdplus \{z1 \mapsto I2\}))$
    []
    /* but if you can't find one that is N then don't worry */
    $\forall z2.(z2 \in \{1,2,3\} \Rightarrow b2(z2) \neq N2) \Longrightarrow skip$
    );
    /* Then, find a buffer that was S and set it to N (It's unique) */
    $@(z3).(z3 \in \{1,2,3\} \wedge b2(z3) = S2 \Longrightarrow b2 := (b2 \lhdplus \{z3 \mapsto N2\}))$
    ;
    /* then find an I and set it to S (there are one or two of these) */
    $@(z4).(z4 \in \{1,2,3\} \wedge b2(z4) = I2 \Longrightarrow b2 := (b2 \lhdplus \{z4 \mapsto S2\}));$

Fig. 2. The original three buffer machine specified in B.

6.3 The "Improved MSMIE" Version

The B machine *snmo* (Figure 3) corresponds to the VDM specification of the 4-buffer MSMIE. (The 3-buffer "inverted map" version has been omitted from this paper, because the same issues arise with this machine.)

At this level, the two notations are once again fairly similar. One difference from the VDM version is that because the generalised substitutions explicitly indicate which variables are to be substituted there is no need for the *Id* clauses that appear in the VDM version.

7 Discussion

As stated in the introduction, this example highlights three areas where the notations encourage different approaches. This closing section gives a brief discussion of some of the points that arose from our study of the MSMIE protocol.

Invariants. In both notations, the invariant is useful for quickly conveying an understanding of the reachable values of the state. However the use of invariants in operation definitions differs. In B, postconditions (in the form of generalised substitutions) have to be written so as to ensure the maintenance of the invariant. In VDM the state invariant is effectively part of the state typing information, and as such is assumed to be maintained in addition to the postcondition.

VDM's implicit maintenance of the invariant led to the choice discussed earlier of how much of the information in the invariant is repeated in a postcondition. There was often some tension between the most concise form that relied on properties of the invariant for its correctness, and a longer, but more explicit form, that included some redundant information. This choice can be seen as an opportunity to prove the stronger forms from the weaker. Which form is chosen may make a significant difference to the complexity of the proofs: the form that most clearly conveys the information may not be the form that will be most usable in proofs. Indeed, the stronger form is more likely to be helpful when the specification is being proved to be a reification of another, and the weaker form when it is itself being reified.

In the B notation, on the other hand, one writes operations so as to imply the preservation of the invariant. This can encourage a tendency to describe *how* the invariant is maintained, which may lead to less abstract specifications.

Operation Definitions. The greater programmatic feel of the B notation is reinforced by the use of generalised substitutions, as opposed to VDM's relational post-conditions. Although the two forms have the same expressive power, in some cases (as for example in *slave* in the *b2* machine) we found it convenient to give greater algorithmic detail in the B version. This would appear to imply that the B notation is more useful for the development of algorithms. Indeed, the process of operation decomposition has been given greater attention in the B methodology than for VDM. By contrast, perhaps VDM's relational postconditions give a greater facility for non-algorithmic specifications of complex operations.

REFINEMENT
 $snmo(MNAME)$

REFINES
 $b0$

VARIABLES
 $sb,\ nb,\ mb,\ ob,$
 $ms4,\ os4$

INVARIANT
 /* typing */
 $sb \in 1..4$ $\wedge$
 $nb \in \text{seq}(1..4)$ $\wedge$
 $mb \in \text{seq}(1..4)$ $\wedge$
 $ob \in \text{seq}(1..4)$ $\wedge$
 $ms4 \in \mathbf{P}(MNAME)$ $\wedge$
 $os4 \in \mathbf{P}(MNAME)$ $\wedge$
 /* subtyping */
 $\text{size}(nb) \in \{0,\ 1\}$ $\wedge$
 $\text{size}(mb) \in \{0,\ 1\}$ $\wedge$
 $\text{size}(ob) \in \{0,\ 1\}$ $\wedge$
 $mb = [] \Leftrightarrow (ms4 = \varnothing)$ $\wedge$
 $ob = [] \Leftrightarrow (os4 = \varnothing)$ $\wedge$
 $[sb] \neq nb$ $\wedge$
 $[sb] \neq mb$ $\wedge$
 $[sb] \neq ob$ $\wedge$
 $nb = mb \Leftrightarrow (nb = [] \wedge mb = [])$ $\wedge$
 $nb = ob \Leftrightarrow (nb = [] \wedge ob = [])$ $\wedge$
 $mb = ob \Leftrightarrow (mb = [] \wedge ob = [])$ $\wedge$
 $mb = [] \wedge nb = [] \Rightarrow ob = []$ $\wedge$
 /* coupling */
 $ms = ms4 \cup os4$ $\wedge$
 $b0 = FALSE \Leftrightarrow$
  $(nb = [] \wedge mb = [] \wedge ob = [])$

INITIALISATION
 $sb := 1$ $\ ||$
 $nb := []$ $\ ||$
 $mb := []$ $\ ||$
 $ob := []$ $\ ||$
 $ms4 := \varnothing$ $\ ||$
 $os4 := \varnothing$

OPERATIONS

 $slave \ \widehat{=}$
  $nb := [sb]$ $\ ||$
  $sb :\in \{1,\ 2,\ 3,\ 4\} - \{sb\}$
    $- \text{ran}(mb) - \text{ran}(ob);$

 $acq(l1) \ \widehat{=}$
  pre
   $l1 \in MNAME$ $\wedge$
   $l1 \notin ms4$ $\wedge$
   $\text{conc}([nb,\ mb]) \neq []$
  then
   select $mb = []$ then
    $mb := nb$ $\ ||$
    $nb := []$ $\ ||$
    $ms4 := \{l1\}$
   when $mb \neq [] \wedge nb \neq [] \wedge$
      $ob = []$ then
    $ob := mb$ $\ ||$
    $mb := nb$ $\ ||$
    $nb := []$ $\ ||$
    $os4 := ms4$ $\ ||$
    $ms4 := \{l1\}$
   else
    $ms4 := ms4 \cup \{l1\}$
   end
  end;

Fig. 3. The four buffer MSMIE as a B refinement

Framing. As stated earlier, the read and write frames are given explicitly in a VDM operation, whereas in B the variable access and modification is implicit in the form of the generalised substitution.

In VDM operations, the semantic role of the read frame is often underplayed. Typically, it is interpreted as merely providing syntactic scoping for variables appearing in the precondition or postcondition. Alternatively, it could be interpreted as a constraint on implementations, restricting which state components can be read. Thus rather than think of the externals clauses as giving information about the variables mentioned in the *specification*, we see them as giving details of what access to state variables an *implementation* of that operation can be allowed to make. (See [Bicarregui93] for further discussion of this point.)

In B, similar restrictions can be given through the hiding principles inherent in the different forms of machine structuring. For instance in this example, where we were able to narrow the read frames in the later VDM specifications, in the B counterparts there is a potential to structure the overall machine as a B "implementation" in terms of simpler machines, one for each status flag.

In the above we have emphasised three areas where our experiments have suggested that the notations of VDM and B encourage different specification styles. Each style may have its own advantages at different stages of the development process. In this example we found that the process of developing implementation code was better addressed in B's abstract machine notation. However, we also found VDM's relational postconditions more convenient for expressing wholly implicit specifications of operations, particularly when the data model involved complex interdependencies.

References

[Abrial92a]   Abrial, J.R. *Introducing B-Technologies* (draft). May 1992.

[Abrial92b]   Abrial, J.R. *The B Method.* Book to appear

[BA91]   Bruns, G. and Anderson, S., *The Formalization of a Communications Protocol.* LFCS Tech. Rep. 91-137 (April 1991).

[BA92]   Bruns, G. and Anderson, S., *The Formalization of a Communications Protocol.* LFCS/Adelard SCCS Tech.Rep. April 6, 1992.

[Bicarregui93] Bicarregui, J.C. *Algorithm refinement with read and write frames,* In this volume.

[BR93]   Bicarregui, J.C. and B. Ritchie. *A Comparison of Two Formal Specification Notations,* RAL Technical Report, 1993.

[Jones90]   Jones, C.B. *Systematic Software Development Using VDM,* second edition. Prentice Hall, 1990.

[Morgan91]   Morgan, C. *Programming from Specifications.* Prentice Hall, 1990.

[Santoline89]   L.L. Santoline *et al. Multiprocessor Shared-Memory Information Exchange.* IEEE Trans. on Nuclear Science. 36(1) 1989, pp.626-633.

The Industrial Take-up of Formal Methods in Safety-Critical and Other Areas: A Perspective

Jonathan Bowen[1] and Victoria Stavridou[2]

[1] Oxford University Computing Laboratory, Programming Research Group,
11 Keble Road, Oxford OX1 3QD, UK. Email: <Jonathan.Bowen@comlab.ox.ac.uk>
[2] Department of Computer Science, Royal Holloway, University of London,
Egham, Surrey TW20 0EX, UK. Email: <victoria@dcs.rhbnc.ac.uk>

Abstract. Formal methods may be at the crossroads of acceptance by a wider industrial community. In order for the techniques to become widely used, the gap between theorists and practitioners must be bridged effectively. In particular, safety-critical systems offer an application area where formal methods may be engaged usefully to the benefit of all. This paper discusses some of the issues concerned with the general acceptance of formal methods and concludes with a summary of the current position and how the formal methods community could proceed to improve matters in the future.

> *"To err is human but to really foul things up requires a computer."*
> Farmers' Almanac for 1978 *(1977) 'Capsules of Wisdom'*

1 Introduction

The software used in computers has become progressively more complex as the size of computers has increased and their price has decreased [36]. Unfortunately software development techniques have not kept pace with the rate of software production and improvements in hardware. Errors in software are renowned and software manufacturers have in general issued their products with outrageous disclaimers that would not be acceptable in any other more established industrial engineering sector.

It has been suggested that formal methods are a possible solution to help reduce errors in software. Sceptics claim that the methods are infeasible for any realistically sized problem. Sensible proponents recommend that they should be applied selectively where they can be used to advantage. More controversially, it has been claimed that formal methods, despite their apparent added complexity in the design process, can actually *reduce* the overall cost of software. The reasoning is that while the cost of the specification and design of the software is increased, this is a small part of the total cost, and time spent in testing and maintenance may be considerably reduced. If formal methods are used, many more errors should be eliminated earlier in the design process and subsequent changes should be easier because the software is better documented and understood.

2 Technology Transfer Problems

The following extract from the BBC television program *Arena* broadcast in the UK during October 1990 graphically illustrates the publicly demonstrated gap between much of the computing and electronics industry, and the formal methods community, in the context of safety-critical systems; these, arguably, have the most potential benefit to gain from the use of formal methods [4].

> Narrator: [On Formal Methods] *"... this concentration on a relatively immature science has been criticized as impractical."*
> Phil Bennett, IEE: *"Well we do face the problem today that we are putting in ever increasing numbers of these systems which we need to assess. The engineers have to use what tools are available to them today and tools which they understand. Unfortunately the mathematical base of formal methods is such that most engineers that are in safety-critical systems do not have the familiarity to make full benefit of them."*
> Martyn Thomas, Chairman, Praxis plc: *"If you can't write down a mathematical description of the behaviour of the system you are designing then you don't understand it. If the mathematics is not advanced enough to support your ability to write it down, what it actually means is that there is no mechanism whereby you can write down precisely that behaviour. If that is the case, what are you doing entrusting people's lives to that system because by definition you don't understand how it's going to behave under all circumstances? ... The fact that we can build over-complex safety-critical systems is no excuse for doing so."*

This repartee is typical not only of the substantial technology transfer problems, but also of the debate between the "reformist" (pro "real world") and the "radical" (pro formal methods) camps in software engineering [42].

2.1 Misconceptions and barriers

Unfortunately formal methods is sometimes misunderstood and relevant terms are even misused in industry (at least, in the eyes of the formal methods community). For example, the following two alternative definitions for *formal specification* are taken from a glossary issued by the IEEE [25]:

1. *A specification written and approved in accordance with established standards.*
2. *A specification written in a formal notation, often for use in proof of correctness.*

The meaning of "formal notation" is not elaborated further in the glossary, although "proof of correctness" is defined in general terms.

Some confuse formal methods with "structured methods". While research is underway to link the two and provide a formal basis to structured methods (e.g., see [26]), the two communities have, at least until now, been sharply divided apart from a few notable exceptions. Many so-called formal "methods" have concentrated on notations and/or tools and have not addressed how they should be slotted into existing industrial best practice. On the other hand, structured methods provide techniques for developing software from requirements to code, normally using diagrams to document the design. While the data structures are often well defined (and easily formalized), the relationships between these structures are often left more hazy and are only defined using informal text (natural language).

Industry has been understandably reluctant to use formal methods since they have been largely untried in practice. There are many methods being touted around the market place and formal methods are just one form of them. When trying out any of these new techniques for the first time, the cost of failure could be prohibitive and the initial cost of training is likely to be very high. For formal methods in particular, few engineers, programmers and managers currently have the skills to apply the techniques beneficially (although many have the ability).

Unfortunately, software adds so much complexity to a system that with today's formal techniques and mechanical tools, it is intractable to analyze all but the simplest systems exhaustively. In addition, the normal concept of tolerance in engineering cannot be applied to software. Merely changing one bit in the object code of a program may have a catastrophic and unpredictable effect. However, software provides such versatility that it is the only viable means of developing many products.

Formal methods have been a topic of research for many years in the theoretical computer science community. However they are still a relatively novel concept for most people in the computing industry. While industrial research laboratories are investigating formal methods, there are not many examples of the use of formal methods in real commercial projects. Even in companies where formal methods are used, it is normally only to a limited extent and is often resisted (at least initially) by engineers, programmers and managers. [20] is an excellent article that helps to dispel some of the unfounded notions and beliefs about formal methods.

Up until quite recently it has widely been considered infeasible to use formal techniques to verify software in an industrial setting. Now that a number of case studies and examples of real use are available, formal methods are becoming more acceptable in some industrial circles [19, 22, 24]. Some of the most notable of these are mentioned in [9], particularly those where a quantitative indication of the benefits gained have been published.

2.2 Modes of use

Formal methods may be characterized at a number of levels of usage and these provide different levels of assurance for the resulting software that is developed. This is sometimes misunderstood by antagonists (and even enthusiasts) who assume that using formal methods means that *everything* has to be proved correct. In fact much current industrial use of formal methods involves no, or minimal, proofs [3].

At a basic level, formal methods may simply be used for a high-level specification of the system to be designed (e.g., using the Z notation). The next level of usage is to apply formal methods to the development process (e.g., VDM), using a set of rules or a design calculus that allows stepwise refinement of the operations and data structures in the specification to an efficiently executable program. At the most rigorous level, the whole process of proof may be mechanized. Hand proofs or design inevitably lead to human errors occurring for all but the simplest systems.

Mechanical theorem provers such as HOL and the Boyer-Moore system have been used to verify significant implementations, but need to be operated by people with skills that very few engineers possess today. Such tools are difficult to use, even for experts, and great improvements will need to be made in the usability of these tools before they can be widely accepted in the computing industry. Tools are now becoming commercially available (e.g., the B tool and Lambda) but there is still little interest in industry at large. Eventually commercial pressures should improve these and other similar tools which up until now have mainly been used in research environments. In particular, the user interface and the control of proofs using strategies or 'tactics', whilst improving, are areas that require considerable further research and development effort.

2.3 Cost considerations

The prerequisite for industrial uptake of formal techniques is a formalism which can adequately deal with the pertinent aspects of computer-based systems. However, the existence of such a formalism is not sufficient; the relevant technology must also be able to address the problems of the industry by integrating with currently used techniques [44], and must do so in a way that is commercially advantageous.

It should be noted that despite the mathematical basis of formal methods, errors are still possible because of the fallibility of humans and, for mechanical verification, computers. However formal methods have been demonstrated to reduce errors (and even costs and time to market) if used appropriately [24, 30]. In general though, formal *development* does increase costs [10]. For example, at the 1992 Z Users Meeting Andrew Bradley of British Aerospace reported the following typical productivity figures for different development approaches in terms of lines of code (LOC) per man year:

Non-safety critical code	1400–1600 LOC/m.y.
Normal safety critical code	700–800 LOC/m.y.
Full formal development	200–400 LOC/m.y.

Even if the use of formal methods incurs higher development costs, this is unlikely to be the predominant factor. The critical considerations to a greater or lesser extent (depending on market growth rates) are development speed and final product cost. Is it, therefore, evident that formal methods can deliver cheaper products rapidly? Given the current technology, the over-zealous use of formal methods can easily slow down rather than speed up the process, although the reverse is also possible if formal methods are used selectively. It is however the case that in specialized markets such as the high integrity sector, other factors such as product quality may be the overriding concern. A further consideration must be whether formal methods can enhance product quality, and even company prestige.

3 Industrial-scale Usage

As has previously been mentioned, the take up of formal methods is not yet great in industry, but their use has normally been successful when they have been applied appropriately [41]. Some companies have managed to specialize in providing formal methods expertise (e.g., CLInc in the US, ORA in Canada and Praxis in the UK), although such examples are exceptional. A recent international investigation of the use of formal methods in industry [13, 14] provides a view of the current situation by comparing some significant projects which have made serious use of such techniques.

[9] provides a survey of selected projects and companies that have used formal methods in the design of safety-critical systems and [1] gives an overall view of this industrial sector in the UK. In critical systems, reliability and safety are paramount. Extra cost involved in the use of formal methods is acceptable, and the use of mechanization for formal proofs may be worthwhile for critical sections of the software. In other cases, the total cost and time to market is of highest importance. For such projects, formal methods should be used more selectively, perhaps only using rigorous proofs or just specification alone. Formal documentation of key components may provide significant benefits to the development of many industrial software-based systems without excessive and sometimes demonstrably decreased overall cost (e.g., see [22, 24, 30]).

3.1 Application areas and techniques

Formal methods are applicable in a wide variety of contexts to both software and hardware. They are useful at a number of levels of abstraction in the development process from requirements capture, through to specification, design, coding, compilation and the underlying digital hardware itself. Some research projects are specification investigating the formal relationships between these different levels [5, 8] which are all important to avoid errors. An example of a suggested overall approach to project organization using formal methods is provided by [37].

The *Cleanroom* approach is a technique that could easily incorporate the use of existing formal notations to produce highly reliable software by means of non execution-based program development [16]. This technique has been applied very successfully using rigorous software development techniques with a proven track record of reducing errors by a significant factor, in both safety-critical and non-critical applications. The programs are developed separately using informal (often just mental) proofs before they are certified (rather than tested). If too many errors are found, the process rather than the program must be changed. The pragmatic view is that real programs are too large to be formally proved correct, so they must be written correctly in the first place! The possibility of combining Cleanroom techniques and formal methods is now being investigated [34].

There is considerable research into object-oriented extensions of existing formal notations such as Z and VDM [40] and the subject is under active discussion in both communities. Object-oriented techniques have had considerable success in their take-up by industry, and such research may eventually lead to a practical method combining the two techniques. However there are currently a large number of different dialects and some rationalization needs to occur before industry is likely to embrace any of the notations to a large degree.

An important but often neglected part of a designed system is its documentation, particularly if subsequent changes are made. Formalizing the documentation leads to less ambiguity and thus less likelyhood of errors [7]. Formal specification alone has proved beneficial in practice in many cases [3]. Such use allows the possibility of formal development subsequently as experience is gained.

The *human-computer interface* (HCI) is an increasingly important component of most software-based systems. Errors often occur due to misunderstandings caused by poorly constructed interfaces [27]. Formalizing an HCI in a realistic and useful manner is a difficult task, but progress is being made in categorizing features of interfaces that may help to ensure their reliability in the future. There seems to be considerable scope for further research in this area, which also spans many other disparate disciplines, particularly with application to safety-critical systems where human errors can easily cause death and injury [21].

4 Motivation for the Use of Formal Methods

4.1 Standards

Up until relatively recently there have been few standards concerned specifically with formal notations and methods. Formal notations are eschewed in many software-related standards for describing *semantics*, although BNF-style descriptions are universally accepted for describing *syntax*. The case for the use of formal notations in standards is now mounting as formalisms become increasingly understood and accepted by the relevant readership [6]. Hopefully this will produce more precise and less ambiguous standards in the future, although there is still considerable debate on the subject and widely differing views across different countries [15]. Formal notations themselves have now reached the level of maturity that some of them are being standardized (e.g., LOTOS, VDM and Z).

An important trigger for the exploitation of research into formal methods could be the interest of regulatory bodies or standardization committees (e.g., the *International Electrotechnical Commission*). Many emerging safety-related standards are at the discussion stage [43]. A major impetus has already been provided in the UK by promulgation of the MoD interim standard 00-55 [2], which mandates the use of formal methods and languages with sound formal semantics.

It is important that standards should not be prescriptive, or that parts that are should be clearly separated and marked as such. Goals should be set and the onus should be on the software supplier that their methods achieve the required level of confidence. If particular methods are recommended or mandated, it is possible for the supplier to assume that the method will produce the desired results and blame the standards body if it does not. This reduces the responsibility and accountability of the supplier. Some guidance is worthwhile, but is likely to date quickly. As a result, it may be best to include it as a separate document or appendix so that it can be updated more frequently to reflect the latest available techniques and best practice. For example, 00-55 includes a separate guidance section.

4.2 Legislation

Governmental legislation is likely to provide increasing motivation to apply appropriate techniques in the development of safety-critical systems. For example, a new piece of European Commission legislation, the Machine Safety Directive, is effective from 1st January 1993 [32]. This encompasses software and if there is an error in the machine's logic that results in injury then a claim can be made under civil law against the supplier. If negligence can be proved during the product's design or manufacture then criminal proceedings may be taken against the director or manager in charge. A maximum penalty of three months in jail or a large fine are possible.

Suppliers will have to demonstrate that they are using best working practice, which could include, for example, the use of formal methods.

However, care should be taken in not overstating the effectiveness of formal methods. In particular, the term *formal proof* has been used quite loosely sometimes, and this has even led to litigation in the law courts over the VIPER microprocessor, although the case was ended before a court ruling was pronounced [29]. If extravagant claims are made, it is quite possible that a similar case could occur again. 00-55 differentiates between *formal proof* and *rigorous argument*, preferring the former, but sometimes accepting the latter with a correspondingly lower level of design assurance. Definitions in such standards could affect court rulings in the future.

4.3 Education and certification

Most modern comprehensive standard text books on software engineering now include a section on formal methods. Many computing science courses, especially in Europe, are now including a significant portion of basic relevant mathematical training (e.g., discrete mathematics such as set theory and predicate logic). In this respect, education in the US seems to be lagging behind.

[35] discusses the accreditation of software engineers by profession institutions. It is suggested that training is as important as experience in that *both* are necessary. In addition, software engineers should be responsible for their mistakes if they occur through negligence rather than genuine error. Safety-critical software is identified as an area of utmost importance where such ideas should be applied first because of the possible gravity of errors if they do occur.

Currently a major barrier to the acceptance of formal methods is that many engineers and programmers do not have the appropriate training to make use of them and many managers do not know when and how they can be applied. This is gradually being alleviated as the necessary mathematics is being taught increasingly in computing science curricula. In the past has been necessary for companies to provide their own training or seek specialist help, although formal methods courses are now quite widely available from both industry and academia in some countries (e.g., for the UK, see [33]). It appears that Europe is leading the US and the rest of the world in this particular battle, and in the use of formal methods in general, so this may be a good sign for the long term development and reliability of software emanating from Europe.

Some standards and draft standards are now recognizing the problems and recommending that appropriate personnel should be used, especially on safety-critical projects. There are suggestions that some sort of certification of developers should be introduced. This is still an active topic of discussion, but there are possible drawbacks as well as benefits by introducing such a 'closed shop' since suitably able and qualified engineers may be inappropriately excluded (and vice versa).

4.4 Bridging the gap

Technology transfer is often fraught with difficulties and is inevitably – and rightly – a lengthy process. Problems at any stage can lead to overall failure [11]. A technology such as formal methods should be well established before it is applied, especially in critical applications where safety is paramount. Awareness of the benefits of formal methods must be publicized to a wide selection of both technical and non-technical people, especially outside the formal methods community (e.g., as in [39]), and the possibilities and limitations of the techniques available must be well understood by the relevant personnel to avoid costly mistakes.

Unfortunately, the rapid advances and reduction in cost of computers in recent years has meant that time is not on our side. However, formal techniques are now sufficiently advanced that they should be considered for selective use in software development, provided the problems of education can be overcome. It is likely that there will be a skills shortage in this area for the foreseeable future and significant difficulties remain to be overcome [12].

Software standards, especially those concerning safety, are likely to provide a motivating force for the use of formal methods, and it is vital that sensible and realistic approaches are suggested in emerging and future standards. 00-55 [2] seems to provide such an example at present and is recommended as guidance for other proposed standards in this area.

5 Conclusions

We conclude with a subjective account of the state of the art and current issues in the formal specification and verification of computer-based systems, both in software and hardware.

5.1 What we have today

Many specification notations and models, although there is scope for improvement, especially in the area of requirements capture. In the words of C.A.R. Hoare [23] models are like seeds scattered in the wind. Most will perish but others will root and flourish. The more seeds the better. A question often asked is "which is the best notation/system to use?" It seems to us that the choice of notation for specifying systems containing both hardware and software are often similar. Although trends come and go, in the end, the answer must relate to the characteristics of the specific product being developed and the background of the individuals involved.

Well developed theorem proving tools. The differences between the quality of such tools produced in the mid-1980s with their counterparts that are being developed today are very marked, particularly through the provision of much improved user interfaces. However further improvements will still need to be made for widespread acceptance in mainstream industry and today's research prototypes will take significant time, resources and, importantly, appropriate marketing to become tomorrow's industrial-strength tools.

Some impressive verification results. Proving the correctness of simple but realistic systems based on small microprocessors is no longer an issue as the work on SACEM [19] and at CLInc [18, 31], for example, illustrates. SACEM is notable for its size, involving around 80 man years effort for a system that is designed for actual use. The work at CLInc is impressive since it considers the linked verification of various levels of abstraction of the system for both software and hardware on a verified microprocessor that has actually been fabricated. However, systems based on widely used programming languages and microprocessors are still problematic and we can only deal with some of their aspects.

Despite these achievements, there are some very real problems hindering widespread use of formal methods. Some of these are articulated elsewhere [13, 14]. We summarize the issues by pointing out that formal methods deployment in the large remains an esoteric, risky and potentially very costly activity whose impact on processes and products of the computer industry has never been properly evaluated. A scientifically sound and objective study of these issues is sorely missing.

5.2 Issues for the future

We must distinguish between the issues relating to technology and those relating to research. By technological issues we mean the problems concerned with the transition from research results to methods and tools which are "fit for purpose" with regard to the needs of industry. Understanding the difference between technology and research results is crucial and can go some way in explaining the reluctance of industry to adopt formal methods. The fact that a highly trained expert proves the correctness of a simple microprocessor-based system in a formal methods laboratory does not imply that a multi-billion dollar manufacturer will have its designers use a theorem prover. Suitable technology must be produced before the process is enabled and as with any other endeavour the user (not the research) community must be the driving force.

Technology issues

Industrial quality tools which are well engineered and have suitable user interfaces. As mentioned earlier, the user interface issue has been the prime beneficiary of theorem proving developments form 1985 onwards. Much remains to be done in improving the efficacy of theorem proving tools by, for instance, incorporating fast decision procedures (such as BDDs) and graph reduction packages where appropriate. Producing industrial quality software of any kind requires levels of funding which are not normally available to research workers. On the other hand, before industry can be convinced to sponsor the development of quality tools they must be persuaded that they have a use for them; but they will not consider such tools useful unless they are well engineered and hence there is a "chicken and egg" situation. The answer must be a level of synergy between the two camps.

Interface to best existing practice. Formal methods are a supplemental *not* a replacement technology. They must therefore work in harmony with existing methods and tools, the purpose of the integration being to strengthen rather than replace existing technology. Happily, there has been a definite trend in this direction by many verification workers. This is happening in two complementary ways. Firstly, the rôle of formal methods as a supplemental technology is being explored by a number of researchers. Secondly, efforts to interface to current technology are exemplified by some investigations into the semantics of industrially used notations and the subsequent provision of formal reasoning frameworks.

So, the verification community has, in the past 5 years or so, gone some way in producing results which enable the transformation of research into technology although much remains to be done in terms of technology transfer. Meetings with a good mix of industry and academia are to be encouraged, such as SAFECOMP [17] and those organized by the UK Safety-Critical Systems Club [38].

Research issues

A concern, separate from ways of transforming research results into technology fit for purpose, is the direction of further research in verification. We believe that much remains to be done in terms of notations and models. Research projects such as the European ESPRIT **ProCoS** project [5] and the UK **safemos** project [8] are attempting to address such issues.

However, a most pressing question is the shape of the future theorem proving activity itself, whether it relates to software, hardware or both. We strongly believe that theorem proving methods have a great deal in common with software engineering and future breakthroughs in the area are likely to originate from recognizing and exploiting this fact.

In our view *proofs are programs* and the evolution of theorem proving closely resembles the evolution of programming practice. Currently, complete low-level proofs look and read like machine code programs with all the consequences for the process of producing such proofs. Proof tactics that largely characterize the writing and execution of proofs closely resemble assembler macros. It seems to us that theorem proving will have to make the difficult transition from an activity of the select few to an engineering discipline in much the same way that software engineering has evolved from the days of machine/assembly coding of the 1950s and the 1960s.

The crucial prerequisite of the evolution of software engineering has been the concept of *abstraction*. Abstraction provided by operating systems, high level programming languages and their compilers, specification languages and the associated machinery such as editors, debuggers, configuration managers and so on. We believe that discovering ways of harnessing abstraction in theorem proving will be exciting and empowering.

Liskov and Guttag argue that abstraction is 2-dimensional [28]. Firstly, it can be obtained via *parameterization*, e.g., the use of procedure parameters so that a piece of code is usable on large, perhaps polymorphic data sets. Secondly, abstraction by *specification* is used to hide details by concentrating on what needs to be achieved by a piece of code rather than describing ways of achieving what is required. Abstraction by parameterization is, to some degree, already exploited in theorem proving through the logical framework ideas of including the object logic as a parameter of a theorem prover rather than "hard-wiring" it into the system. Abstraction by specification, however, is largely unresearched. We believe that such abstraction is urgently in need of research and holds great promise for the future, if the experience of software engineering is to be heeded. Proof specification languages and proof refinement, automatic or not, are aims well worth striving towards. Once these methods have been understood and developed, the theorem provers of today will become the proof compilers of tomorrow.

Acknowledgements

Jonathan Bowen is funded by the collaborative UK Information Engineering Directorate **safemos** project (IED3/1/1036).

References

1. *Safety related computer controlled systems market study.* A review for the Department of Trade and Industry by Coopers & Lybrand in association with SRD-AEA Technology and Benchmark Research (HMSO, London, 1992)
2. *The Procurement of Safety Critical Software in Defence Equipment* (Part 1: Requirements, Part 2: Guidance). Interim Defence Standard 00-55, Issue 1, Ministry of Defence, Directorate of Standardization, Kentigern House, 65 Brown Street, Glasgow G2 8EX, UK (5 April 1991)
3. Barden, R., Stepney, S., Cooper, D.: The use of Z. In Nicholls, J.E. (ed.): Z User Workshop, York 1991 (Springer-Verlag, Workshops in Computing, 1992) pp. 99–124
4. Barroca, L., McDermid, J.: Formal methods: use and relevance for the development of safety critical systems. *The Computer Journal* **35** 6 (December 1992)
5. Bjørner, D.: Trusted computing systems: the ProCoS experience. *Proc. 14th International Conference on Software Engineering (ICSE)*, Melbourne, Australia (11–14 May 1992)
6. Blyth, D., Bolddyreff, C., Ruggles, C., Tetteh-Lartey, N.: The case for formal methods in standards. *IEEE Software* (September 1990) 65–67
7. Bowen, J.P.: Formal specification in Z as a design and documentation tool. *Second IEE/BCS Conference, Software Engineering 88*, Conference Publication No. 290 (July 1988) pp. 164–168
8. Bowen, J.P.: Towards verified systems (Elsevier, Real-time Safety-critical Systems Series, 1993) In preparation
9. Bowen, J.P., Stavridou, V.: Safety-critical systems, formal methods and standards. Technical Report PRG-TR-5-92, Programming Research Group, Oxford University Computing Laboratory, UK (1992) Revised version to appear in the *Software Engineering Journal*
10. Bowen, J.P., Stavridou, V.: Formal methods and software safety. In [17] (1992) pp. 93–98
11. Buxton, J.N., Malcolm, R.: Software technology transfer. *Software Engineering Journal* **6** 1 (January 1991) 17–23
12. Coleman, D.: The technology transfer of formal methods: what's going wrong? *Proc. 12th ICSE Workshop on Industrial Use of Formal Methods*, Nice, France (March 1990)
13. Craigen, D., Gerhart, S., Ralston, T.J.: An international survey of industrial applications of formal methods. Atomic Energy Control Board of Canada, U.S. National Institute of Standards and Technology, and U.S. Naval Research Laboratories (1993) To appear
14. Craigen, D., Gerhart, S., Ralston, T.J.: Formal methods reality check: industrial usage. In *Formal Methods Europe Symposium (FME'93)* (Springer-Verlag, LNCS, 1993) In this volume
15. Deransart, P.: Prolog standardisation: the usefulness of a formal specification, on comp.lang.prolog, comp.specification and comp.software-eng electronic USENET newsgroups (October 1992)
16. Dyer, M.: The Cleanroom approach to quality software development (Wiley Series in Software Engineering Practice, 1992)

194

17. Frey, H.H. (ed.): Safety of computer control systems 1992 (SAFECOMP'92). Computer Systems in Safety-critical Applications, Proc. IFAC Symposium, Zürich, Switzerland, 28–30 October 1992 (Pergamon Press, 1992)

18. Good, D.I., Young, W.D.: Mathematical methods for digital system development. In Prehn, S., Toetenel, W.J. (eds.): *VDM '91, Formal Software Development Methods*, Volume 2: Tutorials (Springer-Verlag, LNCS **552**, 1991) pp. 406–430

19. Guiho, G., Hennebert, C.: SACEM software validation. *Proc. 12th International Conference on Software Engineering (ICSE)* (IEEE Computer Society Press, March 1990) pp. 186–191

20. Hall, J.A.: Seven myths of formal methods. *IEEE Software* (September 1990) 11–19

21. Harrison, M.D.: Engineering human error tolerant software. In Nicholls, J.E. (ed.): Z User Workshop, York 1991 (Springer-Verlag, Workshops in Computing, 1992) pp. 191–204

22. Hill, J.V.: Software development methods in practice. *Proc. COMPASS '91: 6th Annual Conference on Computer Assurance* (1991)

23. Hoare, C.A.R.: Let's make models. In Baeten, J.C.M., Klop, J.W. (eds.): *Proc. CONCUR '90* (Springer-Verlag, LNCS **458**, 1990)

24. Houston, I., King, S: CICS project report: experiences and results from the use of Z in IBM. In Prehn, S., Toetenel, W.J. (eds.): *VDM '91, Formal Software Development Methods* (Springer-Verlag, LNCS **551**, 1991) pp. 588–603

25. IEEE standard glossary of software engineering terminology. In *IEEE Software Engineering Standards Collection* (Elsevier Applied Science, 1991)

26. Josephs, M.B., Redmund-Pyle, D.: Entity-relationship models expressed in Z: a synthesis of structured and formal methods, Technical Report PRG-TR-20-91, Programming Research Group, Oxford University Computing Laboratory, UK (July 1991)

27. Learmount, D.: Airline safety review: human factors. *Flight International* **142** 4238 (22–28 July 1992) 30–33

28. Liskov, B., Guttag, J.: Abstraction and Specification in Program Development (MIT Press, 1986)

29. MacKenzie, D.: Computers, formal proof, and the law courts. *Notices of the American Mathematical Society* **39** 9 (November 1992) 1066–1069

30. May, D., Barrett, G., Shepherd, D.: Designing chips that work. In Hoare, C.A.R., Gordon, M.J.C. (eds.): *Mechanized reasoning and hardware design* (Prentice Hall International Series in Computer Science, 1992) pp. 3–19

31. Moore, J.S. et al., Special issue on system verification. *Journal of Automated Reasoning* **5** 4 (1989) 409–530

32. Neesham, C.: Safe conduct. *Computing* (12 November 1992) 18–20

33. Nicholls, J.E.: A survey of Z courses in the UK. In Nicholls, J.E. (ed.), *Z User Workshop, Oxford 1990* (Springer-Verlag, Workshops in Computing, 1991) pp. 343–350

34. Normington, G.: Cleanroom and Z. In Bowen, J.P., Nicholls, J.E. (eds.), *Z User Workshop, London 1992* (Springer-Verlag, Workshops in Computing, 1993) To appear

35. Pyle, I.: Software engineers and the IEE. *Software Engineering Journal* **1** 2 (March 1986) 66–68

36. Potocki de Montalk, J.P.: Computer software in civil aircraft. *Microprocessors and Microsystems*. In Cullyer, W.J. (ed.): Special issue on safety critical systems (1993) To appear

37. Ravn, A.P., Stavridou, V.: Project organisation. In Bjørner, D., Langmaack, H., Hoare, C.A.R.: *Provably Correct Systems*, chapter 9, part 1, ESPRIT BRA 3104 ProCoS Technical Report (1992) Available from Department of Computer Science, DTH, Lyngby, Denmark

38. Redmill, F., Anderson, T.: Safety-critical systems – current issues, techniques and standards (Chapman and Hall, 1993)
39. Stein, R.M.: Safety by formal design. *BYTE* (August 1992) p. 157
40. Stepney, S., Barden, R., Cooper, D. (eds.): Object orientation in Z (Springer-Verlag, Workshops in Computing, 1992)
41. Thomas, M.C.: The industrial use of formal methods. *Microprocessors and Microsystems*. In Cullyer, W.J. (ed.): Special issue on safety critical systems (1993) To appear
42. Tierney, M.: The evolution of Def Stan 00-55 and 00-56: an intensification of the "formal methods debate" in the UK. *Proc. Workshop on Policy Issues in Systems and Software Development*, Science Policy Research Unit, Brighton, UK (July 1991)
43. Wallace, D.R., Kuhn, D.R., Ippolito, L.M.: An analysis of selected software safety standards. *IEEE AES Magazine* (August 1992) 3–14
44. Wing, J.M., Zaremski, A.M.: Unintrusive ways to integrate formal specifications in practice. In Prehn, S., Toetenel, W.J. (eds.), *VDM '91, Formal Software Development Methods* (Springer-Verlag, LNCS **551**, 1991) pp. 547–569

A Proof Environment for Concurrent Programs

Naïma BROWN and Dominique MERY*

CRIN-CNRS & INRIA Lorraine, BP 239
54506 Vandœuvre-lès-Nancy, France.
email: brown@loria.fr, mery@loria.fr

Abstract. Unity [CM88, Mer92, Kna90], as *action systems* approach [BS91], is a formal method that attempts to decouple a program from its implementation. Therefore, Unity separates logical behaviour from implementation, it provides predicates for specifications, and proof rules for deriving specifications directly from the program text. This type of proof strategy is often clearer and more succinct than argument about a program's operational behaviour. Our research fits into *Unity*'s methodology. Its aims to develop a proof environment suitable for mechanical proof of concurrent programs. This proof is based on Unity [CM88], and may be used to specify and verify both safety and liveness properties. Our verification method is based on theorem proving, so that an axiomatization of the operational semantics is needed. We use Dijkstra's *wp*-calculus to formalize the *Unity* logic, so we can always derive a sound relationship between the operational semantics of a given *Unity* specification and the axiomatic one from which theorems in our logic will be derived.

Automated theorem proving, concurrency, program verification, formal specifications, Unity, B

1 Introduction

In a mechanically verified proof, all proof steps are validated by a computer program called a theorem prover. Hence, whether a mechanically verified proof is correct is really a question of whether the theorem prover is sound. The theorem prover used in our research is *B-Tool* [BT91a, BT91b, BT91c]. B provides a platform for solving the problem specification and correct construction of software systems. It is a flexible inference engine which forms the basis of a computer-aided system for the formal construction of provably correct software. Using a mechanized theorem prover to validate a proof presents an additional burden for the user, since machine validated proofs are longer and more difficult to produce. However, if one trusts the theorem prover, one may then focus attention on the specification that was proved. This analysis may be facilitated by

---

* on sabbatical leave at the Department of Computing Science University of Stirling under the European Science Exchange Programme Royal Society - CNRS

consulting the mechanized proof script. The proof environment for concurrent programs presented in this paper is based on Unity, which has two important characteristics:

◇ Unity provides predicates for specifications, and proof rules to derive specifications directly from the program text. This type of proof strategy is often clearer and more succinct than argument about a program's operational behaviour. David Goldschlag in [Gol90] described how to mechanically verify a Unity program with the Boyer-Moore prover[BM88].

◇ Unity separates the concern of algorithm from that of architecture. It defines a general semantics for concurrent programs that encourage the refinement of architecture-independent programs to architecture-specific ones. In a paper presented at the European Workshops on Parallel Computing [BM92], we have already described a systematic method for mapping (implementing) a Unity specification into the programming language Occam.

2 Unity

This section is a brief discussion of the *Unity* notation and programming logic. The section described the logic defined by Chandy and Misra together with the modification suggested by Sanders to incorporate the notion of *strongest stable predicate* and *weakest stable predicate*.

2.1 A Programming Notation

A Unity program consists of a declaration of variables, a specification of their initial values, and a set of multiple-assignment statements. A program execution starts from a state satisfying the initial condition and loops forever; in each step of execution some assignment statement is selected non-deterministically and executed (Fig.1). Non-deterministic selection is constrained by the rule of *fairness*. A state of a program is called a *fixed point* if and only if execution of any statement of the program, in this state, leaves the state unchanged. Proofs

Fig. 1. Execution of a Unity progam

in Unity are based on assertions of the type {p}s{q}, where s represents the Unity assignment statement, p the precondition that must be validated before the execution of s, and q the post-condition that results from the execution of

s. Our proof system is designed to reason about a set of *Unity* actions. A *Unity* action represents a *Unity* assignment statement. So, to apply our proof method to a *Unity* program, we must first compute, using the algorithm given next, the set of *Unity* actions associated to this program.

---

input:

– U, the Unity program

output:

– SA, set of actions of the *Unity* program U

algorithm

$SA \leftarrow \emptyset$
While $S \neq \emptyset$ (*S represents the set of statements of the program U*) *do*
  Take $s \in S$
  $CASE$

$$s == (x := E) \qquad then\ SA \leftarrow SA \cup \{x := E\}$$
$$s == (x, y := E_1, E_2) \qquad then\ SA \leftarrow SA \cup \{x, y := E_1, E_2\}$$
$$s == (x, y := E_1, E_2\ if\ b)\ then\ SA \leftarrow SA \cup \{x, y := E_1, E_2\ if\ b\}$$
$$s == (x := E)\ if\ g \qquad then\ SA \leftarrow SA \cup \{x := E\ if\ g\}$$
$$s == (x := E_1\ if\ g_1 \sim$$
$$\qquad\qquad E_2\ if\ g_2 \sim$$
$$\qquad\qquad \vdots$$
$$\qquad\qquad E_n\ if\ g_n) \qquad then\ SA \leftarrow SA \cup \{x := E_1\ if\ g_1,$$
$$\qquad\qquad\qquad\qquad\qquad\qquad\qquad x := E_2\ if\ g_2,$$
$$\qquad\qquad\qquad\qquad\qquad\qquad\qquad \vdots$$
$$\qquad\qquad\qquad\qquad\qquad\qquad\qquad x := E_n\ if\ g_n\}$$

2.2   A Programming Logic

Interesting properties of concurrent programs are safety and liveness (progress) [Lam77]. Safety properties state that *something bad will never happen*; examples are *invariance* properties such as *mutual exclusion* and *deadlock-freedom* [GT90]. Liveness properties guarantee that something good will eventually happen; examples are termination and freedom from starvation. Unity defines predicates that permit the specification of subsets of these properties. Stable properties, a subset of safety properties, are specified using the predicate *unless*; progress properties, a subset of liveness properties, are specified using the predicates *ensures* and *leads-to*.

p unless q

$\overset{def}{=}$ {definition of unless in Unity, PRG stands for a Unity program.}

$< \forall s \ : \ s \ in \ PRG \ :: \ \{p \wedge \neg q\} \ s \ \{p \vee q\} >$

$\equiv$ {by using the definition of wlp,

   wlp stands for weakest liberal precondition[Dij76]}

$< \forall s \ : \ s \ in \ PRG \ :: \ \{p \wedge \neg q\} \ \rightarrow wlp(s, p \vee q) >$

$\equiv$ {all statements in a Unity program are guaranteed to terminate}

$< \forall s \ : \ s \ in \ PRG \ :: \ \{p \wedge \neg q\} \ \rightarrow wp(s, p \vee q) >$.

The reader may have noticed that the properties one can specify the operator *unless* are limited to *Safety* properties, i.e, properties that disallow certain transition between program states. When specifying concurrent programs, however, we are often interested in stating that a certain predicate holds at some point in the future. In *Unity*, this requirement is expressed using the operators *ensures* and *leads-to*.

p ensures q

$\overset{def}{=}$ {definition of ensures in Unity}

p unless $q \ \& \ < \exists s \ : \ s \ in \ PRG \ :: \ \{p \wedge \neg q\} \ s \ \{q\} >$

$\equiv$ {by using the definition of wlp}

p unless $q \ \& \ < \exists s \ : \ s \ in \ PRG \ :: \ \{p \wedge \neg q\} \ \rightarrow wlp(s, q) >$

$\equiv$ {all statements in a Unity program are guaranteed to terminate}

p unless $q \ \& \ < \exists s \ : \ s \ in \ PRG \ :: \ \{p \wedge \neg q\} \ \rightarrow wp(s, q) >$.

P *leads-to* Q states that if P holds in some state of the program, then a state is eventually reached where Q holds. The *leads-to* predicate is transitive. Formally, *leads-to* is defined by the following rules (see [CM88]:

(1) $\dfrac{p \ ensures \ q}{p \ leads - to \ q}$

(2) $\dfrac{p \ leads - to \ q, \ q \ leads - to \ r}{p \ leads - to \ r}$

(3) $\dfrac{(p \ leads - to \ q), \ (r \ leads - to \ q)}{(p \vee r) \ leads - to \ q}$

(4) *All* p *leads* $-$ *to* q *are obtained by finite use of the above rules.*

The complete *Unity* programming logic is based on the temporal operators *unless*, *ensures* and *leads-to*, plus the substitution axiom. Combining the substitution axiom with the defined temporal operators gives an unsound proof system [San91, Mis90]. A. Sanders in [San91] modifies the *Unity* logic by eliminating the substitution axiom from this logic and by giving a new definition of the operator *unless*, *ensures* and *leads-to* using the predicate transformers **sst** and **wst**, standing respectively for *strongest stable predicate* and *weakest stable predicate*. Instead of changing the *Unity* logic, as Sanders did in [San91], and in order to capture the semantic completeness of the *Unity* logic, we can be guided by the *feps* [Mer86] system that has been proved correct and semantically complete, by adding the two following rules:

$$\frac{p \; ensures \; q, \mathcal{I}nv(i), \; r \wedge i \Rightarrow p, p \Rightarrow r \wedge i}{r \; ensures \; q}$$
$$\frac{p \; leads-to \; q, \mathcal{I}nv(i), \; r \wedge i \Rightarrow p}{r \; leads-to \; q}$$

However, we must be able to encode the *feps* system in the obtained logic, to provide a full proof of the semantic completeness.

3 The Implementation of Unity in B

This section is a presentation of the Proof Environment. Proof in this Proof Environment resemble *Unity* hand proofs, except that every concept must be defined and every theorem proved in order to have the proof mechanically verified by the *B* prover.

3.1 A brief introduction to B

First, we present the syntax of some symbols representing the main logical operators of the *Unity* logic into *B*.

formal operator	Implementation in B	Meaning
$\neg p$	$\neg p$	negation
$p \wedge q$	$p \; \& \; q$	conjunction
$p \vee q$	$p \mid q$	disjunction
$p \rightarrow q$	$p \Rightarrow q$	implication
$p = q$	$p == q$	equality
$\forall x$	$!x$	universal
$\exists x$	$\#x$	existence

B is a rule-based inference engine with *rule-rewriting* and *pattern matching* facilities. Its behaviour is controlled by rule bases known as *theories*. The application of theories is guided by tactics. Specific proof strategies may be prescribed using appropriate combinations of theories and tactics, a proof can be completely automated. *B* has no pre-defined encoding of any logical laws; these are supplied in the form of theories and tactics wherever appropriate. As a result, *B* can be configured to support a large variety of different logics. However, *B* does have a number of basic built-in mechanisms which are common to most formal proofs regardless of the underlying logic. These mechanisms support the idea of carrying out a proof *under certain hypotheses*, the notion of *variables and their scopes and freeness*, *quantifiers*, *substitution*, *equality*, ... The addition of these mechanisms greatly facilitates the practice of proving theorems encountered in the formal software development process without sacrificing B's generality and flexibility.

When building a proof, B constructs its proof tree dynamically; as a consequence, the state of a proof in construction is characterized by an *incomplete* proof tree. There are two modes for building proofs: one is called the *normal* mode and the other is called the *forward* mode. The *forward* mode is only used when a new hypothesis is generated. It consists of generating other hypotheses that are derived not only from the one just generated, but also from the ones that are already *visible* and from some rule. The *visible hypotheses* are simply those which are members of the sets of hypotheses of the *ascending* nodes of the *current* node. Let's now present some useful B tactics which we will use for the proofs of *Unity* programs.

◇ Proof that construct hypothesis *DED*:

> *Goal to prove* : $f_1 \& f_2 \& \ldots \& f_n \Rightarrow g$
>   *Application of DED*
> *New goal to prove* : g
> *Hypothesis* : $\{f_1, \; f_2, \; \ldots, \; f_n\}$

◇ Proof using hypothesis *INHYP*:

> *Goal to prove* : P
> *visible hypothesis* : $\{\ldots, \; P, \; \ldots\}$
> *Application of INHYP*
> *New goal to prove* :   *Nothing*

◇ Proof by Generalization *GEN*:

> *Goal to prove* : $\forall x.P$
>   *x has no free occurrence in the visible hypothesis.*
> *Application of GEN*
> *New goal to prove* : P

◇ Proof by Generalization *GEN*:

> *Goal to prove* : $\forall x.P$
>   *x has some free occurrences in the visible hypothesis.*
> *Application of GEN*
> *New goal to prove* : $[x := y]P$, *where y is not free in the visible hypothesis nor in formula P.*

3.2 Defining the Proof Environment under Centaur

CENTAUR is used mainly for two purposes: firstly, to develop a programming environment for *Unity*, secondly to consolidate the new development environment with a proof method (Fig.2). The CENTAUR system [Cen91, Cen92] may be used to design a programming language, experiment with syntax, types, and semantics or to construct a specialized language environment. CENTAUR features several *specification formalisms* with which one defines various aspects of programming languages, and compilers that transform specifications in these formalisms into part of a generated environment:

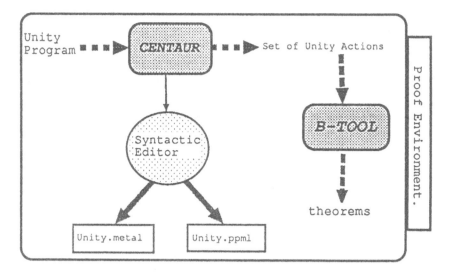

Fig. 2. The Proof Environment

METAL is a meta-language for defining concrete and abstract syntax. The distinguishing feature of METAL is the great flexibility that it allows for mapping between concrete and abstract syntax.

SDF (Syntax Definition Formalism) is also a formalism for defining concrete and abstract syntax. SDF establishes a fixed mapping between concrete and abstract syntax.

PPML a pretty printing meta-language used for defining the mapping from abstract syntax trees to a textual (pretty printed) representation.

TYPOL is a specification language based on inference rules used for the definition of static and dynamic semantics of programming languages.

The design of the programming environment consists of several steps that are either automatic, or semi-automatic. A first step consists of writing a METAL specification of the *Unity* language. This specification defines the concrete syntax, the abstract syntax and the rules of trees formation that express the correspondence between abstract and concrete syntax. The METAL-PPML generates tables and programs used for parser generation from this specification. The generation of a parser is not completely automatic and the user has to supply some files along with those generated by METAL-PPML. The semantics of the language is treated by the TYPOL environment. A second step consists of writing the PPML specification of the rules of textual representation (or unparsing) for the *Unity* formalism from its abstract syntax. The unparser for the *Unity* formalism is generated using the *compile* command of the METAL-PPML environment. The *Unity* environment comprises two kinds of editors: textual and structural. The user can easily write a *Unity* program in a textual form. A parser checks it. If the program is syntactically correct, the parser generates the internal representation.

The user can run an interface to the theorem prover that allows him to prove the correctness of *Unity* program using the set of its actions (statements). The interface ensures the interaction between the *Unity* environment and the proof system implemented under *B*. The interface operates on the internal representation. The prover is designed according to the *enrichment principle* (Fig.3).

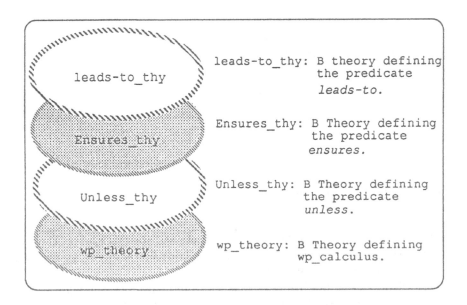

leads-to_thy: B theory defining the predicate *leads-to*.

Ensures_thy: B Theory defining the predicate *ensures*.

Unless_thy: B Theory defining the predicate *unless*.

wp_theory: B Theory defining wp_calculus.

Fig. 3. Structure of the Proof System

A basic layer represents the Dijkstra's *wp*-calculus [Dij76]. This is successively enriched with other theories for reasoning about *Unity* programs. To *wp-theory*, we have supplied another layer for deriving *safety* properties which we denote by *unless-thy*. *ensures-thy* and *leads-to-thy*, defines the most interesting progress properties.

3.3 Implementation of *Wp*-Calculus into *B* prover

The first level of the proof system formalizes the definitions of *wp*-calculus for the assignment statements in the *B* prover. Let x denote a list of program variables, and E a list of expressions, possibly depending on x and matching the variables in x in number and type. An assignment statement is of the form $x := E \ if \ b$, where $x:=E$ is a multiple assignment satement and B is a boolean expression. With *wp* standing for Dijkstra's weakest precondition[Dij76], we define the predicate transformer semantics of such a statement as follows:

$$wp(x := E \ if \ b, Q) \equiv (b \Rightarrow wp(x := E, Q)) \wedge (\neg b \Rightarrow Q)$$
$$\equiv (b \Rightarrow [x := E]Q) \wedge (\neg b \Rightarrow Q)$$

where [x:=E]Q stands for Q with all occurrences of variables in x simultaneously replaced by the matching expressions in E. The second part of the definition above could be omitted when we are dealing with invariant properties.

B-definition

$\diamond$ *THEORY wp − theory IS*

    $\star$ $wp(x := E, p) == [x := E]p,$

    $\star$ $wp((x := E \; if \; b), p) == (b \Rightarrow wp(x := E, p)\&(\neg b \Rightarrow p)),$

    $\star$ $wp((x, y := E, F), p) == [x, y := E, F]p,$

    $\star$ $wp((x, y := E, F \; if \; b), p) == (b \Rightarrow wp((x, y := E, F), p))\&(\neg b \Rightarrow p)$

END

3.4 Implementation of the predicate *unless* in the B prover

unless(PRG, p, q) states that every statement in the program PRG executed in states, where p holds but q does not, will lead to states where p or q holds. Intuitively, this means that once p holds in a computation, it continues to hold, at least until q (this may occur immediately). Notice that if *unless(PRG, p, False)* is true for program PRG and p holds on the initial state, then p is an invariant of PRG. The predicate *unless* is defined as follows:

$\diamond$ **Hypothesis**

    PRG is a Unity program, *wp* weakest precondition[Dij76, Lam90, DS90]

    unless-thy, the name of the *B* theory that contains the definition of unless.

    $PRG \stackrel{def}{=}_B Cons(a_1, Cons(a_2, \ldots, Cons(a_{n-1}, a_n) \ldots))$, *where* $a_{i(n \geq i \geq o)} \in$ *SA*.

    SA, set of actions of the program *PRG*.

$\diamond$ **B-definition**

    THEORY unless-thy IS

        unless(a,p,q) == ((p & ¬(q)) $\Rightarrow$ wp(a,p | q))

        unless(Cons(a,l), p, q) == unless(a,p,q) & unless(l,p,q)

    END

$\diamond$ **comment**

    We implement the predicate *unless* in a recursive manner.

3.5 Implementation of the predicate *ensures* in the B prover

The ensures relation (over predicates) defines the most basic *progress* properties of programs. *p ensures q* states that if p is true at some point in the computation, p remains true as long as q is false, and q eventually becomes true. For a given program PRG, *ensures(PRG, p, q)* is defined as follows:

$\diamond$ **Hypothesis**

    PRG is a Unity program.

    ensures-thy, the name of the *B* theory that contains the definition of *ensures*.

◇ **B-definition**

    THEORY ensures-thy IS
       ensures(a,p,q) == exists-test(a,p,q) & unless(a,p,q)
       ensures(Cons(a,l),p,q) == exists-test(Cons(a,l),p,q) & unless(Cons(a,l),p,q)
       exists-test(a,p,q) == ((p & ¬(q)) ⇒ wp(a,q));
       exists-test(Cons(a,l),p,q) == Or-Else(((p & ¬(q)) ⇒ wp(a,q)),exist-test(l,p,q))
    END

◇ **comment**
    The predicate *ensures* is defined in a recursive manner.
    exists-test(PRG,p,q) == $\exists s \in PRG. (p \wedge \neg q) \Rightarrow wp(s,q)$, this predicate is also
    defined recursively.
    Or-Else(a,b) = a|b.

To complete the definition of ensures, we define the predicate Or-Else as follows:

◇ **Hypothesis**
    bcall, dynamic change of tactics and backtracking in *B*.
    a,b: B formulae.
    t,r: tactics.

◇ **B-definition**

    Or-Else(a,b) == bcall(t:a | r:b)
    Or-Else(a,Or-Else(b,c)) == a | Or-Else(b,c)

◇ **comment**
    The interpretation of bcall($t_1 : f_1 | t_2 : f_2$) goes as follows: we start proving
    the goal f1 using the tactic t1, if this proof fails, then *B* backtracks to the bcall
    node, and f2 becomes the formula to prove using the tactic t2. If this proof
    does not succeed, *B* backtracks to the previous ascending bcall, if any, etc.

3.6 Implementation of the predicate *leads-to* in the B prover

Informally, p *leads-to* q means that if p becomes true q is or will be true. However,
we cannot assert that p will remain true as long as q is not. This is the major
difference between *ensures* and *leads-to*.

◇ **B-definition**

    THEORY leads-to-thy IS
    ensures(s,P,Q) ⇒ leadsto(s,P,Q);
    leadsto(s,P,Q) & leadsto(s,Q,R) ⇒ leadsto(s,P,R);
    leadsto(s,P,Q) & leadsto(s,R,Q) ⇒ leadsto(s,(P|R),Q)
    END

4   Derived Rules

Unity's *unless, ensures* and *leads-to* predicates provide a simple and powerful vocabulary to specify and reason about the behaviour of concurrent programs. Proof rules facilitates the proof of program properties in much that some way that lemmas aid a mathematical proof. In fact, the proof rules presented in this section are theorems about computation. The theorems presented below have been proved correct in our Proof System, by using, both the definition of *unless* and *ensures* given in the previous section, and the assertion theory. Hence, these theorems can be used to prove the correctness of any *unity* program, if necessary.

Consequence Weakening	SimpleDisjunction	Disjunction
$$\dfrac{\begin{array}{c}ensures(p,q)\\ q \Rightarrow r\end{array}}{ensures(p,r)}$$	$$\dfrac{\begin{array}{c}unless(p,q)\\ unless(p\prime,q\prime)\end{array}}{unless(p \vee p\prime, q \vee q\prime)}$$	$$\dfrac{ensures(p,q)}{ensures(p \vee r, q \vee r)}$$

Simple Conjunction	Cancellation	Impossibility
$$\dfrac{\begin{array}{c}unless(p,q)\\ unless(p\prime,q\prime)\end{array}}{unless(p \wedge p\prime, q \vee q\prime)}$$	$$\dfrac{\begin{array}{c}unless(p,q)\\ unless(q,r)\end{array}}{unless(p \vee q, r)}$$	$$\dfrac{ensures(p, false)}{\neg(p)}$$

4.1   Proof of the Consequence Weakening rule

The proof of the consequence weakening for the predicate *ensures* necessitates the use of the definition of *unless* and *ensures*. From p *unless* q, we have for all statements s in the program, $\{p \wedge \neg q\}\ s\ \{p \vee q\}$, and from $q \Rightarrow r$ we can deduce $\neg r \Rightarrow \neg q$. Hence, we have $p \wedge \neg r \Rightarrow p \wedge \neg q$ and $p \vee q \Rightarrow p \vee r$. Therefore, we deduce $\{p \wedge \neg r\}\ s\ \{p \vee r\}$ from which the results follow for the predicate *unless*. We must now show that there exists a statement s such that $\{p \wedge \neg q\}\ s\ \{q\}$ implies $\{p \wedge \neg r\}\ s\ \{q\}$. The proof follows from $p \wedge \neg r \Rightarrow p \wedge \neg q$, because $\neg r \Rightarrow \neg q$. B is able to print a proof tree by *decorating* and *traversing* its nodes in *post-fixed* mode, that is from left to right, from the leaves upward. The B proof of the theorem of consequence weakening described above is *pretty-printed* as follows:

PROOF

```
 1   p and not(q) => wp(s,(p | q))          HYP
 2   p and not(q) => wp(s,q)                HYP
 3   q => r                                 HYP
 4     p and not(q) => wp(s,(p | q))        INHYP
 5     p and not(r)                         HYP
 6       p and not(r)                       INHYP
 7       q => r                             INHYP
 8       not(r) => not(q)                   7 proposition.33
 9       p and not(q)                       6 8 proposition.34
10     p and not(r) => p and not(q)         DED
11     q => r                               INHYP
```

12	(p | q) => (p | r)	11 proposition.32
13	p and not(r) => wp(s,(p | r))	4 10 12 Unity_logic.1
14	p and not(q) => wp(s,(p | q))	INHYP
15	p and not(r)	HYP
16	p and not(r)	INHYP
17	q => r	INHYP
18	not(r) => not(q)	17 proposition.33
19	p and not(q)	16 18 proposition.34
20	p and not(r) => p and not(q)	DED
21	q => r	INHYP
22	(p | q) => r	21 proposition.31
23	p and not(r) => wp(s,r)	14 20 22 Unity_logic.1
24	(p and not(r) => wp(s,(p | r))) & (p and not(r) => wp(s,r))	13 23 AND
25	(p and not(q) => wp(s,(p | q))) & (p and not(q) => wp(s,q)) & (q => r) => (p and not (r) => wp(s,(p | r))) & (p and not(r) => wp (s,r))	DED
26	(p and not(q) => wp(s,(p | q))) & (p and not(q) => wp(s,q)) & (q => r) => unless(s,p ,r) & (p and not(r) => wp(s,r))	25 Forall_test.2
27	(p and not(q) => wp(s,(p | q))) & (p and not(q) => wp(s,q)) & (q => r) => ensures(s, p,r)	26 Forall_test.1
28	unless(s,p,q) & (p and not(q) => wp(s,q)) & (q => r) => ensures(s,p,r)	27 Forall_test.2
29	ensures(s,p,q) & (q => r) => ensures(s,p,r)	28 Forall_test.1

END OF PROOF

5 An Example

The purpose of this section is to describe, by means of an example, how to mechanically verify a concurrent program using our Proof System.

5.1 Proof Format

Most of our proofs are purely computational in the sense that they consist of a number of syntactic transformations instead of semantic reasoning steps. We use a proof format that was first proposed by Feijen, Dijkstra, and others, and that greatly facilitate this kind of proof.

For example, a proof that $A \equiv D$ may be rendered in our format as

$$A$$
$$\equiv \{hint\ why\ A \equiv B\}$$
$$B$$
$$\equiv \{hint\ why\ B \equiv C\}$$
$$C$$
$$\equiv \{hint\ why\ C \equiv D\}$$
$$D$$

5.2 A simple program

The goal of this program [CM88] is to divide M by N, where M and N are integers. $M \geq 0$ and $N > 0$; the quotient is stored in x, and the remainder in y. The specification of the program is that the predicate $x \times N + y = M \wedge 0 \leq y < N$ holds at any fixed point, and that a fixed point is reached eventually.

```
Program Division
declare   x, y, z, k : integer
initially  x, y, z, k = 0, M, N, 1
assign     z, k := 2 × z, 2 × k if y ≥ 2 × z  ~
           N, 1 if y < 2 × z
           [x, y := x + k, y − z if y ≥ z
```

Proof of an Invariant:

We prove that $(I \equiv (y \geq 0) \wedge (k \geq 1) \wedge (z = N \times k) \wedge (x \times N + y = M))$ is an invariant for the Unity program described above. Therefore, we prove that:

- (init $\Rightarrow$ I), i.e: $x = 0 \ \& \ y = M \ \& \ z = N \ \& \ k = 1 \ \& \ M \geq 0 \ \& \ N > 0 \ \Rightarrow y \geq 0 \ \& \ k \geq 1 \ \& \ z = N \times k \ \& \ x \times N + y = M$.
- I is *stable*, i.e:
  $\{I\} \ z, k := 2 \times z, 2 \times k \ if \ y \geq 2 \times z \ \{I\}$
  $\{I\} \ z, k := N, 1 \ if \ y < 2 \times z \ \{I\}$
  $\{I\} \ x, y := x + k, y - z \ if \ y \geq z \ \{I\}$

The complete B proof for all statements of the program is summarized in the Appendix A. In the following, we comment the proof for the first statement of the program.

$\{I\} \ z, k := 2 \times z, 2 \times k \ if \ y \geq 2 \times z \ \{I\}$
$\equiv$ {I invariant of the program **P** :

   $\text{invariant}(P, I) \ \overset{\text{def}}{=} \ \text{stable}(P, I) \ \& \ \text{init}(P) \ \Rightarrow \ I\}$

   Goals : step 39 $x = 0 \ \& \ y = M \ \& \ z = N \ \& \ k = 1 \ \& \ M \geq 0 \ \& \ N > 0 \Rightarrow$
   $y \geq 0 \ \& \ k \geq 1 \ \& \ z = N \times k \ \& \ x \times N + y = M.$
   step 19 $stable(z, k := 2 \times z, 2 \times k \ if \ y \geq 2 \times z,$
   $y \geq 0 \ \& \ k \geq 1 \ \& \ z = N \times k \ \& \ x \times N + y = M).$
$\equiv$ {Proof of the first subgoal init $\Rightarrow$ I, we apply the B atomic tactic DED}

   Hypothesis : $\{x = 0, \ y = M, \ z = N, \ k = 1, \ M \geq 0, \ N > 0\}$
   $\{\text{steps} : \ 20, \ 21, \ ..., \ 25\}$
   Goal : $y \geq 0 \ \& \ k \geq 1 \ \& \ z = N \times k \ \& \ x \times N + y = M.$
   $\{\text{step} : \ 38\}$
$\equiv$ {We apply the B atomic tactic AND}

   Goals : step 27 $y \geq 0$
   step 29 $k \geq 1$
   step 33 $z = N \times k$
   step 37 $x \times N + y = M$

$\equiv \{$Proof of $y \geq 0\}$

From the hypothesis $y = M$ and $M \geq 0$, we deduce that $y \geq 0$.

$\equiv \{$Proof of $k \geq 1\}$

From the hypothesis $k = 1$, we deduce $k \geq 1$, **step 28**

$\equiv \{$Proof of $z = N \times k\}$

From the hypothesis $z = N$ and $k = 1$, we deduce $z = N \times k$, **step 32, 31, 30**

$\equiv \{$Proof of $x \times N + y = M\}$

From the hypothesis $x = 0$ and $y = M$, we deduce $x \times N + y = M$,
step 36, 35, 34

$\equiv \{$Proof of the subgoal stable($z, k := 2 \times z, 2 \times k$ if $y \geq 2 \times z, I)$
Recall that we implement a program in **B** as a sequence of actions.
stable(PRG, I) $\overset{\text{def}}{=}$ I $\Rightarrow$ wp(PRG, I)$\}$

$(y \geq 0 \;\&\; k \geq 1 \;\&\; z = N \times k \;\&\; x \times N + y = M) \;\Rightarrow$
$wp\big(z, k := 2 \times z, 2 \times k \;if\; y \geq 2 \times z,$
$\quad (y \geq 0 \;\&\; k \geq 1 \;\&\; z = N \times k \;\&\; x \times N + y = M)\big)$, **step 18**

$\equiv \{$definition of wp, **step 17**$\}$

$(y \geq 0 \;\&\; k \geq 1 \;\&\; z = N \times k \;\&\; x \times N + y = M) \;\Rightarrow$
$(y \geq 2 \times z \Rightarrow [z, k := 2 \times z, 2 \times k](y \geq 0 \;\&\; k \geq 1 \;\&\; z = N \times k \;\&\; x \times N + y = M)$

$\equiv \{$We apply the **B** atomic tactic DED$\}$

Goal (step 16) $(y \geq 2 \times z \;\Rightarrow$
$\qquad\qquad [z, k := 2 \times z, 2 \times k](y \geq 0 \& k \geq 1 \& z = N \times k \& x \times N + y = M)$
Hypothesis: step 1, $y \geq 0$
$\qquad\qquad$ step 2, $k \geq 1$
$\qquad\qquad$ step 3, $z = N \times k$
$\qquad\qquad$ step 4, $x \times N + y = M$

$\equiv \{$We apply the **B** atomic tactic SUB, **step 15**$\}$

$y \geq 2 \times z \;\Rightarrow\; y \geq 0 \;\&\; 2 \times k \geq 1 \;\&\; 2 \times z = N \times (2 \times k) \;\&\; x \times N + y = M$

$\equiv \{$We apply the **B** atomic tactic DED$\}$

Goal (step 14) $y \geq 0 \;\&\; 2 \times k \geq 1 \;\&\; 2 \times z = N \times (2 \times k) \;\&\; x \times N + y = M$
Hypothesis: step 5 $y \geq 2 \times z$.

≡ {We apply the B atomic tactic AND}

    Goals : step 6 $y \geq 0$
           step 8 $2 \times k \geq 1$
           step 11 $2 \times z = N \times (2 \times k)$
           step 12 $x \times N + y = M$
≡ {For the proof of the subgoals $y \geq 0$ and $x \times N + y = M$,
    we apply the B atomic tactic INHYP
    because $y \geq 0$ and $x \times N + y = M$ are hypothesis.
    Proof of the subgoal $2 \times z = N \times (2 \times k)$.}

From the hypothesis $z = N \times k$, we must then prove that
$2 \times (N \times k) = N \times (2 \times k)$, *which is true by applying the B atomic tactic EQL.*
steps 10, 9

≡ {Proof of the subgoal $2 \times k \geq 1$}

    From the hypothesis $k \geq 1$, we deduce that $2 \times k \geq 1$, step **7**

B is able to print a proof tree by *decorating* and *traversing* its nodes in *post-fixed* mode, that is from left to right, from the leaves upward. The B proof of the theorem of consequence weakening described above is *pretty-printed* as follows:

PROOF

```
 1  y>=0                                         HYP
 2  k>=1                                         HYP
 3  z = N*k                                      HYP
 4  x*N+y = M                                    HYP
 5    y>=2*z                                     HYP
 6      y>=0                                     INHYP
 7      k>=1                                     INHYP
 8      2*k>=1                                   7 proposition.16
 9        2*(N*k) = 2*(N*k)                      EQL
10        2*z = 2*(N*k)                          9 HYP.3
11      2*z = N*(2*k)                            10 proposition.20
12      x*N+y = M                                INHYP
13      y>=0 & 2*k>=1 & 2*z = N*(2*k) & x*N+y =
          M                                      6 8 11 12 AND
14    y>=2*z => y>=0 & 2*k>=1 & 2*z = N*(2*k) &
          x*N+y = M                              DED
15    y>=2*z => [z,k:=2*z,2*k](y>=0 & k>=1 & z
          = N*k & x*N+y = M)                     14 SUB
16  y>=0 & k>=1 & z = N*k & x*N+y = M => (y>=2*
      z => [z,k:=2*z,2*k](y>=0 & k>=1 & z = N*k &
      x*N+y = M))                                DED
17  y>=0 & k>=1 & z = N*k & x*N+y = M => (y>=2*
```

```
        z => wp((z,k:=2*z,2*k),(y>=0 & k>=1 & z = N
    *k & x*N+y = M)))                           16 wp_theory.4
18  y>=0 & k>=1 & z = N*k & x*N+y = M => wp(
    Cond_ass((z,k:=2*z,2*k),y>=2*z),(y>=0 & k>=
    1 & z = N*k & x*N+y = M))                    17 wp_theory.5
19  stable(Cond_ass((z,k:=2*z,2*k),y>=2*z),(y>=
    0 & k>=1 & z = N*k & x*N+y = M))             18 Stable_theory.1
20  x = 0                                        HYP
21  y = M                                        HYP
22  z = N                                        HYP
23  k = 1                                        HYP
24  M>=0                                         HYP
25  N>0                                          HYP
26      M>=0                                     INHYP
27      y>=0                                     26 HYP.21
28      k = 1                                    INHYP
29      k>=1                                     28 proposition.23
30      N = N                                    EQL
31      N = N*1                                  30 proposition.24
32      N = N*k                                  31 HYP.23
33      z = N*k                                  32 HYP.22
34      y = M                                    INHYP
35      0+y = M                                  34 proposition.26
36      0*N+y = M                                35 proposition.25
37      x*N+y = M                                36 HYP.20
38      y>=0 & k>=1 & z = N*k & x*N+y = M        27 29 33 37 AND
39  x = 0 & y = M & z = N & k = 1 & M>=0 & N>0
    => y>=0 & k>=1 & z = N*k & x*N+y = M         DED
40  Inv(y>=0 & k>=1 & z = N*k & x*N+y = M)       19 39 lect_param_i
nv.1
```

END OF PROOF

6   Conclusion

The Proof Environment presented in this paper is based on *Unity* and has been implemented in *B*. Proofs in this Proof Environment resemble *Unity* hand proofs, except that every concept must be defined and every theorem proved in order to have the proof mechanically verified by the *B* prover. This process of mechanical verification allows us to place greater trust in the correction of a proof. This trust comes at the expense of the extra work required to mechanically check a proof. However, if the theorem prover is sound, then one can simply believe the mechanically verified proof and focus attention on the more difficult issue of analysing whether the specification that was proved is appropriate for the problem being solved, refering to the validated proof script, when appropriate. The Proof Environment is the second step of our project. The first was the study of mapping *Unity* programs to *Occam* programs but it requires a sound *Unity* program. The correctness can be verified using our implementation but we need to integrate it into a general tool for manipulating formal texts and refining specifications to programs. This tool will be useful to experiment specific case studies. We have defined a mapping to *Occam* but we can explore other programming languages. Further investigations will use the B toolkit environment to model the refinement of concurrent programs.

References

[BM88] R.S. Boyer and J.S. Moore. *A Computational Logic Handbook.* Academic Press, 1988.

[BM92] N. Brown and D. Mery. Deriving Occam Programs through the Refinement of Unity-like Specifications . In W. Joosen and E. Milgrom, editors, *Proceedings European Workshop on Parallel Computing.* IOS PRESS, 1992.

[BS91] R.J.R. Back and K. Sere. Deriving an occam implementation of action systems. In C. Morgan and J.C.P. Woodcock, editors, *4rd Refinement Workshop.* Springer-Verlag, January 1991. BCS-FACS, Workshops in Computing.

[BT91a] BP Innovation Centre and Edinburgh Portable Compilers Ltd. *B-Tool Version1.1, Reference Manual,* 1991.

[BT91b] BP Innovation Centre and Edinburgh Portable Compilers Ltd. *B-Tool Version1.1, Tutorial,* 1991.

[BT91c] BP Innovation Centre and Edinburgh Portable Compilers Ltd. *B-Tool Version1.1, User Manual,* 1991.

[Cen91] Centaur. *Version1.1, Reference Manual,* 1991.

[Cen92] Centaur. *Version1.2, Reference Manual,* 1992.

[CM88] K.M. Chandy and J. Misra. *Parallel Program Design A Foundation.* Addison-Wesley Publishing Company, 1988. ISBN 0-201-05866-9.

[Dij76] E.W. Dijkstra. *A Discipline of Programming.* Prentice-Hall, 1976.

[DS90] E.W. Dijkstra and C.S. Scholten. *Predicate Calculus and Program Semantics.* Texts and Monographs in Computer Science. Springer Verlag, 1990.

[Gol90] D.M. Goldschlag. Mechanically verifying concurrent programs with the boyer-moore prover. *IEEE Transactions on Software Engineering,* 16(9):1005–1023, september 1990.

[GT90] A.J.M. Van Gasteren and G. Tel. Comments on "on the proof of a distributed algorithm": always true is not invariant. *Information Processing Letters,* 35:277–279, 1990.

[Kna90] E. Knapp. An exercise in the formal derivation of parallel programs: Maximum flows in graphs. *Transactions On Programming Languages and Systems,* 12(2):203–223, 1990.

[Lam77] L. Lamport. Proving the correctness of multiprocess programs. *Trans. on Software Engineering 1,* 1977.

[Lam90] L. Lamport. A temporal logic of actions. Technical Report 57, DEC Palo Alto, april 1990.

[Mer86] D. Mery. A proof system to derive eventuality properties under justice hypothesis. In *LNCS,* number 233. Mathematical Foundations of Computer Science, 1986. Bratislava, Tchecoslovaquie.

[Mer92] D. Mery. The $\mathcal{NU}$ system as a development system for concurrent programs: $\delta\mathcal{NU}$. *Theoretical Computer Science,* 94(2):311 – 334, march 1992.

[Mis90] J. Misra. Soundness of the substitution axiom. *Notes on Unity,* pages 14–90, 1990.

[San91] B.A. Sanders. Eliminating the substitution axiom from unity logic. *Formal Aspects of Computing*, 3:189–205, 1991.

A   APPENDIX A: Proof of Invariance

```
PROOF

  1  y>=0                                              HYP
  2  k>=1                                              HYP
  3  z = N*k                                           HYP
  4  x*N+y = M                                         HYP
  5    y>=2*z                                          HYP
  6      y>=0                                          INHYP
  7      k>=1                                          INHYP
  8      2*k>=1                                        7 proposition.16
  9      2*(N*k) = 2*(N*k)                             EQL
 10      2*z = 2*(N*k)                                 9 HYP.3
 11      2*z = N*(2*k)                                 10 proposition.20
 12      x*N+y = M                                     INHYP
 13      y>=0 & 2*k>=1 & 2*z = N*(2*k) & x*N+y =
         M                                             6 8 11 12 AND
 14      [z,k:=2*z,2*k](y>=0 & k>=1 & z = N*k &
         x*N+y = M)                                    13 SUB
 15      wp((z,k:=2*z,2*k),(y>=0 & k>=1 & z = N*
         k & x*N+y = M))                               14 wp_theory.4
 16      y>=2*z => wp((z,k:=2*z,2*k),(y>=0 & k>=1
         & z = N*k & x*N+y = M))                       DED
 17    wp(Cond_ass((z,k:=2*z,2*k),y>=2*z),(y>=0
       & k>=1 & z = N*k & x*N+y = M))                  16 wp_theory.5
 18  y>=0 & k>=1 & z = N*k & x*N+y = M => wp(
     Cond_ass((z,k:=2*z,2*k),y>=2*z),(y>=0 & k>=
     1 & z = N*k & x*N+y = M))                         DED
 19  stable(Cond_ass((z,k:=2*z,2*k),y>=2*z),(y>=
     0 & k>=1 & z = N*k & x*N+y = M))                  18 Stable_theory.1
 20  y>=0                                              HYP
 21  k>=1                                              HYP
 22  z = N*k                                           HYP
 23  x*N+y = M                                         HYP
 24    y<2*z                                           HYP
 25      y>=0                                          INHYP
 26      1 = 1                                         EQL
 27      1>=1                                          26 proposition.23
 28      N = N                                         EQL
 29      N = N*1                                       28 proposition.24
 30      x*N+y = M                                     INHYP
 31      y>=0 & 1>=1 & N = N*1 & x*N+y = M            25 27 29 30 AND
 32      [z,k:=N,1](y>=0 & k>=1 & z = N*k & x*N+
         y = M)                                        31 SUB
```

```
33    wp((z,k:=N,1),(y>=0 & k>=1 & z = N*k &
      x*N+y = M))                                    32 wp_theory.4
34    y<2*z => wp((z,k:=N,1),(y>=0 & k>=1 & z =
      N*k & x*N+y = M))                              DED
35    wp(Cond_ass((z,k:=N,1),y<2*z),(y>=0 & k>=
      1 & z = N*k & x*N+y = M))                      34 wp_theory.5
36    y>=0 & k>=1 & z = N*k & x*N+y = M => wp(
      Cond_ass((z,k:=N,1),y<2*z),(y>=0 & k>=1 & z
      = N*k & x*N+y = M))                            DED
37    stable(Cond_ass((z,k:=N,1),y<2*z),(y>=0 & k
      >=1 & z = N*k & x*N+y = M))                    36 Stable_theory.1
38    y>=0                                           HYP
39    k>=1                                           HYP
40    z = N*k                                        HYP
41    x*N+y = M                                      HYP
42      y>=z                                         HYP
43        y>=z                                       INHYP
44        y-z>=0                                     43 arithmetique.14
45        k>=1                                       INHYP
46        z = N*k                                    INHYP
47        x*N+y = M                                  INHYP
48        x*N+N*k-N*k+y = M                          47 arithmetique.11
49        x*N+N*k-z+y = M                            48 HYP.40
50        x*N+k*N-z+y = M                            49 arithmetique.1
51        x*N+k*N+(y-z) = M                          50 arithmetique.4
52        (x+k)*N+(y-z) = M                          51 arithmetique.5
53        y-z>=0 & k>=1 & z = N*k & (x+k)*N+(y-z)
          = M                                        44 45 46 52 AND
54        [x,y:=x+k,y-z](y>=0 & k>=1 & z = N*k &
          x*N+y = M)                                 53 SUB
55        wp((x,y:=x+k,y-z),(y>=0 & k>=1 & z = N*
          k & x*N+y = M))                            54 wp_theory.4
56      y>=z => wp((x,y:=x+k,y-z),(y>=0 & k>=1 &
        z = N*k & x*N+y = M))                        DED
57      wp(Cond_ass((x,y:=x+k,y-z),y>=z),(y>=0 &
        k>=1 & z = N*k & x*N+y = M))                 56 wp_theory.5
58    y>=0 & k>=1 & z = N*k & x*N+y = M => wp(
      Cond_ass((x,y:=x+k,y-z),y>=z),(y>=0 & k>=1
      & z = N*k & x*N+y = M))                        DED


59    stable(Cond_ass((x,y:=x+k,y-z),y>=z),(y>=0
      & k>=1 & z = N*k & x*N+y = M))                 58 Stable_theory.1
60    stable(Cons(Cond_ass((z,k:=N,1),y<2*z),
      Cond_ass((x,y:=x+k,y-z),y>=z)),(y>=0 & k>=1
      & z = N*k & x*N+y = M))                        37 59 Stable_theor
y.2
61    stable(Cons(Cond_ass((z,k:=2*z,2*k),y>=2*z)
      ,Cons(Cond_ass((z,k:=N,1),y<2*z),Cond_ass((
```

```
       x,y:=x+k,y-z),y>=z))),(y>=0 & k>=1 & z = N*
       k & x*N+y = M))                              19 60 Stable_theor
y.2
   62  x = 0                                        HYP
   63  y = M                                        HYP
   64  z = N                                        HYP
   65  k = 1                                        HYP
   66  M>=0                                         HYP
   67  N>0                                          HYP
   68    M>=0                                       INHYP
   69    y>=0                                       68 HYP.63
   70    k = 1                                      INHYP
   71    k>=1                                       70 proposition.23
   72    N = N                                      EQL
   73    N = N*1                                    72 proposition.24
   74    N = N*k                                    73 HYP.65
   75    z = N*k                                    74 HYP.64
   76    y = M                                      INHYP
   77    0+y = M                                    76 proposition.26
   78    0*N+y = M                                  77 proposition.25
   79    x*N+y = M                                  78 HYP.62
   80    y>=0 & k>=1 & z = N*k & x*N+y = M          69 71 75 79 AND
   81  x = 0 & y = M & z = N & k = 1 & M>=0 & N>0
       => y>=0 & k>=1 & z = N*k & x*N+y = M         DED
   82  Inv(P)                                       61 81 lect_param_i
nv.1


END OF PROOF
--------------------------------------------------------------------------------
```

A *VDM*♣ Study of Fault-Tolerant Stable Storage — Towards a Computer Engineering Mathematics

Andrew Butterfield

Department of Computer Science, Trinity College, Dublin 2, Ireland

Abstract. This paper presents early results of research work being carried out on applying formal methods to the analysis of Stable Storage (Lampson 1981), which is a particular form of Fault Tolerance (Johnson 1989) adopted for data storage systems A prime concern is the development of the methods of the *Irish School of VDM* (*VDM*♣) (Mac an Airchinnigh 1990) as applied to this application as an effective engineering mathematics discipline. Early results of the modelling are reported involving both the use of the formalism and understanding of the application area gained from the modelling. Also emerging from the research are suggestions of possible new operators that might be added to the calculus to make it a more effective modelling tool, as well as new extensions to the formal method itself.

1 Introduction

This paper presents early results of research work being carried out on applying formal methods to the analysis of *fault-tolerance* (Johnson 1989) in general, and *Stable Storage* (Lampson 1981) in particular. The goals of the research are to produce adequate models of such fault tolerance to assist the FASST research project[1] and to improve and develop the formal method employed, which is the *VDM* (Bjørner and Jones 1978, Bjørner et al. 1987) as modified by the *Irish School* (Mac an Airchinnigh 1990, 1991). The *Irish School of VDM* (*VDM*♣) places VDM in a framework of Applied Constructive Mathematics, basing its reasoning on proving the equality of expressions by substitution of equals, as used in conventional engineering mathematics. This should be contrasted with the approach of Jones (1990) which uses the Logic of Partial Functions (LPF) as its underlying mathematical base. It is the main contention of the Irish School that the constructive mathematics approach, having many similarities to conventional engineering mathematics, is easier to use and henceforth more effective than those formal methods which rely on some form of logic.

Both goals are seen as synergistic — the development of the stable storage subsystem is hard industrial research and development that requires very rigourous reasoning if it is to succeed — while the goal of developing a truly industrial strength set of models and methods will be assisted considerably by the fact that they are being developed in tandem with such a project.

Before proceeding with the details of concern in this paper, it is worthwhile mentioning various aspects of the VDM that are not mentioned here. This paper

---

[1] ESPRIT P 5212 Fault Tolerant Architectures using Stable Storage

has no examples of reification (Andrews, 1987, Jones 1990, Ch. 8., p179) as it has been discussed elsewhere and is not the *present* focus of this work which involves the construction of high level abstractions. Nor do pre-conditions play a major rôle here as the intention of modelling fault tolerant systems is to come up with models valid under all circumstances. The absence of reification or pre-conditions must not be interpreted as meaning that they are absent from $VDM^{\clubsuit}$. They exist and are used in the same fashion as those found in other "Schools".

The notation used is largely that of VDM, except where it clashes with established mathematical notations. The $VDM^{\clubsuit}$ tends to adopt conventional notation where a clash arises, in keeping with its philosophy which eschews the use of automated tools and favours much use of hand-written analysis. A guide to the notation used here is given in Appendix A at the end of this paper.

2 Ideal Memory

We start with a brief description of an abstract model of ideal memory, complete with read and write operations. A more detailed discussion can be found in (Butterfield 1992b). The precise nature of addresses and the stored values is not important at this level of detail, so they will be treated simply as being drawn from appropriate sets, which are considered to be *finite*. In particular, values could be bytes or pages, in solid-state memory or on magnetic media. Memory is modelled as a mapping from addresses to values, with Read (R) and Write (W) operations modelled as map application and override respectively:

$$a \in ADDR, \quad v \in VAL$$
$$\mu \in MEM = ADDR \xrightarrow{m} VAL$$

$$R : ADDR \to MEM \to VAL$$
$$R(a)\mu \triangleq \mu(a) \tag{1}$$

$$W : ADDR \times VAL \to MEM \to MEM$$
$$W(a,v)\mu \triangleq \mu + \{a \mapsto v\} \tag{2}$$

Note 1. As we are considering general memory systems, that we hope will run correctly all the time, all of the the memory accessing operators defined in this paper are considered to have a TRUE pre-condition. Any erroneous events leading to some form of failure will be explicitly modelled as will be seen later, and will always be defined, regardless of the state of the memory.

Note 2. The operators are defined using constructive post-conditions which specify the results as expressions. This should be contrasted with post-conditions expressed in the form of predicates which must be satisfied by the outputs. This latter approach gives rise to a *proof obligation* (Jones 1987, 1990) to show that outputs meeting post-condition do in fact exist. The former approach, as adopted by the $VDM^{\clubsuit}$ incorporates just such a proof, as the post-condition has been *constructed*.

Note 3. value The address (a) and data (v) arguments of these operators have been been separated from the memory arguments (μ) by the technique of *currying* (Schonfinkel 1924, Curry 1958). This allows use to interpret $R(a)$ as an operation that reads from address a of any memory, and $W(a, v)$ as an operator that writes v into address a of any memory.

Given this model it is easy to show some key properties regarding the effects of multiple Writes to the same or different addresses and the effect of Writes on subsequent Reads:

$$(R(a) \circ W(a', v))\mu = \textbf{if } a' = a \textbf{ then } v \textbf{ else } R(a)\mu \tag{3}$$
$$(W(a, v) \circ W(a', v'))\mu = \tag{4}$$
$$\textbf{if } a' = a \textbf{ then } W(a, v)\mu \textbf{ else } (W(a', v') \circ W(a, v))\mu$$

These properties are fairly obvious, but are presented here so that they can be contrasted and compared with later results.

2.1 Error Detecting Memory

2.2 The Model

The key feature of error-detecting memories is some form of encoding that builds in redundant error detection data, with an associated decoder that extracts the original data along with some indication of possible errors. Our first model of *error-detecting memory* (*EDM*) avoids any explicit mention of an encoding scheme—it presumes that the *VAL* component of perfect memory is replaced by a $\mathbf{B} \times VAL$ pair, where the boolean flag is set to TRUE if no error has been *detected* in the data. In all that follows it is important to note that the flag models the knowledge the memory has of the condition of its data. A TRUE flag does not necessarily signify that no error has occurred, and indeed won't do so if an undetected error has taken place.

$$\mu \in EDM = ADDR \xrightarrow{m} (\mathbf{B} \times VAL)$$

The relationship between *MEM* and *EDM* is not one of reification involving abstraction and representation. Error Detecting Memory is viewed within the $VDM^{\clubsuit}$ as an *Elaboration* of the *MEM* model (Mac an Airchinnigh 1990). The "perfect" Read and Write operators are replaced by Lampson (1981) with "imperfect" analogues called Get (G) and Put (P). These take additional *event* parameters which model the possible changes that might occur to data during memory operations. These events are modelled as *total functions* which express how the data actually stored or retrieved is related to the original specified data.

$$\varepsilon_r \in R\_EVT = (\mathbf{B} \times VAL) \rightarrow (\mathbf{B} \times VAL)$$
$$\varepsilon_w \in W\_EVT = VAL \rightarrow R\_EVT$$

Note 4. An instance of ε_w has the form $\varepsilon_w [\![v]\!](b, w) \triangleq (b', v')$ where the single value v represents the new value being written to the memory, while the $\mathbf{B} \times VAL$ pair (b, w) denotes the previous contents. The result (b', v') of the event function is the (boolean,value) pair that is actually written. The brackets used ($[\![\ ]\!]$) are simply intended to highlight the curried arguments.

The reason for choosing functions, rather than erroneous values, to represent events is that functions can capture context-dependent errors (such as bit-toggling) which cause the erroneous value to depend on the previous value.

$$G \; : \; R\_EVT \to ADDR \to EDM \to \mathbf{B} \times VAL$$
$$G[\![\varepsilon_r]\!](a)\mu \triangleq \varepsilon_r(\mu(a)) \tag{5}$$

$$P \; : \; W\_EVT \to ADDR \times VAL \to EDM \to EDM$$
$$P[\![\varepsilon_w]\!](a,v)\mu \triangleq \mu + \{a \mapsto \varepsilon_w[\![v]\!](\mu(a))\} \tag{6}$$

Note 5. The choice of the signatures of the Put and Get operator is dictated by a desire to separate the events from the specifics of the data and addresses being used as much as possible, as one aim of the model is to be able to consider events in isolation. However there some key areas where this is not straightforward or possible as will be discussed shortly.

Comparison with *MEM.* In practice, we hope that errors are few and far between! We need to be able to model situations when no errors are taking place within the same framework. This is very straightforward—Error-free Puts and Gets will use *Identity Event* functions ($\varepsilon_w^{\mathcal{I}}$ and $\varepsilon_r^{\mathcal{I}}$ respectively).

$$\varepsilon_w^{\mathcal{I}} \; : \; W\_EVT$$
$$\varepsilon_w^{\mathcal{I}}[\![v]\!](b,w) \triangleq (\text{TRUE}, v) \tag{7}$$

$$\varepsilon_r^{\mathcal{I}} \; : \; R\_EVT$$
$$\varepsilon_r^{\mathcal{I}} \triangleq \mathcal{I} \tag{8}$$

The first thing that should be shown is that error-free Gets and Puts in *EDM* behave just like the Reads and Writes of *MEM*. The full detail of this is to be found in (Butterfield 1992b) and presents no great difficulties, as long as we restrict *EDM* to those cases where only TRUE occurs in the stored tuples, thus denoting memories where no errors have been *detected*. We just sketch the details here. Essentially we introduce the notion of a *Restricting Invariant* ($inv-D_r$) which limits a domain D to some subset (D_r) that has desirable properties. We also introduce a *Partial Retrieve* function ($retr_p$–E) from D_r to another domain (E) with which the intended comparison is being made. In effect, the restricting invariant acts as a pre-condition for the partial retrieve function.

$$inv-EDM_r \; : \; EDM \to \mathbf{B}$$
$$inv-EDM_r(\mu) \triangleq (^\wedge\!/ \circ \mathcal{P}(\pi_1) \circ \text{rng})\mu \tag{9}$$

$$retr_p-MEM \; : \; EDM_r \to MEM$$
$$retr_p-MEM(\mu_r) \triangleq (\mathcal{I} \xrightarrow{m} \pi_2)\mu_r \tag{10}$$

The problem then reduces to proving the following identities (Butterfield 1992b):

$$W(a,v) \circ retr_p\text{--}MEM = retr_p\text{--}MEM \circ P[\![\varepsilon_w^{\tau}]\!](a,v) \qquad (11)$$

$$R(a) \circ retr_p\text{--}MEM = \pi_2 \circ G[\![\varepsilon_r^{\tau}]\!](a) \qquad (12)$$

What is of interest here is the notion that an *elaboration* of a model can be mapped back onto the original model if a suitable *Restricting Invariant* is found. However, it must also be stressed that the relationship here is not of reification. In particular, there is no requirement to show how elements of *EDM* that contain FALSE flags are related to elements of *MEM* as there is no correspondence in *MEM* to such erroneous values.

Properties of the Model. We now proceed to examine the *EDM* model in more detail. First note that the model does not include scope for addressing errors—other than by explicitly using an address that is declared to be 'wrong'. This is not a serious omission at present because address errors, are a disaster, as far as the fault tolerant stable storage systems in this paper are concerned.

Event Examples. Two important examples of Write Events are the Null Write (ε_w^{ϕ}), where no data is changed at all, and the set of Decay Events (ε_w^{δ}) which indicate the corruption of data while sitting in memory. Decay can be modelled by a Put operation with a Write Event that ignores the Put's *VAL* parameter

$$\varepsilon_w^{\phi}[\![v]\!](b,w) \triangleq (b,w) \qquad (13)$$

$$\varepsilon_w^{\delta}[\![v]\!](b,w) \triangleq \delta(b,w) \text{ where } \delta \in R\_EVT \qquad (14)$$

The Null Write event during a Put operation illustrates an important point regarding the interpretation of the *EDM* model. Such an event will normally be considered an error by any observer, even though the resulting contents of memory may be flagged with TRUE and actually be the previously correct data that was stored before the Put occurred. This data is incorrect as the correct outcome of the Put operation should have been a TRUE flag with the *new* data. To re-iterate: *the value of the flag only models the error detecting memory's own perception of the state of the data.*

Note that both examples above show that some classes of Write Event functions make use of existing values in memory, rather than overriding them the fashion an ideal Write operation. We have here a first classification of Write Events which distinguishes between *History-Preserving* and *History-Breaking* Write Events. A History Breaking event is one where the resulting data is independent of the previous contents of memory, and can always be expressed in the form $\varepsilon_w[\![v]\!](b,w) \triangleq \varepsilon_r(\text{TRUE},v)$ where ε_r is the equivalent Read Event. The Identity Write function (ε_w^{τ}) is the most obvious (and hopefully most frequent) example of a History Breaking Event.

Operator Composition. As with the ideal memory model, it is now necessary to investigate the effects of composing Puts and Gets, with the expectation that the presence of Write Event functions that are history-preserving will complicate matters. We find that the effect of Get after Put is much the same as observed for Reads and Writes (3):

$$(G[\![\varepsilon_r]\!](a) \circ P[\![\varepsilon_w]\!](a', v))\mu$$
$$= \textbf{if}\ a' \neq a\ \textbf{then}\ G[\![\varepsilon_r]\!](a)\mu\ \textbf{else}\ (\varepsilon_r \circ \varepsilon_w[\![v]\!])\mu(a) \tag{15}$$

However, the relationship between successive Puts to the same address is more complex. Using the definition of Put twice with events ε_w and ε_w' gives the following identity:

$$(P[\![\varepsilon_w]\!](a, v) \circ P[\![\varepsilon_w']\!](a, v'))\mu = P[\![\varepsilon_w]\!](a, v)(P[\![\varepsilon_w']\!](a, v')\mu) \tag{16}$$

However, the desired result is of the form

$$(P[\![\varepsilon_w]\!](a, v) \circ P[\![\varepsilon_w']\!](a, v'))\mu = P[\![\varepsilon_w'']\!](a, v)\mu \tag{17}$$

where ε_w'' is the single event that is equivalent to the afore-mentioned two. To achieve this we introduce a version of function composition that is generalised to handle the presence of curried arguments. The *General Function Composition* operator ($\odot$) is ternary, taking the two functions to be composed as well as the curried argument of the first function to be applied (Butterfield, 1992a). The following equations give a definition of this operator and illustrates one of its key properties (a form of Associativity):

$$(f \odot_{x'} g)[\![x]\!]y \triangleq (f[\![x]\!] \circ g[\![x']\!])y \tag{18}$$
$$f \odot_x (g \odot_{x'} h) = (f \odot_x g) \odot_{x'} h \tag{19}$$

This operator enables us to produce a combination of event functions and some context values in such a way as to produce an expression that is itself an event function (i.e. has the same signature). This allows us to maintain the desired separation of events from the data being inserted into memory. Given this operator we can then describe the effect of two successive Puts to the same address as follows:

$$P[\![\varepsilon_w]\!](a, v) \circ P[\![\varepsilon_w']\!](a, v') = P[\![\varepsilon_w \odot_{v'} \varepsilon_w']\!](a, v) \tag{20}$$

where we can say now, that $\varepsilon_w'' = \varepsilon_w \odot_{v'} \varepsilon_w'$. This should be compared to (5). The key result of all of this is that the effect of a sequence of Puts to one address is given by a single Put with the appropriate composition of event functions:

$$P[\![\varepsilon_w^n]\!](a, v_n) \circ P[\![\varepsilon_w^{n-1}]\!](a, v_{n-1}) \circ \cdots \circ P[\![\varepsilon_w^2]\!](a, v_2) \circ P[\![\varepsilon_w^1]\!](a, v_1)$$
$$=$$
$$P[\![\varepsilon_w^n \odot_{v_{n-1}} \varepsilon_w^{n-1} \odot_{v_{n-2}} \cdots \odot_{v_2} \varepsilon_w^2 \odot_{v_1} \varepsilon_w^1]\!](a, v_n) \tag{21}$$

Note that the composition depends on both the events $\varepsilon_w^1 \ldots \varepsilon_w^n$ and the context $(v_1 \ldots v_{n-1})$ in which they occur. This context dependence is important, and the use of the $\odot$ operator highlights precisely what this dependence is. Despite an desire, expressed earlier, to separate the events from the data and addresses involved with Put operators, we see that cannot be achieved for successive Puts to one address. The outcome of a sequence of general events depends intimately on the values present in memory before the events occur. This is most clearly seen in the expression

$\varepsilon_w^n \odot v_{n-1} \varepsilon_w^{n-1} \odot v_{n-2} \cdots \odot v_2 \varepsilon_w^2 \odot v_1 \varepsilon_w^1$ which suggests visually the interleaving of the composition of the write events with the values that the Puts are attempting to write to the memory Adding a new operator should always be approached with care, lest it be too specialised to be of any use outside the problem domain for which it was devised. An indication of other possible uses for $\odot$ is given in Appendix C.

2.3 Careful Memory

In (Lampson 1981), the next step was to define "Careful" versions of Put and Get. There, they are viewed as more fault-tolerant versions implemented using Get and Put as building blocks, but we will treat them as additional operators over the same *EDM* model.

CarefulGet. The following quote describing CarefulGet is from Lampson (1981).

> "*CarefulGet* repeatedly does *Get* until it gets a *good* status, or until it has tried n times"

Note that this implementation makes no explicit mention of errors. To model the fault tolerant aspects of CarefulGet (CG) we need to introduce the notion of a *sequence of Read Events* which will be an extra argument to the CarefulGet operation. It is then straightforward to give a recursive definition of the CarefulGet operator in terms of Get, that matches the above implementation description, except that the premature exhaustion of the read events is interpreted as meaning that a crash occurred before the CarefulGet operation could return any results. This is indicated by $\perp$, which is used in the *VDM*♣ to denote a "do not care" situation, as well as "undefined" (Mac an Airchinnigh 1990). The use of a pre-condition to exclude $\perp$ results is not appropriate, as this would exclude crash conditions from those deemed as "valid inputs" to CG. As the data returned is not defined should the flag be FALSE, this situation is denoted here by the form (FALSE, _). This is the equivalent to the non-deterministic post-condition of more conventional *VDM* (Jones, 1990, p104 for example) as the '_' marker indicates a slot where any value (of the appropriate type) will suffice.

$$\varsigma_r \in R\_EVTS = R\_EVT^\star \tag{22}$$

$$CG \ : \ R\_EVTS \rightarrow ADDR \rightarrow EDM \rightarrow \mathbf{B} \times VAL$$
$$CG[\![\varsigma_r]\!](a) \triangleq CG'[\![n, \varsigma_r]\!](a) \tag{23}$$

$$CG'[\![0, \varsigma_r]\!](a)\mu \triangleq (\text{FALSE}, \_) \tag{24}$$
$$CG'[\![k, \Lambda]\!](a)\mu \triangleq \perp \tag{25}$$
$$CG'[\![k, \varepsilon_r : \varsigma_r]\!](a)\mu \triangleq \tag{26}$$
$$\text{let } (b, v) = G[\![\varepsilon_r]\!](a)\mu \text{ in}$$
$$\text{if } b \text{ then } (b, v) \text{ else } CG'[\![k - 1, \varsigma_r]\!](a)\mu$$

A key property (whose proof is straightforward) can be immediately stated:

$$CG[\![\varsigma_r]\!](a) = CG[\![\varsigma_r[1 \ldots n]\!]\!](a) \tag{27}$$

where $[1\dots n]$ selects the first n elements of a sequence.

A more important property, that is discussed in more detail here, is that the result of a CarefulGet operation with a given Read Event Sequence can be reduced to that of a Get operation with an single equivalent Read Event. This equivalent Read Event is called the *Get-Equivalent Form (GEq)* of the sequence and is derived from the given sequence, as well as a consideration of the actual contents of memory. The only difference is the treatment of crashes, which will be discussed later.

We already have one result regarding the fact that only the first n elements of the sequence matter. The next result is obtained by noting that the address being read during a CG operation is always the same as is the (b, v) value being handled by the read events. So each event in the sequence has the same context. We also note that the following occasions when CG will terminate:

- at the first occurrence of an event that results in $(\text{TRUE}, \_)$.
- if the first n events result in $(\text{FALSE}, \_)$.

A case that needs to be examined is one where all the events result in $(\text{FALSE}, \_)$, but the number of those events is less than n. In other words what has occurred is a crash, after (so-far) persistent read errors. It can be shown that, in the event of a crash, there is no single read event equivalent to the sequence. We can define a predicate *Crsh* that indicates if a sequence will result in a crash, given the existing contents of memory:

$$Crsh \ : \ \mathbf{B} \times VAL \to R\_EVTS \to \mathbf{B}$$

$$Crsh[\![b, v]\!]\varsigma_r \triangleq \operatorname{len}\varsigma_r < n \tag{28}$$
$$\wedge$$
$$\operatorname{elems}((Done_G[\![b, v]\!])^\star \varsigma_r) \subseteq \{\text{FALSE}\}$$
$$\mathbf{where} \ Done_G[\![b, v]\!]\varepsilon_r = \pi_1 \varepsilon_r(b, v)$$

Note 6. When applied to a read event, $Done_G[\![b, v]\!]$ returns TRUE if CarefulGet would terminate after that event.

The *Crsh* predicate serves to act as a pre-condition for *GEq*. The Get-Equivalent Form is defined as follows:

$$GEq \ : \ \mathbf{B} \times VAL \to R\_EVTS \to R\_EVT$$

$$pre\text{-}GEq[\![b, v]\!]\varsigma_r \triangleq \neg Crsh[\![b, v]\!]\varsigma_r \tag{29}$$
$$GEq[\![b, v]\!]\varsigma_r \triangleq \varsigma_r[\min\{n, f_T\}] \tag{30}$$
$$\mathbf{where} \ f_T = \mathit{fstloc}[\![\{\text{TRUE}\}]\!]\beta$$
$$\mathbf{where} \ \beta = (Done_G[\![b, v]\!])^\star \varsigma_r'$$
$$\mathbf{where} \ \varsigma_r' = \varsigma_r[1\dots n]$$

Note 7. When applied to a sequence, $\mathit{fstloc}[\![S]\!]$ returns the index of the first occurrence of a member of S in the sequence. If none are found it returns the sequence length plus one.

Note 8. The sequence β consists of booleans indicating whether each event would cause CarefulGet to halt. It is produced by mapping $Done_G[\![b,v]\!]$ onto every element of ς_r'.

The result is the single error which, if it occurred when a G was attempted, would have the same result as the CG attempted with the sequence of errors

The key property of Get-Equivalent Forms is as follows:

$$\neg Crsh[\![\mu(a)]\!]\varsigma_r \Rightarrow CG[\![\varsigma_r]\!](a)\mu = G[\![GEq[\![\mu(a)]\!]\varsigma_r]\!](a)\mu \tag{31}$$

The proof of this is quite extensive, by induction on n and ς_r, and can be found in (Butterfield 1993b).

CarefulPut. The following quote describing CarefulPut is from Lampson (1981).

> *"CarefulPut* repeatedly does *Put* followed by *Get* until the *Get* returns *good* with the data being written"

The most important thing to note here is the complete absence of the parameter n. CarefulPut keeps trying until it succeeds *or crashes.*

Question 9. How should errors and events be modelled here ? We have *alternating* Puts and Gets with the possibility of a crash inbetween at any point!

Various alternatives are discussed in (Butterfield 1993b), with the method of choice being to use sequences of Write Events. When the Write Events are being fed into the Get operator (every second event in the sequence), they are first applied to the value (v) that the CarefulPut (CP) is trying to write. This results in a Read Event which is context sensitive and can depend on both the existing memory contents *and* the value v. Given sequences of Write and Read Events, it is possible to produce such a single Write Event Sequence denoting their combined effect during a CarefulPut operation by:

1. "Lifting" every Read Event to produce an equivalent Write Event. Such lifted Read Events will be denoted by ε_r^w or ε_r^p: $\varepsilon_r^w[\![v]\!](b,w) \triangleq \varepsilon_r(b,w)$
2. Zipping together the lists, but alternating elements from each, starting with the original Write Events.

For the Get operator in general there is no "context" (what *VAL* entity would act as the first argument ?). However, in the case of CarefulPut, a natural choice for such an argument *is* present.

$$\varsigma_w \in W\_EVTS = W\_EVT^*$$
$$CP : W\_EVTS \to ADDR \times VAL \to EDM \to EDM$$

$$CP[\![\Lambda]\!](a,v)\mu \triangleq \mu \tag{32}$$

$$CP[\![<\varepsilon_w>]\!](a,v)\mu \triangleq P[\![\varepsilon_w]\!](a,v)\mu \tag{33}$$

$$CP[\![<\varepsilon_w,\varepsilon_r^w>\frown\varsigma_w]\!](a,v)\mu \triangleq \text{let } \mu' = P[\![\varepsilon_w]\!](a,v)\mu \text{ in} \tag{34}$$
$$\text{if } G[\![\varepsilon_r^w[\![v]\!]]\!](a)\mu' = (\text{TRUE},v)$$
$$\text{then } \mu'$$
$$\text{else } CP[\![\varsigma_w]\!](a,v)\mu'$$

It might appear that CarefulPut is non-terminating, as a reading of the Lampson quote above would seem to imply. This is not the case however, as the specification presented above encodes explicitly what Lampson assumes implicitly, that CarefulPut, when faced with persistent errors, will run until a crash occurs *and that such a crash will always eventually happen.* The specification of CP above shows this simply because the parameter ς_w is a *finite* sequence of events, and two of them are consumed for each recursive iteration.

The goal here is to find a Put-Equivalent Form (*PEq*) for W_EVTS, that determines the single Put which has the same effect as CarefulPut, as already shown for CarefulGet. We introduce a binary version of the $\odot_x$ operator introduced earlier, that can be used when the curried arguments are the same (the subscript decoration denoting a curried argument is dropped). This is called the *Same Argument Composition* operator and is also discussed in (Butterfield 1992a) It has the following definition:

$$(f \odot g)[\![x]\!]y \triangleq (f[\![x]\!] \circ g[\![x]\!])y \tag{35}$$

We proceed by noting the condition under which CP terminates, in the absence of crashes. This can be shown to be the following:

$$\text{if } (\varepsilon_r^w \odot \varepsilon_w)[\![v]\!]\mu(a) = (\text{TRUE},v) \tag{36}$$

The CP algorithm will iterate until this condition is met, where μ denotes the state of the memory at the start of each iteration. The state of memory at the end of each iteration is given by:

$$\mu' = \mu + \{a \mapsto \varepsilon_w[\![v]\!](\mu(a))\} \tag{37}$$

Assume a call of CP that iterates many times, due to some persistent combination of erroneous events $(<\varepsilon_w^1,\varepsilon_r^1,\dots>)$. The successive contents of $\mu(a)$, originally u (say), will appear as follows:

$$\mu^0(a) = u \tag{38}$$

$$\mu^1(a) = \varepsilon_w^1[\![v]\!](u) \tag{39}$$

$$\mu^2(a) = (\varepsilon_w^2 \odot \varepsilon_w^1)[\![v]\!]u \tag{40}$$

$$\vdots \quad \vdots$$

$$\mu^k(a) = (\varepsilon_w^k \odot \dots \odot \varepsilon_w^2 \odot \varepsilon_w^1)[\![v]\!]u \tag{41}$$

The derivation of a Put-Equivalent Form involves the recognition of the fact that, unlike CarefulGet, CarefulPut does return a meaningful result in the event of a crash—namely the state in which the memory is left by that crash. We therefore anticipate that an equivalent form will be found for any instance of W_EVTS, even if it denotes a crash situation. In particular, we discover that appending any arbitrary "lifted" Read Error (ε_r^w) to the end of a sequence that denotes a crash between a Put and a Get (odd number of errors), will have no net effect on the resulting contents of memory:

$$\text{odd}(\text{len}\varsigma_w) \Rightarrow CP[\![\varsigma_w]\!](a,v) = CP[\![\varsigma_w \frown <\varepsilon_r^w>]\!](a,v) \qquad (42)$$

The proof is presented as Appendix B of this paper. In effect, we have converted the situation to one in which the crash occurs just after the Get, which of course has no effect on the resulting contents of memory.

Note 10. We have assumed here that Gets cannot side-effect memory, regardless of what fault occurs. This assumption would not hold valid for memory technology like Integrated Circuit dynamic memories that perform destructive read and the restore on a whole row of memory as well as the periodic read and refresh of every row[2]. In the presence of faults this could lead to memory changes on read as well as changes to bits at other addresses.

However, introducing this issue at the level of abstraction presented in this paper will introduce implementation features that are inappropriate at this point. The proper way to handle such issues is as they arise during the data reification process, which is where such details start to emerge.

An even more important response to the above note arises when we observe that the effect of such erroneous writes to data other than at the addressed location is likely to produce faults that cannot be tolerated by the stable storage system. In many ways these events are analogous to addressing errors. A key feature of the stable storage algorithms seems to be that the error-detection mechanism must cover all the data that could be affected during a Get or Put operation.

We can now proceed to illustrate the Put-Equivalent Form:

$$PEq : VAL \times (\mathbf{B} \times VAL) \rightarrow W\_EVTS \rightarrow W\_EVT$$

$$\text{pre}-PEq[\![v,(b,w)]\!]\varsigma_w \triangleq \text{even}(\text{len}\varsigma_w) \qquad (43)$$

$$PEq[\![v,(b,w)]\!]\Lambda \triangleq \varepsilon_w^\phi \qquad (44)$$

$$PEq[\![v,(b,w)]\!]\varsigma_w \triangleq \pi_1(\varsigma_w'[i]) \qquad (45)$$

$$\text{where } i = \min\{\text{len}\varsigma_w, f_T\}$$

$$\text{where } f_T = (\text{fstloc}[\![\{\text{TRUE}\}]\!] \circ Done_p[\![v,b,w]\!]^*)\varsigma_w'$$

$$\text{where } \varsigma_w' = (\Pi^\circ \circ \langle,\rangle)\varsigma_w$$

Note 11. We are excluding sequences of odd length, as they can be extended by appending any lifted Read Event.

Note 12. The equivalent of a null event sequence is the Null Write event, as nothing changes.

This description is best understood by observing how it was constructed. Assume that $\varsigma_w = <w_1, r_1, w_2, r_2, \ldots, w_m, r_m>$.

---

[2] Thanks must be given to an anonymous referee for pointing this out

The $\langle,\rangle$ operator simply converts an list of even length $(2m)$ into one of half the length containing pairs thus:

$$\langle,\rangle < w_1, r_1, w_2, r_2, \ldots, w_m, r_m > = < (w_1, r_1), (w_2, r_2), \ldots, (w_m, r_m) > \qquad (46)$$

Note that this step indicates that we could have chosen this form of pair-sequence to represent the events during CarefulPut, as was discussed earlier, without any radical difference in the underlying operator properties.

We want to replace every w_i by the composition of itself with every write event that occurs earlier. This reflects the fact that the effect of that event may depend on previous ones. We wish to convert

$$< (w_1, r_1), (w_2, r_2), \ldots, (w_m, r_m) > \qquad (47)$$

to

$$< (w_1, r_1), (w_2 \odot w_1, r_2), \ldots, (w_m \odot \cdots \odot w_2 \odot w_1, r_m)) > \qquad (48)$$

To do this we introduce a binary operator $\diamond$ defined as follows:

$$(w_1, r_1) \diamond (w_2, r_2) \triangleq (w_2 \odot w_1, r_2) \qquad (49)$$

Another operator we introduce is Π which is a combination of mapping and reduction. Given a binary operator $\oplus$ then $\Pi^{\oplus}$ converts a list of the form:

$$< x_1, x_2, x_3, \ldots, x_n > \qquad (50)$$

to the following list:

$$< x_1, x_1 \oplus x_2, x_1 \oplus (x_2 \oplus x_3), \ldots, x_1 \oplus (x_2 \oplus \cdots \oplus x_n) > \qquad (51)$$

This operator and its properties are discussed in more detail in (Butterfield 1993a) Applying $\Pi^{\diamond}$ has the desired effect.

We finally need a predicate to check to see if a Put-Get sequence was successful:

$$Done_P[\![v, b, w]\!](\varepsilon_w, \varepsilon_r^w) \triangleq (\varepsilon_r^w \odot \varepsilon_w)[\![v]\!](b, w) = (\text{TRUE}, v) \qquad (52)$$

Applying this to every element of the sequence produced in the last step results in a sequence of booleans which indicates which event pairs would have resulted in termination

fstloc is used to obtain an index in a similar manner to *GEq*.

The key property that we required for the Put-Equivalent Form is now stated:

$$CP[\![\varsigma_w]\!](a, v)\mu = P[\![PEq[\![v, \mu(a)]\!]\varsigma_w]\!](a, v)\mu \qquad (53)$$

The proof is trivial for null sequences (Λ), while that for non-null sequences proceeds by a variant of structural induction with a somewhat counter-intuitive inductive step:

1. Base Case: $\varsigma_w = <\varepsilon_w, \varepsilon_r^w >$
2. Inductive Step: We assume that if it holds for an instance of ς_w of the form: $<\varepsilon_w \odot \varepsilon_w', \varepsilon_r^w > \frown \varsigma_w$
   that from this it is possible to deduce that it holds for the following instance: $<\varepsilon_w', \varepsilon_r^p, \varepsilon_w, \varepsilon_r^w > \frown \varsigma_w$

We will justify the induction step here by pointing out that it is possible, given any error list (of even length), to construct a chain of lists of decreasing length, matching the induction step, until the base case is reached. The proof details are omitted here but can be found in (Butterfield 1993b).

2.4 Degree of Coverage

As we have seen, the equivalence operators reduce the sequences of events used by CarefulGet and CarefulPut to the single event that would produce the same result if used by Get or Put. The natural question to ask here is:

Question 13. Is the set of events that can result from finding the equivalents all possible sequences a proper subset of the set of all possible events ? In other words, has the introduction of the Careful operators eliminated some events (hopefully the erroneous ones) ?

The answer is *NO*, as can be seen by the following identities — Let ε_r be such that it produces (FALSE, _) when its context is some instance of $\mathbf{B} \times VAL$, denoted by (b, w). Then the following always holds: $GEq[\![b, w]\!] < \varepsilon_r, \varepsilon_r, \ldots, \varepsilon_r >= \varepsilon_r$ where there are n occurrences of ε_r. For a given value v, let $\varepsilon_r^w [\![v]\!](b, w) = (\text{TRUE}, v)$ be the lifted read event that always returns that value flagged as OK. The the following always holds for any ε_w: $PEq[\![v, (\_, \_)]\!] < \varepsilon_w, \lambda v \cdot \lambda(b, w) \cdot (\text{TRUE}, v) >= \varepsilon_w$.

The Careful operators provide *quantitative* fault tolerance, in that they reduce the probability of some errors occurring. They do not provide *qualitative* fault tolerance, which requires the probability of some errors to be reduced to zero, thus indicating that they have been eliminated. It must be stressed that the model as presented here does not itself handle the quantitative aspects of Stable Storage. Work has been done on introducing probability into the model, but as this raises considerable foundational issues, there is no room here to give it the coverage required. Details of this modelling will be published separately.

2.5 Stable Memory

There is no room here to present a detailed discussion of the work done in applying the $VDM^{\clubsuit}$ to the Stable operations from (Lampson 1981). A salient point of the material presented in this paper is that it justifies a radical set of simplifications to the StableGet and StablePut models. This is a much desired outcome as the complexity of the model, if continued in the same vein, undergoes a considerable increase when the Stable operators are examined.

The radical simplifications are summarised below with a brief justification for each:

- Our studies examine the effect of sequences of Writes and Reads on *independent* memory locations. The independence was demonstrated earlier, and allows us to ignore the aspect of memory modelling that views memory as a mapping from addresses to values. We can concentrate instead on the contents of a single memory location, and examine what happens to it as a result of varying combinations of Puts and Gets (Careful, Stable or otherwise).
- The Careful operators only provide quantitative fault tolerance and so can be replaced by the conventional Put and Get, for the purposes of qualitative analysis.
- The aspects of the Careful operators that matter for *quantitative* analysis (such as assessing the likelihood of certain errors occurring) are encapsulated in the Equivalent Form operators, and can be considered separately.

- The definitions of the Put and Get operators are extended to return *the list of remaining errors*, as well as what is presently returned. This is to allow the use of a single error sequence to describe the events occurring during sequences of operations, and is the main motivation for using a single uniform sequence to represent both Read and Write Events.

The notion of separating out various parts of a complex model into several simpler but interrelated models is considered one of the key requirements for any tractable industrial strength formal method. The examples here are the separation of addressing and quantitative issues out of the original model to leave a simpler core which can be used to assess the qualitative (correctness) properties of Stable Storage.

3 Summary

3.1 Results to Date

The results produced by this research to the present date centre on the demonstration of memory models incorporating conventional (error-prone) operations as well as Careful and Stable analogues. These models have been developed and analysed using the constructive equational reasoning that is characteristic of the $VDM^{\clubsuit}$ (Mac an Airchinnigh 1991).

The emphasis here has been on *elaborating* existing models (Mac an Airchinnigh 1990) at a given level of abstraction rather than following the conventional *VDM* style of reification which involves examining successively more concrete versions of a starting model. A key achievement here is the extension of the VDM concepts of invariant and retrieval into areas where elaboration, not reification, is taking place.

The rigourous examination of the equivalence between single errors and sequences of errors has highlighted a key distinction between between qualitative and quantitative fault tolerance. This distinction was not apparent to the author before the research work had begun. It is important as it stresses the fact that the usefulness of the Stable Storage concepts hinges on the (hoped for) rarity of certain patterns of errors which would cause it to fail. It does not work by eliminating the possibility of certain errors. The discovery of this distinction also contributes to the issue of reducing complexity, because it allows the qualitative and quantitative aspects of the various operators to be considered separately.

From the point of view of developing the mathematical ideas needed for studying fault tolerance, the research has led to the "discovery" of two operators, $\odot_x$ and II which play an important rôle in the models.

3.2 Future Work

Much work remains to be done. The elaboration process has to be continued until all the key features described in (Lampson 1981) have been modelled at the abstract level presented in this paper.

A phase of conventional *VDM* reification is also required, to examine how the concepts carry over to more concrete models of fault tolerance, with particular emphasis on looking at real-world coding schemes used to implement the boolean flag in the abstract model, as well as complications such as pattern faults in memory that affect distinct but related words.

In the longer term, there is a need to collate and rationalise the resulting collection of "discovered" operators. The danger here is that every stage of the modelling process will throw up more convenient operators, or shorthand notations, until the users are swamped by the sheer variety available. A regrouping phase will be required to prune the set of discovered operators down to those that are really fundamental and worth studying in their own right.

4 Acknowledgements

Particular thanks must be given to Dr. Mícheál Mac an Airchinnigh of the University of Dublin, Trinity College for his continual support and assistance with the $VDM^{\clubsuit}$. Thanks is also especially due to the the anonymous referees whose comments helped improve the clarity and focus of this paper.

5 Appendix A - Notation

5.1 $VDM^{\clubsuit}$ Notation

Symbol	Meaning
$X \xrightarrow{m} Y$	Map from X to Y
$f[\![x]\!]y$	Function f applied to (curried) x, applied to y
$+$	Map Override operator
$\mu(x)$	Map Lookup, returning the element in the range mapped to by x
$\mathcal{I}$	The Identity Function
$\oplus/$	Reduction w.r.t. binary operation $\oplus$
$\wedge$	Logical And
$\circ$	Function Composition
$\mathcal{P}(f)$	Mapping function f
π_n	nth Projection Function
rng	Map Range
$(f \xrightarrow{m} g)$	Maps f and g to Domain and Range resp. of a Map
$X^{\star}$	*Finite* Sequences over X
Λ	The Null Sequence
$:$	The Sequence 'Cons' Operator
$[l \ldots h]$	Sequence Subrange operator
$f^{\star}$	Maps f into a Sequence (Kleene Star functor)
len	The Sequence Length operator
$\subseteq$	The Subset relation
$\neg$	Logical Negation
$\Rightarrow$	Logical Implication
$<x>$	Singleton sequence containing x.
$<x, \ldots, y>$	Sequence notation
$\frown$	Sequence Concatenation operator

5.2 Possible extensions to $VDM^{\clubsuit}$ Notation

Symbol	Meaning
$\odot_x$	Context-Dependent Curried-Function Composition, with context x
$fstloc[\![S]\!]$	Returns index of first occurrence of a member of S in a sequence
$\odot$	Context-Free (Same Argument) Curried-Function Composition operator
$\langle,\rangle$	Adjacent Sequence Element Pairing operator
$\amalg$	Map/Accumulate operator (hybrid of Mapping and Reduction)

5.3 Stable Storage Model Notation

Symbol	Meaning
$ADDR, a$	Domain of Addresses, typical member
VAL, v	Domain of Stored Values, typical member
MEM, μ	Domain of Ideal Memory, typical member
W	Write operation on Ideal Memory
R	Read operation on Ideal Memory
EDM, μ	Domain of Error Detecting Memory, typical member
R_EVT, ε_r	Domain of Read Events, typical member
W_EVT, ε_w	Domain of Write Events, typical member
P	Put operation on Error Detecting Memory
G	Get operation on Error Detecting Memory
$\varepsilon_r^{\mathcal{I}}$	Identity Read Event, $\varepsilon_r^{\mathcal{I}} = \mathcal{I}$
$\varepsilon_w^{\mathcal{I}}$	Identity Write Event, $\varepsilon_w^{\mathcal{I}}[\![v]\!](b,w) = (\text{TRUE}, v)$
ε_w^{ϕ}	Null Write Event, $\varepsilon_w^{\phi}[\![v]\!](b,w) = (b,w)$
ε_w^{δ}	Decay Write Event, $\varepsilon_w^{\delta}[\![v]\!](b,w) = \delta(b,w)$
R_EVTS, ς_r	Domain of Read Event sequences, typical member
CG	CarefulGet operation on Error Detecting Memory
$Done_G$	Successful Get predicate $Done_G[\![b,v]\!]\varepsilon_r = \pi_1\varepsilon_r(b,v)$
GEq	Get-Equivalent Form function
$Crsh$	Read Crash predicate
W_EVTS, ς_w	Domain of Write Event sequences, typical member
CP	CarefulPut operation on Error Detecting Memory
$\varepsilon_r^{w}, \varepsilon_r^{p}$	'Lifted' Read Events (converted to Write Events)
$\diamond$	Write Event Accumulation operator
$Done_P$	Successful Put-Get predicate
PEq	Put-Equivalent Form function

6 Appendix B - Proof

The following is the proof that:

$$\text{odd}(\text{len}\varsigma_w) \Rightarrow CP[\![\varsigma_w]\!](a,v) = CP[\![\varsigma_w \frown <\varepsilon_r^w>]\!](a,v) \qquad (54)$$

Proofs in $VDM^{\clubsuit}$ are similar to conventional mathematics in that it involves proving em identities of the form $lhs\text{-}expr = rhs\text{-}expr$, by the process of *substitution of equals*

(Mac an Airchinnigh 1990, 1991). Either one of the *lhs-expr* or the *rhs-expr* are transformed until they equal the other, or both are transformed into an identical third expression.

The proof is by structural induction with a base case of $<\varepsilon_w>$ and an induction step from ς_w to $<\varepsilon_w, \varepsilon_r^w> \frown \varsigma_w$ This enables us to ignore the cases when $\neg odd(len\varsigma_w)$, and remove the implication. The identity being proved here is in fact:

$$CP[\![\varsigma_w]\!](a,v) = CP[\![\varsigma_w \frown <\varepsilon_r^?>]\!](a,v) \tag{55}$$

First we restate the recursive case of the definition of CP (34), by replacing calls to Put and Get by their expansions, and simplifying where possible:

$$CP[\![<\varepsilon_w, \varepsilon_r^w> \frown \varsigma_w]\!](a,v)\mu \tag{56}$$
$$=$$
if $(\varepsilon_r^w \odot \varepsilon_w)[\![v]\!](\mu(a)) = (\text{TRUE}, v)$
then $\mu + \{a \mapsto \varepsilon_w[\![v]\!](\mu(a))\}$
else $CP[\![\varsigma_w]\!](a,v)(\mu + \{a \mapsto \varepsilon_w[\![v]\!](\mu(a))\})$

Case $<\varepsilon_w>$:

$$CP[\![<\varepsilon_w>]\!](a,v)\mu = CP[\![<\varepsilon_w, \varepsilon_r^w>]\!](a,v)\mu \tag{57}$$
$$= \ldots \text{expand } CP \text{ in lhs:}$$
$$\quad \textbf{if } (\varepsilon_r^w \odot \varepsilon_w)[\![v]\!](\mu(a)) = (\text{TRUE}, v) \tag{58}$$
$$\quad \textbf{then } \mu + \{a \mapsto \varepsilon_w[\![v]\!](\mu(a))\}$$
$$\quad \textbf{else } CP[\![\Lambda]\!](a,v)(\mu + \{a \mapsto \varepsilon_w[\![v]\!](\mu(a))\})$$
$$= \ldots \text{expand } CP[\![\Lambda]\!] \text{ in lhs:}$$
$$\quad \textbf{if } (\varepsilon_r^w \odot \varepsilon_w)[\![v]\!](\mu(a)) = (\text{TRUE}, v) \tag{59}$$
$$\quad \textbf{then } \mu + \{a \mapsto \varepsilon_w[\![v]\!](\mu(a))\}$$
$$\quad \textbf{else } \mu + \{a \mapsto \varepsilon_w[\![v]\!](\mu(a))\}$$
$$= \ldots \text{collapse } \textbf{if}\text{-expression as both arms are identical:}$$
$$\mu + \{a \mapsto \varepsilon_w[\![v]\!](\mu(a))\} \tag{60}$$

The lhs is equal to the rhs above, by the definition of CP (33), thus completing this case.

Case ς_w to $<\varepsilon_w, \varepsilon_r^p> \frown \varsigma_w$: We assume that

$$CP[\![\varsigma_w]\!](a,v) = CP[\![\varsigma_w \frown <\varepsilon_r^w>]\!](a,v)$$

and then show that

$$CP[\![<\varepsilon_w, \varepsilon_r^p> \frown \varsigma_w]\!](a,v)\mu = CP[\![<\varepsilon_w, \varepsilon_r^p> \frown \varsigma_w \frown <\varepsilon_r^w>]\!](a,v)\mu \tag{61}$$

where ε_r^p is another lifted Read Event. We first reduce the lhs:

$$CP[\![<\varepsilon_w, \varepsilon_r^p> \,^\frown\varsigma_w]\!](a,v)\mu \tag{62}$$

$$= \ldots \text{expand } CP:$$

$$\textbf{if } (\varepsilon_r^p \odot \varepsilon_w)[\![v]\!](\mu(a)) = (\text{TRUE}, v) \tag{63}$$

$$\textbf{then } \mu + \{a \mapsto \varepsilon_w[\![v]\!](\mu(a))\}$$

$$\textbf{else } CP[\![\varsigma_w]\!](a,v)(\mu + \{a \mapsto \varepsilon_w[\![v]\!](\mu(a))\})$$

We then reduce the rhs:

$$CP[\![<\varepsilon_w, \varepsilon_r^p> \,^\frown\varsigma_w\,^\frown <\varepsilon_r^w>]\!](a,v)\mu \tag{64}$$

$$= \ldots \text{expand } CP:$$

$$\textbf{if } (\varepsilon_r^p \odot \varepsilon_w)[\![v]\!](\mu(a)) = (\text{TRUE}, v) \tag{65}$$

$$\textbf{then } \mu + \{a \mapsto \varepsilon_w[\![v]\!](\mu(a))\}$$

$$\textbf{else } CP[\![\varsigma_w\,^\frown <\varepsilon_r^w>]\!](a,v)(\mu + \{a \mapsto \varepsilon_w[\![v]\!](\mu(a))\})$$

$$= \ldots \text{use induction hypothesis on } \textbf{else}\text{-clause:}$$

$$\textbf{if } (\varepsilon_r^p \odot \varepsilon_w)[\![v]\!](\mu(a)) = (\text{TRUE}, v) \tag{66}$$

$$\textbf{then } \mu + \{a \mapsto \varepsilon_w[\![v]\!](\mu(a))\}$$

$$\textbf{else } CP[\![\varsigma_w]\!](a,v)(\mu + \{a \mapsto \varepsilon_w[\![v]\!](\mu(a))\})$$

We see that the condition, then-clauses and the else-clauses in the lhs and rhs are the same. This completes the proof.

7 Appendix C - The $\odot$ Operator

There are some reasons for considering this operator in more depth. The first is the observation already made, that it generalises function composition from the standard case:

$$\_\circ\_ : (A \to B) \times (B \to C) \to A \to C \tag{67}$$

to one where some curried arguments are carried through:

$$\_\odot\_\_ \quad : \quad (XAB \times X \times YBC) \to YAC$$
$$\textbf{where } XAB = X \to A \to B$$
$$\textbf{and } YBC = Y \to B \to C$$
$$\textbf{and } YAC = Y \to A \to C$$

This operator and related ones are discussed at length in (Butterfield 1992a)

The second reason for considering the operator concerns describing the behaviour of Mealy finite-state machines (Holcombe, 1982 §2.5) in the following way: Let Q denotes the set of states, Σ the set of inputs and Θ the set of outputs. We denote the next-state function as $N : \Sigma \to Q \to Q$ and the output function as $Y : \Sigma \to Q \to \Theta$. Given the current state q and input σ, then the next state and output are given by

$$(q', \theta) = (N[\![\sigma]\!]q, Y[\![\sigma]\!]q) \tag{68}$$

The $\odot$ operator can be used to describe the next output (θ) of the machine resulting from inputting σ after a sequence of inputs $< \sigma_1, \ldots, \sigma_n >$ applied to some starting state q_0, as follows:

$$\theta = (Y \odot_{\sigma_n} N \odot_{\sigma_{n-1}} \cdots \odot_{\sigma_1} N)[\![\sigma]\!]q_0 \qquad (69)$$

What is interesting here is that the expression in parentheses has the signature of, and behaves like the output function Y, except that it refers to a earlier state and takes account of the intervening input sequence.

References

Andrews, D.: Data Reification and Program Decomposition, in *VDM '87 VDM — A Formal Method at Work*, Volume 252 of *Lecture Notes in Computer Science*, pp 389–422, Springer Verlag, 1987.

Bjørner, D., Jones, C. B. Eds: *The Vienna Development Method: The Meta-Language*, Volume 61 of *Lecture Notes in Computer Science*, Springer Verlag, 1978.

Bjørner, D., et al. Eds: *VDM '87 VDM — A Formal Method at Work*, Volume 252 of *Lecture Notes in Computer Science*, Springer Verlag, 1987.

Butterfield, A.: on Curried Function Composition. Technical Report TCD-CS-92-15, Dept. of Comp. Science, Trinity College, Dublin, May 1992.

Butterfield, A.: Formal memory models — a formal analysis using $VDM^{\clubsuit}$. Technical Report TCD-CS-92-27, Dept. of Comp. Science, Trinity College, Dublin, April 1992.

Butterfield, A.: on Mapped Reduction. Technical Report, Dept. of Comp. Science, Trinity College, Dublin, to appear 1993.

Butterfield, A.: The Careful Memory abstraction in Stable Storage. Technical Report, Dept. of Comp. Science, Trinity College, Dublin, to appear 1993.

Curry, H. B., Feys, R. *Combinatory Logic*, Volume 1. North Holland, Amsterdam, 1958.

Holcombe, W., M., L.: *Algebraic automata theory*, Cambridge University Press, 1982.

Johnson, B. W.: *Design and Analysis of Fault Tolerant Digital Systems*. Series in Electrical and Computer Engineering. Addison Wesley, 1989.

Jones, C. B.: VDM Proof Obligations and their Justification, in *VDM '87 VDM — A Formal Method at Work*, Volume 252 of *Lecture Notes in Computer Science*, pp 260–286, Springer Verlag, 1987.

Jones, C. B.: *Systematic Software Development using VDM, 2nd Ed.*. Series in Computer Science. Prentice Hall, 1990.

Lampson, B. W.: Atomic transactions. In *Distributed Systems, Architecture and Implementation: an Advanced Course*, Volume 105 of *Lecture Notes in Computer Science*, Chapter 11, pages 246–265. Springer Verlag, 1981.

Mac an Airchinnigh, M.: Mathematical Structures and their Morphisms in META-IV, in *VDM '87 VDM — A Formal Method at Work*, Volume 252 of *Lecture Notes in Computer Science*, pp 287–320, Springer Verlag, 1987.

Mac an Airchinnigh, M.: *Conceptual Models and Computing*. PhD thesis, Dept. of Comp. Sci,, Trinity College Dublin, Ireland, 1990.

Mac an Airchinnigh, M.: The Irish School of VDM. In *VDM '91*, Volume 552 of *Lecture Notes in Computer Science*. Springer Verlag, 1991.

Schonfinkel, M.: Über die bausteine der mathematischen logik. *Mathematische Annalen*, 92:305–16, 1924.

Applications of Modal Logic for the Specification of Real-Time Systems*

Liang Chen and Alistair Munro

Centre for Communications Research
University of Bristol
Queen's Building
Bristol BS8 1TR, Great Britain

Abstract. We propose a real-time modal logic with recursion for the specification of real-time systems. All modalities of Timed Computational Tree Logic (TCTL) are definable in it. We also present a model checker, a tableau system, which allows us to test whether or not a real-time system expressed as a timed transition system has or satisfies a property given by a formula in a finite model. The tableau system is independent of the choice of time domain, allowing time to be discrete or dense.

1 Introduction

In real-time systems, the interactions with the environment must satisfy some hard time constraints. It is not sufficient only to say events occur or eventually occur, there are lower and upper bounds on when events can occur relative to other events. Typical examples of real-time systems are fault-tolerant systems, including protocols, and safety critical systems, such as radiation exposure or flight control systems. However, traditional methods for reasoning about nondeterministic or concurrent systems, such as [HM85, Mil89, Lar88, SW89], do not consider hard time aspects of systems. Instead they deal with the quantitative aspects of time in a qualitative way and abstract away explicit time information. Clearly, purely qualitative specification and analysis of real-time systems are inadequate. In this paper, we extend these techniques by incorporating time explicitly to reason about quantitative as well as qualitative timing behaviour of systems.

Transition systems are used as models for nondeterministic and concurrent systems. By augmenting them with explicit time information, we obtain timed transition systems for modelling real-time systems. We make no assumption about the underlying nature of time, allowing it to be discrete, for example the natural numbers, or dense, such as the non-negative real numbers. In order to present timed transition systems succinctly, we may appeal to languages of real-time process algebras [Che92, MT90].

Hennessy-Milner Logic is intended to specify the desired properties of nondeterministic or concurrent systems. However, every individual formula of it is only

---

* The work is supported by grant GR/G54399 of the Science and Engineering Research Council of the UK.

capable of describing properties of a certain finite behaviour of systems. By extending Hennessy-Milner Logic with recursion [Lar88], the resulting language is very powerful and allows us to describe temporal properties, such as safety and liveness properties, of systems. In this paper, we augment Hennessy-Milner Logic further with explicit time information and the resulting language (called TML) allows us to specify the desired properties, such as bound-response and bound-invariance properties, of real-time systems. Again, we have no assumption about the underlying nature of time, allowing it to be discrete or dense.

One of the most successful techniques for automatic verification of finite state systems is model checking: testing whether or not a particular state or process has or satisfies a property given as a formula. We present a model checker, a tableau system, which allows us to determine the truth of a formula of TML with respect to a timed transition system. Our tableau system is an extension of that of [SW89] with time constraint lists. The time constraint lists of the tableau system are used to deal with free time variables of processes and formulas. The tableau system is independent of the choice of time domain.

In section 2, we define timed transition systems to model real-time systems. To simplify the presentation of timed transition systems, we appeal to a sublanguage of Timed CCS. We describe its syntax together with rules for generating transitions. In section 3, we describe the syntax and semantics of TML, a timed extension of Hennessy-Milner logic with recursion. We show in section 4 that the formulas of TML can be used to specify the typical properties of real-time systems, such as the bound-response and bound-invariance properties. All modalities of TCTL [ACD90] are definable in TML. In section 5, we present the model checker as a tableau system and show by an example how to use it in the analysis of real-time systems.

2   Computational Model

Our computational model is absolutely timed transition systems which are extensions of transition systems with time, where an absolutely timed transition system

$$\mathcal{S} = (S, s_0, t_0, \cup\{\xrightarrow{a}_t \ : \ a \in Act \ \& \ t \in \mathcal{T}\})$$

consists of the following components:

1. A set S of states.
2. A time domain $(\mathcal{T}, \leq)$. We make no assumption about the time domain, allowing it to be discrete or dense. For example, we allow $\mathcal{T}$ to be $\aleph$, the set of natural numbers, or $\Re^{\geq 0}$, the set of non-negative real numbers.
3. An initial state $s_0 \in S$.
4. An initial time $t_0 \in \mathcal{T}$ of a global clock which represents the starting time of the machine.
5. A set Act of actions which the machine under consideration may perform.
6. For each $a \in Act$ and each $t \in \mathcal{T}$, there is a transition relation $\xrightarrow{a}_t$ over the set $S \times \mathcal{T}$ of timed states. A timed state (s, t) is a pair of a state and a clock. We write $(s, t) \xrightarrow{a}_{t''} (s', t')$ in place of $((s, t), (s', t')) \in \xrightarrow{a}_{t''}$. For any transition of the form $(s, t) \xrightarrow{a}_{t''} (s', t')$, we require that $t \leq t'' \leq t'$, which means that time

always progresses. Note that we use a weak condition $t'' \leq t'$ instead of $t' = t''$ here, as some machines need some time to evolve to next states after actions. The understanding of the transition $(s, t) \xrightarrow{a}_{t''}(s', t')$ is that when the machine under consideration is in state s and at time t, it can perform an action a at some future time t'', where $t \leq t''$, and after performing action a at time t'' it evolves to a state s' at another future time t', $t'' \leq t'$, i.e. it evolves to a timed state (s', t').

Sometimes it is convenient to use relatively timed transition systems, especially when we want to use diagrams to represent timed transition systems. A relatively timed transition system

$$S = (S, s_0, \cup\{\xrightarrow{a}_t \ : a \in Act \ \& \ t \in T\})$$

contains the following components:

1. A set S of states.
2. A time domain $(T, \leq)$.
3. An initial state $s_0 \in S$.
4. A set Act of actions.
5. For each $a \in Act$ and $t \in T$, there is a transition relation $\xrightarrow{a}_t$ over S. The understanding of transition $s \xrightarrow{a}_t s'$ is that the machine under consideration can perform action a at a relative time t when it is in a state s and then evolves to a new state s' after doing so.

There is a close relation between absolutely and relatively timed transition systems. For any relatively timed transition system, we can construct its corresponding absolutely timed transition system for any initial time. For example, for a relatively timed transition system

$$S = (S, s_0, \cup\{\xrightarrow{a}_t \ : a \in Act \ \& \ t \in T\})$$

its corresponding absolutely timed transition system for any initial time $t_0 \in T$

$$S' = (S, s_0, t_0, \cup\{\xrightarrow{a}_t \ : a \in Act \ \& \ t \in T\})$$

is the least transition system which satisfies that

- for any transitions $s_0 \xrightarrow{a}_t s$ of S, there is a transition $(s_0, t_0) \xrightarrow{a}_{t+t_0}(s, t + t_0)$ in S';
- for any transition $s' \xrightarrow{a}_{t''} s''$ of S and transition $(s, t) \xrightarrow{a}_{t'}(s', t')$ of S', there is a transition $(s', t') \xrightarrow{a}_{t'+t''}(s'', t' + t'')$ in S'

Timed transition systems (of limited states and branches) may also be presented diagrammatically. As an example, Fig.1 depicts a relatively timed transition system for a vending machine V, with the set of states $\{s_0, s_1, s_2, s_3\}$, the set of labels $\{coin, refund, collect, choice\}$, and transition relations which satisfy

- for each $t \in [0, \infty)$, we have $s_0 \xrightarrow{coin}_t s_1$;
- for each $t \in [0.1, 5]$, we have $s_1 \xrightarrow{choice}_t s_2$;

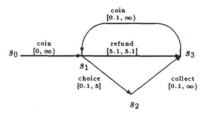

Fig.1. Vending Machine V

- $s_1 \xrightarrow{refund} {}_{5.1} s_3$;
- for each $t \in [0.1, \infty)$, we have $s_2 \xrightarrow{collect} {}_t s_3$; and
- for each $t \in [0.1, \infty)$, we have $s_3 \xrightarrow{coin} {}_t s_1$.

The vending machine V can receive a coin at any time whenever it is in the initial state s_0 or at any time $t \geq 0.1$ whenever it is in state s_3. After accepting a coin from a user, the machine evolves to state s_1 and waits for the user to press a choice button (for tea or coffee). If the user does not press the choice button within 5 minutes, the machine refunds the coin at 5.1 minutes and then evolve to state s_3. If, however, the user presses the choice button within 5 minutes, he can collect his tea or coffee at any time $t \geq 0.1$ (the machine needs 0.1 minutes to prepare the drink). After the user collects his drink, the machine evolves to state s_3 and waits to serve other people.

Pictures of timed transition systems can become very large and unwieldy. It is therefore necessary to have succinct presentations of them. A general technique for achieving this is to have a language of expressions for states, together with rules for generating transitions between states. For instance, to describe the vending machine V we could appeal to the language of Timed CCS [Che92]

$$V \overset{\text{def}}{=} coin(r)_0^\infty . V_1$$

$$V_1 \overset{\text{def}}{=} choice(s)_{0.1}^5 . collect(t)_{0.1}^\infty . V_2 + refund(s)_{5.1}^{5.1} . V_2$$

$$V_2 \overset{\text{def}}{=} coin(r)_{0.1}^\infty . V_1$$

We are employing here a sublanguage of Timed CCS. To give a formal description for the language, we presuppose a set Act of actions, ranged over by a, b. We also suppose a set V_t of time variables which is ranged over by x, y. The process expressions of the language are defined by the following BNF expression:

$$P ::= \delta \mid a(x)_e^{e'} . P \mid P + Q \mid U$$

where e, e' are time expressions or e' is the infinite time ∞, and U is a constant. For each constant U, there is an associated equation of the form $U \overset{\text{def}}{=} P$. Our time expressions are those arithmetic expressions over T which only contain the operators

$+$, $-$, min and max (see [Che92] for the definition). The decidability result of real-time calculi [Che92] has justified our decisions on the choice of time expressions.

The prefix operator $a(x)_e^{e'}$ in $a(x)_e^{e'}.P$ binds all free occurrences of time variable x in P. This gives us, in the usual sense, the notions of free and bound occurrences of time variables.

Process δ is a dead process which cannot engage in any action. Prefix $a(x)_e^{e'}.P$ represents a process which can perform action a at (relative) time t, where $e \leq t \leq e'$, and then evolves to process $P\{t/x\}$, where $P\{t/x\}$ represents the result of substituting all free occurrences of x in P by t. Note that time expressions e and e' express the lower bound and upper bound of action a, respectively. As an example, process $a(x)_0^\infty. b(y)_5^{25}. \delta$ can perform action a followed by action b. Action a can occur at any time t, where $0 \leq t \leq \infty$. After action a occurs, action b can occur at any time of the interval $5 \leq t \leq 25$. The time interval $5 \leq t \leq 25$ of action b is relative to the happening time of action a. For prefix, we have the following transition relation

$$a(x)_e^{e'}. P \xrightarrow{a}_t P\{t/x\} \quad \text{where} \quad e \leq t \leq e'$$

Time variables of the language allow us to express a notion of time dependency, which means that time for some actions depend on the happening time of their previous actions. For example, a machine which can perform action a at any time and if a occurs at time t, then action b must occur within another t time, can be expressed as process $a(x)_0^\infty. b(y)_0^x. \delta$. Summation $P + Q$ represents a process which can behave as processes P or Q. The choice is made at the time of the first action of P or Q. For summation, we have the following transition rules

$$\frac{P \xrightarrow{a}_t P'}{P + Q \xrightarrow{a}_t P'} \qquad\qquad \frac{P \xrightarrow{a}_t P'}{Q + P \xrightarrow{a}_t P'}$$

Constant declaration $U \stackrel{\text{def}}{=} P$ declares that the process constant U to be the process P. It allows us to define infinite processes. For constant declaration, we have the following transition rule

$$\frac{P \xrightarrow{a}_t P'}{U \xrightarrow{a}_t P'} \qquad U \stackrel{\text{def}}{=} P$$

A process Q is said to be a derivative of a process P if there is a sequence of transitions of the form

$$P \xrightarrow{a_1}_{t_1} \cdots \xrightarrow{a_n}_{t_n} Q$$

We use $\mathcal{D}(P)$ to represent the set of all derivatives of P. Note that any process is a derivative of itself, i.e. $P \in \mathcal{D}(P)$. It is easy to see that for any process P, there is a relatively timed transition system

$$(\mathcal{D}(P), P, \cup\{\xrightarrow{a}_t \ : a \in Act \ \& \ t \in T\})$$

where $\xrightarrow{a}_t$ is the least transition relation over $\mathcal{D}(P)$ which is defined by the above transition relation and transition rules, to correspond to it.

3 Modal Logic

3.1 A Timed Modal Logic

Hennessy-Milner Logic [HM85] is used to describe behaviour of nondeterministic and concurrent systems. By extending it with time, we obtain a timed modal logic, called TML, which can be used to describe behaviour of real-time systems. We still make no assumption about the underlying nature of time, allowing it to be discrete or dense. The formulas of the modal language are defined by the following BNF expression:

$$A ::= tt \mid ff \mid A \vee B \mid A \wedge B \mid \langle a \rangle x.(e \triangleright x \triangleleft e' \wedge A) \mid [a]x.(e \triangleright x \triangleleft e' \longrightarrow A)$$

where e is a time expression, e' is a time expression or ∞, x is a time variable, $\triangleright$ and $\triangleleft$ are $<$ or $\leq$, and $a \in Act$. We use ∞ to represent the infinite time. By convention, we have $t < \infty$ for any $t \in T$.

For convenience, we will write A in place of $tt \wedge A$ or $ff \vee A$. For any variable x, we always have $0 \leq x < \infty$. As a result, we will write tt in place of $0 \leq x < \infty$. We further write A in place of $tt \longrightarrow A$.

The intended meaning of the formula $\langle a \rangle x.(e \triangleright x \triangleleft e' \wedge A)$ is that there is an action a which occurs at time x, where $e \triangleright x \triangleleft e'$, and after that the formula A holds. The formula $[a]x.(e \triangleright x \triangleleft e' \longrightarrow A)$ means that after every a action which occurs at time x, where $e \triangleright x \triangleleft e'$, A holds. For the formulas $\langle a \rangle x.(e \triangleright x \triangleleft e' \wedge A)$ and $[a]x.(e \triangleright x \triangleleft e' \longrightarrow A)$, all free occurrences of time variable x in A are bound by $\langle a \rangle x$ and $[a]x$, respectively. These give, in the usual sense, the notions of free and bound occurrences of time variables of formulas. We identify those formulas which are the same up to the change of bound time variables. We say a formula is a sentence if it contains no free occurrences of time variables. Let $\mathcal{L}$ be the set of all sentences defined by the above BNF expression which is still ranged over by A, B.

An important feature of the TML is that its operators are monotonic with respect to subset inclusion. This feature will be exploited when we consider recursively defined formulas based on modal equations.

The formulas of $\mathcal{L}$ are interpreted over absolutely timed transition systems. Given an absolutely timed transition system

$$\mathcal{S} = (S, s_0, t_0, \cup\{\xrightarrow{a}_t \; : \; a \in Act \, \& \, t \in T\})$$

we say $\mathcal{S}$ has a property $A \in \mathcal{L}$ if the initial timed state (s_0, t_0) has or satisfies the property A. A timed state (s, t) of $S \times T$ is said to have the property $A \in \mathcal{L}$, written as $s, \, t \models A$, if $(s, t) \in \|A\|$, where $\|A\|$ is inductively defined as follows:

1. $\|tt\| = S \times T$;
2. $\|A \wedge B\| = \|A\| \cap \|B\|$;
3. $\|A \vee B\| = \|A\| \cup \|B\|$;
4. $\|\langle a \rangle x.(e \triangleright x \triangleleft e' \wedge A)\| = \{(s,t) \in S \times T \; : \; \exists (s',t') \in S \times T \exists t'' \in T.e \triangleright t'' \triangleleft e'$
   $\wedge (s,t) \xrightarrow{a}_{t''} (s',t') \wedge (s',t') \in \|A\{t''/x\}\|\}$; and
5. $\|[a]x.(e \triangleright x \triangleleft e' \longrightarrow A)\| = \{(s,t) \in S \times T \; : \; \forall (s',t') \in S \times T \forall t'' \in T.$
   $((s,t) \xrightarrow{a}_{t''} (s',t') \wedge e \triangleright t'' \triangleleft e' \longrightarrow (s',t') \in \|A\{t''/x\}\|)\}$.

The formulas of $\mathcal{L}$ can also be interpreted over relatively timed transition systems. Given a relatively timed transition system $\mathcal{S}$, let $\mathcal{S}_t$ represent its corresponding absolutely timed transition system for an initial time t. We say a relatively timed transition system $\mathcal{S}$ has a property $A \in \mathcal{L}$ if its corresponding absolutely timed transition system $\mathcal{S}_t$ for any initial time $t \in T$ has the property A.

We will also allow slightly generalized formulas of the form $\langle K \rangle x.(e \rhd x \lhd e' \wedge A)$ and $[K]x.(e \rhd x \lhd e' \longrightarrow A)$, where $K \subseteq Act$. The meaning of $\langle K \rangle x.(e \rhd x \lhd e' \wedge A)$ is that there is some action of K which occurs at time x, where $e \rhd x \lhd e'$, and after that the formula A holds. Similarly, the meaning of the formula $[K]x.(e \rhd x \lhd e' \longrightarrow A)$ is that after every action of K which occurs at time x, where $e \rhd x \lhd e'$, the formula A holds. So $(s,t) \in \|\langle K \rangle x.(e \rhd x \lhd e' \wedge A)\|$ if and only if there are some $a \in K$, $t'' \in T$ and $(s',t') \in S \times T$ such that $(s,t) \xrightarrow{a}_{t''} (s',t')$, $e \rhd t'' \lhd e'$ and $(s',t') \in \|A\{t''/x\}\|$. In contrast, $(s,t) \in \|[K]x.(e \rhd x \lhd e' \longrightarrow A)\|$ if and only if for any $a \in K$, $t'' \in T$ and $(s',t') \in S \times T$, if $(s,t) \xrightarrow{a}_{t''} (s',t')$, where $e \rhd t'' \lhd e'$, then $(s',t') \in \|A\{t''/x\}\|$. Intuitively, the formula $\langle K \rangle x.(e \rhd x \lhd e' \wedge A)$ is logically equivalent to the formula

$$\bigvee_{a \in K} \langle a \rangle x.(e \rhd x \lhd e' \wedge A)$$

and the formula $[K]x.(e \rhd x \lhd e' \longrightarrow A)$ is equivalent to the formula

$$\bigwedge_{a \in K} [a]x.(e \rhd x \lhd e' \longrightarrow A)$$

For simplicity, we will write $[a_1, \cdots, a_n]$ (or $\langle a_1, \cdots, a_n \rangle$) in place of $[\{a_1, \cdots, a_n\}]$ (or $\langle\{a_1, \cdots, a_n\}\rangle$), $[-K]$ (or $\langle -K \rangle$) in place of $[Act - K]$ (or $\langle Act - K \rangle$) and $[\cdot]$ (or $\langle \cdot \rangle$) in place of $[Act]$ (or $\langle Act \rangle$).

The simple formula $\langle a \rangle x.(e \rhd x \lhd e')$ expresses a capability of performing the action a at time x, where $e \rhd x \lhd e'$. In contrast, the formula $[a]x.(e \rhd x \lhd e' \longrightarrow ff)$ expresses an inability of performing the action a at any time x, where $e \rhd x \lhd e'$. For the vending machine of Fig.1, its property that it can only receive a coin as a start and it must receive a coin as a start can be defined by

$$s_0, t \models \langle \cdot \rangle x.tt \wedge [-coin]x.ff$$

for any initial time $t \in T$.

3.2   Temporal Properties and Modal Equations

Clearly any single formula of $\mathcal{L}$ only describes a certain finite part of a system. Temporal properties, like safety and liveness properties, are not expressible by individual formulas of the modal logic. A safety property amounts to nothing bad ever happens while a liveness property expresses something good does eventually happen. The crucial safety property of a mutual exclusion algorithm is that no two processes are ever in their critical section at the same time. An important liveness property is that whenever a process requests execution of its critical section, it will eventually be granted.

In order to capture those temporal properties, we need infinite sets of formulas of $\mathcal{L}$. For instance, to capture a typical bound response property of the bound response machine M of Fig.2, we need an infinite set of formulas: $\{\langle a \rangle x.tt \wedge [a]x.\langle b \rangle y.x \leq y \leq 15 + x, [a]x.[b]y.(x \leq y \leq 15 + x \longrightarrow \langle a \rangle x.tt) \wedge [a]x.\langle b \rangle y.x \leq y \leq 15 + x, \cdots\}$. So we extend the timed modal logic by allowing recursively defined formulas based on modal equations. The resulting timed modal logic, still called TML, is very powerful. We examine this logic and show how it can be used to express properties of real-time systems.

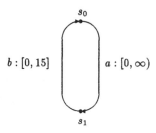

Fig.2. Bound-Response Machine M

Consider a modal equation of the form $Z = A$ which can be viewed as expressing various properties of timed transition systems. Each of these properties is determined by a solution of the equation. There are in general infinitely many solutions for the above equation. However we are especially interested in its maximal solution, the largest solution with respect to subset relation $\subseteq$, and the minimal solution, the smallest one.

Given a modal equation $Z = A$ and a timed transition system S, let

$$Z_0 = ff \qquad Z_{n+1} = A\{Z_n/Z\} \quad n = 0, 1, \cdots$$

where $A\{Z_n/Z\}$ is the modal formula resulted by replacing all free occurrences of Z in A by Z_n. We say a timed state (s,t) of S has the property which is expressed by the minimal solution of $Z = A$ if (s,t) has a property expressed by Z_n for some $n \geq 0$. In contrast, let

$$Z^0 = tt \qquad Z^{n+1} = A\{Z^n/Z\} \quad n = 0, 1, \cdots$$

We say a timed state (s,t) of S has the property expressed by the maximal solution of $Z = A$ if (s,t) has the property expressed by Z^n for all $n \geq 0$.

It is easy to see that any modal equation of the form $Z = A$ has solutions. Therefore it has the minimal solution, the intersection of all its solutions, and the maximal solution, the union of all its solutions. For convenience, we will use $\mu Z.A$ and $\nu Z.A$ to represent the minimal and maximal solutions of the modal equation $Z = A$, respectively.

To interpret the extended formulas (extended with recursively defined formulas) over absolutely timed transition systems, we need a notion of valuations to deal with propositional variables. Given an absolutely timed transition system S, a valuation V

assigns a set of timed states of $\mathcal{S}$ to each propositional variable. For any valuation $\mathcal{V}$, we use $\mathcal{V}[S'/Z]$ to represent a new valuation which agrees with $\mathcal{V}$ at all propositional variables except Z, where it has the value S'.

We say a timed state (s, t) of $\mathcal{S}$ satisfies or has a property A under a valuation $\mathcal{V}$, written as $s,\ t \models_{\mathcal{V}} A$, if $(s, t) \in \|A\|_{\mathcal{V}}$ where $\|A\|_{\mathcal{V}}$ is inductively defined as follows:

1. $\|Z\|_{\mathcal{V}} = \mathcal{V}(Z)$;
2. $\|tt\|_{\mathcal{V}} = S \times T$;
3. $\|A \wedge B\|_{\mathcal{V}} = \|A\|_{\mathcal{V}} \cap \|B\|_{\mathcal{V}}$;
4. $\|A \vee B\|_{\mathcal{V}} = \|A\|_{\mathcal{V}} \cup \|B\|_{\mathcal{V}}$;
5. $\|\langle a \rangle x.(e \triangleright x \triangleleft e' \wedge A)\|_{\mathcal{V}} = \{(s, t) \in S \times T \ : \ \exists (s', t') \in S \times T \exists t'' \in T.$
   $\quad (e \triangleright t'' \triangleleft e' \wedge (s, t) \xrightarrow{a}_{t''} (s', t') \wedge (s', t') \in \|A\{t''/x\}\|_{\mathcal{V}})\}$;
6. $\|[a]x.(e \triangleright x \triangleleft e' \longrightarrow A)\|_{\mathcal{V}} = \{(s, t) \in S \times T \ : \ \forall (s', t') \in S \times T \forall t'' \in T.$
   $\quad (e \triangleright t'' \triangleleft e' \wedge (s, t) \xrightarrow{a}_{t''} (s', t') \text{ implies } (s', t') \in \|A\{t''/x\}\|_{\mathcal{V}})\}$;
7. $\|\mu Z.A\|_{\mathcal{V}} = \bigcap \{P' \subseteq S \times T \ : \ \|A\|_{\mathcal{V}}[P'/Z] \subseteq P'\}$; and
8. $\|\nu Z.A\|_{\mathcal{V}} = \bigcup \{P' \subseteq S \times T \ : \ P' \subseteq \|A\|_{\mathcal{V}}[P'/Z]\}$

An absolutely timed transition system is said to have a property under a valuation if its initial timed state has the property under the same valuation. A relatively timed transition system has a property under a valuation if its corresponding absolutely timed transition system for any initial time has the property under the same valuation. For the closed formulas, i.e. those without free occurrences of propositional variables, their meanings are independent of valuations. In other words, if A is a closed formula, then $\|A\|_{\mathcal{V}} = \|A\|_{\mathcal{V}'}$ for any valuations $\mathcal{V}$ and $\mathcal{V}'$. So we can use the notation $s,\ t \models A$ to represent that the timed state (s, t) satisfies or has the property A under any valuation $\mathcal{V}$ whenever A is a closed formula.

The bound response property of the bound-response machine M of Fig.2, which says that after every occurrence of action a the action b will eventually occur with 15 minutes, can be defined recursively as

$$s_0, t_0 \models \nu Z.[a]x.\langle b \rangle y.(x \leq y \leq x + 15) \wedge [.]x.Z$$

for any initial time $t_0 \in T$.

4 Specifications of Real-Time System

The formulas of TML can be used to describe behaviour of real-time systems. We can express capabilities and necessities of a system performing some actions as formulas. As an example, a simple formula $\langle a \rangle x.e \triangleright x \triangleleft e'$ expresses a capability of performing the action a at some time x of the interval $e \triangleright x \triangleleft e'$ while a simple formula $[a]x.(e \triangleright x \triangleleft e' \longrightarrow ff)$ expresses an inability of performing the action a within the time interval $e \triangleright x \triangleleft e'$. If we think of safety as that no bad states, which has the undesired property A, will be reached, then the safety can be expressed as a formula $\nu Z.\neg A \wedge [\cdot]x.Z$. A typical example of safety for a system is that it never evolves to a deadlocked state. A liveness property of a system that it will eventually evolve to some good state which has a desired property A can be expressed as a formula

$$\mu Z.A \vee (\langle \cdot \rangle x.tt \wedge [\cdot]x.Z)$$

More important properties for real-time systems are bound-response and bound-invariance properties. A bound-response property asserts that something will occur within a certain amount of time. A typical example is to express the requirement of the timed response of an action b to an action a within at most time e, which can be expressed as a modal formula:

$$\nu X.([a]x.\mu Y.(\langle b\rangle y.x \le y \le e + x \wedge [-b]y.Y) \wedge [\cdot]x.X)$$

A bound invariance property asserts that something will hold continuously for a certain amount of time. A typical example is that after an action a occurs, action b cannot occur within time e. We can express this property by the modal formula:

$$\nu X.[a]x.\nu Y.([b]y.(x \le y \le e + x \longrightarrow f\!f) \wedge [\cdot]y.(y \le x + e \longrightarrow Y)) \wedge [\cdot]x.X$$

Example: A general property of the vending machine V of Fig.1 is that whenever a coin is deposited and the choice button is pressed at a right time then tea or coffee can eventually be collected. This property can be expressed as a formula:

$$\nu Z.[coin]x.([choice]y.(x + 0.1 \le y \le x + 5 \longrightarrow A)) \wedge [\cdot]x.Z$$

where $A = \mu Y.\langle collect\rangle z.(z \ge y + 0.1) \wedge [-collect]z.Y$

The TML is a very powerful specification language for real-time systems. We can define all modalities of Timed Computational Tree Logic (TCTL) of [ACD90]. To do so, we first introduce a notion of computations of a transition system. Given an absolutely timed transition system $S = (S, s_0, t_0, \bigcup\{\stackrel{a}{\longrightarrow}_t : a \in Act \,\&\, t \in T\}$, we say a sequence of timed states of the form

$$(s_0, t_0)\stackrel{a_1}{\longrightarrow}_{t_1'} \cdots \stackrel{a_n}{\longrightarrow}_{t_n'}(s_n, t_n)\stackrel{a_{n+1}}{\longrightarrow}_{t_{n+1}'} \cdots$$

is a computation if it is a maximal one. The maximality means that if the sequence is finite then the final timed state (s_n, t_n) is deadlock, i.e. there are no $a \in Act$ and $t \in T$ such that $(s_n, t_n)\stackrel{a}{\longrightarrow}_t(s', t')$ for some timed state (s', t').

1. $\forall\Box_e A$: which states the invariance of A up to time e under all computations. We can define the property $\forall\Box_e A$ of S as:

$$\nu Z.A \wedge [\cdot]x.(x \le e + t_0 \longrightarrow Z)$$

2. $\forall\Diamond_e A$: which means that A eventually holds within time e under all computations. We can define property $\forall\Diamond_e A$ of S as:

$$\mu Z.A \vee ([\cdot]x.(x \le e + t_0 \longrightarrow Z) \wedge [\cdot]x.(x \le e + t_0) \wedge \langle\cdot\rangle x.(x \le e + t_0))$$

3. $\exists\Box_e A$: which means that there are some computations on which the formula A holds up to time e:

$$\nu Z.A \wedge (\langle\cdot\rangle x.(x \le e + t_0 \wedge Z) \vee [\cdot]x.(x \le e + t_0 \longrightarrow f\!f))$$

4. $\exists\Diamond_e A$: which means that there are some computations such that the formula A will hold eventually within time e:

$$\mu Z.A \vee \langle\cdot\rangle x.(x \le e + t_0 \wedge Z)$$

5. $\exists A\mathcal{U}_e B$: which means that there are some computations such that the formula B will hold eventually within time e, and the formula A will continuously hold until B holds:

$$\mu Z.B \vee (A \wedge \langle \cdot \rangle x.(x \le e + t_0 \wedge Z))$$

6. $\forall A\mathcal{U}_e B$: which means that for all computations the formula B will hold eventually within time e and the formula A holds continuously until B holds:

$$\mu Z.B \vee (A \wedge [\cdot]x.(x \le e + T \longrightarrow Z) \wedge [\cdot]x.(x \le e + T) \wedge \langle \cdot \rangle x.(x \le e + T))$$

5 The Model Checker

The model checker is a tableau system for testing whether or not a state or a process has the property expressed by a formula in a finite model, where a model is finite if its set of state is finite. In the tableau system, all rules are inverse natural deduction type rules of the form

$$\frac{P,\ t \vdash_{\Delta}^{\Sigma} A}{P_1,\ t_1 \vdash_{\Delta_1}^{\Sigma_1} A_1 \quad \cdots \quad P_{n+1},\ t_{n+1} \vdash_{\Delta_{n+1}}^{\Sigma_{n+1}} A_{n+1}}$$

possibly with some side conditions. The premise sequent $P,\ t \vdash_{\Delta}^{\Sigma} A$ is the goal to be achieved while the consequents are the subgoals. The definition list Δ is a sequence of declarations of the form $U_1 = A_1, \cdots, U_n = A_n$, where $U_i \neq U_j$ whenever $i \neq j$ and each constant occurring in A_i is one of $U_1, \cdots, U_{i-1}$. We let $dem(\Delta) = \{U_1, \cdots, U_n\}$ and $\Delta(U_i) = A_i$. If $U \notin dom(\Delta)$ and every constant occurring in A is in $dem(\Delta)$, then $\Delta \cdot U = A$ is a new definition list resulted by appending $U = A$ to Δ. The definition lists, which were introduced by Stirling and Walker [SW89], are used to keep track of dynamically changing subformulas as fixpoints are unrolled. We will omit Δ when it is empty. The time constraint list Σ is a sequence of time constraints of the form $e_1 \le x_1 \le e_1', \cdots, e_m \le x_m \le e_m'$, where $x_i \neq x_j$ whenever $i \neq j$ and for any $i = 1, \cdots, m$, e_i and e_i' may only contain time variables $x_1, \cdots, x_{i-1}$. Similarly, we let $dem(\Sigma) = \{x_1, \cdots, x_m\}$ and $\Sigma \cdot e \le x \le e'$, where all free time variables of e and e' are in $dem(\Sigma)$, represents a new time constraint list resulted by appending $e \le x \le e'$ to Σ. Time constraint lists are used to deal with time variables of processes and formulas. A similar idea to was used in [Che91] to give a complete proof system for real-time processes. The intended meaning of sequent $P, t \vdash^{\Sigma} A$, where Σ is the sequence $e_1 \le x_1 \le e_1', \cdots, e_m \le x_m \le e_m'$, is that for any $x_1, \cdots, x_m$, if $e_1 \le x_1 \le e_1' \wedge \cdots \wedge e_m \le x_m \le e_m'$ holds and process P starts from an absolute time t, then P has the property A. Similarly, we will drop Σ in the sequent $P, t \vdash_{\Delta}^{\Sigma} A$ when there are no free time variables in process P and formula A.

To present the rules of the tableau system, we first introduce two notations. We use $\|A_\Delta\|_V$ to represent the semantics (or meaning) of the formula A under the valuation V and the definition list Δ. Note that the formula A may contain constants defined in the definition list Δ. We further generalise $\|A_\Delta\|_V$ to formulas which may contain free time variables. We say $(P, t) \in \|A_\Delta^{\Sigma}\|_V$ if for any time instances $u_1, \cdots, u_n$ (we assume $dem(\Sigma) = \{x_1, \cdots, x_n\}$) which satisfy all time constraints in Σ, we have $(P\{u_1/x_1, \cdots, u_n/x_n\}, t) \in \|A\{u_1/x_1, \cdots, u_n/x_n\}_\Delta\|_V$.

Definition 5.1 *If Δ is $U_1 = A_1, \cdots, U_n = A_n$, then $\|A_\Delta\|_V$ is defined to be $\|A\|_{V_n}$, where $V_0 = V$ and $V_{i+1} = V_i[\|A_{i+1}\|_{V_i}/U_{i+1}]$.*

Definition 5.2 *If Σ is $e_1 \leq x_1 \leq e_1', \cdots, e_n \leq x_n \leq e_n'$, then we say $(P, t) \in \|A_\Delta^\Sigma\|_V$ when for all $u_1, \cdots, u_n$, where $(e_1 \leq x_1 \leq e_1' \wedge \cdots \wedge e_n \leq x_n \leq e_n')\{u_1/x_1, \cdots, u_n/x_n\}$ holds, we have $(P\{u_1/x_1, \cdots, u_n/x_n\}, t) \in \|A\{u_1/x_1, \cdots, u_n/x_n\}_\Delta\|_V$.*

To simplify the presentation of the tableau system, we assume in the sequel of this section that for any process of the form $a(x)_e^{e'}.P$ and formula of the form $\langle a \rangle x.(e \rhd x \lhd e' \wedge A)$ or $[a]x.(e \rhd x \lhd e' \longrightarrow A)$ expressions e and e' do not contain time variable x. We also suppose that both $\rhd$ and $\lhd$ are $\leq$. The case for $\rhd$ or $\lhd$ to be $<$ is similar. The rules of the tableau system are given based on the structures of process P and formula A.

– booleans:

1. $$\frac{P,\ t \vdash_\Delta^\Sigma A \vee B}{P,\ t \vdash_\Delta^\Sigma A}$$

2. $$\frac{P,\ t \vdash_\Delta^\Sigma A \vee B}{P,\ t \vdash_\Delta^\Sigma B}$$

3. $$\frac{P,\ t \vdash_\Delta^\Sigma A \wedge B}{P,\ t \vdash_\Delta^\Sigma A \qquad P,\ t \vdash_\Delta^\Sigma B}$$

– summation of processes:

1. $$\frac{P + Q,\ t \vdash_\Delta^\Sigma \langle a \rangle x.(e \leq x \leq e' \wedge A)}{P,\ t \vdash_\Delta^\Sigma \langle a \rangle x.(e \leq x \leq e' \wedge A)}$$

2. $$\frac{P + Q, t \vdash_\Delta^\Sigma \langle a \rangle x.(e \leq x \leq e' \wedge A)}{Q, t \vdash_\Delta^\Sigma \langle a \rangle x.(e \leq x \leq e' \wedge A)}$$

3. $$\frac{P + Q, t \vdash_\Delta^\Sigma [a]x.(e \leq x \leq e' \longrightarrow A)}{P,\ t \vdash_\Delta^\Sigma [a]x.(e \leq x \leq e' \longrightarrow A) \qquad Q,\ t \vdash_\Delta^\Sigma [a]x.(e \leq x \leq e' \longrightarrow A)}$$

– constant declaration:

$$\frac{W,\ t \vdash_\Delta^\Sigma A}{P,\ t \vdash_\Delta^\Sigma A} \qquad W \stackrel{\text{def}}{=} P$$

– prefix and modal operators:

1. $$\frac{a(x)_e^{e'}.P,\ t \vdash_\Delta^\Sigma [a]t.(f \leq y \leq f' \longrightarrow A)}{P\{y - t/x\},\ y \vdash_\Delta^{\Sigma'} A} \qquad \text{where } max(e + t, f) \leq$$

$min(e' + t, f')$ and Σ' is $\Sigma \cdot max(e + t, f) \leq y \leq min(e' + t, f')$

2.
$$\frac{a(x)_e^{e'} \cdot P, \; t \vdash_\Delta^\Sigma \langle a \rangle y.(f \leq y \leq f' \wedge A)}{P\{y - t/x\}, \; y \vdash_\Delta^{\Sigma'} A}$$
where Σ' is $\Sigma \cdot u \leq y \leq u$ for

some u such that $max(e + t, f) \leq u \leq min(e' + t, f')$.

- fixpoint of formulas:

1.
$$\frac{P, \; t \vdash_\Delta^\Sigma \sigma Z.A}{P, \; t \vdash_{\Delta'}^\Sigma U}$$
Δ' is $\Delta \cdot U = \sigma Z.A$ where $\sigma \in \{\mu, \nu\}$

2.
$$\frac{P, \; t \vdash_\Delta^\Sigma U}{P, \; t \vdash_\Delta^\Sigma A\{U/Z\}}$$
$\mathcal{C}$ and $\Delta(U) = \sigma Z.A$ where $\sigma \in \{\mu, \nu\}$

A tableau for $P, \; t \vdash^\Sigma A$ is a maximal proof tree with the root labelled by the sequent $P, \; t \vdash^\Sigma A$. The sequents labelling the immediate successors of a node are determined by applying one of the rules, dependent on the structures of P and A. Maximality here means that no rule applies to a sequent labelling a leaf of the tableau. We say a node labelled by sequent $P, \; t\vdash_\Delta^\Sigma A$ is true if $(P, t) \in \|A_\Delta^\Sigma\|$.

The rules for booleans, summation of processes and fixpoint of processes are straightforward. The rules for prefix and modal operators follow from the transition rules of timed processes. New constants are introduced in the case of fixpoint formulas, while the rules for constants unroll the fixpoints they abbreviate when condition $\mathcal{C}$ holds. The condition $\mathcal{C}$ is just that no node above the current premise, say $P, t\vdash_\Delta^\Sigma U$, in the proof tree is labelled by $P, t' \vdash_{\Delta'}^{\Sigma'} U$ for some t', Δ' and Σ'. Failure of the condition enforces termination. So the presence of condition $\mathcal{C}$ guarantees that any tableau for $P, \; t \vdash^\Sigma A$ is of finite depth. Moreover all rules are backwards sound and if all leaves of a tableau are true, then so is the root.

A successful tableau for $P, t \vdash^\Sigma A$ is a finite tableau which only contains successful leaves, where a leaf labelled by $Q, s\vdash_\Delta^\Sigma B$ is successful if one of the following conditions holds

- B is tt;
- B is $[b]x.(f \leq x \leq f' \longrightarrow C)$; and
- $B = U$ and $\Delta(U) = \nu Z.C$.

The proof of the following two important theorems are similar to that of [SW89]. These two theorems together say that the problem of a timed state (P, t) has some property A is decidable. The decidability is independent of the choice of time domains.

Theorem 5.3 *Every tableau for $P, \; t \vdash^\Sigma A$ is finite.*

Theorem 5.4 *$P, \; t \vdash_\Delta^\Sigma A$ has a successful tableau if and only if $(P, t) \in \|A_\Delta^\Sigma\|$.*

For any closed process P and formula A, we say a process P has a property A if for any starting time $t \geq 0$, sequent $P, \; t \vdash A$ has a successful tableau. Clearly the problem is decidable and the decidability is independent of the choice of time domain.

Example: In this example, we show by using the tableau system that the bound-response machine $M \overset{\text{def}}{=} a(t)_0^\infty . b(s)_0^{15}$. M has the bound response property

$$\nu Z.[a]x.\langle b \rangle y.(x \leq y \leq x + 15) \wedge [\cdot]x.Z$$

i.e. after action a, an action b must occur within another 15 minutes (if we measure time in minutes).

Let A represent formula $\nu Z.[a]x.\langle b \rangle y.(x \leq y \leq x + 15) \wedge [\cdot]x.Z$. To show the process M has the property A, we only need to show that the sequent $P, t_0 \vdash A$, for any starting time $t_0 \geq 0$, has a successful tableau.

To simplify the presentation of a successful tableau for the sequent $P, t_0 \vdash A$, we let T_1 represent the tableau

$$\frac{b(s)_0^{15}. M, x \vdash_\Delta^{\Sigma_3} [\cdot]x.U}{M, y \vdash_\Delta^{\Sigma_4} U} \qquad \Sigma_4 \text{ is } \Sigma_3 \cdot x \leq y \leq x + 15$$

T_2 represent the tableau

$$\frac{M, t_0 \vdash_\Delta [a]x.\langle b \rangle y.(x \leq y \leq x + 15)}{a(t)_0^\infty . b(s)_0^{15}. M, t_0 \vdash_\Delta [a]x.\langle b \rangle y.(x \leq y \leq x + 15)}$$

$$\frac{b(s)_0^{15}. M, \ x \vdash_\Delta^{\Sigma_1} \langle b \rangle y.(x \leq y \leq x + 15 \wedge tt)}{M, \ y \vdash_\Delta^{\Sigma_2} tt}$$

where Σ_1 is $t_0 \leq x \leq \infty$ and Σ_2 is $\Sigma_1 \cdot x + 10 \leq y \leq x + 10$, and T_3 represent the tableau

$$\frac{M, t_0 \vdash_\Delta [\cdot]x.U}{\dfrac{a(t)_0^\infty . b(s)_0^{15}. M \ t_0 \vdash_\Delta [\cdot]x.U}{b(s)_0^{15}. M, \ x \vdash_\Delta^{\Sigma_3} U}} \qquad \Sigma_3 \text{ is } t_0 \leq x \leq \infty$$

$$\frac{b(s)_0^{15}. M, x \vdash_\Delta^{\Sigma_3} [a]x.\langle b \rangle y.(x \leq y \leq x + 15) \wedge [\cdot]x.U}{b(s)_0^{15}. M, x \vdash_\Delta^{\Sigma_3} [a]x.\langle b \rangle y.(x \leq y \leq x + 15) \qquad T_1}$$

It is easy to see that

$$\frac{M, t_0 \vdash A}{M, t_0 \vdash_\Delta U} \qquad \Delta \text{ is } U = A$$

$$\frac{M, t_0 \vdash_\Delta [a]x.\langle b \rangle y.(x \leq y \leq 15 + x) \wedge [\cdot]x.U}{T_2 \qquad\qquad T_3}$$

is a successful tableau for the sequent $P, t_0 \vdash A$ for any initial time $t_0 \in \mathcal{T}$.

6 Related Work

There have been several attempts of extending temporal logic with time [ACD90, AH90, HLP90, Koy89]. Most of these works are based on linear-time temporal logic or discrete time domains. In [ACD90], Alur, Courcoubetis and Dill propose a timed extension of computational tree logic TCTL, which allows quantitative temporal operators of the forms $\exists A\mathcal{U}_{\sim c}B$ and $\forall A\mathcal{U}_{\sim c}B$. TCTL also makes no assumption about the underlying nature of time, allowing it to be discrete or dense. In this paper, we have shown that all modalities of TCTL are definable in TML. On the other hand, there are time variables in TML which allow us to record different happening time for different actions. It is possible to specify a property "actions a, b and c can happen one by one within 10 *seconds*" as a formula

$$\langle a\rangle x.\langle b\rangle y.\langle c\rangle z.0 \le x + y + z \le 10$$

in TML, but we believe that no formula in TCTL specifies this property.

Acknowledgement: We would like to thank Julian Rose for carefully reading a draft of the paper.

References

[ACD90] R. Alur, C. Courcoubetis and D. L. Dill, *Model Checking for Real-Time Systems*, in Proc. of the 5th Annual Symp. on Logic in Computer Science, pp 414-425, 1990

[AH90] R. Alur and T. A. Henzinger, *A Really temporal Logic*, in Proc. of the 30th Annual Symp. on Foundations of Computer Science, pp 164-169, 1989

[BB91] J.C.M. Baeten and J.A. Bergstra, *Real Time Process Algebra*, Formal Aspects of Computing, 3(2), pp142-188, 1991

[Che91] L. Chen, *Decidability and Completeness in Real-Time Processes*, Technical Report ECS-LFCS-91-185, University of Edinburgh, 1991

[Che92] L. Chen, *An Interleaving Model for Real-Time Systems*, in Proc. of Symp. of Logical Foundations of Computer Science, Lecture Notes in Computer Science 620, pp 81-92, 1992

[HLP90] E. Harel, O. Lichtenstein and A. Pnueli, *Explicit-clock Temporal Logic*, in Proc. of the 5th Annual Symp. on Logic in Computer Science, pp 402-413, 1990

[HM85] M. Hennessy and R. Milner, *Algebraic Laws for Nondeterministic and Concurrency*, Journal of the Asso. for Comp. Machinery, vol 32, pp 137-161, 1985

[Koy89] R. L. C. Koyman, *Specifying Message Passing and Time-Critical Systems with Temporal Logic*, Ph.D thesis, Technical University Eindhoven, 1989

[Lar88] K. Larsen, *Proof Systems for Hennessy-Milner Logic with Recursion*, in Proc. of CAAP, Lecture Notes in Computer Science 299, 1988

[Mil89] R. Milner, **Communication and Concurrency**, Pretice-Hall international, 1989

[MT90] F. Moller and C. Tofts, *A Temporal Calculus of Communicating Systems*, in Proc. of Concur'90, Lecture Notes in Computer Science 458, pp 401-415, 1990

[Sti91] C. Stirling, *Modal and Temporal Logics*, in Handbook of Logic in Computer Science, eds by S. Abramsky, D. Gabbay and T. Maibaum, 1991

[SW89] C. Stirling and D. Walker, *Local Model Checking in the Modal Mu-Calculus*, in Proc. Intl. Joint Conf. on Theory and Practice of Software Development, Lecture Notes in Computer Science 351, 1989

Formal Methods Reality Check: Industrial Usage

Dan Craigen,[1] Susan Gerhart[2] and Ted Ralston[3]

[1] ORA Canada (dan@ora.on.ca)
[2] National Science Foundation (sgerhart@nsf.gov)
[3] Ralston Research Associates (ralston@cli.com)

Abstract. Based on a systematic survey and analysis of the use of formal methods in the development of a dozen industrial applications, we summarize the methods being used, characterize the styles of industrial usage, and provide recommendations for evolutionary enhancements to the technology base of formal methods.

The industrial applications ranged from reverse engineering to system certification; code scale ranges from 1 KLOC to 10 KLOCs. Applications included a software infrastructure for oscilloscopes; a shutdown system for a nuclear generating station; a train protection system; an airline collision avoidance system; an engine monitoring system for shipboard engines; attitude control of satellites; security properties of both a smartcard device and a network; arithmetic units; transaction processing; a real-time database for a medical instrument; and a restructuring program for COBOL.

1 Introduction

This paper discusses the formal methods techniques used in twelve industrial applications, characterizes the use of formal methods, and recommends potentially fruitful areas for research into formal methods. The paper is based on an extensive study [1] that investigated applications in a diverse set of domains, distributed across North America and Europe.

Our definition of "industrial application" stipulates that the subject is a commercial product or a regulated system (completed or under development), that developers be involved in the application (not solely researchers), and that the process used be comparable to other practices in development organizations.

We define "formal methods" as "the application of mathematical synthesis and analysis techniques to the development of computer-controlled systems."

A companion paper [2] provides key observations, in software engineering terms, about formal methods practice, but without emphasizing the particular formal methods techniques used. A second paper [3] discusses briefly the applications that used Z.

2 The Survey Methodology

The methodology was a common sense approach (as opposed to a specific, rigorously defined, social science approach), driven by the need for both a general context of how methods were used and the specific aspects of why formal methods were chosen and how they were used. Appendix B outlines the information gathered and analyzed.

The goals of the study were to

1. better inform industry and governments on standards and regulations.
2. provide an authoritative record on the practical experience to date.
3. provide pointers to future needs and requirements for research and technology transfer.

Cases were selected for coverage of methods and applications, previous notoriety, availability of subjects within our budgetary constraints, and coverage for our target audiences.

A two-phase questionnaire was designed. The first phase asked the interviewees to provide a brief (2 page) description of their project from their own perspective as background for a more detailed interview. Typically, at each interview, two members of the survey team probed further using a background questionnaire, with an emphasis on the most interesting aspects of the case and within the time constraints of the interview.

A total of 23 interviews involved about 50 individuals, ranging in time from half an hour to 11 hours, in both North America and Europe. Each case involved interviewing at least two individuals and ranged up to five. Background material (e.g., papers in the literature) was read before the interview and was collected as the study progressed. The working documents of the projects (e.g., actual specifications) were studied cursorily.

As the interviews were concluding, several forms of analysis were proposed and the following adopted: Feature analysis, R&D Summary, and Timing.

Feature Analysis. A feature analysis forced us to review the data from different perspectives, particularly to address issues considered important for industrial practice. We identified 14 features (see Appendix C) and a rather coarse rating system, with the goal of identifying where formal methods paid off. In some cases, some features were not applicable or we were unable to obtain adequate data (e.g., the effects of formal methods on the cost of a product). However, all cases had subsets of significant features which characterized the general level of success.

R&D Summary. An R&D summary was provided for each case. This information was then abstracted to provide general recommendations and observations to formal methods researchers. The R&D summary is the basis for this paper.

Timing. Intrigued by the progress and duration of the cases, the interesting episodes and the variety of events across the cases, we attempted to capture these key factors as starter-booster-status: starters, what got the case going; boosters, what pushed it along or saved it from failing; and status, what level of use is seen currently in the organizations involved.

To aid the survey, we assembled a distinguished committee of reviewers (see acknowledgments). The committee read report drafts, commented on our methodology, questioned our analyses, identified problems of understandability and credibility in the case summaries, and generally forced us to clarify our exposition.

It is important to recognize the limits of this survey effort:

1. The level of effort of the survey was 1.5 person-years, although background studies had been accumulating.
2. The authors, sponsors and subjects have vested interests in applying the techniques of formal methods. Objectivity was sought by providing multiple views of the data, and by external critiquing.
3. The general methodology was "common sense": that is, common sense to a technologist with an interest in process and applications.
4. The case selection omitted important classes of methods (e.g., the protocol languages SDL and LOTOS) and domains. Some cases bordered on areas considered more hardware than software, but the techniques were similar and every case was dominated by system characteristics.
5. We did not seek examples of outright failure. Such cases would likely be caused by departures and dispersion of personnel.

3 Cases

Within the scope of this paper, it is impossible to describe the twelve cases in detail. The study report [1] requires an average of fifteen pages to describe a case (including data from the questionnaires, interviews and background reading; observations; and analysis). In Appendix A we describe for each case the application, the methods and tools used, and suggested areas of improvement as pertains to the formal methods used. Appendix A is a crucial section of this report and should be read before continuing with the remainder of the main text. The reader is referred to Appendix A for the definitions of the acronyms.

4 Clusters

The report clusters the cases into three categories that share common features:

Regulatory cluster An agency of some government requires a certification for the product and/or its development process. **Cases:** DNGS, MGS, SACEM, TCAS.

Commercial cluster A firm is producing a product in which quality requirements or productivity are of concern. In essence, this cluster refers to attempts to improve profit margins. **Cases:** CICS, Cleanroom, Inmos, SSADM, Tektronix.

Exploratory cluster An organization is exploring the efficacy of formal methods on a specific product or in its development process. **Cases:** HP, LaCoS, TBACS.

Much of our case analysis is based on these clusters. However, the amount of information arising from the three exploratory cases was insufficient for an independent analysis. Consequently, for this paper, we will view TBACS as part of the regulatory cluster; and HP and LaCoS as part of the commercial cluster.

5 Formal Methods Usage

In this section, we discuss the uses of formal methods within the three clusters. On a cluster-by-cluster basis, our discussion will describe the methods used, the tools used, and the improvements required or "needs" of the existing technology. The needs (described in Appendix A) are those identified by the participants in our survey. We also provide our own interpretations of these needs.

5.1 Regulatory Cluster

Some background comments are necessary to set the general context for regulatory cases. In the regulatory arena, government agencies are involved in certification. Such agencies may chose to certify either the product being developed or the process by which a product is developed. In our case studies, MGS and SACEM were a mix of these approaches. TCAS is product certification. DNGS is also product certification (since AECB was uncomfortable with the processes being used).

Note that certification is also a *process*. There is substantial interplay between researchers, developers and certifiers. What is unclear at this point is how formal methods will be used: will they be used for product certification or as process evidence?

Methods.

Conceptual and logical frameworks. First-order logic was used on all the projects and state machine formalisms predominated as a conceptual framework. For example, in SACEM, the B Abstract Machine approach clearly incorporates the "state machine" perspective. Similarly, the Formal Development Methodology (TBACS) explicitly used state machine representations for specifications; specification is defined in terms of state transitions and invariant properties. We felt that most individuals involved with these cases were comfortable with the "state machine" mind-set. Code proofs generally followed the approach of Hoare Logic or a closely related method (strongest postconditions and equivalence with specifications). The use of abstraction and "blackbox" specifications was also fundamental to the cases.

Although different methods are being used (A-7 specifications and strongest post conditions; Gypsy; Hoare Logic and B; Statecharts; and Hoare Logic for the programming languages associated with FDM), there are strong similarities with the underlying mind-sets for specification and proof.

Code proofs and refinement. One of the distinguishing traits of the regulatory cluster is the demonstration that code conforms with requirements. This is characterized by the presence of code proofs and/or refinement in three of the cases. It is also characterized, in some instances, by substantial effort. A particular example is the DNGS case. Here, the regulator, AECB. had substantial concerns about the software. As a consequence, a labour intensive activity (as there was no tool support) proceeded with manual justification that the code (written in Pascal, Fortran or assembler) was equivalent to the requirements. Three independent teams were involved: the requirements team, who reverse engineered the system requirements; the code team, who developed the proof function tables; and the proof team, who were responsible for the equivalence proofs. Four million dollars (Canadian) have been attributed to the verification effort and, at one point, approximately 30 individuals were involved in different aspects of the verification. Similarities can be seen with SACEM: even prior to the use of B, they were performing code proofs using Hoare Logic. For SACEM, around 120,000 hours were used on V&V efforts (this includes analyses in addition to formal methods). Yet, the amounts of code for the DNGS and SACEM cases were quite small. For one of the DNGS shutdown systems (SDS1) there were about 2,500 LOC (FORTRAN and assembler); for SACEM, there were 9,000 LOC.

These code efforts are in addition to the use of formal methods to remove or inhibit the addition of errors to requirements and specifications. In the regulatory cases, formal methods are not used solely to capture requirements; they are also used to assure that code conforms.

Effective Communication. Effective communication of specifications and requirements to individuals not knowledgeable in formal methods was an important characteristic of the regulatory cluster. TCAS and MGS provide cautionary tales for those of us who are familiar with mathematical notation and, perhaps, no longer recognize the potential impediments of improperly chosen notations.

With TCAS, Leveson and her group chose a notation that was a simplified form of Statecharts,[4] augmented with tabular representations of Disjunctive Normal Form predicates describing state transitions. The combination of graphical notation and "decision tables" that were close to the notations used by the engineers on a TCAS committee provided an effective means of communication. Earlier efforts used common predicate calculus notations, which were impediments and thus unsatisfactory. Similarly, with the MGS, there was difficulty using Gypsy to communicate with the developers; instead, a graphical notation was provided.

The ergonomics of language design and the ease with which the underlying semantics can be described cannot be underestimated in developing a successful formal method. Developing computer-controlled systems is already complex; we do not need to augment the problem with needlessly complex languages.

Tools.

Tool impoverishment. From the perspective of the early nineties, the use of tools must be viewed as impoverished. Mostly, this is a result of the newness of the technologies being used and, perhaps, a lack of recognition of what tools are available. Neither TCAS nor DNGS made any use of formal methods tools. We have already noted the effect this had with the DNGS. It is the view of the authors that much of the tool support needed for the DNGS already existed; however, the developers did not have the time to investigate availability or to modify the tools that might have been used. With TCAS, the language being developed is still so new that it has not yet been an object of tool development. The one tool TCAS did use, LaTeX, was in support of their primary goals of readability and reviewability of the specification. Careful consideration was given to the presentation of the specification and to cross-referencing between related concepts.

---

[4] A simplified subset was chosen since 'broadcast communication' was not appropriate to their modelling approach and they did not require the additional modelling approaches provided by Statecharts.

SACEM used the B tool and MGS used the Gypsy Verification Environment to handle proof and specification. With respect to the MGS, the use of the GVE was necessary because of the U.S. National Computer Security Center mandate to use an "endorsed tool" to achieve a high level of certification. From our perspective, the proof checking capabilities of the GVE are weak and are surpassed by a number of existing systems (primarily in North America). Furthermore, there were worries about the soundness of the prover; though as used in the project, the developers of the MGS have confidence in the GVE. (Similar comments may be directed at the FDM prover.) Both B and the GVE were research prototypes, used in industrial contexts. This is a good means for experimenting with the prototypes but may not be the best means for completing a project.

Needs.

Integration of validation techniques. We found from these cases that substantial work is required on how to best integrate formal methods with other assurance (validation) and software engineering activities. From the four cases in the regulatory cluster, it appears that the SACEM developers are on the forefront. They have developed a set of techniques that have not only been used on SACEM but also on two successor efforts (for the French SNCF and for a system in Calcutta, India). It is time for multi-disciplinary projects.

Improved automated deduction systems. It is the view of the authors that the regulatory cluster of cases has demonstrated a greater need for automated deduction support, proof obligation generators and refinement (from specification to code) than the other clusters.

Extension of formal methods capabilities. Formal techniques for handling concurrency, real-time and asynchronous processes were suggested as areas of future research.[5] Currently, other means (such as simulation) are being used. We are puzzled as to why those we interviewed were not particularly bothered by the absence of such formal techniques.

5.2 Commercial Cluster

Methods.

Conceptual and logical frameworks. Our commercial cases predominately used Z, either to specify systems (CASE, CICS, and Inmos) or as a mathematical language to analyze and model various design choices (Tektronix). As with the regulatory cluster, the languages used are first-order and state-machine based. The language used with LaCoS is Raise, which is an exception in that it is a complex, wide-spectrum language that allows for different modes of use.

---

[5] However, we note that there is a substantial body of literature in this area. The problem may not be one of research only, but of technology transition.

We asked ourselves why Z currently predominates industrial use of formal methods. In brief, the predominance appears to result from the (i) choice of set theory; (ii) the development of an accessible (readable and writable) notation; (iii) reasonable support for state machine specifications; (iv) close interaction between the developers of Z and industrial concerns; and (v) a substantial pedagogical literature. Of these five points, we feel that the last two are instrumental to the success of Z.

Code proofs and refinement. Refinement and code proofs had less impact in the commercial cluster when compared with the regulatory cluster, being limited primarily to the Cleanroom and Inmos case studies. Proof, at least at the informal level, is fundamental to the Cleanroom methodology. Inmos used refinement (as supported by the Occam Transformation System) and proved correctness properties for finite state machines. A main reason for the reduced interest for refinement appears to be cost. The use of formal methods to formally describe requirements and specifications has been found to be beneficial with respect to improved quality and, in some instances, demonstrable reduction in costs.

Modelling and communication. The main uses of formal methods in the commercial cluster have been for modelling and communication. The usual attributes of improved precision, conciseness and mathematical modelling were important to all the cases. An example of the use of formal methods in "communication" is the use of Z in round-table discussions as clients and developers discuss the adequacy of specifications. A modelling example is the oscilloscope work performed at Tektronix (and reported at VDM'91) to develop a reusable software infrastructure.

Development processes. Process issues are important to the Raise and HP cases. Interestingly, while HP-SL is not being adopted by the Waltham Medical Instruments Group, there is intent to use the Rigorous Engineering Methodology developed at Bristol. The Raise project has produced a method manual, outlining their approach. Cleanroom has also emphasized process by separating the development and testing teams, and by using statistical testing to infer quality measurements.

Tools. The tool support used by the commercial cluster was (with two exceptions) limited to language well-formedness checkers. Since four of the cases involved Z, the tools were generally Z editors, type checkers, pretty-printers and cross-referencers. All the tools were prototypes.

The two exceptions were Cleanroom and Inmos. Cleanroom accentuates the use of "mental" reasoning and has avoided the use of tools. Fundamental to Cleanroom are group involvement and discussion of specifications. The group, not an individual, is responsible for delivered specifications and software. To an extent, the avoidance of tools echoes comments the authors have heard from researchers involved with the development of Z. It does, however, go against the grain of what industry perceives as its needs.

In addition to using Z, Inmos used the Occam Transformation System and an in-house refinement checker. For example, with the Floating Point Unit, they used Z to specify the unit; manually derived an Occam "specification-level" description of the unit; and used the transformation system to develop an "implementation-level" microcode description.

Unique in the commercial cluster, Inmos used an automatic "correctness-checking" tool for finite state machines on the T9000 Virtual Channel Processor. Interestingly, this correctness-checking tool was limited to a decidable fragment of a theory of proof of correctness of state machines. By doing this, the T9000 engineers could apply the tool automatically to their designs. It also had cost benefits: some of the advantages of formal methods accrued, but the engineers did not need to work through mathematical proofs. Such a tool becomes one of a repertoire that can be used by engineering staff.

Needs.

Formal techniques for real-time. As with the regulatory cluster, there was interest in timing and concurrency. While Inmos, for example, used CCS and CSP to handle concurrency issues, simulators were still used to analyze real-time issues.

Improved Z tools. Perhaps because most of our cases had used Z, there were expressed interests in having various Z-related tools such as schema expansion. Other interests included tools to navigate through specifications, such as browsing and cross-referencing tools.

Improved design methodologies. There was interest in developing design methodologies that encompassed formal methods technologies.

Notation and proof. Problems with notation arose in the HP case: there were difficulties finding people within HP (Waltham) who were willing to learn the notation and mind-set so that HP-SL specifications could be reviewed by domain experts. Improved automated deduction systems and additional experience with such tools were noted. There is also interest in furthering the experience with the wide-spectrum Raise language and determining whether such a large language is a benefit or a detriment to using formal methods?

6   Reality Check and Observations

The "reality check" for formal methods involved identifying the aspects of formal methods research that are important to industry. Below, we summarize our findings.

Integrated Techniques. There is a clear need for improved integration of formal methods techniques with other software engineering practices. We have seen interest in such integration in at least two guises during our study: (i) inclusion of formal methods assurance techniques (such as Hoare Logic proofs) with other assurance techniques (e.g., hazard analysis, trajectory testing); and (ii) integration of formal methods with existing (or new) design methods (e.g., Jackson System Design). Successful integration is important to the long-term success of formal methods. Industry will not abandon its current practices, but it is willing to augment and enhance its practices. So, the use of formal notations (like Z) to replace some informal notations such as English and pseudo-code is an effective transition practice. But there are ancillary issues. We need to understand better how the assurance arising from formal methods analysis augments that from more traditional assurance techniques. Can we quantify such augmentation?

The Inmos and SACEM cases were important examples of what can be achieved with integration, even at this early stage. The SACEM developers have put in place a set of techniques that they are now commercializing and applying to subsequent railway systems (such as a system in Calcutta and a country-wide system for the French national rail system, SNCF). The SACEM developers have spent substantial effort in integrating various assurance practices. The Inmos case is important for analytically demonstrating the power of mathematics. While informal notations are in a number of applications of formal methods, these informal notations are being replaced with formal notations, with clear resulting benefits. With the Inmos case, our impression is that the power of mathematics has been applied, non-trivially, to design and analyze complex components, such as the Virtual Channel Processor. Inmos used formal methods in a strong engineering and opportunistic manner; when critical problems arose, the best techniques to be found were used to resolve the problems and, moreover, some of the techniques were refined so that they were cost effective in their domain of usage.

There are problems, however, with the large scale integration of techniques. For example, in critical applications, regulators need to understand the techniques being used and the limitations.

Cost effective tools. Formal methods tools have been in circulation since the 1970s; yet few, if any, have found substantial application in industrial contexts. The limited dissemination of the tools is due to numerous facts including, but not limited to (i) the research and prototype nature of the tools, making them inappropriate for industrial usage; (ii) the steep learning curves associated with their use; and (iii) governmental limitations on usage.

One cannot expect an industrial firm that has realized that pseudo-code and English specifications are not state of the art, and are inadequate for the development of systems of increasing complexity, to jump into an advanced formal methods tool based on algebraic datatypes, proof editors and mathematical logic. The firm will not have the staff educated for such a transition. In addition, we cannot yet estimate the costs of application developments that use these new techniques. Using existing practice, some measures for costing a project exist; such is not the case with formal methods where we know that the amounts of effort spent at various stages of development are substantially different.

From the case studies, it is clear that industry wants rugged versions of specification language well-formedness checkers. In addition, these tools need to be integrated with other tools used in software development and should support configuration management, cross-referencing and browsing. (Maybe there is a role for hypertext with some of these formal methods tools.)

It is also clear, especially in the regulatory cluster, that improved automated deduction support is essential. We are convinced that such support must have substantial automated support and there is a strong argument that checkers for decidable fragments of theories is one particularly fruitful area. Examples of such decidable fragments are the various model checking techniques (e.g., by Clarke's group at Carnegie-Mellon), finite state machine analysis (e.g., in the protocol area and as used by Inmos), and the simplifiers in a number of automated deduction systems (such as EVES and the new versions of Boyer-Moore). Inmos made particularly effective use of a correctness tool for demonstrating equivalence between state machines, which did not require the engineers to have in-depth understanding of how to perform the logical reasoning. (However, with such tools, and automated deduction tools in general, it is important to provide useful feedback when proofs fail. This is a sadly neglected area of automated deduction.) We are not convinced that the current research on "proof editors" will be useful to industry. There are useful pedagogical tools but these are too labour intensive for industrial practice. Remaining within the axiomatic framework is constraining, especially when there are non-axiomatic techniques (such as Linear Programming) that can be used effectively. The current work on proof editors reminds us of the proof capabilities of the seventies generation of program verification systems developed in the United States (and exemplified in our survey by the MGS and TBACS cases).

At present, automated deduction tools do not provide the same amount of aid to software engineers as, perhaps, symbolic computations systems (e.g., REDUCE, MACSYMA, MATHEMATICA) provide to scientists in their work, or finite state machine analysis tools provide to protocol engineers.

Notational issues. One of the impediments to using formal methods with mathematical notations, based on logic, has been the difficulty in communicating with clients that are not comfortable with these notations. Various methods, such as animation, have been tried to overcome this hurdle. Perhaps, we need to distinguish between the notations (and underlying ideas) that are used amongst formal methods experts and those that we use to communicate with individuals who are not expert in formal methods. This issue arose in a number of our case studies; TCAS and MGS were prime indicators. In both those cases, substantial effort was required to present ideas in a notation understandable to the uninitiated. Similar issues arose in the Tektronix and HP cases. In Tektronix, the Z was replaced by object-oriented code. For the HP case, insurmountable problems arose because no-one at the medical instruments group (outside of the interested parties) was willing or able to review the HP-SL specifications. Much of formal methods notation is based on the original work, from the thirties, on Logic. This notation was never developed ergonomically, and probably was not viewed as having wide-scale industrial application.

Other trends. Of all our case studies, it seems that only TCAS used graphics. Yet, technology advances in graphics, virtual reality, and multi-media are all progressing rapidly. How will formal methods evolve with these new ways of understanding and explaining our environment?

Transition difficulties. No matter how positive we might want to be, we cannot say that the use of formal methods has taken industry by storm. There are a few organizations where the technology has been assimilated and is being applied fruitfully, but, for the most part, industry has been slow to assimilate formal methods. Why is this the case?

A number of potential reasons come to mind, and they are not unique to formal methods: (i) a sophisticated technology is hard to transfer; (ii) new technologies need to be integrated with existing practice; (iii) minimization of risk associated with using new technologies; and (iv) need for expertise.

7 Conclusions

Based on a systematic survey and analysis of the use of formal methods in twelve industrial applications of formal methods, we have summarized the methods being used, characterized the styles of usage, and provided various recommendations and observations for enhancements to formal methods. This paper has taken one particular perspective on the information acquired from the survey. We recommend that our readers acquire the full report [1] for in-depth discussions on the cases and for other our analyses.

Acknowledgments

This study was sponsored by the U.S. National Institute for Standards and Technology, the U.S. Naval Research Laboratory, and the Atomic Energy Control Board of Canada. NSF also provided independent research time for the second author. Previous studies of trends in commercial and regulatory applications of formal methods were performed in conjunction with the organization of the FM89 conference and the MCC Formal Methods Transition Study.

The authors wish to thank the interviewees for their time, professional information, and openness. The advisory committee was also exceptionally helpful: Adele Goldberg, John Marciniak, Morven Gentleman, Lorraine Duvall, and John Gannon.

A Case Descriptions

In this appendix we summarize the 12 cases. The general form of the case descriptions is as follows:

Who The parties involved.

What Description of application.

Why Reason for development of application.

Formalisms Formalisms used.

Uses How the formalisms were used.

Tools The (formal methods) tools used.

Needs Suggested R&D directions (primarily as expressed by the participants).

A.1 Regulatory Cases

Darlington Trip Computer Software (DNGS).

Who Ontario Hydro (OH), AECL, Atomic Energy Control Board of Canada (AECB), David Parnas, and Nancy Leveson.

What Decision-making logic for the shutdown systems at DNGS were implemented in software and proven to be in conformance with requirements.

Why Shutdown system is safety-critical. Use of formal methods to assure regulators (AECB). AECB would not license DNGS in the absence of a convincing demonstration of the correctness of the code.

Formalisms A-7 specification style with program function tables (PFTs) describing strongest post conditions of code routines.

Uses (i) Specification of "systems," not solely "software." (ii) PFTs represent strongest post conditions tabularly. (iii) Specifications may be an object of review. (iv) Equivalence proofs between routine PFT and specification (performed by hand).

Tools Microsoft Excel (TM) was used to manipulate some of the tables.

Needs (i) Tools for automated deduction, developing functional descriptions of code routines, bookkeeping. (ii) Clarification of methodology and underlying mathematics.

Multinet Gateway System (MGS).

Who Ford Aerospace (now part of Loral).

What Secure Internet device for transmission of datagrams.

Why The Multinet Gateway system is security critical. To attain appropriate security rating, formal methods were used to explicate security model.

Formalisms Gypsy and Trust Domains.

Uses (i) Gypsy. To describe security model and for imperative design code. (ii) Trust domains (a graphical notation) for describing networks. (iii) Security model described in terms of information flow. (iv) Proofs that security properties are met (using Gypsy Verification Environment).

Tools (i) Gypsy Verification Environment (GVE). (ii) Separate "extractor" to determine minimal information needed for a proof.

Needs (i) Improved automated deduction. (ii) Better capabilities, in the GVE, to handle industrial-scale projects. (iii) Soundness demonstration of GVE proof system. (iv) Improved specification language expressibility. (v) Notation which is more acceptable to engineering staff.

SACEM.

Who GEC Alsthom and RER (the Paris regional train network) through RATP (Rapid Transit Authority)

What Automated train protection system.

Why To increase train throughput, by decreasing train separation times (from 2min 30sec to 2min), but maintaining safety levels. Success eliminated need to build a new railway line.

Formalisms Hoare assertion augmented with B Abstract Machines.

Uses (i) Abstract Machines to describe system components. (ii) Refinement is defined and used. (iii) Verification is performed at the top-level and lower by proving invariants and refinement obligations. (iv) Newly developed tools are capable of generating code from a low-level specification. (v) Concurrency and timing handled separately. (vi) Validation activities include extensive simulation and operational scenario generation.

Tools (i) Substitution processor for Hoare assertions. (ii) B tool used for theorem proving and specification management. (iii) Based on SACEM experience, the FORSE toolset is being commercialized to support the methodology used.

Needs Better integration of formal specification and proof with other validation activities.

Air Traffic Alert and Collision Avoidance System (TCAS).

Who UC Irvine, U.S. Federal Aviation Administration, members of an aviation working group.

What Formal description of TCAS II collision avoidance logic and surveillance system. TCAS is to reduce risk of mid-air and near mid-air collisions.

Why Clarification of requirements for a complex digital avionics system.

Formalisms A modification of Statecharts, state machines

Uses (i) Handles concurrency as parallel state machines. (ii) Tabular notation (embodying Disjunctive Normal Form) for transition conditions. (iii) Specifications subject to review and IV&V. (iv) CAS Logic formalism being determined from pseudo-code and English. Surveillance Logic from English.

Tools LaTeX

Needs (i) Safety analysis tool. (ii) Automated deduction and model checking support. (iii) Well-formedness checker. (iv) Development and description of underlying mathematics.

A.2 Commercial Cases

Customer Information Control System (CICS).

Who IBM Hursley Laboratory (responsible for CICS product) and Oxford Programming Research Group.

What CICS is a large transaction processing system.

Why Re-engineering of a number of modules and addition of new features; improve quality and reduce development costs.

Formalisms Z with English annotations

Uses Z used to specify module interfaces.

Tools PS/2 based toolset with editor, typechecker and semantic analyzer.

Needs Schema expander, enhanced semantic analyzer and configuration management.

COBOL/SF (Cleanroom). **Note:** A secondary case study was the use of Cleanroom at NASA Goddard in the development of a satellite attitude control system.

Who IBM Federal Systems Division (Gaithersburg, Maryland).

What COBOL/SF, a restructuring facility for COBOL.

Why COBOL/SF was used as a technical challenge in the use of Cleanroom.

Formalisms Functions and box structures (state machines) plus whatever other formalisms (e.g., grammars) are needed.

Uses (i) Functions are decomposed and box structures have state structure added. (ii) Specifications are extensively reviewed for completeness to stabilize requirements before design proceeds. (iii) Usage profiles for testing add context to specification. (iv) Verification is a review process lead by "correctness questions." (v) A reliability model is used in testing to predict and control quality objectives. (vi) A continual objective is simplification–of designs, data structures, algorithms, etc.

Tools (i) Simple editors are used for text management. (ii) Proof checkers are less desirable because Cleanroom emphasizes the review process and its mental group correctness checking. (iii) The most often used tool is the wastebasket for overly complex designs.

Needs Tools for extracting and tracking verification steps are under consideration.

Software Infrastructure (Tektronix).

Who Tektronix R&D lab and engineers in business unit (Beaverton, Oregon).

What Software infrastructure for a family of oscilloscope products.

Why Shorten time-to-market through a reusable software platform.

Formalisms Z

Uses Abstract specification of system operations and user interface in Z; Z specification translated into lower-level representation that is closer to implementation.

Tools Fuzz editor/typechecker/pretty printer;

Needs Proof tool for refinement, pre-condition calculator, and schema expander.

Transputer (Inmos).

Who Inmos Ltd. (Bristol England) developers (with input from Oxford Programming Research Group).

What Components of three generations of commercial microprocessors (including floating point unit and virtual channel processor).

Why Starting as a tractable example for research, evolved into a way to reduce testing and improve confidence in products.

Formalisms Z, Occam and HOL

Uses High-level abstract specification of microprocessor components in Z and Occam; HOL used for proof checking of microcode-controlled hardware (still experimental).

Tools Occam Transformation System; an in-house "refinement checker" that compares specification and implementation.

Needs Verified VHDL semantics and enhanced refinement checker to handle very large state spaces.

SSADM toolset (SSADM).

Who Praxis plc. (of Bath, England)

What A toolset supporting the SSADM (a structured analysis method)

Why Contract development for external client.

Formalisms Z with English annotations

Uses Z used for formal high-level specification of the infrastructure (management facilities) and some of the tools.

Tools Prototype Z parser and typechecker from Forsite project (with added "ascii" screen based editor), plus troff.

Needs Re. method, an ability to handle concurrency. Re. tools, a Z schema expander, enhanced editor, and browsing and x-ref facility.

A.3   Exploratory Cases

Large Correct Systems (LaCoS).

Who ESPRIT project consisting of CRI (Denmark), Lloyds Register, Matra Transport and four others.

What Experimental application of Raise with tool development.

Why (i) evaluate and improve industrial utility of Raise, and (ii) formal methods experiments on the part of Lloyds Register, Matra Transport, et al.

Formalisms RSL, a wide-spectrum specification language supporting different styles (applicative, data types, imperative) and refinement with proof obligations. A prescribed process is also developed in a Method Manual.

Uses (i) Both organizations interviewed were using RSL for modelization: the development of a model for exploring requirements, but not necessarily serving as the base for design. (ii) Concurrency specification is needed but not considered satisfactory in RSL. (iii) Refinement down to code is considered quite important, but difficult. (iv) Justification, i.e., the discharging of proof obligations, is being explored using tools.

Tools (i) The Raise toolset is based on the Cornell Synthesizer Generator, both as editor and for processing language objects. The editor capability is not widely used, but the CSG controls the semantics of RSL. (ii) Automated reasoning tools are just becoming available, specifically a Justification Editor to permit experimentation with justification proofs using different styles and underlying support tools, such as simplifiers. (iii) Configuration and object management are supported.

Needs (i) Better understanding of the complex RSL language. (ii) Experience with automated reasoning tools.

Token Based Access Control System (TBACS).

Who U.S. National Institute of Standards and Technology (NIST) Software Engineering and Security Technology groups.

What Specified and proved security properties of a smartcard.

Why To gain experience in using formal methods and underlying tools. Formalisms] State transition model with assertions expressing the security policy. Language used was InaJo.

Uses (i) C code was the base language for the simulator from which the state transition model was derived. It was matched with the security policy. (ii) The spec was used for informal communication with the smartcard designer. (iii) Errors were discovered and used to improve the manufactured version and the overall design.

Tools (i) Selected functions were verified used the FDM theorem prover. (ii) External paper-and-pencil cross-reference were used. (iii) Scrolling was used to overcome interface problems.

Needs (i) Better understanding of this reverse engineering process into a state transition specification is worthy of investigation. (ii) Improved interface for managing large expressions and long series of proof steps.

Analytical Information Base (HP).

Who HP Bristol Applied Methods Group and Waltham Medical Instruments Division.

What An application (the analytical information base) of an HP patient monitoring system. Real-time database.

Why Evaluate utility of formal methods (in general and with the HP Rigorous Engineering Methodology and HP-SL.

Formalisms Rigorous Engineering Methodology and HP-SL

Uses (i) HP-SL is a VDM-like specification language. (ii) State machine and abstract data types.

Tools HP-SL syntax checker.

Needs (i) HP-SL well-formedness checker. (ii) Notation which is more acceptable to engineering staff.

B Questionnaire Outline

Organizational Context Please describe, in general terms, the organization in which this project was conducted: its goals, products, structure, and composition at the time of the project.

Project Content and History Describe the application involved. Please provide a timeline of the start, major milestones, and level of effort over the history of the project.

Application Drivers Why was this product developed and what were the major concerns that had an impact on the directions of the product development?

Formal Methods Factors Why did you choose to use formal methods? Which formal method(s) did you choose? What criteria did you use in your selection process?

Formal Methods and Tools Usage Describe how you used the method and what tool support you utilized.

Results What advantages and disadvantages did you find using formal methods and tools on this application? What would you have done differently?

C Features

We identified two sets of features: product and process. The product features pertain to the actual product being produced by the application. Process features pertain to the process used in developing the product. We further subdivide process features by considering specific and general features.

C.1 Product features

Client satisfaction. Were clients happier with the product? (Happiness is, of course, due to many aspects of the product, including, for example, enhanced reliability and reduced cost.)

Cost of product. Was the overall cost of the product reduced, or the profit increased?

Impact of product What was the effect of the production of the product on the organization? For example, was the product important to the company's profit margin or an organization's reputation?

Quality. Was the quality of the product improved? By "quality" we include concerns pertaining to safety and security properties, enhanced functionality and performance, and reduction in errors.

Time to market. Was the product, or family of products, made available for marketing more rapidly?

C.2 Process features (General process effects)

Cost of process. Perhaps duplicating the product feature, but as measured through reduction in effort.

Impact of process. What effect did the process used to develop the product have on the organization? For example, was the process important to the company's profit margin or an organization's reputation?

Pedagogical. As a learning opportunity, what did the organization make of the opportunity? Was there a steep learning curve?

Tools. Did the formal methods tools help or hinder the development of the product? Were the tools reliable?

C.3 Process features (Specific process effects)

Design. Were the designs produced using formal methods fundamentally better or worse in some respect? For example, were the designs simpler?

Reusable components. Did the use of formal methods ease the development and/or use of reusable hardware or software components, designs, abstractions, etc.?

Maintainability. Is it easier to maintain the product? Maintenance includes incremental updates to the product and fixing errors.

Requirements capture. Was the acquisition of requirements simplified?

V&V. What impact was there on the V&V aspects of the process? Observe that V&V includes, for examples, testing, proofs, and reviews.

References

1. Dan Craigen, Susan Gerhart, Ted Ralston: An International Survey of Industrial Applications of Formal Methods. Reports to be published by NIST, NRL, and AECB, 1993.
2. Susan Gerhart, Dan Craigen, Ted Ralston: Observations on Industrial Practice Using Formal Methods. In Proceedings of the 15th International Conference on Software Engineering, Baltimore, Maryland, (May 1993).
3. Dan Craigen, Susan Gerhart, Ted Ralston: Comments on the Industrial Usage of Z. In Proceedings of the 7th Z User Meeting, London, England, (December 1992).

Automating the Generation and Sequencing of Test Cases from Model-Based Specifications

Jeremy Dick[1] and Alain Faivre[2]

[1] Bull Information Systems, Maxted Road, Hemel Hempstead, HP2 7DZ, UK
[2] Bull Corporate Research Centre, 78450 Les Clayes-sous-Bois, France

Abstract. Formal specifications contain a great deal of information that can be exploited in the testing of an implementation, either for the generation of test-cases, for sequencing the tests, or as an oracle in verifying the tests. This papers presents automatic techniques for partition analysis in state-based specifications, specifically VDM. Test domains for individual operations are calculated by reduction of their mathematical description to a Disjunctive Normal Form. Following this, a partition analysis of the system state can be performed which permits the construction of a Finite State Automaton from the specification. This, in turn, can be used to sequence the required tests in a valid and sensible way. A tool has been developed based on the techniques applied to VDM, which has been used to develop the examples presented in the paper.

1 Introduction

Formal methods promise high product confidence through mathematical proof of system correctness. The ultimate aim is to do away with the typically large amount of effort spent *a posteriori* in error detection, and replace it by effort spent *a priori* in the construction of systems which are error-free by design.

With the current state-of-the-art, however, there are reasons why the need for post-developmental validation cannot be eliminated. One such reason is that formally developed systems are seldom created and operated in total isolation, being dependent on compilers, operating systems and run-time environments that may not be trustworthy. It also frequently occurs that the cost of performing completely proven refinement steps is only warranted in exceptional cases of high financial or human risk, leading to systems that are formally specified, but whose development was, at least in part, informal. A similar scenario arises with reverse engineering, where a formal specification has been created for an existing system whose development is obscure.

The work reported here is an attempt to add further value to the existence of a formal specification by allowing it to be used in the testing process. We show how the partition analysis of individual operations can be automated, and how valid sequences of operations which cover all the necessary tests can be constructed. The key to this is to exploit the mathematics inherent in the specification in various constraint solving activities. There are four main aspects:

- *the partition analysis of individual operations.* This involves reducing the mathematical expression defining an operation into a Disjunctive Normal Form (DNF), which gives disjoint partitions representing domains of the operation that should be tested in the implementation;

- *the partition analysis of the system state.* Again, the mathematical expression defining the system state, viewed in the light of the pre- and postconditions of operations, is reduced into DNF, which yields disjoint partitions of state values which can be used to construct a Finite State Automaton (FSA) from the specification;

- *the scheduling of tests of different operations to avoid redundancy in the testing process.* This involves finding paths through the FSA which cover all the required tests, and composing the constraints resulting from the composition of these sequences to detect inconsistencies;

- *the generation of test values for use in the validation of the implementation.* This involves the selection of values relating to the operation *input* for each case. These test values must satisfy the constraints imposed by the mathematical definition of the specification in the given case. Once input values have been selected, the constraints describing the case can be simplified, leaving an expression constraining just the *result* values;

- *the verification of the results of an individual test against the specification.* This involves using the residual constraints to verify the values relating to the operation *results* under the test.

Our approach draws on ideas from other work. Initial inspiration came from [BGM1], which reports on test-case extraction from algebraic specifications. A generally applicable framework for the generation of sets of test data is described, in which one is required to state the hypotheses used to justify both the choice of a finite set of test data, and the existence of an oracle for verifying the results. A form of partition analysis is carried out by unfolding equations in the specification.

An earlier paper, [S1], uses case analysis of VDM specifications to partition the test domains. No precise details of how the case analysis could be performed and automated were given.

Reading [HH1] introduced us to the problem of sequencing the tests. This useful survey paper, and others by the same authors, [H1] [H2], discuss a wide range of issues in the use of formal specifications in testing. Hall and Hierons [HH1] suggest the construction of an FSA from model-based specifications, but give no method of doing so. They indicate that, given such an FSA, classical graph traversal algorithms can be used to find the required sequences of operations.

As a vehicle for exploring methods of partition analysis and test-case sequencing, we have chosen the specification language VDM-SL ([D1]), used in the Vienna Development Method ([J1]). We intend, however, the underlying method to be generally applicable to the model-based (sometimes called state-based) approach, which encompasses other notations, such as Z [S2], RSL [R1] and COLD [FJ1].

We use the ideas of [BGM1] to create a more precise formulation of the approach introduced in [S1]. In our approach, the formulae of the specification are the relations on states described by operations, and are expressed in first-order predicate calculus. These relations are reduced to a DNF, creating a set of disjoint sub-relations. Each sub-relation yields a set of constraints which describe a single test domain. The approach of reduction to DNF is a state-oriented equivalent of the case analysis of the algebraic approach. We also transfer the use of uniformity and regularity hypotheses from the algebraic work to our situation.

When applied to the most abstract level of specification, the test domains generated correspond to pure black-box testing; no information concerning the nature of the implementation is taken into consideration. If applied, however, to various levels of refinement, which is possible in the wide spectrum notation VDM-SL, more and more detail can be introduced into the partition analysis, leading, potentially, to complete white-box analysis.

We also describe a method of extracting an FSA from a state-based specification. This method uses the results of the partition analysis of individual operations, to perform a further partition analysis of the system state. The result is a set of disjoint states, each of which is either the before-state or the after-state of at least one of the tests to be performed. From these analyses, an FSA can be constructed.

Unlike in [BGM1] where the kind of formulae treated is more constrained, we cannot, in general, hope to be able to generate solutions to sets of constraints automatically in every possible case; we are working in the semi-decidable logic of the first-order predicate calculus. Despite this inherent limitation, we feel that in practice many specifications can be treated, and our goal is to create a practical approach that offers the maximum of assistance in exploiting a formal specification in the testing process.

We have developed a tool to assess the practicality of the approach, which is briefly outlined in the paper, but described more fully in [DF1] . Except where indicated, the examples shown in Sections 2 and 3 were calculated using this tool.

The paper is organised as follows. Section 2 describes the approach adopted for partition analysis of individual operations with an example. Section 3 describes a method of extracting an FSA, and finding appropriate sequences of tests, again with an example. Section 4 briefly describes the tool we have developed. Section 5 discusses limitations of the approach, and draws conclusions.

2   Partition Analysis

In this section we present our approach to the partition analysis of individual operations. We use VDM-SL, but make reference to how the approach may differ slightly for other notations.

In the state-based approach, operations describe a partial relation between system states. They are specified by giving a logical expression, *Spec-OP*, which characterises that relation. We can express this relation as a set of pairs of states as follows:

```
{ (before, after)
| before:State, after:State
• inv-State(before) ∧ pre-OP(before) ∧
  post-OP(before,after) ∧ inv-State(after)
}
```

where *pre-OP*, *post-OP* and *inv-State* are the expressions that characterise the pre- and postconditions of the the operation *OP* and the state invariant, respectively.

In other notations, such as Z, the precondition may not be explicitly stated, but can be calculated if needed from the specification (see, for instance, [W1]), and the invariant may be made accessible by unfolding the state definitions into the operation.

It will also help us if all types defined in the specification can be decomposed into the basic types, such as Natural numbers, and Booleans, or sets, sequences and maps of basic types. Where types carry invariants, or characterising expressions, these too will then become an explicit part of the operation definition.

This formulation of *spec-OP* corresponds to the idea that, whilst we are only interested in creating tests for the operation for cases in which the precondition (and before-state invariant) is true, we wish to make use of valuable information contained in the structure of the postcondition which leads to a further decomposition into cases. This is important for a number of reasons:

- it may permit the specifier to discover, by examination of the test domains generated, combinations of input and before-state values for which the specification is not satisfiable;
- if the specification is in an advanced state of refinement, it is the structure of the postcondition that will allow us to create, in effect, a white-box test-suite;
- information in the post-condition can provide constraints on the possible results of the operation, to be used later in the validation process.

We continue by splitting the above relation into a set of smaller relations, the union of which is equivalent to the original. This splitting is achieved by transforming its propositional structure into a Disjunctive Normal Form (DNF). The particular formulation is based on a treatment of *or* in which $A \vee B$ is transformed into three disjoint cases: $A \wedge B$, $\neg A \wedge B$ and $A \wedge \neg B$. This in turn transforms $A \Rightarrow B$ into two cases: $\neg A$ and $(A \wedge B)$. This allows us to treat each sub-relation entirely independently. If the ordinary rules for *or* are used, the separate treatment of each sub-relation has to be justified by the use of an appropriate hypothesis.

To illustrate reduction to DNF, consider the following example of a simple VDM operation, MAX, which sets a state component *max* to the larger of its two integer arguments, a and b:

$$MAX(a : \mathbb{Z}, b : \mathbb{Z})$$
$$\textbf{wr } max : \mathbb{Z}$$
$$\textbf{post } (\ max = a \vee max = b \ ) \wedge$$
$$max \geq a \wedge$$
$$max \geq b$$

Since there is no precondition or state-invariant, the characterising expression to be normalised in this example is simply the postcondition:

$$(\ max = a \vee max = b \ ) \wedge$$
$$max \geq a \wedge$$
$$max \geq b$$

Distributing the $\vee$ gives:

$$(\ max = a \wedge max \geq a \wedge max \geq b \ ) \vee$$
$$(\ max = b \wedge max \geq a \wedge max \geq b \ )$$

This gives rise to the following set of three disjoint cases:

$$\{ \; max = a \wedge max = b \wedge max \geq a \wedge max \geq b,$$
$$max = a \wedge max \neq b \wedge max \geq a \wedge max \geq b,$$
$$max \neq a \wedge max = b \wedge max \geq a \wedge max \geq b \; \}$$

These in turn simplify to:

$$\{ \; max = a \wedge max = b,$$
$$max = a \wedge max > b,$$
$$max = b \wedge max > a \; \}$$

For each disjoint case, we have an expression which characterises a sub-relation, *sub-spec-OP*, describing a single test domain.

To summarise, and add other incidental details:

Partition Analysis of an Operation

Step 1: Extract the definition of *spec-OP*, by collecting together all the relevant parts (pre/postconditions, invariants ...).

Step 2: Unfold all definitions, to eliminate all auxiliary predicate calls, and introduce basic types where possible. (The unfolding of recursive function and type definitions has, of course, to be limited. This is discussed below.)

Step 3: Transform the definition into DNF to obtain disjoint sub-relations.

Step 4: Simplify each sub-relation, possibly splitting it into further sub-relations, by using inference rules based on the first order predicate calculus. (How this is achieved in our tool will be briefly described in Sect. 5, and in detail in [DF1].)

Our treatment of recursion is motivated by what we are trying to achieve. Transformation into DNF is akin to the path-coverage analysis of a program. Typically, where loops are encountered in the program, paths that traverse the body of the loop up to a fixed number of times are selected. By analogy, we have chosen to unfold the body of every recursive definition a fixed number of times in every different context in which a call to it appears. This allows us to exploit the propositional structure of every definition, without getting lost in infinite structures. This approach is similar to the use of regularity hypotheses in [BGM1]. Each time such a limit is placed on unfolding, the underlying hypothesis should be justified.

We now illustrate partition analysis by an example. The *Triangle Problem* is becoming a classical example for test-case generation ([N1]). This is perhaps because it gives rise to a simple formal specification, and yet requires a good number of tests to be accurately validated.

The Triangle Problem consists in determining if three lengths given as input constitute the three sides of a triangle, and if the triangle is scalene, isosceles or equilateral.

The formal specification in VDM-SL of the Triangle Problem is given as follows:

types
Triangle $= \mathbb{Z}*$
    inv $t \underline{\triangle} \; \textbf{len} \; t = 3 \wedge (\forall \; i \in \textbf{elems} \; t \bullet (2 \times i) < sum(t))$
TriangleType $=$ SCALENE | ISOSCELES | EQUILATERAL | INVALID

functions
$sum : \mathbb{Z}* \to \mathbb{Z}$
$sum(seq) \underline{\Delta}$ if $seq = []$ then 0 else (hd seq) + sum(tl seq)

$classify : \mathbb{Z}* \to TriangleType$
$classify(sides) \underline{\Delta}$ if *is-Triangle*($sides$) then *variety*($sides$) else INVALID

$variety : Triangle \to TriangleType$
$variety(sides) \underline{\Delta}$

> **cases card(elems** *sides*) :
>> (1) $\to$ EQUILATERAL,
>> (2) $\to$ ISOSCELES,
>> (3) $\to$ SCALENE
> **end**

operations
$CHARACTERISATION(sides : \mathbb{Z}*)$ type : $TriangleType$
   post $type = classify(sides)$

The function *sum* is recursive, and we have chosen to unfold it just once in every context. However, as will be seen below, in most of the cases generated, we know the exact length of its argument, which permits us to unfold *sum* completely.

Note that the specification of the Triangle Problem contains no system state. This means that the further treatment of specifications to be discussed in the Sect. 3 is irrelevant, since it works on the system state.

For convenience, we have specified the main functionality as an operation, *CHARACTERISATION*, with no state component. After extracting and unfolding the definition of the operation, partition analysis produces 22 cases at the end of Step 3. Using the deeper knowledge of the predicate calculus at Step 4, 14 of these cases turn out to be false, due to conflicting constraints not detectable during simple reduction into DNF, such as:

$$len\ sides' = 3\ \wedge\ sides' = []$$

This leaves the 8 following subdomains:

Case 1: Scalene.
$3 = $ **card** { $sides'(1), sides'(2), sides'(3)$ }
$type = $ SCALENE
elems $sides' = $ { $sides'(1), sides'(2), sides'(3)$ }
inds $sides' = $ { 1, 2, 3 }
$sides'(2) + sides'(3) > sides'(1)$
$sides'(1) + sides'(3) > sides'(2)$
$sides'(1) + sides'(2) > sides'(3)$
$sides'(1) \in \mathbb{N}_1$
$sides'(2) \in \mathbb{N}_1$
$sides'(3) \in \mathbb{N}_1$

Case 2: Isosceles with sides 1 and 2 equal.
$2 = $ **card** { $sides'(2), sides'(3)$ }
$type = $ ISOSCELES
elems $sides' = $ { $sides'(2), sides'(3)$ }
inds $sides' = $ { 1, 2, 3 }
$sides'(1) = sides'(2)$
$sides'(2) + sides'(2) > sides'(3)$
$sides'(2) \in \mathbb{N}_1$
$sides'(3) \in \mathbb{N}_1$

Case 3: Isosceles with sides 2 and 3 equal.
$2 = $ **card** { $sides'(1), sides'(3)$ }
$type = $ ISOSCELES

elems *sides'* = { *sides'*(1), *sides'*(3) }
inds *sides'* = { 1, 2, 3 }
sides'(2) = *sides'*(3)
sides'(3) + *sides'*(3) > *sides'*(1)
sides'(1) ∈ $\mathbb{N}_1$
sides'(3) ∈ $\mathbb{N}_1$

Case 4: Isosceles with sides 1 and 3 equal.
2 = **card** { *sides'*(2), *sides'*(3) }
type = ISOSCELES
elems *sides'* = { *sides'*(2), *sides'*(3) }
inds *sides'* = { 1, 2, 3 }
sides'(1) = *sides'*(3)
sides'(3) + *sides'*(3) > *sides'*(2)
sides'(2) ∈ $\mathbb{N}_1$
sides'(3) ∈ $\mathbb{N}_1$

Case 5: Equilateral.
1 = **card** { *sides'*(3) }
type = EQUILATERAL
elems *sides'* = { *sides'*(3) }
inds *sides'* = { 1, 2, 3 }
sides'(1) = *sides'*(3)
sides'(2) = *sides'*(3)
sides'(3) ∈ $\mathbb{N}_1$

Case 6: Invalid with sides not satisfying triangle property.
type = INVALID
sides' ≠ []
∃i ∈ **elems** *sides'* • *sides'*(1) + *sum*(**tl** *sides'*) ≥ 2 × i
elems *sides'* ⊆ $\mathbb{Z}$

Case 7: Invalid with wrong number of sides satisfying triangle property.

type = INVALID
3 ≠ **len** *sides'*
sides' ≠ []
∀i ∈ **elems** *sides'* • 2 × i < *sides'*(1) + *sum*(**tl** *sides'*)
elems *sides'* ⊆ $\mathbb{Z}$

Case 8: Invalid with no sides.
type = INVALID
sides' = []

These 8 cases represent test domains from which test-cases can be selected, taking into account boundary cases, minimum and maximum integers, etc. We could automate the generation of such boundary cases by a further inference step in which domains containing, for instance, $x \in \mathbb{Z}$, are further partitioned by

$$0 < x \leq MAXINT \qquad x = 0 \qquad 0 > x \geq MININT$$

3 Test Sequencing

We have so far considered the treatment of operations in isolation from one another: partition analysis is used to determine cases for which individual operations should be tested. There are, however, a number of important theoretical and practical issues to be addressed in the use of formal specifications in the testing process after partition analysis. These mainly relate to the problems involved in scheduling the sequence of tests to be performed so as to achieve the right internal state of the system to be tested. These issues have implications for the design of test-beds for systems.

Our motivation is to be able to place the physical system in the states required by the test domains. One solution is to provide test-bed functions which can place the system directly into any desired state, and use the partition analysis of individual operations to test operations directly. In many systems, this just will not be practical, perhaps because it has inaccessible imported components without the necessary functionality, or perhaps due to the sheer expense or complexity involved. In these cases, it is probably only achievable by the execution of sequences of operations, which could themselves be tests. The problem therefore becomes closely related to the issue of how best to sequence the tests to avoid unnecessary repetition. Here an analysis of the formal specification can help.

Suppose that we have already performed partition analysis on individual operations, giving rise to a set of subcases of each operation, which we call sub-operations. In this we should include a partition analysis of the initial state specification, treated as an operation without a before state. What interests us is an FSA whose transitions are precisely this set of sub-operations. A complete traversal of the FSA will then give us a complete sequence of the tests we wish to perform. The states of such an FSA, then, are those in which the pre- or postcondition of at least one sub-operation is satisfied.

We propose the following method of finding the FSA:

Calculating an FSA from a State-based Specification

Step 1. Perform partition analysis on all individual operations and initial state to obtain the set of sub-operations.

Step 2. Extract from each sub-operation two sets of constraints, one describing its before state, and the other describing its after state. This is done by existentially quantifying every variable external to the state in question, and simplifying.

Step 3. Perform partition analysis, by reduction to DNF, of the disjunction of the sets of constraints found in Step 2. The resulting partitions will describe disjoint states in which at least one sub-operation either creates the state (corresponding to the post-condition) or is executable in that state (corresponding to the pre-condition).

Step 4. Step 1 has provided the transitions of the FSA, and Step 3 has provided its states. The FSA can now be constructed by resolving the constraints of sub-operations against states. A transition labeled OP is created from $S1$ to $S2$ for every sub-operation OP and every state $S1$ and $S2$ satisfying

$$(S1, S2) \in rel\text{-}OP$$

where $rel\text{-}OP$ is the relation on states defined by the constraints on OP resulting from partition analysis.

Step 5. If possible, simplify the FSA using classical FSA reduction techniques.

Since partition analysis always gives a finite number of partitions, we can always find an FSA corresponding to a specification. The result is an FSA of exactly the right level of abstraction for the task in hand. But, since it is a finite state abstraction of the, in general, infinite number of states allowable by the specification, we must allow for the FSA to be non-deterministic; that is, two arcs with the same label (same sub-operation) lead from the same before state to different after states. This non-determinacy considerably increases the complexity of solving the sequence-finding problem, and will be discussed later.

For the purposes of testing, we need to find a path through the FSA which traverses every transition with the *minimum number of repetitions*. Sequences will start with an "initial" sub-operation, which places the system into a valid initial state, as defined by the specification, and will proceed by the composition of successive sub-operations until all sub-operations have been covered. More than one sequence may be necessary, branching in different directions, to cover all of the cases. For this reason, the duplication of some tests may be unavoidable. It may not be possible to select a single path that traverses all the arcs; or it may be better not to do so when several shorter paths will do.

Since there may be several transitions for each sub-operation, this means that each sub-operation may be used several times in different contexts. This corresponds to a finer partition of operations than is obtained from the partition analysis of individual operations.

As a path through the FSA is found, a sequence of operations is formed. As each new operation is added to the sequence, the composition of resulting constraints must be resolved. These constraints may then be used to resolve non-determinism in the FSA. Where the non-determinism cannot be disambiguated as the constraints are resolved, it is because there is looseness in the specification which can only be resolved by execution of the implementation. The effect of this is that a complete path through the FSA can only be found as the tests are performed, the remaining path being recalculated after each test. For this reason, it is not obvious that classical path-finding algorithms (see for instance [ADLU1]) could be easily adapted to assist.

Similar problems arise when a test fails. The test process may suddenly find the system in an unexpected state. One option would be simply to stop, and let the error be corrected. But this is not desirable, because it fragments the test process; it is better to push on to find as many errors as possible in a single test run. In this case, a recalculation of the remaining sequence will have to take place, leaving out the erroneous case, and as many as possible of those tests already performed.

The following procedure suggests itself for sequencing tests in a complete test suite.

Performing Tests

Step 1. Using the FSA, chart several paths (or perhaps just one), from some initial state, in which every test appears a minimum number of times, but at least once, in the set of paths selected. As the paths are constructed, the composition of the constraints is resolved at each stage, to ensure a valid and unambiguous path;

Step 2. Choose test data values for all the operations in the sequence which satisfy the composed constraints.

Step 3. Perform the first (next) test, and check the result against the specification. If the test is successful, then

- if the system is in the expected state for the currently selected sequence, continue the test sequence with the next test at Step 3;

– if the system is not in the expected state for the currently selected sequence (due to non-determinism), repeat from Step 1, assuming the current state as the initial state, omitting where possible the tests already performed.

Otherwise, if the test is unsuccessful, check the after-state of the system, and

– if it matches the current composite constraints (*i.e.* the operation failed in relation to its result value, but left the system in the correct state), continue the test sequence;

– if it does not satisfy the current composite constraints, but does correspond to another state in the FSA, repeat from Step 1, assuming the current state as the initial state, omitting the erroneous case, and taking into account the tests already performed;

– else repeat from Step 1, restarting from an initial state, omitting the erroneous case, and taking into account the tests already performed;

Step 4. Repeat from Step 2 for another sequence.

In this way, the maximum number of tests can be performed in a single test run, despite the occurrence of non-determinism and failure, and the formal specification is used to a maximum in scheduling the sequence of tests.

Important issues from a testing point of view arise from this approach. It may be desirable to test the system for all possible valid sequences of operations, giving rise to testing very much like that carried out in the process algebra world for protocols [SL1], and a different analysis of the FSA. Quite independently of this, as soon as operations are chained together, possible dependencies become visible which could give rise to further test cases, or the elimination of some suggested by partition analysis of the individual operations. The latter situation will arise when it is found that it is just not possible to put the system, using the given operations, into a state appropriate for a particular test. For an example of operation dependencies, what if the result of one operation is identified with the input of the next?

The main implication of these issues for an automated testing environment based on formal specifications is that the analysis tool must be fully integrated with the testing environment. It must provide the facility of solving logical constraints during the execution of the tests, for

– finding appropriate test sequences;
– the selection of appropriate test data;
– the verification of the result of the operation;
– the comparison of the state of the physical system with abstract states in the FSA.

We should also briefly mention the problem of relating the abstract values of the specification to the concrete values of the implementation. If testing from the formal specification is to be automated, the test-bed will have to be equipped with the means of converting between these abstract and concrete values. In ideal circumstances, retrieval functions could be implemented as part of the test-bed to expose the state of the system in terms relating to the specification. Such functions may even correspond to those used during a formal development. Even if these are true functions, in the sense that a concrete value has a single abstract representation, it cannot be guaranteed that they are implementable, or even calculable. Moving in the other direction, an abstract value could have many concrete representatives (possibly an infinite number). A means of selecting an appropriate concrete value will have to be provided.

At the time of writing, the tool we have developed allows the user to compose a sequence of tests, and checks at each stage that the composition is satisfiable. An implementation of the calculation of an FSA by partition analysis is planned in the very near future. In the example that now follows, the FSA was calculated by hand, and the tool was used to verify the selected sequence by operation composition.

The example concerns a system process scheduler. At any one time, the system may have some processes *ready* to be scheduled, some processes *waiting* for some external action before they become *ready* and, optionally, a single *active* process. Each process is identified by a unique *Pid* (process identifier). There is a state invariant indicating that the two sets *ready* and *waiting* are always disjoint (a process cannot be both ready and waiting), that the active process is not ready or waiting, and that the only time there is no active process is when there are none ready to be scheduled. It also contains an auxiliary function definition, *schedule*, which characterises the scheduling algorithm very abstractly: it simply chooses any process from the provided set.

There are three operations: *NEW* which introduces a new process into the system in waiting state, *READY* which moves a waiting process into a ready state, making it active if the system is idle, and *SWAP* which swaps the currently active process for a ready one, leaving the system idle if there are no ready processes. The initial state of the system is idle and empty of processes:

```
state System of
        active  : [Pid]
        ready   : Pid-set
        waiting : Pid-set
inv mk-System(active,ready,waiting) △
                ready ∩ waiting = ∅   ∧
                active ∉ (ready ∪ waiting)   ∧
                (active = nil) ⇒ (ready = ∅)
init mk-System(active,ready,waiting) △
                ready ∪ waiting = ∅   ∧
                active = nil

end


types
    Pid = ℕ


functions
    schedule(from:Pid-set)sel:Pid
    pre     from ≠ ∅
    post    sel ∈ from


operations
    NEW(p:Pid)
    wr waiting:Pid-set
    rd active:[Pid]
    pre     p ≠ active ∧
            p ∉ (ready ∪ waiting)
    post    waiting = waiting' ∪ { p }

    READY(q:Pid)
    wr waiting:Pid-set
```

wr *ready:Pid*-set
wr *active:[Pid]*
pre $q \in waiting$
post $waiting = waiting' - \{ q \} \wedge$
     if $active' = $ nil
     then
             ($ready = ready' \wedge$
              $active = q$)
     else
             ($ready = ready' \cup \{ q \} \wedge$
              $active = active'$)

$SWAP()$
wr *active:[Pid]*
wr *ready:Pid*-set
wr *waiting:Pid*-set
pre $active \neq $ nil
post **if** $ready' = \emptyset$
     then ($active = $ nil $\wedge ready = \emptyset$)
     else   ($active = schedule(ready') \wedge$
                   $ready = ready' - \{active\}$) $\wedge$
     $waiting = waiting' \cup \{active'\}$

The result of partition analysis on the individual operations gives the obvious set of 7 sub-operations, two for each operation, and one for the initial state:

$INIT$-1	$active = $ nil	$READY$-2(q')	$active = active'$
	$ready = \emptyset$		$ready = ready' \cup \{ q' \}$
	$waiting = \emptyset$		$waiting = waiting' - \{ q' \}$
			$ready' \cap waiting' = \emptyset$
NEW-1(p')	$active = $ nil		$active' \neq $ nil
	$ready = \emptyset$		$active' \notin ready'$
	$waiting = waiting' \cup \{ p' \}$		$active' \notin waiting'$
	$active' = $ nil		$waiting' \subseteq \mathbb{N}$
	$ready' = \emptyset$		$active' \in \mathbb{N}$
	$p' \notin waiting'$		$q' \in waiting'$
	$p' \in \mathbb{N}$		$ready' \subseteq \mathbb{N}$
	$waiting' \subseteq \mathbb{N}$		
NEW-2(p')	$waiting = waiting' \cup \{ p' \}$		
	$active' = active$		
	$ready' = ready$	$SWAP$-1()	$active = $ nil
	$ready \cap waiting' = \emptyset$		$ready = \emptyset$
	$active \neq p'$		$waiting = waiting' \cup \{ active' \}$
	$active \notin ready$		$ready' = \emptyset$
	$active \notin waiting'$		$active' \notin waiting'$
	$p' \notin ready$		$active' \in \mathbb{N}$
	$p' \notin waiting'$		$waiting' \subseteq \mathbb{N}$
	$active \in \mathbb{N}$	$SWAP$-2()	$ready = ready' - \{ active \}$
	$ready \subseteq \mathbb{N}$		$waiting = waiting' \cup \{ active' \}$
	$waiting' \subseteq \mathbb{N}$		$ready' \cap waiting' = \emptyset$
			$active' \notin ready'$
$READY$-1(q')	$active = q'$		$active' \notin waiting'$
	$active' = $ nil		$active \in ready'$
	$ready = \emptyset$		$active' \in \mathbb{N}$
	$waiting = waiting' - \{ active \}$		$ready' \subseteq \mathbb{N}$
	$ready' = \emptyset$		$waiting' \subseteq \mathbb{N}$
	$active \in \mathbb{N}$		
	$active \in waiting'$		
	$waiting' \subseteq \mathbb{N}$		

Partition analysis of the system state for finding the FSA gives the following 6 states:

1 $active = nil$	4 $active \neq nil$
$ready = \emptyset$	$ready = \emptyset$
$waiting = \emptyset$	$waiting \neq \emptyset$

2 $active = nil$	5 $active \neq nil$
$ready = \emptyset$	$ready \neq \emptyset$
$waiting \neq \emptyset$	$waiting = \emptyset$

3 $active \neq nil$	6 $active \neq nil$
$ready = \emptyset$	$ready \neq \emptyset$
$waiting = \emptyset$	$waiting \neq \emptyset$

The associated FSA is therefore as shown in Fig. 1.

This FSA cannot be reduced by classic reduction techniques. Note that it is non-deterministic in states 2, 5 and 6. In fact the choice of arc to follow is always determined by the composed constraints of the operations that lead to non-deterministic states. What has happened here, in effect, is that the partition analysis that takes into account all the operations has resulted in a finer partitioning of individual operations. This is not only manifest in the above non-determinacy, but also in the duplicated arcs for NEW-1 on states 1 and 2, and for NEW-2 on states 4 and 6, for example. For a complete test, every arc should be traversed, including the duplicates.

The sequence of operations we have chosen is given below:

$init$-1 ; NEW-1(p-1) ; $READY$-1(p-1) ; NEW-2(p-3) ; $READY$-2(p-3) ; $SWAP$-2 ; $READY$-2(p-7) ; NEW-2(p-7) ; $READY$-2(p-7) ; $SWAP$-2 ; NEW-2(p-7) ; $READY$-2(p-7) ; $SWAP$-2 ; $SWAP$-2 ; $SWAP$-1 ; NEW-1(p-1) ; $READY$-1(p-7) ; $SWAP$-1 ; $READY$-1(p-7) ; NEW-2(p-7)

This sequences traverses all of the 18 arcs in 20 transitions. The duplicated transitions are $READY$-1 between states 2 and 3, and $READY$-2 between 4 and 5.

When test data has been randomly selected, the constraints associated with this sequence of tests is as follows:

Operation	Constraints
1 $INIT()$	$active$-1 $=$ nil $\wedge$ $ready$-1 $= \emptyset$ $\wedge$ $waiting$-1 $= \emptyset$
2 NEW-1(15)	$active$-2 $=$ nil $\wedge$ $ready$-2 $= \emptyset$ $\wedge$ $waiting$-2 $= \{ 15 \}$
3 $READY$-1(15)	$active$-3 $= 15 \wedge ready$-3 $= \emptyset \wedge waiting$-3 $= \emptyset$
4 NEW-2(9)	$active$-4 $= 15 \wedge ready$-4 $= \emptyset \wedge waiting$-4 $= \{ 9 \}$
5 $READY$-2(9)	$active$-5 $= 15 \wedge ready$-5 $= \{ 9 \} \wedge waiting$-5 $= \emptyset$
6 $SWAP$-2()	$active$-6 $= 9 \wedge ready$-6 $= \emptyset \wedge waiting$-6 $= \{ 15 \}$
7 $READY$-2(15)	$active$-7 $= 9 \wedge ready$-7 $= \{ 15 \} \wedge waiting$-7 $= \emptyset$
8 NEW-2(4)	$active$-8 $= 9 \wedge ready$-8 $= \{ 15 \} \wedge waiting$-8 $= \{ 4 \}$
9 $READY$-2(4)	$active$-9 $= 9 \wedge ready$-9 $= \{ 4, 15 \} \wedge waiting$-9 $= \emptyset$
10 $SWAP$-2()	$active$-10 $\in \{ 4, 15 \} \wedge ready$-10 $= \{ 4, 15 \} - \{active$-10$\} \wedge waiting$-10 $= \{ 9 \}$
11 NEW-2(67)	$active$-11 $= active$-10 $\wedge ready$-11 $= \{ 4, 15 \} - \{active$-10$\} \wedge waiting$-11 $= \{ 9, 67 \}$
12 $READY$-2(9)	$active$-12 $= active$-10 $\wedge ready$-12 $= \{ 4, 9, 15 \} - \{active-10\} \wedge waiting$-12 $= \{ 67 \}$
13 $SWAP$-2()	$active$-13 $\in \{ 4, 9, 15 \} \wedge ready$-13 $= \{ 4, 9, 15 \} - \{ active$-10, $active$-13 $\} \wedge$ $waiting$-13 $= \{ active$-10, 67 $\} \wedge active$-13 $\neq active$-10
14 $SWAP$-2()	$active$-14 $\in \{ 4, 9, 15 \} \wedge ready$-14 $= \emptyset \wedge waiting$-14 $= \{ active$-10, $active$-13, 67 $\} \wedge$ $active$-14 $\neq active$-13 $\wedge active$-14 $\neq active$-10 $\wedge active$-13 $\neq active$-10
15 $SWAP$-1()	$active$-15 $=$ nil $\wedge ready$-15 $= \emptyset \wedge waiting$-15 $= \{ 4, 9, 15, 67 \}$
16 NEW-1(12)	$active$-16 $=$ nil $\wedge ready$-16 $= \emptyset \wedge waiting$-16 $= \{ 4, 9, 12, 15, 67 \}$
17 $READY$-1(15)	$active$-17 $= 15 \wedge ready$-17 $= \emptyset \wedge waiting$-17 $= \{ 4, 9, 12, 67 \}$
18 $SWAP$-1()	$active$-18 $=$ nil $\wedge ready$-18 $= \emptyset \wedge waiting$-18 $= \{ 4, 9, 12, 15, 67 \}$
19 $READY$-1(12)	$active$-19 $= 12 \wedge ready$-19 $= \emptyset \wedge waiting$-19 $= \{ 4, 9, 15, 67 \}$
20 NEW-2(26)	$active$-20 $= 12 \wedge ready$-20 $= \emptyset \wedge waiting$-20 $= \{ 4, 9, 15, 26, 67 \}$

Note the looseness in the specification which is manifest in steps 10 and 13. In this example, the looseness does not lead to non-determinism in the FSA. All of the

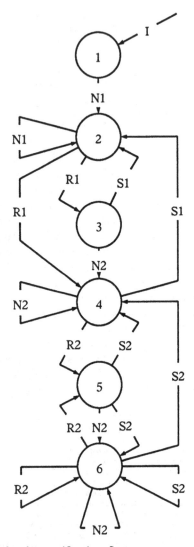

Fig. 1. The FSA created for the specification *System*.

non-determinism is resolved by composed constraints during the path construction.

4 The Tool

The test case generation tool has been written in SEPIA Prolog with KEGI, an XView interfacing tool, and amounts to about 9000 lines of code. It has been integrated in the Atmosphere VDM tool-set [L1] which includes:

– a VDM multi-font editor;

- a VDM type checker;
- "VDM through Pictures", [DL1] a tool which allows specifications to be represented as diagrams, with transformations between text and visual notations.

The tool hooks onto the back of the VDM parser to extract representations of VDM specifications. Reduction to DNF is performed in Prolog, and VDM knowledge is encoded as a set of about 200 inference rules, which are used in Step 4 of partition analysis. This specialised theorem-proving capability does not aspire to be complete, since it is handling the full first-order predicate logic. The set of inference rules may be extended to treat particular cases as needed. As the tool "gains experience" in this way, the range of problems treatable is expanded.

At the time of writing, the techniques in the paper are all implemented except the generation of FSAs and test values. In addition, we have a tool which allows sequences of operations to be composed, and their combined constraints resolved.

The tool is described in detail in [DF1].

5 Conclusions

We have presented techniques for automatic partition analysis of model-based specifications with a view to the generation and sequencing of test-cases. We have implemented a tool specialising these techniques for VDM. The main novelty lies in the use of a special DNF for partition analysis, and in the technique described for extracting an FSA from the specification.

The work is in its early stages. Many more experiments will have to be done to assess the theoretical and practical viability of the techniques. The tool in its present form cannot treat very large specifications. This is because of the size of expressions generating during reduction to DNF. There are now, however, very efficient techniques for treating this problem, which can rapidly handle huge expressions [CM1].

One limitation inherent to this approach is the fact that with VDM-like specification languages, we are working in a semi-decidable logic, which in general cannot be fully automated. This incompleteness problem, as briefly mentioned in the previous section, is handled in our tool by using an extendible set of inference rules. The implications of the incompleteness are, however, as follows:

- same test domains may not be reduced to false, resulting in test cases that will (should) always fail. This is moderated a little by the fact that the falsehood of the domain will almost certainly be detected when actual test values are substituted into the constraints;
- the partition analysis may not be as detailed as possible, since the deeper propositional structure of some test domains may not have been exploited to the full in generating further sub-domains. To notice this problem may require a considerable amount of expertise and careful observation on the part of the practitioner.

Another limitation is our treatment of recursion. Whilst being adequate for the partition analysis that we perform, it does require prior reflection and intervention from the user. The absence of a full treatment of recursion in the theorem-proving aspects of the tool will also severely restrict the use of the techniques in any more general theorem proving domain.

There are other potential advantages of partition analysis in formal specifications. The generation of test cases is for internal verification of a product, *i.e.* is the implementation correct with respect to the specification? The analysis techniques described may also useful as a means of external validation, *i.e.* is the specification correct with respect to requirements? This is because the presentation of the specification as a set of cases provides an alternative view of its implications, and can help the specifier reflect on its meaning. Moreover, the ability to generate an FSA corresponding to a specification may provide valuable insight into its dynamic aspects. Indeed, it would be interesting to link the generation of the FSA to the Operation State Diagrams used in [DL1] in the visualisation of VDM.

Another interesting line of study here, would be to look at the effect of refinement on partition analysis. Does refining a specification create a super-set of the partitions of the previous level? Can partition analysis be used to guide the refinement process?

Acknowledgements: We wish to thank Bruno Marre and Marie-Claude Gaudel for useful discussions during the early stages of this work, Pat Hall for his very encouraging letter, Dick Hamlet for his comments as a referee on a previous incarnation of the paper, and the FME'93 referees for their constructive critisms, particularly for the suggestion of the *MAX* example. Alain Faivre conducted his part of this work whilst studying for his Diplôme d'Ingénieur at the Conservatoire National des Arts et Metiers, Paris, supervised by Prof. Philippe Facon.

References

[ADLU1] Aho A. V., Dahbura A. T., Lee D., Uyar M.U., *An Optimisation Technique for Protocol Conformance Test Generation Based on UIO Sequences and Rural Chinese Postman Tours*, Proc. Protocol Specification, Test and Verification VIII, 1988

[BGM1] Bernot G, Gaudel M-C, Marre B, *Software Testing Based on Formal Specifications: a Theory and a Tool*, Software Eng. Journal, Nov 1991

[CM1] O. Coudert, J. C. Madre, "Towards a Symbolic Logic Minimization Algorithm", in Proc. of *VLSI Design'93*, Bombay, India, January 1993.

[D1] John Dawes, *The VDM-SL Reference Guide*, Pitman, 1991.

[D2] Tim Denvir, *Introduction to Discrete Mathematics for Software Engineering*, Mac Millan, 1986.

[DF1] Jeremy Dick, Alain Faivre, *Automatic Partition Analysis of VDM Specifications*, Research Report RAD/DMA/92027, Bull Research Centre, Les Clayes-sous-Bois, France, Oct 1992

[DL1] Jeremy Dick, Jérôme Loubersac, *Integrating Structured and Formal Methods: A Visual Approach to VDM*, Proc. ESEC'91, Milan, Springer-Verlag LNCS 550, pp.37-59, Oct 1991

[FJ1] L.M.G. Feijs, H.B.M. Jonkers. *Specification and Design with COLD-K*, Philips Research Laboratories, Eindhoven, The Netherlands.

[H1] Hall, Patrick A. V., *Towards a Theory of Test Data Selection*, Second IEE/BCS Conf. Software Engineering 88. IEE Conf. Publication Number 290. pp. 159-163. 1988

[H2]	Hall, Patrick A. V., *Relationship between specifications and testing*, Information and Software Technology, Jan/Feb 1991
[HH1]	Hall P. A. V., Hierons R., *Formal Methods and Testing*, The Open Univ. Computing Dept. Tech Report No 91/16, August 1991
[J1]	Cliff B. Jones, *Systematic Software Development using VDM*, Second Edition, Prentice Hall Int., 1990.
[L1]	J. Loubersac, *VtP Users' Guide*, Atmosphere deliverable No. I4.1.4.2.3.1, Bull Research Centre, 1992.
[N1]	N. D. North, *Automatic Test Generation for the Triangle Problem*, National Physical Laboratory Report DITC 161/90, February 1990.
[P1]	M. Phillips, *CICS/ESA 3.1 Experience*, Procs. Z Users' Group, Oxford, 1989.
[S1]	G. T. Scullard, *Test Case Selection using VDM*, In Proc. VDM'88, LNCS 328, Springer Verlag.
[SL1]	Sidhu D. P., Lenung T. K., *Formal Methods in Protocol Testing: a Detailed Study*, IEEE Trans. SE Vol 15 No 4, 1989
[S2]	J. M. Spivey, *The Z Notation*, Prentice Hall, 1989.
[R1]	The RAISE Language Group, *The RAISE Specification Language*, Report No. CRI/RAISE/DOC/1/v1, CRI, Denmark 1991.
[W1]	J. Woodcock, M. Loomes *Software Engineering Mathematics* Pitman, 1988.

The Parallel Abstract Machine : A Common Execution Model for FDTs [*]

Guillaume Doumenc[1] and Jean-Francois Monin[2]

[1] Soft Mountain
Ophira 2, route des Dolines
Sophia-Antipolis
06565 Valbonne, France
email: gdo@cma.cma.fr
[2] C. N. E. T.
Centre Lannion A
2, route de Trégastel - BP 40
22 301 LANNION CEDEX
email: monin@lannion.cnet.fr

Abstract. We introduce a new execution model for implementing FDTs based on the reactive approach. In this model, called the *PAM*, systems are divided into several reactive entities communicating by an activation mechanism. This paper introduces the *PAM* approach and shows how different communication mechanisms such as asynchronous fifo in *ESTELLE* or multiple rendez-vous in *LOTOS* can be implemented. It then presents the analysis of an implementation of a transport protocol (CCITT T70).

1 Presentation

The *Parallel Abstract Machine* was first introduced in the RACE-SPECS project as a model for implementing the CRL language [SPECS]. This language and its semantics are constructed on the process calculus algebra paradigms [Mi80]. In such formalisms, the behaviour of a process is defined by Plotkin rules : the behaviour of a system is synthetized from the behaviours of its subsystems by a proof construction ([Pl81]).

This mecanism is used at compile time to transform an expression or even a specification into such a finite representation, such as finite sate machine or automaton. Unfortunately, such a transformation is not always feaseable and a more general model, where parallelism and communication still exist, has to be defined. We must point out that we call parallelism, the *logical* modularity and concurrence, but not the *physical* distribution.

Instead of adding parallelism into these classical formalisms, such as Petri Nets or derived approaches ([Ta89], [GaSi90]), we prefer *an operating system* point of view : in the*PAM*, a system is a net of virtual processes calculating at run-time the proof of a behaviour. More precisely, each node of the net is a behavioural operator, and the execution "simulates" the construction of the proof of the behaviour.

---

[*] This work has been realized at the Centre de Mathématiques Appliquées de l'École des Mines de Paris, place Sophie Laffitte, 06 560 SOPHIA ANTIPOLIS

In the *PAM* approach, each process is viewed as a *"black box"*, transforming input behaviours into a new output behaviour. The real implementation formalism for each process is not relevant to the model; only the behaviour transformation has to be described. The *PAM* is a machine in the configuration/move sense : from one configuration, a step represents the construction of a proof, the move is the realisation of the behaviour derived from this proof and then a new configuration is obtained.

In order to evaluate the *PAM* approach, the CNET decided to study the implementation of a real protocol defined in different specification languages. This study had two targets :

1. Illustrating how the *PAM* approach allows concurrent implementation of heterogeneous FDTs such as *ESTELLE* or *LOTOS*,
2. Evaluating the usefullness of such an approach to a real protocol specification.

This paper is a presentation of this evaluation. After a description of the reactive approach and of the *PAM* structure, we study how *ESTELLE* and *LOTOS* concepts can be implemented on the *PAM* model.

2 Presentation of the *PAM* model

2.1 The reactive approach

The reactive approach was developed in the early 80's for describing systems wich must interact continuously with their environment [HaPn85], [Be89]. When activated with some input events, a reactive system *reacts* by producing output events. The life of a reactive system is divided into *instants*, that are the moments where it reacts. Accordingly, one can speak of the first instant of a reactive program, the second instant, and so on. These instants are not related to physical time, which is why we often speak about *logical time* in reactive systems.

One basic hypothesis of the reactive approach is that reactions are *atomic* that is, a particular reaction does not interfere with other reactions. In other words, program reactions cannot overlap : there is no possibility to activate a system while it is still reacting to the current activation. This hypothesis simplifies reasoning about reactive systems as concurrency between reactions doesn't have to be considered. This hypothesis is called the *perfect synchrony hypothesis* in the *ESTEREL* or *LUSTRE* languages ([BeGo88], [CaPiHaPl87]).

2.2 The Parallel Abstract Machine

Since a process in the *PAM* model, is modeled as an operator, synthetizing behaviour of its children (in the net) to produce a new behaviour, the reactive property is then immediate : a process is a transducer of behaviours. The reactive approach is then the natural framework for implementing the *PAM* model. As a first consequence, the main difference between a *PAM* and other parallel machines is that a *PAM* has no notion of proper time. Another important feature of a *PAM* is that it needs an environment to execute.

Classically, processes are independant calculation units, with their own notion of clock and time. They interact with each other using communication mechanisms which synchronize them. By contrast, in the *PAM* model, processes are asleep until they are activated. Hence, the notion of clock and time are defined by the environment : *each new activation is a new instant.* In the sequel, *PAM* processes are called *rprocesses* (for reactive processes) to underline this particularity.

Activation gates The activation of a rprocess is performed through a structure called an *activation gate.* When activated a rprocess can also activate other rprocesses, so there are *input gates* and *ouput gates.* Conceptually, each rprocess is thought as a separate thread so that it cannot communicate with any other rprocess except through an activation gate. A configuration of a *PAM* consists of a one-to-one association of output gates and input gates.

A gate which is not linked to any other is called *observable,* and represent the interface with the environment. Theses observable gates of a given *PAM* allow us to consider this all *PAM* as a new rprocess of a bigger *PAM* with these observable gates as activation ones. If each node of the *PAM* is an operator, the whole *PAM* is a derived operator.

A *PAM* may be visualised as a directed graph where nodes represent rprocesses and edges represent links between activation gates. This graph may be decomposed in a top-down fashion : a node may be replaced by a sub-graph, provided this subgraph can be appropriately pasted into the behavioural transducer functionality of the original node.

The abstraction of an entire *PAM* into a single rprocess is the heart of our approach. An execution step of a *PAM* results from the reactions of the rprocesses each being activated at most once. The *atomicity hypothesis* of the execution steps defines the new abstract *PAM reaction.*

The execution model The execution model of the *PAM* arises from the abstraction of a rprocess into an operator : since the *PAM* is a *part of a theorem prover,* the execution will be the construction a proof.

The construction of this proof (to determine a possible behaviour) is not always deterministic and cannot be found in a straightforward way. In order to avoid a backtrack mechanism, which would be too slow at run-time, the proof construction is decomposed into two phases : *proposition* and *validation.*

1. At the end of each step, every rprocess puts in the *proposition channel* of its output gate, the list of possible activations it can perform (1). Some of them could result from a run-time calculation depending on values read on the proposition channel of its input gates.
2. At an observable gate of the *PAM*, a possible activation is then validated, i.e. one of the activations present in the proposition channel is chosen and put in the *validation channel* (2). Then the rprocess reacts and can perform validation of its own input gates in a similar way (3).

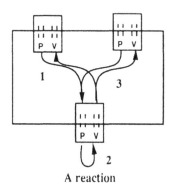

A reaction

The main problem is to ensure that this propagation of reactions will not diverge. For this purpose, we impose, for the moment, that :

1. Every rprocess has only one output gate,
2. Every input gate of a rprocess is linked to an output gate of another rprocess,
3. The configuration is always a tree.

In this case, propagation of propositions and validation is defined in a unique way by the structure. Accordingly, the first implementation of the CRL language (i.e. the kernel process algebra in the SPECS project) used directly the syntactic representation (syntactic tree) as configuration.

A formal definition We will now give a more formal definition of the PAM to describe without ambiguity how programs behave. In the sequel, we denote by $p, q, \ldots$ the rprocesses, and by $a, b, \ldots$ the activations. An activation gate is composed of a list of proposed activations and a validated one, i.e. $ag = (P, v)$. We will denote by $ag.P$ the list of proposed activations, and $ag.v$ the validated one. A rprocess is represented by a state s, a list of input gates I and one output gate o, hence $p = (s, I, o)$. As before, we denote the state s of p by $p.s$ and so on.

As is described above, a rprocess behaves like an algebraic operator on behaviours. Using a *behavioural semantics* is then quite natural. This semantics manipulates operational transitions having the following format :

$$s \xrightarrow{\{a_i\}_I / a} s'$$

This rewriting rule must be read as follows : from the state s, the rprocess can perform the activation a if the activations a_i belong respectively to its input gate $i \in I$. When activated by a, the rprocess moves to the new state s' (at the next instant, this rprocess will react from s').

Abstractly, we consider the PAM as a list of oriented and indexed connected rprocesses $\mathcal{PAM} = \{(p, n, q)\}$ (q is the nth child of p). The execution steps can be expressed more formally :

– The proposition step rule :

$$\frac{\{a_i \in p.i.P\} \ \& \ p.s \stackrel{\{a_i\}/a}{\rightarrow} p.s'}{p.o.P = p.o.P \cup \{a\}}$$

– The validation step rule :

$$\frac{p.o.v = a \ \& \ p.s \stackrel{\{a_i\}/a}{\rightarrow} p.s'}{p.s \rightarrow p.s' \ \& \ \{p.i.v = a_i\}}$$

These rules describe the behaviour of one rprocess. We now give the rule describing the propagation of propositions and validations in the *PAM* :

– The propagation rule :

$$\frac{(p, i, q) \in \mathcal{PAM}}{p.i.P = q'.o.P \ \& \ q.o.v = p'.i.v}$$

The synchronisation of the reactions is defined by the following algorithm :

1. First use the proposition step and propagation rules,
2. Wait for an external activation (the *PAM* is a rprocess of a bigger *PAM*...),
3. Then use the validation step and propagation rules,
4. Redo this calculation.

To be complete, we should say that some actions can modify dynamiquely the configuration of the net (in respect with the topologic constraints). This modification occurs at the end of every step, and doesn't disturb the construction of the proof.

3 Implementation of *ESTELLE* and *LOTOS*

In order to assess the adequacy of the PAM model to telecommunication protocols, we tested this approach on a case study. The aim was twofold :

1. first, testing if differents FDT's can be implemented on this execution model,
2. second, evaluating if this approach, with dynamic evaluation, is realistic for a real protocol.

We chose the CCITT T70 protocol – a videotex transport protocol –, because a description of this protocol is available in each of the standard FDTs.

More precisely, we arbitrarily chose to implement the T70 sender from the *ES-TELLE* description, and the receiver from the *LOTOS* description. In order to simulate the behaviour of the whole system, a medium was described using directly a reactive language RC [BoDo91].

Optimisation in the case of protocols However let us begin by a preliminary remark. The PAM model has been designed for giving a simple and common model for communicating systems specified using a combination of process algebras and of extended automatas. These formalisms, especially process algebras like LOTOS, allow quite abstracts ways of specification, e.g. "specification by constraints". Such styles are quite elegant, but are not intended to provide much information related to the order of events occuring during execution. Implementation has to go further, and this is why the proposition phase is needed in the PAM model.

Now it turns out that "real" telecommunication protocols, such as T70, are specified in a quite operationnal way. Moreover, a protocol entity should be able to accept any SDU or PDU at almost any time – of course, an incorrect SDU could occur, but a real protocol should be able to handle this abnormal situation.

This implies that the set of possible interactions is *known in advance*. In other words, the proposition phase of the PAM model becomes unnecessary for implementing such protocols.

Note however that the proposition phase remains of interest during the debugging phase, since it provides an interactive way of running an implementation.

Actual executions show that these implementations work satisfactorily for this kind of protocol. Response times range typically from 0.1 to 1 ms to etablish a connection, send a message and disconnect.

Instead of describing our implementation of T70, we prefer to give the guidelines we followed for implementing an *ESTELLE* or *LOTOS* specification using the *PAM* model.

LOTOS The implementation of the *LOTOS* specification language on our model can be done in two ways :

1. *LOTOS* can be considered as a process algebra and then each operator implemented directly as a rprocess. The configuration of the PAM after each step is exactly the same as the residual specification at each instant.
2. This notion of one operator/one rprocess can be enlarged to obtain the derived operator approach as in LOTOMATON [Na90]. In this approach, somre parts of a specification are viewed as derived operators and are compiled into extended automata; these automata represent the semantics of these derived operators. In this case the configuration is a sub-tree of the specification syntactic tree.
3. The synthetizers of behaviours can be considered to be the gates. In this case the gates are denoted by rprocesses which force or refuse the communication. In contrast to the classical approach, where communication are define under processes, here, a node gate is defined as a parent of the communication entities. At the top level, the observable gates are the output activation gates of observable *LOTOS* gates.

   In our implementation of the T70 test, we have represented the gates as operators, and processes as rprocesses. The actions proposed on gates are associated with data equations allowing unification in communication and representing the transfer of data. At each validation, these equations are resolved and variables are bounds.

ESTELLE The basic idea for implementing *ESTELLE* specifications using the PAM model is quite simple. An *ESTELLE* module hierarchy corresponds naturally to a tree of rprocesses, with one rprocess $transl(M)$ for each module instance M. When a transition t is offered by M, a corresponding reaction $r(t)$ is proposed by $transl(M)$ to $transl(P(m))$, where $P(M)$ is the parent module of M. Firing t corresponds to validating $r(t)$.

In the general case, parent/children conflicts can occur in the selection phase for finding the transitions to be fired in a module. The double propagation of propositions/validations of the *PAM* is used for implementing such situations in a fairly natural way. A parent module handles special reactions in order to take into account reactions corresponding to offered transitions of its children. However, these reactions are validated only when no transition of the parent is validated.

For implementing the no-blocking communication semantics of *ESTELLE*, one also has to introduce a rprocess for each FIFO queue handling an *ESTELLE* interaction point (or handling a set of common queued interaction points). These rprocesses are described in such a way that they continuously propose to accept any interaction [3]. An interaction output is represented in the *PAM* model by the validation of the activation of the FIFO transition corresponding to the reaction "enqueue this interaction". As these reactions are always considered as proposed, they can be validated without additional calculation, and hence without considering intermediate reactions. This allows an atomic implementation of transition firing in the *PAM* model, even in the case of transitions involving several outputs.

Let us now consider another interesting feature of *ESTELLE*, namely time handling via delay clauses. Recall that no explicit notion of time is provided in the *PAM* model. This issue is dealt with by introducing several rprocesses called *clock*, containing a data structure $C_{M,tr}$ for each pair (M, tr), where M is a module instance and tr a delayed transition of M. $C_{M,tr}$ represents the status of transition tr, denoted by `delays(tr,sit)` in the semantics of *ESTELLE* (see [ISO89], p. 87). Intuitively, each $C_{M,tr}$ is a little timer which is turned on as soon as tr is enabled, and is turned off when an enabling clause of tr is violated, or when the specified time has elapsed. In each case, a parametered activation is put on the corresponding validation channel of the rprocess implementing M, where the parameter is tested in order to decide whether tr has really to be fired. Each rprocess *clock* also proposes a implicit activation to increment the local current time. This reaction is validated by an external process, provided by the underlying operating system for instance.

4 Results of the implementation

The most important result of our evaluation is that this approach is not too slow for implementing high level protocols of the ISO layers (higher than the net layer). In addition, the top-down abstraction allows encapsulation of classical efficient formalisms.

---

[3] Of course they should in fact accept only well-typed interactions, but this typing information is not relevant at run time, since it could have been checked at compile time.

It is difficult to express a significative benchmark since the code was produced on workstation on which outer levels were simulated. On a Sony 68030 station, 500 connections followed by a transfert of one caracter and a deconnection takes about of 3.95 secondes.

One another positive result is that the automatic implementation of a specification into a net of rprocesses is not very difficult. It can be produced directly from the syntatic tree and from the operational semantics of the langage. Unfortunately it gives no idea of a distributed implementation of the parallelism.

5 Conclusion

We have presented a common execution model for heterogeneous FDTs such as *ESTELLE* and *LOTOS*. This model, called the *PAM*, has its origins in a reactive approach of Plotkin's semantic theory : *a process is a derived algebraic operator which transforms input behaviours into a synthetized output one.*

To evaluate this model, we have implemented a real protocol (CCITT T70) with the sender described in *ESTELLE* and the receiver in *LOTOS*. We have shown how asynchronous communication and multiple rendez-vous can be implemented on it. We have also shown that it can be reasonably used for upper layer ISO protocols.

We now study how the *PAM* can be distributed on different physical processors and how the model can be extended to cover powerful configurations.

References

[Be89] G. BERRY, 'Real Time Programming : special purpose or general languages', IFIP Congress (1989).

[BeGo88] G. BERRY AND G. GONTHIER, 'The Esterel Synchronous Programming Language : Design, semantics, implementation', INRIA RR-842 (1988).

[Bo91] F. BOUSSINOT, 'Réseaux de processus réactifs', Rapport de Recherche ENSMP-CMA 12/91 (1991).

[BoDo91] F. BOUSSINOT AND G. DOUMENC, 'Le langage Reactive C', Rapport de Recherche ENSMP-CMA 09/91 (1991).

[CaPiHaPl87] P. CASPI AND D. PILAUD AND N. HALBWAKS AND J. PLACE, 'LUSTRE, a Declarative Language for Programming Synchronous System', *Proceeding ACM Conference on Principles of Programming Languages*, Munich (1987).

[GaSi90] H.GARAVEL AND J. SIFAKIS, 'Compilation and Verification of LOTOS specification', *Proc. of the 10th Int. Symposium on Protocol, Specification, Testing and Verification*, IFIP North Holland (1990)

[HaPn85] D. HAREL AND A. PNUELI, *On the Development of Reactive Systems*, Logic and Models of Concurent Systems, Springer-Verlag, pp. 477-498 (1985).

[Na90] E. NAJM, '*LOTOMATON : A Wide Spectrum Transformation Framework For LOTOS*', LOTOSPHERE, Lo/WP11/T1.2/N0019 (1990).

[ISO89] ISO IS 9074. Estelle - A formal Description Technique Based on an Extended State Transition Model (1989).

[Pl81] G.D. PLOTKIN, "A structural approach to operational semantics', Lecture Notes, Aarhus Univ. (1981).

[Mi80] R. MILNER, '*A Calculus of Communicating Systems*', LNCS 92, SPRINGER-VERLAG (1980).

293

[SPECS] RACE Project, SPECS-Semantics, 'Code Generation: Presentation of the PAM and ASA models' MP.A61.1 (1990).

[Ta89] D.A.TAUBNER, *'Finite Representations of CCS and TCSP programs by automata and Petri nets'*, LNCS 369, Springer (1989).

Generalizing Abadi & Lamport's Method to Solve a Problem Posed by A. Pnueli

Kai Engelhardt* and Willem-Paul de Roever**

Christian-Albrechts-Universität zu Kiel, Institut für Informatik, W 2300 Kiel 1, Germany

Abstract. By adding a new technique and a simple proof strategy to Abadi & Lamport's 1988 method [1] for proving refinement between specifications of distributed programs correct, the inherent limitation of their method, occurring when the abstract level of specification features so-called infinite invisible nondeterminism or internal discontinuity, can be sometimes overcome. This technique is applied to the cruel last step of a three step correctness proof for an algorithm for communication between migrating processes within a finite network due to Kleinman, Moscowitz, Pnueli & Shapiro [5].

1 Introduction

In this paper we suggest a generalization of the method developed by Abadi & Lamport in [1] and utilize it to prove a refinement step in the derivation of a protocol that provides a mechanism analogous to message passing between possibly migrating processes in a fixed finite network of nodes.

This protocol is described in [5], and concerns a three step refinement of a specification of a distributed algorithm, hence, in all, concerning four layers of abstraction.

The challenge in proving refinement between these implementations correct is that Amir Pnueli posed us this problem as a typical illustration of the kind of implementations for which a straightforward proof using the method developed by Abadi & Lamport in 1988 would not be possible, because the method would not be powerful enough.

In particular, the protocol is developed in layers DV_{OS}, DV_N, DV_I, and finally, DV_{FC}. Now the authors of [5], Kleinman, Moscowitz, Pnueli, and Shapiro, do succeed to prove correctness of each of the three lower levels, DV_N, DV_I, and DV_{FC} with respect to DV_{OS}, all using A&L's method, but were not able, according to Pnueli, to give a chain of refinement proofs in which the next (concrete) layer is proved correct w.r.t. the previous (abstract) layer due to limitations seemingly inherent in the completeness result contained in A&L's method.

These limitations concern hidden, unbounded nondeterminism and internal discontinuity within the upper (abstract) level of the specification, a typical situation arising when the invisible parts of the implementation increase with implementation depth.

---

* email: ke@informatik.uni-kiel.dbp.de
** email: wpr@informatik.uni-kiel.dbp.de, supported by ESPRIT BRA projects 'SPEC' and 'REACT' (no. 6021)

We shall demonstrate that only a minor generalization of A&L's method is sufficient to give a refinement proof for such situations, by observing that there is neither intrinsic need to hide so much of the state space nor a necessity to require internal continuity for the upper level specification in the refinement proofs.

If we want to prove a more-than-one-step refinement, it may occur that the overall observable component of the state, i.e. the part which should essentially be preserved by all refinements, is too small to prove refinement using A&L's method, since the hidden part of the state of some levels may cause infinite invisible nondeterminism. Therefore we try to maximize, for each refinement proof, the observable component of the state, the only constraint being that the original observable component should be part of it. So, in case of the 3-step refinement of the algorithm in [5], it can happen that we have three different observable state components depending on which proof level we are considering. That we are allowed to change these observable parts follows from a simple proof rule, stating that if we have refinement w.r.t. an increased portion of the observable state, one has also refinement when using any subcomponent of this observable state as new observable part of the state.

Specifications aim besides at defining the observable behaviour of a system also at dealing responsibly with system resources as e.g. memory. Therefore, it can happen that fairness is required for some transitions that do not have any externally observable impact, e.g. that are part of a system for garbage collection. This may cause internal discontinuity but should not be considered harmful. Thus, contrary to A&L's method, our method should be able to handle internal discontinuity (on the higher level of specification). The internal continuity requirement can be dropped because there is a simple way to find an equivalent specification that is internally continuous and can substitute the original one in the refinement proof.

Besides the two steps proposed by Abadi and Lamport, namely adding history or prophecy variables, there is a third possibility to construct an intermediate specification to anneal the higher level specification from the lower level one. One is allowed to restrict the supplementary property of a specification in such a way that e.g. additional fairness requirements are posed onto transitions that have no externally visible effect. This enables us to prove an example of Abadi and Lamport that they can not prove within their method.

2 Browsing through A&L's Method

We adopt the notion of specifications and refinement presented in [1]. This section provides a small reminder of these notions and related terms. For A&L's formal definitions, consult Appendix A.

2.1 Refinement and Specifications

We take a behavioural view of the specified systems, namely, we consider a specification as a characterization of a certain set of allowed *behaviours*, where the behaviours are infinite sequences of states. A behaviour $\sigma = \langle\!\langle s_0, s_1, s_2, \ldots \rangle\!\rangle$ is called *terminating* iff it reaches a *final state*, i.e. a state in which it stutters forever. $\natural(\sigma)$, the stutterfree behaviour equivalent to σ, is obtained by removing all finite amounts of stuttering from σ. Two behaviours σ and τ are *stuttering equivalent* $(\sigma \simeq \tau)$ iff $\natural(\sigma) = \natural(\tau)$. Stuttering ranges below our level of abstraction. Hence we consider specifications describing sets of behaviours which contain a behaviour iff an element of its $\simeq$ equivalence class is also contained. These stuttering closed sets are called *properties*.

Suppose we would like to express refinement between a lower level specification S_C and a higher level specification S_A which characterize properties P_C and P_A, respectively.

The first attempt is $P_C \subseteq P_A$. This appears quite natural but forces us unfortunately to stick to the same set of variables on both levels of abstraction. Since we want to use local variables we have to make the following distinction. A state is partitioned into an observable component which should be preserved by refinement and an unobservable internal component containing the above mentioned local variables which need not occur on the other level.

Our second attempt employs the projection function Π_E which maps states onto their observable components, and complete behaviours onto externally visible behaviours. Note that the image of a complete property under Π_E need not be stuttering closed. $\Pi_E(P_C) \subseteq \Pi_E(P_A)$ as requirement for refinement is still too strong since it may rule out situations in which the lower level system needs less internal steps than the higher level system to expose an observable step.

So our final expression for refinement is $\Gamma(\Pi_E(P_C)) \subseteq \Gamma(\Pi_E(P_A))$, where $\Gamma(\sigma)$ is the set of all behaviours stuttering equivalent to σ. $\Gamma(\Pi_E(P))$ is called *externally visible property* and denoted by O (for observable). Two specifications are called *equivalent* iff they induce the same externally visible property. Thus, equivalence means refinement in both directions.

Safety properties are closed and *liveness properties* are dense sets in the domain of infinite state sequences.

Every property can be expressed as the intersection of a safety property and a liveness property. (Proof: $X = \overline{X} \cap \Sigma^\omega \setminus (\overline{X} \setminus X)$)

A specification is defined in terms of a state automaton (Σ, Φ, T) and a so-called *supplementary property* L (for liveness), where Σ denotes the state space, $\Phi \subseteq \Sigma$ the initial states, and $T \subseteq \Sigma \times \Sigma$ the transition relation, respectively. The machine property M of such an automaton consists of those behaviours that start in an initial state and where each step is either allowed by the transition relation or a stuttering one. M is a safety property. S is said to induce the complete property $P = M \cap L$. Sometimes, we describe the supplementary property of a specification as fairness constraints for classes of transitions.

Definition 1. Let σ be a computation sequence and C be a set of transitions. σ is *weakly fair for* C iff it is not the case that from a certain index i in σ on there are always enabled transitions in C but none of them is ever taken. σ is *strongly fair for* C iff it is not the case that from a certain index i in σ on there are infinitely often enabled transitions in C but none of them is ever taken.

Refinement mappings are functions from concrete states to abstract states. They preserve observable state machine behaviour and the supplementary property. The existence of a refinement mapping between two specifications implies refinement.

2.2 Internal Continuity

We use the standard mapping extensions, e.g. refinement mappings are extended to map complete behaviours to abstract behaviours by the following rule:

$$f(\langle\!\langle s_0, s_1, \ldots \rangle\!\rangle) = \langle\!\langle f(s_0), f(s_1), \ldots \rangle\!\rangle$$

It is easy to prove that refinement mappings are continuous. It is this continuity that imposes the restriction of internal continuity on the higher level specification. A complete property P is called *internally continuous* iff the decision whether a behaviour σ belongs to P is based only on its observable part $\Pi_E(\sigma)$ and finite prefixes of σ. Consider the following situation where the abstract level specification is not internally continuous:

Example 1 (inspired by [1]). Let $\sigma_C, \sigma_C^{(i)} \in \Sigma_C$ and $\sigma_A, \sigma_A', \sigma_A^{(i)} \in \Sigma_A$ such that the following holds. Assume f is a refinement mapping from Σ_C to Σ_A such that

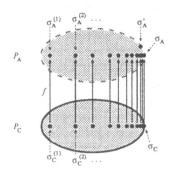

$$\Pi_E(\sigma_C) = \Pi_E(\sigma_A) = \Pi_E(\sigma_A')$$
$$\Pi_E(\sigma_C^{(i)}) = \Pi_E(\sigma_A^{(i)}) \text{ for } i \geq 0$$
$$\sigma_A = \lim \sigma_A^{(i)}$$
$$\sigma_A', \sigma_A^{(i)} \in P_A$$
$$\sigma_A \notin L_A$$
$$\sigma_C = \lim \sigma_C^{(i)}$$
$$\sigma_C, \sigma_C^{(i)} \in P_C$$

Fig. 1. internal continuity

$f(\sigma_C^{(i)}) = \sigma_A^{(i)}$. Since refinement mappings are continuous $f(\lim \sigma_C^{(i)}) = f(\sigma_C)$.

Hence, if $f(\sigma_C^{(i)}) = \sigma_A^{(i)}$ then $f(\sigma_C) \in P_A$ since f is a refinement mapping and $\sigma_C \in P_C$. But, by continuity of f, we have:

$$f(\sigma_C) = f(\lim \sigma_C^{(i)}) = \lim f(\sigma_C^{(i)}) = \lim \sigma_A^{(i)} = \sigma_A \notin P_A, \text{ contradiction!}$$

Hence f can not be a refinement mapping but this can not be deduced by looking only at O_A all finite prefixes of behaviours in P_A.

2.3 Machine Closure and Finite Invisible Nondeterminism

Adding auxiliary variables to a specification should be sound, i.e. if S is a specification with machine property M and supplementary property L, and S^{aux} is obtained from S by adding an auxiliary variable then the following should hold:

$$(*)\ \Gamma(\Pi_E(M \cap L)) \subseteq \Gamma(\Pi_E(M^{\mathrm{aux}} \cap L^{\mathrm{aux}}))$$

A&L's requirements on auxiliary variables are:

$$(1)\ M = \Pi_{[\text{aux}]}(M^{\text{aux}})$$
$$(2)\ L^{\text{aux}} = \Pi_{[\text{aux}]}^{-1}(L)$$

where $\Pi_{[\text{aux}]}$ projects S^{aux}-states onto S-states, namely removes the value of the auxiliary variable.

Lemma 2. *A&L's requirements imply the soundness requirement stated above, viz.* $(1) \wedge (2) \Rightarrow (*)$.

A&L's requirements are motivated by the wish to introduce a separation of concerns such that the safety properties of the lower and higher level specifications, i.e. their state machines, and the supplementary properties can be handled separately. This is the price they have to pay:

Consider two specifications $S_A = (M_A, L_A)$ and $S_C = (M_C, L_C)$ such that $S_C \sqsupseteq S_A$. If $\Pi_E(M_C) \not\subseteq \Pi_E(M_A)$ then refinement can not be proven using A&L's method. There are two cases in which $S_C \sqsupseteq S_A$ but $\Pi_E(M_C) \not\subseteq \Pi_E(M_A)$:

1. L_C specifies safety properties not already specified by M_C.
2. M_A specifies liveness properties.

The first case implies that S_C is not machine closed, and the second case implies that S_A is not fin (and even not gfin as defined in Definition 4).

2.4 Abadi and Lamport's Auxiliary Variables

The machine property M of a specification $S = (\Sigma, \Phi, T, L)$ could equivalently be defined as the stuttering closure of the set of paths of the directed graph with nodes Σ and edges T that start in Φ. This interpretation of machine properties as graphs helped us when we tried to understand the intuitive meaning of A&L's auxiliary variable constructions.

Assume $S_C = (\Sigma_C, \Phi_C, T_C, L_C)$ refines $S_A = (\Sigma_A, \Phi_A, T_A, L_A)$ is provable using A&L's method, and one has already a specific refinement relation f in mind when trying to prove this. Unfortunately it turns out that f is no mapping, e.g. there exists a state s_C such that f relates it to two different abstract states s_A, s_A'. This can have two reasons:

1. Two paths are unified at s_C on the lower level while related paths on the higher level are still separated.
2. A single path is split up into two before reaching s_A and s_A' on the higher level while the single related lower level one is still unsplit in s_C.

A&L use two kinds of auxiliary variables to transform the lower level specification into an equivalent one: history variables and prophecy variables. They help us finding a functional refinement relation, namely a refinement mapping, by blowing up the state space, and thereby the graph, of the lower level specification such that the two reasons given above do not hold anymore.

1. Adding a history variable to the lower level specification that records the path leads to a specification whose graph is a forest because every junction of paths in the original lower level specification is split up according to the different histories.
2. Adding a prophecy variable to the lower level specification splits paths which are only distinguished by a different future also with respect to their past.

3 Problem

Essentially, we would like to prove refinement between an abstract and a concrete specification of the distributed system described below.

This system concerns message passing between migrating processes within a finite network of nodes communicating over, on the most concrete level unreliable, channels and is described in [5].

At the most abstract level of description, DV_{OS}, communication is direct and instantaneous. At the next naive level of specification, DV_N, messages chase processes along their migration paths, using forwarding addresses left by their migrating processes in each node visited. At the third, improved level, DV_I, the path a message takes while chasing a migrating addressee process may be dynamically shortened, while at the fourth level, DV_{FC}, the unreliability of message transmission, due to getting lost along a communication channel, is taken care of by introducing simple fault tolerance techniques.

Contrary to what is done in [5], we prove in particular that DV_{FC} refines DV_I to demonstrate the applicability and power of our method.

Next we describe these layers in more detail.

3.1 Description of the Systems

DV_{OS}: Consider a finite network of nodes, each containing separate processes. Processes communicate with each other by sending messages. Processes can travel from one node to another. However, each node has (global) knowledge about the node where a process resides. A message between processes is forwarded directly by the originating process to the globally available address of the destination process. Assumption: the transmission of a message and the updating of the global knowledge upon process migration is instantaneous.

DV_N: In the naive implementation DV_N the global knowledge in DV_{OS} is substituted by local knowledge in every node. Message transmission progresses in jumps, as does process migration. Usually processes which want to communicate lived once in the same node, and left behind a forwarding address in a routing table. So now a message may chase a process along the path it migrated along through the network of nodes. Therefore it is in principle possible that a message chases its destination process indefinitely because that process switches nodes (although from a finite network) an infinite amount of times. Conclusion: when a process eventually stops migrating, messages chasing it will reach it eventually.

DV_{I}: When a message reaches its destination process, that process sends an acknowledgement to the originator of that message whose address at the moment of sending is attached to that message. Upon reception of an acknowledgement the sender's routing table is updated. Messages may be discarded at intermediate nodes[3]. Hence copies of messages are sent until the acknowledgement arrives.

DV_{FC}: Nodes are not connected directly to each other anymore, but are connected via a network consisting of faulty links. Fairness assumption: a copy of a message eventually passes the network.

3.2 Description of the Problem

The observable part of these four systems (i.e. the state component that should be preserved by refinement) is the set of all sent messages. It is already shown in [5] that each implementation refines the specification DV_{OS} with respect to the observability criterion chosen by the authors:

$$DV_{\mathrm{OS}}$$

$$DV_{\mathrm{N}} \qquad DV_{\mathrm{I}} \qquad DV_{\mathrm{FC}}$$

But this is not what the development of layered systems is about. It would be more interesting to prove a chain of refinements:

$$DV_{\mathrm{FC}} \ \sqsupseteq \ DV_{\mathrm{I}} \ \sqsupseteq \ DV_{\mathrm{N}} \ \sqsupseteq \ DV_{\mathrm{OS}}$$

We can not prove this directly with the method provided in [1] since, as we will see in Sect. 6, DV_{I} is neither fin nor internally continuous with respect to the observability criterion chosen in [5].

There are at least two ways to tackle problems like the one described above:

- Choose a different observability criterion such that the infinite invisible nondeterminism becomes visible (except for a finite part) or the internal discontinuity disappears.
- Generalize the proof method of Abadi & Lamport such that it handles some cases of infinite invisible nondeterminism and internal discontinuity.

Both ways are formalized and justified in Sect. 4 and used together in Sect. 6 to prove that DV_{FC} refines DV_{I}.

---

[3] It can happen that a copy of a message chasing a process is discarded by an intermediate node because that one does not know where to send the message to. This depends on details of the implementation which are of no relevance to the refinement problem above.

4 Generalizations

4.1 Choice of the Set of Observable States Σ_E

Since we assume that DV_{FC} and DV_I have much more in common than only the set of sent messages we prove refinement with respect to a higher degree of observability.

Let Σ_E refer to the set of observable states (of all levels), Σ_I' refer to the set of hidden state components of DV_I and Σ_I denote DV_I's state space.

Then we change the definition of Σ_E and Σ_I' with $\Sigma_I \subseteq \Sigma_E \times \Sigma_I'$ in such a way that Σ_E contains for this level components which previously belonged to Σ_I'.

The following lemma justifies the soundness of this approach. It states that refinement with respect to some degree of observability implies refinement with respect to smaller degrees of observability.

Lemma 3. *If a specification S_C refines another specification S_A with respect to their common observable state component Σ_E, i.e. $S_C \sqsupseteq S_A$ holds, then $S_C \sqsupseteq S_A$ holds also with respect to any component of Σ_E.*

4.2 Generalized Fin Properties

As already stated in [1], a complete property P, viz. the set of all allowed behaviours including hidden state components, need not necessarily be fin to achieve that its induced externally visible property is a safety property, i.e. does not specify any liveness. It would be sufficient if each infinite invisible nondeterminism would be eventually externally displayed.

Definition 4. Let P be a property and O its induced externally visible property $\Gamma(\Pi_E(P))$. We say that P is *gfin* (for *generalized fin*) iff for all $\eta \in O$ and all $n \geq 0$ there exists $n' \geq n$ such that the set

$$\{ \natural(\sigma|_m) \mid (m > 0) \wedge (\sigma \in P) \wedge (\Pi_E(\sigma|_m) \simeq \eta|_n) \wedge \exists m' : (\Pi_E(\sigma|_{m'}) \simeq \eta|_{n'}) \}$$

is finite. We say that a specification is gfin iff the complete property of the specification is gfin.

Proposition 5. *If a safety property P is gfin, then its induced externally visible property $\Gamma(\Pi_E(P))$ is also a safety property.*

We will need stronger prophecy variables if we want to weaken the prerequisites about the higher level specification in the completeness theorem of [1] from fin to gfin. We only have to change the last point in the definition of prophecy variables (in Appendix A), that is P6, to P6' as defined below to get *strong prophecy variables*.

P6': For all reachable $s \in \Sigma$:

1. The set $\Pi_{[P]}^{-1}(s)$ is non-empty.
2. If $\Pi_{[P]}^{-1}(s)$ is infinite then for each occurrence σ_i of s in an externally visible behaviour $\sigma \in O^P$ there exists an $i' \geq i$ such that $\Pi_{[P]}^{-1}(\sigma_{i'})$ is finite.

In a slightly different setting this is already observed in [3].

4.3 Achieving Internal Continuity

The techniques presented above were not sufficient to prove the cruel last step of the three step refinement under consideration. We did succeed in circumventing the infinite invisible nondeterminism but failed to reach internal continuity by maximizing the observable part of the systems' state spaces. The following lemma allows one to drop the internal continuity requirement. It does so by showing that each specification has an easily definable internally continuous equivalent.

Lemma 6. *Let $S = (\Sigma, \Phi, T, L)$ be a specification with induced externally visible property O and define $S^{\mathrm{ic}} = (\Sigma, \Phi, T, L^{\mathrm{ic}})$ where $L^{\mathrm{ic}} = L \cup \Pi_{\mathrm{E}}^{-1}(O)$. Then the following holds:*

1. *S and S^{ic} are equivalent.*
2. *S^{ic} is internally continuous.*

S^{ic} *is called* internally continuous equivalent of S.

With the aid of the techniques presented in this section, A&L's completeness theorem can be extended to the following one.

Theorem 7. *If the machine-closed specification S_{C} implements the specification S whose internally continuous equivalent S^{ic} is gfin, then there is a specification $S_{\mathrm{C}}^{\mathrm{h}}$ obtained from S_{C} by adding a history variable and a specification $S_{\mathrm{C}}^{\mathrm{hp}}$ obtained from $S_{\mathrm{C}}^{\mathrm{h}}$ by adding a strong prophecy variable such that there exists a refinement mapping from $S_{\mathrm{C}}^{\mathrm{hp}}$ to S^{ic}.*

Example 1 demonstrated that internal continuity in the upper level specification is required for proving refinement with refinement mappings. Now, we can simply prove refinement correct using our method.

Example 2 (cf. Example 1). Let $S = (\Sigma, \Phi, T, L)$, $S_{\mathrm{C}} = (\Sigma_{\mathrm{C}}, \Phi_{\mathrm{C}}, T_{\mathrm{C}}, L_{\mathrm{C}})$, and $\Sigma_{\mathrm{E}} = \mathbb{N}$, where

- $\Sigma = \Sigma_{\mathrm{E}} \times \{\mathbf{t}, \mathbf{f}\}$
- $\Phi = \{(0, \mathbf{t})(0, \mathbf{f})\}$
- $T = \{ (i, b) \to (i + 1, b) \mid i \in \mathbb{N} \wedge b \in \{\mathbf{t}, \mathbf{f}\} \}$
- L consists of all behaviours except those behaviours of S's state machine which have one of the two forms:
  - terminating, internal component is always $\mathbf{f}$
  - nonterminating, internal component is always $\mathbf{t}$
- $\Sigma_{\mathrm{C}} = \Sigma_{\mathrm{E}}$
- $\Phi_{\mathrm{C}} = \{0\}$
- $T_{\mathrm{C}} = \{ i \to i + 1 \mid i \in \mathbb{N} \}$
- $L_{\mathrm{C}} = \Sigma_{\mathrm{C}}^{\omega}$

As shown in [1] $S_{\mathrm{C}} \sqsupseteq S$ is true but, since S is not internally continuous, this example is not covered by their completeness result.

The supplementary property of S's internally continuous equivalent S^{ic} is $L^{\mathrm{ic}} = \Sigma^{\omega}$.

Furthermore, we observe that S^{ic} also could have been obtained from S_C by adding a (simple) prophecy variable that guesses the value of S_A's internal state component in the initial state. (Check P1–P6 from Definition 18 in the appendix.) Hence $S_\mathrm{C} \sqsupseteq S$ is provable within our method and covered by the completeness result in Theorem 7.

5 Toy Example

Before we finally solve the problem stated in Sect. 3, we present a toy example which displays the same kind of difference in communication modelling as there is between DV_I and DV_FC.

We model a very simplistic network of only a single node that communicates with itself.

The set $\mathcal{M}ess$ of messages the buffers involved in the specifications in this example is the disjoint union of the set $\mathcal{M}$ of normal messages (with typical elements m, m_0, ...), the corresponding set of acknowledgement messages (with typical element ack_m, ack_{m_0}, ...), and the corresponding set of reception messages (with typical element M, M_0, ...). There is no predefined order in the transmission of messages.

The externally visible state component of the two specifications described below is a message buffer S representing the union of a system utilizing the communication protocol with an output buffer

$$\Sigma_\mathrm{E} \quad = \quad \mathcal{M}ess^\star$$

On both levels there is also an input buffer I while only on the concrete level a so called network buffer N is plugged in between S and I (as in the previous two examples).

5.1 Abstract Level

The behaviour of the abstract specification can be described as follows: Transmission of a fresh message (a message such that neither itself nor a corresponding acknowledgement or reception message already occurs in any of the system's buffers) is initiated by adding this message to the system buffer S. Each normal message contained in the system buffer can be transmitted (copied) to the input buffer. The system receives a normal message from the input buffer by converting it into the appropriate reception message M and leaving an acknowledgement message ack_m behind. To handle an acknowledgement message ack_m it is moved from the input buffer to the system buffer where it replaces the original message m. Superfluous copies of normal messages m can be discarded from the input buffer if the corresponding reception message M is already contained in the system buffer S.

Let S_A be $(\Sigma_\mathrm{A}, \Phi_\mathrm{A}, T_\mathrm{A}, L_\mathrm{A})$ where:

$\Sigma_\mathrm{A} = \Sigma_\mathrm{E}$, S_A's internal state component is its input buffer

$\Phi_\mathrm{A} = \{(\emptyset, \emptyset)\}$, initially no message is present

$$T_{\mathrm{A}} = \quad \{ \ (\mathcal{S}, I) \to (\mathcal{S} \oplus m, I) \mid m \in \mathcal{M} \setminus (\mathcal{S} \cup I) \ \} \qquad , \mathbf{Send}_m$$
$$\cup \{ \ (\mathcal{S}, I) \to (\mathcal{S}, I \oplus m) \mid m \in \mathcal{M} \cap \mathcal{S} \ \} \qquad , \mathbf{Transmit}_m$$
$$\cup \{ \ (\mathcal{S}, I) \to (\mathcal{S} \oplus M, I \oplus ack_m \ominus m) \mid m \in I \wedge M \notin \mathcal{S} \ \}$$
$$, \mathbf{Receive}_m$$
$$\cup \{ \ (\mathcal{S}, I) \to (\mathcal{S} \oplus ack_m \ominus m, I \ominus ack_m) \mid ack_m \in I \wedge m \in \mathcal{S} \ \}$$
$$, \mathbf{Ack}_m$$
$$\cup \{ \ (\mathcal{S}, I) \to (\mathcal{S}, I \ominus m) \mid m \in I \wedge M \in \mathcal{S} \ \} \qquad , \mathbf{Discard}_m$$
$$L_{\mathrm{A}} = \text{weak fairness for all classes except } \mathbf{Send}_m$$

The above definition of L_{A} grants that once a normal message m is put into the system buffer eventually the corresponding reception message M and the corresponding acknowledgement message ack_m will enter the system buffer, and eventually these two messages will be the only messages related to m occurring in the specification's state.

Figure 2 illustrates the impact of transitions on the two buffers of the abstract level specification S_{A}.

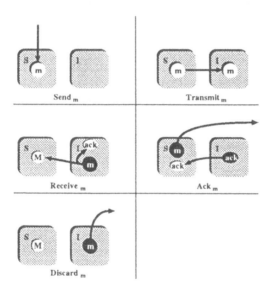

Fig. 2. transitions of S_{A}

5.2 Concrete Level

The network buffer of the concrete specification may loose messages, but we can prove with the fairness assumptions in L_{C} below that once a message is put into the output buffer the corresponding reception message eventually reaches the system buffer.

Let S_{C} be $(\Sigma_{\mathrm{C}}, \Phi_{\mathrm{C}}, T_{\mathrm{C}}, L_{\mathrm{C}})$ where:

$\Sigma_C = \Sigma_E \times \mathcal{Mess}^\star$

$\Phi_C = \{(\emptyset, \emptyset, \emptyset)\}$, initially no message is present

$T_C = \ \{ (\mathcal{S}, N, I) \rightarrow (\mathcal{S} \oplus m, N, I) \mid m \in \mathcal{M} \setminus (\mathcal{S} \cup N \cup I) \}$, $\mathbf{Send}_m$

$\cup \{ (\mathcal{S}, N, I) \rightarrow (\mathcal{S}, N \oplus m, I) \mid m \in \mathcal{M} \cap \mathcal{S} \setminus (N \cup I) \}$, $\mathbf{Transmit}_m$

$\cup \{ (\mathcal{S}, N, I) \rightarrow (\mathcal{S} \oplus M, N \oplus ack_m, I \ominus m) \mid m \in I \wedge M \notin \mathcal{S} \}$
, $\mathbf{Receive}_m$

$\cup \{ (\mathcal{S}, N, I) \rightarrow (\mathcal{S} \oplus ack_m \ominus m, N, I \ominus ack_m) \mid ack_m \in I \wedge m \in \mathcal{S} \}$
, $\mathbf{Ack}_m$

$\cup \{ (\mathcal{S}, N, I) \rightarrow (\mathcal{S}, N \oplus ack_m, I \ominus m) \mid m \in I \wedge M \in \mathcal{S} \}$
, $\mathbf{Discard}_m$

$\cup \{ (\mathcal{S}, N, I) \rightarrow (\mathcal{S}, N \ominus X, I \oplus X) \mid X \in N \}$, $\mathbf{Move}_X$

$\cup \{ (\mathcal{S}, N, I) \rightarrow (\mathcal{S}, N \ominus X, I) \mid X \in N \}$, $\mathbf{Fault}_X$

$\cup \{ (\mathcal{S}, N, I) \rightarrow (\mathcal{S}, N, I \ominus ack_m) \mid ack_m \in \mathcal{S} \}$, $\mathbf{Ignore}_m$

L_C = strong fairness for all classes $\mathbf{Receive}_m$ and $\mathbf{Ack}_m$, and weak
fairness for all other classes except $\mathbf{Send}_m$ and $\mathbf{Fault}_X$

Figure 3 illustrates the effect of transitions of the concrete level specification S_C that differ from the corresponding transitions on the abstract level.

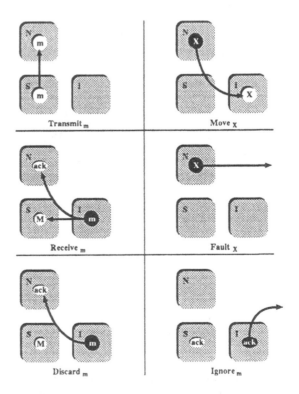

Transmit $_m$ Move $_X$

Receive $_m$ Fault $_X$

Discard $_m$ Ignore $_m$

Fig. 3. transitions of S_C

5.3 S_C Refines S_A

We need three steps to prove refinement between the two specifications under consideration, with respect to the system buffer $\mathcal{S}$.

1. Augment S_C with a prophecy variable p that forecasts S_A's input buffer to achieve a specification S_C^p.
2. Strengthen S_C^p's supplementary property L_C^p such that the externally visible property remains unchanged but some fairness requirements for transitions only influencing the prophecy variable are met and reach an equivalent specification S_C^{pf} (which is not internally continuous any more).
3. Find a refinement mapping from S_C^{pf} to S_A.

N.B. S_A is not internally continuous with respect to the above defined Σ_E since fairness is required e.g. for the externally invisible **Discard**$_m$ transitions.

Define $S_C^p = (\Sigma_C^p, \Phi_C^p, T_C^p, L_C^p)$ such that:

$$\Sigma_P = \mathcal{M}ess \qquad \text{, another message buffer}$$
$$\Sigma_C^p \subseteq \Sigma_C \times \Sigma_P \qquad \text{(exactly: all reachable states)}$$
$$\Phi_C^p = \Phi_C \times \{\emptyset\} \qquad \text{, initially empty prophecy buffer}$$
$$L_C^p = \Pi_{[P]}^{-1}(L_C)$$

Each class of S_C-transitions has a corresponding class of S_C^p-transitions. Classes of S_C^p-transitions are marked by superscript p. Let $(\mathcal{S}, N, I) \to (\mathcal{S}', N', I') \in T_C$ then we define the corresponding class of transitions in T_C^p by giving only its additional impact on the prophecy variable p.
$(\mathcal{S}, N, I, p) \to (\mathcal{S}', N', I', p') \in T_C^p$:

$$
\begin{array}{lll}
\textbf{Transmit}_m^p & : & p' = p \oplus m \\
\textbf{Receive}_m^p & : & p' = p \oplus ack_m \ominus m \\
\textbf{Ack}_m^p & : & p' = p \ominus ack_m \\
\textbf{Discard}_m^p & : & p' = p \ominus m \\
\textbf{Send}_m^p, \textbf{Ignore}_m^p, \textbf{Move}_X^p, \textbf{Fault}_X^p & : & p' = p
\end{array}
$$

See Fig. 4 for an illustration of those four classes of S_C^p-transitions which alter the prophecy variable and correspond to transitions in S_C. We also add a class of transitions that change only the prophecy variable. If an **Ack**$_m^p$ or **Ignore**$_m^p$ is taken in state (s, p) where m does not occur any more in the input or network buffer, S_C^p shall discard m from the prophecy buffer. This has to be done because a copy of an already acknowledged message that was removed from N by the **Fault**$_m^p$ transition may leave a surviving copy (called *zombie*) in p behind. These zombies would stay forever in p while handling of the message is completed which could be disturbing when looking for a refinement mapping from S_C^p to S_A because the weak fairness requirement for **Discard** would not be met. The new class of transitions is the set (see Fig. 5):

$$\{ (\mathcal{S}, N, I, p) \to (\mathcal{S}, N, I, p \ominus m) \mid m \in p \setminus (\mathcal{S} \cup N \cup I) \} \quad , \quad \textbf{PDiscard}_m^p$$

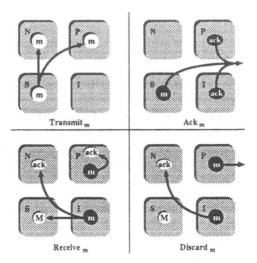

Fig. 4. some transitions of S_C^p

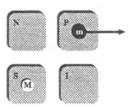

Fig. 5. PDiscard$_m^p$

Proposition 8. S_C^p *is obtained from* S_C *by adding a prophecy variable that adds stuttering.*

By assuming weak fairness also for the class of **PDiscard**$_m^p$ transitions to ensure removal of zombies we obtain S_C^{pf} from S_C^p. This preserves the externally visible property of S_C^p since these transitions influence neither the flow of control nor the observable state component Σ_E. Hence

$$S_C \sqsupseteq S_C^p \sqsupseteq S_C^{pf}$$

Proposition 9. *In each complete behaviour of* S_C^{pf}: *If* m *enters* p *it is eventually removed.*

Proof. If such a copy becomes a zombie it is eventually removed by a cleanup transition. If this copy is caught up by a copy of the same message entering I then it is eventually (re)moved from I and p by **Discard**$_m^p$, **Transmit**$_m^p$, or **Receive**$_m^p$. If this copy neither becomes a zombie nor is removed nor is caught up then m is never acknowledged. In this case m will be transmitted forever. This means that copies of m infinitely often get lost in the network buffer, but this contradicts the strong fairness requirement for the **Move**-transitions.   □

Proposition 10. *In each complete behaviour of S_C^{pf}: If ack_m enters p it is eventually removed.*

Proposition 11. $f : \Sigma_C^{pf} \to \Sigma_A$ *defined by* $f(S, N, I, p) = (S, p)$ *is a refinement mapping from S_C^{pf} to S_A.*

Proof. **R1–R3**: by definition.
R4: Assume there exists a complete behaviour $\sigma \in P_C^{pf}$ of S_C^{pf} such that $f(\sigma) \notin L_A$. That means since L_A is weak fairness for some classes of S_A-transitions there exists an index $v > 0$ such that for all indices $w \geq v$ a certain class $t \subseteq T_A$ is enabled in $f(\sigma_w)$ without being taken. Consider the cases of t:

Transmit$_m$: then, in contradiction to the definition of L_C^{pf}, **Transmit$_m^P$** is continuously enabled in σ from index v on.
Receive$_m$, Discard$_m$: then m stays forever in p without being removed. This contradicts proposition 9.
Ack$_m$: then ack_m stays forever in p without being removed. This contradicts proposition 10.

□

By transitivity we have $S_C \sqsupseteq S_A$ with respect to Σ_E.

6 Solution

The systems concerned in the original problem of proving $DV_{FC} \sqsupseteq DV_I$ as described in Sect. 3 are closely related to the previous example. Proofs in this section have been sacrificed for the sake of space limitations and can be found in the full version [2].

6.1 Specification of DV_I

We take DV_I as a somehow given specification $(\Sigma_I, \Phi_I, T_I, L_I)$ and assume that $s \in \Sigma_I$ is an n-tuple of DV_I-node states $s = (s_1, \ldots, s_n)$ where $s_i = (S_i, I_i, O_i)$ denoting the node's internal state, input buffer, and output buffer, respectively.[4] The internal states of a node represent at least: the set of all messages this node successfully received, a routing table, and a system that utilizes this communication protocol. Initially the buffers I_i and O_i are empty. The DV_I-transitions T_I are partitioned into classes (for each node i):

Local$_i$:   Only S_i is changed.
Send$_i(m)$:   A fresh message (m, i) is placed in O_i initiated by a request from the internal part of the node i.

---

[4] Readers familiar with the paper [5] may complain that routing tables are not explicitly introduced in this presentation of DV_I. The routing tables and their administration are hidden in the internal state components S_i because they are handled simultaneously in both specifications, DV_I and DV_{FC}.

Receive$_i$(m):   Node i decides that it can handle m and picks (m, j) out of I_i to change S_i accordingly and acknowledges this by putting (ack_m, i) into the input buffer of node j which was the originator of the message.

Forward$_i$(m):   Node i decides to forward (m, j) and moves it from I_i to some other input buffer I_k depending on internal information in S_i (e.g. a routing table).

Discard$_i$(m):   Node i can not handle the message m at all so it removes (m, j) from I_i. This is also the case when node i has already received a copy of m.

Transmit$_i$(m):   The message (m, i) is copied from the output buffer O_i to the appropriate input buffer I_j (node i consults its routing table to decide which node is the correct addressee).

Ack$_i$(m):   This transition removes a message (m, i) from node i's output buffer O_i together with an acknowledgement message (ack_m, j) from the input buffer I_i.e

Send$_i$, **Receive$_i$**, and **Ack$_i$** also update the internal state S_i. Note that at most one of **Receive$_i$(m)**, **Forward$_i$(m)**, and **Discard$_i$(m)** is enabled.

L_I = weak fairness for all the above defined classes of transitions.

6.2 Specification of DV_{FC}

The state s_i of a DV_{FC}-node is given as (S_i, I_i, O_i, N_i) where the first three components are similar to a DV_I-node state and the last component represents that part of the faulty network that passes messages to node i. N_i is interpreted as an initially empty buffer between the rest of DV_{FC} and node i's input buffer. These network components are faulty, that is, they may loose messages of any kind; but we assume strong fairness for transitions moving messages out of network components into input buffers. All this should remind the reader to the example in the previous section.

DV_{FC}-transitions are of course closely related to DV_I-transitions. The following additions and changes are required.

- Each DV_I-transition (**Transmit$_i$(m)**, **Forward$_i$(m)**, or **Receive$_i$(m)**) that adds a message to an input buffer I_k is replaced be one that adds this message only to the network component N_k.
- Each DV_I-transition **Discard$_i$(m)** that removes a message $t = (m, j)$ from I_i because node i has already received t earlier additionally places an acknowledgement message (ack_m, i) in node j's network component N_j to prevent endless retransmission of t in case the first acknowledgement became victim of a network fault.
- **Ignore$_i$(ack_m)** removes an acknowledgement message (ack_m, j) from node i's input buffer if m has been acknowledged before.
- Transitions **Move$_i$(x)** that move a message from a network component N_i to the same node's input buffer I_i are added.
- To simulate network faults we introduce transitions **Fault$_i$(x)** that simply remove a message x from a network component N_i.

L_{FC} = weak fairness for all classes of transitions except for **Fault** and strong fairness for all classes $\mathbf{Move}_i(x)$

6.3 DV_{FC} Refines DV_I

As in the toy example we will pursue a certain strategy to prove refinement between the two specifications under consideration with respect to the set of all sent messages:

1. Take Σ_I without the input buffers I_i as observable state component Σ_E. (Thus, Σ_E has elements of the form $((\mathcal{S}_1, O_1), \ldots, (\mathcal{S}_n, O_n))$.)
2. Augment DV_{FC} with a prophecy variable $\mathbf{p} = (p_1, \ldots, p_n)$ that forecasts DV_I's input buffers to achieve a specification DV_{FC}^P.
3. Strengthen DV_{FC}^P's supplementary property L_{FC}^P such that the externally visible property remains unchanged but some fairness requirements for transitions only influencing the prophecy variable are met and reach an equivalent specification DV_{FC}^{pf} (which is not internally continuous any more).
4. Find a refinement mapping from DV_{FC}^{pf} to DV_I.
5. Apply Lemma 3 resulting in $DV_{FC}^{pf} \sqsupseteq DV_I$ with respect to the set of all sent messages which is a subcomponent of the chosen observable state component Σ_E.

N.B. DV_I is not internally continuous with respect to the above defined Σ_E since fairness is required e.g. for the externally invisible transmission of superfluous acknowledgements of an already acknowledged message.

Define $S_{FC}^P = (\Sigma_{FC}^P, \Phi_{FC}^P, T_{FC}^P, L_{FC}^P)$ such that:

$$
\begin{aligned}
\Sigma^P &= \times_{i=1}^n \mathcal{T\!Mess} & &\text{an } n\text{-tuple of message buffers} \\
\Sigma_{FC}^P &\subseteq \Sigma_{FC} \times \Sigma^P & &\text{(exactly: all reachable states)} \\
\Phi_{FC}^P &= \Phi_{FC} \times \{(\emptyset, \ldots, \emptyset)\} & &\text{initially empty prophecy buffers} \\
L_{FC}^P &= \Pi_{[P]}^{-1}(L_{FC})
\end{aligned}
$$

Each class of DV_{FC}-transitions corresponds with a class in T_{FC}^P having the same name plus superscript p. Let $(s, \mathbf{p}) \rightarrow (s', \mathbf{p}') \in T_{FC}^P$, $\mathbf{p} = (p_1, \ldots, p_n)$, and $\mathbf{p}' = (p'_1, \ldots, p'_n)$. Define its principal impact on the prophecy variable $\mathbf{p}$ as follows (assume $s \rightarrow s' \in T_{FC}$):

$\mathbf{Receive}_i^P(m)$: if $I_i \setminus I'_i = \{(m, j)\}$ then $\mathbf{p}' = \mathbf{p}[{}^{p_i \ominus (m,j)}/_{p_i}, {}^{p_j \oplus (ackm, i)}/_{p_j}]$

$\mathbf{Forward}_i^P(m)$: if $N'_k \setminus N_k = \{(m, j)\}$ then $\mathbf{p}' = \mathbf{p}[{}^{p_k \oplus (m,j)}/_{p_k}, {}^{p_i \ominus (m,j)}/_{p_i}]$

$\mathbf{Discard}_i^P(m)$: if $I_i \setminus I'_i = \{(m, j)\}$ then $\mathbf{p}' = \mathbf{p}[{}^{p_i \ominus (m,j)}/_{p_i}]$

$\mathbf{Transmit}_i^P(m)$: if $N'_k \setminus N_k = \{(m, i)\}$ then $\mathbf{p}' = \mathbf{p}[{}^{p_k \oplus (m,i)}/_{p_k}]$

$\mathbf{Ack}_i^P(m)$: if $I'_i \setminus I_i = \{(ackm, j)\}$ then $\mathbf{p}' = \mathbf{p}[{}^{p_i \ominus (ackm,j)}/_{p_i}]$

$\mathbf{Local}_i^P, \mathbf{Send}_i^P(m), \mathbf{Ignore}_i^P(ackm), \mathbf{Move}_i^P(x), \mathbf{Fault}_i^P(x)$: $\mathbf{p}' = \mathbf{p}$

As in the toy example a problem with so-called zombie messages in $\mathbf{p}$ arises and is solved analogously. Define $zomb_i(t) = (t \in p_i \setminus (\bigcup_{l=1}^n (I_l, O_l)))$, then the classes of cleanup transitions look like:

$\mathbf{PForward}_i^P(m)$: if $zomb_i((m, j))$ then $\mathbf{p}' = \mathbf{p}[{}^{p_i \ominus (m,j)}/_{p_i}, {}^{p_k \oplus (m,j)}/_{p_k}]$

$\mathbf{PDiscard}_i^P(m)$: if $zomb_i((m, j))$ then $\mathbf{p}' = \mathbf{p}[{}^{p_i \ominus (m,j)}/_{p_i}]$

where node k in the description of **PForward**$_i^p$ was the next node on the route the successfully received copy of m travelled along. **PDiscard**$_i^p(m)$ can only be taken if i is the node that successfully received a copy of m.

Proposition 12. DV_{FC}^p *is obtained from* DV_{FC} *by adding a prophecy variable that adds stuttering.*

We obtain DV_{FC}^{pf} from DV_{FC}^p by assuming weak fairness also for the classes of cleanup transitions **PForward**$_i^p(m)$ and **PDiscard**$_i^p(m)$ to ensure the completion of cleanup phases. This preserves the externally visible property of DV_{FC}^p since these transitions influence neither the flow of control nor the observable state component Σ_E. Hence

$$DV_{FC} \sqsupseteq DV_{FC}^p \sqsupseteq DV_{FC}^{pf}$$

Proposition 13. *In each complete behaviour of* DV_{FC}^{pf}: *If* (m, j) *enters* p_i *it is eventually removed.*

Proposition 14. *In each complete behaviour of* DV_{FC}^{pf}: *If* (ack_m, j) *enters* p_i *it is eventually removed.*

Proposition 15. $f : \Sigma_{FC}^{pf} \rightarrow \Sigma_I$ *defined by*

$$f((\mathcal{S}_1, I_1, O_1, N_1), \ldots, (\mathcal{S}_n, I_n, O_n), (\mathbf{p})) = ((\mathcal{S}_1, p_1, O_1), \ldots, (\mathcal{S}_n, p_n, O_n))$$

is a refinement mapping from DV_{FC}^{pf} *to* DV_I.

By transitivity we have $DV_{FC} \sqsupseteq DV_I$ with respect to Σ_E. Finally, an application of Lemma 3 results in $DV_{FC} \sqsupseteq DV_I$ with respect to the set of all sent messages.

Acknowledgements. Amir Pnueli, Bengt Jonsson and Yassine Lakhneche are thanked for clarifying A&L's method, suggesting problems involved with it, and convincing us that is is worthwhile to work on them. BRA project SPEC made this cooperation possible.

References

1. M. Abadi and L. Lamport. The existence of refinement mappings. In *Proceedings* 3rd *Annual Symposium on Logic in Computer Science*, pages 165–175, Edinburgh, 1988.
2. K. Engelhardt and W.-P. de Roever. Generalizing Abadi & Lamport's Method to Solve a Problem Posed by A. Pnueli. Technical report, Institut für Informatik und Praktische Mathematik, Christian-Albrechts-Universität zu Kiel, 1993.
3. B. Jonsson. Simulations between specifications of distributed systems. In J. C. M. Baeten and J. F. Groote, editors, *Proceedings CONCUR '91, 2nd International Conference on Concurrency Theory, Amsterdam, The Netherlands*, volume 527 of *LNCS*, pages 346 – 360. Springer, Aug. 1991.
4. A. Kleinmann, Y. Moscowitz, A. Pnueli, and E. Shapiro. Communication with directed logical variables. 48 pages, Oct. 1990.
5. A. Kleinmann, Y. Moscowitz, A. Pnueli, and E. Shapiro. Communication with directed logical variables. In *Conference Record of the Eighteenth Annual ACM Symposium on Principles of Programming Languages*, pages 221 – 232. ACM, Jan. 1991.

A   Refinement Mappings & Auxiliary Variable Constructions

Definition 16 (taken from [1]). A *refinement mapping* from a specification $S_C = (\Sigma_C, \Phi_C, T_C, L_C)$ to a specification $S_A = (\Sigma_A, \Phi_A, T_A, L_A)$ is a mapping $f : \Sigma_C \to \Sigma_A$ such that

R1: $\forall s \in \Sigma_C (\Pi_E(f(s)) = \Pi_E(s))$ (f preserves the externally visible state component.)

R2: $f(\Phi_C) \subseteq \Phi_A$ (f maps initial states into initial states.)

R3: $s \to t \in T_C \Rightarrow f(s) \to f(t) \in T_A \vee f(s) = f(t)$ (f maps transitions of S_C into (possibly stuttering) allowed transitions of S_A)

R4: $f(P_C) \subseteq L_A$ (f maps behaviours of S_C into behaviours that are not forbidden by S_A's supplementary property.)

Definition 17 (taken from [1]). A specification $S^h = (\Sigma^h, \Phi^h, T^h, L^h)$ *is obtained from* another specification $S = (\Sigma, \Phi, T, L)$ *by adding a history variable* iff:

H1: $\Sigma^h \subseteq \Sigma \times \Sigma_H$ **H2:** $\Pi_{[H]}(\Phi^h) = \Phi$

H3: $(s, h) \to (s', h') \in T^h \Rightarrow s \to s' \in T \vee s = s'$

H4: $s \to s' \in T \wedge (s, h) \in \Sigma^h \Rightarrow \exists h' \in \Sigma_h((s, h) \to (s', h') \in T^h)$

H5: $L^h = \Pi_{[H]}^{-1}(L)$

Definition 18 (taken from [1]). A specification $S^p = (\Sigma^p, \Phi^p, T^p, L^p)$ *is obtained from* another specification $S = (\Sigma, \Phi, T, L)$ *by adding a simple prophecy variable* iff:

P1: $\Sigma^p \subseteq \Sigma \times \Sigma_P$ **P2':** $\Phi^p = \Pi_{[P]}^{-1}(\Phi)$

P3: $(s, p) \to (s', p') \in T^p \Rightarrow s \to s' \in T \vee s = s'$

P4': $s \to s' \in T \wedge (s', p') \in \Sigma^p \Rightarrow \exists p \in \Sigma_P((s, p) \to (s', p') \in T^p)$

P5: $L^p = \Pi_{[P]}^{-1}(L)$

P6: For all $s \in \Sigma$ the set $\Pi_{[P]}^{-1}(s)$ is finite and non-empty.

resp. *by adding a prophecy variable (that adds stuttering)* iff we replace P2' and P4' from above with the following:

P2: (a) $\Pi_{[P]}(\Phi^p) \subseteq \Phi$.

(b) For all $(s, p) \in \Pi_{[P]}^{-1}(\Phi)$ there exist $p_0, p_1, \ldots, p_n = p$ such that $(s, p_0) \in \Phi^p$ and, for $0 \le i < n, (s, p_i) \to (s, p_{i+1}) \in T^p$.

P4: If $s \to s' \in T$ and $(s', p') \in \Sigma^p$ then there exist $p, p'_0, \ldots, p'_n = p'$ such that $(s, p) \to (s', p'_0) \in T^p$ and, for $0 \le i < n, (s', p'_i) \to (s', p'_{i+1}) \in T^p$

Definition 19 (taken from [1]). A specification S having machine property M and supplementary property L is *machine closed* iff $M = \overline{M \cap L}$.

Definition 20. Let P be a property and O its induced externally visible property $\Gamma(\Pi_E(P))$. We say that P is *fin* (for *finitely invisibly nondeterministic*) iff for all $\eta \in O$ and all $n \ge 0$, the set
$\{ \natural(\sigma|_m) \mid (m > 0) \wedge (\sigma \in P) \wedge (\Pi_E(\sigma|_m) \simeq \eta|_n) \}$ is finite. We say that a specification is *fin* iff the complete property of the specification is fin.

Definition 21 (taken from [1]). A Σ-property P with induced externally visible property O is *internally continuous* iff, for any Σ-behaviour σ, if $\Pi_E(\sigma) \in O$ and $\sigma \in \overline{P}$, then $\sigma \in P$. A specification is internally continuous iff the (complete) property it defines is internally continuous.

Real-Time Refinement

Colin Fidge

Software Verification Research Centre,
The University of Queensland, QLD 4072, Australia

Abstract. The refinement calculus is extended for real-time system development. Heuristic rules for deriving high-level designs from Z specifications are also given. A detailed example of real-time refinement is presented.

1 Introduction

Formal methods have long been touted as a solution to industry's software development problems. Unfortunately many practical issues faced by 'real-world' software developers remain beyond the reach of formal techniques. Foremost among these are the 'hard real-time' requirements of applications with precise and inviolate timing constraints. Although numerous real-time specification and programming notations have been proposed, practical design and development methodologies for real-time systems are lacking.

This paper extends the refinement calculus to make it suitable for derivation of real-time systems. This is done by adding time-based side-conditions to the refinement rules which must be provably satisfied for the refinement step to be valid, thus guaranteeing that the resultant system adheres to its timing constraints. Furthermore, a set of heuristic rules is given for directly converting from Z specifications into a high-level system design.

2 Background

Our real-time refinement methodology builds on a number of established techniques.

2.1 Z

Z is a specification language for defining, and reasoning about, a wide range of systems [9]. The Z notation consists of two parts: the schema language (a specification structuring technique) and a mathematical language.

When used to define a system consisting of a number of distinct operations there are typically two distinct uses of schemata, state and operation:

Declare a number of variables and express invariants on them in the predicate.

```
┌─ Operation ─────────────────
│  declarations
│  ──────────────
│  predicate
└─────────────────────────────
```
Change the declared variables as per pre and post-conditions defined by the predicate.

By convention, an operation schema that includes a state schema name in its declaration part as $\Delta State$ may change the value of the variables declared in $State$. An undecorated variable name v appearing in an operation schema refers to the value of the variable before the operation occurs and v' refers to its value after the operation has been performed.

Schemata may be composed using a number of special operators. For instance, schema conjunction,

$$Op \triangleq Op_1 \wedge Op_2 ,$$

is used to merge the declarations of operations Op_1 and Op_2 and take the logical 'and' of their predicates.

The mathematical notation used within schemata is based on set theory and includes numerous operators.

2.2 The Refinement Calculus

The refinement calculus is a rigorous method for deriving executable programs from abstract specifications [5]. The calculus operates on Dijkstra's guarded command language (GCL) augmented with specification statements. In this way partly refined algorithms can be expressed in a 'mixed' notation of concrete GCL code and abstract behavioural specifications.

A specification statement,

$$w : [pre, post] ,$$

says that, executed in a state satisfying its pre-condition, it will terminate in a state satisfying the post-condition, while modifying only those variables listed in the 'frame' w. In the post-condition an undecorated variable name v refers to the value of the variable in the post-state and v_0 refers to its value in the pre-state.

System development involves repeatedly applying refinement laws, expressed using a refinement relation, denoted $\sqsubseteq$. For instance, a law for decomposing a specification statement into two sequentially composed statements is

$$w : [pre, post] \sqsubseteq w : [pre, mid] ; w : [mid, post]$$

(assuming v_0 variables are not used). These laws guarantee that the right-hand side is a valid 'implementation' of the left.

When considering the practicalities of real-time programming we need to extend the guarded command language slightly. Assume the existence of **output**(c, E) and **input**(c, v) statements for sending the value of an expression E to, or receiving a value into variable v from, some external channel c, and an **idle**(t) statement for effecting an idle delay of exactly t time units.

2.3 Heuristic Rules

Attempting to refine a Z specification into code can be a long and tedious process. Furthermore, as seen above, the Z notation differs from that of the specification statements used by the refinement calculus. King [3] recognised that these problems hinder the acceptance of these formal methods in industry. He proposed using a number of heuristic "change of notation" rules, operating on commonly occurring Z constructs, to (i) change the Z notation into refinement calculus notation and (ii) directly translate Z schemata into 'mixed notation' system designs in which some structure is already present, thus bypassing intermediate steps.

For instance, given a Z operation defined using disjunction,

$$Op \cong Op_1 \vee Op_2 ,$$

it may be expressible in GCL as

> **if** pre $Op_1 \rightarrow Op_1{}^*$
> [] pre $Op_2 \rightarrow Op_2{}^*$
> **fi** ,

where 'pre Op_x' is the pre-condition extracted from the predicate part of schema Op_x, and $Op_x{}^*$ is the specification statement corresponding to the schema. (The resulting system typically reflects the structure of the specification. Such direct correspondence has practical benefits for system maintenance, although it may limit possible implementations.)

As shown in Sect. 3.2, we adopt King's approach but extend the number of rules as well as introducing real-time constraints.

2.4 Timing Prediction

Timing prediction techniques estimate the real-time behaviour of high-level language program segments from their source code and a knowledge of the target operating environment. Herein we assume the target language is GCL itself and adapt rules defined by Shaw [8] and Puschner & Koza [7].

For a GCL statement s, let $T(s)$ return a non-empty set of its possible execution times. Selected timing prediction rules are given below; they are used later as the basis for timing side-conditions.

T1 Primitive times. Execution time estimates must be made available for primitive actions, using knowledge of the target system. Herein we assume that estimates are known for: $T(.v)$, the time to get the address of variable v; $T(v)$, the time to load the value of variable v; $T(c)$ the time to load the value of a constant c; $T(:=)$ the time to perform an assignment, i.e., the 'store' time; $T(\text{op})$, the time to perform an arithmetic or logical operation; $T(\text{io})$, the time to perform an input or output operation; $T(\text{br})$, the time to branch to a new code segment.

T2 Expressions. For an expression E consisting of i operators, j variable operands and k constant operands (and assuming sufficient registers are available),

$$T(E) = \sum_i T(\text{op}) + \sum_j T(v) + \sum_k T(c) .$$

T3 Assignment.

$$T(v := E) = T(.v) + T(:=) + T(E) .$$

T4 Sequence. For two statements s_1 and s_2,

$$T(s_1 ; s_2) = T(s_1) + T(s_2) .$$

We assume that sequential composition takes no time, i.e., $T(;) = \{0\}$.

T5 Alternatives. For an **if** statement,

$$T(\mathbf{if} \, (\![]i \bullet G_i \rightarrow s_i) \, \mathbf{fi}) = \bigcup_i (T(\mathbf{if}_i) + T(G_i) + T(s_i)) ,$$

where $T(\mathbf{if}_i)$ is the time required to reach the ith alternative, $T(G_i)$ is the time needed to evaluate the ith guard and $T(s_i)$ is the execution time for the ith alternative. $T(\mathbf{if}_i)$ includes the time taken to evaluate preceding false guards (if any) and branch to the appropriate point.

T6 Iteration. Similarly, in a **do** statement, let $T(\mathbf{do}_i)$ be the time taken to reach the ith alternative since the beginning of this iteration.

Shaw uses time intervals to express the inevitable uncertainty in execution times. We generalise this to time *sets* to allow for the possibility that there are two distinct ways to perform an action, with widely differing execution times, but where an 'intermediate' execution time is impossible. For example, loading the value of a variable may take 1 time unit if it is in primary memory, or 4 time units if it is in secondary storage. However to say that the possible execution time is the interval [1 .. 4] is nonsensical because the load operation can never take 3 time units. We extend arithmetic operations pointwise to sets; the set additions above operate on *every pair* of values from the two operands and return a set of values, e.g., $\{7, 10\} + \{2, 3\} = \{9, 10, 12, 13\}$.

3 Real-Time Refinement Methodology

This section presents the real-time refinement methodology.

3.1 A Timing Notation

Firstly, a notation for expressing timing requirements in Z is needed. We adopt a minimal approach and simply allow each operation schema Op to have a non-empty set D of possible execution times associated with it, denoted

$$Op \odot D .$$

The $\odot$ operator takes a schema and a set of times and returns a new schema. Some laws describing its behaviour are given in appendix A and its formal definition is outlined in appendix B.

We can think of D as specifying the possible durations of Op or, if it is considered better to treat transitions as indivisible, then D may be thought of as the possible delays between the occurrence of Op and its predecessor.

We also allow the $\odot$ notation to be used with refinement calculus specification statements and GCL code so that the timing requirements are carried through into system development. (This is in keeping with the philosophy that timing constraints must persist as permanent reminders of timing obligations. Even after a constraint has been satisfied it should be retained in the program code as a comment to act as documentation in case of future system maintenance or modification.)

3.2 Real-Time Heuristic Rules

The following heuristic rules allow direct conversion from a "timed" Z specification into a high-level system design expressed using GCL and specification statements. The timing conditions following each rule are based on those in the formal refinement calculus introduced in Sect. 3.3.

H1 Basic change of notation. Given a schema of the form

$$Op \odot D \ ,$$

it can be expressed as a specification statement

$$w : [pre, post] \odot D \ ,$$

where the following notational changes are made:
1. variable names are shortened to one or two characters to conform with refinement calculus convention,
2. the Z dashed/undashed variable decorations are translated into refinement calculus subscripted 0 form and other syntactic changes made (e.g., the Z sequence concatenation operator $\frown$ becomes the equivalent specification statement operator $+\!\!+$),
3. the 'implicit precondition' rule [3] is used to extract the pre and post-conditions from the Z predicate (the predicate becomes the post-condition and the precondition is created from the predicate by existential quantification over the initial variables, removal of conjuncts referring to final variables, and name substitution to remove subscripted variable names), and
4. the resultant expressions are simplified, if necessary.

Let Op^* be the specification statement produced by applying these changes to a Z operation schema Op. King [3] gives further details but notes that, with practice, converting from Z to the specification statement notation can be done directly.

H2 Introduce 'top-level' iteration. The operational interpretation of a Z specification is that one of the operations whose pre-condition is satisfied is performed until no such operation remains. Where more than one operation can be performed the choice is nondeterministic. Therefore, given a Z specification consisting of a distinguished initialisation schema $Op_0 \odot D_0$ and n 'top-level' operation schemata (i.e., those not used in the definition of any other schema), $Op_1 \odot D_1 \ \cdots \ Op_n \odot D_n$, then the entire specification can be expressed as

$$(Op_0 \odot D_0)^*;$$
$$\textbf{do pre } Op_1 \rightarrow (Op_1 \odot D_{1'})^*$$
$$\cdots$$
$$[] \text{ pre } Op_n \rightarrow (Op_n \odot D_{n'})^*$$
$$\textbf{od},$$

where $\forall 1 \leqslant i \leqslant n \bullet (T(\textbf{do}_i) + T(\text{pre } Op_i) + D_{i'}) \subseteq D_i$ to account for the time taken to evaluate guards and branch to the appropriate point in the code. This rule allows us to introduce non-terminating iteration, a common feature of embedded real-time applications.

H3 Introduce alternation. Given a schema that can be expressed using disjunction,

$$Op \cong Op_1 \odot D_1 \vee Op_2 \odot D_2 ,$$

where the pre-conditions of the operations can be directly expressed in the target language [3], then it can be rewritten as

$$\textbf{if pre } Op_1 \rightarrow (Op_1 \odot D_{1'})^*$$
$$[] \text{ pre } Op_2 \rightarrow (Op_2 \odot D_{2'})^*$$
$$\textbf{fi},$$

where $(T(\textbf{if}_1) + T(\text{pre } Op_1) + D_{1'}) \subseteq D_1$ and $(T(\textbf{if}_2) + T(\text{pre } Op_2) + D_{2'}) \subseteq D_2$.

H4 Introduce sequencing 1. Given a schema that can be expressed using conjunction,

$$Op \cong Op_1 \odot D_1 \wedge Op_2 \odot D_2 ,$$

where Op_1 and Op_2 act on disjoint parts of the state-space [3], then it can be expressed either as

$$(Op_1 \odot D_3)^* ; (Op_2 \odot D_4)^*$$

or

$$(Op_2 \odot D_4)^* ; (Op_1 \odot D_3)^* ,$$

where $D_3 + D_4 \subseteq D_1 \cap D_2$ (see law L2, appendix A).

H5 Introduce sequencing 2. Given a schema that can be expressed using schema composition as

$$Op \cong Op_1 \odot D_1 \,\text{\S}\, Op_2 \odot D_2 ,$$

then it can be rewritten as

$$(Op_1 \odot D_3)^* ; (Op_2 \odot D_4)^* ,$$

where $D_3 + D_4 \subseteq D_1 + D_2$ (see law L3, appendix A).

3.3 The Real-Time Refinement Calculus

The real-time refinement calculus gives formal rules for deriving GCL code from specification statements. Each rule is followed by timing requirements acting as side-conditions that must be formally proven correct for the refinement step to be valid. Selected laws are shown below.

R1 Increase predictability.

$$w\colon [pre, post] \odot D \sqsubseteq w\colon [pre, post] \odot D_1 \;,$$

where $D_1 \subseteq D$ and $D_1 \neq \{\}$.

R2 Introduce (single) assignment. If $pre \Rightarrow post[E/w][x/x_0]$ (for every x_0),

$$w\colon [pre, post] \odot D \sqsubseteq w := E \;,$$

where $(T(.w) + T(:=) + T(E)) \subseteq D$.

R3 Introduce sequential composition. For fresh constants X,

$$w, x\colon [pre, post] \odot D$$
$$\sqsubseteq \; \mathbf{con}\, X \bullet$$
$$x\colon [pre, mid] \odot D_1 \;;\; w, x\colon [mid[X/x_0], post[X/x_0]] \odot D_2 \;,$$

where $D_1 + D_2 \subseteq D$ and mid contains no initial variables other than x_0 [5].

R4 Introduce trailing skip.

$$w\colon [pre, post] \odot D \sqsubseteq w\colon [pre, post] \odot D_1 \;;\; [\text{true}, \text{true}] \odot D_2 \;,$$

where $D_1 + D_2 \subseteq D$.

R5 Introduce idling.

$$[\text{true}, \text{true}] \odot D \sqsubseteq \mathbf{idle}(d) \;,$$

where $d \in D$.

R6 Introduce alternation.

$$w\colon [pre \wedge (\vee i \bullet G_i), post] \odot D$$
$$\sqsubseteq \; \mathbf{if}\, ([]i \bullet G_i \rightarrow w\colon [pre \wedge G_i, post] \odot D_i)\, \mathbf{fi} \;,$$

where $\bigcup_i (T(\mathbf{if}_i) + T(G_i) + D_i) \subseteq D$.

R7 Introduce input.

$$\alpha, x\colon [\alpha \neq \langle\rangle, \alpha_0 = x\colon\alpha] \odot D \sqsubseteq \mathbf{input}(\alpha, x) \;,$$

where $(T(.x) + T(\text{io})) \subseteq D$.

R8 Introduce output.

$$\omega\colon [pre, \omega = \omega_0 \dblplus \langle E\rangle] \odot D \sqsubseteq \mathbf{output}(\omega, E) \;,$$

where $(T(E) + T(\text{io})) \subseteq D$.

Rules R2, R3 and R6 are familiar from the untimed calculus [5] with obvious timing annotations. R1 is an important rule that is often appealed to implicitly during refinement. It says that an implementation with *stricter* timing bounds than those specified is always acceptable. Rules R4 and R5 allow introduction of idle delays as long as they fit within the timing constraints.

When considering real-time behaviour, we must account for the time taken to receive and send values and therefore use rules R7 and R8 to generate inputs and outputs. We have followed Morgan's approach [5] in which Greek variable names, e.g., α and ω, represent sequences of incoming and outgoing values.

4 Example

This section illustrates, in detail, the derivation of a real-time program from a Z specification.

4.1 Specification

Consider that subsystem of a ground-based vehicle dedicated to displaying the current speed and total distance travelled. A hardware device attached to one of the wheels generates pulses as the wheel rotates. This information is used to update two 6-digit displays, showing speed in kilometres per hour and distance travelled in kilometres. Furthermore, if the vehicle's speed exceeds 100 km/h, a speed limiting device must be activated.

Functional Description. The following schemata define the functional behaviour of the system. Its timing requirement is given below.

$\_State$ _____
$HowFar, TotalDist : \mathbb{N}$
$\alpha, \omega, \psi : \mathrm{seq}_\infty \mathbf{Z}$

TotalDist is the total distance the vehicle has ever travelled, *HowFar* is the distance travelled during the last period, both in centimetres. Sequence α is the inputs from the pulse generator and ω and ψ are the outputs to the speed and distance displays, respectively.

To represent the repetitive i/o of an embedded system we have used unbounded sequences to represent i/o streams. There is no *Init* schema in this example. The initial value of *TotalDist* is assumed to be carried over from the last journey. Similarly for the output streams. The value of input stream α is supplied by the environment.

In each period the system must read the number of pulses and then use this information to update the display:

$$Display \,\,\widehat{=}\,\, ReadPulses \,\,{}_9^\circ\,\, Update$$

$\begin{array}{|l}
\text{\underline{ReadPulses}} \\
\Delta State \\
\hline
HowFar' = 20 * (head\ \alpha) \\
\alpha' = (tail\ \alpha) \\
\omega' = \omega \\
\psi' = \psi \\
TotalDist' = TotalDist
\end{array}$

Each value in stream α returns the number of pulses since the stream was last accessed. *HowFar* is updated based on the assumption that the wheel hub generates 10 pulses per revolution and the wheel has a circumference of 2 metres.

Updating the display consists of updating both the distance travelled and the current speed:

$$Update \,\hat{=}\, Distance \land Speed$$

$\begin{array}{|l}
\text{\underline{Distance}} \\
\Delta State \\
\hline
TotalDist' = TotalDist+ \\
\qquad\qquad HowFar \\
\psi' = \psi \,^\frown \langle \lfloor TotalDist'/100000 \rfloor \\
\qquad\qquad \text{mod } 1000000 \rangle \\
\alpha' = \alpha
\end{array}$

Stream ψ writes to the distance travelled display. Modulo arithmetic is used to allow for the limited number of digits on the display device.

Updating the speed display consists of one of two possible actions, depending on whether the vehicle is within the speed limit or not:

$$Speed \,\hat{=}\, TooFast \lor WithinLimit$$

$\begin{array}{|l}
\text{\underline{TooFast}} \\
\Delta State \\
\hline
HowFar > 277 \\
\omega' = \omega \,^\frown \langle -1 \rangle
\end{array}$

Sending special value -1 to the speed display is assumed to display a warning message and activate the speed-limiting hardware. The value 277 is explained below.

$\begin{array}{|l}
\text{\underline{WithinLimit}} \\
\Delta State \\
\hline
HowFar \leqslant 277 \\
\omega' = \omega \,^\frown \langle \lfloor (HowFar * 36)/100 \rfloor \rangle
\end{array}$

Send the speed, converted to kilometres per hour, to the speed display.

Timing Requirement. To operate correctly the functional specification above relies upon an assumption that the incoming stream is updated 10 times per second. The figure '277' used in the pre-condition of *Speed* is based on the knowledge that 100 kilometres per hour is equivalent to 277 centimetres per decisecond. (We have used many explicit constants in this example to shorten the presentation and to emphasise the often rigid requirements of embedded systems, but acknowledge that these could be named to improve readability and maintainability.)

The system thus has a timing requirement to cycle every tenth of a second. One way to express this is to redefine the repetitive 'top-level' action *Display* with an expected duration as follows:

$$TDisplay \mathrel{\widehat{=}} Display \odot \{95 \mathrel{.\,.} 105\} \ .$$

All time values are in milliseconds. A five percent cumulative error has been allowed. (To simplify the presentation, we take $\{m \mathrel{.\,.} n\}$ to mean the set of all integers between m and n, inclusive. However, the techniques are equally applicable to a continuous time domain.)

The functional specification is intimately linked to this timing requirement; the arithmetic in schema *Speed* is meaningless if it is not achieved.

4.2 High-Level System Design

Initially system development proceeds by developing an overall design via the heuristic rules in Sect. 3.2. Each step imposes a timing obligation that must later be satisfied.

Step 1. Applying H2 to the system described in Sect. 4.1 generates

> **do** pre *TDisplay* $\rightarrow$ (*TDisplay* $\odot$ D_{a})*
> **od** ,

where $(T(\mathbf{do}_1) + T(\text{pre } TDisplay) + D_{\mathrm{a}}) \subseteq \{95 \mathrel{.\,.} 105\}$.

Step 2. Applying H5 to *TDisplay* $\odot$ D_{a} generates

> $(ReadPulses \odot D_{\mathrm{b}})^{*}$; $(Update \odot D_{\mathrm{c}})^{*}$,

where $D_{\mathrm{b}} + D_{\mathrm{c}} \subseteq D_{\mathrm{a}}$ (heeding law L3, appendix A).

Step 3. Applying H4 to *Update* $\odot$ D_{c} generates

> $(Distance \odot D_{\mathrm{d}})^{*}$; $(Speed \odot D_{\mathrm{e}})^{*}$,

where $D_{\mathrm{d}} + D_{\mathrm{e}} \subseteq D_{\mathrm{c}}$ (using law L2, appendix A).

Step 4. Applying H3 to $Speed \odot D_e$ generates

> **if** pre $TooFast \rightarrow (TooFast \odot D_f)^*$
> [] pre $WithinLimit \rightarrow (WithinLimit \odot D_g)^*$
> **fi** ,

where $((T(\mathbf{if}_1) + T(\text{pre } TooFast) + D_f) \cup (T(\mathbf{if}_2) + T(\text{pre } WithinLimit) + D_g)) \subseteq D_e$
(using law L4, appendix A).

Step 5. Combining the results of these steps yields a complete high-level design,

> **do** pre $TDisplay \rightarrow ((ReadPulses \odot D_b)^*;$
> $\qquad\qquad\qquad\quad ((Distance \odot D_d)^*;$
> $\qquad\qquad\qquad\quad (\textbf{if} \text{ pre } TooFast \rightarrow (TooFast \odot D_f)^*$
> $\qquad\qquad\qquad\quad\ [] \text{ pre } WithinLimit \rightarrow (WithinLimit \odot D_g)^*$
> $\qquad\qquad\qquad\quad \textbf{fi}) \odot D_e) \odot D_c) \odot D_a$
> **od** ,

which, by application of rule H1, can be rewritten as

> **do** true $\rightarrow (hf, \alpha \colon [\text{true}, hf = 20 * (\text{hd } \alpha_0) \wedge \alpha = (\text{tl } \alpha_0)] \odot D_b;$
> $\qquad\qquad (td, \psi \colon [\text{true}, td = td_0 + hf \wedge$
> $\qquad\qquad\qquad\qquad\qquad \psi = \psi_0 \mathbin{+\!\!+} \langle \lfloor td/100000 \rfloor \bmod 1000000 \rangle] \odot D_d;$
> $\qquad\qquad (\textbf{if } hf > 277 \rightarrow \omega \colon [hf > 277, \omega = \omega_0 \mathbin{+\!\!+} \langle -1 \rangle] \odot D_f$
> $\qquad\qquad\ [] \ hf \leqslant 277 \rightarrow \omega \colon [hf \leqslant 277,$
> $\qquad\qquad\qquad\qquad\qquad\qquad \omega = \omega_0 \mathbin{+\!\!+} \langle \lfloor (hf * 36)/100 \rfloor \rangle] \odot D_g$
> $\qquad\qquad \textbf{fi}) \odot D_e) \odot D_c) \odot D_a$
> **od** .

4.3 Detailed Design

The design is completed using the refinement calculus to derive GCL code for each of the specification statements above (the guards are already in a satisfactory form).

Step 6. By R3 and re-expressing the *mid* condition, then R7 and R2,

$$hf, \alpha \colon [\text{true}, hf = 20 * (\text{hd } \alpha_0) \wedge \alpha = (\text{tl } \alpha_0)] \odot D_b$$

$\sqsubseteq$ **con** $X \bullet$
$\qquad hf, \alpha \colon [\text{true}, \alpha_0 = hf \colon \alpha] \odot D_h;$
$\qquad hf, \alpha \colon [X = hf \colon \alpha, hf = 20 * (\text{hd } X) \wedge \alpha = (\text{tl } X)] \odot D_i$

$\sqsubseteq$ **input**(α, hf) ; $hf := 20 * hf$,

where $D_h + D_i \subseteq D_b$ and $T(.hf) + T(\text{io}) \subseteq D_h$ and $T(.hf) + T(:=) + T(20 * hf) \subseteq D_i$. (For brevity, it is assumed that the pulse generator reliably produces values; the need to check for "eof" on α is therefore omitted.)

Step 7. Let Y represent "$\lfloor td/100000 \rfloor$ mod 1000000". By R3 and then R2 and R8,

$$td, \psi \colon [\text{true}, td = td_0 + hf \wedge \psi = \psi_0 +\!\!+ \langle Y \rangle] \odot D_d$$

$$\sqsubseteq \text{ con } X \bullet$$
$$\qquad td \colon [\text{true}, td = td_0 + hf] \odot D_j;$$
$$\qquad \psi \colon [td = X + hf, td = X + hf \wedge \psi = \psi_0 +\!\!+ \langle Y \rangle] \odot D_k$$

$$\sqsubseteq \; td := td + hf \; ; \mathbf{output}(\psi, (td \div 100000) \bmod 1000000) ,$$

where $D_j + D_k \subseteq D_d$ and $T(.td) + T(:=) + T(td + hf) \subseteq D_j$ and $T((td \div 100000) \bmod 1000000) + T(\text{io}) \subseteq D_k$.

Step 8. By R8,

$$\omega \colon [hf > 277, \omega = \omega_0 +\!\!+ \langle -1 \rangle] \odot D_f \sqsubseteq \mathbf{output}(\omega, -1) ,$$

where $T(-1) + T(\text{io}) \subseteq D_f$.

Step 9. By R8,

$$\omega \colon [hf \leqslant 277, \omega = \omega_0 +\!\!+ \langle \lfloor (hf * 36)/100 \rfloor \rangle] \odot D_g$$
$$\sqsubseteq \mathbf{output}(\omega, (hf * 36) \div 100) ,$$

where $T((hf * 36) \div 100) + T(\text{io}) \subseteq D_g$.

4.4 Timing Analysis

Although the steps above have derived a detailed system design it is not considered complete until the timing conditions associated with each step have been formally satisfied. To do this some knowledge of the timing behaviour of the intended operating environment is needed.

Firstly, either via experimentation, formal analysis or from the manufacturer's specifications, primitive times for the target architecture (in milliseconds) are determined:

A1 As required by rule T1, assume that

$$
\begin{aligned}
T(.v) &= \{0, 1, 2\}, \\
T(c) &= \{0, 1\}, \\
T(v) &= \{0, 1, 4\}, \\
T(:=) &= \{0, 1, 4\}, \\
T(\text{op}) &= \{3\}, \\
T(\text{io}) &= \{9\}, \\
T(\text{br}) &= \{2\}.
\end{aligned}
$$

Notice that some of the values are uncertain. For instance, the time $T(v)$ needed to load the value of a variable v may be 0, if it can be determined at compile-time that the value of v will already be in a register, 1, if the variable is in RAM, or 4, if the value must be fetched from secondary storage.

Further information allows us to reduce timing uncertainty, so we then determine as much as we can about the target compiler:

C1 The compiler can recognise an infinite loop due to a 'do true → ... od' construct and hence the true guard will incur no run-time overhead.

C2 The compiler is found not to keep track of which constants are in registers, so $T(c)$ will never be 0.

C3 The compiler generates deterministic code for **if** and **do** statements, evaluating the guards in their textual order until a true one is found.

Finally, our knowledge of the application program under development also allows reductions in timing uncertainty:

P1 Addresses of variables can all be determined at compile time so $T(.v)$ will incur no run-time overhead.

P2 Given the small number of variables in this example they can always be held in primary memory so $T(v)$ and $T(:=)$ will never be 4. (In fact, it is likely that the variables will never need to be moved from the registers at all, but we will err on the side of caution in the absence of more information about the optimisation strategy used by the compiler).

Given these assumptions we can now determine the time required to evaluate the **if** guards:

$$\begin{aligned}
T(\text{pre } TooFast) &= T(hf > 277) \\
&= T(v) + T(\text{op}) + T(c) \\
&= \{0,1\} + \{3\} + \{1\} = \{4,5\} \ ,
\end{aligned}$$

$$\begin{aligned}
T(\text{pre } WithinLimit) &= T(hf \leqslant 277) \\
&= T(v) + T(\text{op}) + T(c) \\
&= \{0,1\} + \{3\} + \{1\} = \{4,5\} \ .
\end{aligned}$$

Execution times for the simple actions, i.e., assignments, reads and writes, can be computed routinely, making use of rules T1 to T3:

$$D_{\mathrm{f}} = T(\mathbf{output}(\omega, -1)) = T(c) + T(\text{io}) = \{1\} + \{9\} = \{10\} \ ,$$

$$\begin{aligned}
D_{\mathrm{g}} &= T(\mathbf{output}(\omega, (hf * 36) \div 100)) \\
&= T(v) + T(\text{op}) + T(c) + T(\text{op}) + T(c) + T(\text{io}) \\
&= \{0,1\} + \{3\} + \{1\} + \{3\} + \{1\} + \{9\} = \{17,18\} \ ,
\end{aligned}$$

$$D_{\mathrm{h}} = T(\mathbf{input}(\alpha, hf)) = T(.v) + T(\text{io}) = \{0\} + \{9\} = \{9\} \ ,$$

$$\begin{aligned}
D_{\mathrm{i}} &= T(hf := 20 * hf) \\
&= T(.v) + T(:=) + T(c) + T(\text{op}) + T(v) \\
&= \{0\} + \{0,1\} + \{1\} + \{3\} + \{0,1\} = \{4,5,6\} \ ,
\end{aligned}$$

$$\begin{aligned}
D_{\mathrm{j}} &= T(td := td + hf) \\
&= T(.v) + T(:=) + T(v) + T(\text{op}) + T(v) \\
&= \{0\} + \{0,1\} + \{0,1\} + \{3\} + \{0,1\} = \{3..6\} \ ,
\end{aligned}$$

$$D_k = T(\textbf{output}(\psi, (td \div 100000) \bmod 1000000))$$
$$= T(v) + T(\text{op}) + T(c) + T(\text{op}) + T(c) + T(\text{io})$$
$$= \{0, 1\} + \{3\} + \{1\} + \{3\} + \{1\} + \{9\} = \{17, 18\} \ .$$

From step 1 we can re-state our timing goal by accounting for the time taken for each iteration, i.e.,

$$T(\textbf{do}_1) + T(\text{pre } TDisplay) + D_a = \{2\} + \{0\} + D_a$$

(using assumption C1 and letting $T(\textbf{do}_1) = T(\text{br})$). Thus, from steps 2 and 3, we must demonstrate that

$$\{2\} + D_b + D_d + D_e \subseteq \{95 \ .. \ 105\}$$

to satisfy the periodic constraint.

Using the durations calculated above let us adopt some preliminary times. From step 6, let

$$D_b = D_h + D_i = \{9\} + \{4, 5, 6\} = \{13, 14, 15\} \ .$$

From step 7, let

$$D_d = D_j + D_k = \{3 \ .. \ 6\} + \{17, 18\} = \{20 \ .. \ 24\} \ .$$

To evaluate D_e we rely on assumption C3 above to determine that

$$T(\textbf{if}_1) = T(\text{br}) = \{2\} \ ,$$

whereas the second alternative cannot be reached without having evaluated the first guard, i.e.,

$$T(\textbf{if}_2) = T(\text{br}) + T(\text{pre } TooFast) + T(\text{br})$$
$$= \{2\} + \{4, 5\} + \{2\} = \{8, 9\} \ .$$

Now, from steps 4, 8 and 9, let

$$D_e = (\{2\} + \{4, 5\} + \{10\}) \cup (\{8, 9\} + \{4, 5\} + \{17, 18\})$$
$$= \{16, 17, 29 \ .. \ 32\} \ .$$

Thus, using these figures, $\{2\} + D_b + D_d + D_e = \{51 .. 58, 64 .. 73\}$ rather than $\{95 .. 105\}$ and we must conclude that our system does *not* satisfy the timing requirement!

4.5 Redesign

The set of possible execution times above shows that the design fails in two distinct ways: (i) the range of values is much broader than the allowable five percent uncertainty, and (ii) the system iterates too quickly for the arithmetic used in schema *Speed*.

To solve the first problem we need to reduce the range of possible execution times. An obvious starting point is the "loosest" execution time D_e. The problem is that the two alternative branches take greatly differing execution times, the first $\{16, 17\}$ and the second $\{29 .. 32\}$. This uncertainty can be reduced by making the shorter first alternative take longer by inserting an idle delay.

Steps 4' and 8'. By appealing to rule R1 (with respect to $Speed \odot D_e$), and using rules R4 and R5, we can replace $(TooFast \odot D_f)^*$ with

$$\omega : [hf > 277, \omega = \omega_0 + \langle -1 \rangle] \odot D_f$$
$$\sqsubseteq \omega : [hf > 277, \omega = \omega_0 + \langle -1 \rangle] \odot D_l \, ; [\text{true}, \text{true}] \odot D_m$$
$$\sqsubseteq \text{output}(s, -1) \, ; \text{idle}(d_m) \, ,$$

where $D_l + D_m \subseteq D_f$ and $d_m \in D_m$.

We must now ensure that the possible execution times for the first branch are a subset of those for the second, i.e.,

$$\{16, 17\} + D_m \subseteq \{29 .. 32\} \, ,$$

which has solution set

$$D_m = \{13, 14, 15\} \, .$$

Selecting $d_m = 13$ and recalculating the execution times yields

$$D_e = \{29 .. 32\}$$

and hence $\{2\} + D_b + D_d + D_e = \{64 .. 73\}$, (barely) within the necessary tolerance.

To solve the second problem, and prevent the system from iterating too quickly, we elect to introduce another idle delay, this time at the end of the cycle.

Steps 1' and 10. Again using rules R1, R4 and R5 we can replace $(TDisplay \odot D_a)^*$ with

$$(TDisplay \odot D_{a'})^* \, ; [\text{true}, \text{true}] \odot D_n$$
$$\sqsubseteq (TDisplay \odot D_{a'})^* \, ; \text{idle}(d_n) \, ,$$

where $D_{a'} + D_n \subseteq D_a$ and $d_n \in D_n$.

$D_{a'}$ is the time required to execute the original loop body, i.e., $D_b + D_d + D_e = \{62 .. 71\}$. Therefore, from our original timing goal, we must show that

$$\{2\} + \{62 .. 71\} + D_n \subseteq \{95 ... 105\} \, ,$$

which has solution set

$$D_n = \{31, 32\} \, .$$

Selecting $d_n = 31$ and recalculating the execution time for the loop body now yields $\{2\} + D_b + D_d + D_e + D_n = \{95 .. 104\}$, as required.

We can now give a complete implementation, proven correct with respect to time:

```
do true → input(α, hf);
          hf := 20 * hf;
          td := td + hf;
          output(ψ, (td ÷ 100000) mod 1000000);
          if hf > 277 → output(ω, -1);
                        idle(13)
          [] hf ≤ 277 → output(ω, (hf * 36) ÷ 100)
          fi;
          idle(31)
od .
```

5 Conclusions

We have presented a refinement calculus for formal derivation of real-time systems. Further, a complete software development methodology has been defined with functional and timing specification in an extended Z notation, high-level system design via heuristic rules, detailed design via the real-time refinement calculus and timing validation using timing prediction rules. Coupled with some knowledge of the intended operating environment, this allows us to generate programs that are guaranteed to satisfy their timing requirements.

System development proceeds by routine application of the rules. The only creative input required is in selecting which possible refinement rule to apply at each step. The potential for automating subsequent application of the rule and checking of time-based side-conditions is obvious.

The work closest to ours is that of Mahony and Hayes [4]. Their specification methods have the advantage of greater abstraction, although our use of the operational interpretation of Z is, arguably, more conducive to immediate industrial application.

Not all timing problems can be solved by simply introducing delays, as was the case in Sect. 4.5. Many timing problems necessitate a major redesign of the system. In this situation we benefit from the standard refinement calculus discipline, which rigorously documents all design decisions, and our timing side-conditions, which allow new designs to be rapidly assessed for timing correctness.

Of course, many timing problems stemming from code that is too slow can be solved by introducing parallelism. Indeed, the major weakness of our work to date is the failure to consider parallelism. It is trivial to introduce refinement rules for non-communicating concurrency (to generate **pardo** and **parif** statements [1]) but the problem of communicating parallelism is much harder. However, given that this issue is far from being resolved for the *untimed* refinement calculus [2, 6], we feel no embarrassment in not (yet) being able to handle it in the *timed* case!

Acknowledgements. Thanks to members of the UQ CS refinement group for their numerous suggestions, especially David Carrington, Ian Hayes, Brendan Mahony, Mark Utting and Nigel Ward. Thanks also to the anonymous referees for many helpful comments. This work was primarily supported by an Australian Postdoctoral Research Fellowship.

References

1. V.K. Haase. Real-time behavior of programs. *IEEE Transactions on Software Engineering*, SE-7(5):494–501, September 1981.
2. C.B. Jones. Interference resumed. In *Proc. 6th Australian Software Engineering Conference*, pages 31–55, Sydney, July 1991.
3. S. King. Z and the refinement calculus. In D. Bjørner, C.A.R. Hoare, and H. Longmaack, editors, *Proc. VDM'90*, volume 428 of *Lecture Notes in Computer Science*, pages 164–188. Springer-Verlag, April 1990.
4. B.P. Mahony and I.J. Hayes. A case-study in timed refinement: A mine pump. *IEEE Transactions on Software Engineering*, 18(9):817–826, September 1992.

5. C. Morgan. *Programming from Specifications*. Prentice-Hall, 1990.

6. E.-R. Olderog. Towards a design calculus for communicating programs. In J.C.M. Baeten and J.F. Groote, editors, *Concur'91*, volume 527 of *Lecture Notes in Computer Science*, pages 61–77. Springer-Verlag, 1991.

7. P. Puschner and Ch. Koza. Calculating the maximum execution time of real-time programs. *Journal of Real-Time Systems*, 1(2):159–176, September 1989.

8. A.C. Shaw. Reasoning about time in higher-level language software. *IEEE Transactions on Software Engineering*, 15(7):875–889, July 1989.

9. J.M. Spivey. *The Z Notation: A Reference Manual.* Prentice Hall International, 1989.

A   Laws for Duration Operator

The following selected laws define valid uses of the $\odot$ notation and show how it interacts with standard schema operators.

L1 $Op \odot D_1 \odot D_2 = Op \odot (D_1 \cap D_2)$.
L2 $Op_1 \odot D_1 \wedge Op_2 \odot D_2 = (Op_1 \wedge Op_2) \odot (D_1 \cap D_2)$.
L3 $Op_1 \odot D_1 \, \S \, Op_2 \odot D_2 = (Op_1 \, \S \, Op_2) \odot (D_1 + D_2)$.
L4 $Op \odot D_1 \vee Op \odot D_2 = Op \odot (D_1 \cup D_2)$.
L5 $Op_1 \odot D \vee Op_2 \odot D = (Op_1 \vee Op_2) \odot D$.

Law L1 shows how adding timing annotations progressively constrains the possible times for an operation. Law L2 tells us that taking the conjunction of two operations also restricts the allowable timing behaviours (because the resultant schema must satisfy the requirements of both components). Law L3 shows how schema composition adds the durations. It thus acts like *sequential* composition.

Laws L4 and L5 illustrate two aspects of schema disjunction. In general, however,

$$Op_1 \odot D_1 \vee Op_2 \odot D_2 \neq (Op_1 \vee Op_2) \odot (D_1 \cup D_2)$$

because, e.g., $Op_1 \odot D_2$ may not be a possible behaviour of the left-hand side. (This means that schema disjunction can create behaviours that cannot be expressed as a single schema using the $\odot$ notation. The notation is, in fact, expressively weak, but suffices for the example considered herein. Suggested improvements to the notation have included a causality based model, absolute timing expressions, and timing expressions based on values of variables.)

When no timing constraint is associated with an operation then it has the broadest possible timing constraint, i.e., $\{0 .. \infty\}$.

B   Definition of Duration Operator

The '$\odot$' operator introduced in Sect. 3.1 is formally defined in standard Z as a shorthand for an auxiliary time variable. Let 't' be some variable name not used in a Z specification. To convert this specification to a "timed" specification we firstly add t to the *State* schema and then, for every $Op \odot D$, assert that $(t' - t) \in D$ in the predicate of Op. (The type of t can be $\mathbb{N}$, if discrete time is assumed, or $\mathbb{R}$, if a continuous time model is desired.)

The laws for schemata with attached timing constraints in appendix A then follow immediately. For example, law L2 holds because

$$Op_1 \odot D_1 \wedge Op_2 \odot D_2$$
$$= [\text{decs } Op_1 \mid \text{pred } Op_1 \wedge (t' - t) \in D_1] \wedge$$
$$[\text{decs } Op_2 \mid \text{pred } Op_2 \wedge (t' - t) \in D_2]$$
$$= [\text{decs } (Op_1 \wedge Op_2) \mid \text{pred } Op_1 \wedge \text{pred } Op_2 \wedge (t' - t) \in D_1 \cap D_2] \ .$$

Laws L4 and L5 hold because

$$Op_1 \odot D_1 \vee Op_2 \odot D_2$$
$$= [\text{decs } Op_1 \mid \text{pred } Op_1 \wedge (t' - t) \in D_1] \vee$$
$$[\text{decs } Op_2 \mid \text{pred } Op_2 \wedge (t' - t) \in D_2]$$
$$= [\text{decs } (Op_1 \wedge Op_2) \mid$$
$$(\text{pred } Op_1 \wedge (t' - t) \in D_1) \vee (\text{pred } Op_2 \wedge (t' - t) \in D_2)] \ .$$

Similarly for law L3.

The auxiliary variable is then carried through into the refinement calculus where it defines valid refinements.

Different FDT's Confronted with Different ODP-Viewpoints of the Trader

Joachim Fischer, Andreas Prinz and Andreas Vogel *

Department of Informatics
Humboldt-University Berlin
Unter den Linden 6
P.O. Box 1297
Germany, Berlin D-O-1086
{fischer, prinz, avogel}@informatik.hu-berlin.de

Abstract. The Reference Model of Open Distributed Processing (ODP RM) is intended to create an international standard for the design and realization of open distributed systems by both ISO and CCITT.
The use of formal methods in the design process of ODP systems is explicitly required. In this article the use of the Formal Description Techniques (FDT's) Z, LOTOS and SDL'92 is investigated and evaluated. These three FDT's are considered as representatives of the classes of formal techniques characterized by their structuring concepts and their underlying models, logic (set theory), process algebras and finite state machines, respectively.
The ODP trader which is intended to be a standard as well is selected as case study.

1 Introduction

1.1 Open Distributed Processing

The Reference Model of Open Distributed Processing (ODP RM) is intended to create an international standard for the design and realization of open distributed systems by both ISO and CCITT.

The ODP RM is organized in five parts, three defining and two giving explanations. The three defining parts are

- part 2 Descriptive model,
- part 3 Prescriptive model, and
- part 5 Architectural Semantics, Specification Techniques and Formalisms.

Whereas the descriptive model defines concepts for modeling of distributed systems in general, the prescriptive model defines the constraints which an ODP-system has to fulfill. Specification techniques and styles are investigated with respect to their suitability in the ODP context in part 5.

Rather than to deal with a distributed system in its full complexity, five viewpoints, abstractions on different levels, are defined in the ODP RM. These are the enterprise, information, computation, engineering and technology viewpoint.

---

* supported by a postgraduate grant of the Deutscher Akademischer Austauschdienst

Enterprise Viewpoint. The enterprise viewpoint is concerned with the following objectives:

- the rules and activities that exist within the enterprise,
- the interaction between the system and its environment,
- organizational structure of the enterprise,
- artifacts used in the enterprise rules,
- types of processing done in the enterprise, and
- security and management policies used in the enterprise.

The system is modeled in terms of enterprise objects. These objects represent the user rules, the business and management policies, the ODP system itself and its environment. The behaviour is defined by sequencing enterprise activities.

Information Viewpoint. From the information viewpoint are visible:

- information elements, their structure, their quality attributes and the relationships between them,
- the information flow,
- how information and information processing is visible to the user, and
- logical partitions of the ODP system.

An ODP system from the information viewpoint has to be modeled in terms of (information) objects, templates and classes. An object is defined by its states.

Computation Viewpoint. From this viewpoint, processing functions (instantiation, assignment, invocation, synchronization, communication, etc.) and data types are visible. A specification from the computation viewpoint describes a system independently of computers and networks.

The system is modeled by computation objects. Computation objects offer computation operations through computation interfaces. These operations are defined by one initial and a finite set of termination events. The invocation of an operation is of type interrogative or announcement.

Engineering Viewpoint. Engineering viewpoint specifications deal with control and transparency mechanisms, processors, memory, and communication networks. The distribution of behaviour and data is specified.

The main modeling concept are engineering objects. Computation objects are templates for the engineering ones. Furthermore, transparency and nucleus objects are visible.

- nucleus objects: provide a basic set of processing, storage and communication functions.
- transparency objects: provide transparency functions; there are transparency functions with respect to access, location, migration, concurrency and livelyness.
- engineering objects: interact with each other via transparency and nucleus objects.

Technology Viewpoint. The technical artifacts realizing the ODP system are visible from the technology viewpoint. These mean local operating systems, I/O devices, storage, access points to communications, etc.
The prescriptive part about the technology viewpoint is still undefined.

1.2 The ODP Trader

The trader is the main application of ODP RM and will become a standard too. The trader appears as an object from which another object can import its needs and export its interfaces in a distributed environment. A trader realizes at least the six operations for exporters (servers) and importers (clients).

Operations for Exporters:

- export: makes an interface available
- withdraw: withdraws the exported interface
- modify: modifies the attributes of an exported interface

Operations for Importers:

- list: lists the attributes of an interfaces
- search: searches interfaces of a given interface type fulfilling certain requirements
- select: selects the interface which is best with respect to certain selection requirements

Furthermore, there are operations to realize internal administration of a trader. For the sake of clearness we restrict ourselfes within this paper to the three operations export, withdraw and search.
These operations have the following parameters (their semantic can be found in [7]):

Export

- name of exporter
- name of interfacetype
- name of context
- values of necessary attributes
- values of optional attributes
- The return parameter is an identifier for the exported service or an error message

Withdraw

- name of exporter
- name of context
- name of exported entity
- The return parameter is OK or an error message.

Search

- name of importer
- name of context
- name of interfacetype
- predicates over attributes
- list of attributes to be returned
- search limitations
- The return parameter is a list of requested attributes of available services.

2 Motivation

The standardisation of ODP explicitely requests the application of FDT's, but the philosophy of ODP is much more complex as those of OSI. This becomes obvious, if we have a look e.g. at the need for support of the various viewpoints and for support of object-oriented concepts such as composition, inheritance and genericity. Currently there are no formal specifications of ODP concepts which are widely accepted. One interesting question concerns the suitability of the existing FDT's for their use in ODP.

The ODP trader is chosen as case study because it appears as a first main application of ODP. Furthermore, there are (informal) specifications of the five viewpoints given in the standardization documents of the ODP trader. For the specification of the ODP trader we used the specification languages LOTOS [4], Z [9], and SDL (in it's new object-oriented version SDL'92 [1]). Because of the differences of these techniques first of all in their underlying mathematical models and their structuring facilities different evaluations will be expected. Figure 1 shows the relations between the three techniques with regard to their degree of abstraction and their suitability for generating target code in the sense of rapid prototyping.

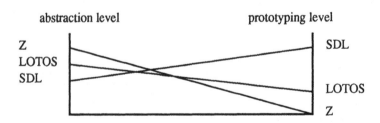

Fig. 1. Confrontation of Z, LOTOS and SDL

The languages LOTOS and SDL as executable techniques are special forms of so-called labelled transition systems. They provide the same abstract data type concept ACT ONE. Furthermore enhancements of SDL and LOTOS offer the usage of ASN.1 data types. The possibility to execute specifications is the base for testing of specifications. But a complete analysis of complex specifications using the interleaving semantic leads to the well-known problem of state explosion. The situation in

SDL is much harder compared to that in LOTOS because of the asynchronous communication with no restriction of buffer bounds and of time consumption of basic sequential actions. That's why testing is the only practical way for the evaluation of the specifications in many real applications. Even more dramatic is the fact that both languages are not powerful enough for the description of properties of the specification. Lets have a look at the simple Sliding-Window-Protocol [2]: the request for the correct ordering of the received messages can be described only in an informal manner. Moreover it is impossible to proof the validity of this property using a transmission channel as abstraction of an underlying network with such phenomena like message lost, duplication of messages, and reordering of messages.

It is only possible to test the corresponding specification. These disadvantages are compensated by the possibility to generate target code automatically. The underlying model of SDL provides the best initial position here.

Almost contrary is the situation with Z. Using a version of typed set theory Z specifications concentrate on pre- and post-conditions of operations rather than temporal ordering. Data type facilities of Z are considered easier to use, more versatile and more intuitive than those of ACT ONE. In particular, one can express in Z data type invariants. Z is well suited for information modelling, especially for the description of systems interacting with their environment through request-reply operations. Moreover, Z provides means to formulate and to proof properties of specifications [8].

After these general remarks we want to concentrate on the suitability of the FDT's in ODP. One of the new challenges is the request for the support of such object-oriented concepts like inheritance and generic object classes. Objects in LOTOS can be constructed as process instantiations. In SDL this could be done as system, block and process instantiations, where for each of them one can define object classes with possibilities for describing inheritance, virtual and generic concepts. This is not possible in LOTOS. Genericity is possible in Z only for abstract data types. The same is true for ACT ONE as a sublanguage of LOTOS and SDL. Dynamic configurations and aggregations of objects can be defined well-suited in SDL. In LOTOS only some forms of dynamic configuration can be specified. Further concepts requested by ODP like refinement, behavioural compatibility, modularity, design engineering, human use etc. are compared in [5].

Another interesting question concerns the suitability to describe the various ODP viewpoints. A summary of our case study for the ODP trader is found in the following table

	Z	LOTOS	SDL'92	
EntVP	−	−	−	
InfVP	+	±(with extensions [11])	±(partial)	− impossible
ComVP	±	+	+	± possible, but inconvenient
EngVP	±	+	+	+ well-suited
TecVP	−	±	±	

Last but not least the problem of the relations between specifications of the ODP viewpoints should be discussed. While SDL provides the inheritance concept which guarantees an interface compability, LOTOS is well-suited for behavioural compatibility.

An obvious conclusion is the fact, that no FDT is well-suited for all. We think that it is not useful to play one traditional FDT off against the other. Finding out possible transformations between them would be better because that could support the development and evaluation of specifications under various viewpoints.

In the following sections we want to give an impression of the indivual advantages of the various FDT's describing some viewpoints of the ODP trader:

- Z : compact specification of the information viewpoint,
- LOTOS: behavioural equivalence between computation viewpoint and engineering viewpoint,
- SDL : interface compatibility and modular refinement by inheritance.

3 Z

Since Z is the most abstract of the three specification languages in consideration, it is used to model the information viewpoint, which is considered to be the most abstract but formalizable one. A Z-specification describes possible state changes and input-output-relations but says nothing about any concrete computation nor about distribution. So, Z is well suited for modelling the information viewpoint. The information viewpoint takes the trader to be something like an abstract data type. This leads to another approach of formalizing the information viewpoint of the trader by using ADT's (as offered by both SDL'92 and LOTOS).

Z is a FDT just being standardized. Its semantic is stable since some years. Z is based on pure mathematics like set theory and logics. Special constructs are provided to formulate state changes. These constructs of Z are all again mapped onto the underlying mathematics. This makes it possible for Z to formulate all kinds of parallel, concurrent and sequential processes. But since Z is mainly descriptive, its use to formulate programs is not appropriate. Rather it should be used to formulate properties of programs and to relate them to each other.

It should be noted, that there exists an object-oriented extension of Z, namely Object-Z [3]. Object-Z can express temporal ordering and concurrency constraints because of its use of temporal logic operators, such that specifications of more ODP viewpoints could be supported.

A Z-specification of the trader has to deal first of all with the data types involved. Let $[Name]$ and $[Value]$ be given sets and $Boolean \cong \{False, True\}$ be a predefined type. For the sake of clearness we restrict ourself to the three trader operations $Operation \cong \{Export, Withdraw, Search\}$. Furthermore, we need a data type consisting of error messages $Errormsg \cong \{noerror, opninvalid, ...\}$. Next we define some records:

```
┌─ Usage ──────────────         ┌─ AttrCounts ──────────────
│ entity : Name                 │ necAttrC, OptAttrC : N
│ op : Operation
                                ┌─ dbEntry ──────────────
┌─ dbKey ──────────────         │ interface, entity : Name
│ context, service : Name       │ necAttr, optAttr : seq Value
```

Now we are able to define the traders state consisting of a validity function to check if incoming requests are permitted, a set of known interfaces with attributes belonging to them, a set of known contexts and a set of available operations.

$$
\begin{array}{|l}
\hline
\textit{Validity} : \textit{Usage} \rightarrow \textit{Boolean} \\
\textit{Interfaces} : \textit{Name} \nrightarrow \textit{AttrCounts} \\
\textit{Contexts} : \mathbf{P}\,\textit{Name} \\
\textit{AvailOps} : \textit{dbKey} \nrightarrow \textit{dbEntry} \\
\textit{Reachable} : \textit{Contexts} \rightarrow \mathbf{P}\,\textit{Contexts} \\
\hline
(\text{ran } \textit{AvailOps}).\textit{interface} \subseteq \text{dom } \textit{Interfaces} \\
(\text{dom } \textit{AvailOps}).\textit{context} \subseteq \textit{Contexts} \\
\forall\, x : \text{ran } \textit{AvailOps} \bullet \textit{Validity}(x.\textit{entity}, \textit{Export}) = \textit{True} \\
\hline
\end{array}
$$

This trader-state should be initializied properly.

$$
\begin{array}{|l}
\hline
\_\,\textit{INIT}\,_____ \\
\textit{AvailOps} = \varnothing \\
\hline
\end{array}
$$

Now we define all possible error cases in order to prevent the trader from change in such cases.

$$
\begin{array}{|l}
\hline
\_\,\textit{OpnInvalid}\,_____ \\
\textit{ReqEntity?} : \textit{Name} \\
\textit{Op?} : \textit{Operation} \\
\textit{Error!} : \textit{Errormsg} \\
\hline
\neg\, \textit{Validity}(\textit{ReqEntity?}, \textit{Op?}) \\
\textit{Error!} = \textit{opninvalid} \\
\hline
\end{array}
\qquad
\begin{array}{|l}
\hline
\_\,\textit{ServiceNotFound}\,_____ \\
\textit{Context?}, \textit{Service?} : \textit{Name} \\
\textit{Error!} : \textit{ErrorMsg} \\
\hline
\langle \textit{Service?}, \textit{Context?}\rangle \notin \\
\quad \text{dom } \textit{AvailOps} \\
\textit{Error!} = \textit{servicenotfound} \\
\hline
\end{array}
$$

$$
\begin{array}{|l}
\hline
\_\,\textit{WrongContext}\,_____ \\
\textit{Context?} : \textit{Name} \\
\textit{Error!} : \textit{Errormsg} \\
\hline
\textit{Context?} \notin \textit{Contexts} \\
\textit{Error!} = \textit{wrongcontext} \\
\hline
\end{array}
\qquad
\begin{array}{|l}
\hline
\_\,\textit{WrongInterface}\,_____ \\
\textit{InterfaceType?} : \textit{Name} \\
\textit{Error!} : \textit{Errormsg} \\
\hline
\textit{InterfaceType} \notin \text{dom } \textit{Interfaces} \\
\textit{Error!} = \textit{wronginterface} \\
\hline
\end{array}
$$

$$
\begin{array}{|l}
\hline
\_\,\textit{WrongParameterCount}\,_____ \\
\textit{NecAttributes?}, \textit{OptAttributes?} : \text{seq } \textit{value} \\
\textit{InterfaceType?} : \textit{Name} \\
\hline
\textit{Interfaces}(\textit{InterfaceType}).\textit{necAttrC} \neq \#\textit{NecAttributes?} \;\vee \\
\quad \textit{Interfaces}(\textit{InterfaceType}).\textit{optAttrC} < \#\textit{OptAttributes?} \\
\textit{Error!} = \textit{wrongparametercount} \\
\hline
\end{array}
$$

After the error cases we specify the correct case. This operation should only occur in the absence of errors.

```
┌─ PureExport ─────────────────────────────────────────────
│ ΔAvailOps
│ ReqEntity?, InterfaceType?, Context?, Result! : Name
│ NecAttributes?, OptAttributes? : seq Value
├──────────────────────────────────────────────────────────
│ ⟨Result!, Context?⟩ ∉ dom AvailOps
│ AvailOps' = AvailOps∪
│     {⟨Result!, Context?⟩ ↦ ⟨InterfaceType?, ReqEntity?,
│               NecAttributes?, OptAttributes?⟩}
└──────────────────────────────────────────────────────────
```

The above definitions lead to the following compound specification of the *Export*-operation. Note at this point, that there is no problem to add some further error conditions later on.

$ExportNotOk \mathrel{\hat=} (op! = Export \gg OpnInvalid) \lor WrongInterface$
$\quad \lor WrongContext \lor WrongParameterCount$
$ExportOk \mathrel{\hat=} \neg ExportNotOk \land Error! = noerror \land PureExport$
$Export \mathrel{\hat=} ExportOk \lor ExportNotOk$

Let us proceed with the operation *Withdraw*. We first specify a pure (correct) case operation and then put together all the things needed to specify the whole operation.

```
┌─ PureWithdraw ───────────────────────────────────────────
│ ΔAvailOps
│ ReqEntity?, Context?, ExportedService? : Name
├──────────────────────────────────────────────────────────
│ AvailOps' = AvailOps ◁ ExportedService?
└──────────────────────────────────────────────────────────
```

$WithdrawNotOk \mathrel{\hat=}$
$\quad (op! = Withdraw \gg OpnInvalid) \lor WrongContext \lor ServiceNotFound$
$WithdrawOk \mathrel{\hat=} \neg WithdrawNotOk \land Error! = noerror \land PureWithdraw$
$Withdraw \mathrel{\hat=} WithdrawOk \lor WithdrawNotOk$

In order to specify the *Search*-operation, we first need an additional record-type and three additional types. Furthermore, other kinds of errors may occur. As in the previous cases, we define a pure variant of *Search* and put the partial operations together afterwards.

```
┌─ dbRecord ───────────────────────────────────────────────
│ service, entity, context : Name
│ attr : seq Value
└──────────────────────────────────────────────────────────
```

$Predicate \mathrel{\hat=} seq\ Value \times seq\ Value \to Boolean$
$AttributeNumber \mathrel{\hat=} \mathbb{N}_1$
$LimitationFunction \mathrel{\hat=} dbKey \to Boolean$

___ *ServiceUnAvailable* _____
Context?, Service? : *Name*
Error! : *ErrorMsg*
LimitationsSet : **P** *LimitationFunction*
_____
$\forall\, c : Reachable(Context?)\ \bullet$
$\quad\langle Service?, c\rangle \notin \mathrm{dom}\ AvailOps\ \vee$
$\qquad \exists\, l : LimitationSet \bullet l(\langle Service?, c\rangle) = True$
$Error! = servicenotfound$

___ *TooManyAttrRequired* _____
ReturnAttr? : seq *AttributeNumber*
InterfaceType? : *Name*
_____
$\mathbf{let}\ i \mathrel{\widehat{=}} Interfaces(InterfaceType)\ \mathbf{in}$
$\quad \exists\, x : \mathrm{ran}\ ReturnAttr? \bullet x > i.necAttr + i.optAttr$
$Error! = wrongparametercount$

___ *PureSearch* _____
Context?, InterfaceType? : *Name*
Constraints? : seq *Predicate*
ReturnAttr? : seq *AttributeNumber*
LimitationSet? : **P** *LimitationFunction*
_____
$Result!.context \in Reachable(Context?)$
$\forall\, l : LimitationSet? \bullet l(\langle Result!.service, Result!.context\rangle) = False$
$\mathbf{let}\ dbval \mathrel{\widehat{=}} AvailOps(\langle Result!.service, Result!.context\rangle)\ \mathbf{in}$
$\quad dbval.interface = InterfaceType?$
$\quad Result!.entity = dbval.entity$
$\quad \#Result!.attr = \#ReturnAttr?$
$\quad \mathbf{let}\ na \mathrel{\widehat{=}} Interfaces(InterfaceType?).necAttr\ \mathbf{in}$
$\qquad na < ReturnAttr?(i) \Rightarrow$
$\qquad\quad Result!.attr(i) = dbval.optAttr(ReturnAttr?(i) - na)$
$\qquad na \geq ReturnAttr?(i) \Rightarrow$
$\qquad\quad Result!.attr(i) = dbval.necAttr(ReturnAttr?(i))$

$SearchNotOk \mathrel{\widehat{=}} (op! = Search \gg OpnInvalid) \vee WrongContext\ \vee$
$\qquad WrongInterface \vee ServiceUnavailable \vee TooManyAttributesRequired$
$SearchOk \mathrel{\widehat{=}} \neg\, SearchNotOk \wedge Error! = noerror \wedge PureSearch$
$Search \mathrel{\widehat{=}} SearchOk \vee SearchNotOk$

This completes the partial specification of the information viewpoint as far as the trader is concerned. The definition offered is very compact and neither over- nor underspecified. Operations are specified by stating pre- and postconditions.

Since this viewpoint does not have any specifications of parallelism or concurrency, one could also try to define the behaviour of the trader by means of equations like the standard abstract data type approach does. Means for specifying abstract data types are supplied by both LOTOS and SDL. They differ only in syntax.

This kind of specification is also very compact. Nevertheless the term structure of the equations introduces an implicit queue-outfit of the trader, that means, the equations handle the trader like a queue. This may be regarded to be some kind of overspecification. In fact, the trader may well be a hashtable, but human readers would tend to realize, that it is a queue. So this is a (marginal) drawback of this kind of specification.

4 LOTOS

4.1 Introduction

LOTOS is one of the Formal Description Techniques (FDT) standardized by the ISO. Its formal semantic of the behaviour and of the data descriptions is based on process algebras and many sorted algebras, respectively. There are different styles of LOTOS specifications. According to them, LOTOS can be used to describe both abstract requirements (constraint oriented style) and implementations (resource oriented style) of distributed systems. The underlying mathematical models allow transformations between specifications of different styles fulfilling equivalence relations.

4.2 An ODP Design Methodology

A methodology has been worked out which is based on the ODP concepts and formulated in LOTOS. The main idea is to define a set of LOTOS specifications with elements being related to a certain viewpoint. Each specification is defined as a restriction of the LOTOS syntax and leaves the LOTOS semantics unchanged. It yields an explicit relationship between the LOTOS constructs and the ODP concepts. Because of the LOTOS semantics, rules for the transformation between viewpoints and for code generation can be given.

Subsets of LOTOS w.r.t. ODP Viewpoints. In order to specify ODP systems from different viewpoints, subsets of LOTOS are introduced [11]. They define a special structure of behaviour corresponding to the architectural remarks in the RM. Furthermore, mappings between the ODP concepts and LOTOS constructs are given for each viewpoint.

Enterprise Viewpoint. In the opinion of the authors, the enterprise viewpoint specifications are understood as informal. The view from the information viewpoint is considered as the formalization of an enterprise viewpoint specification.

Information Viewpoint. The related LOTOS subset defines a structure which supports the constraint oriented specification style. LOTOS processes describe constraints which are identified as information objects. Information objects are composed from other ones or specified in the monolithic specification style.

The data type defining the operations provided by the ODP system are specified global and totally independent from any implementation.

Computation Viewpoint. In this viewpoint computational objects are visible. There are three types of them, invoking, operation and combined objects. Operation objects provide operations whereas invoking objects invoke these operations. Combined objects are combinations of both. All are specified as LOTOS processes. The operation signature as well as the starting and termination events are visible in the gate lists of the processes providing and invoking the operation. The types of the parameters of the events - completing the computation interfaces - are defined global to the computation objects.

Engineering Viewpoint. Engineering objects are specified as LOTOS processes. They communicate with each other via the nucleus system using transparency functions. This is reflected by the following structure:

```
( engineering-object ||| ... ||| engineering-object )
||
nucleus-system
```

The nucleus system consists of nucleus objects. They specify the kind of communication. The nucleus objects are described as LOTOS processes, too.

Transparency functions are specified as abstract data types. They are specified local to nucleus objects.

Technology Viewpoint. From the LOTOS point of view, the refinement of the engineering nucleus system has to be specified w.r.t. various domains given by different computer systems and networks. These are defined as the triple implementation environment

< *operating system, programming language, communication routines* >.

Furthermore, a coding function is defined mapping each LOTOS construct of the technology viewpoint specification to the corresponding one of the implementation environment.

Transformation Rules. A set of transformation rules and their application in the design process are given [11]. The rules fulfill the weak bisimulation equivalence.

- Reordering of processes
  to group resources from a logical partition
  use: information to computation viewpoint transformation
- Unplaiting of events and predicates
  to unplait complex constraints
  use: information to computation viewpoint transformation
- Instantiation
  to create communicating instances of an object
  use: computation to engineering viewpoint transformation
- Refinement of communication
  to refine the communication structure
  use: engineering viewpoint
- Hierarchical ordering of data types
  to form objects encapsulating local, hidden data types
  use: computation and engineering viewpoint

4.3 The ODP Trader Specifications

As mentioned above, LOTOS is considered to be the most suitable technique to describe systems from the computation and engineering viewpoint. Consequently, the specifications of the ODP trader from these viewpoints and the use of the given transformation rules are stressed in this section. Within these viewpoints, the structural aspects are emphasized. Finally, some remarks about the other viewpoints and code generation are given.

Computation Viewpoint. From the computation viewpoint, the three computation objects are seen:

- manager: invoking object
- database: operation object
- authentifier: operation object

They are structured as followed:

```
hide auth_req, auth_resp, db_req, db_resp in
manager[export, withdraw, search,
        db_req, db_resp, auth_req, auth_resp]
|[ db_req, db_resp, auth_req, auth_resp ]|
(   database[db_req, db_resp]
    |||
    authentifier[auth_req, auth_resp])
```

The hidden events are the starting (`db_req`, `auth_req`) and termination events (`db_resp`, `auth_res`) of the interfaces of the operation objects `database` and `authentifier`. The types handled at these events are defined global. The operations (or methods) provided by the operation objects are specified local to these objects. The behaviour of the objects is specified monolithically.

Engineering Viewpoint. From the engineering viewpoint, various instances of the trader object are visible. These objects communicate with each other. This is called federation. Following the ODP RM, the communication is hidden in a nucleus system.

In order to achieve a transformation preserving correctness the rule of instantiation is applied. There are several engineering objects of the trader which are instances of the computation object. The engineering objects communicate via the `nucleus_system`.

```
( trader[...](...) ||| ... ||| trader[...](...) )
||
nucleus_system[...]
```

In order to maintain correctness, the engineering objects have to be extended with communication facilities.

On one hand, the `manager` object has to invoke federated operation. This can be expressed by the introduction of a pair of start and termination events:

```
fed_op_req !p;
fed_op_resp ?res: res_sort;
```

On the other hand, the **trader** object itself can be invoked by another **trader** instance via the **nucleus_system**. Therefore a new object **fed_manager** is designed and added to the set of the other subobjects in the following way:

```
(    manager[ ... ]
     |||
     fed_manager[ fed_op_ind, fed_op_conf, ... ] )
|[ db_req, db_resp, auth_req, auth_resp ]|
(    database[db_req, db_resp]
     |||
     authentifier[auth_req, auth_resp] )
```

The object **fed_manager** is quite similar to the **manager** object. The difference is that the requests do not arrive from the environment, but from the **nucleus_system** via the gates **fed_op_ind, fed_op_conf**.

The rule of communication refinement is used to design the **nucleus_system**. It consists of **nucleus** objects and a **communication_platform**.

```
process nucleus_system
    hide cp_req, cp_ind, cp_conf, cp_resp in
    nucleus[ ... ] ||| ... ||| nucleus[ ... ]
    ||
    communication_platform[ cp_req, cp_ind, cp_conf, cp_resp ]
where
    ...
endproc (* nucleus system *)
```

Other Viewpoints and Code Generation. The specification from the computation viewpoint is strictly constraint oriented and appears very compact. The transformation to the computation viewpoint is especially based on the rule *unplaiting*.

A mapping from LOTOS to an implementation environment is given for the technology viewpoint. The triple < *SUN-OS, C, rpc's* > is chosen as example for an implementation environment. A prototype of the trader is running.

5 SDL'92

5.1 SDL'92: an Object-oriented Extension of SDL'88

SDL'92 [1] is an object-oriented extension of the widly used specification language SDL, which has a long tradition within the telecommunication. Besides the object-orientation SDL'92 supports

− generic parameters for structuring types,

- libraries for SDL specifications,
- interfaces for using ASN.1 data types,
- broadcast signal transfer, and
- more possibilities to express nondetermistic behaviour.

SDL'92 offers an unique sharp distinction between type definitions, specific instances and sets of those instances. Specific instances are carriers of state information and behaviour, while type definitions are patterns defining common structure and properties of instances. The instances model the phenomena of the application area, while the type definitions model the concepts. The object-oriented character of SDL'92 is given by notions as

- inheritance for types of system, block, process, procedure, service and signals;
- virtual concept for the types **block**, **process**, **service**, **procedure** and for the concept of state transition;
- polymorphy concept for
  - the instance creation of block, process, service, procedure,
  - the actualization of generic parameters, and
  - returns in procedures;
- late binding for offering a Remote-Procedure-Call-facility.

Using an object-oriented approach, one applies the principle of aggregating data structures together with the interface of operations performed on them, calling the whole a class in form of an abstract datatype definition. From such a class it is possible to generate instances (so-called objects) statically or dynamically. A phenomenon from the real world can be described as a composition of such cooperating objects which have their own life cycles. One of the advantages of this approach is the information hiding principle, which is naturally supported. The application of this concept is necessary for the further object oriented ones.

If we have a look at the old SDL'88 or at LOTOS, we can see that this basic paradigm is already realized by the corresponding process concept. That's why we concentrate upon the application of inheritance, but it is only possible to give an overview here.

5.2 The ODP Trader Specification

The main experience in applying the inheritance concept in order to specify the trader is to clarify the relations between the single ODP viewpoints. In Fig. 2 and 4 these relations are expressed in SDL structure definitions.

The same procedure would be necessary for the definition of the behaviour (which is only indicated here) and the data structures, used by the message handling. The expressive power of SDL for the first two viewpoints are restricted. All in all the structural decomposition is similar to the LOTOS approach.

Enterprise Viewpoint. The SDL specification in Fig. 2a shows a block type definition, whose interface, structure and behaviour could be described only in an informal manner. So the block definition of the trader in the information viewpoint inherits no more than the name. The more precise definitions cannot be proved to match the comments from the enterprise viewpoint.

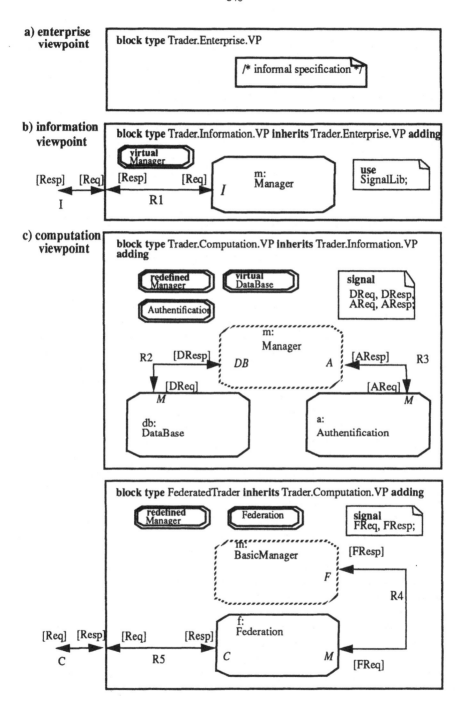

Fig. 2. Architecture correspondence of the enterprise, information and computation viewpoints

Information Viewpoint. The main request consists of the specification of the interface of the trader facility, which is described here only as a black box. Such an interface is described by a formal gate definition I (interface) which is connected with the gate I of the included process type which could represent the trader behaviour in a very abstract manner (Fig. 2b). The behaviour could be described as a single process, where the nondeterministic possibilities of SDL could be used so that the input-output-behaviour could be defined precisely, especially the signal structure and the necessary data types. The specifications to follow could be expressed as separate library units, which could be imported by further refinements. The abstract behaviour is represented by a virtual process type *Manager*. The term virtual means that this component could be redefined in the next design stage.

Computation Viewpoint. The interface definition for the trader of the information viewpoint could be kept by applying the inheritance concept again. But the new derived block type has a modified structure and a more precise behaviour, which is expressed by a new *Manager* process cooperating with two other process types (Fig. 2c). The *Manager* type is a redefinition of the *Manager* of the information viewpoint by inheritance, so that the communication with the trader environment could be kept again. *Database* is a new component which could be modified in the further viewpoints by realization of special data base strategies. In this viewpoint only the communication with the *Manager* and a basic version of data handling is defined which could be redefined. The *Authentification* process type does not have such a virtual identification and cannot be redefined later. The signals necessary for the communication of the three kinds of processes in the trader are also specified here. Figure 3 shows the definition of *Manager* at this level. It's behaviour in form of state transitions is given. *Manager* accepts ordinary requests from the environment (clients) and communicates with its *Authentification* process to check the authentification of the sender. After that the request could be processed by *Database* if the check was positive. The next transition is a virtual one and can be redefined in later refinements. It is concerned with the processing of the *Database* answer. In this version the trader is specified as a non-federated one. The specification of a federated trader is derived by another inheritance step. The block type *FederatedTrader* is an extension of a modified trader. The addition amounts to another process type *Federation*, which communicates with a modified *Manager*. The modification of *Manager* concerns the last virtual state transition. If the local *Database* component cannot process the request, the Manager sends this to it's *Federation*. This process has a table of trader adresses and will pass the request to other traders where the sending trader will be an ordinary client of the receiving ones. The block type *DistributedTrader* is a derived version of the *FederatedTrader*, where the data base of the trader itself is a distributed database. In this case the *DataBase* process has to be redefined as a data base manager communicating with several single data base processes. Following this scheme other refinements may be defined.

Engineering Viewpoint. A concrete realization of a configuration of a trader system could be manifold. Only a simple example is shown in Fig. 5. Three federated

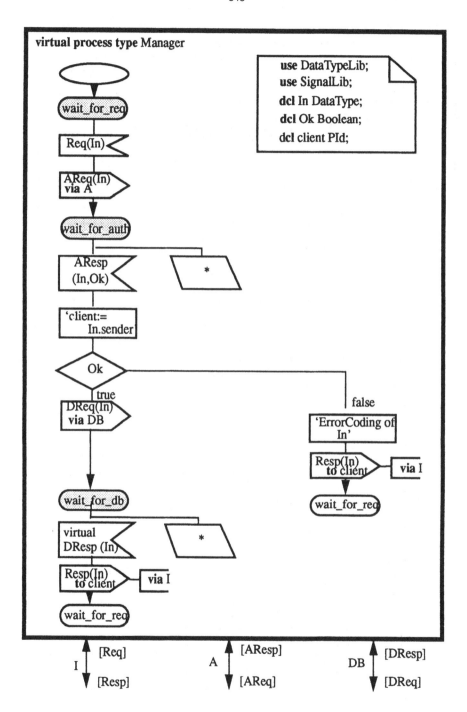

Fig. 3. Behaviour specification of the trader manager

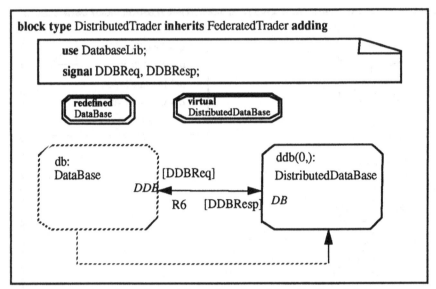

Fig. 4. Computation viewpoint: a federated trader with a distributed database

traders with their client environments are connected, two of them working with a distributed data base. The channels between the traders are abstractions of the underlying network, which could be defined by the well-known channel refinement concept of SDL'88.

References

1. CCITT: *CCITT Specification and description language SDL*. Recommendation Z.100 (SDL'92). Geneva. 1992.
2. CCITT: *Sliding Window Protocol Example*. Study Group X - Report R 29, Document COM X-R 29-E of CCITT. chapter 9. pp 75-134. 1988.
3. Duke, R.; King, P.; Rose, G.; Smith, G.: *The Object-Z Specification Language Version 1*. Technical Report No 91-1. Software Verification Research Centre. Department of Computing Science. The University of Queensland. 1991.
4. ISO: *LOTOS - A formal description technique based on the temporal ordering of observational behaviour*. ISO 8807. International Standard.
5. ISO/IEC: *Proposed Draft Answer to the Question Q7/1 on the Suitability of the Formal Description Technique Z for Use in ODP*. Ottawa. May 1992.
6. ISO/IEC: *Basic Reference Model of Open Distributed Processing - Part 1-5*. ISO/IEC JTC1/SC21. Working Draft.
7. ISO/IEC: *ODP Trader*. ISO/IEC JTC1/SC21. Working Document.
8. Prinz, A.: *The Sliding Window Protocol - correct or not?* internal paper.
9. Spivey, J.M., *The Z notation - a reference manual*. Prentice-Hall International. 1989.
10. Vogel, A.: *LOTOS Design Methodology Based on ODP - Viewpoints*. in Hogrefe, D. (Editor): Formale Beschreibungstechniken für verteilte Systeme. Springer Verlag. 1992.
11. Vogel, A.: *Entwurf, Realisierung und Test von ODP Systemen auf der Grundlage von formalen Beschreibungstechniken*. (in german). Berlin. in preparation.

350

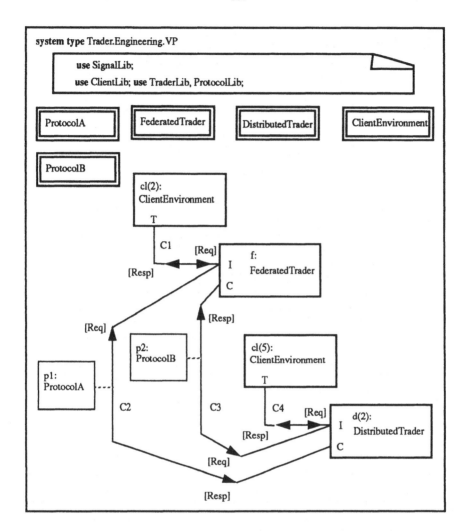

Fig. 5. Engineering viewpoint: a small configuration of federated and distributed traders

12. *Proceedings of Third LOTOSPHERE Workshop.* Pisa. 1992.

On the Derivation of Executable Database Programs from Formal Specifications*

Thomas Günther, Klaus-Dieter Schewe, Ingrid Wetzel

University of Hamburg, Dept. of Computer Science,
Vogt-Kölln-Str. 30, D-W-2000 Hamburg 54, FRG

Abstract. Achieving wide acceptance of formal methods in software development requires a smooth integration with requirements analysis, design and implementation. Especially for database application systems there exist well-known approaches to conceptual modeling as well as a sophisticated implementation technology on the basis of database programming languagues. The work described in this paper is based on a scenario, where the B method is coupled with a conceptual modeling language TDL and a database programming language DBPL. Both these languages can be represented in B. We concentrate on the problem of characterizing those B specifications that are sufficiently refined in order to be transformed into equivalent DBPL programs. This gives rise to some kind of *implementability proof obligation*.
Moreover, we show that the *transformation* itself can be regarded as a term rewriting task based on a representation by term algebras of the languages involved. For this task we exploit order-sorted algebra by using the OBJ system.

1 Introduction

Formal Methods such as B [1], VDM [8], OBJ [4] or Z [14] have often been criticized as being cumbersome, hard to understand, hard to handle and in any case not suitable for real application systems of large size. The core of the problem seems to be that an accompanying methodology is almost always left unclear. How should the user proceed in order to get a first formal specification? Which refinement steps should be applied? Where should one stop the refinement process? Therefore, a smooth integration with requirements analysis, design and implementation is required to enhance the acceptability of formal methods in software development.

Our approach to solve this problem assumes the coupling of a formal method with a "front-end" design language and a "back-end" implementation language. We believe that requirements analysis and first design should be oriented toward the application domain. There will be no loss of formal software safety as long as the semantics of the used design language can be described by the formal method.

On the other hand, formal methods will fail their goals, if they ignore the high-level mechanisms offered by modern programming languages. It should be possible to capture the semantics of such implementation languages by the formal method and to exploit this to combine the safety achieved by the use of a formal method with the efficiency achieved by the use of a sophisticated implementation technology.

* This work has been supported in part by research grants from the E.E.C. Basic Research Action 3070 FIDE: "Formally Integrated Data Environments".

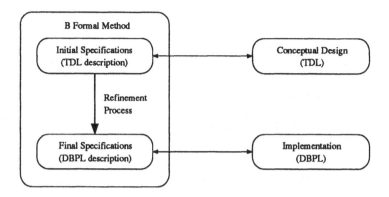

Fig. 1. The Development Process

1.1 A Scenario for the Development of Data Intensive Application Systems

The development of database application systems usually starts with a conceptual design of a database schema. Semantic datamodels [6] are commonly used for this purpose. On the other hand, the implementation is usually done using a relational DBMS or a database programming language such as DBPL [9]. Then the *reification problem* occurs, i.e. to transform a given conceptual design into a running implementation.

The DAIDA project [2, 7] proposed to use formal methods to fill this gap. This is in accordance with the general approach described above, using a slightly revised version (TDL) of TAXIS [10] as a "front-end", DBPL as a "back-end" and a slight revision of the B formal method [12]. Figure 1 illustrates this scenario.

The transformation of TDL designs into a B representation and standard refinement rules directed towards an implementation in DBPL have been described in [13] and will not be repeated here. Then the following problems remain:

- characterize final B specifications that are equivalent to DBPL programs, and
- set up an automatic transformation of final specifications into DBPL syntax.

In order to solve the first problem, we have to show that DBPL programs are indeed equivalent to certain B specifications. We express DBPL language constructs by pieces of B. Then the characterization consists in some general properties such as determinism, termination and consistency that are independent from the specific implementation language and in a specific form required for the data description.

1.2 An Algebraic Approach to Program Generation

In order to solve the second problem we use OBJ, an algebraic specification language and term rewriting system based on order-sorted algebra. It has been pointed out [4] that order-sorted algebra is useful for the specification of programming languages, where terms represent language constructs and conditional equations represent semantic equivalences.

In our case the languages in question are DBPL and B, where constructs of the former one are equivalent to specific constructs of the latter one. We may exploit the ordering on sorts to capture this inclusion. Moreover, the conditional equations are given by the representation of DBPL in B as mentioned above.

Regarding each conditional equation as a rewrite rule and taking a complex term that represents a final B specification OBJ will produce a normal form term, i.e. a term representing a DBPL program.

1.3 The Organization of the Paper

The remainder of the paper is organized as follows. After a short review of the B formal method in Section 2 without discussing refinement we address the derivation of an implementability proof obligation in Section 3. We briefly describe the implementation language DBPL and then show the representation of selected language constructs using B. On this basis we are able to characterize sufficiently refined formal specifications.

Section 4 is devoted to the transformation task. After a brief introduction into order-sorted algebra on the basis of OBJ, we proceed to describe in part the algebra associated with B and DBPL. For selected language constructs this sets up the term rewriting rules used for the transformation. We conclude with a short valuation of what has been gained by our approach focussing on the suitability of the chosen formal method for our problem.

2 Specifications Using the B Formal Method

B is a model-based formal method developed by J. R. Abrial [1]. Basically a B specification is composed of a specification of structure and behaviour. The main difference to its forerunners VDM [8] and Z [14] are the style of operation specification and the coupling of structure and behaviour specification in basic units called *abstract machines*.

2.1 Specification of Structure

The structural part of a B specification consists of a collection of abstract machines and contexts that are used to specify state spaces. A state space is given by a list of variable names, called the *state variables* and by a list of well-founded formulas of a many-sorted first-order language $\mathcal{L}$ called the *invariant* and denoted by $\mathcal{I}$. Free variables occurring in $\mathcal{I}$ must be state variables.

Each state variable belongs to a unique *basic set*, which has to be declared in some context. Hence, in order to complete the state space specification we must give a list of *contexts* that can be seen by the machine.

Such a context is defined by a list of *basic sets*, a list of *constant names* and a list of closed formulae over the language $\mathcal{L}$ called *properties*. A basic set may be either the set of natural numbers, an abstract set given only by its name, a set given by the enumeration of its elements or a constructed set, where cartesian product, powerset and partial function space are the only allowed constructors. We may then assume to have a fixed preinterpretation of these sorts s by sets $\mathcal{D}_s$.

Then the state space of an abstract machine with state variables $x_1, \ldots, x_n$ is semantically denoted by the set

$$\Sigma = \{\sigma : \{x_1, \ldots, x_n\} \to \mathcal{D} \mid \sigma(x_i) \in \mathcal{D}_{s_i} \text{ for all } i\},$$

where each s_i is the sort of the variable x_i and $\mathcal{D}$ denotes the union of the sets $\mathcal{D}_s$.

The language $\mathcal{L}$ associated with an abstract machine can then easily be formalized. The basic sorts of $\mathcal{L}$ are NAT and the other non-constructed basic sorts. The set of sorts is recursively defined using the basic sorts and the sort constructors pow, $\times$, $\mapsto$ denoting powerset construction, cartesian products and partial functions.

Since we use a fixed preinterpretation of the sorts as sets, one may regard the elements of these sets as constant symbols in $\mathcal{L}$ of the corresponding sort. Other function symbols are given by the usual functions $+$, $*$ on NAT, $\cup$, $\cap$, $\setminus$ on powersets or by the constant declarations in some context. The terms and formulas in $\mathcal{L}$ are defined in the usual way. The semantics of $\mathcal{L}$ is given by an interpretation $(\mathcal{A}, \sigma)$, where $\mathcal{A}$ is a structure extending the preinterpretation on sorts and σ is a variable binding.

We assume $\mathcal{A}$ to be fixed and write $\models_\sigma \mathcal{R}$, iff $\mathcal{R}$ is true under the interpretation $(\mathcal{A}, \sigma)$.

A well-formed formula $\mathcal{R}$ of $\mathcal{L}$ such that the free variables of $\mathcal{R}$ are state variables denotes a subset of Σ, namely

$$\Sigma_{\mathcal{R}} = \{\sigma \mid \models_\sigma \mathcal{R}\}.$$

Hence the invariant serves as a means to distinguish legal states in Σ_I from others.

2.2 Specification of Behaviour

The dynamic part of a B specification is given through an *initialization* assigning initial values to each of the state variables of an abstract machine and *transitions* that update this state space. Both parts are associated with abstract machines. Both kinds of state transitions are specified using guarded commands introduced by Dijkstra [3] and generalized by G. Nelson [11].

The semantics of a transition S is given by means of two specific predicate transformers $wlp(S)$ and $wp(S)$, which satisfy the *pairing condition*, i.e. for all predicates $\mathcal{R}$

$$wp(S)(\mathcal{R}) \equiv wlp(S)(\mathcal{R}) \wedge wp(S)(true)$$

and the *universal conjunctivity condition*, which states for any family $(R_i)_{i \in I}$ of predicates

$$wlp(S)(\forall i \in I \cdot R_i) \equiv \forall i \in I \cdot wlp(S)(R_i).$$

These conditions imply the conjunctivity of $wp(S)$ over non-empty families of predicates. As usual $wlp(S)$ will be called the *weakest liberal precondition* of S, and $wp(S)$

will be called the *weakest precondition* of S. The notation f^*, which we shall use later, denotes the *conjugate predicate transformer* of f. It is defined by

$$f^*(\mathcal{R}) \equiv \neg f(\neg \mathcal{R}) .$$

The definitions of $wlp(S)$ and $wp(S)$ for all the guarded commands are given in [11].

3   The Formal Description of Database Programs

Let us now proceed to characterize sufficiently refined B specifications with respect to a follow-on implementation in the relational database programming language DBPL. First we give a brief overview on DBPL and then outline its representation in B. We focus on selected DBPL language constructs. On this basis we give a proof obligation for finalizing the refinement process.

3.1   An Overview on the Language DBPL

The language DBPL [9] integrates an extended relational view of database modeling into the programming language Modula-2. Basically the extension comprises new *data types*, new expressions called *access expressions* used for queries and orthogonal *persistence*.

- DBPL provides a new data type *relation* which allows relational database modeling to be coupled with the expressiveness of the programming language. This new datatype is orthogonal to the existing types of Modula-2, hence sets of arrays, arrays of relations, records of relations, etc. can be modeled.
- Complex *access expressions* as usual in relational databases allow to express complex queries on a database without using iteration.
- Persistence is added allowing modules to be qualified as database modules, keyword *DATABASE*, which turns the variables in them to be persistent and shared. Specific procedures are characterized to be *transactions* denoting atomic state changes on persistent data. For these transactions DBPL provides mechanisms for controlled concurrent access to such data and for recovery.

Example 1. Let us illustrate DBPL taking an example from [13].

DATABASE MODULE ResearchCompaniesModule;

   IMPORT Identifier, String;

   TYPE

     Agencies = (ESPRIT, DFG, NSF, ...);

     CompNames, EmpNames, ProjNames = String.Type;

     EmpIds = Identifier.Type;

     ProjIdRecType =

        RECORD projName : ProjNames; getsGrantFrom : Agencies END;

     ProjIdRelType = RELATION OF ProjIdRecType;

     CompRelType = RELATION compName OF

        RECORD compName : CompNames; engagedIn : ProjIdRelType END;

```
EmpRelType = RELATION employee OF
      RECORD employee : EmpIds; empName : EmpNames;
          belongsTo : CompNames; worksOn : ProjIdRelType END;
ProjRelType = RELATION projId OF
      RECORD projId : ProjIdRecType;
          consortium : RELATION OF CompNames END;

VAR compRel : CompRelType;
    empRel : EmpRelType;
    projRel : ProjRelType;

TRANSACTION hireEmployee (name:EmpNames;
      belongs:CompNames; works:ProjIdRelType) : EmpIds;
    VAR tEmpId : EmpIds;
    BEGIN
    IF SOME c IN compRel (c.compName = belongs) AND
      ALL w IN works (SOME p IN compRel[belongs].engagedIn (w = p))
    THEN tEmpId := Identifier.New;
        empRel :+ EmpRelType{{tEmpId,name,belongs,works}};
        RETURN tEmpId
    ELSE RETURN Identifier.Nil
    END
    END hireEmployee;
END ResearchCompaniesModule  □
```

3.2   The Formal Representation of Selected DBPL Constructs

Let us now represent language constructs of DBPL as above in B. We concentrate on
those types, expressions and procedures that are essential in the database context.

Type Representation. In general a type is an algebra, hence consists of a fixed
set of values and fixed operations on that set. Thus, a DBPL type corresponds to
a basic set in a context plus additional functions that can also be represented in a
context using constants and properties.

Let us first examine *record types* in DBPL that are heterogenous aggregates of
the form

$$T = RECORD\, tag_1 : D_1; \ldots; tag_n : D_n\ END;$$

For concrete record types see Example 1.

Since $D_1 \ldots D_n$ are also types, we may assume that there are basic sets also
denoted $D_1 \ldots D_n$ represented them. Then the underlying set of the *record type* T
can simply be represented by the cartesian product

$$T = D_1 \times \cdots \times D_n . \tag{1}$$

The tags $tag_1 \ldots tag_n$ are used as designators for the components of the type T,
hence give rise to functions $(i = 1, \ldots, n)$

$$tag_i \in T \to D_i \qquad\qquad \text{defined as} \tag{2}$$

$$tag_i = \lambda x \cdot (x \in T \wedge x = (d_1, \ldots, d_n) \mid d_i) . \tag{3}$$

Then (1), (2) and (3) in a context – more precicely in the **basic sets**, **constants** and **properties** sections respectively – define a B representation of the record type T.

Example 2. Let us take the type declaration

$ProjIdRecType =$
$\qquad RECORD\ projName : ProjNames;\ getsGrantFrom : Agencies\ END;$

from Example 1. Then a representation in a B context would be

Basic Sets $ProjIdRecType = ProjNames \times Agencies$
Constants $projName \in ProjIdRecType \rightarrow ProjNames$
$\qquad getsGrantFrom \in ProjIdRecType \rightarrow Agencies$
Properties $projName = \lambda x \cdot (x \in ProjIdRecType \wedge x = (y, z) \mid y)$
$\qquad getsGrantFrom = \lambda x \cdot (x \in ProjIdRecType \wedge x = (y, z) \mid z)$ $\qquad\qquad$ □

There exists an alternative representation of record types using functions. We omit the details here [5]. Moreover, the tags are used in expressions and hence also in transactions, e.g. on the left or right hand side of an assignment such as $v.projName :=$ .... In B this has to represented by applying the function $projName$ to v, i.e. $projName(v)$. We also omit the details.

Let us now turn to the representation of *relation types* – for concrete relation types see Example 1 – such as

$T = RELATION\ key_1 , \ldots, key_n\ OF\ D ;$

Basically each element of this type is a finite set of elements of type D with unique values of the attributes $key_1, \ldots, key_n$. Assume that the type D has been introduced and named explicitly – the general case can be easily reduced to this. Then also functions $key_i : D \rightarrow D_i$ are defined ($i = 1, \ldots, n$), and the set underlying T is representable as

$$T = \{x \mid x \in 2^D \wedge \forall d, e \in x \cdot$$
$$key_1(d) = key_1(e) \wedge \ldots \wedge key_n(d) = key_n(e) \Rightarrow d = e\} \tag{4}$$

If r is a variable of type T, then $r[k_1, \ldots, k_n]$ denotes in DBPL the selection of an element from r with key values $k_1, \ldots, k_n$. This selection function can be represented in a context as

$$sel_T \in T \times D_1 \times \cdots \times D_n \rightarrow D \qquad\qquad \text{defined as} \tag{5}$$

$$sel_T = \lambda x, y_1, \ldots, y_n \cdot (z \in x \wedge key_1(z) = y_1 \wedge \ldots \wedge key_n(z) = y_n \mid z) . \tag{6}$$

The DBPL expression $r[k_1, \ldots, k_n]$ then corresponds to $sel_T(r, k_1, \ldots, k_n)$. Then the representation of the relation type T comprises (4), (5), (6) and the representation of operations : +, : − and : & for the *insertion*, *deletion* and *update*. As an alternative, relations could also be represented by partial functions as done in [13]. For further details see [5].

Example 3. Take the type declaration

CompRelType = RELATION compName OF
    RECORD compName : CompNames; engagedIn : ProjIdRelType END;

from Example 1, which can be represented (in part) as follows in a context:

Basic Sets
    CompRelType =
      $\{x \mid x \in 2^{CompNames \times ProjIdRelType} \wedge \forall d, e \in x \cdot$
      compName(d) = compName(e) \wedge \ldots \wedge engagedIn(d) = engagedIn(e)
                          $\Rightarrow d = e\}$

Constants
    $compName \in CompNames \times ProjIdRelType \rightarrow CompNames$
    $engagedIn \in CompNames \times ProjIdRelType \rightarrow ProjIdRelType$
    $sel_{CompRelType} \in CompRelType \times CompNames \times ProjIdRelType$
        $\rightarrow CompNames \times ProjIdRelType$

Properties
    $compName = \ldots$
    $engagedIn = \ldots$
    $sel_{CompRelType} =$
      $\lambda x, y, z \cdot (\, v \in x \wedge compName(v) = y \wedge engagedIn(v) = z \mid v \,)$ ☐

The Representation of Access Expressions. In DBPL queries can be formulated through *access expressions* that are either *constructive* or *selective*. Constructive access expressions describe derivation rules that take the values of some given relations and produce another relation using the operations of relational algebra. Selective access expressions can only produce subsets of one given relation. The main difference is the possibility to update relations derived by selective expressions.

Let us concentrate on a selective access expression of the form

EACH e IN R : *P* ,

where *e* is a variable, *R* a relational expression and *P* a first-order formula with free variable *e*. In B this corresponds to a set expression of the form

$$\{x \mid x \in R \wedge P(x)\} \, . \tag{7}$$

Access expressions can be used in relational expressions of the form $T\{exp\}$, where T is a relation type and exp is an access expression. This can be represented by the identity function

$$id_T \in T \rightarrow T \qquad \text{with} \qquad id_T = \lambda x \cdot (\, x \in T \mid x \,) \tag{8}$$

applied to *exp*. The generalization of (7) and (8) to constructive access expressions is straightforward. For details see [5].

Example 4. Take the type *CompRelType* of Examples 1 and 3 and the relational expression

$$CompRelType \ \{ \ EACH \ e \ IN \ compRel : e.compName = \text{``}MyCompany\text{''} \ \} \ .$$

This can be represented by

$$id_{CompRelType}(\{x \mid x \in compRel \wedge compName(x) = \text{``}MyCompany\text{''}\}\Box$$

Transaction Representation. Since transition specifications in abstract machines use parameterized guarded commands and transactions in DBPL are mostly written procedurally, there is in general no problem to formally represent transactions. Therefore, let us focus on insertions, deletions and updates on relations. We already mentioned these operations when we discussed the representation of relation types.

If r is a variable and R is a relational expression, both of relation type T, then $r :+ R$ denotes the insertion into r of all those elements of R that have key values not already in r. Analogously $r :- R$ and $r :\&R$ are used for deletions and updates respectively.

Insertion can be represented in B specifications by

$$r := id_T(r \cup \{x \mid x \in R \wedge \forall e \in r \cdot (key_1(e) \neq key_1(x) \vee \cdots \vee key_n(e) \neq key_n(x))\}) \ . (9)$$

The representation of deletions and updates is analogous.

Example 5. Take the insertion operation

$$empRel :+ EmpRelType\{\{tEmpId, name, belongs, works\}\}$$

from Example 1 which is representable as

$$empRel := id_{EmpRelType} (\ empRel \ \cup \ \{x \mid x = (tEmpId, name, belongs, works)$$
$$\wedge \ \forall e \in empRel \cdot employee(e) \neq tEmpId\} \ ) \ .\Box$$

3.3   A Characterization of Implementable Specifications

The representation of DBPL constructs in B specifications sets up a semantic equivalence between DBPL programs and specific B specifications. However, our original problem was just to find a transformation the other way round. Since this is not possible for every B specification, we have to characterize those specifications that are equivalent to DBPL programs. This gives us a proof obligation that indicates whether the refinement process has to be continued or not.

Before we give this characterization, we make the assumption that there is only one abstract machine in our specification and that all contexts have been collapsed into one seen by the one and only machine. This assumption is due to the fact that we did not yet consider modularization.

Under these assumptions final specifications can be characterized by seven properties. The first three concern the data structures and are DBPL specific, whereas the last four are general conditions on operations [12].

Completeness. In the final context all basic sets and all constants are unambiguously defined. In particular there are no more abstract sets.

Covering. In the final context all basic sets have the structure of a DBPL type and all operations corresponding to such a type are defined as constants.

Typing. For each state variable x of the final machine there exists a typing condition $x \in T$ in the invariant section such that T is a type defined in the final context.

Consistency. Each operation S in the final machine is consistent with respect to the invariant $\mathcal{I}$, i.e. $\mathcal{I} \Rightarrow wlp(S)(\mathcal{I})$ holds. The initialization S_0 satisfies $wp(S_0)(\mathcal{I}) \Leftrightarrow true$.

Totality. Each operation S in the final machine is total, i.e. $wp(S)(false) \Leftrightarrow false$ holds.

Termination. Provided the invariant holds each operation S in the final machine always terminates, i.e. $\mathcal{I} \Rightarrow wp(S)(true)$ holds. The initialization S_0 satisfies $wp(S_0)(true) \Leftrightarrow true$.

Determinism. Provided the invariant holds each operation S in the final machine is deterministic, i.e. $\mathcal{I} \wedge wlp(S)^*(\mathcal{R}) \Rightarrow wp(S)(\mathcal{R})$ holds for all well-formed formulae $\mathcal{R}$. For the initialization we must have $wlp(S_0)^*(\mathcal{R}) \Rightarrow wp(S_0)(\mathcal{R})$.

4 Database Program Generation as a Term Rewriting Process

Let us now address our main problem how to transform a final B specification into executable DBPL code. Since we neglected modularization aspects in Section 3, it should be clear that the result will be just one *module* in DBPL. Moreover, this should be a *database module*, i.e. all variables in it are considered to be persistent.

It has been exemplified in [4] that *order-sorted algebra* is useful for the specification of programming languages or even more general for a specification language such as B. Hence the idea to apply this algebraic approach to our problem, i.e. to represent B and DBPL in order-sorted algebra. Moreover, in the previous section we demonstrated that DBPL is representable in B. Thus, each DBPL program may be considered as a syntactic variant of a specific B specification. In order-sorted algebra this can be represented by using a unified algebra with the sorts from DBPL being subsorts of corresponding sorts from B and (conditional) equations that relate DBPL and B expressions. This is our approach here, where we use the OBJ system to accomplish the task.

A collection of (conditional) equations can also be regarded as a term rewriting system as OBJ does. Then the reduction of a complex term that represents a final B specification will result in the required DBPL code.

The rewrite rules that are presented in this section are simpler than the representation of DBPL in B suggests. This simplification is due to the fact that we assume them to be applied only to final specifications.

```
obj AM is protecting ID .
  ...
  sort set .
  subsort identifier enumset rangeset < set .
    op INT        : -> set .
    op POW        : set -> set .
    op _ /\ _     : set set -> set [assoc comm prec 30] .
  sort substitution .
    op (_ := _)   : lambda expression -> substitution [prec 43] .
    op (_ || _)   : substitution substitution
                    -> substitution [assoc comm prec 70] .
  sort command .
  subsort substitution < command .
    op SKIP       : -> command .
    op _ ; _      : command command -> command [assoc prec 70] .
    op _ [] _     : command command -> command [assoc comm prec 70] .
    op _ ==> _    : predicate command -> command [prec 60] .
    op VAR_IN_END : identifier-list command -> command .
    op DO_==>_OD  : predicate command -> command .
  ...
endo
```

Fig. 2. The OBJ module AM

4.1 An Overview on OBJ

OBJ is an algebraic specification language based on order-sorted algebra. The basic building block of an OBJ specification is the *object* or *module*. Each such object consists of a *signature* and *axioms*. In a signature *sorts* and *operators* are declared. Sorts are arranged in a *subsort hierarchy*. Each operator has an arity in $S^* \times S$, where S is the set of sorts. Figure 2 gives an example of an object called AM.

The axioms on an OBJ object are expressed as (conditional) equations with terms built from the constants and operators and an S-indexed family of variables. Associativity, commutativity, idempotency and neutral elements can be specified by specific keywords and need not be specified as axioms.

We may assign an order-sorted algebra A with a signature. Doing this we associate with each sort s a set A_s called the *carrier* of the sort such that subsorts correspond to subsets and the carriers are disjoint otherwise. Moreover, each operator f with arity $s_1 \cdots s_n \to s$ corresponds to some function $f_A : A_{s_1} \times \cdots \times A_{s_N} \to A_s$. If all (conditional) equations are satisfied when interpreted in the usual way in A, we may associate A with the specification.

In OBJ the semantics of an object is given by an initial order-sorted algebra. This algebra can be built as a quotient of the order-sorted term algebra constructed from the constants and the operators of the object with respect to the equivalence relation defined by the axioms. See [4] for more details.

OBJ supports modular specifications. An object may be built from others using three different modes called *proctecting*, *extending* and *uses*. The protecting mode assures that the initial semantics of all old sorts and operators remains completely unchanged, i.e. no additional closed terms occur (*no junk*) and no terms are identified by new equations (*no confusion*). The extending mode only assures that there is no confusion, whereas *uses* assures nothing.

In addition to modularization OBJ also supports parameterization in a sophisticated way. However, this feature will not be used for our problem. Therefore, we dispense with describing it.

OBJ is supported by a software system that is built around a term rewriting engine. For term rewriting each (conditional) equation is interpreted as a rewrite rule in order to replace the left hand side by the right hand side. The OBJ rewrite engine supports AC and ACI rewriting. Rewriting of a term t is done by running $reduce(t)$ in the OBJ system.

4.2 Language Representation by Term Algebras

In order to apply OBJ to our problem we define four OBJ modules. The first one is called ID and contains general identifier and number symbols. We omit the details.

The module AM which protects ID contains the specification of the B syntax. It is illustrated in part in Figure 2. For a complete description see [5].

In AM we have sorts *enumset, rangeset* and *set* that are used for enumerated sets, for sets defined as subsets of others and for arbitrary (basic) sets. Clearly *enumset* and *rangeset* are subsorts of *set*. Thus, INT occurs as a constant of sort *set* and the intersection ∩ as an associative and commutative operator.

In order to represent guarded commands the sorts *substitution* and *command* are introduced with *substitution* being a subsort of *command* containing only the assignment commands.

The module DBPL which also protects ID contains the specification of the DBPL syntax. In this module we have among others the sort *Type* with some subtypes and the sort *Assignment*. *Type* contains the specifications of types. *Assignment* contains the specifications of specific operations on relations. The module DBPL is illustrated in part in Figure 3.

The last module is TRANS without new sorts. It only contains the sorts from AM (extended) and DBPL, some few new operations and the equations representing the equivalence between final B specifications and DBPL. The equations are illustrated in part in Figure 4 with primary focus on record and relation types, access expressions and transactions. Figure 5 illustrates the complete sort hierarchy in TRANS.

5 Conclusion

The work described in this paper is based on a three stage scenario for the development of database application systems.

- The first stage consists in building a conceptual design in some high-level design language. In our case this language is the dynamically enriched semantic data model TDL. A conceptual design should be automatically translatable into an initial formal specification.

```
obj DBPL is protecting ID .
  ...
  sort SimpleType .
  subsort Ident Enumeration SubrangeType < SimpleType .
  sort Type .
  subsort SimpleType < Type .
    op INTEGER   : -> Type .
  sort FieldList .
    op (_ :´ _)  : IdentList Type -> FieldList [prec 60] .
    op (_ ;´ _)  : FieldList FieldList -> FieldList [assoc prec 70] .
    op RECORD_END : FieldList -> Type .
  sort RelationKey .
  subsort KeyDesignator IdentList < RelationKey .
    op _ ,´ _ : RelationKey RelationKey -> RelationKey [assoc prec 40] .
    op RELATION OF_ : Type -> Type .
    op RELATION _ OF_ : RelationKey Type -> Type .
  sort Assignment .
    op (_ :=´_) : Designator Expression -> Assignment [prec 60].
    op (_ :+ _) : Designator Expression -> Assignment [prec 60].
    op (_ :- _) : Designator Expression -> Assignment [prec 60].
    op (_ :& _) : Designator Expression -> Assignment [prec 60].
  sort Statement .
  subsort Assignment < Statement .
  ...
endo
```

Fig. 3. The OBJ module DBPL

- The second stage comprises standard refinement rules that direct the completion and modification of the initial formal specification towards an implementation in a specific implementation language. In our case the formal method is B and the implementation language is the relational database programming language DBPL.
- The last stage consists in a characterization of sufficiently refined specifications and their automatic transformation into executable database programs.

While the first two stages were discussed in [13] we concentrate on the last stage. The characterization of implementable specifications could be achieved by representing DBPL language constructs in B which defines a semantic equivalence. The transformation was achieved by representing both the B and the DBPL language in a unified order-sorted algebra such that the semantic equivalences could be used as (conditional) rewrite rules. For this purpose we used OBJ.

Although we made some restrictive assumptions it could be shown that the automatic generation of DBPL programs is possible. However, two severe problems arise.

- B does not provide any notion of orthogonal persistence. Our approach here made everything persistent, which is possible, but not useful in practice. Therefore,

```
obj TRANS is extending AM . extending DBPL . extending TRUTH .
  var X Y Z : Ident . var E E1 E2 : Expression . var F F1 F2 : Designator .
  var K : KeyDesignator . var T : Type . var A A1 A2 : AccessExpressionList .
  ...
  op subdesignator : Designator -> KeyDesignator .
  eq subdesignator(X [E]) = [E] .
  eq subdesignator(F [E]) = (subdesignator(F) [E]) .
  eq subdesignator(X . Y) = Y .
  eq subdesignator(F . Y) = (subdesignator(F) . Y) .
  eq (POW(T)).set = (RELATION OF T).Type .
  eq { X | (X : RELATION OF T) & ALL X1 IN X (ALL X2 IN X ((F1 =´ F2) <=´
    (X1 =´ X2))) } = { X | (X : RELATION subdesignator(F1) OF T) } .
  eq { X | (X : RELATION OF T) & ALL X1 IN X (ALL X2 IN X ((F1 =´ F2) AND
    E <=´ (X1 =´ X2))) } = { X | (X : RELATION subdesignator(F1) OF T)
    & ALL X1 IN X (ALL X2 IN X (E <=´ (X1 =´ X2))) } .
  eq { X | (X : RELATION K OF T) & ALL X1 IN X (ALL X2 IN X ((F1 =´ F2) AND
    E <=´ (X1 =´ X2))) } = { X | (X : RELATION K ,´ subdesignator(F1) OF T)
    & ALL X1 IN X (ALL X2 IN X (E <=´ (X1 =´ X2))) } .
  eq { X | (X : RELATION K OF T) & ALL X1 IN X (ALL X2 IN X ((F1 =´ F2) <=´
    (X1 =´ X2))) } = { X | (X : RELATION K ,´ subdesignator(F1) OF T) } .
  eq ({ X | X : RELATION OF T }).set = (RELATION OF T).Type .
  eq ({ X | X : RELATION K OF T }).set = (RELATION K OF T).Type .
  eq RELATION subdesignator(X) OF T = RELATION OF T .
  ...
  eq SOME X IN E1 (E2 =´ X) = E2 IN E1 .
  eq ALL  X IN E1 (X IN E2) = E1 <=´ E2 .
  eq { X | (X =´ E1) AND E2 & (Y : E).predicate } =
    { X | (X =´ E1) AND E2 & (EACH Y IN E).ElementDenotation } .
  eq { X | (X =´ E1) AND E2 & Q & (Y : E).predicate } =
    { X | (X =´ E1) AND E2 & Q & (EACH Y IN E).ElementDenotation } .
  eq (B1 & B2).predicate = (B1 ,´ B2).ElementDenotation-list .
  eq { X | (X =´ E1) AND E2 & B } = { E1 OF B :´ E2 } .
  eq { X OF EACH X IN E1 :´ E2 } = { EACH X IN E1 :´ E2 } .
  eq { A1 } \/ { A2 } = { (A1 ,´ A2).AccessExpressionList } .
  eq (% X . (X : Z | X) { A }).lambda = (Z{ A }).Expression .
  ...
  eq (F := E).substitution = (F :=´ E).Assignment .
  eq (F :=´ (Z{ EACH Y  IN F :´ NOT (Y IN E) }).Expression) = (F :- E) .
  eq (F :=´ (Z{ EACH Y  IN F :´ TRUE ,´
                EACH Y1 IN E :´ NOT (Y1 IN F) }).Expression) = (F :+ E) .
  eq (F :=´ (Z{ EACH Y1 IN F :´ NOT (Y1 IN E) ,´
                EACH Y2 IN E :´ (Y2 IN F) }).Expression) = (F :& E) .
  ...
endo
```

Fig. 4. The OBJ module TRANS

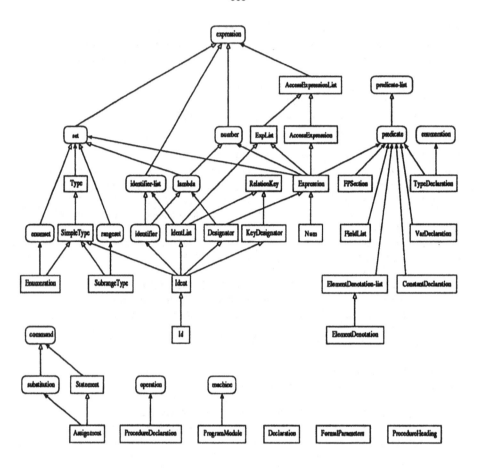

Fig. 5. The sort hierarchy in the OBJ module TRANS

formal methods that are suitable for database application systems should at least offer the user to declare parts of the state description being persistent.
- While the operations in final specifications could be nicely characterized by abstract logical formulae involving predicate transformers, the characterization of final data structures is cumbersome. The reason for this is that DBPL is strongly typed, whereas B is untyped. Further investigations in formal methods should solve this mismatch by introducing typed specifications as proposed in [12]. Otherwise we risc to specify on a lower level of abstraction than we implement which would make formal methods inacceptable.

Despite these outstanding problems it has been made apparent that formal methods combined with conceptual design as a "front-end" and sophisticated implementation as a "back-end" enhances the benefits of formal methods, eases their use and at the same time fills the gap between the conceptual design and the implementation on a safe mathematical basis.

References

1. J. R. Abrial: *A Formal Approach to Large Software Construction*, in J.L.A. van de Snepscheut (Ed.): *Mathematics of Program Construction*, Proc. Int. Conf. Groningen, The Netherlands, June 89, Springer LNCS 375, 1989
2. A. Borgida, J. Mylopoulos, J. W. Schmidt, I. Wetzel: *Support for Data-Intensive Applications: Conceptual Design and Software Development*, Proc. of the 2nd Workshop on Database Programming Languages, Salishan Lodge, Oregon, June 1989
3. E. W. Dijkstra, C. S. Scholten: *Predicate Calculus and Program Semantics*, Springer-Verlag, 1989
4. J. A. Goguen, T. Winkler: *Introducing OBJ3*, SRI International, Technical Report, August 1988
5. T. Günther: *Charakterisierung und Transformation in DBPL implementierbarer Abstrakter Maschinen* (in German), Master Thesis, University of Hamburg, August 1992
6. R. Hull, R. King: *Semantic Database Modeling: Survey, Applications and Research Issues*, ACM Computing Surveys, vol. 19(3), September 1987
7. M. Jarke, J. Mylopoulos, J. W. Schmidt. Y. Vassiliou: *DAIDA: An Environment for Evolving Information Systems*, ACM ToIS, vol. 10 (1), January 1992, pp. 1 – 50
8. C. B. Jones: *Systematic Software Development using VDM*, Prentice-Hall International, London 1986
9. F. Matthes, J. W. Schmidt: *DBPL Rationale and Report*, FIDE technical report, 1992
10. J. Mylopoulos, P. A. Bernstein, H. K. T. Wong: *A Language Facility for Designing Interactive Database-Intensive Applications*, ACM ToDS, vol. 5 (2), April 1980, pp. 185 – 207
11. G. Nelson: *A Generalization of Dijkstra's Calculus*, ACM TOPLAS, vol. 11 (4), October 1989, pp. 517 – 561
12. K.-D. Schewe, J. W. Schmidt, I. Wetzel, N. Bidoit, D. Castelli, C. Meghini: *Abstract Machines Revisited*, FIDE technical report 1991/11
13. K.-D. Schewe, J. W. Schmidt, I. Wetzel: *Specification and Refinement in an Integrated Database Application Environment*, in S. Prehn, H. Toetenel (Eds.): Proc. VDM 91, Noordwijkerhout, October 1991, Springer LNCS
14. J. M. Spivey: *Understanding Z, A Specification language and its Formal Semantics*, Cambridge University Press, 1988

A Concurrency Case Study Using RAISE

Anne Haxthausen and Chris George

Computer Resources International A/S,
Bregnerødvej 144, DK-3460 Birkerød, Denmark

Abstract. In this paper, a case study concerning specification and development of a concurrent system is presented. The emphasis is on exploring how RAISE may be used to isolate reusable abstraction and provide a basis for separate development. The study comprises four levels of presentation of a gas-burner control system, ranging from a quite abstract applicative specification, to a quite operational, concurrent design.

1 Introduction

During the last decade many formal methods have been researched and developed. However, still, it is very limited how much formal methods are used in industry. Yet, it is by the suitability of their industrial application and the extent of their usage that formal methods will ultimately be judged.

RAISE is a formal method which is aimed at industry and is currently being used by a number of companies. RAISE is hence used on various industrial-sized applications ranging from safety-critical concurrent systems to systems software. Some of the features of RAISE which have shown to be useful for industrial-sized applications are:

- The stepwise development principle together with good abstraction facilities, which makes it possible to cope with details one at a time.
- The separate development principle, by which different teams may work concurrently on developing parts of the system.
- Reusability.
- Tool support, which for instance makes it possible to record and check well-formedness of specifications, to do version control and change propagation, to produce and justify proof obligations, and to automatically translate low-level specifications to programming language code.

It is well-known that it is not easy to write abstract specifications for concurrent systems, allowing separate development. In this paper, we will present how RAISE may tackle this, by reporting on a particular case study concerning the specification and development of the gas-burner control system investigated in the ProCoS basic research action ([SRR90], [HRR91],[RRH93]).

The paper is organised as follows. First, in Sect. 2, a short introduction to RAISE is given. Next, in Sect. 3, an informal description of the gas-burner example is given. Then, in Sect. 4-7, a specification is developed through 3 steps. Finally, in Sect. 8, a conclusion is given. This conclusion will discuss why the techniques used in the example may scale up to industrial-sized applications.

2 RAISE Overview

RAISE stands for *Rigorous Approach to Industrial Software Engineering* and is a product consisting of:

- A software development method.
- A formal specification language, RSL.
- Tools supporting the language as well as the method.
- Technology transfer material (documents, videos and courses).

In the following, first the RAISE background and an ongoing project are described, and then a short description of the language, method and tools is given.

2.1 The RAISE Background

RAISE is the result of an ESPRIT project carried out during 1985 - 1990 by four companies:

- DDC/CRI (DK)
- STC (UK)
- ICL (UK)
- NBB/ABB/SYPRO (DK)

The starting point for RAISE was the Vienna Development Method, VDM ([BJ82], [Jon86]), which had had success in industry, but lacked a number of useful features. Hence, the aim was to enhance VDM with structuring facilities, algebraic specification, concurrency, formal semantics and computer-based tools.

Many languages and methods have been sources of inspiration for the enhancements, e.g. Z ([Abr80]), ML ([Mac85]), Clear ([BG80]), ASL ([SW85]), ACT ONE ([EM85]), LARCH ([GHW85]), OBJ ([FGJM85]), CSP ([Hoa85]) and CCS ([Mil80]).

2.2 The LaCoS Continuation

A new ESPRIT project, called LaCoS — Large Scale Correct Systems Using Formal Methods — follows up on RAISE. The aim of LaCoS is to use RAISE on real industrial applications and, based upon the experience (see [DGPZ93]) from these applications to further evolve the RAISE product. The project runs in the period 1990 - 1995 and is carried out by the following companies:

- CRI (DK)
- CAP PROGRAMATOR (DK)
- BNR Europe (UK)
- Lloyd's Register (UK)
- Bull (F)
- MATRA Transport (F)
- Inisel Espacio (E)
- Space Software Italia (I)
- Technisystems (GR)

2.3 RSL Overview

The RAISE specification language, RSL, is a wide-spectrum language which encompasses and integrates different specification styles in a common conceptual framework. RSL enables the formulation of modular, structured specifications which are model-oriented or algebraic; applicative or imperative; sequential or concurrent.

The language is given a formal semantics in [Mil90] and a collection of proof rules in [Mil90], such that properties of specifications can be proved. The construction of the denotational model and a demonstration of its existence is presented in [BD92a] and [BD92b].

Below a short summary of some basic language constructs is given. A detailed description of RSL may be found in [Rlg92].

An RSL specification consists of module definitions. A module may define types, values, variables, channels and (sub-)modules, and may also present axioms.

Types. Types may be sorts as known from algebraic specification:

type Id

or may be constructed from built-in types and type constructors as known from model-oriented specification:

type Table = Id $\rightarrow$ Int

Types may also be defined as subtypes of other types:

type NegInt = {| i : Int $\cdot$ i < 0|}

RSL additionally provides union and short record type definitions similar to those in VDM, and variant type definitions, which are short-hands for a sort definition, value definitions of constructors, and disjointness and induction axioms. For example the variant type definition

type Colour == black | white

defines a type (*Colour*) containing exactly two values (*black* and *white*).

Values. Values (constants and functions) may be defined in a signature/axiom style as known from algebraic specification:

> **value**
>   x, y : T
> **axiom**
>   x ≠ y

in a pre/post style:

> **value**
>   square_root : **Real** $\overset{\sim}{\to}$ **Real**
>   square_root(x) **as** y
>   **post** y $*$ y $=$ x $\wedge$ y $\geq$ 0.0
>   **pre** x $\geq$ 0.0

or in an explicit (signature/body) style as known from model-oriented specification:

> **value**
>   update : Id $\times$ **Int** $\times$ Table $\to$ Table
>   update(id, i, t) $\equiv$ t † [id $\mapsto$ i]

Variables. In RSL, functions may access, i.e. read or write, declared variables:

> **variable** t : Table
> **value** mk_empty : **Unit** $\to$ **write** t **Unit**

where **Unit** is the type containing the single value, (). The access description in the function signature constrains the allowed side-effects. At early specification stages it is often useful not to decide which variables will eventually be needed. The access descriptions **read any** and **write any** may be used to describe a function that may be developed into a function accessing any variable which may be introduced in a later development.

In RSL there is no distinction between value expressions and statements. Hence, there are value expressions for assigning a value e to a variable t, $t := e$, and for sequencing of two expressions $e1$ and $e2$, $e1$; $e2$.

Channels. Channels are the means by which processes communicate. In RSL, functions may access channels, i.e. input from or output on, declared channels:

> **channel** i : **Int**, o : **Bool**
> **value** test : **Int** $\to$ **in** i **out** o **Unit**

As for variables, channel access descriptions may be recorded in the function signature, and may use **any**.

In RSL there is no distinction between value expressions and process expressions. Concurrency is obtained among expressions of type **Unit** by either the parallel combinator, ||, or by the interlock combinator, ⫴, where the former allows the two expressions to communicate, possibly also with the environment, but where the latter forces the two expressions to communicate, without communication with the environment.

Communication is synchronised: A process may output a value e on a channel o by the output expression $o!e$ when and only when another process accepts this by an input expression $o?$.

Modularity. RSL has two kinds of modules, schemes and objects, as explained below.

Both kinds of modules are built from *class* expressions, where a basic class expression just embraces a set of definitions and axioms by the keywords **class** and **end**. A class expression denotes the set of all models concordant with its definitions and axioms (i.e. it has loose semantics).

RSL provides a number of class-building operators for renaming and hiding entities, for extending one class expression with another, and for instantiating schemes.

A *scheme* is a named class. An example of a scheme definition is:

scheme ELEM = **class type** Elem **end**

An *object* denotes a single model from a class. Examples of object definitions are:

object ElemObj : ELEM, IntObj : **class type** Elem = **Int end**

Objects may additionally be indexed with values, giving arrays.

Schemes may be parameterised with objects as in:

scheme STACK(E : ELEM) =
  class
    type Stack
    value push : E.Elem × Stack → Stack
    ...
  end

Here E is the formal parameter object. Within the scheme, entities from the parameter are referred to by qualification, like *E.Elem*.

Schemes may be instantiated with actual objects which statically implement the formal parameter objects, like in

object IntStack = STACK(IntObj)

The notion of *implementation* is explained in Sect. 2.4.

2.4 Method Overview

The RAISE method is based on the *stepwise development* paradigm according to which the software is developed in a number of steps.

Each step starts with a description of the software and produces a new description which is more detailed. The specifications are formulated in the RAISE specification language, RSL. The first specification is typically very abstract. After a number of steps in which design decisions are taken one may obtain a specification which is conveniently concrete to be (perhaps automatically) translated into a programming language.

The stepwise development is carried out under the *invent-and-verify* approach. That is, in each step first the new specification is invented and then it is verified that it in some way conforms to (is a correct development of) the previous specification. This approach is in contrast to the transformational approach, known from for instance PROSPECTRA ([Kri90]), where the new specification is obtained from the old one by a transformation and thereby is correct by construction.

The exact relationship (conformance) of the specifications in a development step may be a user-defined relation or the pre-defined 'implementation relation', which is described below.

The verification, or *justification* as it is called in RAISE, is *rigorous* (as the 'R' in RAISE indicates). That is, the method allows the verification to be formal but does not require it. The postulation of a certain development relation or a theory about a specification are examples of *justification conditions*.

A module *M2 implements* a module *M1*, $M2 \sqsubseteq M1$, if they are the same kind of modules (schemes or objects), and the class expression of *M2* implements the class expression of *M1*, and for parameterised schemes the parameters of *M1* implement corresponding parameters of *M2*, and for indexed objects if the index type of *M1* is a subtype of the index type of *M2*.

A class expression *C2 implements* another class expression *C1*, $C2 \preceq C1$, if *C2* *statically implements* *C1*, i.e. the signature of *C1* is a subsignature of the signature of *C2*, and if all properties stated (explicitly or implicitly) in *C1* are derivable from the properties stated in *C2*.

As a very import feature, the RSL structuring mechanisms, together with the implementation relation allow for *separate development*. As an example, assume that the following specification is to be developed by two teams.

scheme $P1 = \ldots$, $M1(E:P1) = \ldots$

One team develops *P1* to *P2* such that $P2 \sqsubseteq P1$, and another team develops *M1* to *M2* such that $M2 \sqsubseteq M1$, while still assuming only the properties of *P1*:

scheme $P2 = \ldots$, $M2(E:P1) = \ldots$

then it holds that $M2(O2) \preceq M1(O1)$, where

object $O1 : P1$, $O2 : P2$

It is also possible to allow the team developing *M* to gain more knowledge of the component *P*, by developing more synchronously. In the examples in Sect. 4 - 7 the components are developed synchronously in two steps, and one of the components is developed separately in a third step.

In [BG90] a full exposition of the RAISE method is given.

2.5 Tools Overview

The RAISE method as well as the RAISE specification language are supported by computer-based tools. The RAISE tools consist of:

- A library with full version control for storing and retrieving RAISE entities such as RSL modules, relations between them, theories about them, justification conditions and justifications.
- Interactive, syntax-oriented, type checking editors for the RAISE entities mentioned above.
- Functionality for pretty-printing RAISE entities using LaTeX.
- Translators from low-level RSL to Ada and C++.
- Justification tools for producing and justifying conditions.

All the modules and justifications in this paper have been produced using the tools.

3 Informal Description of The Gas-burner Example

A simplified version of the gas-burner example, which has been studied in the ProCoS basic research action ([SRR90], [HRR91],[RRH93]), may informally be described as follows.

A gas-burner system consists of the following components:

- a gas valve, which may be put on or off
- an ignition device that may ignite the gas
- a flame sensor that indicates if the gas is burning
- a thermostat that indicates whether heating is required or not
- a control system

The main function of the control system is to activate and deactivate the gas valve and ignition device in accordance with signals received from the flame sensor and thermostat. The control system should operate the system cyclically through a number of phases:

idle: The system should start in this phase in which it should remain until heat is required, whereupon it should enter the *required* phase.

required: The gas and ignition should be put on, whereupon the system should enter the *igniting* phase.

igniting: If there is a flame the system should enter the *ignited* phase else it should enter the *not_ignited* phase.

not_ignited: The gas and ignition should be switched off whereupon the system should enter the *idle* phase.

ignited: The ignition should be switched off whereupon the system should enter the *burning* phase.

burning: The system should remain in this phase until no heat is required or there is no flame, whereupon it should enter the *not_burning* phase.

not_burning: The gas should be turned off whereupon the system should enter the *idle* phase.

Note that we have so far ignored any timing requirements as these can not directly be dealt with using RSL.

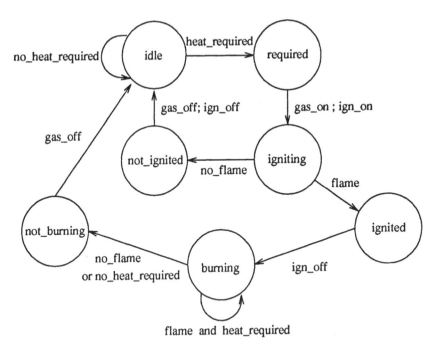

Fig. 1. Phase transitions for the gas burner

4 Level 0 — Applicative Sequential Specification

At this level we will give a formal specification of the control system informally described in previous section. In order to specify the control system we also need to specify its environment: the gas valve, ignition device, flame sensor and thermostat.

We aim at isolating reusable abstractions and on providing a good basis for separate development.

It is characteristic for the example, and for many control systems indeed, that they are understood as control mechanisms that respond to *sensors* and affect *actuators*. We will start the description of the gas-burner by first isolating those two abstractions: sensors and actuators.

So what are the basic properties of sensors? That they may enable measurements of values of a certain type. That is:

scheme ELEM = **class type** Elem **end**

scheme SENSOR0(E : ELEM) =
    class type Sensor   **value** reading : Sensor $\to$ E.Elem $\times$ Sensor **end**

where all we have said is, that a sensor will alow a value to be read, whereby it possibly changes to a new sensor. The totality of the function *reading* guaranties that it is always possible to read a value. At this level nothing is said about how a sensor process is run and interacts with its environment.

An actuator is specified in a similar way; all we have to say is that an actuator may have certain values sent to it, whereby it possibly changes.

scheme ACTUATOR0(E : ELEM) =
class type Actuator   value send : Actuator × E.Elem → Actuator end

The *CONTROL0* module constitutes an abstract specification of the control system and is parameterised with its environment.

scheme CONTROL0(
          H : class type Elem == heat | no_heat end,
          TH : SENSOR0(H),
          F : class type Elem == flame | no_flame end,
          FS : SENSOR0(F),
          G : class type Elem == on | off end,
          GAS : ACTUATOR0(G),
          I : class type Elem == on | off end,
          IGN : ACTUATOR0(I)
) =
hide obs, required, igniting, not_ignited, ignited, burning, not_burning in
class
     type Control, Act
     value
          idle, required, igniting, not_ignited, ignited, burning, not_burning :
            Control,
          obs : (Control × TH.Sensor × FS.Sensor ×
                      GAS.Actuator × IGN.Actuator)
                  → Act
     axiom
          forall th : TH.Sensor, fs : FS.Sensor,
               gas : GAS.Actuator, ign : IGN.Actuator •
          obs(idle, th, fs, gas, ign) ≡
            let (h', th') = TH.reading(th) in
               let
                  c' = case h' of H.no_heat → idle, H.heat → required end
               in
                  obs(c', th', fs, gas, ign)
               end
            end,
          obs(required, th, fs, gas, ign) ≡
            let gas' = GAS.send(gas, G.on), ign' = IGN.send(ign, I.on) in
               obs(igniting, th, fs, gas', ign')
            end,
          obs(igniting, th, fs, gas, ign) ≡
            let (f', fs') = FS.reading(fs) in

```
            let
                c' =
                    case f' of
                        F.flame → ignited, F.no_flame → not_ignited
                    end
            in
                obs(c', th, fs', gas, ign)
            end
        end,
        obs(not_ignited, th, fs, gas, ign) ≡
            let gas' = GAS.send(gas, G.off), ign' = IGN.send(ign, I.off) in
                obs(idle, th, fs, gas', ign')
            end,
        obs(ignited, th, fs, gas, ign) ≡
            let ign' = IGN.send(ign, I.off) in
                obs(burning, th, fs, gas, ign')
            end,
        obs(burning, th, fs, gas, ign) ≡
            let (f', fs') = FS.reading(fs), (h', th') = TH.reading(th) in
                let
                    c' =
                        case (h', f') of
                            (= H.heat, = F.flame) → burning, _ → not_burning
                        end
                in
                    obs(c', th', fs', gas, ign)
                end
            end,
        obs(not_burning, th, fs, gas, ign) ≡
            let gas' = GAS.send(gas, G.off) in
                obs(idle, th, fs, gas', ign)
            end
    end
```

The thermostat and flame sensor components (*TH* and *FS*) are specified as instances of the *SENSOR* module with actual parameter objects (*H* and *F*), which provide suitable element types for the values they can produce.

Similarly, the gas valve and ignition device components (*GAS* and *IGN*) are specified as instances of the *ACTUATOR* module with actual parameter objects (*G* and *I*), which provide suitable element types for the values that can be sent to them.

A standard way of describing possible phase transitions of control systems is to use finite state machines with states corresponding to phases as shown in Fig.1.

This can quite systematically be formalised in RSL by defining a value for each of the states (*idle, ... , not_burning*), and axioms defining the possible state (phase) transitions.

Each of the values represents the control system in a particular state. Their type, *Control*, is a sort, as we will leave it open for later developments to decide what the representation should be.

A *whole* gas-burner system consists of a the control system, the sensors and actuators, each in a particular state. As the time goes the system may change: the state of the control system, sensors and actuators may change.

There is an equivalence relation over gas burner systems which expresses that two systems are related if one may be obtained from the other by a chain of phase transitions, or vice versa. In other words the equivalence relation is the transitive, symmetric closure of the "is reachable from" relation.

At this level we describe the possible phase transitions by defining this relation abstracting away from the number and direction of transitions.

The standard way of describing an equivalence over some entities is to define an observer function over the entities which returns the same value for equivalent elements. Here, *obs* is the observer function, and *Act* is the type of the equivalence classes. The axioms define the *obs* function and thereby express possible phase transitions.

Note that the assumed properties of the environment are very weak — that sensors always send values when asked to, and that actuators always absorb values. Thus properties we prove about *CONTROL0* will hold in any environment just meeting these requirements. Such environments will (we are assuming) include the actual environment of our system, and any "testbeds" we set up as development of the actuators and sensors.

5 Level 1 — Abstract Concurrent Specification

The specification at level 0 was very abstract — no representation was given for the system components (sensors, actuators and control system values). A quite natural choice would be to let the system components be individual processes that can be run in parallel.

We first develop the sensors and actuators to be processes:

scheme SENSOR1(E : ELEM) =
    hide l, r, Act, is_sensor in
        class
            object l : class end, r : class end
            type
                Act = Unit $\overset{\sim}{\rightarrow}$ in r.any out l.any write r.any Unit,
                Sensor = {| s : Act • is_sensor(s) |}
            value
                is_sensor : Act → Bool,
                reading : Sensor → E.Elem × Sensor
        end

The development depends critically on the ability in RSL to implement the previously abstract type *Sensor* as a subtype of a process type. This allows us to develop from applicative specifications to imperative, concurrent ones.

The internal objects *l* and *r* are meant to hold any communication channels and state components needed in an implementation, and we define the sensors (the type *Sensor*) to be some of the *Act* processes that may output to any channels in *l*, and input on any channels and write in any variables in *r*. This use of **any** access descriptors illustrates a technique for abstracting away from (postponing decisions about) details about which channels and variables should be used. This makes event refinement possible.

The justification that SENSOR1 implements SENSOR0 is trivial, since SEN-SOR1 is an extension of SENSOR0 with some new enties, and with more specific details on the type *Sensor* (a sort may be implemented with any concrete type).

The actuator is specified in a similar way:

scheme ACTUATOR1(E : ELEM) =
    hide l, r, Act, is_actuator **in**
      class
        object l : **class end**, r : **class end**
        type
          Act = Unit $\overset{\sim}{\to}$ **in** r.any **out** l.any **write** r.any Unit,
          Actuator = {| s : Act • is_actuator(s) |}
        value
          is_actuator : Act → **Bool**,
          send : Actuator × E.Elem → Actuator
    end

Likewise, the justification that ACTUATOR1 implements ACTUATOR0 is trivial.

Having developed the sensors and actuators to processes we now develop the control system values to be processes. The *idle* process is the initial control system process. From each state it has a continuation which is another control process.

scheme CONTROL1(
          H : **class type** Elem == heat | no_heat **end**,
          TH : SENSOR1(H),
          F : **class type** Elem == flame | no_flame **end**,
          FS : SENSOR1(F),
          G : **class type** Elem == on | off **end**,
          GAS : ACTUATOR1(G),
          I : **class type** Elem == on | off **end**,
          IGN : ACTUATOR1(I)
) =
  hide
    is_control,
    obs, required, igniting, not_ignited, ignited, burning, not_burning
  in class
    type
      Act = Unit $\overset{\sim}{\to}$ **in** any **out** any **write** any Unit,
      Control = {| c : Act • is_control(c) |}
    value
      idle, required, igniting, not_ignited, ignited, burning, not_burning :
        Control,
      obs :

(Control × TH.Sensor × FS.Sensor ×
  GAS.Actuator × IGN.Actuator)
→ Act
obs(c, th, fs, gas, ign) ≡ (λ () • c() ⊬ (th() ‖ fs() ‖ gas() ‖ ign())),
is_control : Act → **Bool**
is_control(a) ≡
  a ∈
{idle, required, igniting, not_ignited, ignited, burning, not_burning}
axiom
  forall th : TH.Sensor, fs : FS.Sensor,
      gas : GAS.Actuator, ign : IGN.Actuator •
  idle() ⊬ (th() ‖ fs() ‖ gas() ‖ ign()) ≡
    let (h′, th′) = TH.reading(th) **in**
      let c′ = **case** h′ **of** H.no_heat → idle, H.heat → required **end**
      in
        c′() ⊬ (th′() ‖ fs() ‖ gas() ‖ ign())
      end
    end,
  required() ⊬ (th() ‖ fs() ‖ gas() ‖ ign()) ≡
    let gas′ = GAS.send(gas, G.on), ign′ = IGN.send(ign, I.on) **in**
      igniting() ⊬ (th() ‖ fs() ‖ gas′() ‖ ign′())
    end,
      . . .
end

Again we use **any** access descriptors in order to abstract away from details about channels and variables.

Note how the possible phase transitions are now expressed by axioms stating what happens when each of the control processes is interlocked with a parallel combination of the other system components (the sensors and actuators). Furthermore, the state function is now explicitly defined using a suitable representation for the equivalence classes.

The justification that instances of CONTROL1 implement corresponding instances of CONTROL0 lies mainly in showing that the axioms from CONTROL0 are true in CONTROL1. In appendix A.1 the second of these axioms is justified.

6 Level 2 — Explicit Concurrent Design

The specification at level 1 was still quite abstract — the processes were implicitly defined by axioms. As a step towards an implementation, we now want to explicitly define the processes.

In order to be do to that we first introduce client (interface) functions, *get* and *put*, for sensors and actuators, respectively.

scheme SENSOR2(E : ELEM) =
  hide l, r, Act, is_sensor **in**

```
class
    object l : class end,  r : class end
    type
        Act = Unit ⥲ in r.any out l.any write r.any Unit,
        Sensor = {| s : Act • is_sensor(s) |}
    value
        is_sensor : Act → Bool,
        get : Unit ⥲ in l.any out r.any E.Elem,
        reading : Sensor → E.Elem × Sensor
    axiom
        ∀ s : Sensor, test_elem : E.Elem ⥲ Unit •
            s() ∦ test_elem(get()) ≡
                let (e′, s′) = reading(s) in s′() ∦ test_elem(e′) end
end
```

The justification that SENSOR2 implements SENSOR1 is trivial.

```
scheme ACTUATOR2(E : ELEM) =
    hide l, r, Act, is_actuator in
        class
            object l : class end,  r : class end
            type
                Act = Unit ⥲ in r.any out l.any write r.any Unit,
                Actuator = {| a : Act • is_actuator(a) |}
            value
                is_actuator : Act → Bool,
                put : E.Elem ⥲ in l.any out r.any Unit,
                send : (Actuator × E.Elem) → Actuator
                send(a, e)() ≡ a() ∦ put(e)
        end
```

The justification that ACTUATOR2 implements ACTUATOR1 is trivial.

With this enriched interface, we can now, quite systematically, explicitly define the control processes.

```
scheme CONTROL2(
            H : class type Elem == heat | no_heat end,
            TH : SENSOR2(H),
            F : class type Elem == flame | no_flame end,
            FS : SENSOR2(F),
            G : class type Elem == on | off end,
            GAS : ACTUATOR2(G),
            I : class type Elem == on | off end,
            IGN : ACTUATOR2(I)
            ) =
    hide
        is_control,
```

obs, required, igniting, not_ignited, ignited, burning, not_burning

in class

  type

    Act = Unit $\overset{\sim}{\to}$ **in any out any write any** Unit,
    Control = {| c : Act • is_control(c) |}

  value

    obs :
        (Control × TH.Sensor × FS.Sensor ×
          GAS.Actuator × IGN.Actuator)
        → Act
    obs(c, th, fs, gas, ign) ≡ (λ () • c() ‖ (th() ‖ fs() ‖ gas() ‖ ign()))),
    is_control : Act → **Bool**
    is_control(a) ≡
        a ∈
    {idle, required, igniting, not_ignited, ignited, burning, not_burning},
    idle : Control
    idle() ≡
        case TH.get() **of** H.no_heat → idle(), H.heat → required() **end**,
    required : Control
    required() ≡ GAS.put(G.on) ; IGN.put(I.on) ; igniting(),
        . . .

  end

The justification that instances of CONTROL2 implement corresponding instances of CONTROL1 lies mainly in showing that the axioms from CONTROL1 are true in CONTROL2. In appendix A.2 the second of these axioms is justified.

7 Level 3 — Efficient Control Process

As a final step, we define a fairly minimal version of CONTROL, containing an explicit operational definition of the *idle* process. This is obtained by unfolding the mutually recursive processes, except *idle*, while eliminating embedded recursion in favour of loops, using standard techniques for recursion removal.

  scheme CONTROL3(
        H : **class type** Elem == heat | no_heat **end**,
        TH : SENSOR2(H),
        F : **class type** Elem == flame | no_flame **end**,
        FS : SENSOR2(F),
        G : **class type** Elem == on | off **end**,
        GAS : ACTUATOR2(G),
        I : **class type** Elem == on | off **end**,
        IGN : ACTUATOR2(I)
) =
    class
      value
        idle : Unit $\overset{\sim}{\to}$ **in any out any write any** Unit

```
idle() ≡
   while true do
      while TH.get() = H.no_heat do skip end ;
      (GAS.put(G.on) ; IGN.put(I.on)) ;
      case FS.get() of
         F.flame →
            IGN.put(I.off) ;
            while
               (TH.get(),FS.get()) = (H.heat,F.flame)
            do skip end ;
            GAS.put(G.off),
         F.no_flame → GAS.put(G.off) ; IGN.put(I.off)
      end end
end
```

The process *idle* is all we are actually interested in translating. However, this is not adequate to show implementation, because things are missing. If we extend the module with the missing entities and include a new axiom for *burning* (using a loop instead of recursion) and all the axioms from CONTROL2 except that for *idle* and *burning*, it would be possible to show implementation.

If we were also further developing the sensors and actuators, we would use explicit channels and output and input expressions for definitions of *put* and *get*. However, the sensors and actuators are probably hardware components with some control software and interface functions. In this case the task is to implement *put* and *get* in terms of these interface functions.

8 Conclusions

A control system for a gas-burner has been stepwise developed using RAISE, starting from a rather abstract, applicative specification, and ending with a detailed concurrent design. The RAISE tools have been used to check the well-formedness of the specifications and to generate and justify the conditions that show the development steps are implementations.

The example has illustrated how modularity and abstraction facilities may be used to isolate and provide a basis for separate and stepwise development of a concurrent system. In particular it has shown how the ability to refine abstract types into process types, allows applicative specifications to be refined to imperative, concurrent ones. Secondly, two very special language constructs, the **any** access descriptor and the interlock combinator (⫲), make it possible to abstract away from which channels and variables should be used and to specify the behaviour of processes axiomatically. By this, state and event refinement is possible. These facilities are, as far as the authors know, not provided by any other languages.

Advantages of developing the system stepwise starting from an abstract specification rather than directly writing an operational design are:

- One need not cope with all design decisions at one time.

- The formulation of an abstract specification is typically easier to make correct, validate and maintain as it is more close to the informal description, the original requirements.
- It is easier to prove properties for abstract specifications like those at level 0 and 1 than for more explicit specifications like those at level 2 and 3, cf. the justifications in appendix A.1 and A.2. (This especially holds for concurrent systems.) Since the RSL implementation relation ensures maintenance of properties, properties that are true in the abstract specification will be true in the concrete ones. Conversely, problems like timing and conformance to safety critical coding standards are more easily dealt with at the concrete level.
- Maintenance (adaptive or corrective) is enabled by the preservation of the design history. For instance, a more realistic gas burner would have a fail state which it should reach if the flame fails to ignite or goes out. Adapting the abstract axioms and redeveloping provides a reliable route to a new implementation; just changing the final definition of *idle* would be much less reliable.

The advantages of reuse and separate development should be obvious.

The principles of reusability, stepwise and separate development illustrated in the example also apply to larger industrial-sized applications in which they are rather important — they are what makes the method scalable.

Acknowledgements.

This work has been carried out within the ESPRIT-II LaCoS project partially supported by the Commission of European Communities.

The original ideas behind this paper were first formulated by Søren Prehn.

The authors would like to thank Jan Storbank Pedersen for useful discussions and proposals.

References

[Abr80]   Abrial, J.R.: The Specification Language Z: Syntax and Semantics. Technical report, Oxford University Computing Laboratory, Programming Research Group, April 1980

[BD92a]   Bolignano, D., Debabi, M.: On the Foundations of the RAISE Specification Language. LACOS Report Bull/DB/27, Bull Corporate Research Center, June 1992

[BD92b]   Bolignano, D., Debabi, M.: Higher Order Communicating Processes with Value-passing, Assignment and Return of Results. In *Proceedings of ISAAC'92*, volume 650 of *Lecture Notes in Computer Science*. Springer-Verlag, 1992

[BG80]   Burstall, R.M., Goguen, J. A.: The Semantics of Clear, a Specification Language. In *Proceedings of Advanced Course on Abstract Software Specifications*, volume 86 of *Lecture Notes in Computer Science*, pages 292–332. Springer-Verlag, 1980

[BG90]   Brock, S., George, C.: RAISE Method Manual. LACOS Report DOC/3, Computer Resources International A/S, August 1990

[BJ82]   Bjørner, D., Jones, C.B.: *Formal Specification & Software Development*. Prentice-Hall Series in Computer Science. Prentice-Hall International, 1982

[DGPZ93] Dandanell, B., Gørtz, J., Storbank Pedersen, J., Zierau, E.: Experiences from Applications of RAISE. In *Proceedings of FME'93, Lecture Notes in Computer Science.* Springer-Verlag, 1993

[EM85] Ehrig, H., Mahr, E.: *Fundamentals of Algebraic Specification 1: Equations and Initial Semantics.* Springer-Verlag, 1985

[FGJM85] Futatsugi, K., Goguen, J. A., Jouannaud, J., Meseguer, J.: Principles of OBJ2. In *Proceedings of POPL'85*, 1985

[GHW85] Guttag, J.V., Horning, J.J., Wing, J.M.: *Larch in Five Easy Pieces.* Digital, Palo Alto, California, 1985

[GP92] George, C., Prehn, S.: The RAISE Justification Handbook. LACOS Report DOC/7, Computer Resources International A/S, 1992

[Hoa85] Hoare, C.A.R.: *Communicating Sequential Processes.* Prentice-Hall Series in Computer Science. Prentice-Hall International, 1985

[HRR91] Hansen, K.M., Ravn, A.P., Rischel, H.: Specifying and Verifying Requirements of Real-Time Systems. In *Proceedings of ACM SIGSOFT'91 Conference on Software for Critical Systems*, volume 16 of *ACM Software Engineering Notes*, pages 44 – 55, 1991

[Jon86] Jones, C.B.: *Systematic Software Development Using VDM.* Prentice-Hall Series in Computer Science. Prentice-Hall International, 1986

[Kri90] PROgram Development by SPECification and TRAnsformation: Technical report, Univ. Bremen, Univ. Dortmund, Univ. Passau, Univ. des Saarlandes, Univ. Strathclyde, Syseca Logiciel, CRI A/S, Alcatel Standard Eléctrica SA, Univ. Pol. de Cataluña, 1990

[Mac85] MacQueen, D.B.: Modules for Standard ML. *Polymorphism*, II(2), 1985

[Mil80] Milner, R.: *A Calculus of Communicating Systems*, volume 92 of *Lecture Notes in Computer Science*, pages 1 – 172. Springer-Verlag, 1980

[Mil90] Milne, R.: The proof theory for the RAISE specification language. RAISE Report REM/12, STC Technology Ltd, 1990

[Rlg92] The RAISE Language Group: *The RAISE Specification Language.* BCS Practitioner Series. Prentice-Hall International, 1992

[RRH93] Ravn, A.P., Rischel, H., Hansen, K.M.: Specifying and Verifying Requirements of Real-Time Systems. *To appear in IEEE Transaction of Software Engineering*, 1993

[SRR90] Sørensen, E.V., Ravn, A.P., Rischel, H.: Control Program for a Gas Burner: Part 1: Informal Requirements, ProCoS Case Study 1. ProCoS Report ID/DTH EVS2, Department of Computer Science, Technical University of Denmark, 1990

[SW85] Sannella, D., Wirsing, M.: A Kernel Language for Algebraic Specification and Implementation. Technical report, Department of Computer Science, University of Edinburgh, 1985

A Appendix

This appendix contains parts of justifications of the implementation relation conditions at level 0 and 1.

The justifications are presented 'backwards', i.e. at the top of a justification the condition to be justified is presented (enclosed by the brackets ⌊ and ⌋). This goal is by application of RSL proof rules stepwise simplified into simpler goals, which are finally reduced to true, whereby the justification is completed. At each step the name of the applied rule is mentioned. Some of the proof rules have side conditions which are shown and justified after the keyword **since**.

Readers who want to study justifications in detail are referred to [GP92], where a full exposition of the syntax for justifications and the RSL proof rules are given.

A.1 Level 1 — Justification of Implementation

'unnamed_1' is an application of the second unnamed axiom from CONTROL1.

justification CONTROL01_TH2_J of CONTROL01_TH2 :
⌊in
    extend
      class
        object
          H : class type Elem == heat | no_heat end,
          TH : SENSOR1(H),
          F : class type Elem == flame | no_flame end,
          FS : SENSOR1(F),
          G : class type Elem == on | off end,
          GAS : ACTUATOR1(G),
          I : class type Elem == on | off end,
          IGN : ACTUATOR1(I)
        end
      with
        CONTROL1(H, TH, F, FS, G, GAS, I, IGN)
    ⊢
      ∀
        th : TH.Sensor,
        fs : FS.Sensor,
        gas : GAS.Actuator,
        ign : IGN.Actuator
      •
        obs(required, th, fs, gas, ign) ≡
          let gas′ = GAS.send(gas, G.on), ign′ = IGN.send(ign, I.on) in
            obs(igniting, th, fs, gas′, ign′)
          end⌋
  class_scope_assumption_inf, all_assumption_inf, application_expr_unfold1 :
  ⌊(λ () • required() ∦ (th() || fs() || gas() || ign())) ≡
    let gas′ = GAS.send(gas, G.on), ign′ = IGN.send(ign, I.on) in
      obs(igniting, th, fs, gas′, ign′)
    end⌋
  unnamed_1 :
    ⌊(
      λ () •
        let gas′ = GAS.send(gas, G.on), ign′ = IGN.send(ign, I.on) in
          igniting() ∦ (th() || fs() || gas′() || ign′())
        end
) ≡
        let gas′ = GAS.send(gas, G.on), ign′ = IGN.send(ign, I.on) in

obs(igniting, th, fs, gas$'$, ign$'$)

    end$_\lrcorner$

lambda_application2, let_expansion, let_function_application5,
let_function_application5, lambda_absorption1 :

  $\llcorner$(

    let gas$'$ = GAS.send(gas, G.on) **in**

      let ign$'$ = IGN.send(ign, I.on) **in**

        λ () • igniting() $\parallel$ (th() $\parallel$ fs() $\parallel$ gas$'$() $\parallel$ ign$'$())

      end

    end

) $\equiv$

    let gas$'$ = GAS.send(gas, G.on), ign$'$ = IGN.send(ign, I.on) **in**

      obs(igniting, th, fs, gas$'$, ign$'$)

    end$_\lrcorner$

application_expr_unfold1, let_expansion :

  $\llcorner$(

    let gas$'$ = GAS.send(gas, G.on) **in**

      let ign$'$ = IGN.send(ign, I.on) **in**

        λ () • igniting() $\parallel$ (th() $\parallel$ fs() $\parallel$ gas$'$() $\parallel$ ign$'$())

      end

    end

) $\equiv$

    let gas$'$ = GAS.send(gas, G.on) **in**

      let ign$'$ = IGN.send(ign, I.on) **in**

        (λ () • igniting() $\parallel$ (th() $\parallel$ fs() $\parallel$ gas$'$() $\parallel$ ign$'$()))

      end

    end$_\lrcorner$

  is_annihilation, qed

end

A.2 Level 2 — Justification of Implementation

justification CONTROL12_TH2_J **of** CONTROL12_TH2 :

  $\llcorner$**in**

    extend

      class

        object

          H : **class type** Elem == heat | no_heat **end**,

          TH : SENSOR2(H),

          F : **class type** Elem == flame | no_flame **end**,

          FS : SENSOR2(F),

          G : **class type** Elem == on | off **end**,

          GAS : ACTUATOR2(G),

          I : **class type** Elem == on | off **end**,

          IGN : ACTUATOR2(I)

        end

with
CONTROL2(H, TH, F, FS, G, GAS, I, IGN)
⊢
∀
 th : TH.Sensor,
 fs : FS.Sensor,
 gas : GAS.Actuator,
 ign : IGN.Actuator

 required() ⫲ (th() ∥ fs() ∥ gas() ∥ ign()) ≡
  let gas′ = GAS.send(gas, G.on), ign′ = IGN.send(ign, I.on) **in**
   igniting() ⫲ (th() ∥ fs() ∥ gas′() ∥ ign′())
  end⌟

class_scope_assumption_inf, all_assumption_inf, application_expr_unfold1,
interlock_commutativity, parallel_associativity, parallel_commutativity,
parallel_associativity, parallel_commutativity, interlock_sequence,
interlock_commutativity, interlock_parallel2 :
 ⌞GAS.send(gas, G.on)() ∥ (th() ∥ fs() ∥ ign()))
 ⫲
 IGN.put(I.on) ; igniting() ≡
  let gas′ = GAS.send(gas, G.on), ign′ = IGN.send(ign, I.on) **in**
   igniting() ⫲ (th() ∥ fs() ∥ gas′() ∥ ign′())
  end⌟
since
  ⌞GAS.put(G.on) ⫲ gas() ≡ GAS.send(gas, G.on)()⌟
  application_expr_unfold1, interlock_commutativity, is_annihilation, **qed**
end

parallel_associativity, parallel_commutativity, interlock_sequence,
interlock_commutativity, interlock_parallel2 :
 ⌞IGN.send(ign, I.on)()
 ∥
 (GAS.send(gas, G.on)() ∥ (th() ∥ fs()))
 ⫲
 igniting() ≡
  let gas′ = GAS.send(gas, G.on), ign′ = IGN.send(ign, I.on) **in**
   igniting() ⫲ (th() ∥ fs() ∥ gas′() ∥ ign′())
  end⌟
since
  ⌞IGN.put(I.on) ⫲ ign() ≡ IGN.send(ign, I.on)()⌟
  application_expr_unfold1, interlock_commutativity, is_annihilation, **qed**
end

let_expansion, let_absorption4, let_absorption4, parallel_commutativity,
parallel_commutativity, interlock_commutativity, application_expansion3,
application_expansion3, is_annihilation, **qed**
end

Specifying a Safety-Critical Control System in Z

Jonathan Jacky

Department of Radiation Oncology RC-08
University of Washington,
Seattle WA 98195, USA

Abstract. This paper presents a formal specification in the Z notation for a safety-critical control system. It describes a particular medical device but is quite generic and should be widely applicable. The specification emphasizes safety interlocking and other discontinuous features that are not considered in classical control theory. A method for calculating interlock conditions for particular operations from system safety assertions is proposed; it is similar to ordinary Z precondition calculation, but usually results in stronger preconditions. The specification is presented as a partially complete framework that can be edited and filled in with the specific features of a particular control system. Our system is large but the specification is concise. It is built up from components, subsystems, conditions and modes that are developed separately, but also accounts for behaviors that emerge at the system level. The specification illustrates several useful idioms of the Z notation, and demonstrates that an object-oriented specification style can be expressed in ordinary Z.

1 Introduction

Safety-critical control systems are often advocated as ideal applications for formal software development methods [1]. However, there are very few published examples of formal specifications for real safety-critical systems that have been built and used. Those few are expressed in notations that are not in wide use (for example, [4]).

The complexity of a real control system confronts the specification writer with problems of style and organization whose solutions are not apparent from most small case studies found in the literature. Examples of formal specifications for realistic control systems might serve as models, or *reusable frameworks* [3], that could be adapted to other projects.

The large literature on control theory (for example, [2]) emphasizes continuous, closed-loop controls. It provides little guidance regarding discontinuous, essentially "open-loop" operations such as turning subsystems on and off, and safety interlocking. Such features dominate the requirements for many safety-critical systems, including our own.

Researchers concerned with safety issues have proposed abstract formal models of process control systems that provide criteria for evaluating specifications for desirable properties such as completeness and safety [9, 12]. This work challenges builders of real systems to provide specifications that are sufficiently formal to support such evaluation.

This paper describes a framework for formal specifications of safety-critical control systems, and demonstrates its application to a real medical device. Some of our preliminary work was reported in [6].

2 A Case Study

The Clinical Neutron Therapy System at the University of Washington is a cyclotron and treatment facility that provides particle beams for cancer treatments with fast neutrons, production of medical isotopes, and physics experiments. The facility was installed in 1984, and includes a computer control system provided by the cyclotron vendor [14]. Devices under computer control include a 900 amp electromagnet and a 30 ton rotating gantry, as well as four terminals at three operator consoles. The control system handles over one thousand input and output signals, and includes six programmable processors as well as some nonprogrammable (hard-wired) controls.

The University is now developing a new, successor control system. This development project is motivated by requirements to make the system easier and quicker to use, easier to maintain, and able to accomodate future hardware and software modifications.

We have mostly completed an informal specification, which is being produced with the participation of the therapists, physicists and engineers who use and maintain the facility. It will comprise about 500 pages of prose and diagrams [7, 8], and documents the requirements expressed in the formal specification. We hope that the formal specification will be much shorter and will serve as the primary guidance for software development.

3 A Framework for Safety-Critical Systems

A *framework* is a formal model that abstracts the central features of a family of applications, which can be adapted or extended to fit the needs of particular projects [3]. Our specification is presented here as a partially complete framework that can be edited and filled in with the specific features of different control systems.

3.1 State Variables, Control Laws and Safety Assertions

Reviewing our prose specifications [7, 8], we find that most of our requirements can be expressed by a quite simple framework: a system is a collection of *state variables* that must obey certain *control laws* and *safety assertions*. This can be modeled by a Z state schema.

The state variables are named in the schema declaration and can be discrete indicators or numeric quantities. The control laws and safety assertions are system invariants which appear as schema predicates. Control laws are formulae that relate state variables in a way that produces the intended system behaviors. In classical control theory [2], control laws are usually differential equations that relate continuous variables, but our control laws also include discrete variables and logical connectives. Safety assertions are formulae that place additional constraints on the state variables, as required by considerations of human safety and equipment protection.

As an example of this framework, here are some definitions and a (much simplified) state schema for our cyclotron. The schema shows a few of the state variables and laws concerned with the radio-frequency (RF) amplifiers that accelerate the particles, the magnet that confines them, and the shielding door that protects staff and visitors from scattered radiation.

$$STATUS ::= disabled \mid off \mid on \mid error$$

$$CURRENT == -100.00 \mathinner{.\,.} 900.00$$

Many more definitions ...

Cyclotron

$mainfld : STATUS$
$mainfld\_setpoint, mainfld\_preset, mainfld\_current : CURRENT$
$rf : STATUS$
$door : DOOR$

Many other state variables ...

$mainfld \in \{disabled, off\} \Rightarrow mainfld\_setpoint = 0.00$
$mainfld \in \{on, error\} \Rightarrow mainfld\_setpoint = mainfld\_preset$
$mainfld = on \Rightarrow \mid mainfld\_setpoint - mainfld\_current \mid \leq \epsilon$

Many other control laws ...

$rf = on \Rightarrow door = closed$
$rf = on \Rightarrow mainfld = on$

Many other safety assertions ...

The particle beam is considered to be on whenever the RF drive amplifiers are on. When the main magnet field is off, its current is zero; when it is on, its current is held at a nominal preset value (this magnet also has a disabled state from which it cannot be turned on, and an error state where it has been turned on but is not running correctly). The safety assertions say that the beam can only be on when the vault door is closed and the main field is running within its nominal range.

This paper does not describe how the state variables are input, output, or transformed between their values in meaningful engineering units and their low-level representation as bit patterns in device registers. Those vital activities are the subject of another report [5].

3.2 Operations

The control system provides a repertoire of *operations* that can change the values of some state variables. These are modeled by Z operation schemas.

For example, this operation turns on the main field power supply, unless it has been disabled.

TurnOnMainfld _____

$\Delta Cyclotron$

$mainfld \neq disabled$

$mainfld\_setpoint' = mainfld\_preset$

Changing *mainfld_setpoint* usually causes *mainfld_current* to follow (the control law for this is rather complicated and is not shown). The control laws require that *mainfld* must change as well; it either becomes *on* or *error*, depending on whether *mainfld_current* approaches *mainfld_setpoint*.

This illustrates a common technique for writing concise operation definitions: the variables explicitly changed in the operation schema drive other variables, as dictated by the control laws. Therefore, operation definitions usually do not include predicates that fix the values of variables that are not explicitly changed.

3.3 Interlocks

A distinguishing feature of safety-critical control systems is that many operations are *interlocked*; they are not allowed to proceed if certain potentially hazardous conditions exist. In our framework, interlocks are preconditions for operation schemas. If a precondition is not satisfied, the interlock is *set* or *active*, and the operation must not proceed; otherwise the interlock is *clear*.

Consider the operation invoked by pressing the BEAM ON button. Here is a naive specification.

TurnOnBeam _____

$\Delta Cyclotron$

$rf \neq disabled$

$rf' \in \{on, error\}$

This schema says that pressing the BEAM ON button when the RF system has not been disabled will attempt turn on the RF drive amplifiers (it cannot be guaranteed that they will turn on; they may indicate an error).

This definition is not consistent with the intent of the system safety assertions. Additional interlocks should prevent the beam from turning on if the vault door is not closed, or the main field current is outside its nominal range.

It seems that it should be possible to calculate the intended interlock conditions from the system safety assertions. However, the ordinary Z precondition [15, 13] is too weak. Despite the safety assertion about *door* in *Cyclotron*, the precondition of *TurnOnBeam* does not include *door* = *closed*. This somewhat surprising result occurs because *door* is an input sensor whose value may change at any time. We cannot write any operation schemas that constrain the final values of such sensors — we can't even say *door'* = *door*. Therefore, we cannot calculate any ordinary Z precondition involving *door*.

However, we do wish to prohibit turning on the beam when the door is open. To achieve this and similar intended effects, the interlock predicates should be chosen to ensure that the "after" state of the operation schema (the state formed by the primed schema variables) will be sure to satisfy the system state invariant when the values of all the sensor variables remain the same in the "before" and "after" states.

We can state this formally, by making a stronger version of the usual Z precondition expression: from the state schema S, extract the schema $Sensor$ that consists only of the declarations of the state variables that represent sensors whose values cannot be directly controlled. This is necessary because safety assertions typically involve these sensors. Then the interlock precondition for operation Op is given by the schema expression $PreSafeOp \mathrel{\widehat{=}} \exists\, S' \bullet Op \wedge \Xi Sensors$. In our example,

$$
\begin{array}{|l}
\hline
\; CyclotronSensors \underline{\hspace{8cm}} \\
\quad mainfld\_current : CURRENT \\
\quad door : DOOR \\
\hline
\end{array}
$$

$$PreSafeTurnOnBeam \mathrel{\widehat{=}} \exists\, Cyclotron' \bullet TurnOnBeam \wedge \Xi CyclotronSensors$$

We obtain

$$
\begin{array}{|l}
\hline
\; PreSafeTurnOnBeam \underline{\hspace{6cm}} \\
\quad Cyclotron \\
\quad \underline{\hspace{3cm}} \\
\quad rf \neq disabled \\
\quad door = closed \\
\quad mainfld = on \\
\hline
\end{array}
$$

These preconditions can be conjoined with the naive operation definition to obtain the intended definition:

$$SafeTurnOnBeam \mathrel{\widehat{=}} TurnOnBeam \wedge PreSafeTurnOnBeam$$

This prevents the beam from being turned on when the door is open. Of course, it still does not prevent the door from being opened immediately after the beam turns on, but in that event the system safety invariant dictates that the beam should turn off immediately.

It is useful to compare the interlock conditions computed from the state schema by this method to the interlocks recommended by the designers, based on their understanding of the system. Disagreement may indicate that the system safety assertions are not complete (or are too restrictive), or the operation is not fully described.

There are legitimate reasons why the computed interlock conditions might not agree with designers' recommendations. It is sometimes necessary to add interlocks beyond those entailed by the system safety assertions, in order to prevent certain transitions between states, even though the states themselves are sometimes permitted.

4 Limitations of the Basic Framework

The basic framework presented in section 3 can describe most of our requirements, but it is not very useful as a practical specification style. Its disadvantages arise because all the system state variables appear in a single state schema. Real process control systems have hundreds or thousands of state variables. Moreover, the number of operations and the specification for each would have to be very large because there are so many variables and conditions to consider.

5 A Framework Based on Components

Most of our system's size derives from repetition of similar components. We can make our specification much shorter and easier to grasp by identifying the components, describing them separately, and then combining them. Each kind of component is specified using the basic framework presented in section 3, with its own state, operations, and interlocks.

Each kind of component can be considered an *abstract data type* or, to use the terminology of the popular object-oriented programming movement, a *class*. Several notations based on Z add constructs intended to support object-oriented programming [16]. We find that ordinary Z [15] serves well as a notation for specifying object-oriented programs.

The following sections describe some components we have found useful for our application. Subsequent sections show how the component specifications are combined into a system specification.

5.1 Analog Control Parameters

The three state variables *mainfld_setpoint*, *mainfld_preset*, *mainfld_current* that appeared in the *Cyclotron* schema in section 3 reveal a pattern that appears in many other contexts. We define a schema for this recurring pattern, which we call a *control parameter* or simply a *parameter* (in this paper we use the word "parameter" in this sense, not the programming languages sense).

$$
\begin{array}{|l}
\hline
\_Param \underline{\hspace{4cm}} \\
\hline
preset, setpoint, value : SIGNAL \\
\hline
\end{array}
$$

It is useful to define a schema for the situation where the parameter's value is nearly equal to the setpoint.

$$
\begin{array}{|l}
\hline
\_Param\ Valid \underline{\hspace{3cm}} \\
Param \\
\hline
|\ setpoint - value\ | \leq \epsilon \\
\hline
\end{array}
$$

5.2 Power Supplies and Servomotors

Many of the state variables in our system are devoted to about forty power supplies that provide current to the magnets that confine, focus and steer the beam. The main field supply discussed in section 3 is just one of these. Here is a slightly more realistic generalization; this model also includes the contactor that connects the supply to its power source, and represents the various faults that induce the *disabled* and *error* states. The control law says that current cannot flow when the contactor is open. The safety assertions say that we must not try to drive current when faults exist or the contactor is open.

$SWITCH ::= open \mid closed$

$FAULT ::= overload \mid line\_voltage \mid overtemp \mid ground\_short$

┌─ *PS* ───
│ *Param*
│ *contactor* : *SWITCH*
│ *faults* : **P** *FAULT*
├───
│ $contactor = open \Rightarrow value \leq \epsilon$
│
│ $faults \neq \emptyset \Rightarrow setpoint = 0$
│ $contactor = open \Rightarrow setpoint = 0$
└───

Explicitly modelling the contactor and faults reveals that the status values of section 3 (*disabled*, *off* etc.) actually indicate different power supply states, so we no longer need an explicit *status* variable. The supply is *Off* when the contactor is open and there are no faults:

┌─ *Off* ───
│ *PS*
├───
│ $contactor = open$
│ $faults = \emptyset$
└───

The supply is *On* when the contactor is closed, there are no faults, and *setpoint* and *value* (nearly) equal *preset*. Note that power supplies can use ("inherit") any properties defined for parameters, such as *Param Valid*.

┌─ *On* ───
│ *PS*
├───
│ *Param Valid*
│ $contactor = closed$
│ $setpoint = preset$
│ $faults = \emptyset$
└───

There are several other states, including an *Error* state. It is easy to define operations in terms of these states.

$$TurnOn \cong \mathit{Off} \wedge (\mathit{On}' \vee \mathit{Error}')$$

Several other kinds of components besides power supplies include control parameters. For example, in servomotors the signals represent position, not current.

```
┌─ Servo ────────────────────────────────────────────────
│ Param
│ enable : MODE
│
│ Other state variables specific to servomotors ...
└──────────────────────────────────────────────────────
```

5.3 Discrete Indicators

It is convenient if every state variable in the system is handled in a uniform way, as part of an instance of some class of components. Those few system-level state variables that do not belong to any obvious component can be handled by defining simple "components" with only one state variable.

```
┌─ Indicator ────────────────────────────────────────────
│ status : INDICATOR
└──────────────────────────────────────────────────────
```

5.4 Combining the Components

With several kinds of components now in hand, we return to the system level. Every component has a name. Each class of components in the system is modelled as a function from names to instances of the state schema for that class. This example shows only three kinds of components; the real system has many more.

$[NAME]$

$$ps, s, i : \mathbf{P}\ NAME$$

```
│ rf, mainfld, door : NAME
├──────────────────────
│ rf ∈ ps ∧ mainfld ∈ ps
│ door ∈ i
```

```
┌─ Cyclotron ────────────────────────────────────────────
│ supply : ps → PS
│ servo : s → Servo
│ indicator : i → Indicator
├──────────────────────────────────────────────────────
│ supply rf ∈ On ⇒ (indicator door).status = closed
│ supply rf ∈ On ⇒ supply mainfld ∈ On
│
│ Other system level laws ...
└──────────────────────────────────────────────────────
```

For each class of component, there is a set that names all the components of that class. The declarations say that the roster of components in the system is fixed. Therefore, each maplet of the form *name* $\mapsto$ θ*Component* can be regarded as a persistent object. This is a central idea in our object-oriented specification style for Z.

All of the state variables and most of the predicates from the basic framework are now inside the various components, so the system state schema can be much smaller. However, laws that relate state variables in different components can only be expressed at the system level. These include the two safety assertions discussed in section 3.

6 Some Useful Idioms

Specifying the operations of a system described this way requires several constructions in the Z notation that are not obvious. We call them *idioms*. These idioms are not described in the reference manual [15] nor taught in textbooks [13]; they must be gleaned from case studies [11] or technical reports [10]. Here are two useful ones.

6.1 Promotion

Much useful behavior can be modeled at the component level. However, methods defined at the component level are not, by themselves, meaningful at the system level. For example, at the system level it makes no sense to merely turn on a power supply; it is necessary to say *which* supply. Component-level operations that must be made available at the system level can be adapted by applying a Z idiom called *promotion* [11, 10].

First, for each type of component we have to define a *framing schema*, where the identifier of the component of interest is an input parameter. For power supplies, the framing schema is $Cyclo\Phi PS$.

```
┌─ CycloΦPS ──────────────────────────────────
│ ΔCyclotron
│ ΔPS
│ ps? : NAME
├─────────────────────────────────────────────
│ ps? ∈ ps
│ θPS = supply ps? ∧ θPS' = supply' ps?
└─────────────────────────────────────────────
```

Then the operation to turn on the main field magnet is:

```
┌─ TurnOnMainfld ─────────────────────────────
│ CycloΦPS
│ TurnOn
├─────────────────────────────────────────────
│ ps? = mainfld
└─────────────────────────────────────────────
```

Other power supply operations can be promoted in the same way.

Sometimes, additional predicates must be added to promoted operations to account for requirements that emerge at the system level.

```
┌─ TurnOnBeam ─────────────────────────────────────────────
│ CycloΦPS
│ TurnOn
├──────────────────────────────────────────────────────────
│ ps? = rf
│ (indicator door).status = closed
│ supply mainfld ∈ On
└──────────────────────────────────────────────────────────
```

The additional interlock preconditions here could have been calculated from the system safety assertions by the method described in section 3.3.

6.2 Operations on Multiple Components

Other system level operations are obtained by performing the same method on multiple components. For example, a common operation is to turn on all the power supplies in some subsystem, say Beam Line A. This is provided at a single button, to save the operator the trouble of switching each supply on individually. It can be expressed by another Z idiom:

```
┌─ TurnOnBLA ──────────────────────────────────────────────
│ ΔCyclotron
├──────────────────────────────────────────────────────────
│ ∀ ps : blaps • ∃ TurnOn • θPS = supply ps ∧ θPS' = supply' ps
└──────────────────────────────────────────────────────────
```

7 Subsystems, Conditions, and Modes

In addition to components, we use a few other ideas to organize the specification. Other authors have noted the usefulness of conditions and modes [4]. Subsystems are also helpful.

7.1 Subsystems

The various subsystems include the RF system, the cyclotron proper, the three beamlines, the two treatment rooms, etc. Each is simply a collection of components, identified by their names.

```
│ rfsys, cyclo, bla, blb, blc, iso, fix : P NAME
```

Our subsystems are not necessarily disjoint — it is convenient to regard certain components as belonging to two or more subsystems.

7.2 Conditions

It is useful to define schemas to abbreviate conditions that appear frequently in the specification. Some conditions are quite simple.

```
┌─ BeamOn ─────────────────────────────────────
│ Cyclotron
├──────────────────────────────────────────────
│ supply rf ∈ On
└──────────────────────────────────────────────
```

Others are more complex; subsystems often appear in these definitions. For example, the cyclotron is ready when the vault door is closed, all of its power supplies have been switched on and are free of faults, and all their currents are near their setpoints.

```
┌─ CycloReady ─────────────────────────────────
│ Cyclotron
├──────────────────────────────────────────────
│ (indicator door).status = closed
│ supply⦇cyclo ∩ ps⦈ ⊆ On
└──────────────────────────────────────────────
```

This is a precondition for many operations. Here is a more realistic specification for turning on the beam.

```
┌─ TurnOnBeam ─────────────────────────────────
│ CycloΦPS
│ TurnOn
├──────────────────────────────────────────────
│ ps? = rf
│ CycloReady
│ BeamOn'
└──────────────────────────────────────────────
```

As this example shows, redundant conditions can be included to help make the intended effect clear to the reader.

7.3 Modes

Our cyclotron can be operated in different *modes*. Each mode is characterized by the destination and purpose of the beam. The beam can be delivered to two treatment rooms or an isotope production station. It can be used to treat patients, or for experiments and testing.

Modes are a kind of condition, for example:

```
┌─ IsoTest ────────────────────────────────────
│ Cyclotron
├──────────────────────────────────────────────
│
│ Isocentric room, test mode ...
│
└──────────────────────────────────────────────
```

Modes are important because the control laws and safety assertions depend on which mode is selected. In order to turn on the beam in a room, the beam line to that room must be ready. Moreover, different safety interlocks must be cleared, depending on whether we are preparing to treat a patient, or, alternatively, run an experiment with no people in the room. This is expressed by using modes and other conditions to write the control laws and safety assertions.

$$
\begin{array}{|l}
\hline\, SafeCyclotron \underline{\hspace{6cm}} \\
\quad Cyclotron \\
\hline
\quad IsoTest \wedge BeamOn \Rightarrow CycloReady \wedge BLAReady \wedge IsoReady \\
\quad IsoTreat \wedge BeamOn \Rightarrow CycloReady \wedge BLAReady \wedge IsoSafe \\[4pt]
\quad \text{Laws for other modes} \ldots \\
\hline
\end{array}
$$

These predicates concisely express many important properties. For example, if any of the conditions included in *IsoSafe* becomes false while the beam is on in *IsoTreat* mode, the beam must turn off.

Modes and conditions also appear in the operation schemas:

$$
\begin{array}{|l}
\hline\, SafeTurnOnBeam \underline{\hspace{5cm}} \\
\quad TurnOnBeam \\
\hline
\quad IsoTest \Rightarrow CycloReady \wedge BLAReady \wedge IsoReady \\
\quad IsoTreat \Rightarrow CycloReady \wedge BLAReady \wedge IsoSafe \\[4pt]
\quad \text{Preconditions for other modes} \ldots \\
\hline
\end{array}
$$

8 User Interface

Our complete specification will include a schema for every operation that users can invoke which might change the values of any state variables. Therefore, we must write a schema for every control panel button and every on-screen menu selection.

Our complete specification will also include some schemas for operations that occur spontaneously when the values of certain sensor variables change. Turning off the beam at the end of a treatment, when integrating sensors indicate that the prescribed dose has been delivered, is one example.

When users attempt operations that are interlocked, the system state does not change. Pressing the BEAM ON button turns on the RF drive if all the interlocks relevant to the selected mode are clear; otherwise, nothing happens. Therefore, the full specification for this and every other operation must be *total*; they must cover both possibilities. This is expressed:

$$
T\_TurnOnBeam \,\widehat{=}\, SafeTurnOnBeam \vee \Xi Cyclotron
$$

The active interlocks, conditions and modes are displayed at the control console so operators can see which operations are enabled.

Our specification implicitly determines that some sequences of operations are permitted and others are not possible, because in most states some variables act as interlocks to inhibit certain operations. Users may select operations in any sequence they wish, subject only to the sequencing constraints imposed by the preconditions. There is no other "flow of control."

Graphical notations such as state transition diagrams can help make sequencing constraints clear, and might be a useful complement to the Z texts.

The translations between internal state variable values and their representations in user interface devices such as analog meters or workstation displays are among the input/output operations that we have formally specified in another report [5]. Other details — whether a particular operation is invoked by pressing a button on a control panel, or selecting a menu option at a workstation — are described in prose and diagrams [8]. We do not believe it would be useful to formally specify the "look and feel" aspects of the user interface.

9 Progress Report and Preliminary Evaluation

At this writing (January 1993) our formal specification is not complete, but we are confident that all functional requirements documented in the informal specification [7, 8] can be formalized using techniques described in this paper (and a few more that we have omitted for brevity). All that remains is to finish filling in the framework.

We have only attempted to formalize the functional aspects of our system. The Z notation does not provide built-in facilities for representing time or concurrency. If we decide to formalize these features we will select a notation suited for them.

Much of the effort in developing large applications like ours is devoted to enumerating the system state variables and describing the operations that must be provided, taking care that nothing is omitted and no inconsistencies are introduced. The Z notation provides a discipline for organizing this work that is supported by a de-facto standard [15], several good textbooks, and robust tools for document preparation, syntax and type checking.

Z is particularly effective for systems whose size derives from repetition of components which are not identical but share many features in common. The Z schema calculus permits recurring features to be described with texts that apply to all, supplemented with brief texts that address the differences. As a result, definitions such as *SafeTurnOnBeam* in section 7.3 can be quite compact even though they actually describe hundreds of state variables.

We have already found the formal texts to be useful as descriptive documentation. We hope their brevity will help us build an economical implementation. The possibility that they might also support safety analyses and formal development of the implementation is an additional bonus.

10 Acknowledgements

The author thanks Norman Delisle, David Garlan and Mike Spivey for explaining some Z idioms and commenting on earlier versions of this work. The author also thanks three anonymous reviewers for suggestions that improved the clarity of this version of the paper.

References

1. Dan Craigen. FM89: Assessment of formal methods for trustworthy computer systems. In *12th International Conference on Software Engineering Proceedings*, pages 233 – 235, IEEE Computer Society, 1990.
2. Gene F. Franklin, J. David Powell, and Abbas Emami-Naeini. *Feedback Control of Dynamic Systems*. Addison-Wesley, second edition, 1991.
3. David Garlan and Norman Delisle. Formal specifications as reusable frameworks. In D. Bjorner, C. A. R. Hoare, and H. Langmaack, editors, *VDM '90: VDM and Z — Formal Methods in Software Development*, pages 150 – 163, Third International Symposium of VDM Europe, Springer-Verlag, Kiel, FRG, April 1990. Lecture Notes in Computer Science number 428.
4. K.L. Heninger. Specifying software requirements for complex systems: new techniques and their application. *IEEE Transactions on Software Engineering*, SE-6(1):2 – 13, 1980.
5. Jonathan Jacky. *Formal Specification and Development of Control System Input/Output*. Technical Report 92-05-02, Radiation Oncology Department, University of Washington, Seattle, WA, May 1992.
6. Jonathan Jacky. Formal specifications for a clinical cyclotron control system. In Mark Moriconi, editor, *Proceedings of the ACM SIGSOFT International Workshop on Formal Methods in Software Development*, pages 45 – 54, Napa, California, USA, May 9 – 11 1990. (also in *ACM Software Engineering Notes*, 15(4), Sept. 1990).
7. Jonathan Jacky, Ruedi Risler, Ira Kalet, and Peter Wootton. *Clinical Neutron Therapy System, Control System Specification, Part I: System Overview and Hardware Organization*. Technical Report 90-12-01, Radiation Oncology Department, University of Washington, Seattle, WA, December 1990.
8. Jonathan Jacky, Ruedi Risler, Ira Kalet, Peter Wootton, and Stan Brossard. *Clinical Neutron Therapy System, Control System Specification, Part II: User Operations*. Technical Report 92-05-01, Radiation Oncology Department, University of Washington, Seattle, WA, May 1992.
9. Matthew S. Jaffe, Nancy G. Leveson, Mats P. E. Heimdahl, and Bonnie E. Melhart. Software requirements analysis for real-time process control systems. *IEEE Transactions on Software Engineering*, 17(3):241 – 258, March 1991.
10. Ruaridh Macdonald. *Z Usage and Abusage*. Technical Report 91003, Royal Signals and Radar Establishment, St. Andrews Road, Malvern, Worcestershire, WR14 3PS, February 1991.
11. Carroll Morgan and Bernard Sufrin. Specification of the UNIX file system. *IEEE Transactions on Software Engineering*, SE-10(2):128 – 142, March 1984.
12. David Lorge Parnas and Jan Madey. *Functional Documentation for Computer Systems Engineering (Version 2)*. Technical Report, Telecommunications Research Institute of Ontario (TRIO), McMaster University, Hamilton, Ontario, L8S 4K1, September 1991. CRL Report No. 237.
13. Ben Potter, Jane Sinclair, and David Till. *An Introduction to Formal Specification and Z*. Prentice Hall International (UK) Ltd, Hemel Hempstead, Hertfordshire, 1991.
14. Ruedi Risler, Jüri Eenmaa, Jonathan P. Jacky, Ira J. Kalet, Peter Wootton, and S. Lindbaeck. Installation of the cyclotron based clinical neutron therapy system in Seat-

tle. In *Proceedings of the Tenth International Conference on Cyclotrons and their Applications*, pages 428 – 430, IEEE, East Lansing, Michigan, May 1984.

15. J. M. Spivey. *The Z Notation: A Reference Manual*. Prentice-Hall, New York, 1989.

16. Susan Stepney, Rosalind Barden, and David Cooper. A survey of object orientation in Z. *Software Engineering Journal*, 7(2):150 – 160, March 1992.

An Overview of the SPRINT Method

H.B.M. Jonkers

Philips Research Laboratories Eindhoven
Information and Software Technology
P.O. Box 80000, 5600 JA Eindhoven, The Netherlands
E-mail: jonkers@prl.philips.nl

Abstract. This paper gives an overview of the SPRINT method, which is a formal method for the development of control software of audio/video systems used in Philips. It is an integrated approach combining three key techniques in software development: specification, prototyping and reuse. The paper discusses the various constituents of the method using a subdivision in five categories: principles, models, languages, tools and guidelines, with focus on models and languages.

1 Introduction

This paper gives an overview of the SPRINT method [14], which is a formal method for the development of control software of audio/video (A/V) systems. It has been developed by the Information and Software Technology (IST) department of Philips Research in cooperation with Philips Consumer Electronics (CE). SPRINT is an acronym for *Specification, Prototyping & Reusability INTegration* and covers the entire software life cycle excluding the requirements analysis and definition phase.

1.1 The Goals of SPRINT

The primary goal of SPRINT is to establish a major improvement of the software development process in the A/V application domain, where improvement means first of all:

1. *Reduction of lead times.* In the consumer market it is particularly important that development times are short. Due to the growing number of features of A/V systems, the complexity of the control software is rapidly increasing. This leads to a situation where software development is becoming the bottleneck in the overall development process.
2. *Elimination of faults.* Failures of A/V control systems are unacceptable. The reason is not so much that A/V systems are safety-critical, but that bug fixes in the field are not feasible due to the quantity of systems (millions). Hence faults in the control software may lead to serious user dissatisfaction and consequently to loss of market.

The secondary goal of SPRINT is to gradually exploit the full potential of formal techniques. This goal is motivated by our conviction that formal techniques are the key to truly systematic software development and that their introduction in the industrial software development process should take place in an *evolutionary* rather than a revolutionary way.

We shall not argue why we advocate the use of formal techniques. The advantages and disadvantages of formal techniques have been discussed extensively in the literature, see e.g. [19, 26]. The reason why we advocate evolution is that we do not believe that the way industrial software developers and managers think and work can be revolutionized. If we want a formal method to work in practice, it should be possible to introduce the method at a level that fits in with relatively traditional concepts and techniques. Once introduced, the method will *educate* its users and lift them to a level where the full benefits of formal techniques can be reaped.

1.2 Specification, Prototyping & Reusability INTegration

It is obvious that the use of formal techniques can help in achieving the goal of eliminating software faults. In particular, the use of formal *specification* techniques allows one to describe unambiguously the required behaviour of systems, to formally reason about their correctness and to support the verification process with powerful tools.

It is not immediately clear that formal techniques can contribute to a reduction of lead times. The myth is widespread that formal methods reduce the productivity of software developers [7], leading to higher costs and longer development times. One of the ways to reduce lead times is by using *prototyping* techniques that support automatic generation of product quality code from executable specifications. This makes it possible to perform a considerable part of the development process by modifications at the specification level only.

Another way to reduce lead times is by exploiting the commonalities of systems. A/V systems come in ranges, where models within a range have the same basic functionality and differ only in a number of features. Even across ranges common functionalities can be identified, providing opportunities for *reuse*. Though there is little available evidence of successful applications of software reuse, there is growing consensus concerning the importance of reuse not only for reducing lead times and development costs but also for increasing software quality. Essential for the successful reuse of software is the availability of good specifications, hence formal techniques have an important role to play here.

As indicated by its acronym, SPRINT is an *integrated* software development method supporting the three key techniques discussed above: specification, prototyping and reuse. The integration is achieved by using a single formal language as the backbone of the method: the COLD specification and design language. COLD is used as the basis of the specification and prototyping formalisms and the reuse mechanisms supported by the method. Many of the methodological notions underlying the method are directly defined in terms of COLD concepts as well. In this respect SPRINT is a true formal method.

A software development method consists of many different constituents. In the discussion of SPRINT below we have tried to classify them more or less systematically in five different categories: principles, models, languages, tools and guidelines. Each category is discussed in a separate section. Since we focus on the formal aspects of the method, the sections on models and languages are the most detailed ones. We restrict ourselves to the technical aspects and do not discuss managerial issues.

2 The Principles

2.1 Productive Use of Formal Techniques

One of the dangers when introducing formal techniques in industry is that they are used on the wrong problems. For example, excessive amounts of time can be spent on formally specifying trivial pieces of software at the highest possible level of abstraction or formally proving non-critical program modules correct. Such use of formal techniques may easily lead managers to qualify formal methods as being counterproductive and to discard them altogether.

Formal techniques are not the answer to all software problems; they are no 'silver bullet' [4]. They should be used only where they are really effective. The SPRINT method differentiates several effective ways of using formal techniques. In concrete terms this means, e.g.: pre- and postcondition specifications and C implementations for the reusable components, executable specifications for control components and generated specifications and implementations for standard components. The emphasis of the method is on rigorous development and not on formal proofs of correctness. Instead of proof tools the method provides advanced compile-time analysis techniques that could later evolve into full support for (semi-)automatic theorem proving.

2.2 Executable Specifications

Using formal techniques productively means being able to choose the appropriate level of abstraction at any time. If all we provide is some very abstract specification formalism, the effort to construct complete specifications and the gap to bridge to a system implementation would be enormous. Executable specification techniques can be used to provide intermediate levels of abstraction. Executable specifications are less abstract than general non-constructive specifications, but they can be much more abstract than e.g. C programs and more precise than e.g. pseudo-code, while having the advantage of executability. As such, they provide a good compromise between the conflicting requirements of abstractness of specifications and speed of development.

The SPRINT method provides executable specification techniques through the PROTOCOLD language. As a specification language, PROTOCOLD can be viewed as a very simple yet powerful language for specifying state transition systems by means of state transition rules. As a programming language,

PROTOCOLD can be viewed as a mixture of classical imperative languages and logic programming languages, without the low level nature of the former and the inefficiencies of the latter.

2.3 Component-Oriented Design

The fundamental notion permeating the entire SPRINT method is that of a *component*. Components are the uniform building blocks of designs; all parts of the system, including hardware, software, environmental entities and the system itself are viewed as components. Components are *not* e.g. program modules, specifications or files, they are *abstractions* that identify units of system design. Though abstract, they have a number of concrete attributes associated with them, formal as well as informal, such as a specification, implementation(s), documentation, test data, instantiation information, review data, etc.

We characterize the SPRINT approach to system development as *component-oriented design*. This term refers to the fact that all development activities are in terms of operations on or with components. This approach is essential for achieving a high level of integration of the various development activities (specification, design, testing, etc.). It is also essential for making reuse work, since components are the natural, though certainly not the only, units of reuse. Components are to SPRINT what objects are to object-oriented design methods. Component-oriented design and object-oriented design have many things in common. One of the main differences is that component-oriented design takes integration of the development process one step further by making formal specifications an integrated part of the development activity.

2.4 Language Design by Subsetting

Formality refers to the use of formal languages. Besides one or more programming languages, which are very formal languages indeed, any formal software development method will support other formal languages, in particular specification languages. When more than one specification language is supported the problem of language interfaces arises: how do we relate specifications written in one specification formalism to specifications written in another formalism? This problem arises anyhow in connection with the specification and programming language(s), but a tower of Babel at the specification level is highly undesirable. The need to make artificial translations from one specification formalism to another creates 'semantic gaps' [22]. It would make the method much harder to use and introduce, and it would negatively affect the level of integration.

The way we deal with this problem in SPRINT is *not* by using a single specification language, but by making sure that all specification formalisms used are embedded within the same common language. The wide-spectrum language COLD, in particular the user-oriented version of the language called COLD-1 [16], is used for this purpose. Apart from full COLD, two specification languages have been developed by subsetting. The first is the SPECICOLD sublanguage, used for specifying application-oriented components, and the second

is the PROTOCOLD language meant for writing executable specifications. The
various languages of SPRINT are indicated in Fig. 1, where the PRINT language
is used for interfacing PROTOCOLD and C.

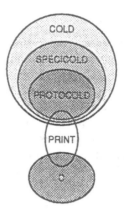

Fig. 1. The SPRINT languages

2.5 Use of Generator Tools

A basic software engineering principle is that dependencies between the various
constituents of a system design should, as far as possible, be maintained
automatically. This reduces the risk of inconsistencies when modifying a design, which becomes essential when dealing with complex systems. Several tools
exist for maintaining such dependencies such as the Unix 'make' facility. The
SPRINT tool support relies heavily on the use of *generator tools* for automating the dependencies. For example, make files are themselves dependent on the
system design, hence they are generated automatically from the system design
using 'makefile makers'. The generator technology used is based on the Elegant
compiler generator system featuring lazy attribute evaluation [1].

Another important dependency is the dependency of a reusable component
on its parameters. When using a reusable component in a system design it
should be *instantiated* by providing values for the parameters. The principle
of component-oriented design implies that instantiation means not only generating the implementation of the component, but also all of its other attributes such
as its specification, documentation, etc. In other words, reusable components are
a kind of higher-order objects that *generate* instantiated components.

In SPRINT we take the idea of reusable components as generators further by
providing a very flexible parameter mechanism for reusable components, even to
the extent that parameters may be provided interactively. This is used for example for generating the data types used in a design (enumerated types, record

types, etc.), since from the SPRINT point of view data types are normal components. A more advanced example is a reusable menu component that is instantiated by 'calling' the component, bringing one into a menu editor where the menus can be designed interactively, and at the end of the session generating a complete operational menu system including specification.

3 The Models

3.1 The Component Model

In Sect. 2.3 we discussed components as the basic building blocks of designs and identified a number of attributes associated with components. In this section we focus on the 'meaning' of components, i.e. the semantic model of components as the functional parts of a system. When we use the word 'component' in this section we shall often mean 'component model'.

SPRINT components are essentially *transition systems*, implying that they consist of the following entitities:

1. a collection of *states*;
2. an *initial state*;
3. a number of mappings from states to values called *observers*;
4. a number of state transition relations called *transformers*.

This model is the same as the semantic model underlying the COLD 'class' concept (see Sect. 4.1).

Note that transformers are *relations* between states. Two concepts that are important in connection with transformers are *success* and *failure*. If S is the set of states and $p \subseteq S \times S$ is a transformer, then p is said to *succeed* in a state s if there is a state t such that $(s, t) \in p$; if there is no such state t then p is said to *fail* in s. The operational intuition is that if p is activated in state s and p succeeds in s, the component will make a transition from state s to some state t with $(s, t) \in p$; if p is activated in s and p fails in s, nothing happens, i.e. the component remains in state s.

The dynamic behaviour of components is modelled in SPRINT by associating *actors* with the operations of components. The sole purpose of an actor is to *activate* operations at specified times, thus making the component move from one state to another. Without actors, a component is as dead as a doornail. In other words: transformers determine which state transitions a component *can* make, while actors determine which state transitions a component *will* make. Actors as used in SPRINT are similar to actors in e.g. the actor-agent-server model of [2] and [12], the difference being that SPRINT actors are not components themselves: they are merely providers of activation stimuli.

The transformers of a component are classified in three different categories:

1. *commands*, that pass information from the external world to the component;
2. *events*, that pass information from the component to the external world;
3. *steps*, that model the autonomous internal actions of the component.

Commands, events and also steps are treated uniformly as transformers and are specified as normal COLD procedures.

Steps play a special role. Autonomous activity in components is modelled by introducing *system actors*. The system actors are supposed to implicitly activate certain transformers, thus generating autonomous behaviour. In reality, the role of system actors is played by e.g. a scheduler or a hardware timer. The transformers directly activated by the system actors are by definition called 'steps'. To a certain extent the role of steps in SPRINT can be compared with the role of the τ operator in process algebras: both are used to model 'silent steps' though in a completely different setting.

A component is graphically represented by a so-called *box diagram* (see Fig. 2). As an example, consider a tuner component of a TV set. The following are examples of all four kinds of operations associated with the component:

1. *observer*: the operation yielding the frequency currently tuned to;
2. *command*: the operation starting a search for the next station on the frequency band;
3. *event*: the operation reporting that a station has been found;
4. *step*: the internal action of incrementing the frequency (when searching).

The 'station found event' would typically fail if no station has been found and succeed otherwise, bringing the system into a state where the event is 'cleared'. Likewise, the 'search step' would fail when the tuner is not in searching mode and succeed otherwise. Not all components have all four kinds of operations. Examples are components with observers only (static data types) and components with observers and commands only (passive state machines).

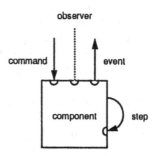

Fig. 2. The SPRINT component model

The above indicates how we deal with *processes* in SPRINT. Neither the actors nor the steps are processes, it is the combination of actors and the steps they trigger that induces processes by generating autonomous activity. Hence we can summarize the SPRINT process model as follows:

$$\text{process} = \text{actor} + \text{step}$$

One of the advantages of this view of processes is that it provides a natural separation of safety and liveness concerns. All safety properties are connected with the transformers (steps) while all liveness properties are associated with the behaviour of the actors.

An essential property of transformers is that they are *atomic*. When activated they either succeed, establishing an 'instantaneous' state transition, or fail without causing a side effect. This property of atomicity derives directly from the model of components as transition systems, but it does *not* imply that operations cannot execute concurrently. The requirement of atomicity translates to the requirement of *serializability* at the implementation level, implying that the operations of components may be executed concurrently and that components may contain internal concurrency (the steps), but that the effect of the concurrent execution of a number of operations is always equivalent to some serial execution of the same operations. Concurrency in components is dealt with in SPRINT in much the same way as in the *atomic data types* of [23, 25] and the *linearizable objects* of [11]. (In fact, what we call 'serializability' above, would be called 'linearizability' in [11].)

3.2 The Control Model

The notion of *control* refers to the coordinating activities that are necessary to make a collection of components behave in some orderly fashion. In SPRINT the control part of a system can be viewed as a special component put on top of the other components of the system in a way as indicated in Fig. 3. Typically, control would detect events in certain components and issue commands to other components as a reaction to these events.

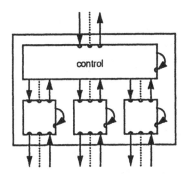

Fig. 3. The SPRINT control model

The SPRINT control model is *rule-based*. This refers to the fact that system control is specified (in PROTOCOLD) by means of a number of *state transition rules*, each rule describing a set of possible state transitions that the system can make. State transition rules are semantically equivalent to transformers of components, the only difference being that they describe simultaneous state transitions of a set of components rather than of a single component. Just like a transformer, a state transition rule will either *succeed* or *fail* in a given state. Whether or not a state transition specified by a state transition rule will ever occur depends on whether or not the rule is ever activated by an actor. The activation of the state transition rules is usually taken care of by introducing one or more system actors and *control steps* that, either directly or indirectly, trigger the rules. With system control described by rules there is no such thing as an implicit 'program counter', as in classical imperative programming. Control is completely stateless: all state information is contained in components.

The fact that the state transition rules for specifying control are semantically equivalent to transformers has a number of consequences. The first is that we may apply *control abstraction*: a collection of components together with a control system coordinating the behaviour of the components can be turned into a new component, where certain state transition rules of the control system become transformers of the new component and certain transformers (and observers) of the old components may be hidden. In other words, Fig. 3 can be viewed as the picture of a component itself. This component creates a *layer of control abstraction* by hiding the internal control details from the user of the component.

The second consequence of state transition rules being transformers is that they are *atomic*. This implies that when activated they either succeed, establishing an 'instantaneous' state transition, or fail without causing a side effect. As with transformers, there is nothing that prevents state transition rules from being executed concurrently. The same requirement of *serializability* applies: state transition rules may be executed concurrently, provided that the effect of the concurrent execution of a number of rules is always equivalent to some serial execution of the same rules. The difference with transformers is that state transition rules perform actions on a number of components rather than on a single component, making it much harder to satisfy the serializability requirement. In other words, state transition rules are like *transactions* on databases, where serializability is a well-known problem [21]. The solution to this problem chosen in SPRINT is based on a decomposition of applications in loosely-coupled processes, but discussion of the details of this solution goes beyond the scope of this paper.

3.3 The Architectural Model

The architectural model of a SPRINT application is schematically indicated in Fig. 4. According to this model, the system as a whole consists of a number of layers of components where the functionality of components in a given layer is based on the functionality of components in lower layers only. The three main layers are indicated in Fig. 4.

The bottom layer, called the *component layer*, consists of a number of self-contained components that are combinations of hardware and software, including components that provide the interfaces with the external world. This layer moulds the bare functionality provided by the hardware into *logical functionality* as required for a proper software design. Each component in this layer can

412

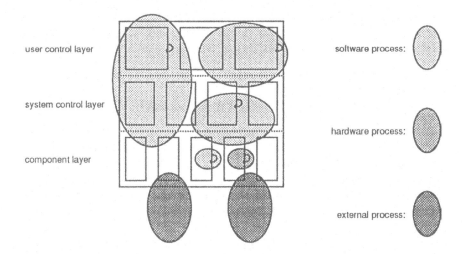

user control layer

system control layer

component layer

software process:

hardware process:

external process:

Fig. 4. The SPRINT system architecture

be viewed as a maximal abstraction of the underlying hardware while retaining the essential functionality of the component. The only interconnections between the components are hardware connections. Due to the modularity of the hardware, the components in this layer are prime candidates for reuse. An example of a component in this layer is a 'video tuner', consisting of tuner hardware and software functionality such as frequency selection and search tuning.

The two higher layers are pure software layers. The *system control layer* combines the functionalities of several components from the component layer and structures them into *subsystems*. Each subsystem constitutes a logical unit from the control software point of view, without incorporating any details of the user interface. The difference with the component layer is that subsystems need not be independent the way components in the component layer are. Hence the system control layer can be viewed as a *software chassis*, providing essentially the same functionality as the hardware chassis, but abstracted and rearranged in a way that fits in with the required software structure. An example of a subsystem is the 'audio system', providing all basic functions related to audio.

The highest layer is the *user control layer* which contains all functionality related to the user interface. The components in this layer determine how the system reacts to user events e.g. by linking remote control commands from the user to actions on the subsystems. An example of a component in this layer is the 'main control' component, containing the step of the main control process that holds sway over the system.

Besides the layering of components discussed above, which is connected with the use-relation of components, the system architecture defines additional structure by identifying the *processes* in the system. As discussed in Sect. 3.1, each step together with its associated actor induces a process. The variables directly or indirectly accessed by the step of a process are called its *process domain.*

Process domains are schematically indicated by ovals in Fig. 4. As can be seen, process domains are disjoint with shared components acting as the interfaces between the processes. The processes can be subdivided into:

1. *external processes* in the environment that are beyond our control;
2. *hardware processes* in the system hardware;
3. *software processes* executed under software control by the system microprocessor.

The layer in which a process is embedded is determined by the component containing the step of the process. By embedding a process as a whole in a component we can achieve *process abstraction*. This mechanism is essentially the same as the control abstraction mechanism discussed in Sect. 3.2 and allows the creation of components or layers of components with autonomous internal activity.

Software processes have an internal architecture as indicated in Fig. 5. The bottom layer, called *basic control*, consists of all components that contain state information in one form or another. The components in this layer can be divided into *state components*, containing the local state information of the process, and *interface components*, containing the state of the interfaces of the process with the external world (the 'communication channels'). The state components belong as a whole to the domain of the process, while the interface components are shared with other processes.

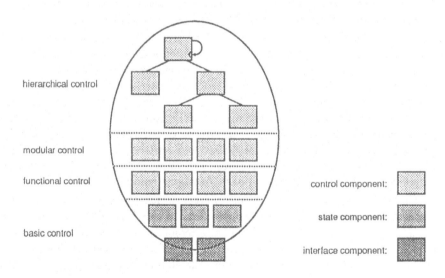

Fig. 5. The SPRINT process architecture

The three higher layers are completely stateless: they define the behaviour of the process by means of state transition rules only, as discussed in Sect. 3.2. The *functional control* layer provides *control functions* that combine functions of the basic control layer into new functions. It defines basic functions only and does not deal with event handling.

The *modular control* layer is the layer where the link between events and the required actions is established. Each component in this layer, called a *control module*, can be viewed as an *event handler* that performs actions in reaction to the occurrence of events. The events are typically user events (e.g. 'volume up') or system events (e.g. a sound signal changing from mono to stereo). The actions are typically control functions defined in the functional control layer.

The *hierarchical control* layer organizes the control system of the process in accordance with the hierarchical structure of its *control states*. Each process has a number of so-called *control state components*, defined in the basic control layer, that are used to represent the states of the process at the interaction points with its environment. These states have a hierarchical structure as exemplified by Fig. 6. This figure indicates, for example, that if the system is in the **standby** state, it is at the same time in the **on** 'superstate'. The hierarchical control layer defines control components for each state and superstate, the top level component containing the step of the process. This is done in such a way that control defined for a superstate applies automatically to all substates. How we deal with this at the language level is discussed in Sect. 4.3. The use of control states in SPRINT is similar to the AND/OR states as used in Statecharts [9].

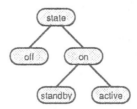

Fig. 6. Control state hierarchy

3.4 The Software Process Model

SPRINT is based on a software process model consisting of two parallel development processes with different life cycles (see Fig. 7). The first process is the product development process which is *project-oriented*. Products are being developed in *product ranges* and individual products within a range are being developed in separate projects under standard project control. The second process is a development process with a much longer life cycle aimed at developing a base of reusable knowledge for use in product development. Though the variety of knowledge that can be reused is large, the most concrete reusable items in the SPRINT development model are *reusable components*. Due to the generality of the component-concept and the component-oriented way of working, reusable components can capture a considerable part of the reusable knowledge. For example, one of the most reusable items in the A/V application domain is the knowledge concerning the various audio and video signals and signal standards. This knowledge is necessary for properly specifying and using A/V components and can be modelled most naturally by value-based components defining signal properties as attributes of signal values. The more concrete purpose of the second process is therefore the development and maintenance of a *library* of reusable components.

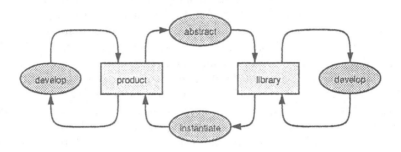

Fig. 7. Product and library development

The library development process will continuously monitor the product development process, identify candidate items for reuse and package them as reusable components. The latter is essentially a process of *abstraction*, where components are decoupled from their design context and parameterized if necessary, implementation details are hidden, functionality is rearranged, etc. Primary requirements for reusable components are that they are *self-contained, coherent* and *generally applicable* within the application domain.

Component flow in the other direction between the processes is established by the product developers selecting and *instantiating* reusable components from the library. Reusable components can be viewed as templates and instantiation as the creation of *instantiated components* from the templates. Instantiated components as such need no longer be reusable since at instantiation time they are specialized to and embedded in a given product design. In Sect. 2.5 we discussed a very general model of instantiation where reusable components are instantiation tools themselves, allowing flexible and individual forms of instantiation.

The SPRINT method also identifies seven generic instantiation mechanisms which can in principle be applied to arbitrary reusable components with a formal specification in SPECICOLD: *application, copying, importing, exporting, renaming, qualifying* and *glueing*. All these operations have a fully formal meaning in terms of the COLD structuring mechanisms. They have the property that if their arguments have implementations, both the specification and implementation of the resulting component can be generated automatically. Reuse in terms of these operations is more flexible than allowing reuse by copying only, as sometimes suggested, while still maintaining the advantage of reliability: no manual steps in the instantiation process are necessary.

The SPRINT model of the product development process can be viewed as a combination of several existing process models. Using the terminology and classification of process models from [24], it contains elements of the following development paradigms:

1. The waterfall approach.
2. Exploratory programming.
3. System assembly from reusable components.

The waterfall approach is used at the start of a product range to develop the system architecture and a global design from the requirements. This leads to specifications for the main system components, where certain components are chosen directly from the library of reusable components. Using (a prototype of) the hardware chassis and software stubs, a working though incomplete system is developed as quickly as possible. The waterfall approach is again used in the development of the individual components identified in the global design, now going all the way to implementation. As soon as a component has been implemented and tested, it is integrated and becomes part of the working system.

During this process the system requirements may still change, in particular with respect to the features of the user interface. Such changes are directly translated to modifications of the product specification at the user control level (see Fig. 4), where new components from the library may be instantiated and added to the specification or old ones removed. The product specification describes the effect of user events in terms of operations on the system components and is written in PROTOCOLD. From the modified specification a new working prototype of the product can be generated automatically, allowing the effect of changes to be observed and evaluated immediately. The same approach is also used for experimenting with new features.

If we have to characterize the SPRINT product development model, the term *incremental development* probably comes closest. The SPRINT model of the product development process is schematically indicated in Fig. 8. This picture shows only the exploratory and reuse aspects of the model while ignoring the waterfall aspects. Note the double role of the reusable components: the developer of the product specification uses them in terms of their specifications (in SPECICOLD) only and never sees their implementations. The tools that generate the prototype may use the specifications as well for verification and optimization purposes, but only the implementations are used for building the executable code.

4 The Languages

4.1 The Wide-Spectrum Language

The formal basis for the SPRINT method is the wide-spectrum language COLD (*Common Object-oriented Language for Design*) developed by Philips Research in the framwork of ESPRIT projects METEOR and ATMOSPHERE. COLD is a state-based, model-oriented specification and design language in the tradition of

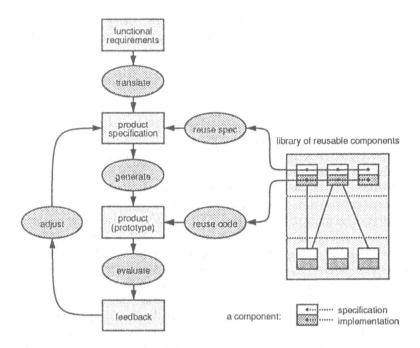

Fig. 8. Product development process

VDM, but with a clear algebraic background and a stronger focus on techniques for 'design in the large'.

The *kernel language* COLD-K as defined in [5] provides the semantic primitives of COLD. For an introduction to COLD-K see [13], and for a more extensive treatment see [6]. For practical use, the *user-oriented language* COLD-1 has been defined [16] as a kind of user-friendly 'shell' around the kernel language COLD-K. COLD-1 is essentially a macro-extension of COLD-K and does not add new expressive power. In SPRINT, and also in this paper, we use COLD-1 only and when we refer to COLD we usually mean COLD-1.

The semantic objects described by COLD specifications are called *classes.* Classes are transition systems as discussed in 3.1, where the observers are (state-dependent) *predicates* and *functions* and the transformers are called *procedures.* Algebraic data types are viewed as degenerate classes consisting of state-independent sorts, predicates and functions only. This view allows a completely uniform treatment of all static, dynamic, mutable and immutable data types and lies at the basis of the SPRINT component concept.

The wide-spectrum nature of COLD is reflected by its support for several styles of description such as algebraic specifications, axiomatic specifications, inductive definitions, pre- and postcondition specifications and abstract algorithmic descriptions. In SPRINT the language is for example used in the standard library to define the usual data types such as sets, sequences, tuples, maps, etc. that are built-in in most other specification languages. A typical definition taken from the library is the inductive definition of the concatenation operator on sequences:

```
FUNC cat : Seq # Seq -> Seq
IND  cat( empty, s ) = s
   ; cat( cons( i, s), t ) = cons( i, cat( s, t) )
```

Design in the large is supported by the COLD component concept and the structuring mechanisms associated with components. The SPRINT component concept discussed in Sect. 3.1 can be viewed as a method-oriented extension of the COLD component concept. A typical COLD specification of a component is given below:

```
COMPONENT PRESET_LIST[Preset] SPECIFICATION

ABSTRACT
   PRESET
EXPORT
   FUNC preset      : Preset -> Frequency
   PROC set_preset : Preset # Frequency ->
IMPORT
   FREQUENCY
CLASS
   ...
END
```

It specifies a 'preset table' with the sort Preset (usually some enumerated type) acting as a parameter. The parameter and any restrictions on it are specified by the PRESET component in the ABSTRACT clause. The EXPORT clause defines which operations of the component are public while the IMPORT clause defines which components are used internally in the specification. The specifications of the exported operations are given between the CLASS and END brackets. COLD supports various techniques for manipulating and combining components such as renaming, copying, exporting, importing, etc. which are the basis of the reuse mechanisms of SPRINT (see Sect. 3.4).

4.2 The Specification Language

In developing specifications of application-oriented components, the full power of a wide-spectrum language is neither required nor desirable. If newcomers first have to master the full complexity of a wide-spectrum language before they can start using formal specifications in their application domain, this will create a serious obstacle to the introduction of formal techniques. That is the reason why SPRINT uses a sublanguage of COLD, called SPECICOLD [18], as its specification language (see Fig. 1). This sublanguage is tailored to the use of the pre- and postcondition style and omits constructs uncommon to this style of specification. Furthermore, the language imposes syntactical restrictions such that the interfaces of components are compatible with components specified in PROTOCOLD (see Sect. 4.3).

An example of a pre- and postcondition specification in SPECICOLD is the following specification of the search step of a tuner:

```
PROC search_step : ->
PRE  searching_mode = on
SAT  MOD frequency, searching_mode, station_found
POST frequency = next( frequency' )
   ; carries_signal( frequency )      => ( searching_mode = off
                                         ; station_found
                                         )
   ; NOT carries_signal( frequency ) => ( searching_mode = on
                                         ; NOT station_found
                                         )
```

A detailed discussion of the (SPECI)COLD pre- and postcondition technique can be found in [15].

Another typical application of SPECICOLD is for specifying hardware-based components, since many A/V system components are hardware-based (tuner, amplifier, teletext unit, etc.). Suppose we have a simple hardware component with one input and one output as indicated in Fig. 9. The input and output

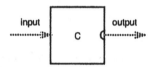

Fig. 9. A hardware component

of the component would be modelled as normal observers (see Fig. 2), with arrow heads added to the dotted lines representing the observers to indicate the direction of the signal flow. The specification of the component in SPECICOLD would read something like:

```
COMPONENT C SPECIFICATION

EXPORT
   FUNC input  : -> Signal
   FUNC output : -> Signal
IMPORT
   SIGNAL
CLASS
   FUNC input  : -> Signal    FREE
   FUNC output : -> Signal    DEP input, ...
   ...
END
```

If we want to specify a new component that is the composition of a number
of hardware components, such as the component indicated in Fig. 10, it is not

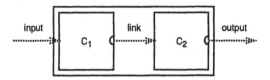

Fig. 10. A composite hardware component

always worthwhile to try and specify the new component as a pure black box.
It is often more effective and even clearer to specify the component directly in
terms of its subcomponents. For the component indicated in Fig. 10 this can be
achieved in SPECICOLD as follows:

```
COMPONENT CC SPECIFICATION

EXPORT
   FUNC input  : -> Signal
   FUNC output : -> Signal
IMPORT C' RENAMING output TO link END
     , C' RENAMING input  TO link END
END
```

This shows how hardware interconnections can be modelled in SPECICOLD.
The notation C' denotes a fresh copy of the component C. Note that the internal
interconnection between the two copies of C is hidden to the external world.

4.3 The Prototyping Language

As argued in Sect. 2.2 executable specifications are an essential element in the
productive use of formal techniques. They provide an automatic prototyping
facility and can in certain situations even be used for generating the final product
code. In SPRINT executable specifications are provided by the PROTOCOLD
language [17], which is meant for specifying system control. PROTOCOLD is a
sublanguage of full COLD as well as SPECICOLD (see Fig. 1).

As discussed in Sect. 3.2 the SPRINT control model is rule-based. System
behaviour is controlled by state transition rules and the PROTOCOLD language provides the formalism for specifying these rules. State transition rules
are specified by a restricted form of COLD procedures. The definition of each
state transition rule has the following general form:

```
PROC rule : T_1 # ... # T_n ->
IN    x_1,...,x_n
DEF   declaration; expression
```

Here $x_1, \ldots, x_n$ are the *parameters* of the rule and $T_1, \ldots, T_n$ are the types of the parameters. The *declaration* may introduce object names local to the rule and the *expression* defines the actual state transition rule. This may all seem much like a normal procedure definition as in Pascal or C, but there are essential differences as discussed below. Note that as remarked in Sect. 3.2 state transition rules and transformers are semantically equivalent, hence the above definition can also be viewed as the definition of a transformer.

The complete collection of PROTOCOLD expressions is indicated in Fig. 11, where A is an assertion, i.e. a test on the system state, E, E_1, E_2 are expressions,

$$
\boxed{
\begin{array}{l}
A \; ? \\
E_1 \; ; \; E_2 \\
E_1 \; | \; E_2 \\
E \; * \\
p(t_1, \ldots, t_n) \\
x := t
\end{array}
}
$$

Fig. 11. The PROTOCOLD expressions

p is the name of a rule or transformer, $t, t_1, \ldots, t_n$ are terms denoting objects and x is an object name introduced in the parameter list or in the declaration part of a rule.

Each expression denotes a relation between states which may either *succeed* or *fail* in a given state, as defined in Sect. 3.1. The first four expressions in Fig. 11 are the *regular programs* from dynamic logic and they have the standard meaning, see [8]. This is no wonder since the assertion language of COLD is based on dynamic logic. So, for example, the *sequential composition operator* ';' denotes relation composition and the *choice operator* '|' denotes union of relations. The fifth expression is a call (or 'activation') of the rule or transformer p with actual parameters $t_1, \ldots, t_n$ and the last construct, the *binding expression*, plays a special role to which we will come back.

The choice operator provides support for a 'conjunctive style' of specification. Suppose, for example, that we have specified two rules: `volume_control` and `program_control`, describing the handling of volume control and program control events respectively. That is, `volume_control` succeeds if and only if some volume-related event (e.g. 'volume down') has occurred and `program_control` succeeds if and only if some program-related event (e.g. 'select program 1') has occurred, where both rules take the appropriate measures to handle the event. A 'handler' of volume control *and* program control events can now be defined by the expression:

```
volume_control | program_control
```

If no volume or program control event occurs, the expression will fail. If a volume or program control event occurs, the expression will succeed and the first or second alternative will be chosen, depending on the event. This gives a glimpse of the simple way PROTOCOLD allows 'features' to be added and removed.

PROTOCOLD also supports hierarchical control specifications, as exemplified by the following state transition rule defining the behaviour in the on state of an A/V system with hierarchical control states as indicated by Fig. 6:

```
PROC on_control : ->
DEF ( general_on_control
    | state_is_standby ?; standby_control
    | state_is_active  ?; active_control
    )
```

Here we assume that `standby_control` and `active_control` are state transition rules that handle the events specific to the `standby` and `active` states respectively, while `general_on_control` handles the events that require the same reaction in the `standby` and `active` states. The 'guard' containing the assertion `state_is_standby` succeeds in the `standby` state only, hence it 'deactivates' the `standby_control` transition rule when the system is not in the `standby` state.

Modularity of control is supported in a natural way by PROTOCOLD because complete event handlers can be defined as transition rules. An example of such a control module is the following rule, handling events related to program selection:

```
PROC program_control : ->
DEF LET d:Digit;
    ( digit_event( d ) ; select_program( d )
    | search_next_event; start_searching
    )
```

This example also demonstrates the use of declarations and object names. The declaration of the object name d after the LET symbol should *not* be interpreted as the declaration of a programming variable but as the introduction of an existentially quantified *logical variable*. That is, `program_control` succeeds if and only if *there is* a digit d such that the expression following the declaration succeeds.

In operational terms the above means that the declaration of d introduces d as a 'single-assignment' variable which is initially 'free'. If `digit_key_event(d)` succeeds, it will *bind* a value to the variable d which can subsequently be used in `select_program(d)`. Values may be bound explicitly to object names by means of the binding expression, e.g.:

```
d := 0
```

Just like other expressions, such bindings may succeed or fail. For example, the following expression always fails:

```
d := 0; d := 1
```

The reason is that there is no d such that d is equal to both 0 and 1. The rules and object names of PROTOCOLD are similar to the clauses and variables of PROLOG, with at least three important differences. The first is that side effects in rules are allowed in PROTOCOLD. Object names in a rule are nevertheless referentially transparent: they denote the same value all over the rule. The second difference is that object names are used in PROTOCOLD in a much more restricted way than variables in PROLOG. Object names are either completely free or bound to a unique value, thus avoiding unification problems. Finally, the required backtracking in the evaluation of a rule is limited to the first point where a side effect occurs. As soon as a side effect occurs, the rest of the rule should succeed unconditionally. (Note: bindings have no side effects!) In other words, a side effect in PROTOCOLD has the same effect as the cut operator in PROLOG. The last two differences from PROLOG guarantee that PROTOCOLD can be implemented efficiently and with predictable execution times.

PROTOCOLD is used in SPRINT to specify the upper three control layers of processes (see Fig. 5). The on_control, program_control and select_program rules occurring in the above examples are typical examples of rules defined in the hierarchical, modular and functional control layers respectively. As discussed in Sect. 3.2, the transitions specified by a rule are executed only if the rule is, directly or indirectly, activated by an actor. The activation is carried out in the top level component of a process, which contains the 'step(s)' that are activated by the system actor(s).

4.4 The Programming Languages

The idea of using formal specifications productively implies not trying to specify formally every low-level detail of the implementation of a component. Once a component of a reasonable size has been formally specified in SPECICOLD, a good programmer should be able to produce a correct implementation of the component in a standard programming language without the need to introduce additional levels of formality. In such a situation the level of abstraction provided by a programming language is the most appropriate and productive choice.

The SPRINT method recognizes the above role of programming languages. The method is completely open-ended with respect to the programming language(s) used for implementing the components. In principle any general-purpose programming language can be used, though current SPRINT applications use mainly C. This is true not only for the implementation but also for the reverse engineering of components (the converse of implementation). Due to the generality of the component concept, an external piece of code, such as a device driver that comes with a piece of hardware, can easily be encapsulated in such a way that it behaves as a proper SPRINT component. Developing a proper specification matching the implementation may be much harder, but this is a general problem of reverse engineering.

4.5 The Interface Languages

The PROTOCOLD compiler supports separate compilation of PROTOCOLD components. Since a PROTOCOLD component may import other components implemented in either PROTOCOLD or some other programming language, the compiler should be provided with sufficient information about the imported components. It is not sufficient to provide the SPECICOLD specification of the imported components, because the compiler may need implementation details of the imported components. For example, if the implementation language L of an imported component does not support overloading of operation names, the compiler must know what the representation of a given overloaded SPECICOLD name in the language L is.

In order to pass the required information about a component to the compiler, a separate *interface description* of the component is necessary. Interface descriptions are written in a simple language called PRINT (*PRotocold INterface Templates*) and put in separate files. The function of these PRINT files is similar to that of .h files in C. A PRINT file is the description of the signature of a component extended with additional information that can be separated into implementation-independent and implementation-dependent information. The former provides semantic information about the component, allowing the compiler to make optimizations and perform a more elaborate static analysis. The latter is concerned with name conversions, representation of data types, etc. The implementation-dependency implies that there is a separate PRINT language for each implementation language, though the differences between the languages can be small.

5 The Tools

Due to the formal and integrated nature of the SPRINT approach, the possibilities for developing useful support tools are almost unlimited. The SPRINT Software Development Environment (SDE) as currently used exploits only a small proportion of these possibilities. Besides the usual tools found in programming-support environments, such as project management, version management, configuration management and documentation tools, compilers, assemblers, debuggers, etc. the SPRINT SDE contains a number of tools that are more specific to the SPRINT approach, such as:

- *Specification tools:* tools that help in constructing formal specifications, such as a COLD parser, unparser, type checker and cross reference generator.
- *Prototyping tools:* the PROTOCOLD compiler and makefile makers to automate the system building process.
- *Reusability tools:* a library of standard components and basic component generators.
- *Integrated tools:* a design browser allowing a complete design, including specifications, implementations and documentation to be inspected and visualized.

The tool set indicated above is sufficient for the operational use of the SPRINT method. Additional tools that are conceivable in the near future are e.g. library management facilities, hypertext support, improved component generators and advanced compile-time and run-time analysis tools for specifications and designs.

6   The Guidelines

No matter how beautiful the languages and tools, no software development method is complete without sufficient directions for its use. This holds even more for formal methods than for informal methods, since the proper and effective use of formal techniques is not always that obvious. As part of the further evolution of the SPRINT method, considerable effort is therefore spent on developing informal guidelines and standards for the various development activities such as specifying, implementing, testing, documenting, etc.

The (not so) surprising thing in developing such informal guidelines is that, more or less by themselves, they become much more concrete and precise than comparable guidelines of informal software development methods such as structured methods (e.g. [27, 10]) and object-oriented approaches (e.g. [20, 3]). This is of course due to the underlying formal framework that allows methodological concepts to be defined in precise terms. An example is the concept of an 'invariant' that is not always a clear-cut notion, even in object-oriented methods. The fact is that there are many different types of invariants and in SPRINT we can define precisely which type we mean.

7   Conclusion

The SPRINT method discussed in this paper distinguishes itself from existing formal and informal software development methods by the following combination of features:

- it is aimed at *fast* development of *fault-free* control systems;
- it applies formal techniques in a selective way to optimize productivity;
- it provides a synergy of formal specification and prototyping technology;
- it is based on a uniform notion of *component* and supports advanced techniques for reusing components;
- it features a simple yet powerful executable specification language, allowing automatic code generation from specifications;
- it is based on the use of a formal, high-level specification and design language as the backbone of the method.

The last point in this list is perhaps the most important. The fact that we had a wide-spectrum language with sufficient expressive power was the key to the development of SPRINT. It made it possible to give the methodological concepts a firm basis and to achieve a high level of integration.

SPRINT has been influenced by many different software development methods, both formal and informal, and most of the ingredients of SPRINT can be found in other methods as well. As usual, it is the combination of features that makes the novelty. Other formal methods based on wide-spectrum languages are e.g. VDM, CIP, SPEC, RAISE and Larch. Some technical points where SPRINT differs from all of these methods are:

- the component model;
- the modelling of concurrency;
- the use of success and failure concepts.

One could also say that SPRINT is a more dedicated method than any of the above general-purpose methods since it was developed for the A/V application domain. There is little or nothing in the method, however, that is specific to the A/V application domain. The requirement of applicability in the A/V domain has guided many choices made in the development of SPRINT, but none of these choices has led to the introduction of A/V-specific concepts in the method. There is e.g. no built-in 'volume' concept in the language, since it can be specified as a normal data type. We therefore believe that the method is applicable in a much wider domain, in particular to the development of control systems in general.

SPRINT is currently being used in the Business Group Television (BG-TV) of Philips Consumer Electronics. This indicates that the method has reached industrial strength. There are nevertheless several points where the method can be augmented and improved, in particular in the area of tool support and guidelines. Further development of SPRINT is therefore required. SPRINT as currently used exploits only a part of the potential that lies hidden in its formal backbone, so it could be said that the best is yet to come.

Acknowledgements

SPRINT is the result of a fruitful cooperation between the IST department of Philips Research and the Business Group Television of Philips Consumer Electronics. Much of the credit for the evolution of SPRINT to an industrial-strength method goes to the members of the joint IST/BG-TV team who were the first to apply the method to real products and gave valuable feedback.

References

1. L. AUGUSTEIJN, *The Elegant Compiler Generator System*, in: P. Deransart, M. Jourdan (eds.), Attribute Grammars and their Applications, LNCS 461, Springer-Verlag (1990), 238–254.
2. G.S. BOOCH, *Object-oriented Development*, IEEE Transactions on Software Engineering 12, 2 (1986), 211–221.
3. G.S. BOOCH, *Object-oriented Design with Applications*, Benjamin/Cummings (1991).
4. F.P. BROOKS Jr., *No Silver Bullet – Essence and Accidents of Software Engineering*, in: H.-J. Kugler (ed.), Information Processing 86, Elsevier Science Publishers (1986), 1069–1076.
5. L.M.G. FEIJS, H.B.M. JONKERS, C.P.J. KOYMANS, G.R. RENARDEL DE LA-VALETTE, *Formal Definition of the Design Language COLD-K*, Technical Report, ESPRIT project 432 (1987).
6. L.M.G. FEIJS, H.B.M. JONKERS, *Formal Specification and Design*, Cambridge University Press (1992).

427

7. A. HALL, *Seven Myths of Formal Methods*, IEEE Software 7, 9 (1990), 11–19.
8. D. HAREL, *First-order Dynamic Logic*, Lecture Notes in Computer Science 68, Springer-Verlag (1979).
9. D. HAREL, *Statecharts: A Visual Formalism for Complex Systems*, Science of Computer Programming 8 (1987), 231–274.
10. D.J. HATLEY, I.A. PIRBHAI, *Strategies for Real-Time System Specification*, Dorset House Publishing (1987).
11. M.P. HERLIHY, J.M. WING, *Linearizability: A Correctness Condition for Concurrent Objects*, ACM Transactions on Programming Languages and Systems 12 (1990), 463–492.
12. HOOD Working Group, *HOOD Reference Manual*, European Space Agency Document WME/89-173/JB (1989).
13. H.B.M. JONKERS, *An Introduction to COLD-K*, in: M. Wirsing, J.A. Bergstra (eds.), Algebraic Methods: Theory, Tools and Applications, LNCS 394, Springer-Verlag (1989), 139–205.
14. H.B.M. JONKERS, *The SPRINT Method*, Technical Note Nr. 183/90, Philips Research (1990).
15. H.B.M. JONKERS, *Upgrading the Pre- and Postcondition Technique*, in: S. Prehn and W.J. Toetenel (eds.), VDM '91, Formal Software Development Methods, Volume 1, LNCS 551, Springer-Verlag (1991), 428–456.
16. H.B.M. JONKERS, *Description of COLD-1*, Report RWR-513-hj-91020-hj, Philips Research, Information and Software Technology (1991).
17. H.B.M. JONKERS, *PROTOCOLD 1.1 User Manual*, Report RWR-513-hj-91080-hj, Philips Research, Information and Software Technology (1991).
18. H.B.M. JONKERS, *Description of SPECICOLD 1.0*, Report RWB-508-re-92271, Philips Research, Information and Software Technology (1992).
19. B. MEYER, *On Formalism in Specifications*, IEEE Software 2, 1 (1985), 6–26.
20. B. MEYER, *Object-oriented Software Construction*, Prentice Hall (1988).
21. C.H. PAPADIMITRIOU, *The Serializability of Concurrent Database Updates*, Journal of the ACM 26 (1979), 631–653.
22. D.A. PENNY, R.C. HOLT, M.W. GODFREY, *Formal Specification in Metamorphic Programming*, in: S. Prehn and W.J. Toetenel (eds.), VDM '91, Formal Software Development Methods, Volume 1, LNCS 551, Springer-Verlag (1991), 11–30.
23. P.M. SCHWARZ, A.Z. SPECTOR, *Synchronizing Shared Abstract Types*, ACM Transactions on Computer Systems 2 (1984), 223–250.
24. I. SOMMERVILLE, *Software Engineering*, Fourth Edition, Addison-Wesley Publishing Company (1992).
25. W.E. WEIHL, *Local Atomicity Properties: Modular Concurrency Control for Abstract Data Types*, ACM Transactions on Programming Languages and Systems 11 (1989), 249–282.
26. J.M. WING, *A Specifier's Introduction to Formal Methods*, IEEE Computer 23, 9 (1990), 8–24.
27. E.N. YOURDON, L.L. CONSTANTINE, *Structured Design*, Prentice Hall (1979).

Application of Composition Development Method for definition of SYNTHESIS information resource query language semantics

Leonid Kalinichenko,[1] Nikolaj Nikitchenko[2] and Vladimir Zadorozhny[1]

[1] Institute of Problems of Informatics
Russian Academy of Sciences
Vavilova 30/6, Moscow, V-334, 117900
e-mail: leonidk@ipian15.ipian.msk.su
[2] Faculty of Cybernetics
Kiev University
Vladimirskaja 64, Kiev-17, Ukraine
e-mail: kib.uni.kiev@p6.f23.n463.z2.fidonet.org

Abstract. This paper presents the main ideas of the Composition Development Method and its application to the semantics definition of the query language for *SYNTHESIS* – a system for heterogeneous information resource interoperation. This definition is used for implementation of the query language compiler.

1 Introduction

The purpose of this paper is to present the main ideas of the Composition Development Method (CDM) and its application to the semantics definition of the query language for *SYNTHESIS* – a system for heterogeneous information resource interoperation [14, 17]. This definition is used as a basis for implementation of the query language compiler components. As an example we consider programs admissibility checker.

This work is chiefly based on the researches which have been carried out in the former Soviet Union on formal methods of program development through the last decades. Among the first should be mentioned the method of microprogram construction using Systems of Algorithmic Algebras [10]. This method in its main ideas anticipated structural programming. Then different methods of software development which were based on algebraic [11, 8], operational [27] and logical [26] approaches appeared. At first the main efforts were concentrated on the formal definitions of programming languages and the development of their processors.

The results obtained in the formalization of programming and database languages allowed to construct their unified formal models and propose several development methods of corresponding software. The CDM is such a method which is based on special formal program models [5]. This method was used in the development of multilanguage system DEFIPS [28] and DBMS COMBAD [4].

This paper exemplify an attempt of application of the basic CDM ideas to the *SYNTHESIS* project. The project investigates principal methods and tools for information resource management integrating preexisting heterogeneous data, knowledge and program repositories [13]. A collection of various information resources interoperating in computer networks for application problem solving constitutes an *interoperable information resource environment (IIRE)*. A basic research for the project is concentrated around formally interoperable heterogeneous information resource environment.

The paper is built as follows: first we briefly introduce CDM, then we describe the main features of *SYNTHESIS* query language and construct its formal model using CDM. Finally we illustrate the application of this formalization for the implementation of the query language compiler components, namely for the block of programs admissibility checking.

2 Composition development method

The CDM, like the majority of software development methods, is based on the stepwise refinement paradigm and supports the development phases from specification to implementation. The main difference consists in choosing of formal models for program representations. These models are built in accordance with general and special principles of composition programming [20, 21], the main ones being the principles of subordination, separation, functionality and compositionality.

The subordination principle suggests that the pragmatic aspect is of primary importance among the three main aspects of programs; the semantic aspect is subordinated to the pragmatic aspect, while the syntactic aspect is derived from the other two aspects. The separation principle makes it possible to focus separately on the semantic aspect, abstracting from the syntactic aspect. The functionality principle treats the program semantics as a function that associates results with input data. The compositionality principles reduces tools of program construction to algebraic operations (compositions) on certain functions.

Specific systems are thus determined by 1) the set of data that the programs manipulate, 2) the set of functions representing the program semantics, 3) the set of composition formalizing the program construction tools. Therefore, the semantics aspects of programs are specified in the CDM by algebras of programs and the method itself may be considered as an algebraic one. The advantages of such methods are simple semantics, clear hierarchical structure of programs and wide applicability of algebraic methods to program analysis and construction.

A distinctive feature of the CDM is the goal-directed and conscious use of naming relations in the construction of data, functions and compositions. Data are specialized as named data, which adequately represent data structures of programming languages and databases [5, 18, 22, 23]. Data management functions are considered as special named functions. Thus functions over named data (named functions) represent semantics of program. Algebras of named functions are studied. Composition models of different programming and query languages are built and their various properties are investigated. These properties of program transformation and refinement allow to develop software components from the top level specification to the correct implementation.

The application of the CDM to the definition of the *SYNTHESIS* query language semantics demands its adaptation to deductive object-oriented databases.

3   An overview of SYNTHESIS language features

In the *SYNTHESIS* project constructing of the interoperable information resource environment (IIRE) for the information system design and nonprocedural problem solving is considered as a *knowledge-intensive activity* .

The IIRE metainformation (knowledge base) should include generalized information resource specifications, rules of transformation of primary resources into the equivalent generalized ones, clean separate description of a real world (application domain) model as the basic semantic reference point, information resource semantic specifications establishing correspondence of resources to the application entities and activities. The last point constitutes the cornerstone of the semantic interoperability. To treat a resource as the concretization of an application, certain structural, value and behavioral properties of resource should be satisfied [12]. Thus extensional and intentional properties of an application may be preserved and the ground for analysis of resource behavioral semantic discrepancy and reconciliation may be created.

Such specifications should be well-defined to make possible static provable checking of database invariant preservation by the database operations [7] as well as the provable treatment of the application behavior (expressed by functions and assertions) concretization by a resource [12]. The model-based specifications using pre-, postconditions and predicate transformers provide such possibility [2, 25]. This model is well-agreed with the choice of the typed first ordered language for the specification of rules in the definitions of functions and transactions, specification of assertions, specification of axioms and theorems establishing connections between resource and application descriptions.

Recently substantial research and technological advances were reached in the area of models and languages supporting data and knowledge bases leading to creation of:

- paradigms of the application domain representation models and information resource requirement specifications;
- models and languages providing for the information system conceptual design;
- object-oriented data models;
- deductive database models and languages;
- generalized data models for heterogeneous multidatabase systems [24];
- predicative specification technique for data intensive applications.

Each of these models or languages is not adequate in itself for the interoperable environment support. The cost of usage of different language environments for different levels of description is high due to the necessity of special methodologies and tools for the mappings between representational formalisms.

The *SYNTHESIS* language [14] incorporates necessary facilities for IIRE support. It was specified as a common platform suitable for all levels of the metadefinitions listed above. The language basic facilities look as follows:

- *Frame representation facilities.* Frames are treated as typeless objects. They are introduced for description of conceptual and weakly structured information on application domain, for information resource metadata representation, for definition of arbitrary semantic associations of frames, for representation of temporal associations.

– *Unifying type system.* The unifying type system is chosen on the basis of the type completeness requirement. The comprehensive set of basic types as well as a universal type constructor (*abstract data type* specifier) are included. A generic parameterized type definition is provided. Different programming language procedure interfaces for various environments could be uniformly specified. Types are treated as a special kind of value and may be passed as parameters of functions. Categories of types provide a flexible specification of polymorphic programming interfaces.

– *Class representation facilities.* Class hierarchies and inheritance mechanisms make it possible to define generalization relationships. Metaclasses provide for introducing of classification relationships. Class attributes may be typed by classes or by types from the unifying type system. Declarative logic assertions and functions may be associated with classes and their attributes. Events associated with such assertions define conditions of their enforcement. Encapsulation benefits are made available in the system.

– *Activity representation facilities.* These are used for specification of transactions conforming to various transaction models and of multiactivities in the form of a script.

– *Assertion definition facilities.* Mainly, components of assertions associated with objects may be formulated using typed first-order language formulae. The basic components are: assertion enforcement predicate in terms of event predicates, constraint predicate, function expressing necessary action. The collection of assertions may be well structured: part of the assertions may be defined inside of a class specification; another part may be defined in the module where the information resources (with which assertions are associated) are specified, and parts of them may be collected in separate modules (e.g., global assertions).

– *Query facilities.* Formally the query language is treated as a declarative deductive language in an object-oriented / frame-oriented environment. The expressiveness of separate queries or right parts of rules is comparable to the level achieved in query languages for conventional databases. The usage of the "query" language goes beyond query formulation and includes: specification of rules in functions and transactions; specification of assertion components; predicative specification of functions and transactions; specification of axioms and theorems expressing properties of resource / application mapping.

In this paper we address the problems of formal specification of the semantics of the *SYNTHESIS* query language.

The description of the *SYNTHESIS* language and its semantics definition one can find in [14, 17]. Here we consider the language subset which allows to demonstrate the main ideas of the approach proposed.

Logical formulae (or simply formulae) in the *SYNTHESIS* query language are used for defining rules which constitutes body of functions, for formulation of assertions as consistency constraints of the information resource base and for expressing queries.

For expressing formulae, a subset of a multisorted first-order predicate language is used. Every predicate, function, constant and variable in the formulae is typed. Predicates in formulae correspond to classes, methods and functions defined in information resource definition modules.

Variables, constants and function symbols may be used as terms. Each term is typed.

An atom (an atomic formula) appears as $p(t_1, ..., t_n)$ where p is a predicate symbol and t_i are terms. A formula is either an atom or has the form:

w_1 & w_2 (w_1 and w_2),

$w_1 \mid w_2$ (w_1 or w_2),

all x/t ($w_1 - > w_2$) (for all x of type t if w_1 then w_2),

ex x/t (w) (for some x of type t w),

$\hat{}w_2$ (not w_2),

where w, w_1, w_2 – formulae, x – a vector of variables, t – a vector of types.

Variables may be bound in formulae by quantifiers. Notation x/t defines that the type of x is t.

Rules are closed formulae of the kind: $a : - w$, where a is an atom and w is a formula: a is a head and w is a body of the rule. If a formula is used as a query for the information resource base (such query is called a filter) and it has free variables $H_1, ..., H_n$ then the answer to such a query is a set of different substitutions of variables $H_1, ..., H_n$ of proper types. On each such substitution the filter should become true under interpretation on an information resource base [11]. The *SYNTHESIS* query language program is a set of rules. The method of the program evaluation is based on the bottom-up computation of the least fixed point for immediate consequence operator defined by the program [11].

Example 1. Consider the following program:

$p(z) : - $ all y $((p_0(y)$ & $p_1(y)) - >$
$\qquad\qquad$ all x $(p_2(x) - > p_3(x, z, y)))$
$p_1(x) : - p_0(x)$ & $\hat{}p_2(x)$.

Let information resource base (database) contains relations p_0, p_2 and p_3:

$p_0(1)$	$p_2(1)$	$p_3(1, 3, 4)$
$p_0(2)$	$p_2(3)$	$p_3(3, 3, 4)$
$p_0(4)$		$p_3(1, 4, 1)$
		$p_3(1, 5, 4)$
		$p_3(3, 5, 4)$
		$p_3(1, 3, 2)$
		$p_3(3, 3, 2)$

Resulted relations p and p_1 will contain the following tuples:

$p(3)$	$p_1(2)$
	$p_1(4)$

□

Example 2. Let the following classes of objects are defined in the information resource base:

part(pname:string, color:string);
supplier(sname:string, city:string);
supply(sp:supplier, pt:part).

Evaluation of the rule

$$red\_supplier(s) \; : - \; all \; p \; (color \; = \; 'red' \; \& \; part(p/self) \; - > $$
$$supply(s/supplier, p/pt.self))$$

will result in forming of a one-attribute relation *red_supplier* containing suppliers (class supplier objects) which supply each red part.
□

It should be noted, that the traditional approach for the interpretation of the universally quantified formula in the body of a rule is unsuitable for our case. Consider the following rule:

$r_1 : \; p(y) \; : - \; all \; x \; (q_1(x) \; - > \; q_2(x, y))$.

By transformation into PROLOG clauses we get the following rules:

$r_2 : \; p(y) \; : - \; not \; g(y)$.

$r_3 : \; g(y) \; : - \; q_1(x), \; not \; q_2(x, y)$.

It is clearly seen that rules r_1 and r_2 cannot be used for getting the value of y because the variable appears only in the negative predicates. The second observation is that these rules under fixpoint evaluation are unsafe.

Additional problems is connected with recursive *SYNTHESIS* programs. In this case the above mentioned transformation may result in unstratifiable [17] programs.

4 Formal definition of SYNTHESIS sublanguages

Definitions are based on principles of subordination and separation. These principles lead to language definitions of semantic-syntactic type. But here we shall use mixed scheme with elements both of semantic-syntactic and syntactic-semantic type.

The stages of the formal definition are:

- construction of semantic algebras,
- definition of syntactic algebras,
- definition of connection between syntax and semantics.

These stages are repeated for each sublanguage from chosen family.

We also prove the equivalence of different sublanguage semantics being constructed.

The simplified version of META-IV [6] which has clear intuitive meaning will be used as a metalanguage.

4.1 Semantics algebras for SYNTHESIS sublanguages

Semantic algebras are constructed step by step choosing relatively independent constructs which are used in different sublanguages.

Algebra of rules (RULES) While constructing this algebra a partially ordered set of data bases DB with partial order relation $\subseteq$ is used as a basic one.

1. DB – set of data bases

Then a set $RULES$ is built.

2. $RULES = DB \rightarrow DB$ – set of rules

The set $RULES$ is chosen for the carrier of the algebra. Certain operations are defined on this set: $\amalg$ (semantic union), $\bar{db}$ (constant), sfp (special fixed point operation).

Definitions of operations.

3. $\theta_1 \amalg \dots \amalg \theta_n(db) \triangleq \theta_1(db) \cup \dots \cup \theta_n(db)$

4. $\bar{db}(db') \triangleq db$

5. $sfp(\theta)(db) \triangleq lfp(\theta \amalg \bar{db})$

Annotation.

5. lfp – least fixed point operator.

Algebra of formula mappings (FORM) This algebra is built on the following basic sets:

1. $VALUES$ – set of values
2. VAR – set of variables
3. DB – set of data bases

Then new sets are constructed:

4. $STATE = VAR \rightarrow VALUES$ – set of states of variables
5. $FORM = DB \rightarrow B(STATE)$ – set of formula mappings

The set $FORM$ is chosen for the carrier of the algebra. Certain operations are defined on this set: $\triangle$ (join operation), ∇ (union operation), res^x (restricting operation), $proj^x$ (projecting operation), neg (negation). These operations reflect the language facilities for formulae construction.

Let us denote the set of all possible states with variables $\bar{x}$ as $STATE^x$. Complement to state st with variables $\bar{x}$ is defined as follows: $\bar{st} = STATE^x \setminus st$.

States st I st' are *compatible* ($st \approx st'$), if $st \cup st' \in STATE$, i.e., the same variables in st and st' have the same values.

For sets of states ST and ST' their *join* is defined as follows:
$ST \sqcup ST' = \{st \cup st' \mid st \in ST, st' \in ST', st \approx st'\}$.

We will also use the following notations:
$st^x = \{(y,d) \mid (y,d) \in st, y \in \bar{x}\}$,
$st^{\neg x} = \{(y,d) \mid (y,d) \in st, y \notin \bar{x}\}$,
$ST^x = \{st^x \mid st \in ST\}$,
$ST^{\neg x} = \{st^{\neg x} \mid st \in ST\}$.

Definitions of operations.

11. $\triangle(\varphi_1, \varphi_2)(db) \triangleq \varphi_1(db) \sqcup \varphi_2(db)$

12. $\nabla(\varphi_1, \varphi_2)(db) \triangleq \varphi_1(db) \cup \varphi_2(db)$

13. $res^x(\varphi_1, \varphi_2)(db) \triangleq$

$$\{s_2^{\neg x} \mid s_2 \in \varphi_2(db), \forall s_1 \in \varphi_1(db)(s_1 \cup s_2^{\neg x} \in \varphi_2(db))\}$$

14. $proj^x(\varphi)(db) \triangleq (\varphi(db))^{\neg x}$

15. $neg(\varphi)(db) \triangleq \sqcup_{st \in \varphi(db)} \bar{s}\bar{t}$

Algebra of atoms (ATOM) This algebra is built on the following basic sets:

1. $PREDNAME$ – set of predicate names
2. $TERM$ – set of terms

The carrier of the algebra:

3. $ATOM = PREDNAME \times TERM^*$ – set of atoms

This carrier will be used while defining operations on different carriers. This algebra connects the algebra of data, algebra of formula mappings and the algebra of rules.

Multicarrier algebra for deductive languages Algebras considered allow constructing of a multicarrier algebra which reflects the semantics of the deductive sublanguages of $SYNTHESIS$. There are three carriers in the algebra: $RULES$, $FORM$ and $ATOM$. Its operations include the operations of algebras **RULES**, **FORM** and a number of new operations which connect different carriers:

$type : cons : ATOM \times FORM \rightarrow RULES$ – immediate consequence operation

$type : match : ATOM \rightarrow FORM$ – matching operation

An exact definition of the operations depends on properties of data.

So we have the multicarrier algebra (fig. 1):

$$\textbf{BUALG} =< RULES, FORM, ATOM, sfp, \sqcup, \bar{db}, \triangle, \nabla, res^x, proj^x, neg,$$
$$cons, match >$$

In the algebra **BUALG** carriers $RULES$ and $FORM$ are independent to some extent. Specific features of the languages concern primarily sets $VALUES$, $TERM$, VAR. We have not included these carriers in **BUALG**, because it is intended for investigation of deductive facilities of the languages.

We construct specific definitions for $cons$ and $match$ for different sublanguages of $SYNTHESIS$. We give a general definition of these mappings using operations $substit$ (substitution) and $bind$ (binding) which are defined on terms. These operations are parameterized with algebra of data **VALUES**. In order to simplify a view of formulae this parameter is not written explicitly. Their types are as follows:

$type : substit : TERM \times STATE \rightarrow VALUES$

$type : bind : TERM \times VALUES \rightarrow B(STATE)$

Then

$$cons(p(t_1, ..., t_n), form)(db) \triangleq$$
$$\{p(substit(t_1, st), ..., substit(t_n, st)) \mid st \in form(db)\}$$

$$match(p(t_1, ..., t_n))(db) \triangleq$$

$$\bigcup_{p(c_1,...,c_n) \in db} (bind(t_1, c_1) \sqcup ... \sqcup bind(t_n, c_n))$$

Operations $substit$ and $bind$ are specified for different sets $VALUES$ and $TERM$.

[t]

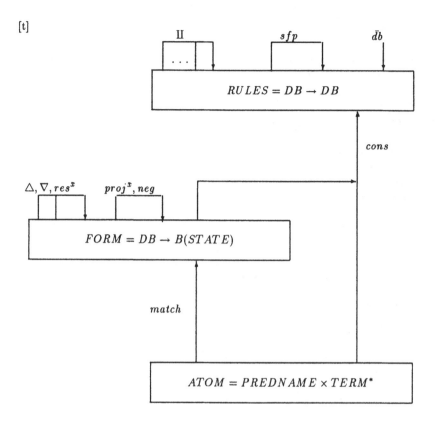

Fig. 1. Multicarrier algebra

4.2 Syntax of considered SYNTHESIS sublanguage

Here we consider rather abstract syntax. In particular semantic sets are used in syntactic rules.

Syntactic rules:

1. $Program = Rule$
2. $Rule = Atom \; : - \; Form \mid Rule^*$
3. $Atom = PREDNAME \; Term^*$
4. $Form = Atom \mid Form \; \& \; Form \mid Form \; "|" \; Form \mid$
   $\qquad all \; \bar{x}(Form \rightarrow Form) \mid ex \; \bar{x}(Form) \mid \; \hat{} Form$
5. $Term = VAR \mid VALUES \mid FUNCNAME \; Term^*$

4.3 Order-independent definition of semantics

Let us define the main semantics of the sublanguage (order-independent with bottom-up least fixed point computation).

Types of semantic functions:

6. $type : sem\text{-}Program : Program \rightarrow RULES$
7. $type : sem\text{-}Rule : Rule \rightarrow RULES$
8. $type : sem\text{-}Form : Form \rightarrow FORM$
9. $type : sem\text{-}Atom : Atom \rightarrow ATOM$
10. $type : sem\text{-}Term : Term \rightarrow TERM$

Here are the definitions of these functions:
11. $sem\text{-}Program(rule) \triangleq$
      $sfp(sem\text{-}Rule(rule))$
12. $sem\text{-}Rule(rule) \triangleq$
      $cases\ rule :$
         $(atom : -form) \rightarrow$
            $cons(sem\text{-}Atom(atom), sem\text{-}Form(form));$
         $(rule_1, ..., rule_n) \rightarrow$
            $sem\text{-}Rule(rule_1)\ \amalg\ ...\ \amalg\ sem\text{-}Rule(rule_n)$
      end
13. $sem\text{-}Form(form) \triangleq$
      $cases\ form :$
         $atom \rightarrow match(sem\text{-}Atom(atom));$
         $form_1\ \&\ form_2 \rightarrow \Delta(sem\text{-}Form(form_1), sem\text{-}Form(form_2));$
         $form_1\ |\ form_2 \rightarrow \nabla(sem\text{-}Form(form_1), sem\text{-}Form(form_2));$
         $all\ \bar{x}\ (form_1 \rightarrow form_2) \rightarrow res^x(sem\text{-}Form(form_1), sem\text{-}Form(form_2));$
         $ex\ \bar{x}\ (form') \rightarrow proj^x(sem\text{-}Form(form'));$
         $\hat{\ }\ form' \rightarrow neg(sem\text{-}Form(form'))$
      end
14. $sem\text{-}Atom(p(t_1, ..., t_n)) \triangleq$
      $(p, (sem\text{-}Term(t_1), ..., sem\text{-}Term(t_n)))$
15. $sem\text{-}Term(term) \triangleq$
      $cases\ term :$
         $var \rightarrow var;$
         $values \rightarrow values;$
         $f(t_1, ..., t_n) \rightarrow (f, (sem\text{-}Term(t_1), ..., sem\text{-}Term(t_n)))$
      end

Specific languages are obtained by rewriting of above mentioned definitions and by redefining *substit* and *bind* operations.

4.4 Sequential (order-dependent) semantics

In the case of sequential semantics (with *sideways information passing*) while evaluating some formula one takes into account the results of the previous evaluation of other formulae. It restricts the amount of the facts extracted from the database and so the evaluation efficiency is increased.

In order to define sequential semantics a particular semantic algebra **BUALG1** is constructed. Denotation of the sets and operations of **BUALG1** coincide with the ones of **BUALG** except that the symbol 1 is added to each denotation of **BUALG1**. Thereat all sets (except *FORM1*) don't change. New formula mappings set is defined as follows:

$FORM1 = B(STATE1) \times B(FACT1) \rightarrow B(STATE1)$.

The first occurrence of $B(STATE1)$ is used for taking into account previously computed states.

The operations depending on *FORM1* should also be changed.

The new (sequential) semantics *sem1-Program: Program* $\rightarrow$ *RULES1* is defined. The theorem of semantic equivalence is proved.

Theorem 1 *For any prog* $\in$ *Prog*
$sem\text{-}Program(prog) = sem1\text{-}Program(prog)$.

Similarly top-down and magic sets semantics definition have been considered too.

4.5 Formalization of object-oriented facilities

The object-oriented facilities formalization is obtained as a natural extension of above mentioned multicarrier algebra. The sequential semantics is built and the equivalence theorem is proved too.

5 Detection of critical query language constructs

The formalization considered was used for the implementation of the *SYNTHESIS* language compiler. It helped to clarify some questions which influenced a number of structural and conceptual decisions. In particular it concerns the special block of compiler – query language pretranslator which provides correctness and efficiency of logic program evaluation. One of the functions of the pretranslator is *programs admissibility checking*. This question is used here as an illustration of application of above mentioned formalization.

The problem is as follows. The method of the program evaluation is based on the bottom-up computation of the least fixed point for immediate consequence operator defined by the program [9]. Generally the immediate consequence operator is not monotonic on non-Horn databases. For example, consider the following rule :

$p(y) \; : - \; (all \; x \; (p(x) \; - > \; b_1(x,y)) \; | \; b_2(y)$
and the database

$b_1(1,2)$ $b_2(1)$
$b_1(2,2)$
$b_1(1,3)$

At the first step of the *lfp-iteration* we get the fact $p(1)$; at the second one the new facts $p(2)$ and $p(3)$ are generated. However, at the third step the new facts which have been generated at the second one are refuted.

Non-monotonicity of the immediate consequence operator may influence the correctness of computation. We will call the language constructs which can violate the monotonicy of this operator as critical constructs. For providing the computational correctness one must consider each construct and conclude whether it is critical or not. Then we can use special policy for treating such constructs. In particular, under *stratification approach* (which is adopted in *SYNTHESIS*) we have to evaluate critical constructs of a rule body *completely* before evaluation the rule head. If it is possible, the program is called *admissible*. Using formula mapping of our formalization we can prove the following theorem.

Theorem 2 *A construct of SYNTHESIS language is critical iff corresponding formula mapping is nonmonotonic.*

Thus we have uniform approach for critical constructs detecting. This theorem is a basis of the programs admissibility checker. The correctness of implementation can be proved using our multilevel formalization of the language.

6 Conclusion

An approach to multilevel formal definition of deductive query languages based on composition development method have been used. This approach and the results obtained may be characterized in the following way:

- High level definitions are the most abstract and reflect the general functional properties of the language. Lower levels definitions deal with specific features of the language. They are used for more detailed investigation of it and for efficient implementation. Correspondence criteria for different language representations are stated and the equivalence of the representations with respect to correspondence criteria is proved.
- A multicarrier algebra is used for language semantics definitions. Such representation allows to extract and investigate particular subalgebras which reflect specific properties of the language.
- Syntax is described with system of rules which define syntactic domains of the language and a special formalism is used to connect syntax and semantics of the language.
- While extending and modifying the language the high level algebras are changed only a little. Specific language features are located in data algebras.

The above mentioned approach was successfully used for the implementation of the *SYNTHESIS* language compiler.

The proposed approach allows to formalize more general languages in a natural way by extending representations previously constructed. Based on the results obtained we may conclude that this approach can be taken as a methodological basis for formalization and implementation of powerful deductive query languages.

References

1. Abiteboul S. Towards a deductive object-oriented database language. DOOD'89, 1989, p. 419-438.

2. Abrial J.R. A formal approach to large software construction. In Mathematics of program construction, Proceedings of the International Conference, LNCS 375, Springer-Verlag, 1989.
3. Atkinson M., et.al. The object-oriented database system manifesto. DOOD'89, 1989, p. 40-57.
4. Basarab N.A., Lisovsky M.S., Gubsky B.V. An interactive information system for table data structures processing. Control automation and mechanization journal, N. 2, 1986, p. 33-36. (In Russian)
5. Basarab I.A., Nikitchenko N.S., Red'ko V.N. Composition databases. Kiev, Lybid' Publ, 1992, p. 192. (In Russian)
6. Bjorner D., Jones C.B., editors. Formal Specification and Software Development. Prentice-Hall International, 1982, p. 501.
7. Borgida A., Mertikas M., Schmidt J.W., Wetzel I. Specification and refinement of databases and transactions. DAIDA Deliverable, ESPRIT 892, Universitaet Hamburg, Germany, 1990, p. 24.
8. Ceitlin G.E., Yuschenko E.L. Multilevel synthesis of structured programs. Kibernetika journal, N. 5, 1982, p. 11-21. (In Russian)
9. Ceri S., Gottlob G., Tanca L. Logic programming and databases. Springer Verlag, 1990, p. 284.
10. Glushkov V.M. Automata theory and formal transformation of microprograms. Kibernetika journal, N. 5, 1965, p. 1-10. (In Russian)
11. Glushkov V.M., Kapitonova Y.V., Letichevskiy A.A. On application of formalized technical jobs method for design of programs for data structures processing. Programmirovanie journal, N. 6, 1975, p. 31-44. (In Russian)
12. Kalinichenko L.A. An Anatomy of Information Resource Semantic Abstraction. ACM SIGMOD Record, vol. 20, N. 4, 1991, p. 21-24.
13. Kalinichenko L.A. The interoperable environment of heterogeneous information resources: a generalization perspective. Proc. of the First International Workshop on Interoperability in Multidatabase System, April 1991, Kyoto, p. 196 - 199.
14. Kalinichenko L.A. SYNTHESIS: a language for description, design and programming of interoperable information resource environment. Technical Report. Institute of Problems of Informatics of the Russian Academy of Sciences, September 1991, p. 101. (In Russian)
15. Kalinichenko L.A. Methods and tools for heterogeneous database integration. Moscow, Science Publ., 1983, p. 423. (In Russian)
16. Kalinichenko L.A., Ryvkin V.M., Chaban I.A. Main features of data manipulation language in SISYPHUS - the system for integrated storage of information. Programmirovanie journal, Moscow, N. 6, 1975. (In Russian)
17. Kalinichenko L., Zadorozhny V. A generalized information resource query language and basic query evaluation technique. Proc. of the Second Int. Conf. on DOOD, Munich, December 1991, LNCS 566, p. 546-566.
18. Nikitchenko N. Composition semantics of programming languages. Programmirovanie journal, N. 6, 1982, p. 9-18. (In Russian)
19. Nikitchenko N., Zadorozhny V. An algebraic approach to deductive databases query languages formalization. Programmirovanie journal, N. 6, 1992, p. 29-47. (In Russian)
20. Red'ko V.N. Composition of programs and composition programming. Programmirovanie journal, N. 5, 1978, p. 3-24. (In Russian)
21. Red'ko V.N. Fundamentals of composition programming. Programmirovanie journal, N. 3, 1979, p. 3-13. (In Russian)
22. Red'ko V. Semantics structures of programs. Programmirovanie journal, N. 1, 1981, p. 3-19. (In Russian)

23. Red'ko V.N., Nikitchenko N.S. Composition aspects of programmology. Kibernetika journal, part 1, N. 5, 1987, p. 49-56, part 2, N. 1, 1988, p. 28-34. (In Russian)
24. Sheth A., Larson J. Federated database systems for managing distributed, heterogeneous, and autonomous databases. ACM Computing Surveys, v. 22, N. 3, 1990, p. 183-236.
25. Spivey J.M. The Z Notation. A reference manual. Prentice-Hall, 1989, p. 155.
26. Tiugu E.H. Conceptual programming. Moscow, Science Publ, 1984, p. 256. (In Russian)
27. Velbitskiy I.V. Technology of programming. Kiev, Tehnika Publ., 1989, p. 279. (In Russian)
28. Volohov V.N., Voronov S.V. DEFIPS: an automated system for language processors design. Control systems and machins journal, N. 3, 1984, p. 69-73. (In Russian)

Verification Tools in the Development
of Provably Correct Compilers

M. R. K. Krishna Rao
P. K. Pandya
R. K. Shyamasundar

Computer Science Group
Tata Institute of Fundamental Research
Homi Bhabha Road, Colaba
BOMBAY 400 005, INDIA
e-mail: {krishna, pandya, shyam}@tifrvax.bitnet

Abstract. The paper presents a practical verification tool that helps in the development of provably correct compilers. The tool is based on the approach of proving termination of PROLOG-like programs using term-rewriting techniques and a technique of testing whether a given PROLOG program can be soundly executed on PROLOG interpreters without the Occur-check test. The tool has been built on top of the theorem prover, RRL (Rewrite Rule Laboratory). The tool is effective for compilers developed using Hoare's refinement algebra approach. The utility of the tool is illustrated through a case study on correctness of a prototype compiler of the **ProCoS** level 0 language PL_0.

1 Introduction

The problem of developing provably correct compilers has been of interest to researchers for many years. It is especially important to use such compilers in safety critical applications, where errors in execution of the program can be disastrous or expensive. Hoare [12] has recently proposed an approach for developing provably correct compilers based on refinement algebra and Bowen *et al* [5] have applied such an approach for the development of prototype compilers in PROLOG. In this paper, we present a practical verification tool for the analysis of logic programs and illustrate its utility in the development of provably correct compilers.

A brief look into the refinement algebra approach will reflect the need and importance of such tools in the design of correct compilers. In Hoare's approach [12], a compiling specification is designed to describe how each construct of the source language is translated into a sequence of object code instructions. A proof that the compiling specification is correct must show that the behavior (or meaning) of the object code is *at least as good as* that of the source program. For this purpose, the meaning of the object code can be defined by an interpreter written in the source language itself so that a source program and its object code can be compared.

Compiling specification consists of a set of theorems which specify the valid object code for each of the constructs of the source language. Hoare [12] shows that such theorems can be proved correct using the algebraic laws governing the source language and the interpreter for the machine programs. Each theorem is in the form of a Horn clause and describes the compilation of a composite program in terms of the compilation of its components. These Horn clauses can be translated into a logic program (say, PROLOG) to get a prototype compiler as demonstrated in [5].

Proving correctness of this prototype compiler amounts to showing that the object code generated by the compiler from a given source program satisfies the compiling specification and that compiler generates object code for every valid source program. Such a correctness proof must show:

1. The compiler is a *refinement* [12] of the compiling specification; this can be done easily. (Compiler is *sound* declaraively).
2. The compiler always terminates for any valid source program.
3. The compiler is sound with respect to the compiling specification in spite of the various non-declarative features of PROLOG such as cut (!) and also the idiosyncracies of the PROLOG interpreters such as omission of occur-check test in the unification algorithm. (Compiler is *sound* procedurally).

In this paper, we are concerned with the development of tools for checking 2 and 3 above. To be more specific, we describe an implementation of a verification system that helps in proving termination of PROLOG programs in a semi-automatic (almost automatic) fashion and proving that a PROLOG program can be soundly executed on an interpreter without occur-check test in an *automatic* fashion. The tool is based on the results of Krishna Rao, Kapur and Shyamasundar [17] and Krishna Rao [16]. The approach proposed in [17] is based on reducing the termination problem of logic programs to the termination problem of term rewriting systems. Such a reduction or transformation makes it possible to use the various termination tools available in the rewriting literature for proving termination of logic programs. We implement the transformation procedure proposed in [17] as a front end to the rewrite rule laboratory RRL [15], where tools for proving termination of term rewriting systems are available. Using this tool, we have successfully proved the correctness of a prototype compiler for **ProCoS** level 0 language PL_0. It may be noted that termination of this compiler cannot be proved using the methods of [25, 21, 22]. It is hoped that the tool will be of help in the development of provably correct compilers in logic programming languages (sequential or parallel).

Even though the main thrust of the paper is applicability of the above tool in the development of provably correct compilers, the tool has many other applications. For example, in the context of developing compilers through partial evaluation as proposed in Jones [14], termination is an important issue and the above tool can be used for proving termination.

Rest of the paper is organized as follows. Next section provides an overview of the refinement algebra approach. Section 3 briefly describes various results on termination of logic programs and explains in detail the termination method based on which, the tool is built. Section 4 explain the problem of occur-check and section 5 describes termination techniques of rewriting. Section 6 describes the implementation of the tool, and explains various modules in the tool and their functionality. Section 7 gives a detailed case study on correctness proof for **ProCoS** PL_0 compiler and section 8 concludes the paper with a discussion.

2 An overview of Refinement Algebra Approach

Hoare [12] has proposed the use of *refinement algebra* in proving correctness of compiling specifications. In this method, the compiling specification takes the form of a set of Horn Clauses, which together describe a **correct-compilation** predicate $\mathcal{C}$. Formula (atom) $\mathcal{C}(p, m, \Psi)$ states that the machine program m is a semantically acceptable translation of the source program p. Here, Ψ is the symbol table mapping a free variable of p to a location in machine memory. Each clause in the specification describes one way of compiling a composite program in terms of compilation of its components. For example,

$$\mathcal{C}(p; q,\ m_1 : m_2,\ \Psi) \quad \Leftarrow \quad \mathcal{C}(p, m_1, \Psi) \wedge \mathcal{C}(q, m_2, \Psi)$$
$$\mathcal{C}(skip, \langle\rangle, \Psi)$$

(Here, we use $(m_1 : m_2)$ to represent a machine program which executes m_1 first and on its completion starts executing m_2. $\langle\rangle$ denotes an empty program which terminates immediately). Each clause is proved correct w.r.t. the definition of $\mathcal{C}$ using refinement algebra.

Refinement algebra for the source programming language PL consists of a set of algebraic laws which allow us to establish relationships of the form $p \sqsubseteq q$. Intuitively, $p \sqsubseteq q$ states that the program q is *at least as good as* the program p in all circumstances (for example, it terminates more often and it is more deterministic) e.g. $x := 1;\ x : = 2;\ P \sqsubseteq x : = 2;\ P$. The behavior of the machine programs is formalized by giving an interpreter I for the machine language. The interpreter I is itself a program of PL. The compiling specification $\mathcal{C}(p, m, \Psi)$ is *defined* to be correct if $p \sqsubseteq_{\Psi} I(m)$; i.e. the interpretation of machine code m has same or better effect as source program p with appropriate translation from the data space of target code to that of the source program (based on Ψ). *Each clause in the compiling specification is proved correct w.r.t. the above definition.* Such a proof can be given entirely through the refinement algebra of PL. The proof of each clause is independent of the other clauses. The advantage of this modularity is that the proof of correctness of a large compiling specification becomes manageable, and that a compiling specification can be easily extended with new clauses. We refer the reader to [12, 13, 5] for more details of the refinement algebra approach.

Bowen *et al* have developed a prototype compiler using this approach for the **ProCoS** PL_0 language [5, 11]. Here, the set of Horn clauses constituting the compiling specification is directly translated into a PROLOG program. Such a program can be used to compile a source program p by executing a query $\leftarrow \mathcal{C}(p, M, \Psi_0)$, where p is a source program and Ψ_0 is the initial symbol table[1] mapping global variables of p to their locations. This query will return the object code of p as binding for variable M.

3 Termination of Logic Programs

Recently, termination analysis of logic programs has attracted attention of many and a good number of results are reported in the literature (see [1, 24] for a brief survey). In general, termination of a recursive program can be proved by showing that some arguments of the recursive procedure decrease (under a well-founded ordering) after every invocation (or call) of it. That is, to show that the arguments of outer call are greater than the arguments of the inner call. Presence of local variables (variable occurring in the body but not occurring in the head of a clause) poses a few problems to this general approach (see [21, 17] for a discussion on local variables). Many approaches are proposed to tackle the presence of local variables. The results proposed so far on termination of logic programs can be broadly classified into two categories.

1. Many characterizations of termination of logic programs are proposed in [26, 4, 1, 24] and others. They give necessary and sufficient conditions for termination. Since logic programming has the full power of Turing machine, these conditions in general are undecidable.
2. Some efforts towards developing mechanizable techniques for proving termination of logic programs are reported in [25, 21, 17, 22, 10] and others. For the same reasons as stated above, these techniques will cater to proper sub-classes of Horn clause programs.

The methods proposed in [25, 21, 22] use linear predicate inequalities and their usefulness is demonstrated through a good number of examples. However, these methods have requirements like, *existence of admissible solution graphs* [21] and *uniqueness* property [25] of clauses. For example, multiplication program (Example 1 in the following subsection) and the **ProCoS** PL_0 compiler do not satisfy these conditions. Krishna Rao, Kapur and Shyamasundar [17] take a different approach and propose to transform given logic program into a term rewriting system and prove termination of rewriting system using many available techniques and tools (such as RRL and REVE [15, 18]) reported in the rewriting literature. This approach does not have restrictions like the ones mentioned above and looks promising (see [17] for a comparison of the two approaches).

In the rest of the section, we introduce the notion of well-modedness and describe the main steps of the method described in [17] for proving termination.

---

[1] Ψ_0 is usually empty. However in some languages there are some predefined variables; e.g. *input* and *output* files in pascal, which must be allocated some predetermined set of locations.

3.1 Well-moded logic programs

A *mode* m of an n-ary predicate p is a function from $\{1, \cdots, n\}$ to the set $\{in,\ out\}$. The set of input positions of p is $\{i \mid m(i) = in\}$ (output positions are defined similarly). Let $c\ :\ A \leftarrow B_1, \cdots, B_k$ be a clause and let Y be a variable in the head A, then A is a *producer* of Y if Y occurs in an input position of A, otherwise A is a *consumer* of Y. Let X be a variable in B_i such that A is not a producer of X, then B_i is a *consumer* of X if X occurs in an input position of B_i, otherwise B_i is a producer of X. The producer-consumer relation of the above clause c is a relation on the atoms in its body and is defined as $\{\ (B_i,\ B_j)\ \mid\ B_i$ a producer and B_j is a consumer of some variable X in $c\ \}$.

A clause c is *well-moded* if (a) its producer-consumer relation is *acyclic* and (b) every variable in c has a producer. A program P is *well-moded* if every clause in it is well-moded. A well-moded query is a well-moded clause without head.

A selection rule [19] (or computation rule) gives the next literal to be resolved among the literals (subgoals) in the current goal. This notion of selection rule can be extended for a clause, as a rule which gives an evaluation order among the literals in the body of the clause [17, 16]. It can be captured by a partial order (if $l_i < l_j$ in the partial order, it means that l_i would be selected before l_j is selected). A selection rule S is *implied* by the moding information of a well-moded program if *for each clause in the program, the evaluation order given by S is an extension of the producer-consumer relation of that clause.*

Example 1: Consider the following multiplication program

```
moding: add (in, in, out)  and  mult (in, in, out)

add(0, Y, Y).
add(s(X), Y, s(Z)) :- add(X, Y, Z).
mult(0, Y, 0).
mult(s(X), Y, Z) :- mult(X, Y, Z1), add(Z1, Y, Z).
```

The producer-consumer relation of all clauses (except the last) is empty. For the last clause, it is $\{\ \langle mult(X, Y, Z1),\ add(Z1, Y, Z)\rangle),\ \}$. It is easy to see that for every clause, (i) the producer-consumer relation is acyclic and (ii) all the variables in it are having at least one producer. So this program is well-moded.

It is easy to see that PROLOG's left-to-right evaluation order on the atoms in body of each clause is a linear extension of its producer-consumer relation. Hence, PROLOG's left-to-right selection rule is implied by the moding information. □

3.2 Method of Proving Termination

The transformational method proposed in [17] contains the following steps:

1. Transforming given logic program into a term rewriting system (TRS).

2. Proving termination of the resulting term rewriting system.

The transformation is based on the idea of eliminating local variables by introducing Skolem functions. For each n-ary predicate p having a moding with k output positions, we introduce k new function symbols $p^1, \ldots, p^k$, each of arity $n - k$ (i.e., number of input positions). These k-function symbols correspond to the k output positions of the predicate p. If the predicate p has no output positions, we introduce a n-ary function symbol p^0. We construct a set of rewrite rules to compute these new functions. In the following, we informally explain the transformation using some examples before giving its formal description.

Example 2: From the multiplication program along with the moding information given above, we obtain the following rewrite rules:

1. Since the output of predicate add for inputs 0 and Y is Y, we get $\mathbf{add}^1(\mathbf{0}, \mathbf{Y}) \to \mathbf{Y}$.

2. The output of mult for inputs 0 and Y is 0. We get $\mathbf{mult}^1(\mathbf{0}, \mathbf{Y}) \to \mathbf{0}$.

3. From the second clause, the output of add for inputs $s(X)$ and Y is $s(Z)$, where Z is the output of add for the inputs X and Y. We get $\mathbf{add}^1(\mathbf{s}(\mathbf{X}), \mathbf{Y}) \to \mathbf{s}(\mathbf{add}^1(\mathbf{X}, \mathbf{Y}))$.

4. From the last clause, the output of mult for inputs $s(X)$ and Y is Z, where Z is the output of add for the inputs $Z1$ and Y, where $Z1$ is the output of mult for inputs X and Y. So we get $mult^1(s(X), Y) \to add^1(Z1, Y)$, where $Z1 = mult^1(X, Y)$. The resulting rule is $\mathbf{mult}^1(\mathbf{s}(\mathbf{X}), \mathbf{Y}) \to \mathbf{add}^1(\mathbf{mult}^1(\mathbf{X}, \mathbf{Y}), \mathbf{Y})$. $\square$

When a nonvariable term appears in an output position of a body literal, we may need to introduce an *inverse function* as illustrated in the following example [17].

Example 3: Consider the following clause:

```
moding: a (in, out);  b (in, out)  and  c (in, out)

a(X, Y) :-  b(X, f(Z)), c(Z, Y)
```

The output of predicate a for input X is Y, where Y is the output of predicate c for input Z. Now, one would have to answer the question: *What is the value of the input argument of predicate c (i.e., Z) ?*. One can answer this question by saying that Z is equal to $f^{-1}(f(Z))$, where $f(Z)$ is output of b for input X. Therefore, we get $\mathbf{a}^1(\mathbf{X}) \to \mathbf{c}^1(\mathbf{f}^{-1}(\mathbf{b}^1(\mathbf{X})))$. And to reduce $f^{-1}(f(Z))$ to Z, a rewrite rule $\mathbf{f}^{-1}(\mathbf{f}(\mathbf{X})) \to \mathbf{X}$ is added. $\square$

In the above two examples, all the variables occurring in output positions in the body are also occurring either in output positions of the head or in input positions of some other literal in the body (ie., they have at least one consumer). When there are some variables occurring only in output positions of a literal in the body, we need to *add additional rewrite rules* as illustrated in [17] for capturing so called unnecessary computations [17] in the logic program. The set $Unsry$ in the following algorithm captures these unnecessary computations (see [17] for more details).

3.3 Formal description of the transformation

In this subsection, we give the formal description of the transformation procedure. Given a well-moded logic program and moding information, the transformation always *terminates* producing a term rewriting system whose termination implies the termination of the given logic program. However, nontermination of the derived term rewriting system does not imply nontermination of the logic program. To be precise, we have proved the following theorem in [17].

Theorem 1: *A well-moded logic program terminates for all well-moded queries under any selection rule implied by the moding information of the predicates, if the derived term rewriting system terminates.*

The main algorithm is given below. Some of the issues related to *inverse-functions* and *built-ins* will be discussed while describing the implementation aspects.

Though input and output positions of a predicate can mix together in all possible ways, for notational convenience, we write all input positions first, followed by all output positions (this is only for notational convenience in describing the algorithm and this is not assumed in the implementation). We write $p(t_{i_1}, \ldots, t_{i_j}, \; t_{o_1}, \ldots, t_{o_k})$ to denote an atom $p(\cdots)$ containing the terms $t_{i_1}, \ldots, t_{i_j}$ in input positions and $t_{o_1}, \ldots, t_{o_k}$ in output positions. For each clause c, the transformation procedure computes the following:

1. $Prod(X) = \{ \; \langle p^l(t_{i_1}, \ldots, t_{i_j}), \; t_{o_l} \rangle \mid X \in Var(t_{o_l}), X \notin Var(\{t_{i_1}, \ldots, t_{i_j}\})$
   and $p(t_{i_1}, \ldots, t_{i_j}, \; t_{o_1}, \ldots, t_{o_k})$ is an atom in the body $\}$ is the set of producers of local variable X.
2. $Consvar = \{X \in Var(c) - in(head) \mid X \in out(head)$ or X occurs in an input position of an atom in the body $\}$ is the set of variables consumed at least once.
3. $Unsry = \{ \; p^l(t_{i_1}, \ldots, t_{i_j}) \mid Var(t_{o_l}) \cap Consvar = \phi \; \} \cup \{ \; q^0(s_{i_1}, \ldots, s_{i_k}) \mid$ predicate q does not have output positions $\}$, where $p(\cdots)$ and $q(\cdots)$ are atoms in the body.

```
algorithm TRANSFORM (P : in; R_P : out);
begin
  R_P := φ;              {* R_P contains rewrite rules *}
  for each clause c: a(t_{i_1}, ···, t_{i_k}, t_{o_1}, ···, t_{o_{k'}}) ← B_1, ... B_n  ∈ P do
    begin  INhead := Var({t_{i_1}, ···, t_{i_k}})
    Compute Consvar and Unsry;
    Compute Prod(X) for every variable in Var(c) − INhead;
    for j := 1 to k' do
        begin T := {t_{o_j}};     { * T is a set of terms *}
              ELIMINATE-LOCAL-VARIABLES(T);
              R_P := R_P ∪ { a^j(t_{i_1}, ···, t_{i_k}) → t | t ∈ T }
        end;
    {* Following code derives rewrite rules corresponding to unnecessary computations. *}
    T := Unsry;
    ELIMINATE-LOCAL-VARIABLES(T);
    R_P := R_P ∪ { a^{k'}(t_{i_1}, ···, t_{i_k}) → $(t) | t ∈ T }
    end
end TRANSFORM.
```

procedure ELIMINATE-LOCAL-VARIABLES(T)
{* *This procedure goes on replacing the* local *variables in the set of terms T by the* terms
*corresponding to their producers as long as there are local varibles. Since producer-consumer
relation of every well-moded clause is acyclic, this procedure is guaranteed to terminate.* *}
begin $V := Var(T) - INhead$;
  while $V \neq \phi$ **do**
   begin
    for each $X \in V$ **do**
     begin $T' := \phi$;
      for each $\langle p^l(\cdots), t \rangle \in Prod(X)$ **do**
       if $t = X$ **then** $T' := T' \cup T.\{X/p^l(\cdots)\}$ {* Replace local var X by its producer-term. *}
       else if $t = f(X)$ **then**
         begin
          $T' := T' \cup T.\{ X/f^{-1}(p^l(\cdots)) \}$;   {* Introduce inverse functions *}
          $R_P := R_P \cup \{ f^{-1}(f(X)) \rightarrow X \}$
         end;
    $T := T'$
    end;
   $V := Var(T) - INhead$
  end;
end ELIMINATE-LOCAL-VARIABLES;

Example 4: Let us illustrate the transformation with the following clause

```
Modings: ce (in, in, out, out, in, in); mt (in, in, out, out);
         ap (in, in, out)

ce(E1 <= E2, S, F, M, P, cons(Loc, 0)) :-
         ce(E1 < E2, S, L1, M1, P, cons(Loc, 0)),
         mt(eqc(0), L1, F, M2),
         ap(M1, M2, M).
```

The predicate ce has two output positions (with variables F and M in those positions in
head). The head ce(E1 <= E2, S, F, M, P, cons(Loc, 0)) has input terms E1 <= E2, S, P
and cons(Loc, 0), hence left-hand-sides of the rewrite rules will be $ce^1(E1 <= E2, S, P, cons(Loc, O))$
and $ce^2(E1 <= E2, S, P, cons(Loc, O))$. To construct right-hand-side term of first rule, algorithm TRANSFORM calls ELIMINATE-LOCAL-VARIABLES with argument $T = \{F\}$. Various
iterations of the while loop in ELIMINATE-LOCAL-VARIABLES are shown below.
$$T = \{F\}$$
Ite. 1   *Replace local variable F by the term corresponding to its producer.*
$$T = \{ mt^1(eqc(0), L1) \}$$
Ite. 2   *Replace local variable L1 by the term corresponding to its producer.*
$$T = \{ mt^1(eqc(0), ce^1(E1 < E2, S, P, cons(Loc, O))) \}$$
Since there are no local variables in T after 2nd iteration, ELIMINATE-LOCAL-VARIABLES
terminates returning this T to TRANSFORM, which produces the following rewrite rule.

$$ce^1(E1 <= E2, S, P, cons(Loc, O)) \rightarrow mt^1(eqc(0), ce^1(E1 < E2, S, P, cons(Loc, O)))$$

Similarly, second rewrite rule can be constructed (it takes 3 iterations).   □

4 Occur-check Problem

The occur-check problem arises from the differences between the formal definition of the unification and its implementations in most of the PROLOG interpreters. A variable X unifies with any term t, provided X does not occur in t. The correct unification algorithm checks for occurrence of the variable in the term with which it is being unified. For efficiency reasons, most of the unification procedures implemented in PROLOG interpreters do not check this condition and unify terms $f(X, g(X))$ and $f(Y, Y)$. Due to this discrepancy,

1. Unsound answers are given by the PROLOG interpreters. For example, most of the PROLOG interpreters (without occur-check test) give answer 'yes' to the query $\leftarrow$ $append([\,], [a|L], L)$ with the usual append program, in contradiction with its declarative semantics.
2. Unification without occur-check test will loop, while trying to unify the following two terms $f(X, g(X), Y, g(Y), X, Y)$ and $f(Z, Z, W, W, S, S)$, which are obviously not unifiable [7].

Two different approaches have been proposed in the literature for handling the problem of occur-check. (1) To find the set of points in the execution of the program at which occur-check test has to performed (to avoid unsound behavior) dynamically [3] or statically [20, 23] and insert code for occur-check at those points. This involves complicated global/local analysis. (2) To give sufficient conditions on the programs and queries, so that occur-check test can be omitted without getting unsound behavior [6, 7, 2, 16]. Such programs are called NSTO (not subjected to occur-check) [7] (or *occur-check free* [2]) programs.

We have implemented the sufficient condition proposed in [16, 2]. The main result of [16] is the following:

A well-moded logic program is *occur-check free* if no variable occurs more than once in the output terms of head of each clause.

This condition can be checked in linear time and is satisfied by a large class of programs. For a lucid discussion on various aspects of occur-check, the reader is refered to [2].

5 Termination of rewrite systems

The termination of term rewriting systems in general is undecidable. However, a wide variety of heuristics and techniques have been proposed for proving termination of classes of term rewriting systems (for a survey of such techniques, see [8]). The key idea is to show that terms decrease under a well-founded ordering after each rewriting step. Many well-founded orderings discussed in [8] exploit the syntactic structure of terms. Simplification orderings [8] such as *recursive path ordering*, and *lexicographic path ordering* are good examples of such orderings and are implemented in theorem provers based on rewriting paradigms such as RRL [15], REVE [18] etc. For proving termination of a rewrite system using a simplification ordering, *it is enough to show that left-hand-side of every rewrite rule is greater than the right-hand-side under that ordering*. In the following, we explain the recursive path ordering and its use.

5.1 Recursive path ordering

Termination of **ProCoS** compiler is proved using recursive path ordering (with status for function symbols). Before giving the definition of recursive path ordering (with status), we describe the two important orderings (called lexicographic and multiset orderings) induced by a given ordering.

Let $\succ$ be an order on set S. The *lexicographic ordering* $\succ^*$ on set of the sequences (or tuples) of elements of S induced by $\succ$ is defined (recursively) as follows.

$(s_1, s_2, \cdots, s_m) \succ^* (t_1, t_2, \cdots, t_n)$ if
$\quad (i) \quad m > n = 0 \quad$ or
$\quad (ii) \quad s_1 \succ t_1 \quad$ or
$\quad (iii) \quad s_1 = t_1$ and $(s_2, \cdots, s_m) \succ^* (t_2, \cdots, t_n)$

Let $>$ be an order on set S. This order induces an ordering $\gg$ on set of finite *multisets* (or bags) of S as follows (here, M_1 and M_2 are two multisets of S):

$$M_1 \gg M_2 \Leftrightarrow M_1 \neq M_2 \text{ and } (\forall y \in M_2 - M_1)(\exists x \in M_1 - M_2) \, x > y$$

Now we are in a position to define the recursive path ordering with status. We allow an operator to have one of the following three statuses: multiset, lexicographic-left-to-right (LR) and lexicographic-right-to-left (RL). Multiset status is taken as default status of an operator if its status is not specified.

Definition 1: Let $>$ be a precedence relation on set $\mathcal{F}$ of function symbols. The *recursive path ordering* $>_{rpos}$ on the set $T(\mathcal{F})$ of terms over $\mathcal{F}$ is defined recursively as follows:
$$s = f(s_1, \ldots, s_m) >_{rpos} g(t_1, \ldots, t_n) = t \quad \text{ if}$$

$(a) \quad s_i \geq_{rpos} t$ for some $i = 1, \ldots, m,$ or
$(b) \quad f > g$ and $s >_{rpos} t_j$ for all $j = 1, \ldots, n,$ or
$(c) \quad f \approx g,$ f, g have *multiset* status and $\{s_1, \ldots, s_m\} \gg_{rpos} \{t_1, \ldots, t_n\},$ or
$(d) \quad f \approx g,$ $s >_{rpos} t_j$ for all $j = 1, \ldots, n$ and
$\quad (i) \quad f$ and g have LR status and $(s_1, \ldots, s_m) >^*_{rpos} (t_1, \ldots, t_n) \quad$ or
$\quad (ii) \quad f$ and g have RL status and $(s_m, s_{m-1}, \ldots, s_1) >^*_{rpos} (t_n, t_{n-1}, \ldots, t_1)$

Example 5: We can prove the termination of the following rewriting system using recursive path ordering with the precedence relation $s_1 > c$ and multiset status for both the operators.

$s_1(nil, Y) \rightarrow nil$
$s_1(c(X, Xs), Y) \rightarrow c(X, s_1(Xs, Y))$
$s_1(c(X, Xs), Y) \rightarrow s_1(Xs, Y)$

First rule is simple (follows from clause (a) of the definition of RPOS).
Let us prove $s_1(c(X, Xs), Y) >_{rpos} c(X, s_1(Xs, Y))$ for the second rule. Here $s_1 > c$, so (by clause b) we have to prove

(1) $s_1(c(X, Xs), Y) >_{rpos} X$, which is again simple and
(2) $s_1(c(X, Xs), Y) >_{rpos} s_1(Xs, Y)$.

Now to prove (2) we have to show $\{c(X, Xs), Y\} \gg_{rpos} \{Xs, Y\}$ (by clause c). This can be easily verified since $c(X, Xs) >_{rpos} Xs$ (by clause a). The proof for the third rule can be given on similar lines. $\qquad\qquad\square$

6 Implementation

In this section, we describe some salient features of our implementation. As mentioned earlier, the transformation procedure and occur-check test are implemented as front-ends to RRL. We explain various modules in our tool and their interconnections and interactions with user. The following block diagram gives the module structure of the tool.

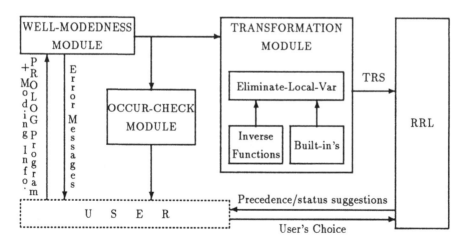

Block-diagram of the modules in the System.

Rewrite Rule Laboratory: RRL

Rewrite Rule Laboratory (RRL) is a theorem proving environment for experimenting with automated reasoning algorithms for equational logic based rewriting techniques as well as for developing new reasoning algorithms [15]. Among the facilities it provides at present are:

1. Automatically proving theorems in first-order predicate calculus with equality.
2. Checking consistency and completeness of equational specifications.
3. Proving theorems using *inductionless-induction*.
4. Generating decision procedures for first-order equational theories using completion (like Knuth-Bendix) procedures. It uses recursive path ordering described above for ensuring termination.

Well-modedness Module

This module checks well-modedness of the given program, applying the following steps on each clause:

1.1 A producer-consumer graph with atoms in the body as nodes is constructed.
1.2 Producer-consumer graph is checked for acyclicity (using depth-first-search).
1.3 If it is not acyclic, a warning is given saying that a particular clause is not well-moded.
2.1 Set of producers of each variable in the clause is computed.
2.2 It is checked whether every variable has at least one producer.
2.3 If any variable has no producer, a warning is given saying that a particular variable has no producer.

Occur-check Module

This module takes well-moded PROLOG programs and checks whether they can be executed soundly on PROLOG interpreters without occur-check test. This module essentially checks whether any variable occurs more than once in output terms of head of any clause. If no variable occurs more than once in output terms of heads, the program is declared not subjected to occur-check (NSTO). If there is a variable occurring more than once in output terms of some head, this module notifies the user of the offending variable and the clause.

Transformation Module

This is the most important module of the system. This module essentially implements the transformation procedure described in the previous section. Foe each clause, it computes the sets *Unsry* and *Consvar* (as defined in the formal transformation given earlier) and the set of producers of each local variable.[2] The major submodule

---

[2] Actually, 'well-modedness' module checks every clause for well-modedness and passes the set of producers of each variable to the 'transformation' module. So there is no repetition of work.

here is 'eliminate-local-variable' which implements the formal procedure described earlier. In addition to this, there are two more modules; one for generating inverse functions and other for *built-ins*. Some of the subtle aspects not explained earlier are detailed below.

Inverse functions

As shown in Example 3, inverse functions are needed when a non-variable term occurs in an output position of an atom in the body. The generation of appropriate inverse functions is done as follows:

1. Tree representation of the nonvariable output term is built.
2. For each variable in this term (and consumed by other atoms in the clause), set of paths from root to the occurrences of that variable in the above tree are identified.
3. Each path is traversed upwards (from leaf to root), collecting suitable inverse function symbols, which will be used in constructing the right-hand-sides of the rewrite rules as illustrated in the following example.

Example 6: Consider the following clause:

```
moding: a (in, out);  b (in, in, out);  c (in, out)

a(X, Y) :- b(X, 0, f(X, g(h(0, Z), X), X, 1)), c(Z, Y).
```

A nonvariable term `f(X, g(h(0, Z), X), X, 1)` is occurring in the output position of `b` and the local variable `Z` occurring in this term is consumed by the atom `c(Z, Y)`. Function symbols `f`, `g` and `h` occur in the path from the root to the variable Z and the appropriate inverse functions are collected as follows:

Since `Z` is second argument of `h`, inverse function $h2^{-1}$ is collected (and a rewrite rule $h2^{-1}(h(X1, X2)) \rightarrow X2$ is added to the rewrite system). Since the subterm `h(0, Z)` is first argument of `g`, inverse function symbol $g1^{-1}$ is collected (and a rewrite rule $g1^{-1}(g(X1, X2)) \rightarrow X1$ is added). Since `g(...)` is second argument of `f`, inverse function symbol $f2^{-1}$ is collected (and a rewrite rule $f2^{-1}(f(X1, X2, X3, X4)) \rightarrow X2$ is added). The transformation procedure derives the following rewrite rules from the above clause.

$$a^1(X) \rightarrow c^1(h2^{-1}(g1^{-1}(f2^{-1}(b^1(X,0)))))$$
$$h2^{-1}(h(X1, X2)) \rightarrow X2$$
$$g1^{-1}(g(X1, X2)) \rightarrow X1$$
$$f2^{-1}(f(X1, X2, X3, X4)) \rightarrow X2 \qquad\qquad \square$$

Built-in predicates

PROLOG has built-in predicates `=, <, <=, >, >=, \=` with moding `(in, in)` and `is` with moding `(out, in)`. According to the definition of *Unsry* in the transformation algorithm, for each built-in atom $b(t1, t2)$, $b \in \{$ `=, <, <=, >, >=, \=`

} in a clause, $b^0(t1, t2)$ is included in $Unsry$ and rewrite rules of the form $lhs \rightarrow \$(b^0(t1, t2))$ will be present in R_p. Since we know that the above built-in atoms always terminate, our implementation does not make rules of the above form (this is achieved by removing the above terms from $Unsry$ before making the \$ rules).

An **is** atom is a producer of the variables occurring in its first argument and the Skolem function is^1 occurs in right-hand-side of the derived rewrite rules. Since, we know the semantics of **is**, we (in implementation) reduce the right-hand-sides of the rules by the rule $is^1(X) \rightarrow X$ before outputting the rules in R_p (i.e., we do not see is^1 functions in the rewrite rules; this enhances the readability of the derived rewrite system).

7 Case Study: Correctness Proof for ProCoS PL₀ Compiler

In this section, we discuss the application of the tool described in the previous sections, for showing the correctness (as discussed earlier) of the prototype compiler for ProCoS level 0 language, developed by Bowen, He and Pandya [5, 11]. This compiler translates a sequential subset of Occam called PL₀ into a subset of transputer instructions called ML_0. We first give a brief description of the compiling specification and the PROLOG program derived from it.

Machine language ML_0 consists of instructions such as $ldc(con)$ which loads the constant con into the register, and $stl(addr)$ which stores the contents of the register into the memory location having address $addr$. Note that ML_0 instructions are of variable length; each such instruction is implemented as a *sequence* of simpler single-byte **transputer** instructions. Function $mtrans(minstr)$ translates an ML_0 instruction into a sequence of **transputer** instructions. Machine program resides in a read only memory denoted by m. Data variables are stored in a read-write memory denoted by M. Notation $m[s : t]$ denotes the sequence $m[s], \ldots, m[t]$. It represents a section of the machine memory between locations s and t. Thus, $m[s : f - 1] = mtrans(stl(x))$ states that the memory section between locations s and $f - 1$ contains the instruction $stl(x)$ where x is a memory address in M. There are two jump instructions: $j(n)$ represents unconditional jump by n bytes, and $cj(n)$ represents jump by n bytes if the register is false, and **skip** otherwise. The argument of a jump instruction is the byte offset from the *end* of the jump instruction to the *start* of the target instruction.

Compiling specification describes the correct compilation predicate $C P s m f \Psi \Omega$. This predicate states that program P is correctly implemented by the sequence of instructions contained in the memory section $m[s : f - 1]$. Here, Ψ is the symbol table and Ω is the set of available (free) locations.

The complete compiling specification is given in [11]. Here, we only give some typical clauses. The first clause below states that **skip** can be compiled into an empty sequence of machine instructions - denoted by the memory section $m[s : s - 1]$. The second clause describes the compilation of the assignment statement **x:=e**. The code for evaluating **e** is put in memory section $m[s : l - 1]$; executing this code leaves the value of e in the register. This code is immediately followed by the instruction stl(Ψx) in the memory section $m[l : f - 1]$. Here Ψx gives the machine address of variable x and execution of this instruction stores the value of the register into memory location having address Ψx. Construct $\text{SEQ}[P_1, \ldots, P_n]$ denotes sequential composition of P_1 to P_n. The third clause states that $\text{SEQ}[\ ]$ behaves like skip. The fourth clause states that statement $\text{SEQ}[P_1, \ldots, P_n]$ can be compiled by putting the code for P_1 in memory section $m[s : l - 1]$ and the code for $\text{SEQ}[P_2, \ldots, P_n]$ between memory locations $m[l : f - 1]$. The last clause describes the compilation of a pascal-like while loop construct.

$$\mathcal{C}(\text{skip})smf\Psi\Omega \quad \textbf{if} \quad s = f \tag{1}$$

$$
\begin{aligned}
&\mathcal{C}(\text{x} := \text{e})smf\Psi\Omega &&\textbf{if} \\
&\quad \exists l. \quad l \leq f \\
&\quad\quad \mathcal{C}(\text{e})sml\Psi\Omega \\
&\quad\quad m[l : f - 1] = mtrans(stl(\Psi(x)))
\end{aligned}
\tag{2}
$$

$$
\begin{aligned}
&\mathcal{C}(\text{SEQ}[])smf\Psi\Omega &&\textbf{if} \\
&\quad \mathcal{C}(\text{SKIP})smf\Psi\Omega
\end{aligned}
\tag{3}
$$

$$
\begin{aligned}
&\mathcal{C}(\text{SEQ}[P_1, \ldots, P_n])smf\Psi\Omega &&\textbf{if} \\
&\quad \exists l. \quad l \leq f \\
&\quad\quad \mathcal{C}(P_1)slf\Psi\Omega \quad \wedge \\
&\quad\quad \mathcal{C}(\text{SEQ}[P_2, \ldots, P_n])lmf\Psi\Omega
\end{aligned}
\tag{4}
$$

$$
\begin{aligned}
&\mathcal{C}(\text{WHILE}(\text{b}, \text{P}))smf\Psi\Omega &&\textbf{if} \\
&\quad \exists l_1, l_2, l_3. \quad l_1 \leq l_2 \leq l_3 \leq f \quad \wedge \\
&\quad\quad m[s : l_1 - 1] = mtrans(j(l_2 - l_1)) \quad \wedge \\
&\quad\quad \mathcal{C}(\text{P})l_1ml_2\Psi\Omega \quad \wedge \\
&\quad\quad \mathcal{C}((\text{NOT b}))\, l_2ml_3\Psi\Omega \quad \wedge \\
&\quad\quad m[l_3 : f - 1] = mtrans(cj(l_1 - f)
\end{aligned}
\tag{5}
$$

Bowen et al [5] have shown that with some minor modifications (such as implementing sets by lists, and memory sections as lists of (address, value) pairs), this compiling specification can be directly implemented as a PROLOG program. The complete PROLOG program can be found in [11]. In the following, we consider two sample clauses for illustrating the termination proof. In these clauses, M denotes the memory section containing the appropriate machine code. $Append(M_1, M_2, M)$ combines two memory sections M_1, M_2 into one larger memory section M.

Well-modedness: PROLOG clauses derived from compiling specifications of various constructs of the language are *naturally well-moded* as illustrated below. From clauses (3) and (4) of the above compiling specification, we obtain the following PROLOG clauses. It is easy to see that these clauses are well-moded with moding: c : (in,in,out,out,in,in) and append : (in,in,out).

```
c(seq([]), S, F, M, Psi, Omega) :-
            c(skip, S, F, M, Psi, Omega).
```

```
c(seq([P1 | Pr]), S, F, M, Psi, Omega) :-
            c(P1, S, L1, M1, Psi, Omega),
            c(seq(Pr), L1, F, M2, Psi, Omega),
            append(M1, M2, M).
```

The PROLOG program can be used to compile a source program p by executing the query :- $c(p, s, M, F, PsiO, Omega)$, where $PsiO$ is the initial symbol table which assigns appropriate memory locations (determined by hardware) to two predefined channels *input* and *output*. $Omega$ is the list of available free memory locations on the target computer. It is easy to verify that this query is well-moded.

Occur-check: By the results of [16, 2], *if no variable occurs more than once in output positions of head of each clause*, the program is not subjected to occur-check (NSTO) and can be run soundly on any PROLOG interpreter. The tool checked each clause for this property and proved that the PL_0 complier is NSTO.

Transformation: Our tool first transforms the given PROLOG program (compiler in this case) into a term rewriting system and then proves the termination of the derived term rewriting system. In the following, we give the rewrite rules derived from the above two clauses and termination proof for the derived rewrite rules.

1. $c1(seq(nnil), xs, x\Psi, x\Omega) \rightarrow c1(skip, xs, x\Psi, x\Omega)$
2. $c2(seq(nnil), xs, x\Psi, x\Omega) \rightarrow c2(skip, xs, x\Psi, x\Omega)$

3. $c1(seq(cons(xp1, xpr)), xs, x\Psi, x\Omega) \rightarrow c1(seq(xpr), c1(xp1, xs, x\Psi, x\Omega), x\Psi, x\Omega)$
4. $c2(seq(cons(xp1, xpr)), xs, x\Psi, x\Omega) \rightarrow$
$$append1(c2(xp1, xs, x\Psi, x\Omega), c2(seq(xpr), c1(xp1, xs, x\Psi, x\Omega), x\Psi, x\Omega))$$

Termination: The recursive path ordering **rpos** (described in the previous section) is used for proving termination of the derived rewrite system. Since **rpos** is a simplification ordering, it is enough to show that left-hand-side of each rule is greater than the right-hand-side of that rule under **rpos**. We illustrate the proofs for rewrite rules 1 and 4 above using **rpos** with precedence: $c1 \approx c2 > append1$ and $seq > skip$ with LR status for $c1$ and $c2$ (this is a part of the precedence/status information *generated by the tool* in proving termination of the whole rewrite system).

To prove $c1(seq(nnil), xs, x\Psi, x\Omega) >_{rpos} c1(skip, xs, x\Psi, x\Omega)$, it is enough (by subclause d.i in the definition of **rpos**) to prove that

(i) $c1(seq(nnil), xs, x\Psi, x\Omega) >_{rpos} skip$
(ii) $c1(seq(nnil), xs, x\Psi, x\Omega) >_{rpos} xs$
(iii) $c1(seq(nnil), xs, x\Psi, x\Omega) >_{rpos} x\Psi$
(iv) $c1(seq(nnil), xs, x\Psi, x\Omega) >_{rpos} x\Omega$ and
(v) $(seq(nnil), xs, x\Psi, x\Omega) >_{rpos}^{*} (skip, , xs, x\Psi, x\Omega)$

It is easy to see that (ii), (iii) and (iv) hold by subterm property (clause (a) in the definition of **rpos**). Since $seq > skip$ in the precedence, $seq(nnil) >_{rpos} skip$ by clause (b) and hence $c1(seq(nnil), xs, x\Psi, x\Omega) >_{rpos} skip$ by clause (a). This completes (i). By the definition of lexicographic ordering, to prove (v) it is enough to prove $seq(nnil) >_{rpos} skip$, which we have already done. This completes the proof for rewrite rule 1.

To prove $c2(seq(cons(xp1, xpr)), xs, x\Psi, x\Omega) >_{rpos}$
$$append1(c2(xp1, xs, x\Psi, x\Omega), c2(seq(xpr), c1(xp1, xs, x\Psi, x\Omega), x\Psi, x\Omega)),$$
by clause (b) and precedence $c2 > append1$, it is enough to prove
(i) $c2(seq(cons(xp1, xpr)), xs, x\Psi, x\Omega) >_{rpos} c2(xp1, xs, x\Psi, x\Omega)$ and
(ii) $c2(seq(cons(xp1, xpr)), xs, x\Psi, x\Omega) >_{rpos} c2(seq(xpr), c1(xp1, xs, x\Psi, x\Omega), x\Psi, x\Omega))$.
We prove (ii) below and proof for (i) is similar (even easier).

To prove (ii), it is enough to prove (by clause d.1)
(1) $c2(seq(cons(xp1, xpr)), xs, x\Psi, x\Omega) >_{rpos} seq(xpr)$
(2) $c2(seq(cons(xp1, xpr)), xs, x\Psi, x\Omega) >_{rpos} c1(xp1, xs, x\Psi, x\Omega)$
(3) $c2(seq(cons(xp1, xpr)), xs, x\Psi, x\Omega) >_{rpos} x\Psi$
(4) $c2(seq(cons(xp1, xpr)), xs, x\Psi, x\Omega) >_{rpos} x\Omega$ and
(5) $seq(cons(xp1, xpr)) >_{rpos} seq(xpr)$
By subterm property, (3) and (4) hold. By clause (a), $cons(xp1, xpr) >_{rpos} xpr$ and hence by clause (c), $seq(cons(xp1, xpr)) >_{rpos} seq(xpr)$, which is same as (5). By clause (a), (5) implies (1).
Since $c1 \approx c2$ in the precedence and have LR status, proving (2) involves proofs of
(6) $c2(seq(cons(xp1, xpr)), xs, x\Psi, x\Omega) >_{rpos} xp1$,
(7) $c2(seq(cons(xp1, xpr)), xs, x\Psi, x\Omega) >_{rpos} xs$ and
(8) $seq(cons(xp1, xpr)) >_{rpos} xp1$ in addition to (3) and (4).
Since variables $xp1$ and xs are occurring in $c2(seq(cons(xp1, xpr)), xs, x\Psi, x\Omega)$, by subterm property (6) and (7) hold. Proof of (8) again follows from subterm property. This completes proof for rewrite rule 4.   □

The above proof illustrates the highly detailed and tedious, mechanical checking that is often necessary in proving termination of the term rewriting system derived from a logic program. We believe that such checking should be largely left to a mechanical tool if errors are to be avoided. We have carried out the termination proof for the whole prototype compiler of the **ProCoS** level 0 langauage PL_0 using our tool in an interactive fashion as described below.

The tool (RRL module) tries to prove termination by showing that left-hand-side term is greater than right-hand-side term of every rule under **rpos**. It incrementally builds up the precedence relation and status information of the operators in the process. For proving lhs $>_{rpos}$ rhs, it (exhaustively) suggests many pairs in the precedence relation (which might be needed in the proof) and asks user to choose some pairs. Once user gives his choice of pairs, it updates the precedence relation and check whether lhs $>_{rpos}$ rhs is true, if so, it picks the next rewrite rule and proceed. If the pairs picked by the user are not enough for proving lhs $>_{rpos}$ rhs, RRL asks him to pick some more. If all the suggested pairs are exhausted and it is unable to prove lhs $>_{rpos}$ rhs, the tool suggests giving status LR or RL to some function symbols.

Experience with the Tool: In the following, we give the details of the effort involved in proving the termination of the prototype compiler.

Number of nonunit PROLOG **clauses** : 32
Number of **rewrite rules** derived :   63
Number of **interactions** needed in the proof : 21

In summary, our tool has proved automatically that the **ProCoS** compiler can be safely executed without occur check and that it is terminating. However, there is another aspect that needs to be considered; the presence of cuts in the program. The effect of cuts is to chop of certain branches from the search space (SLD-tree). If the cuts are not used carefully, they can chop off certain success branches and it is possible that the compiler may not generate any code for some source programs, even though they satisfy the compiling specification. In other words, this would affect the completeness of the compiler. As far as the PL_0 compiler is concerned, we could establish that the compiler generates code for all valid source programs by observing the structure of the clauses. However, in general, there is a *need for further work* for dealing with this aspect in an effective way.

8 Discussion

In this paper, we have described a tool for proving correctness of compilers written in PROLOG. This tool is applied to establish correctness of the **ProCoS** PL_0 compiler developed using refinement algebra approach. The versatility of the system described in the development of compilers based on the refinement algebra approach becomes evident by the following observations about the compiler for PL_0.

-- The clauses are well-moded; thus facilitating the application of our system for proving the termination and occur-check freeness of the compiler.
  It may be noted that even though the methods of [25, 21, 22] are also for well-moded programs, they have further requirements such as *existence of admissible solution graphs* [21] and *uniqueness* property [25] of clauses. There are many clauses in the prototype compiler for PL_0, which do not satisfy these properties. Hence, their methods cannot be used for proving termination of PL_0 compiler.
- Cuts in the clause appear at the end of the body of each clause.

However, as already discussed, *there is a need to develop techniques and tools that aid* in verifying the completeness of the compiler in the presence of cuts (even in the middle of the body of the clauses).

Our experience shows that our system is quite useful in showing the correctness of compilers in PROLOG. Further, our system also helps in proving termination of concurrent logic programs such as GHC on the same lines and hence, would be applicable for compilers in GHC. We are currently working on the enhancement of the system to cater to various other aspects already mentioned and also the applicability of the tools in the context of developing compilers using partial evaluation as proposed in [14].

References

1. K.R. Apt and D. Pedreschi (1991), *Reasoning about Termination of Logic Programs*, Technical report, University of Pisa, September 1991.
2. K.R. Apt and A. Pellegrini (1992), *Why the Occur-check is Not a Problem*, in Proc. of 4th Intl. Symp. on Programming Language Implementation and Logic Programming (PLILP'92), Springer-Verlag LNCS Vol 531.
3. J. Beer (1988), *The Occur-check Problem Revisited*, Journal of Logic Programming, 5, pp. 243-261.
4. M. Bezem (1989), *Characterizing Termination of Logic Programs*, Report CS-R8912, CWI, Amsterdam. Also in Proc. of North American Conf. on Logic Programming NACLP'89.
5. J. Bowen, J. He and P. Pandya (1990), *An Approach to Verifiable Compiling Specification and Prototyping*, in Proc. of 2nd Symp. on Programming Language Implementation and Logic Programming, PLILP'90 springer-Verlag LNCS Vol. 456.
6. P. Deransart and J. Maluszinski (1985), *Relating Logic Programs and Attribute Grammers*, Journal of Logic Programming 2, pp. 119-155.
7. P. Deransart, G. Ferrand and M. Téguia (1991), *NSTO Programs (Not Subjected To Occur-check)*, in Proc. Intl. Logic Programming Symp, ILPS'91, pp. 533-547.
8. N. Dershowitz (1987), *Termination of Rewriting*, J. of Symbolic Computation, 3, pp. 69-116.
9. N. Dershowitz and J.-P. Jouannaud (1990), *Rewrite Systems*, in J. van Leeuwen, editor, *Handbook of Theoretical Computer Science B: Formal Methods and Semantics*, North-Holland, pp. 243-320.
10. D. De Schreye and K. Verschaetse (1992), *Termination Analysis of Definite Logic Programs with respect to Call Patterns*, K.U. Leuven, submitted for publication.
11. Jifeng He, P. Pandya and J. Bowen (1990), *Compiling Specification for ProCoS Programming Language Level 0*, ProCoS Workshop, Malente, April 1990. Also appears as Project Document, OU HJF 4/2.
12. C.A.R. Hoare (1990), *Refinement Algebra Proves Correctness of Compiling Specifications*, Proc. 3rd Refinement Workshop (edited by C.C. Morgan and J.C.P. Woodcock), Springer-Verlag, Workshops in Computing series, pp. 33-48.
13. C.A.R. Hoare, J. He, J. Bowen and P. Pandya (1990), *An Algebraic Approach to Verifiable Compiling Specification and Prototyping of ProCoS level 0 Programming Language*, Proc. of ESPRIT'90, Brussels (ed. Commission of European Communities), Kluwer Acadenuc Publishers, 1990.
14. N.D. Jones (1990), *Partial Evaluation, Self-Application and Types*, Proc. 17th ICALP, Springer-Verlag LNCS 443, pp. 639-59.
15. D. Kapur and H. Zhang (1989), *An Overview of Rewrite Rule Laboratory (RRL)*, Proc. of Rewrite Techniques and Applications conference, RTA'89, Springer-Verlag LNCS vol. 355, pp 559-563.
16. M.R.K. Krishna Rao (1992), *Occur-check in Well-moded Logic Programs*, Proc. 7th Intl. Meeting of Young Computer Scientists, IMYCS'92, Smolenice Castle, Bratislava.
17. M.R.K. Krishna Rao, D. Kapur and R.K. Shyamasundar (1991), *A Transformational Methodology for Proving termination of Logic Programs*, Proc. Computer Science Logic, CSL'91, Springer-Verlag LNCS Vol. 626. pp. 213-216.
18. P. Lescanne (1983), *Computer Experiments with the REVE Term Rewriting Systems Generator*, in proc. 10th ACM POPL (1983), pp. 99-108.
19. J. W. Lloyd (1987), *Foundations of Logic Programming*, Springer-Verlag.
20. D. A. Plaisted (1984), *The Occur-check Problem in Prolog*, in Proc. Intl. Symp. on Logic Programming, pp. 272-280.

21. L. Pluemer (1990), *Termination Proofs for Logic Programs*, Ph. D. Thesis, University of Dortmund, Also appears as Springer-Verlag LNCS vol. 446.

22. L. Pluemer (1991), *Automatic Termination Proofs for Prolog Programs Operating on Nonground Terms*, in proc. Intl. Logic Programming Symposium, ILPS'91, pp. 503-17.

23. H.Sondergaard (1986), *An Application of Abstract Interpretation of Logic Programs: Occur-check Reduction*, in Proc. ESOP'86, LNCS vol. 213, pp. 327-336.

24. R.K. Shyamasundar, M.R.K. Krishna Rao and D. Kapur (1990), *Rewriting Concepts in the Study of Termination of Logic Programs*, Proc. ALPUK'92 conf. (edited by K. Broda), Springer-Verlag, Workshops in Computing series, pp. 3-20.

25. J.D. Ullman and A. van Gelder (1988), *Efficient Tests for Top-Down Termination of Logical Rules*, JACM, 35(2), pp. 345-373.

26. T. Vasak and J. Potter (1986), *Characterization of Terminating Logic Programs*, IEEE Symposium on Logic Programming, pp. 140-147.

Encoding
$\mathcal{W}$: A Logic for Z
in 2OBJ

Andrew Martin

Programming Research Group, Oxford University Computing Laboratory,
11 Keble Road, Oxford OX1 3RQ, UK.

Abstract. A prototype proof system for "$\mathcal{W}$: A Logic for Z" has been produced using the 2OBJ metalogical theorem-prover. 2OBJ permits an encoding which is very similar in structure to that of $\mathcal{W}$, and the details are presented here. Like $\mathcal{W}$ the encoding assumes that all its inputs are well-typed. The structure of the encoding is enhanced by a meta-rule on the *lifting* of proof rules and tactics. There is some discussion of how tactics can make $\mathcal{W}$ more easily usable.

1 Introduction

In modern software engineering, many opportunities for improving one's confidence in a specification or development present themselves as proof obligations. These may arise as proofs of consistency, proofs that a specification satisfies some requirement (e.g. a security requirement), or as refinement proofs.

Many such specifications are expressed using the Z notation [13], which formalises much classical logic and elementary set theory, and does so in a style well-suited to the specification of large computer systems. $\mathcal{W}$ provides a soundly-based formalism for reasoning about such specifications. This leads to proof obligations which are *large*, that is, they are expressed using many heavily nested definitions, but not very *deep*. Proofs which discharge these obligations are, by reason of their size (and in particular, the size of the terms they involve), quite tedious to produce and difficult to check manually. Since relatively little "insight" is needed in their production, they are very suitable for consideration by mechanical theorem-proving assistants. We might hope that such an assistant could have a similar rôle in the development process to that of the compiler/debugger.

A lot of the effort in machine-assisted theorem-proving has concentrated on theoretical considerations. LCF [5, 9], for example, permits reasoning about computable functions, denotational semantics and domain theory. More recent work includes Isabelle [10] which supports a number of formalisms (intuitionistic logic, constructive type theory, classical first-order logic, ZF set theory, etc) none of which are *alone* in use in software engineering. Many other tools, however, are more closely targetted at engineering applications. Gordon's HOL [4] has been used for large-scale hardware verification, and the **B** tool is part of a whole software engineering method [1]. Mural [8] supports reasoning needed for work in VDM, seeking to provide assistance for a familiar "pen-and-paper" style of working.

This paper outlines the result of trying to produce a prototype of a proof system falling into the second of these two groups. The system encodes $\mathcal{W}$ in the 2OBJ system and is tentatively named "Jigsa$\mathcal{W}$". The remainder of this section explains a little about $\mathcal{W}$, and about 2OBJ. Section 2 discusses how Z's syntax has been encoded in OBJ, and Sect. 3 shows how the basic predicate calculus rules are expressed in 2OBJ. Sections 4 and 5 consider two proof-structuring devices; *rule-lifting* and *tactics*. In Sect. 6 the encoding of $\mathcal{W}$'s rules for reasoning about expressions is explained, and in Sect. 7 the rules which enable Z's specification constructs to be used in proof are considered. The paper ends with a discussion outlining some of the proofs thus far produced using the tool, and describing some goals for future work.

1.1 $\mathcal{W}$: A Logic for Z

As Z has grown in popularity, various logics have been proposed for reasoning within it. One such logic is $\mathcal{W}$ [15]. $\mathcal{W}$ has the great benefit of having (largely) been proven sound with respect to the semantics of standard Z [13]. The logic is a sequent calculus in the style of Gentzen; but since it is for reasoning in Z, it is a *typed* logic. Thus the sequents take the following form:

Declarations | Predicates ⊢ Predicates .

The sequent is said to be valid iff, in an environment augmented by the Declarations, by assuming all the Predicates on the left-hand side (the *antecedents*) it is possible to prove one of those on the right (the *consequents*). Any (or all) of these parts of the sequent may be empty.[1] If there are no predicates or no declarations on the left, the bar is omitted. Rules in $\mathcal{W}$ are written

$$\frac{\text{premisses}}{\text{conclusion}} \ (\text{name})$$

where the conclusion is a sequent, and the premisses consist of zero or more sequents. The rule may also have a side-condition (proviso).

The presentation in [15] gives an explicit characterization of bound and free variables, and of substitution, which makes encoding it very straightforward. Also included are rules (axioms) for the basic expressions which occur in Z (rules concerning set membership, cartesian tuple equality, etc), and rules which permit the definitions introduced in a specification (in schemas, generic definitions etc) to be incorporated as antecedents.

1.2 2OBJ: A Metalogical Theorem Prover

In order to support an encoding of $\mathcal{W}$ a suitably general theorem-proving assistant is needed. Tools which provide a built-in logic already—even if very similar to the sequent calculus chosen in $\mathcal{W}$—will not necessarily be useful. This is, then, an ideal task for a so-called *metalogical framework*. Examples of such tools include the Edinburgh Logical Framework [6], Isabelle [10] and 2OBJ [2, 14]. Of these, 2OBJ, whilst

---

[1] Readers unfamiliar with this style will be surprised to see sequents such as $\Phi \vdash$. This is valid only if the predicates in Φ are contradictory (hence, $\Phi \vdash$ is equivalent to $\Phi \vdash$ false).

still being developed, had the advantage of being produced locally and providing a moderately good user interface.

2OBJ consists of a number of OBJ3 (see [3]) modules (the *2OBJ System*), together with an X-windows based user interface to OBJ3 (the *2OBJ Tool*). The tool provides windows for easy interaction with the underlying OBJ system; button presses being converted into OBJ input commands. The output from OBJ is redirected into a number of windows, so that, for example, proofs under construction can be represented as trees in a manner which corresponds to a pencil-and-paper proof.

2OBJ imposes very few assumptions about the logic being encoded. The OBJ3 modules construct an abstract datatype of **Proofs**, together with operations for constructing such proofs from **Goals** and **Rules**. Such **Rules** may be combined to form **Tactics**. The user must supply OBJ modules which define a term algebra for the object language (see below). These are then linked to the 2OBJ system by identifying one form of term (in our case, the *sequent*) with the OBJ sort **Goal**. The inference rules of the system are then described as objects of sort **Rule**. The user describes the behaviour of these rules by giving equations for the built-in operator[2]

```
op _ _ : Rule Goal -> GoalList .
```

Thus rules are viewed as functions from **Goals** to lists of **Goals**.

The encoding is comprised of a few modules containing such equations. The user of JigsaW creates a module containing definitions from a Z specification (see, for example, those in Sect. 7 below), importing these modules too. After this module has been loaded into 2OBJ, the user may specify a goal term (using the 2OBJ tool), and the system uses the user-supplied rules, together with built-in rules for manipulating proof trees, to construct a proof tree. This construction is entirely user-driven; to apply a rule to a particular node in the tree, the user simply has to click on that node and specify the rule/tactic to be applied.

The theory underlying 2OBJ is Hendrik Hilberdink's work [7]. It is intended that the implementation of 2OBJ should be shown to conform to its specification in Hilberdink's formal proof theory. This framework makes possible a proof that the encoding is faithful to W—and thus that proofs produced using JigsaW are indeed sound (that is, as sound as W).

2 Syntax

The first step in producing an encoding of a logic in 2OBJ, then, is to provide an OBJ module defining a term algebra[3] for the logic under consideration. Z has a rich concrete syntax, described using a context-free grammar in the draft Z standard [13]. This can be translated into OBJ in a fairly systematic manner, due to OBJ's order-sorted algebra and arbitrary mixfix operator definitions.

---

[2] The keyword op introduces an operator definition. In this instance, this is a degenerate case of OBJ3's arbitrary *mixfix* syntax. The simple juxtaposition of a Rule and a Goal forms an application of this operator.

[3] That is, the constants and operator symbols for the language, together with laws describing which strings of symbols make valid terms.

Each of the main non-terminal symbols in the grammar becomes an OBJ *sort*. In principle each non-terminal could be an OBJ sort, but since many are not referred to outside the grammar, it suffices to collapse many of the productions in the grammar, using operator precedences to ensure that the same language is described. An example of a part of this encoding is given below. (The expression in square brackets describes the operator precedence; operators with lower numbers bind tighter.)

```
op |A| _ <.> _ : SchemaText Predicate -> Predicate [ prec 40 ] .
op |E| _ <.> _ : SchemaText Predicate -> Predicate [ prec 40 ] .
op |E1| _ <.> _ : SchemaText Predicate -> Predicate [ prec 40 ] .
op _ <=> _ : Predicate Predicate -> Predicate [ prec 35 ] .
op _ => _ : Predicate Predicate -> Predicate [ prec 32 ] .
op _ V _ : Predicate Predicate -> Predicate [ prec 30 ] .
op _ ^ _ : Predicate Predicate -> Predicate [ prec 28 ] .
```

Some of the non-terminals are given by productions with potential repetitions—these are represented using extra sorts. For example, sequence displays are defined as follows:

```
Expression5 = ... | Sequence | ...
Sequence = '⟨' , Expression0, { ',', Expression0},'⟩'
```

In OBJ, this is expressed (with all the Expression classes collapsed into one) by defining the comma as an associative operator which forms lists of expressions from shorter lists; single expressions being the simplest of those lists. Sequences are formed by surrounding such lists of expressions with angle brackets.

```
sort Expressions .
subsort Expression < Expressions .
op _ , _ : Expressions Expressions -> Expressions [ assoc ] .

op < _ > : Expressions -> Expression [ prec 15 ] .
```

The grammar is also careful to specify the rôle of parentheses in Z. This is slightly unfortunate, in that parentheses in OBJ have a built-in meaning—they are used to modify operator precedence. In most cases, Z uses them for the same purpose, and to avoid circularity in the grammar. By explicitly giving operator precedence to the symbols being defined, and collapsing together some of the non-terminals, explicit mentioning of parentheses in the grammar can be avoided. The parentheses defining tuples, though, have genuine syntactic value. Because in OBJ they serve only to group objects, this definition

```
op ( _ ) : Expressions -> Expression .
```

is meaningless. Instead, we write

```
op Tuple( _ ) : Expressions -> Expression .
```

There are few instances of this type of problem, so the result of this activity is a concrete syntax which is tolerably readable. If a standard ASCII format for representing Z is arrived at, it could readily be used here. Good concrete syntax makes the encoding of rules easy to read and so increases confidence in the accuracy of the code.

2.1 Type-Checking

As yet, no attempt has been made to include type-checking in the encoding. This is a significant problem as, clearly, the soundness of the logic is dependent on its input being well-typed. $\mathcal{W}$ ensures that most of the inference rules preserve type-correctness. The only exception is *cut*, which introduces new predicates (*cut* is discussed at greater length in Sect. 5.2 below).

$$\frac{e \mid \Phi \vdash p, \Psi \qquad e \mid p, \Phi \vdash \Psi}{e \mid \Phi \vdash \Psi} \ (cut(p))$$

Therefore, the minimum requirement is that both initial goals and sequents produced by *cut* (in backward reasoning) be type-checked. Having no mechanism available for type inference means that all generics must be fully instantiated at input time (and hence at all points of interaction with the tool)—writing $\varnothing[X]$ instead of merely $\varnothing$ and $(S, T) \in (\_ \subseteq \_)[X]$ instead of $S \subseteq T$, for example.[4]

This is consistent with $\mathcal{W}$'s approach—the logic simply assumes that all the terms it encounters are well-typed, and that all generics are fully instantiated. In "pen-and-paper" reasoning, such details can often be overlooked; this option is not available since the tool must work entirely formally. We could extend the logic to include another form of judgement; one indicating that a particular expression has a particular type. This would permit type-checking to be performed at the same time as proof (generally via automatic tactics, since Z's type system is decidable), allowing generic parameters to be supplied when necessary. However, it would mean that the logic being encoded was far removed from $\mathcal{W}$.

The 2OBJ documentation [14] suggests using *sort constraints* in encoding the grammar, so that terms will be syntactically well-formed only if they are type-correct. This is appealing, but even if it is possible to express the Z type system in this way, performance of the tool is likely to render it useless—parsing is already very slow.

Another possibility is to pre-process the user's OBJ code using a tool similar to *f*UZZ [12], both checking for type-correctness and providing generic parameters. The *cut* rule presents a problem in this scheme. It would be possible to have the rule write its resulting sequents out to a file which could later be type-checked (the soundness of the proof being dependent on the success of the type-checking). This is problematic because *LIFT* (see Sect. 4) introduces nested scopes. When *cut* is used within the lifted proof, the cut term may contain variables which are in scope in the context of the *LIFT*, but not in global scope; their types may not, therefore, be readily apparent unless each application of *LIFT* also makes an entry in the file.

2.2 $\mathcal{W}$ Meta-Functions and Syntax Extensions

Since 2OBJ assumes very little about the logic being encoded, it is necessary explicitly to define the sequent[5] (identifying it with the sort `Goal` mentioned above), and

---

[4] A new version of [13] writes these expressions as $\varnothing_{[X]}$ and $S \subseteq_{[X]} T$. This is yet to be incorporated into the encoding.

[5] Note that whereas in $\mathcal{W}$ missing declarations and predicates are denoted by white space, pattern-matching in the encoding is greatly aided by inclusion of symbols for empty

notions of free variables (ϕ), alphabet of declarations(α), and substitution. These are carefully defined in the presentation of $\mathcal{W}$[15] and/or the semantics[13], using sets of equations.

Substitution, for example (accomplished using explicit bindings) is specified with expressions like

$$b.(\forall d \mid p \bullet q) \equiv \forall b.d \mid (\alpha d \lhd b).p \bullet (\alpha d \lhd b).q$$
$$\text{provided } \alpha d \cap \phi_e(\alpha d \lhd b) = \emptyset$$
$$b.(\neg\, p) \equiv \neg\, b.p$$
$$b.(p \wedge q) \equiv b.p \wedge b.q$$
$$b.(p \vee q) \equiv b.p \vee b.q$$

These equations translate directly into OBJ3 (the keyword **eq** introduces an equation, **ceq** introduces a conditional equation):

```
ceq (b . (|A| d | p <.> q)) = (|A| (b . d) |
      ((alpha(d) \dsub b) . p)<.> ((alpha(d) \dsub b) . q))
   if ((alpha(d) inter phie(alpha(d) \dsub b)) == *nil*) .
eq (b . ( p)) =   (b . p) .
eq (b . (p ^ q) = (b . p) ^ (b . q) .
eq (b . (p V q)) = (b . p) V (b . q) .
```

As immediate substitution is not always required (for example, the presentation of Leibniz' rule requires that there be a predicate present of the form $\langle\!|\ x \rightsquigarrow t\ |\!\rangle.p$) these rules are presented using 2OBJ's ability to "turn off" rewrites; they are only used when the rule *subst* is selected.

The equations for α and ϕ could be presented in a similar manner. However, since they are features common to most logics, 2OBJ provides fast built-in operators for implementing them. The equations then provide a specification against which to test (and prove) this implementation.

3   General Rules

$\mathcal{W}$ is based on a classical sequent calculus, and thus includes a full set of well-known inference rules. For example, the classical rules for *or*-introduction on the right and the left could be written in $\mathcal{W}$ as

$$\frac{d \mid \Phi \vdash \Psi, p, q}{d \mid \Phi \vdash \Psi, p \vee q}\ (\vdash\vee) \qquad \frac{d \mid \Phi, p \vdash \Psi \qquad d \mid \Phi, q \vdash \Psi}{d \mid \Phi, p \vee q \vdash \Psi}\ (\vee\vdash)$$

However, in the presentation of $\mathcal{W}$ [15], rules are presented in a simplified form, together with a theorem on *rule-lifting* (this theorem is reproduced in Sect. 4 below):

$$\frac{\vdash p, q}{\vdash p \vee q}\ (\vdash\vee) \qquad \frac{p \vdash \qquad q \vdash}{p \vee q \vdash}\ (\vee\vdash)$$

---

declarations and empty lists of predicates. As a result, the empty sequent ($\vdash$) is denoted
% | * |- *.

It is convenient to present the encoding in a similar way, with simple rules together with a meta-rule for rule-lifting (also discussed below). Thus two rules above are implemented by |-or and or|- (these are defined as constant operators of sort Rule; recall that a rule juxtaposed with a goal forms an instance of the rule application operator, so these equations are between GoalLists):

```
op |-or : -> Rule .
eq |-or (% | * |- p V q) = (% | * |- p , q) .

op or|- : -> Rule .
eq or|- (% | p V q |- *) = (% | p |- *) , (% | q |- *) .
```

The *assumption* rule is distinctive in that it has no premiss:

$$\frac{}{d \mid p \vdash p} \ (assumption) \ ,$$

and so the 2OBJ rule generates an empty list of subgoals:

```
op assumption : -> Rule .
eq assumption (d | p |- p ) = [] .
```

This implementation leads to a very clean and neat encoding, which is easily seen to be correct, and can also easily be verified correct (that is, faithful to $\mathcal{W}$).

4 Lifting

The theorem on *rule-lifting* serves both to simplify the presentation of $\mathcal{W}$ (by making it easier to read) and to help structure the proof that $\mathcal{W}$ is sound with respect to Z's semantics. It factors-out elements which would otherwise be common to each rule.

Theorem (Rule-lifting).

If the inference rule $\dfrac{e; d' \mid \Psi' \vdash \Phi'}{e; d \mid \Psi \vdash \Phi}$ *is sound,*

then the rule $\dfrac{f; e; d' \mid p, \Psi' \vdash q, \Phi'}{f; e; d \mid p, \Psi \vdash q, \Phi}$ *is also sound,*

providing that $(\alpha d \cup \alpha d') \cap (\phi p \cup \phi q) = \varnothing$.

The theorem could readily be generalised to cover rules (proofs) with more than one premiss.

For similar reasons, it is useful to provide a meta-rule in the encoding (justified by this theorem) which takes a rule, R, and some collection of terms from the current goal, and returns a new goal which is the result of applying R to the selected terms, leaving the other terms unchanged (read $\uparrow$ ($\downarrow$) as selecting (excluding) predicates/declarations indicated by position number, hence $(p, q, r, s) \uparrow (1\,3) \equiv (p, r)$

and $(p, q, r, s) \downarrow (1\,3) \equiv (q, s)$):

$$\frac{d'; d \downarrow i \mid \Phi'; \Phi \downarrow j \vdash \Psi'; \Psi \downarrow k}{d \mid \Phi \vdash \Psi} \ (LIFT(i, j, k, R))$$

$$\text{whenever} \quad \frac{d' \mid \Phi' \vdash \Psi'}{d \uparrow i \mid \Phi \uparrow j \vdash \Psi \uparrow k} \ (R)$$

provided $((\alpha(d \uparrow i) \cup \alpha(d')) \setminus (\alpha(d \uparrow i) \cap \alpha(d'))) \cap (\Phi \downarrow j \cup \Psi \downarrow k) = \varnothing$.[6]

In some languages, this description would almost serve to define rule-lifting. This, however, is merely a specification of some rather ugly OBJ3 code, which is not reproduced here. Proving that this specification of the rule is sound, and proving that the implementation of rule-lifting satisfies it, is one of the major activities in the proof of soundness for JigsaW (see Sect. 8).

The reason why this rule is needed may not be immediately clear. Systems such as LCF [9] have no comparable construction. The problem lies in the fact that 2OBJ is a *logical framework* whereas LCF implements a particular logic. The rule-lifting takes place at a very low level in the latter; in the former it must be defined by the user (the author of the encoding). If the logic under consideration were more unusual (linear logic, for example) the forms of lifting which would produce faithful encodings would be much more restricted; this is why lifting cannot easily be built-in to 2OBJ.

4.1 Possible Variations

In Andrew Stevens' encoding of first order predicate calculus (FOPC) in 2OBJ (the example encoding in [14]), each of the primitive rules is expressed in its full form, with lifting 'built-in', for example:

```
op ore : NzInt -> Rule .
ceq ore (N) (H |- X) =
       ( H ; hyp(N,H) : 1 |- X ),( H ; hyp(N,H) : 2 |- X )
   if matches( Z v Y, hyp(N, H) ) .
```

which simply makes this inference:

$$\frac{H; Z \vdash X \qquad H; Y \vdash Z}{H \vdash X} \ (ore(N)) \quad \text{whenever } H \uparrow N = Z \vee Y .$$

This makes the rule hard to read—and verify—and tends to make tactics hard to write. Moreover, the side condition present in the rule-lifting theorem would need to be duplicated in several rules.

By contrast, if it were seen as desirable to have a rule such as the above in JigsaW, it could readily be defined (as a tactic) using *LIFT* (a 0 is used as an argument to LIFT to denote parts of the sequent from which nothing is to be lifted):

---

[6] Note that this is a slightly stronger condition than the one in the theorem. It requires that the changing declarations have disjoint alphabets; this happens to be easier to check.

```
op OR|- : NzNat -> Tactic .
eq OR|- (n) Seq = LIFT(0,n,0,or|-) .
```

The use of lifting within tactics leads to some interesting results; see Sect. 5 below.

This form of rule lifting is tied closely to counting the positions of predicates (and declarations) in lists. Another approach might be to make use of associative/commutative matching, writing patterns which would match lists (sets) of predicates containing one to which the rule would apply. A problem here would be that in the case of multiple matches, one would need a means of indicating to which predicate the rule is to be applied.

Again, if a rule of this sort—one which matches any applicable part of the goal—is needed, it can be written using $LIFT$, with an auxiliary function $find$ which finds a match (using the 2OBJ built-in $matches$) in a list of predicates and returns its position number:

```
op |-OR : -> Tactic .
eq |-OR (d | PHI |- PSI) = LIFT(0,0,find(p V q,PSI),|-or) .
```

Thus the high-level $LIFT$ meta-rule appears to be a very general formulation, both making derived rules and tactics very easy to write and making any proofs about the encoding easy to structure, since it corresponds well with the original presentation. It would also appear to be slightly novel. In encoding a sequent calculus for first-order logic in Isabelle [11], Paulson uses associative unification, and so presents his inference rules in "lifted" form. A formulation which seems broadly similar to the one given here comes in the Edinburgh LF [6, Chapter 4] presentation of first-order logic, using a natural deduction style. (The details are very different, but a consequence is that rules are expressed in a simple, "un-lifted" form, like those above.)

The greatest problem with this approach is that there is much potential for inefficiency. Having the selection of predicates from goals as a high-level operation (on a par with tactic interpretation) rather than as a fast built-in, hidden from the user, leaves the user free to write very inefficient tactics which frequently pull sequents apart and then put them back together again. However, the judicious combination of $LIFT$ with tactics can lead to very efficient tactics where each rule is directly applicable to the goal at hand, with no need for searching or selection (see below, example on page 12).

Whilst lifting aids the construction of tactics, it can be rather difficult to use interactively: counting predicates as they are printed on the screen is very error-prone. A good user interface would permit clicking on the predicates to which a rule is to be applied. The rule could be wrapped in a $LIFT$ whenever the form of the selected goal demanded it.

5 Tactics

Tactics can be thought of as programs which perform proofs. A tactic captures the essence of a formal proof, in some sense, and thus storing the tactic enables the proof to be repeated at a later date, maybe in differing circumstances. This is an important software engineering consideration since a system specification may be expected to change from time to time, and it should be possible to check that theorems are still provable without unnecessary additional effort. The proof performed by a tactic may be very general, in which case the tactic is available as a derived inference rule.

The fact that the tactic is built from primitive rules means that the proof will succeed only if the side-conditions on those rules are met, even though they are not (usually) mentioned explicitly in the tactic. By virtue of being built solely from sound inference rules, tactics may make large inference steps without any need for additional proofs of soundness beyond those necessary for the primitive rules. In making reasoning steps, the user need not be aware which are the result of rules, and which are implemented by tactics. Thus, for example, although the definitions from the Z mathematical toolkit are provided, the user will not generally need to be concerned with the details of the rules for applying generic definitions; instead a toolkit tactic will bring the relevant definition into the antecedent, apply it to the selected term, and remove any unwanted definitions. An example of such a tactic is given below.

5.1 Tactic Language

In 2OBJ the tactic language is an extension of the language of rules. All rules can be considered as tactics, and tactics can be combined using the following LCF-style *tacticals* (t_1 and t_2 are tactics, ts is a list of tactics):

t_1 *THEN* t_2 (sequential composition) applies t_1 to the goal then applies t_2 to the resulting subgoal(s).

t_1 *THENL* ts (parallel composition) applies t_1 to the goal, then applies the tactics in ts *zip*-wise to the resulting goals. Thus, for example, if t_1 produces three subgoals, ts must consist of three tactics; $ts[1]$ is applied to the first subgoal, $ts[2]$ to the second, etc.

t_1 *ELSE* t_2 applies t_1 to the goal; if it succeeds, the tactic terminates, otherwise t_2 is applied *to the initial goal*.

As the tactics are written in OBJ they may be arbitrarily complex. Tactics may call other tactics, in a functional programming style, and recursion is available, making the language very powerful. Thus these tacticals may be used to construct various other familiar programming language features. The 2OBJ documentation [14] suggests tactics for iteration (*REPEAT*) and exhaustive application of rules (*EXHAUST*). Both are recursive, *REPEAT* applying the supplied tactic and then calling itself with an index which is the predecessor of the original index; and *EXHAUST* using *ELSE* to continue execution until application of the supplied tactic fails.

```
op REPEAT : Nat ProofTactic -> Tactic .
eq REPEAT( N, PT ) Seq = if N == 0 then idtac
                else PT THEN REPEAT(p(N) , PT) fi .
op EXHAUST : ProofTactic -> Tactic .
eq EXHAUST( PT ) Seq = (PT THEN EXHAUST(PT)) ELSE idtac .
```

(idtac is an identity tactic; it always succeeds, leaving the goal to which it is applied unchanged. Seq is a place-holder denoting any sequent—see below for tactics defined as applying to more specific goals.)

5.2 Often-used forms

Tactics are made more general by being parametrised. CUT takes a parameter which gives the predicate to be cut into the goal. The "raw" cut rule in $\mathcal{W}$ is only applicable to a goal consisting of an empty sequent, an unlikely goal:

$$\frac{p \vdash \qquad \vdash p}{\vdash} \ (cut(p))$$.

However, writing

```
op CUT : Predicate -> Tactic .
eq CUT (p) Seq = LIFT(0,0,0,cut(d)) .
```

yields the more useful rule

$$\frac{e \mid \Phi \vdash p, \Psi \qquad e \mid p, \Phi \vdash \Psi}{e \mid \Phi \vdash \Psi} \ (CUT(p))$$.

Often, cut is used to introduce a lemma (or theorem, or axiom) for which a proof (tactic) already exists. CUT can be used to construct a tactic which introduces the predicate p to a goal's hypothesis list, proving $\vdash p$ using the provided tactic, PT.

```
op CUTLEM : Predicate ProofTactic -> Tactic .
eq CUTLEM (p, PT) Seq = CUT(p) THENL(LIFT(0,0,1,PT), idtac) .
```

Many axioms (see below) are expressed in the form $\vdash p \Leftrightarrow q$ from which it is a simple matter to prove, for example, the validity of the following inference rule

$$\frac{\vdash q}{\vdash p}$$.

The transformation from an equivalence to an inference rule is accomplished by the tactic `|-EQULIFT=>`. As the goal must match one side of the equivalence (the left-hand side, in this case), this tactic uses pattern matching on the goal to ensure that it is only applied where appropriate. 2OBJ's tactics are defined using an equation involving a goal (in the above, any goal `Seq` is satisfactory) so that the tactic's action can be conditional on the form of the goal.

`|-EQULIFT=>` uses `CUTLEM` (above) to introduce $p \Leftrightarrow q$ to the hypothesis list, and then splits it apart using $\Leftrightarrow\vdash$ and $\Rightarrow\vdash$. The latter produces two subgoals: the first is the required sequent (reduced to $\vdash q$ by $thin$) and the second is of the form $p, \ldots \vdash p$; which is discharged by $assumption$.

```
op |-EQULIFT=> : Predicate ProofTactic -> Tactic .
eq |-EQULIFT=> (p <=> q, PT) (% | * |- p) =
   ( CUTLEM (p <=> q, PT) THEN LIFT(0,1,0,equ|-) THEN LIFT(0,2,0,imp|-)
   THENL (THIN(0,1,2), LIFT(0,1,1,assumption) ) ) .
```

The goal-term is not necessary in this case; it simply avoids the inefficiency of applying the tactic when it is certain to fail. It also serves to ensure that the position numbers supplied to $LIFT$ are correct (i.e. that there are no spurious predicates present which might become involved in the proof); the tactic will, in general, need to be $lift$-ed before use. The tactic could be more concisely written, with the user merely supplying q, and the tactic forming the predicate $p \Leftrightarrow q$ to be supplied to $CUTLEM$. This is of little consequence, as `|-EQULIFT=>` will generally be used within other tactics, as illustrated below.

5.3 Tactic Transformation

With such a rich tactic language, there will be many tactic forms which will be functionally equivalent. It has already been noted that lifting can be used with tactics to create efficient new tactics. *CUTLEM*, for example, can be more efficiently expressed with the *THENL* within the scope of the *LIFT*:

```
eq CUTLEM (p, PT) Seq = LIFT(0,0,0,(cut(p) THENL(PT, idtac))) .
```

This uses only one instance of *LIFT* instead of the two above. A more concrete example is this derivation involving the axiom of extension (expressed here as an inference. See page 13)

$$
\cfrac{\cfrac{d \mid \varPhi \vdash \forall x : t \bullet x \in u, \varPsi \qquad d \mid \varPhi \vdash \forall x : u \bullet x \in t, \varPsi}{d \mid \varPhi \vdash \forall x : t \bullet x \in u \land \forall x : u \bullet x \in t, \varPsi}\ {\scriptstyle (\vdash \land)}}{d \mid \varPhi \vdash t = u, \varPsi}\ {\scriptstyle (\vdash\ EXTENSION(x))}
$$

which could be programmed as

```
LIFT(0,0,1,|-EXTENSION(x)) THEN LIFT(0,0,1,|-and)
```

but is better written as

```
LIFT(0,0,1,|-EXTENSION(x) THEN |-and) .
```

It seems that rule lifting frequently distributes through *THEN*. Similarly some tactics expressed using pattern matching to take different actions depending on the form of the goal could also be written using *ELSE*. Some ways of expressing tactics will be much more efficient than others. It should be possible to construct some transformational rules which will take tactics to their most efficient form. It may even be worthwhile to have OBJ3 undertake this transformation before applying the tactic.

Some general-purpose tactics have been developed for our particular problem domain—for example, for commencing the proof of the initialisation theorem for a Z specification.

6 Expressions

In order to reason about Z specifications, $\mathcal{W}$ provides a number of axioms which describe how sets and functions and the predicate calculus are related. There is also a theorem which permits axioms to be expressed as premiss-free inference rules, so that, for example, the axiom concerning binding membership becomes a premiss-free inference rule.

$$\vdash b \in S \Leftrightarrow b.S \qquad \text{becomes} \qquad \cfrac{}{\vdash b \in S \Leftrightarrow b.S}\ (bindingMem)\ .$$

Such rules are readily implemented as rules which produce no new subgoals, but to apply them in this form would be tedious in the extreme. Fortunately, it is easy to incorporate them in a tactic which makes the rule very usable:

$$\cfrac{\vdash b.S}{\vdash b \in S}\ (\vdash\ BINDINGMEM)\ .$$

```
op |-BINDINGMEM : -> Tactic .
eq |-BINDINGMEM (% | * |- b \in S) =
    |-EQULIFT=>(b \in S <=> b . S, bindingMem) .
```

This scheme also allows parameters to be provided to the inference rules. For example, the axiom of extension quantifies over a variable, with certain freeness conditions:

$$\vdash t = u \Leftrightarrow \forall x : t \bullet x \in u \wedge \forall x : u \bullet x \in t \qquad \text{provided } x \notin (\phi_e u \cup \phi_e t) .$$

The tactic |-EXTENSION implements this axiom as an inference rule, allowing the user to choose the bound variable (its freeness being assured by the rule **extension**).

```
op extension : -> Rule .
cq extension (% | * |- (t = u) <=>
      ((|A| (x : t) <.> (x \in u)) ^ (|A| (x : u) <.> (x \in t)))) = []
    if (((x) inter (phie(u) union phie(t))) == *nil*) .
op |-EXTENSION : Word -> Tactic .
eq |-EXTENSION(x) (% | * |- t = u) =
    |-EQULIFT=>(t = u <=> |A| x : t <.> x \in t ^
              |A| x : u <.> x \in t, extension) .
```

Section 6 illustrates the use of this tactic. Moreover, application of |-EXTENSION will invariably be followed by ⊢∧ and ⊢ ∀, so it may be bundled into a tactic which does precisely this, and automatically chooses a fresh bound variable:

```
op |-EXT-TAC : -> Tactic .
eq |-EXT-TAC (% | * |- t = u) =
    |-EXTENSION(new(x,x)) THEN |-and THEN |-all .
```

So this tactic makes a (relatively) large reasoning step:

$$\frac{x_1 : t \vdash x \in u \qquad x_1 : u \vdash x \in t}{\vdash t = u} \; (\text{|-EXT-TAC}) \quad .$$

Rules which are expressed using ellipses present the greatest difficulty. Their presentation in $\mathcal{W}$ is essentially informal. Before they can be encoded, they must be formalised. Thus

$$\vdash (t_1, \ldots, t_n) = (u_1, \ldots, u_n) \Leftrightarrow t_1 = u_1 \wedge \ldots \wedge t_n = u_n$$

is more precisely expressed as

$$\vdash ts = us \Leftrightarrow \xi(ts, us)$$
where $\xi(t, u) \equiv (t = u)$ and $\xi((t, ts), (u, us)) \equiv (t = u) \wedge \xi(ts, us) .$

Once the axiom is expressed in this form, an OBJ3 implementation becomes natural:

```
op cartProdEqu : -> Rule .
op mkeqconj : Expressions Expressions -> Predicate .
eq mkeqconj (t,u) = (t = u) .
eq mkeqconj ((t,ts),(u,us)) = (t = u) ^ mkeqconj(ts,us) .

cq cartProdEqu (% | * |- (Tuple(ts) = Tuple(us)) <=> p) = []
    if (p == mkeqconj(ts,us)) .
```

and, again, a tactic makes it usable:

```
op |-CARTPRODEQ : -> Tactic .
eq |-CARTPRODEQ (% | * |- Tuple(ts) = Tuple(us)) =
   |-EQULIFT=>((Tuple(ts) = Tuple(us)) <=>
                  mkeqconj(ts,us) , cartProdEqu) .
```

7 Declarations

$\mathcal{W}$ includes rules for making use of the large structuring constructs in a Z specification: schemas, axiomatic/generic definitions, etc. These inference rules are implemented as 2OBJ **Rules** with schemas etc. as parameters.

7.1 Schemas

This schema

permits this inference to be made:

$$\frac{S = [d \mid p] \vdash}{\vdash} .$$

Which is expressed in 2OBJ as

```
op schdef : SchemaDef -> Rule .
eq schdef (SCH S IS d ST p END) (% | * |- *) = (% | S = [ d | p ] |- *) .
```

Clearly the user does not want to type out the schema definition each time it is used, so we encode the definitions from a given Z specification in an OBJ module. By defining an auxiliary operator

```
op _ -def : SchemaName -> SchemaDef .
```

we enable the user to make definitions like

```
eq S -def = SCH S IS x : T ST x \in U END .
```

and refer to S **-def** in invoking the rule. In fact, this is made still easier by a tactic:

```
op SCHDEF : SchemaName -> Tactic .
eq SCHDEF (S) Seq = LIFT(0,0,0,schdef(S -def)) .
```

This encoding also makes alphabet calculations very straightforward: when the **alpha** function encounters a schema name S as part of a declaration, it tries to expand S **-def**.

The primitive inference rules are not particularly useful, in that the predicates introduced to the sequent will invariably be used with an application of Leibniz' rule. So, for schemas, for example, we have a tactic:

```
op APPLY-SCHDEF : SchemaName -> Tactic .
eq APPLY-SCHDEF (S) (% | * |- p) = ( SCHDEF(S) THEN |-LEIBNIZ
   THEN THIN(0,1,0) THEN subst THEN EXHAUST(|-and) ) .
```

This brings the schema equality into the assumptions, uses it to rewrite the right-hand side, removes the definition again, applies subst (as |-LEIBNIZ introduces a binding, rather than actually rewriting the right-hand side) and then exhaustively applies ⊢∧ to split the goal into its constituent parts. For example, given

$$S \mathrel{\hat{=}} [x : \mathsf{N} \mid x \le 6] \ ,$$

we infer

$$\frac{\vdash x \in \mathsf{N} \qquad \vdash x \le 6}{\vdash S} \ (\text{APPLY-SCHDEF(S)}) \quad .$$

The tactic AUTO-SCHDEF uses APPLY-SCHDEF, choosing the schema name from the form of the goal.

```
op AUTO-SCHDEF : -> Tactic .
eq AUTO-SCHDEF (% | * |- S) = APPLY-SCHDEF(S) .
eq AUTO-SCHDEF (% | * |- b . S) = APPLY-SCHDEF(S) .
```

Since schemas are often nested, application of EXHAUST(AUTO-SCHDEF) is a common paradigm in tactics where schema definitions need to be expanded, for example in the tactic for initial state theorem proofs.

7.2   Generic Definitions

In a similar way, whilst the generic definitions which comprise the Z mathematical toolkit are available to the user of Jigsa$\mathcal{W}$, they will generally be used via tactics which hide the instances of GenDef (the equivalent for generic definitions of schdef for schemas). For example, dom has the following definition

```
let domdef = ( GEN [ X , Y ] BAR
      (dom : (PP(X \cross Y) --> PP(X)))
   ST
      (|A| R : PP(X \cross Y) <.> dom R =
         { (x : X) ; (y : Y) | ((x |-> y) \in R) <.> x })
   END ) .
```

and the tactic below makes, for example, the inferences shown in Fig. 1.

```
op |-DOM-TAC([ _ ], _) : Expressions Expression -> Tactic .
eq |-DOM-TAC([X,Y], S) (% | * |- p) =
(  GENDEF(domdef,[X,Y]) THEN CUT(<| R > S |> \in [ R : PP(X \cross Y) ])
   THENL
   (
      ( THIN(0,1 2,2) THEN |-BINDINGMEM THEN subst THEN
         |-POWERSET(x) THEN |-all )
   ,
      ( LIFT(0,1 3,0,all|-) THEN THIN(0,1 2 4,0) THEN subst THEN
         LIFT(0,1,1,|-LEIBNIZ) THEN THIN(0,1,0) )
   )
) .
```

The aim is to simplify a goal of the form $\vdash z \in \operatorname{dom}[X, Y]S$. Application of *GenDef* introduces the signature and predicate from the definition of dom as antecedents. The *cut* rule introduces a binding which can be used to specialise the universal quantifier from the definition of dom (i.e. it identifies R in the definition with S in the goal). This produces two subgoals. The first asserts that the chosen binding belongs to the correct (schema) type. This is simplified, using *bindingMem* etc., to an assertion that S is a subset of $X \times Y$. The second subgoal is rewritten using $\forall \vdash$, *thin* and *subst* so that the antecedent contains a definition of $\operatorname{dom}[X, Y]S$ using a set comprehension. *Leibniz'* rule is used to instantiate that definition, and then the rule of *thin* is used to remove the definition from the antecedent.

$$
\cfrac{
\cfrac{
\cfrac{
\cfrac{
\cfrac{
\cfrac{
\cfrac{
\cfrac{
\cfrac{
\begin{array}{c}
\cfrac{
\cfrac{
\cfrac{
\cfrac{x : S \vdash x \in X \times Y}{\vdash \forall x : S \bullet x \in X \times Y}\,(\vdash \forall)
}{\vdash S \in \mathbf{P}(X \times Y)}\,(powerset)
}{\vdash (\!|\, R \leadsto S\, |\!).[R : \mathbf{P}(X \times Y)]}\,(subst)
}{\vdash (\!|\, R \leadsto S\, |\!) \in [R : \mathbf{P}(X \times Y)]}\,(b'Mem) \\
\begin{array}{c}
\operatorname{dom} \in \mathbf{P}(X \times Y) \to \mathbf{P}(X), \\
\forall R : \mathbf{P}(X \times Y) \bullet \operatorname{dom}[X, Y]R = \\
\{x : X; y : Y \mid x \mapsto y \in R \bullet x\} \\
\vdash \\
(\!|\, R \leadsto S\, |\!) \in [R : \mathbf{P}(X \times Y)], \\
z \in \operatorname{dom}[X, Y]S
\end{array}
\end{array}
}{}
\quad \text{(thin)}
\qquad
\cfrac{
\cfrac{
\cfrac{
\cfrac{
\cfrac{
\begin{array}{c}
\vdash z \in \{x : X; y : Y \mid x \mapsto y \in S \bullet x\}
\end{array}
}{\begin{array}{c}
\operatorname{dom}[X, Y]S = \\
\{x : X; y : Y \mid x \mapsto y \in S \bullet x\} \\
\vdash
\end{array}}\,(thin)
}{\begin{array}{c}
z \in \{x : X; y : Y \mid x \mapsto y \in S \bullet x\} \\
\operatorname{dom}[X, Y]S = \\
\{x : X; y : Y \mid x \mapsto y \in S \bullet x\} \\
\vdash
\end{array}}\,(Leib)
}{\begin{array}{c}
z \in \operatorname{dom}[X, Y]S \\
(\!|\, R \leadsto S\, |\!).(\operatorname{dom}[X, Y]R = \\
\{x : X; y : Y \mid x \mapsto y \in R \bullet x\}) \\
\vdash
\end{array}}\,(subst)
}{\begin{array}{c}
z \in \operatorname{dom}[X, Y]S \\
(\!|\, R \leadsto S\, |\!) \in [R : \mathbf{P}(X \times Y)], \\
\forall R : \mathbf{P}(X \times Y) \bullet \operatorname{dom}[X, Y]R = \\
\{x : X; y : Y \mid x \mapsto y \in R \bullet x\}, \\
(\!|\, R \leadsto S\, |\!).(\operatorname{dom}[X, Y]R = \\
\{x : X; y : Y \mid x \mapsto y \in R \bullet x\}), \\
\operatorname{dom} \in \mathbf{P}(X \times Y) \to \mathbf{P}(X) \\
\vdash
\end{array}}\,(thin)
}{\begin{array}{c}
z \in \operatorname{dom}[X, Y]S \\
(\!|\, R \leadsto S\, |\!) \in [R : \mathbf{P}(X \times Y)], \\
\operatorname{dom} \in \mathbf{P}(X \times Y) \to \mathbf{P}(X), \\
\forall R : \mathbf{P}(X \times Y) \bullet \operatorname{dom}[X, Y]R = \\
\{x : X; y : Y \mid x \mapsto y \in R \bullet x\} \\
\vdash \\
z \in \operatorname{dom}[X, Y]S
\end{array}}\,(\forall \vdash)
}{}
}{
\begin{array}{c}
\operatorname{dom} \in \mathbf{P}(X \times Y) \to \mathbf{P}(X) \\
\forall R : \mathbf{P}(X \times Y) \bullet \operatorname{dom}[X, Y]R = \\
\{x : X; y : Y \mid x \mapsto y \in R \bullet x\}, \\
\vdash \\
z \in \operatorname{dom}[X, Y]S
\end{array}
}\,(cut)
}{\vdash z \in \operatorname{dom}[X, Y]S}\,(GenDef(\operatorname{dom}))
$$

Fig. 1. Application of |-DOM-TAC

7.3 Abbreviations

One further class of definitions found in Z is the abbreviation definitions:

$$\varnothing[X] == \{x : X \mid false\} \ .$$

$\mathcal{W}$ has, so far, given no rule for dealing with such definitions, but in order to accomplish useful proofs, a way is needed of dealing with them (for example, the definition of $\varnothing$ is essential in many initial state theorem proofs). The abbreviation is intended as shorthand for the generic definition

```
┌─[X]══════════════════════════════
│ ∅ : P X
├──────────────────────────────────
│ ∅ = {x : X | false}
└──────────────────────────────────
```

but to make this translation, type inference is needed—which we do not have. The encoding used, for the time being, keeps to the spirit of the abbreviation; it is implemented as a direct OBJ3 rewrite:

```
[axiom emptydef] eq \empty [ t ] = (<| X  > t |> . { x : X | False }) .
```

The binding is used to prevent any problems of variable capture: it allows substitution to remain in the $\mathcal{W}$ scheme, rather than conforming to OBJ3's ideas of rewriting. The labels "axiom" and "emptydef" serve respectively to prevent the rule from being used as a general rewrite, and to identify the rule when the user wishes to apply it. (The rule is applied using |-apply, which is implemented using the 2OBJ operation namedred.) A common use of this definition is to discharge goals of the form $x \in \varnothing[X] \vdash$ by reducing the left-hand side to *false*. This is accomplished by EMPTY-TAC|-.

```
op EMPTY-TAC|- : -> Tactic .
eq EMPTY-TAC|- (% | t \in \empty [ u ] |- *) =
    ( apply|-('emptydef) THEN subst THEN SETCOMP|- THEN
    exist|- THEN LIFT(0,1,0,and|-) THEN LIFT(0,1,0,false|-) ) .
```

This tactic exhibits a subtle problem: the definition of $\varnothing$ mentions a variable, x. Following the application of $(\exists \vdash)$, x is present in the declaration part of the schema, so to satisfy the side condition on $LIFT$, x must not appear free in the goal sequent, otherwise the tactic fails. Since the tactic does not produce any new subgoals, this problem could be avoided by beginning the tactic with a $TRY(chHypVars\langle\!| \ x \rightsquigarrow x_1 \ |\!\rangle)$. For a tactic which returns a new goal, however, such a renaming might be disconcerting for the user. $\mathcal{W}$ allows for α-conversion under the quantifier, but this has not been implemented yet.

8 Discussion

8.1 Achievements

The system which has been produced has been of considerable benefit in exploring how to reason in $\mathcal{W}$; indeed, it has brought to light several infelicities in the original presentation of $\mathcal{W}$. 2OBJ seems to be well-suited to this task. The chief benefit has been the ability to construct with relative ease a (probably) faithful encoding which *looks* rather similar to the "pencil-and-paper" presentation of the logic. Such a presentation has the advantage of being easy to verify correct (informally, at least), and one's intuition continues to apply. In the places where the encoding does not look like usual Z concrete syntax, in particular in dealing with fully instantiated generics, the intuition vanishes. This is not really a problem with the encoding, rather a feature of $\mathcal{W}$ (and probably any reasonable logic for Z): in order to reason with complete formality, the generic parameters must be present. Such formality is not usually necessary when producing proofs by hand, so the ability to elide this material from the user interface would be most useful.

If a system less general than 2OBJ were to have been used, many more problems can be forseen. If, for example, the form of the sequent were prescribed (and it were not the same as $\mathcal{W}$'s) notational tricks would be needed, which would necessarily render the encoding less readable. Since 2OBJ is intended to support many logics, it is not surprising that Jigsa$\mathcal{W}$ has not used all the features available. As 2OBJ continues to be developed, there may be opportunities for improving the encoding in future.

Some modest proofs have been completed using the tool; the proof of an initialisation theorem for a specification having about five schemas contributing to its state, and a precondition proof for an operation on that state. Many of the largest problems that have been encountered are those which one could imagine at the outset; the problems that any general-purpose system is likely to suffer when compared to a (perhaps hypothetical) specialised one. The implementation is very slow—taking about one hour on an otherwise idle large-memory SPARCstation to complete the proof of the initialisation theorem, and the user interface, though good for small terms, is far from being suitable for viewing the very large sequents which arise when, for example, generic definitions are brought into the antecedent. Moreover, the tool lacks standard input/output formats, so that the user must write some OBJ code in order to enter a Z specification, and the proof which is produced can be output only as a poor ASCII reduction of the proof tree, or a screen dump.

One major lack in 2OBJ (and hence Jigsa$\mathcal{W}$) at present is that it cannot support schematic proofs—i.e. proofs containing meta-variables (variables denoting predicates, for example). This is because rules' side conditions are all fully evaluated as the rule is applied; and freeness conditions are generally satisfied (x does not occur free in the literal "p", even if p denotes a predicate); so unsound inferences may follow. However, if such a proof is reduced to a tactic (and for the time being, at least, this is the only way to re-use proofs in 2OBJ) then whenever the tactic is applied (to ground terms), the side-conditions will be properly checked, and only sound inferences can result.

8.2 Future Work

Some work has been begun which aims to show that the encoding is faithful to $\mathcal{W}$— that is, that all the theorems it proves are theorems of $\mathcal{W}$. This is clearly important, as a reasoning system which makes no pretence at soundness is likely to be of little use to anyone.

"Raw" $\mathcal{W}$ is not seen as a practical tool for reasoning in Z, more as a foundation on which other reasoning systems may be constructed. The proofs constructed thus far have given some insight into the sorts of tactics which will be needed in order to make proving mundane theorems an easy task. Construction and refinement of these tactics is the obvious next step. It may be possible to exploit 2OBJ's rôle as a *meta-logical* theorem-prover in such refinements. Certainly, tactic transformations could be used to improve efficiency, and arranging for OBJ to make such transformations automatically should not be too hard.

Acknowledgements

$\mathcal{W}$ is the work of Jim Woodcock and Stephen Brien. Both have been very patient in answering my questions about the logic—and occasionally agreeing that new rules are needed. Andrew Stevens and Keith Hobley, as the main implementors of 2OBJ, have likewise been very quick at implementing enhancements that I suggested, and fixing bugs as they arose. Andrew made several important suggestions about how to do the encoding; in particular how to implement rule-lifting. Three anonymous referees also made some helpful comments. My work is being carried out under a research studentship from the UK Science and Engineering Research Council.

References

1. Jean-Raymond Abrial. A formal introduction to mathematical reasoning. Technical report, BP Research International, 1991.
2. Joseph Goguen, Andrew Stevens, Hendrik Hilberdink, and Keith Hobley. 2OBJ: A Metalogical Theorem Prover based on Equational Logic. *Philosophical Transactions of the Royal Society, Series A*, 1992.
3. Joseph Goguen and Timothy Winkler. Introducing OBJ3. Technical Report SRI-CSL-88-9, SRI International, Computer Science Lab, August 1988.
4. M. J. C. Gordon. HOL: A proof generating system for higher-order logic. In G. Birtwistle and P. A. Subrahmanyam, editors, *VLSI Specification, Verification and Synthesis*. Kluwer Academic Publishers, 1988.
5. M. J. C. Gordon, R. Milner, and C. P. Wadsworth. *Edinburgh LCF: A Mechanised Logic of Computation*, volume 78 of *LNCS*. Springer-Verlag, 1979.
6. Robert Harper, Furio Honsell, and Gordon Plotkin. A framework for defining logics. Report series, LFCS, Department of Computer Science, University of Edinburgh, 1991.
7. Hendrik B. Hilberdink. Oxford DPhil Thesis, To appear.
8. C. B. Jones, K. D. Jones, P. A. Lindsay, and R. Moore. *mural: A Formal Development Support System*. Springer Verlag, 1991.
9. Lawrence C. Paulson. *Logic and Computation—Interactive Proof with Cambridge LCF*. CUP, 1987.
10. Lawrence C. Paulson. The foundation of a generic theorem prover. Technical report, Computer Laboratory, University of Cambridge, 1988.
11. Lawrence C. Paulson. A preliminary user's manual for Isabelle. Technical report, Computer Laboratory, University of Cambridge, 1988.
12. J. Michael Spivey. *The ʃuzz Manual*. Computing Science Consultancy, 2 Willow Close, Garsington, Oxford OX9 9AN, UK, 1988.
13. Z Base Standard, March 1992. Version 0.5.

14. Andrew Stevens and Keith Hobley. *Mechanized Theorem Proving with 2OBJ: A Tutorial Introduction*, 1992.
15. J. C. P. Woodcock and S.M. Brien. *W: A Logic for Z*. In *Proceedings 6th Z User Meeting*. Springer-Verlag, 1992.

Formal Verification for Fault-Tolerant Architectures: Some Lessons Learned*

Sam Owre, John Rushby,
Natarajan Shankar, Friedrich von Henke**

Computer Science Laboratory
SRI International
Menlo Park CA 94025 USA

Abstract. In collaboration with NASA's Langley Research Center, we are developing mechanically verified formal specifications for the fault-tolerant architecture, algorithms, and implementations of a "reliable computing platform" (RCP) for digital flight-control applications.

Several of the formal specifications and verifications performed in support of RCP are individually of considerable complexity and difficulty. But in order to contribute to the larger goal, it has often been necessary to modify completed verifications to accommodate changed assumptions or requirements, and people other than the original developer have often needed to build on, modify, or cannibalize an intricate verification.

Accordingly, we have been developing and honing our verification tools to better support these large, difficult, iterative, and collaborative verifications. Our goal is to reduce formal verifications as difficult as these to routine exercises, and to maximize the value obtained from formalization and verification. In this paper, we describe some of the challenges we have faced, lessons learned, design decisions taken, and results obtained.

1 Introduction

Catastrophic failure of digital flight-control systems for passenger airplanes must be "extremely improbable"; a requirement that can be interpreted as a failure rate of less than 10^{-9} per hour [6, paragraph 10.b]. This must be achieved using electronic devices such as computers and sensors whose individual failure rates are several orders of magnitude worse than this. Thus, extensive redundancy and fault tolerance are needed to provide a computing resource of adequate reliability for flight-control applications. Organization of redundancy and fault-tolerance mechanisms for ultra-high reliability is a challenging problem. Redundancy management can account for half the software in a flight-control system and, if less than perfect, can itself become the *primary* source of system failure [11].

There are many candidate architectures for the ultra-reliable "computing platform" required for flight-control applications, but a general approach based on rational foundations was established in the late 1970s and early 1980s by the SIFT

---

* This work was performed for the National Aeronautics and Space Administration Langley Research Center under contracts NAS1 17067 and NAS1 18969.
** Von Henke's main affiliation now Fakultät für Informatik, Universität Ulm, Germany.

project [28]: several independent computing channels operate in approximate synchrony; single source data (such as sensor samples) are distributed to each channel in a manner that is resistant to "Byzantine" faults[3] [8], so that each good channel gets exactly the same input data; the channels run the same application tasks on the same data at the same time and the results are submitted to exact-match majority voting before being sent to the actuators. Failed sensors are dealt with by the sensor-conditioning and diagnosis code that is common to every channel; failed channels are masked by the majority voting of actuator output.

Experimental data shows that the large majority of faults are *transient* (typically single event upsets caused by cosmic rays, and other passing hazards): the device temporarily goes bad and corrupts data, but then restores itself to normal operation. The potential for lingering harm remains, however, from the corrupted data that is left behind. This contamination can gradually be purged if the computing channels vote portions of their internal state data periodically and replace their local copies by majority-voted versions. This process provides *transient recovery*; after a while, an afflicted processor will have completely recovered its health, refreshed its state data, and become a productive member of the community again. The viability of this scheme depends on the recovery rate (which itself depends on the frequency and manner in which state data are refreshed with majority voted copies, and on the pattern of dataflow dependencies among the application tasks) and on the fault arrival rate. Markov modeling shows that a nonreconfigurable architecture with transient recovery can provide fully adequate reliability even under fairly pessimistic assumptions.

We mentioned earlier that the distribution of single-source data must be done in a manner that is resistant to Byzantine faults. The same is true of the clock synchronization that keeps the channels operating in lock-step. Byzantine fault-tolerant algorithms suitable for both problems are known, but suffer from some disadvantages. First, the classic Byzantine fault-tolerant clock-synchronization algorithms do not provide transient recovery: there is no fully analyzed mechanism that allows a temporarily disturbed clock to get back into synchronization with its peers. Second, Byzantine fault-tolerant algorithms treat all faults as Byzantine and therefore tolerate *fewer* simple faults than less sophisticated algorithms. For example, a five-channel system ought to be able to withstand two simultaneous symmetric faults by simple majority voting, and as many as four crash faults. Yet a standard Byzantine fault-tolerant algorithm is only good for one fault of *any* kind in a five-channel system. To overcome this, the MAFT project introduced the idea of *hybrid* fault models and of algorithms that are maximally resistant to simultaneous combinations of faults of various types [25].

Although the principles just sketched for a "reliable computing platform" (RCP) for flight-control applications are understood, fully credible analysis of the necessary algorithms and their implementations (which require a combination of hardware and software), and of their synthesis into a total architecture, has been lacking.

---

[3] Byzantine faults are those that manifest asymmetric symptoms: sending one value to one channel and a different value to another, thereby making it difficult for the receivers to reach a common view. Symmetric faults deliver wrong values but do so consistently. Crash faults are as if the failed channel had simply ceased to exist.

In 1989, NASA's Langley Research Center began a program to investigate use of formal methods in the design and analysis of an RCP. We supplied our EHDM and (later) PVS verification systems to NASA Langley, and have collaborated closely with researchers there. The overall goal of the program is to develop mechanically checked formal specifications and verifications for the architecture, algorithms, and implementations of a nonreconfigurable RCP with transient recovery.

This is a rather ambitious goal, since the arguments for correctness of some of the individual Byzantine fault-tolerant algorithms are quite intricate, and their synthesis into an overall architecture is of daunting complexity. Because mechanized verification of algorithms and fault-tolerance arguments of the difficulty we were contemplating had not been attempted before, we did not have the confidence to simply lay out a complete architecture and then start verifying it. Instead, we first isolated some of the key challenges and worked on those in a relatively abstracted form, and then gradually elaborated the analysis, and put some of the pieces together. The process is still far from complete and we expect the program to occupy us for some time to come.[4] The verifications performed with our tools are described in Section 2, the lessons we have learned in Section 3, and brief conclusions are presented in Section 4. Before describing the verifications performed with them, we briefly introduce our tools.

1.1 Our Verification Systems

EHDM, which first became operational in 1984 [12] but whose development still continues, is a system for the development, management, and analysis of formal specifications and abstract programs that extends a line of development that began with SRI's original Hierarchical Development Methodology (HDM) of the 1970's. EHDM's specification language is a higher-order logic with a rather rich type system and facilities for grouping related material into parameterized modules. EHDM supports hierarchical verification, so that the theory described by one set of modules can be shown to interpret that of another; this mechanism is used to demonstrate correctness of implementations, and also the consistency of axiomatizations. The EHDM tools include parser, prettyprinter, typechecker, proof checker, and many browsing and documentation aids, all of which use a customized Gnu Emacs as their interface. Its proof checker is built on a decision procedure (due to Shostak [23]) for a combination of ground theories that includes linear arithmetic over both integers and rationals. EHDM's proof-checker is not interactive; it is guided by proof descriptions prepared by the user and included as part of the specification text [20].

Development of PVS, our other verification system, started in 1991; it was built as a lightweight prototype for a "next generation" verification system and in order to explore ideas in interactive proof checking. Our goal was considerably greater productivity in mechanically-supported verification than had been achieved with other systems. The logic of PVS is similar to that of EHDM, but has an even richer

---

[4] CLI Inc., and ORA Corporation also participate in the program, using their own tools. Descriptions of some of their work can be found in [1] and [24], respectively. The overall program is not large; it is equivalent to about three full-time staff at NASA, and slightly less than one each at CLI, ORA, and SRI.

type system. Its proof theorem prover includes the same decision procedures as EHDM, but in an interactive environment that uses a presentation based on the sequent calculus [15]. The primitive inference steps of the PVS prover are rather powerful and highly automated, but the selection and composition of those primitive steps into an overall proof is performed interactively in response to commands from the user. Theorem proving techniques prototyped in PVS are now being incorporated into EHDM.

Specifications in EHDM and PVS can be stated constructively using a number of definitional forms that provide conservative extension, or they can be given axiomatically, or a mixture of both styles can be used. Although a notion of implicit program "state" is supported in EHDM, it is not used in the specifications considered here; algorithms and computations are described functionally. The built-in types of EHDM and PVS include the booleans, integers, and rationals; enumerations and uninterpreted types can also be introduced, and compound types can be built using (higher-order) function and record constructors (PVS also provides tuples). The type systems of both languages provide features (such as predicate subtypes) that render typechecking algorithmically undecidable. In these cases, proof obligations (called type-correctness conditions, or TCCs) are generated and must be discharged before the specification is considered type correct. The specification languages of EHDM and PVS are built on very different foundations than those of, say, Z and VDM, but, in our experience, provide similar convenience and expressiveness.

2 Formal Verifications Performed

The first verification we undertook in NASA's program was of Lamport and Melliar-Smith's Interactive Convergence Algorithm (ICA) for Byzantine fault-tolerant clock synchronization. At the time, this was one of the hardest mechanized verifications that had been undertaken and we began by simply trying to reproduce the arguments in the journal paper that introduced the algorithm [7]. Eventually, we succeeded, but discovered in the process that the proofs or statements of all but one of the lemmas, and the proof of the main theorem, were flawed in the journal presentation. In developing our mechanically-checked verification we eliminated the approximations used by Lamport and Melliar-Smith and streamlined the argument. We were able to derive a journal-style presentation from our mechanized verification that is not only more precise than the original, but is simpler, more uniform, and easier to follow [19]. Our mechanized verification in EHDM took us a couple of months to complete and required about 200 lemmas (most of which are concerned with "background knowledge," such as summation and properties of the arithmetic mean, that are assumed in informal presentations).

We have modified our original verification several times. For example, we were unhappy with the large number of axioms required in the first version. Later, when definitional forms guaranteeing conservative extension were added to EHDM, we were able to eliminate the large majority of these in favor of definitions. Even so, Bill Young of CLI, who repeated our verification using the Boyer-Moore prover [29], pointed out that one of the remaining axioms was unsatisfiable in the case of drift-free clocks. We adopted a repair suggested by him (a substitution of $\leq$ for $<$), and also an improved way to organize the main induction. We have since verified the consistency of the axioms in our current specification of ICA using the theory interpretation mechanism of EHDM.

Our colleague Erwin Liu developed a design for a hardware circuit to perform part of the clock-synchronization function, and formally verified the design [10] (this was his first exposure to formal hardware verification). During circuit design, it became apparent that one of the assumptions of the clock-synchronization verification (i.e., that the initial clock corrections are all zero) is very inconvenient to satisfy in an implementation. We explored the conjecture that this assumption is unnecessary by simply eliminating it from the formal specification and re-running all the proofs (which takes about 10 minutes on a Sun SparcStation 2) in order to see which ones no longer succeeded. We found that the proofs of a few internal lemmas needed to be adjusted, but that the rest of the verification was unaffected.

We are now contemplating further adjustments to the verification. Dan Palumbo and Lynn Graham of NASA built equipment for experimenting with clock-synchronization circuitry and found that the observed worst-case skews were better than predicted by theory. They showed that a slight adjustment to the analysis can bring theory into closer agreement with observation [16]. We intend to incorporate this improved bound into our mechanically-checked verification, and will also expand the analysis to incorporate a hybrid fault model (an informal derivation has already been developed).

There are alternatives to ICA that seem more attractive from the implementation point of view. Also, there is a choice in formalizations of clock synchronization whether clocks are modeled as functions from "clock time" to "real time" or the reverse. ICA does it the first way, but the other appears to fit better into the arguments for an overall architecture. Accordingly, we next embarked on a mechanized verification of Schneider's generalized clock-synchronization protocol, which gives a uniform treatment that includes almost all known synchronization algorithms [21], and models clocks in the "real time" to "clock time" direction. As before, we found a number of small errors in the original argument and were able to produce an improved journal-style presentation as well as the mechanically-checked proof [22].

This verification included a proof that the "convergence function" of ICA satisfies Schneider's general conditions (thereby providing an independent formal verification of ICA). Paul Miner of NASA took a copy of our EHDM verification and extended it to verify that the more attractive convergence function characterizing the Welch-Lynch fault-tolerant mid-point algorithm [27] also satisfies these conditions. In addition, he identified improvements in the formulations of some of the conditions. In continuing work, he is verifying a significant extension to the algorithm that provides for transient recovery [14].

Turning from fault-tolerant clock synchronization to sensor distribution, we next focussed on the "Oral Messages" algorithm for Interactive Consistency [8].[5] Bevier and Young at CLI, who had already verified this algorithm, found it "a fairly difficult

---

[5] Interactive consistency is the problem of distributing consistent values to multiple channels in the presence of faults. It is the symmetric version of the Byzantine Generals problem, and should not be confused with interactive convergence, which is an algorithm for clock synchronization.

exercise in mechanical theorem proving" [1]. We suspected that their treatment was more complex than necessary, and attempted an independent verification. We were able to complete this in less than a week, and found that one of the keys to simplifying the argument was to focus on the symmetric formulation (which is actually the form required), rather than the asymmetric Byzantine Generals form [18].

Because of its manageable size and complexity (it is an order of magnitude smaller than the clock-synchronization proofs), we used verification of the Oral Messages algorithm as a test-case in the development of the theorem prover for PVS. Eventually we were able to construct the necessary proofs (starting from the specification and a couple of minor lemmas) in under an hour. Thus equipped, we turned to an important variation on the algorithm due to Thambidurai and Park [25] that uses a hybrid fault model, and thereby provides greater fault tolerance than the classical algorithm. Here we found not merely that the journal-style argument for the correctness of the algorithm was flawed, but that the algorithm contained an outright bug. We proposed a modified algorithm and our colleague Pat Lincoln formally verified its correctness—and then found that it, too, was flawed.

How could we verify an incorrect algorithm? The explanation is that our axiomatization of a certain "hybrid majority" function required "omniscience": it had to be able to exclude faulty values from the vote, whereas the source of all the difficulty in Byzantine fault-tolerant algorithms is that it is not known which values are faulty. Thus our algorithm was "correct" but unimplementable. Pat Lincoln detected this problem by thinking carefully about the specification, and we were then able to develop and formally verify a new and correct algorithm for Interactive Consistency under a hybrid fault model [9]. This work took less than two weeks, and was primarily undertaken by Pat Lincoln (using PVS) as his first exercise in mechanized formal verification. We believe that the discipline of formalism and the mechanical support provided by PVS were instrumental in developing a correct algorithm and argument for this tricky problem.

A model for the main fault-masking and transient-recovery architecture of RCP, and the argument for its correctness, were developed by Rick Butler, Jim Caldwell and Ben Di Vito at NASA. Their model and verification were formal, in the style of a traditional presentation of a mathematical argument [5]. Working in parallel, we developed a formal specification and verification of a slightly simplified, but also rather more general model [17]. Before formally specifying and verifying our model in EHDM, we developed a description and proof with pencil and paper. This description was developed with specification in EHDM in mind; it was built from straightforward mathematical concepts and was transliterated more or less directly into EHDM in a matter of hours. The formal verification took about three weeks of part-time work. Some of this time was required because the formal verification proves a number of subsidiary results that were glossed over in the pencil and paper version, and some of it was required because EHDM's theorem prover lacked a rewriter at that time. However, the mechanically verified theorem is also stronger than the pencil and paper version. The stronger theorem requires a proof by Noetherian induction (as opposed to simple induction for the weaker theorem), which is rather tricky to state and carry out in semi-formal notation, but no more difficult than simple induction in a mechanized setting.

The most ambitious formal verification carried out in the program so far was performed by Rick Butler and Ben Di Vito at NASA: it connects fault masking with clock synchronization. The models for fault masking (and also those for interactive consistency) assume totally synchronous execution of the redundant computing channels (and instantaneous communication), whereas the clock-synchronization algorithms guarantee only that the channels are synchronized within some small bound. The reconciliation of these different models involves a hierarchical verification with two intermediate levels. The topmost level is called the uniprocessor synchronous (US) model: it is essentially the correctness criterion—a single computer that never fails. The level below this is the fault-masking model, now called the replicated synchronous (RS) model; below this is the distributed synchronous (DS) model, which introduces the fact that communication between channels takes time; and at the bottom is the distributed asynchronous (DA) model, which connects to the clock synchronization conditions and recognizes that the channels are only approximately synchronized. The US to RS verification is similar to ours, the other two are new and involve quite large specifications and proofs (well over 300 lemmas) [4].

3 Lessons Learned

We summarize here some of the main characteristics observed and conclusions drawn from the verifications described above. First, most of the proofs we have been interested in checking, not to mention many of the theorems, and some of the algorithms, were incorrect when we started. Thus, we find it at least as important that a verification system should assist in the early detection of error as that it should confirm truth. Second, our axiomatizations were occasionally unsound, and sometimes they were sound but didn't say what we thought they did. Mechanisms for establishing soundness of axiomatizations are clearly desirable (purely definitional specifications are often too restricting), as are habits and techniques for reviewing the content of formal specifications. Third, our verifications are seldom finished: changed assumptions and requirements, the desire to improve an argument or a bound, and simple experimentation, have led us to revise some of our verifications several times. We believe that investment in an existing verification should assist, not discourage discovery of simplifications, improvements, and generalizations. But this means that the method of theorem proving must be robust in the face of reasonably small changes to the specification. Fourth, our formal specifications and verifications were often used by someone other than their original developer. These secondary users sometimes carry off just a few theories (or ideas) for their own work, sometimes they substantially modify or extend the existing verification, and sometimes they build on top of it; in all cases, they need to understand the original verification. These activities argue for specifications and proofs that are structured or modularized in some way, and that are sufficiently perspicuous that users other than the original authors can comprehend them well enough to make effective use of them.

In the following subsections we expand on these points and describe some of the design decisions taken in our languages, support tools, and theorem provers, in light of these experiences.

3.1 Specification Language

In this section we describe some of the choices made in the design of our specification languages, and discuss some of the changes we have made in the light of experience. The main constraints informing our design decisions have been the desire for a language that is powerfully expressive, yet that nonspecialists find comfortable, that has a straightforward semantics, and that can be given effective mechanized support—this includes very stringent (and early) detection of specification errors, as well as powerful theorem proving.

The domain of problems that we have investigated involves asynchronous communication, distributed execution, real-time properties, fault tolerance, and hierarchical development. One question that arises is the degree of support for these topics that should be built-in to the specification language and its verification system. Our viewpoint here is pragmatic rather than philosophical: we have found that a classical, simply-typed higher-order logic is adequate for formalizing all the concepts of interest to us in a perspicuous and effective way. We have also found that the computational aspects of the systems of interest to us are adequately modeled in a functional style and we have not found it necessary to employ Hoare logic or other machinery for reasoning about imperative programs.

We do use specialized formalisms, such as temporal logic, when it seems appropriate, but we do so by formalizing them within higher-order logic. The advantage of embedding such formalisms within a single logic is that it is then easier to combine them with others and easier to share common theories, such as datatypes, arithmetic, and other prerequisite mathematics. Furthermore, we are not restricted to a fixed selection of formalisms, but can develop specialized notations to suit the problem at hand—rather in the way that productive pencil and paper mathematics is done.

We have taken some pains to allow formal specifications to be rendered in a natural syntactic form. For example, we provide rich sets of propositional connectives (including a polymorphic *if-then-else*) and of arithmetic and relational operators, and we allow set-notation for predicates.[6] Several conveniences that appear syntactic actually require semantic treatment. For example, we allow the propositional connectives such as "or" and the arithmetic and relational operators such as $+$ and $\leq$ to be overloaded with new definitions (while retaining their standard ones). This allows the propositional connectives to be "lifted" to temporal formulas (represented as predicates on the natural numbers), for example, so that if x and y are temporal formulas, $x \vee y$ could be defined to denote their pointwise disjunction. These usages correspond to informal mathematical practice, but their mechanized analysis requires rather powerful strategies for type inference and name resolution.

Just as the syntactic aspects of our languages have been enriched over the years, so have their semantic attributes—and in particular the type systems. Initially we had just the "ground" types (i.e., uninterpreted, boolean, and integer and rational numbers) and (higher-order) function types. We soon found it convenient to add record and enumeration types, and then—the most significant step of all—predicate subtypes. In PVS we also provide tuple types, and dependent type constructions.

---

[6] In higher-order logic, sets are represented by their characteristic predicates, which are themselves simply functions with range type "boolean."

As their name suggests, predicate subtypes use a predicate to induce a subtype on some parent type. For example, the natural numbers are specified (in PVS) as:

$$nat : \mathbf{type} = \{n : int \,|\, n \geq 0\} \ .$$

More interestingly, the signature for the division operation (on the rationals) is specified by

$$/ : [rational, nonzero\_rational \rightarrow rational]$$

where

$$nonzero\_rational : \mathbf{type} = \{x : rational \,|\, x \neq 0\}$$

specifies the nonzero rational numbers. This constrains division to nonzero divisors, so that a formula such as

$$x \neq y \supset (y - x)/(x - y) < 0$$

requires the typechecker to discharge the proof obligation (or TCC)

$$x \neq y \supset (x - y) \neq 0$$

in order to ensure that the occurrence of division is well-typed. Notice that the "context" ($x \neq y$) of the division appears as an antecedent in the proof obligation. These proof obligations establish that the value of the original expression does not depend upon the value of a type-incorrect term. The arithmetic decision procedures of our theorem provers generally dispose of such proof obligations instantly (if they are true!), and the user usually need not be aware of them. This use of predicate subtypes allows certain functions that are partial in some other treatments to remain total (thereby avoiding the need for logics of partial terms or three-valued logics).

Proof obligations that are not discharged automatically by the theorem prover are added to the specification text and can be proved later, under the user's control. Untrue proof obligations indicate a type-error in the specification, and have proved a potent method for the early discovery of specification errors. For example, the injections are specified as a subtype of the functions:

$$injection : \mathbf{type} = \{f : [t_1 \rightarrow t_2] \,|\, \forall(i, j : t_1) : f(i) = f(j) \supset i = j\}$$

(here t_1 and t_2 are uninterpreted types introduced in the module parameter list). If we were later to specify the function *square* as an injection from the integers to the naturals by the declaration

$$square : injection[int \rightarrow nat] = \lambda(x : int) : x \times x : nat$$

then the PVS typechecker would require us to show that the body of *square* satisfies the *injection* subtype predicate.[7] That is, it requires the proof obligation $i^2 = j^2 \supset i = j$ to be proved in order to establish that the *square* function is well-typed. Since this theorem is untrue (e.g., $2^2 = (-2)^2$ but $2 \neq -2$), we are led to discover a fault in this specification.

---

[7] We would also be required to discharge the (true) proof obligation generated by the subtype predicate for *nat*: $\forall(x : int) : x \times x \geq 0$.

Notice how use of predicate subtypes here has automatically led to the generation of proof obligations that might require special-purpose checking tools in other systems. Yet another example of the utility of predicate subtypes arises when modeling a system by means of a state machine. In this style of specification, we first identify the components of the system state; an invariant specifies how the components of the system state are related, and we then specify operations that are required to preserve this relation. With predicate subtypes available, we can use the invariant to induce a subtype on the type of states, and can specify that each operation returns a value of that subtype. Typechecking the specification will then automatically generate the proof obligations necessary to ensure that the operations preserve the invariant.

Dependent types increase the expressive convenience of the language still further. We find them particularly convenient for dealing with functions that would be partial in simpler type systems. The standard "challenge" for treatments of partial functions [3] is the function $subp$ on the integers defined by

$$subp(i,j) = \mathbf{if}\ i = j\ \mathbf{then}\ 0\ \mathbf{else}\ subp(i, j+1) + 1\ \mathbf{endif}\ .$$

This function is undefined if $i < j$ (when $i \geq j$, $subp(i, j) = i - j$) and it is often argued that if a specification language is to admit such a definition, then it must provide a treatment for partial functions. Fortunately, examples such as these do *not* require partial functions: they can be admitted as total functions on a very precisely specified domain. *Dependent types*, in which the *type* of one component of a structure depends on the *value* of another, are the key to this. For example, in the language of PVS, $subp$ can be specified as follows.

$$subp((i\ :\ int),\ (j\ :\ int\ |\ i \geq j))\text{: } \mathbf{recursive}\ int =$$
$$\mathbf{if}\ i = j\ \mathbf{then}\ 0\ \mathbf{else}\ subp(i,\ j+1) + 1\ \mathbf{endif}$$
$$\mathbf{measure}\ \lambda\ (i\ :\ int),\ (j\ :\ int\ |\ i \geq j)\text{: }i - j^8$$

Here, the domain of $subp$ is the dependent tuple-type $[i : int, \{j : int\ |\ i \geq j\}]$ (i.e., the pairs of integers in which the first component is greater than or equal to the second) and the function is total on this domain.

The earliest versions of EHDM required almost all concepts to be specified axiomatically thereby raising the possibility of inadvertently introducing inconsistencies. Our decisions to support very powerful type-constructions and to embrace the consequence that theorem-proving can be required during typechecking were motivated by a desire to increase the expressive power of those elements of the language for which we could guarantee conservative extension. On the other hand, we do not wish to exclude axiomatic specifications; these are often the most natural way to specify assumptions about the environment, and top-level requirements. Axioms can be proved consistent by exhibiting a model—a process that is closely related to verification of hierarchical developments.

The established way to demonstrate that one level of specification "implements" the requirements of another is to exhibit an "abstraction" (also called "retrieve") function that induces a homomorphism between the concrete and the abstract specification. The required constructions can easily be specified within our specification languages, but we have found the process to be tedious and error-prone (for example,

---

[8] The **measure** clause specifies a function to be used in the termination proof.

it is easy to overlook the requirement that the abstraction function be surjective). Accordingly, we have provided mechanized support for hierarchical verification since the earliest versions of EHDM.[9] Our mechanization is based on the notion of *theory interpretations*; the basic idea is to establish a translation from the types and constants of the "source" or abstract specification to those of a "target" or concrete specification, and to prove that the axioms of the source specification, when translated into the terms of the target specification, become provable theorems of that target specification. The difference between the use of theory interpretation to demonstrate correctness of an implementation and to demonstrate consistency of a specification is that for the latter, the "implementation" does not have to be useful, or realistic, or efficient; it just has to exist.[10]

The basic mechanism of theory interpretation is quite easy to implement: a "mapping" module specifies the connection between a source and a target module by giving a translation from the types and constants of the former to those of the latter, and a "mapped" module of proof obligations is then generated. Special care is needed when the equality relation on a type is interpreted by something other than equality on the corresponding concrete type.[11] This construction requires proof obligations to ensure that the mapped equality is a congruence relation (i.e., has the properties of equivalence and substitutivity).

These straightforward mechanisms have become somewhat embellished over time, as the stress of real use has revealed additional requirements. For example, we originally assumed that source modules would be specified entirely axiomatically. This proved unrealistic: modules generally contain a mixture of axiomatic and definitional constructions, and it is necessary for the mapping mechanism to translate definitions (and theorems) into the terms of the target specification. Next, we found that our users wished to interpret not just single modules, but whole chunks of specification in which both source and target spanned several modules. This is quite straightforward to support, except that care needs to be taken to exclude modules common to both source and target (these often include modules that specify mathematical prerequisites common to both levels). As the size of specifications increases, it becomes necessary to introduce more layers into the hierarchical verification. For example, in demonstrating the consistency of the axiomatization used to specify assumptions about clocks [19], we have a module *algorithm* that uses (imports) the module *clocks*. An interpretation for *algorithm* will normally generate interpretations for the types and constants in *clocks* as well. But if we have already established an interpretation for *clocks*, we will want the interpretation for *algorithm* to refer to it, not generate a new one. Supporting these requirements in a reasonable way is not difficult once the requirements have been understood. Our experience has been that it takes some real-world use to learn these requirements.

---

[9] PVS does not support this at the moment; we are examining a slightly different approach involving quotient types.

[10] What is demonstrated here is *relative* consistency: the source specification is consistent if the target specification is. Generally, the target specification is one that is specified definitionally, or one for which we have some other good reason to believe in its consistency.

[11] For example, if abstractly specified stacks are implemented by a pair comprising an array and a pointer, then the equality on abstract stacks corresponds to equality of the implementing arrays *up to* the pointer; this is not the standard equality on pairs.

3.2 Support Tools

The previous few paragraphs have outlined some of the complicating details that must be addressed in the support environment for a specification language that provides a rich type system and theory interpretations. A consequence of the design decision that typechecking can require theorem proving is that the support environments for EHDM and PVS provide a far closer integration between the language analysis and theorem proving components than is usual. We discuss this in more detail in the section on theorem proving. More mundane, but no less important, engineering decisions concern the choice of interface, style of interaction, and functions provided by the support tools.

Our specifications have been quite large, typically involving hundreds of distinct identifiers and dozens of separate modules. We have found facilities for cross-referencing and browsing essential to productive development of large specifications and verifications, especially when returning to them after an absence, or when building on the work of others. Browsing is an on-line capability that allows the user to instantly refer to the definition or uses of an identifier; cross-reference listings provide comparable information in a static form suitable for typeset documentation.

Our specifications and verifications are developed over periods of days or weeks and we have found it imperative that the system record the state of a development (including completed and partial proofs) from one session to the next, so that work can pick up where it left off. We have found it best to record such information continuously (so that not everything will be lost if a machine crashes) and incrementally (so that work is not interrupted while the entire state is saved in a single shot).

We have also found it necessary to support version management and careful analysis of the consequences of changes. Version management is concerned with the control of changes to a formal development (ensuring that two people do not modify a module simultaneously, for example) and with tracking the consequences of changes. Not all verification systems police these matters carefully. For example, some implementations of HOL, which is often praised as a system with very sound foundations, can still consider a theorem proved after some of its supporting definitions have been changed.

EHDM at one time had quite elaborate built-in capabilities for version management, maintenance of shared libraries, and so on. These proved unpopular (users wanted direct access to the underlying files), so we have now arranged matters so that EHDM and PVS monitor, but do not attempt to control, access to specification files. Changes to specification files are detected by examining their write-dates, and internal data structures corresponding to changed files are invalidated. Users who wish to exercise more control over modification to specification files can do so using a standard version control package.

Tracking the propagation of changes can be performed at many levels of granularity. At the coarsest level, the state of an entire development can be reset when any part of it is changed; at a finer level, changes can be tracked at the module level; and at the finest level of granularity, they can be tracked at the level of individual declarations and proofs. Once the consequences of changes have been propagated, another choice needs to be made: should the affected parts be reprocessed at once, or only when needed? EHDM originally propagated changes at the module level (so that if a module was changed and its internal data structures invalidated, that invalidation would propagate transitively up the tree of modules). Reprocessing (i.e., typechecking and proving) took place under user control and reconstructed the internal data structures of the entire tree of modules. This proved expensive when large specifications were involved. An unsuccessful proof in a module at the top of a tree of modules might necessitate a change to an axiom in a module at the bottom. Re-typechecking the entire tree could take several minutes, with consequent loss of concentration and productivity. EHDM now propagates the consequences of changes at the level of individual declarations, and re-typechecking is done incrementally and lazily (i.e., only when needed), also at the level of declarations. This requires a far more complex implementation, but the increase in human productivity is enormous, as the user now typically waits only seconds while the relevant consequences of a change are propagated. Because it can take several seconds, or even minutes, to replay a proof, this is only done on request. "Proof-tree analysis" (described below) identifies the state of a proof during an evolving verification.

3.3 Theorem Proving

Theorem proving in support of fairly difficult or large verifications requires a rather large range of capabilities and attributes on the part of the theorem prover or proof checker. Furthermore, we have found that each formal verification evolves through a succession of phases, not unlike the lifecycle in software development, and that different requirements emerge at different phases. We have identified four phases in the "verification lifecycle" as follows.

Exploration: In the early stages of developing a formal specification and verification, we are chiefly concerned with exploring the best way to approach the chosen problem. Many of the approaches will be flawed, and thus many of the theorems that we attempt to prove will be false. It is precisely in the discovery and isolation of mistakes that formal verification can be of most value. Indeed, the philosopher Lakatos argues similarly for the role of proof in mathematics. According to this view, successful completion is among the least interesting and useful outcomes of a proof attempt at this stage; the real benefit comes from failed proof attempts, since these challenge us to revise our hypotheses, sharpen our statements, and achieve a deeper understanding of our problem: proofs are less instruments of justification than tools of discovery.

The fact that many putative theorems are false imposes a novel requirement on theorem proving in support of verification: it is at least as important for the theorem prover to provide assistance in the discovery of error, as that it should be able to prove true theorems with aplomb. Most research on automatic theorem proving has concentrated on proving true theorems; accordingly, few heavily automated provers terminate quickly on false theorems, nor do they return useful information from failed proof attempts. By the same token, powerful heuristic techniques are of questionable value in this phase, since they require the user to figure out whether a failed proof attempt is due to an inadequate heuristic, or a false theorem.

Development: Following the exploration phase, we expect to have a specification that is mostly correct and a body of theorems that are mostly true. Although debugging will still be important, the emphasis in the development phase will be on *efficient* construction of the overall verification. Here we can expect to be dealing with a very large body of theorems spanning a wide range of difficulty. Accordingly, efficient proof construction will require a wide range of capabilities. We would like small or simple theorems to be dealt with automatically. Large and complex theorems will require human control of the proof process, and we would like this control to be as straightforward and direct as possible.

In our experience, formal verification of even a moderately sized example can generate large numbers of lemmas involving arithmetic. Effective automation of arithmetic, that is the ability to instantly discharge formulas such as

$$x \leq y \ \wedge \ x \leq 1 - y \ \wedge \ 2 \times x \geq 1 \ \supset \ F(2 \times x) = F(1)$$

(where x and y are rational numbers), is therefore essential to productive theorem proving in this context.

Our proof checkers include decision procedures for linear arithmetic (including uninterpreted function symbols) over both integer and rational numbers, and propositional calculus [23]. It would, in our view, be quite infeasible to undertake verifications that involve large amounts of arithmetic (such as clock synchronization) without arithmetic decision procedures. However, it has also been our experience that seemingly non-arithmetic topics (such as fault masking) require a surprising quantity of elementary arithmetic (for example, inequality chaining, and "+1" arguments in inductions). Verification systems that lack automation of arithmetic and propositional reasoning require their users to waste inordinate amounts of effort establishing trivial facts.

Other common operations in proofs arising from formal verification are to expand the definition of a function and to replace one side of an equation by the corresponding instance of the other. Both of these can be automated by rewriting. But it is not enough for a prover to have arithmetic and rewriting capabilities that are individually powerful: these two capabilities need to be tightly integrated. For example, the arithmetic procedures must be capable of invoking rewriting for simplification—and the rewriter should employ the arithmetic procedures in discharging the conditions of a conditional equation, or in simplifying expanded definitions by eliminating irrelevant cases. Theorem provers that are productive in verification systems derive much of their effectiveness from tight integration of powerful primitives such as rewriting and arithmetic decision procedures—and the real skill in developing such provers is in constructing these integrations [2]. More visibly impressive capabilities such as automatic induction heuristics are useful (and we do provide them), but of much less importance than competence in combining powerful basic inference steps including arithmetic and rewriting.

An integrated collection of highly effective primitive inference steps is one requirement for productive theorem proving during the proof development phase; another is an effective way for the user to control and guide the prover through larger steps. Even "automatic" theorem provers need some human guidance or control in the construction and checking of proofs. Some receive this guidance indirectly in the order and selection of results they are invited to consider (the Boyer-Moore prover is like this), or in the form of a program that specifies the proof strategy to be used (the "tactics" of LCF-style provers such as HOL are like this). We have found that direct instruction by the user seems the most productive and most easily understood method of guidance, provided the basic repertoire of operations is not too large (no more than a dozen or so). And we find that a style of proof based on Gentzen's Sequent Calculus allows information to be presented to the user in a very compact but understandable form, and also organizes the interaction very conveniently.

A large verification often decomposes into smaller parts that are very similar to each other and we have found it useful if the user can specify customized proof control "strategies" (similar to LCF-style tactics and tacticals) that can automate the repetitive elements of the proof.

Presentation: Formal verification may be undertaken for a variety of purposes; the "presentation" phase is the one in which the chosen purpose is satisfied. For example, one important purpose is to provide evidence to be considered in certifying that a system is fit for its intended application. We do not believe the mere fact that certain properties have been formally verified should constitute grounds for certification; the *content* of the verification should be examined, and human judgment brought to bear. This means that one product of verification must be a genuine proof—that is a chain of argument that will convince a human reviewer. It is this proof that distills the insight into why a certain design does its job, and it is this proof that we will need to examine if we subsequently wish to change the design or its requirements. Many powerful theorem-proving techniques (for example, resolution) work in ways that do not lend themselves to the extraction of a readable proof, and are unattractive on this count. On the other hand, heuristic methods can generate "unnatural" proofs, while low-level proof checkers overwhelm the reader with detail. It seems to us that the most promising route to mechanically-checked proofs that are also readable is to allow the user to indicate major steps, while routine ones are heavily automated.

Generalization and Maintenance: Designs are seldom static; user requirements may change with time, as may the interfaces and services provided by other components of the overall system. A verification may therefore need to be revisited periodically and adjusted in the light of changes, or explored in order to predict the consequences of proposed changes. Thus, in addition to the human-readable proof, a second product of formal verification should be a description that guides the theorem prover to repeat the verification without human guidance. This proof description should be robust—describing a strategy rather than a line-by-line argument—so that small changes to the specification of lemmas will not derail it.

In addition to the modifications and adjustments that may be made to accommodate changes in the original application, another class of modifications—generalizations—may be made in order to support future applications, or to distill general principles. For example, we may extract and generalize some part of the specification as a reusable and verified component to be stored in a library.

Consequences for Prover Design: The evolution of our theorem proving systems to best serve the various requirements described above has followed two main tracks: increasingly powerful automation of low-level inference steps, such as arithmetic reasoning and rewriting, and increasingly direct and interactive control by the user for the higher level steps. We have found this combination to provide greater productivity than that achieved either with highly automated provers that must be kept on a short leash, or with low level proof checkers that must be dragged towards a proof.

We have made a number of design decisions in the interests of enhancing productivity for the human user that have entailed complex implementation strategies. For example, we allow the user to invent and introduce new lemmas or definitions during an ongoing proof; this flexibility is very valuable, but requires tight integration between the theorem prover and the rest of the verification system: the prover must be able to call the parser and typechecker in order to admit a new definition (and also when substitutions are proposed for quantified variables), and typechecking can then generate further proof obligations.

A yet more daring freedom is the ability to modify the statement of a lemma or definition during an ongoing proof. Much of what happens during a proof attempt is the discovery of inadequacies, oversights, and faults in the specification that is intended to support the theorem. Having to abandon the current proof attempt, correct the problem, and then get back to the previous position in the proof, can be very time consuming. Allowing the underlying specification to be extended and modified during a proof (as we do in PVS) confers enormous gains in productivity, but the mechanisms needed to support this in a sound way are quite complex.

One of the greatest advantages provided by interactive theorem provers is the ability to back out of (i.e., undo) unproductive lines of exploration. This can often save much work in the long run: if a case-split is performed too soon, then many identical subproofs may be performed on each of the branches. A user who recognizes this can back up to before the case-split, do a little more work there so that the offending subproof is dealt with once and for all, and then invoke the case-split once more.

Interactive theorem provers must avoid overwhelming the user with information. Ideally, the user should be expected to examine less than a screenful of information at each interaction. It requires powerful low level automation to prune (only) irrelevant information effectively. For example, irrelevant cases should be silently discarded when expanding definitions—so that expanding a definition of the form

$$f(x) = \text{if } x = 0 \text{ then } A \text{ else } B \text{ endif}$$

in the context $f(z+1)$ where z is a natural number should result in simply B. Such automation requires tight integration of rewriting, arithmetic, and the use of type information.

An interactive prover should allow the user to attack the subcases of a proof in any order, and to use lemmas before they have been proved. Often, the user will be most interested in the main line of the proof, and may wish to postpone minor cases and boundary conditions until satisfied that the overall argument is likely to succeed. In these cases, it is necessary to provide a macroscopic "proof-tree analyzer" to make sure that all cases and lemmas are eventually dealt with, and that all proof obligations arising from typechecking are discharged. In addition to this "honesty check," our systems can identify all the axioms, definitions, assumptions and lemmas used in the proof of a formula (and so on recursively, for all the lemmas used in the proof). Such information helps eliminate unnecessary axioms and definitions from theories, and identifies the assumptions that must be validated by external means.

4   Conclusions

We have described our experiences in developing mechanically-checked formal verifications of several quite difficult arguments arising in fault-tolerant systems. As well as ourselves, verifications were performed by colleagues at SRI who had not been involved in the development of our tools, and by collaborators 3,000 miles away at NASA Langley Research Center. The evolution of our languages and tools in response to the lessons learned took us in the direction of increasingly powerful type systems, and increasingly interactive and powerfully automated theorem proving. Powerful type systems allow many constraints to be embedded in the types, so that the main specification is uncluttered and typechecking can provide a very effective consistency check. Effectively automated and user-guided theorem proving also assists early detection of error, and the productive development of proofs whose information content can assist in the certification of safety-critical systems.

Most of the techniques we employ were pioneered by others. For example, Nuprl and Veritas provide predicate subtypes and dependent types; theory interpretations were used in Iota and, later, Imps; our theorem proving techniques draw on LCF, the Boyer-Moore prover, and on earlier work at SRI. Our systems differ from others in tightly integrating capabilities that usually occur separately; this has allowed us to provide expressive specification languages and powerful and very effective mechanization within a classical framework. It should be noted that many of the design choices we have made are tightly coupled: for example, predicate subtypes and dependent types bring great richness of expression to a logic of total functions but require theorem proving to ensure type correctness, which is only feasible if the theorem prover is highly effective; effective theorem proving needs decision procedures for arithmetic and equality over uninterpreted function symbols, which require that functions are total.

We consider these design choices to have served us well and, at some risk of complacency, we are satisfied with them; although we plan to improve on the details of our languages and their mechanizations, we do not expect to change the main decisions. Direct comparisons with alternative approaches would support objective evaluation, but will not be possible until more verification systems are capable of undertaking mechanically checked verifications of the scale and difficulty described here.

Although this paper has concentrated on our experiences with verification of fault-tolerance properties, EHDM and PVS are also being applied to designs for secure systems, to hardware, and to real-time applications. In other collaborative projects, PVS is being used in requirements analysis for the "Jet Select" function of the Space Shuttle flight control system, and for microprogram verification of a commercial avionics computer.

Acknowledgments: The work reported here owes a very great deal to our collaborators at NASA Langley Research Center: Rick Butler, Jim Caldwell, Paul Miner, and Ben Di Vito. We also thank colleagues at SRI: Pat Lincoln and Erwin Liu, who performed some of the verifications, and David Cyrluk, who contributed to the tools development.

References

1. W. R. Bevier and W. D. Young. The design and proof of correctness of a fault-tolerant circuit. In Meyer and Schlichting [13], pages 243–260.
2. R. S. Boyer and J S. Moore. Integrating decision procedures into heuristic theorem provers: A case study with linear arithmetic. In *Machine Intelligence*, volume 11. Oxford University Press, 1986.
3. J. H. Cheng and C. B. Jones. On the usability of logics which handle partial functions. In Carroll Morgan and J. C. P. Woodcock, editors, *Proceedings of the Third Refinement Workshop*, pages 51–69. Springer-Verlag Workshops in Computing, 1990.
4. Ben L. Di Vito and Ricky W. Butler. Formal techniques for synchronized fault-tolerant systems. In *3rd IFIP Working Conference on Dependable Computing for Critical Applications*, pages 85–97, Mondello, Sicily, Italy, September 1992.
5. Ben L. Di Vito, Ricky W. Butler, and James L. Caldwell. High level design proof of a reliable computing platform. In Meyer and Schlichting [13], pages 279–306.
6. *System Design and Analysis*. Federal Aviation Administration, June 21, 1988. Advisory Circular 25.1309-1A.
7. L. Lamport and P. M. Melliar-Smith. Synchronizing clocks in the presence of faults. *Journal of the ACM*, 32(1):52–78, January 1985.
8. Leslie Lamport, Robert Shostak, and Marshall Pease. The Byzantine generals problem. *ACM Transactions on Programming Languages and Systems*, 4(3):382–401, July 1982.
9. Patrick Lincoln and John Rushby. Formal verification of algorithm for interactive consistency under a hybrid fault model. Technical report, Computer Science Laboratory, SRI International, Menlo Park, CA, February 1993.
10. Erwin Liu and John Rushby. Formal verification of a clock synchronization support circuit. Technical report, Computer Science Laboratory, SRI International, Menlo Park, CA, 1993. Forthcoming.
11. Dale A. Mackall. Development and flight test experiences with a flight-crucial digital control system. NASA Technical Paper 2857, NASA Ames Research Center, Dryden Flight Research Facility, Edwards, CA, 1988.
12. P. Michael Melliar-Smith and John Rushby. The Enhanced HDM system for specification and verification. In *Proc. VerkShop III*, pages 41–43, Watsonville, CA, February 1985. Published as ACM Software Engineering Notes, Vol. 10, No. 4, Aug. 85.
13. J. F. Meyer and R. D. Schlichting, editors. *Dependable Computing for Critical Applications—2*, volume 6 of *Dependable Computing and Fault-Tolerant Systems*, Tucson, AZ, February 1991. Springer-Verlag, Wien, Austria.
14. Paul S. Miner. A verified design of a fault-tolerant clock synchronization circuit: Preliminary investigations. NASA Technical Memorandum 107568, NASA Langley Research Center, Hampton, VA, March 1992.
15. S. Owre, J. M. Rushby, and N. Shankar. PVS: A prototype verification system. In Deepak Kapur, editor, *11th International Conference on Automated Deduction (CADE)*, volume 607 of *Lecture Notes in Artificial Intelligence*, pages 748–752, Saratoga, NY, 1992. Springer Verlag.
16. Daniel L. Palumbo and R. Lynn Graham. Experimental validation of clock synchronization algorithms. NASA Technical Paper 2857, NASA Langley Research Center, Hampton, VA, July 1992.

17. John Rushby. Formal specification and verification of a fault-masking and transient-recovery model for digital flight-control systems. In Vytopil [26], pages 237–257.

18. John Rushby. Formal verification of an Oral Messages algorithm for interactive consistency. Technical Report SRI-CSL-92-1, Computer Science Laboratory, SRI International, Menlo Park, CA, July 1992. Also available as NASA Contractor Report 189704, October 1992.

19. John Rushby and Friedrich von Henke. Formal verification of algorithms for critical systems. In *SIGSOFT '91: Software for Critical Systems*, pages 1–15, New Orleans, LA, December 1991. Expanded version to appear in *IEEE Transactions on Software Engineering*, 1993.

20. John Rushby, Friedrich von Henke, and Sam Owre. An introduction to formal specification and verification using EHDM. Technical Report SRI-CSL-91-2, Computer Science Laboratory, SRI International, Menlo Park, CA, February 1991.

21. Fred B. Schneider. Understanding protocols for Byzantine clock synchronization. Technical Report 87-859, Department of Computer Science, Cornell University, Ithaca, NY, August 1987.

22. Natarajan Shankar. Mechanical verification of a generalized protocol for Byzantine fault-tolerant clock synchronization. In Vytopil [26], pages 217–236.

23. Robert E. Shostak. Deciding combinations of theories. *Journal of the ACM*, 31(1):1–12, January 1984.

24. Mandayam Srivas and Mark Bickford. Verification of the FtCayuga fault-tolerant microprocessor system, volume 1: A case-study in theorem prover-based verification. Contractor Report 4381, NASA Langley Research Center, Hampton, VA, July 1991.

25. Philip Thambidurai and You-Keun Park. Interactive consistency with multiple failure modes. In *7th Symposium on Reliable Distributed Systems*, pages 93–100, Columbus, OH, October 1988. IEEE Computer Society.

26. J. Vytopil, editor. *Formal Techniques in Real-Time and Fault-Tolerant Systems*, volume 571 of *Lecture Notes in Computer Science*, Nijmegen, The Netherlands, January 1992. Springer Verlag.

27. J. Lundelius Welch and N. Lynch. A new fault-tolerant algorithm for clock synchronization. *Information and Computation*, 77(1):1–36, April 1988.

28. John H. Wensley et al. SIFT: Design and analysis of a fault-tolerant computer for aircraft control. *Proceedings of the IEEE*, 66(10):1240–1255, October 1978.

29. William D. Young. Verifying the Interactive Convergence clock-synchronization algorithm using the Boyer-Moore prover. NASA Contractor Report 189649, NASA Langley Research Center, Hampton, VA, April 1992.

Conformity Clause for VDM-SL

Graeme I. Parkin and Brian Wichmann

National Physical Laboratory,
Teddington, Middlesex, England.
e-mail: gip@seg.npl.co.uk, baw@seg.npl.co.uk

Abstract. Some of the often quoted barriers to the use of formal methods
have been the lack of standardised formal methods and the lack of associated
tools. The Vienna Development Method Specification Language (VDM-SL)
is being standardised by ISO/IEC. It has become clear from this work that
we need to clarify what we mean by conformity of a specification or a tool to
such standards. In this paper we define what conformity to such standards
means and also highlight some of the problems that arise from this. This
work is also applicable to other language standards.

1 Introduction

Most international computing language standards now have what we shall call a
conformity clause. These international language standards use a variety of different
names for this clause such as conformance and compliance, but conformity is the
ISO approved term. In attempting to write one for the Vienna Development Method
Specification Language (VDM-SL) [1, 2] it became clear that we were not sure what
a conformity clause is nor how to write one. This paper describes the information
we have found on conformity clauses and gives one for VDM-SL. It concludes with
possible developments and uses for this work.

2 Conformity

A conformity clause for an international language standard is a statement within
that standard clearly stating which objects conform to that standard and how. We
have used the word objects in place of products, processes or services which is used in
the ISO/IEC Directives [3, 4, 5]. In the following sections we look at how conformity
clauses have been defined in the ISO/IEC directives [3, 4, 5], programming languages
[6, 7, 8, 9], specification languages [10, 11] and open systems interconnection [12].
We then summarise these by answering two questions: a) why is a conformity clause
needed and b) when one is needed what should a conformity clause contain?

2.1 ISO/IEC Directives

The ISO/IEC JTC 1 Directives [3, 4, 5] are published in three parts:

- Part 1: Procedures for the technical work [3]
- Part 2: Methodology for the development of international standards [4]

– Part 3: Drafting and presentation of international standards [5]

These documents outline the way that standards committees should work, what should be in a standard and how it should be presented.

We expected to find a definition of what a conformity clause is in one of these documents but there is none. The implication seems to be that a standard is a set of requirements with which it is necessary to conform to be able to claim conformity to that standard (section 2.1 [5]), that is, there is no need for a conformity clause.

However some statements made in these documents have a bearing on conformity. These are:

– The principle of 'verifiability' (section 5.3 [4]) which is that only such requirements shall be included in the standard that can be verified. Also it states (section 5.3.2 [4]) that a requirement should not be specified if no test method is known by means of which compliance with this requirement can be verified in a reasonably short time.
– Section 6 of [4] on test methods implies that all requirements should be testable.
– For each requirement there should be a test method (section 2.4.3 [5]). This is reinforced (section 2.4.5 [5]) by stating that the test methods should ensure reproducibility.
– A system of classification of how an object may conform to the stated requirements (section 2.4.6 [5]).

Summary

The directives give no definition of what a conformity clause is but indicate that conformity is linked with testability and perhaps with a system of classification.

2.2 Programming Languages

The following sections examine: a technical report which provides guidelines for conformity clauses for programming languages and the conformity clauses in some existing programming language standards.

Guidelines

In the area of programming languages a technical report [8] has been produced which gives guidelines for the preparation of conformity clauses in programming language standards. These guidelines state:

– "Conformity clauses ... aid the user of the standard in assessing conformity of processors[1] and programs[2] for adherence to the language standard". That is there are two types of users of a language standard: those who want to write programs and those who want to use or build compilers or tools. Both will want to conform to the standard and will have to satisfy different requirements.

---

[1] Defined in [8] as: Compiler, translator or interpreter working in combination with a configuration. In turn a configuration is defined as: Host and target computers, any operating system(s) and software used to operate a language processor.
[2] See [13] for a definition of this.

– "If conformity requirements are imprecise, testing for compliance can be difficult and potentially impossible". This clearly links the conformity clause with testing which is reinforced by another technical report specifically on test methods for programming language processors [14].

The guidelines covers what might be included in a conformity clause. For the processor this could cover correct translation of a conforming program, documentation, processor dependencies, errors, extensions, subsets and deprecated language elements, while for a program it gives some possible wordings of a conformity clause.

Pascal

The Pascal standard [7] has a conformity clause (clause 5 Compliance) which is divided in two parts, one for processors and the other for programs. For both processors and programs it allows two levels of conformity which have been defined in terms of the language constructs which are allowed.

The conformity clause for programs is defined purely in terms of the language constructs which are allowed (extensions being excluded). Also it does not allow a program to rely on any particular interpretation of implementation-dependent features.

The conformity clause for processors is much more complex, it covers:

– extensions, which the standard allows;
– implementation-defined features;
– violations which have to be reported if not errors, the Pascal standard defines an error: as a violation by a program of the requirements of the Pascal standard that a processor is permitted to leave undetected;
– documentation; and
– subsets which it allows.

C

The C standard [6] has a conformity clause (clause 4 Compliance) which distinguishes between programs (conforming programs) and processors (conforming implementations), both of which have two levels.

The conforming programs can have extensions.

The conformity clause for conforming implementations covers:

– extensions, which are allowed provided they do not alter the meaning of language constructs in the standard;
– subsets of which only one is allowed; and
– documentation.

Ada

The Ada standard [9] has a conformity clause (clause 1.1.2 Conformity of an implementation with the standard and clause 1.6 Classification of errors) which is divided up between two clauses. Both of these clauses deal with a processor (conforming implementation), although one refers only to a conforming implementation while the other refers only to an Ada compiler. A conforming program does not seem to be mentioned except implicitly.

The conformity clause for conforming implementations covers:

- correct translation of programs;
- errors;
- extensions which it does not allow;
- subsets which it does not allow; and
- documentation which it mentions in terms of permitted variations.

Summary

A conformity clause for programming languages usually distinguishes between two types of users, those that write programs and those that use or build processors (compilers).

The guidelines provide a useful checklist of topics to be covered in the conformity clause and link conformity with testing for it. The examples in the existing standards given in this paper cover most of those topics.

2.3 Specification Languages

As far as we know there exist no guidelines for writing conformity clauses for formal description techniques (specification languages), so we consider two existing standards.

LOTOS

The LOTOS standard [10] has a conformity clause (clause 3, Conformance) which only considers what a conforming specification[3] means. It does not mention what a conforming tool[4] should or should not do. A conforming specification is defined to be one that satisfies the requirements as stated in the standard.

Estelle

The Estelle standard [11] has a conformity clause (clause 4, Conformance) which considers both specifications and tools.

A conforming specification is defined as one that satisfies the requirements stated in the standard.

It states that the standard does not specify requirements for compilers or tools.

Summary

The existing formal description techniques standards[5] only consider conformity with respect to a specification. They do not give any requirements for a conforming tool which means that tools based on these standards will be unable to claim conformity to these standards.

---

[3] We shall for specification languages use specification in place of program.

[4] We shall for specification languages use tool in place of processors.

[5] There is only one other formal description techniques standard for SDL (Specification and Description Language, CCITT Z.100-Z.104, Geneva, 1988) which we have not yet looked at.

2.4 ISO/IEC 9646

The standard ISO/IEC 9646[6] [12] specifies a general methodology for testing for conformity (conformance) of products to International Standards or CCITT Recommendations that specify OSI protocols or transfer syntaxes which the products are claimed to implement. The purpose of conformity testing is to increase the inter-operability of different OSI protocols. The conformity testing is also set up to minimise the need for repeated testing of the same system.

The steps of conformity assessment outlined in the standard are:

1. For each System Under Test (SUT) there will be a System Conformance Statement (SCS) which summarises which standards are implemented.
2. For each standard for which conformity is claimed in the SCS there will be a Protocol Implementation Conformance Statement (PICS) which gives the capabilities, a set of functions in the relevant protocols, that have been implemented.
3. For the PICS an appropriate Abstract Test Method (ATM) and Abstract Test Suite (ATS) can be chosen. The ATMs which are allowed are defined in the ISO/IEC 9646 standard and are basically black box test methods. The ATS is defined in a test language which is defined in the ISO/IEC 9646 standard.
4. The SUT is then prepared for testing based on the ATSs and ATMs.
5. Testing takes place by executing the Parameterised Executable Test Suites which has been generated from the ATSs.
6. Finally an analysis of the test results takes place and reports are produced (which are again defined in the ISO/IEC 9646 standard).

It is stated that conformity testing is not intended to include assessment of the performance, robustness or reliability of a system. Testing cannot guarantee conformity to a specification since it detects errors rather than their absence. It does give some degree of confidence that the implementation has the required capabilities and that its behaviour conforms consistently in representative instances of communication.

The conformity requirements can be mandatory, conditional or options in an International Standard or CCITT Recommendation. They come in one of two types: static and dynamic. The static requirements are those that specify the allowable capabilities of a system. The dynamic requirements define the allowable behaviour of a system.

Summary

In OSI conformity is clearly related to testing and the ISO/IEC 9646 standard provides an excellent framework for setting up conformity testing facilities.

2.5 Summary

A language standard consists of a set of requirements which define the syntax and semantics of the language. A conformity clause for a language standard is then needed for the following reasons:

---

[6] The standard is in five parts of which we have referenced the first as this contains information relevant to conformity.

- The standard is read by different types of users[7] with different conformity needs: those who want to write programs/specifications and those who want to use or build processors/tools. These different requirements need to be clearly stated.
- It can cover topics not covered by the language definition such as extensions and subsets.
- It can define different levels of conformity to the standard. This allows processors/tools of different complexity to conform to the standard and yet to be clear about what they can or cannot do.
- It can make it very clear what requirements need to be conformed with.

A conformity clause for a language standard needs to consider the following:

- Testability, i.e. can the requirements be tested.
- Who will use the standard, usually writers of the language and users or builders of tools.
- Levels of conformity.
- The checklist given below for processors/tools which has been derived from the guidelines [8]:
  - correct translation of a conforming program;
  - documentation;
  - processor dependencies;
  - errors;
  - extensions;
  - subsets;
  - deprecated language elements.

3 Conformity Clause for VDM-SL

Having now discussed what a conformity clause is we will show how we have developed one for VDM-SL. Appendix C contains the proposed conformity clause for the VDM-SL standard while appendices A and B contain the proposed Scope and Definition clauses. Note some terms used in this section will be defined in appendix B and this will be indicated by using the sans serif style.

3.1 VDM-SL

The Vienna Development Method Specification Language (VDM-SL) is in the process of being standardised by ISO, a version exists in document *ISO/IEC JTC1/SC22/WG19, Document Reference IN9* [1] and also in [15, 16, 17]. For an introduction to standard VDM-SL see [2].

When building a system you need to know what you want to build, i.e. you need a specification. VDM-SL is a language which has been designed to help you to describe *what* you want to build rather than *how* to build it, although it can do both. A programming language can be used to describe what you want to build but can

---

[7] This point was introduced by D Rayner, Protocols Group, National Physical Laboratory, in a talk he gave on the use of ISO/IEC 9646 standard for non-OSI uses.

only do this by telling you how to build it. A specification of a system described in VDM-SL is not usually executable whereas if described in a programming language it will always be executable.

The method part of VDM-SL is the process of transforming your original specification into an executable one (i.e. one that can be implemented in some programming language), while at the same time preserving functionality (see [18] for more details). This is known as reification and could involve a considerable amount of proof work.

VDM-SL is a model-based specification language, i.e. specifications are explicit system models[8] constructed out of either abstract or concrete primitives. Also VDM-SL is formal in the sense that its semantics have been mathematically defined.

At the time of writing there exists no ISO model-based specification language standard.

3.2 Content and Structure of the VDM-SL Standard

We shall briefly describe the contents of the ISO VDM-SL standard by using the structure of the standard which is given in Table 1. This is correct at the time of writing although the element numbers may change or elements may be coalesced into one.

The definition of the contents of the Foreword, Introduction, Scope, Normative References and Definitions are defined in [5]. The annexes of the standard, Index and Cross References are all informative, i.e. published with the standard but are not part of the requirements of the standard. Annex A of the standard on modules may become normative but we will assume to be informative for this paper.

The element of the standard with title Conformity is being defined in this paper while the rest of the elements are requirements on VDM-SL.

A VDM-SL specification has two means of representation, Mathematical Concrete Syntax (MCS) and ISO 646 Concrete Syntax (ICS). The MCS allows the usual representation of mathematical symbols but does not define how it is to be represented electronically whereas the ICS does not always give the usual representation but does define how it is to be represented electronically. The MCS is to be used for presentation of VDM-SL on paper while the ICS is meant for electronic information exchange.

The Outer Abstract Syntax (OAS) is derived, approximately, from the MCS (or ICS) by the removal of the keywords and punctuation. It gives the structure of the language with details of its concrete representation stripped away and is used as the basis of the definition of VDM-SL.

The Syntax Mapping (SM) takes the OAS and derives the Core Abstract Syntax (CAS) from this. This basically simplifies the OAS and so makes the Dynamic Semantics (DS), which is defined on the CAS, easier to define.

The DS defines a function, called *SemSpec* whose signature is $Definitions \rightarrow \mathcal{P}(\mathcal{ENV}_{\mathcal{PURE}})$, from the CAS to a set of models. The semantics of a specification is this set of models. The DS is defined using mathematics based on set theory.

---

[8] The word model is used here with its usual dictionary meaning, that is not as defined in Appendix B.

508

Table 1. Structure of the VDM-SL standard

Element	Title	Acronym (for use in this paper)
	Foreword	
	Introduction	
1	Scope	
2	Normative References	
3	Definitions	
4	Conformity	
5	Basic Mathematical Notation	
6	Core Abstract Syntax	CAS
7	Dynamic Semantic Domains	
8	Dynamic Semantics	DS
9	Mathematical Concrete Syntax	MCS
10	ISO 646 Concrete Syntax	ICS
11	Outer Abstract Syntax	OAS
12	Syntax Mapping	SM
13	Static Semantic Domains	
14	Static Semantics	SS
Annex A	Modules	
Annex B	Language Survey	
Annex C	Examples	
Annex D	Bibliography	
	Index	
	Cross References	

A specification is said to be a meaningless specification if it is not correct with respect to the representation, MCS or ICS, it is written in and also if it does not satisfy the requirements e.g. uniqueness of identifiers within types, needed for it to be transformed into the CAS by the SM. A specification is said to be an inconsistent specification if it is not a meaningless specification and the DS produces an empty set of models. A specification is said to be a consistent specification if it is not a meaningless specification and the DS produces a non empty set of models for it.

To determine whether a given specification has a semantics with respect to the DS is undecidable. The Static Semantics (SS), which is decidable, will for a particular subset of the specifications determine whether they are consistent specifications or inconsistent specifications. The SS is written in VDM-SL. The SS defines various types of analysis on a given specification called basic (BASIC), local context (LOCALCONTEXT), total functions (TOTALFUNC) and union close (UNIONCLOSE). For each analysis it determines whether a specification is a consistent specification, an inconsistent specification or does not know. The SS has been written in such a way that it is clear which analysis is being done and whether it is checking for a consistent specification or an inconsistent specification. It is assumed that, when the SS is implemented, a basic analysis is always done. The SS covers all the checks done by the SM. We have attempted below to say what these analyses are trying to do:

basic This covers the use of identifiers not defined or not visible. It includes all the checks needed for the SM (duplication of identifiers). It also checks that function types are used correctly in recursive type equations, set types, map types, the state and the arguments to imperative functions.

local context Checks that a type of an expression is valid when the types of identifiers in that expression are given.

total functions Checks for the well formedness of total functions without preconditions (explicit or hidden) in terms of the types of the formal parameters, the body and the result of the function.

union close Uses the fact that if an expression holds for two types it holds for the union of those types.

The above brief description of the VDM-SL standard highlights the main difference from that of a programming language standard: it is always decidable whether a program written in a particular programming language has semantics whereas this is not true for a specification written in VDM-SL. This means that for a conventional programming language, if the static semantics are satisfied (i.e. the program can compile), it is meaningful to start execution of the program.

3.3 Tools for VDM-SL

We have classified the tools for VDM-SL in terms of the functionality they offer, this classification comes from [19], three different types are distinguished:

Syntactic support These are tools mainly concerned with grammar of the language and what can be checked automatically, e.g. pretty printers, structured editors, type checkers and cross reference generators.

Semantic support These tools can be used to manipulate the semantics of specifications. This will include developing one specification from another, generating proof obligations or prototyping specifications, e.g. prototypers, proof editors and proof checkers.

Pragmatic support These are tools that support the management of the development of a specification, e.g. version control and configuration control.

It is not yet clear to us whether tools for pragmatic support would come within the scope of the VDM-SL standard.

When comparing the above tools with those for programming languages there are many similarities. The main differences are that there are many more commercially available tools for programming languages. They are concentrated in the area of semantic support and the majority, by far, are compilers.

3.4 Rationale behind the Conformity Clause for VDM-SL

Appendix C contains the proposed version while in the following sections we give the rationale behind it. The conformity clause for the VDM-SL standard was developed based on the summary in Sect. 2.5.

There are two types of users of the VDM-SL standard those writing specifications[9] and those using or developing tools. The conformity clause has therefore been split in two, one for specification conformity and one for tool conformity.

Specification Conformity

The aim of the specification conformity clause is to make it clear which parts of the VDM-SL standard a users written VDM-SL specification must conform to.

An argument put forward for extensions is that formal methods have been developed using mathematics and when some new mathematical construct is needed you would like to include it since it could make your work considerably easier. Extensions are not allowed for three reasons:

- A language standard is a standard for a particular language and if extensions are needed they should be proposed for future revisions of that standard.
- If extensions were allowed it is not clear when you have a completely new language.
- It is difficult to define formally what you mean by an extension.

Subsets, which use some of the syntax of the VDM-SL standard and do not change their meaning, are still within the VDM-SL standard, while anything else we would classify as an extension, so that the above discussion would then apply.

The specification conformity clause is based on that of LOTOS and Estelle and requires conformity to either clause 9 or 10 and clauses 6, 7, 8, 11 and 12 of the VDM-SL standard. A specification will conform if it is consistent specification or it is not a meaningless specification. A specification which is not a meaningless specification will be allowed to conform because the DS is undecidable and so it will be impossible in some cases to prove that it is a consistent specification.

Tool Conformity

The aim of the tool conformity clause is to make it clear which parts of the standard a user or developer of VDM-SL tools must conform to.

The following discussion follows the points in the summary, not necessarily in the same order, given in Sect. 2.5 which are relevant to tools.

Testability

Requirements specified in an ISO standard must be testable and a practical test method specified (see Sect. 2.1). At the moment no practical test method exists that can test all the requirements for compilers (processors) or of protocols (see Sect. 2.4) because of the combinatorial explosion that occurs. Consider a programming language with say two types of statement and assume there is no limit on the number of consecutive statements: to test all possible sequences of n statements would mean 2^n tests! There are similar problems for protocols and specification languages. The tests that are done can only give some degree of confidence that the compiler

---

[9] We have, in the context of conformity of programming languages, replaced the word program by the newly defined word specification and similarly processor by tool.

(protocol) is implemented correctly. This forms the basis of language compiler validation suites, see, for example, the details of the Pascal compiler validation suite [20]. For how this type of testing might be extended see [21] on the Ada program test generator which generates self checking Ada programs to a specified complexity to test the code generation aspects of a compiler. It will be assumed that similar testing methods will be used to check conformity of tools for VDM-SL although this will be more difficult because of the undecidability of the semantics of VDM-SL. The advantage to users of a validation service is that it gives then some degree of confidence that a tool for VDM-SL is implemented correctly.

Existing programming language standards seemed to have assumed that there is only one type of tool for programming languages that is a compiler. They have also assumed, but not usually stated, certain characteristics of compilers, these are that they accept a concrete syntax stored in electronic form, error messages produced by the compiler can be captured by the environment it is being run in and it can be run in batch mode.

The tests in a validation suite for VDM-SL need to be stored in a common electronic interchange format to enable practical testing of VDM-SL tools and so we have chosen the ICS of VDM-SL. To further enable practical testing we need to remove as much human interaction as possible so we require that the tools under test can be run in batch mode and report their results in a form that can be captured by the test harness.

Therefore these assumed characteristics of compilers have been made as specific requirements for VDM-SL tools. This is made more necessary for VDM-SL tools because it is difficult to:

- develop a testing methodology for the the wide range of possible VDM-SL tools, of which no one type is dominant;
- test the WIMP (Windows, Icons, Menus, Pointing) like interfaces, for tools which, for example, only accept MCS;
- see how the developers of WIMP interfaces for language-based tools go about testing them.

It is also true that this should be done in the programming language conformity clauses for processors.

It should also be pointed out that formal methods like VDM-SL tend to be used in highly critical applications which demand a high degree of assurance of their correctness which in turn means that tools for such methods used in this environment need to be validated with ease.

An attempt has been made here to develop a conformity clause which covers all types of VDM-SL tools and really means that we only test the front end of tools and not what they produce. This is probably acceptable for existing VDM-SL tools but may need to be reconsidered when it becomes clearer what the main types of commercial VDM-SL tools are. This may lead to the tool part of the conformity clause being subdivided to cope with the different types of tools.

All the above discussion is based on the testing of tools but because of the mathematics underlying formal methods there exists the possibility of proving that tools for such methods conform to their language standards. This could be particularly relevant for prototyping tools where you would want to show that the semantics of the specification was equivalent to the semantics of the implementation language of the prototype. At the moment this does not seem very practical because of the size of proofs, lack of proof checkers and the need to set up some mechanism for independently checking proofs.

Extensions

The wide range of possible extensions makes it impossible to develop validation services to take these into account. Tools that accept extensions which do not affect the existing standard can be considered to be acceptable because the validation services can test only for the existing standard. A conforming tool will be one that conforms in terms of the existing standard but can accept extensions. If a conforming tool accepts extensions it must be capable of being run in a mode which rejects all such extensions. Extensions which are allowed by the tool should not invalidate any part of the existing standard except by prohibiting the use of one or more particular spellings of identifiers.

Subsets

The range of possible subsets makes it difficult to develop validation services to take these into account. If subsets were allowed then they could remove some aspects expected of VDM-SL or create a new language for example an executable subset would be more like a programming language. The VDM-SL standard does not specify any allowable subsets of itself and it is difficult to see how we could define a set of rules to define sensible allowable subsets (although it would be quite easy to define subsets for the implicit and explicit styles of VDM-SL). Therefore a conforming tool will not be allowed to accept only a subset of VDM-SL. The only problem with this is that developers of VDM-SL tools may consider the VDM-SL standard difficult to implement due to its size. We do not believe that this is the case.

Errors

A specification may be a meaningless specification, an inconsistent specification or a consistent specification. A meaningless specification or an inconsistent specification will be said to have an error. The static semantics of VDM-SL can tell you whether a specification has an error, is a consistent specification or is an undefined specification, an undefined specification meaning when the static semantics cannot determine whether a specification is a consistent specification or an inconsistent specification.

The above is different for programming languages where compilers determine both static semantic errors and at run time dynamic semantic errors.

Levels of Conformity

Some existing language standards do have levels of conformity, e.g. Pascal (see Sect. 2.2) but these are at the level of subsets (extensions) of the language. These would not be applicable to VDM-SL (see above) since we have ruled out subsets for VDM-SL.

Having only one level of conformity of VDM-SL tools would, because of the wide range of VDM-SL tools, ranging from syntactic to pragmatic (see Sect. 3.3), rule out too many such tools. The levels of conformity we are introducing are on the semantic level. We are proposing three general levels: syntactic, static semantic and dynamic semantic, of which the static semantic will be divided into four as summarised in Table 2.

The six tool conformity levels range from 0 to 5 where each level i, $0 \leq i \leq 4$ is also implemented by the next level $i+1$ above. The documentation of the conforming tool must clearly state which level it conforms to or the conforming tool must report the level.

The syntactic level accepts syntactically correct VDM-SL specifications, i.e. they are undefined specifications, but gives an error for syntactically incorrect ones. We have also included in this level the checks for uniqueness of identifiers.

The static semantics has been written in such a way as to allow a wide range of possible levels (see Sect. 3.2), but because of the confusion this may cause the user of such a conforming tool we have restricted the number of levels to 4, corresponding to the number of possible checks. Each level will determine whether a specification has an error, is a consistent specification or is an undefined specification. These will all have to be reported by a conforming tool.

All the levels from 0 to 4 are testable in some way. For the final level 5, dynamic semantics, it is much more difficult to define what we mean by a conforming tool. For example taking a prototyping tool which converts VDM-SL to a programming language, you would like the derived programming language program to have equivalent semantics to each given specification. If you consider $\mathbf{Z}$ or $\mathbf{R}$ arithmetic in the specification then when this is translated into the programming language program there would usually be some limitation on the range of the allowed arithmetic. This sort of problem comes about because the translator is doing some reification which needs to be communicated to the user of the tool. We propose that either the tool or the accompanying documentation to the tool makes it clear when such deviations from the semantics are taking place.

Miscellaneous

Briefly we will just cover the other items in the checklist of Sect. 2.5 which we have not mentioned above.

Deprecated language elements is not currently relevant to VDM-SL.

At the time of writing, the VDM-SL standard makes no mention of tool dependent features and so this will not feature in the conformity clause.

Table 2. Levels of conformity

Classification /Level		Part of standard implemented (refers to clauses of the standard)	Brief description
Syntactic	0	Clauses 10 and 12.	Mainly syntactic and deals with the uniqueness of identifiers.
Static Semantic	1	From clauses 13 and 14 $wf–Spec(mk–DEF(\{\ \}))$ and $wf–Spec(mk–POS(\{\ \}))$	This covers the use of identifiers not defined or not visible. It also checks that function types are used correctly in recursive type equations, set types, map types, the state and the arguments to imperative functions.
	2	From clauses 13 and 14 $wf–Spec(mk–DEF(\{\textbf{LOCALCONTEXT}\}))$ and $wf–Spec(mk–POS(\{\textbf{LOCALCONTEXT}\}))$	Checks that a type of an expression is valid when the types of identifiers in that expression are given.
	3	From clauses 13 and 14 $wf–Spec(mk–DEF(\{\textbf{LOCALCONTEXT},$ $\textbf{TOTALFUNC}\}))$ and $wf–Spec(mk–POS(\{\textbf{LOCALCONTEXT},$ $\textbf{TOTALFUNC}\}))$	Checks for the well-formedness of total functions without preconditions (explicit or hidden) in terms of the types of the formal parameters, the body and the result of the function.
	4	From clauses 13 and 14 $wf–Spec(mk–DEF(\{\textbf{LOCALCONTEXT},$ $\textbf{TOTALFUNC}, \textbf{UNIONCLOSE}\}))$ and $wf–Spec(mk–POS(\{\textbf{LOCALCONTEXT},$ $\textbf{TOTALFUNC}, \textbf{UNIONCLOSE}\}))$	Uses the fact that if an expression holds for two types it holds for the union of those types.
Dynamic Semantics	5	Clauses 7 and 8.	Documentation with the tool describes for the user the possible problems of interpretation of the semantics.

4 Conclusion

An explanation of the use of a conformity clause and a checklist of its contents has been derived from existing standards documentation and language standards. The most significant points being: it is aimed at different types of users and it should be testable. It has been shown in some cases that the conformity clause for some language standards has not been understood and has been ill used. The ISO/IEC 9646 standard seems to warrant investigation for its use in the area of computer languages and perhaps software engineering in general.

A conformity clause is proposed for VDM-SL. This has highlighted several problems: the difficulty of testing conforming tools which attempt to preserve the semantics of the specification language, that test methods need to be developed for WIMP interface tools, and that there exist few commercially available VDM-SL tools (and of these none at the current time would conform to the standard as the static semantics has only recently become available). As a result of these problems the conformity clause for conforming tools only deals with the front end of VDM-SL tools. It would be useful to see how far one could develop the concept of showing conformity by proof using the current technology and then see what further work needs to be done to make it a practical method. The above work would also be applicable to other specification languages like Z [22, 23] or RAISE [24] when standardised.

Acknowledgements

We would like to thank the members of the the ISO VDM-SL Standardisation Working Group, Software Engineering Group (National Physical Laboratory), Open Systems Group (National Physical Laboratory) and Vic Stenning (Consultant) for their many useful comments and discussions.

References

1. Document Reference ISO/IEC JTC1/SC22/WG19 IN9. *VDM Specification Language Proto-Standard, Draft*, 1991. Available from: D Andrews, Department of Computing Studies, University of Leicester, University Road, Leicester, LE1 7RH.
2. J. Dawes. *The VDM-SL Reference Guide*. Pitman, 1991. ISBN 0-273-03151-1.
3. DIRECTIVES. *Procedures for the technical work of ISO/IEC JTC 1 on Information Technology*. International Organization for Standardization/International Electrotechnical Commission, first edition, 1990.
4. DIRECTIVES Part 2. *Methodology for the development of International Standards*. International Electrotechnical Commission/International Organization for Standardization, first edition, 1989.
5. DIRECTIVES Part 3. *Drafting and presentation*. International Electrotechnical Commission/International Organization for Standardization, second edition, 1989.
6. ISO/IEC 9899: 1990. *Programming Languages – C*. International Organization for Standardization/International Electrotechnical Commission, 1990.
7. ISO/IEC 7185: 1990. *Information technology – Programming languages – Pascal*. International Organization for Standardization/International Electrotechnical Commission, 1990.
8. ISO/IEC TR 10034: 1990. *Guidelines for the preparation of conformity clauses in programming language standards*. International Organization for Standardization/International Electrotechnical Commission, 1990.
9. ANSI/MIL-STD-1815A-1983. *Reference manual for the Ada programming language*, 1983.
10. ISO 8807. *Information processing systems — Open systems interconnection — LOTOS - A formal description technique based on the temporal ordering of observational behaviour*. International Organization for Standardization, 1989.
11. ISO 9074. *Information processing systems - Open systems interconnection - Estelle: A formal description technique based on an extended state transition model*. International Organization for Standardization, 1989.

12. ISO/IEC 9646-1. *Information technology – Open Systems Interconnection – Conformance testing methodology and framework – Part 1: General concepts.* International Organization for Standardization/International Electrotechnical Commission, version 7.12 – 14 march 1991 edition, 1991.

13. ISO 2382/15-1985(E/F). *Data processing – Vocabulary – Part 15: Programming languages.* International Organization for Standardization, first edition, 1985.

14. ISO/TR 9547: 1988 (E). *Programming language processors – Test methods – Guidelines for their development and acceptability.* International Organization for Standardization, 1988.

15. Peter Gorm Larsen. The Dynamic Semantics of the BSI/VDM Specification Language. Technical report, The Institute for Applied Computer Science, Denmark, February 1992.

16. Hans Bruun, Bo Stig Hansen, and Flemming Damm. The Static Semantics of VDM-SL. Technical report, Technical University of Denmark, April 1992.

17. Nico Plat and Hans Toetenel. A formal transformation from the BSI/VDM-SL concrete syntax to the core abstract syntax. Technical Report 92-07, Delft University of Technology, 1992.

18. C.B. Jones. *Systematic Software Development Using VDM - Second Edition.* Prentice Hall International Series in Computer Science. Prentice-Hall International, 1990. ISBN 0-13-880733-7.

19. Nico Plat and Hans Toetenel. Tool support for VDM. Technical Report 89-81, Delft University of Technology, 1989.

20. Brian A. Wichmann and Z. J. Ciechanowicz. *Pascal Compiler Validation.* John Wiley & Sons, 1983. ISBN 0 471 90133 4.

21. S M Austin, D R Wilkins, and B A Wichmann. An ada program test generator. In *TriAda Conference Proceedings.* ACM, October 1991.

22. J.M. Spivey. *The Z Notation - A Reference Manual.* Prentice Hall International Series in Computer Science. Prentice-Hall International, 1989. ISBN 0-13-983768-X.

23. J.M. Spivey. *Understanding Z - A Specification language and its formal semantics.* Cambridge Tracts in Theoretical Computer Science 3. Cambridge University Press, 1988. ISBN 0-521-33429-2.

24. The RAISE Language Group. *The RAISE Specification Language.* The BCS Practitioner Series. Prentice Hall, 1992. ISBN 0-13-752833-7.

25. ISO Standards Handbook 10. *Data Processing – Vocabulary.* International Organization for Standardization, first edition, 1982.

26. C.L.N. Ruggles. *Formal Methods in Standards.* Springer-Verlag, 1990. ISBN 3-540-19577-7, ISBN 0-387-19577-7.

27. ISO/IEC TR 10176: 1991. *Information Technology – Guidelines for the preparation of programming language standards.* International Organization for Standardization/International Electrotechnical Commission, 1991.

A   Scope

The following is intended for the Scope clause of the VDM-SL standard. The note (introduced by NOTE –) will not be part of this clause but has been left in for this paper to explain how the scope clause was derived.

1 Scope

This International Standard specifies the model based specification language the Vienna Development Method Specification Language. It specifies:

- two representations: the mathematical and ISO 646;
- the syntax;
- the static semantics;
- the dynamic semantics;
- conformity for specifications and tools.

It does not specify:

- the proof obligations;
- the reification rules;
- the size or complexity of a specification that will exceed the capacity of any specific data processing system or the capacity of a particular tool, nor the actions to be taken when the corresponding limits are exceeded;
- the minimal requirements of a data processing system that is capable of supporting an implementation of a tool;
- the method that tools use for reporting errors.

NOTE – The above scope clause has been derived by looking at how scope clauses have been defined in specification languages, programming languages and the ISO/IEC directives.

The scope clauses of LOTOS [10] and Estelle [11] are rather similar in that they both state that they cover syntax and semantics, they then give an overview of its use and application. Estelle differs from LOTOS by adding:

This International Standard does not define methods for the verification of specifications written in Estelle.

This is interpreted[10] to mean that the Estelle standard does not define methods of checking an Estelle specification for undesirable properties such as deadlock. VDM-SL will need to say if it specifies proof obligations and reification rules.

The scope clauses for C [6] and Pascal [7] divide the scope into aspects they do specify and those they do not. They both mention syntax, semantics and conformity in aspects specified. C also includes in aspects specified representation of: programs, input data and output data. The aspects which they claim not to specify are mainly to do with the processor. Pascal also includes in aspects not specified the method of reporting errors and the typographical representation of a program.

Scope as defined in the ISO Directives 3 [5] should contain the subject and the aspects of the subject covered. The subject of the VDM-SL standard will be the model based specification language the Vienna Development Method Specification Language while the aspects will cover representations, syntax, semantics, conformity clause, proof obligations and reification rules. We shall discuss each of these aspects for VDM-SL:

Representations *For VDM-SL there are two representations mathematical and concrete. The mathematical is used for human reading and the concrete for storing a portable representation of a specification. The concrete could also be used for human reading but the mathematical cannot be used for storing (except on paper). These are both specified.*

---

[10] Interpretation from D Rayner, Protocols Standards Group, DITC.

Syntax and Semantics *Both are specified. The semantics is split up into the dynamic semantics and the static semantics.*
Conformity *This needs to be specified as explained in Sect. 2.5.*
Proof rules and Reification rules *Neither of these are specified in VDM-SL.*

B Definitions

The following is intended for the Definitions clause of the VDM-SL standard. The notes (introduced by *NOTE –*) will not be part of this clause but have been left in for this paper to explain how the definitions were derived.

3 Definitions

For the purposes of this International Standard, the following definitions apply.

3.1 batch mode: The processing of specifications by a tool in such a manner that a user does not have to further influence its processing.
NOTE – Modified version of the definition of **batch processing** *contained in [25].*

3.2 conforming specification: A specification which is written in the language defined by this International Standard and which obeys all the conformity clauses for specifications in this International Standard.
NOTE – This has been derived from the definition of **conforming program** *contained in [8], replacing program by specification.*

3.3 conforming tool: A tool which processes conforming specifications and which obeys all the conformity clauses for tools in this International Standard.
NOTE – This has been derived from the definition of **conforming processor** *contained in [8], replacing processor by tool.*

3.4 consistent specification: A specification which is not meaningless and for which there exists a model.
NOTE – This definition is contained in [16].

3.5 dynamic semantics: The meaning of a specification.

3.6 error: A fault in a specification which means it could be a meaningless specification or an inconsistent specification.

3.7 extension: An addition to the requirements of this International Standard that does not invalidate any conforming specification with this standard except by prohibiting the use of one or more particular spellings of identifiers.
NOTE – This is a modified version of the definition for **extension** *contained in [7].*

3.8 inconsistent specification: A specification which is not meaningless and for which there does not exist a model.
NOTE – This definition is contained in [16].

3.9 meaningless specification: A specification for which no semantics can be given.
NOTE – This definition is contained in [16].

3.10 model: A mathematical construction designated as the meaning of a specification or part of such specification.
NOTE – This is a modified version of the definition for **denotation** *contained in [11].*

3.11 proof obligations: The set of proofs that are necessary to show that a specification is semantically correct.

3.12 reification rules: A set of rules which, for two specifications can be shown to be applicable and in which by doing, you will have shown that certain properties of those two specifications have been preserved (these are used in developing a specification into an implementation).

3.13 specification: A description of an object in a formal language.
NOTE – This is a modified version of the definitions of **specification** *contained in [26] and The Concise Oxford Dictionary, Sixth Edition.*

3.14 static semantics: A subset of the dynamic semantics that can checked automatically (by tools).

3.15 system: Software for controlling the execution of tools.
NOTE – Modified version of the definition of **operating system** *contained in [25].*

3.16 tool: The entire computing system which enables the specification user to manipulate specifications, in general consisting both of hardware and of the relevant associated software.
NOTE – This has been derived from the definition of **programming language processor** *contained in [27].*

3.17 undefined specification: A specification which is not a meaningless specification but it has not yet been determined whether it is a consistent specification or an inconsistent specification.

C Conformity

The following is intended for the Conformity clause of the VDM-SL standard.

4 Conformity

4.1 Tools

There are six levels of conformity for conforming tools, level i, $0 \leq i \leq 5$.
A tool conforming with the requirements of this International Standard shall

a) for level 0, be able to determine whether a specification is in error or is an undefined specification and report this to the system;
NOTE 1 – This is the only level at which it is not possible to determine whether a specification is a consistent specification.

b) for all levels except level 0, be able to determine whether a specification is a consistent specification, in error or an undefined specification and report this to the system;

c) for all levels be able to be run in batch mode;

d) if it conforms at level i, $1 \leq i \leq 5$, conform to level $i - 1$;

e) if it conforms at level 0, accept all the features of clause 10 and determine any errors as specified in clause 12;
NOTE 2 – This implies that all conforming tools are required to accept all the features of the language specified in clause 10. It also means they are not allowed to accept a subset.

f) if it conforms at level 1, implement all the features specified in clause 14 by the functions
   $wf\text{-}Spec(mk\text{-}DEF(\{\,\}))$ and $wf\text{-}Spec(mk\text{-}POS(\{\,\}))$;

g) if it conforms at level 2, implement all the features specified in clause 14 by the functions
   $wf\text{-}Spec(mk\text{-}DEF(\{LOCALCONTEXT\}))$ and
   $wf\text{-}Spec(mk\text{-}POS(\{LOCALCONTEXT\}))$;

h) if it conforms at level 3, implement all the features specified in clause 14 by the functions
   $wf\text{-}Spec(mk\text{-}DEF(\{LOCALCONTEXT, TOTALFUNC\}))$
   and $wf\text{-}Spec(mk\text{-}POS(\{LOCALCONTEXT, TOTALFUNC\}))$;

i) if it conforms at level 4, implement all the features specified in clause 14 by the functions
   $wf\text{-}Spec(mk\text{-}DEF(\{LOCALCONTEXT, TOTALFUNC,$
   $UNIONCLOSE\}))$
   and
   $wf\text{-}Spec(mk\text{-}POS(\{LOCALCONTEXT, TOTALFUNC,$
   $UNIONCLOSE\}))$;

j) if it conforms at level 5, report to the system when it deviates from the features specified in clause 8 by the function $SemSpec$ and have an accompanying document which provides details of the features specified in clause 8 by the function $SemSpec$, which it has implemented;

k) be accompanied by a document that separately describes, in the same style as the requirements specified in this International Standard any extensions accepted by the tool and be capable of running in a mode which treats all extensions as errors;

l) report to the system the level to which it conforms or be accompanied by documentation describing that level.

4.2 Specifications

A specification conforms to the requirements of this International Standard if and only if it is derivable according to the syntactic rules of either clause 9 or clause 10 and is consistent or not meaningless with respect to clauses 6, 7, 8, 11 and 12.

Process Instances in LOTOS Simulation*

Simon Pickin[1], Yan Yang[2], Wiet Bouma[2], Sylvie Simon[3] and Tanja de Groot[4]

[1] Centre National d'Etudes des Télécommunications, 22301 Lannion CEDEX, France
[2] PTT-Research, P.O. box 421, Leidschendam, the Netherlands
[3] IBM Scientific Center, Paris, France[‡]
[4] Alcatel Alsthom Recherche, Route de Nozay, 91460 Marcoussis, France

Abstract. We introduce a slight modification of the usual operational semantics for LOTOS based on preserving history information. We then show how we can use the history information in each state to define state-oriented properties and features. By means of an example we show how these properties and features can be used to enhance the usual simulation methods for LOTOS specifications. An implementation is then sketched and some extensions are suggested.

1 Introduction

LOTOS, Language Of Temporal Ordering Specification, is standardized by ISO as a language for formal specification of communication protocols. The basic idea is that systems can be described in terms of the temporal ordering of events which are externally observable. The language has two components, one dealing with the algebraic description of data based on the algebraic specification language ACT ONE [EM] and one for the description of process behaviours and interactions based on a modification of CCS [M] with elements from CSP [H]. The language is defined in [B] and a tutorial appears in [BB].

The semantics of a LOTOS specification is defined by a *labelled transition system* in [B] with states consisting of behaviour expressions and labels consisting of events. This labelled transition system is derived from the specification using the LOTOS inference rules. In general, when simulating a LOTOS specification, one only obtains information about event offers and possibly also about values that variables are instantiated to. However, properties such as the status of process instances or the value of variables in given process instances are also of interest, since the specifier may often reason in terms of these concepts. The semantics of a LOTOS system is global and the notion of process remains a syntactic one. Thus information concerning process instantiation is not represented in the usual transition system semantics and is therefore lost in simulation using this semantics. In order to preserve the process information and other information concerning the specification structure, this paper introduces a more distinguishing execution-oriented semantics, by modifying the usual LOTOS inference rules, and then uses it to define some state-oriented properties.

---

* This work was supported by the SPECS project. It represents the view of the authors.
[‡] Sylvie Simon is now working at SEPT, 42 Rue des Coutures, Caen, France

The idea of the execution-oriented semantics for LOTOS defined in this paper can be summarised as follows. The behaviour expression being simulated does not change between states, but instead an *execution history*, a representation of the inference rules used in previous steps, is maintained. It is this execution history which changes from state to state. The idea of recording the inference rules used in a transition also appears in the "proved transitions" of Boudol and Castellani, see for example [BC]. However, the objectives of these authors in keeping this information, namely to use it to define a non-interleaving semantics, were very different from ours and for this reason the manner in which the information is recorded in our semantics (state based) is also quite different. The motivation here for recording derivation information is to enable us to see which process instances offer which actions and to permit the calculation of dynamic properties of behaviour expression instances such as whether they are terminated or not. It also enables us to easily keep track of the parallelism structure of the specification as well as the hierarchy of process creation. In this paper we concentrate on those additional LOTOS simulation features permitted by the execution history semantics. Other features of LOTOS simulation and simulator functionalities are only discussed when relevent to the presentation of the possibilities offered by this semantics.

In section 2, the execution history and the idea of instances are defined. In section 3 the simulation enhancements permitted by the execution history semantics are presented, in particular, the dynamic state-oriented properties of instances. The use of these properties is illustrated with an example in section 4. Some implementation issues are treated briefly in section 5. In sections 2 and 3 we have assumed data is treated in a non-symbolic manner though we define our concepts in such a way that they can be easily extended to the symbolic data case. The ability to treat data in a symbolic manner is a powerful feature. Accordingly, in section 6 we discuss the extension of the execution history ideas to the symbolic data case. In this section also we discuss the incorporation of these properties in a temporal framwork and its subsequent use in simulation. The first appendix contains the formal definitions of the *unrolling* relation together with that of the *Unroll* function. The second contains a sample of the execution history semantic rules.

2 Definition of the Execution History

In order to simplify the presentation of the execution history semantics we assume that we are dealing with flat specifications. In the rest of the article we will use a kind of vector notation for lists of variable and gate names, defined at the beginning of appendix B.

2.1 Variable Instances

For each (flat) process identifier P in the LOTOS specification under study we suppose a (potentially infinite) list of process instances $P.p$, where p ranges over the natural numbers. For each (flat) variable identifier x in the LOTOS specification under study, we suppose a (potentially infinite) list of variable instances[6] $x.p$, for p a natural number. When calculating the next possible

---

[6] multiple instances due to multiple instantiations of the surrounding process

steps, instead of substituting values, we dynamically relabel variables, that is to say we substitute them by variable instances. This also enables us to keep track of the relation between formal parameter instances and (earlier instantiated) variable instances. In each state we maintain a set of the variable instantiations (or assignments), denoted I, carried out thus far. Note that the terms on the r.h.s. of such equations may themselves contain variable instances but such instances will already occur on the l.h.s. of some other equation in I. We will denote by $B[\bar{x}.p/\bar{x}]$ the behaviour expression B with the free variables $\bar{x}$ substituted by the variable instances $\bar{x}.p$. Behaviour expressions which may contain such substitutions, which will be referred to as *relabelled behaviour expressions*, must be interpreted w.r.t. a set of instantiations giving the value of the variable instances. We treat formal gate identifers in exactly the same way as variable identifiers, maintaining the record of their instantiations in the set I. Thus for each gate identifier h in a formal gate list, we suppose a potentially infinite family of gate variable instances $h.p$, where p is a natural number. As we are also keeping track of instances of process definitions our allocation of instance numbers ensures that the number given to a particular variable instance coincides with that given to its containing process instance.

2.2 LOTOS Execution History Terms

We suppose a set $LRCT$ of constants l, r, c and t for *left, right, communicating* and *terminated* respectively. We denote by VI the set of variable instances, by GI the set of gate variable instances and by PI the set of process instances. Now we build inductively a set $HIST$ of LOTOS *execution history* terms:

1. The constants *init* (not yet begun), *term* (terminated) are execution history terms.
2. If $\mathcal{L}$ is a list of variable instances, $suffix(\mathcal{L}, ex)$, $sum(\mathcal{L}, ex)$ are execution history terms. They represent action denotation resp. sum over data involving variable instances $\mathcal{L}$.
3. If ex is an execution history term, so are $choice_l(ex)$ and $choice_r(ex)$. They represent the left resp. right branch of a choice expression.
4. If μ is a list of constants l, r, c, and ex, ex' are execution history terms, then so is $par_\mu(ex, ex')$, representing a parallel-expression with a list of synchronisation choices.
5. If ex and ex' are execution history terms, then so are $disable_l(ex)$, $disable_t(ex)$ and $disable_r(ex, ex')$. They represent the three possible states of a disable expression, where t is a constant representing the termination of the left-hand side of a disable-expression (and therefore of the whole expression).
6. If ex and ex' are execution history terms, $\mathcal{L}$ a list of variable instances, then $enable_l(ex)$ and $enable_r(\mathcal{L}, ex, ex')$ are also execution history terms. They represent the two possible states of an enable expression, the list $\mathcal{L}$ being the variable instances involved.
7. If $\mathcal{L}$ is a list of variable instances, $\mathcal{G}$ a list of gate variable instances, $P.p$ a process instance, and ex an execution history term, then $apply(P.p, \mathcal{L}, \mathcal{G}, ex)$ is also an execution history term representing process instantiation involving variable resp. gate instances $\mathcal{L}$ resp. $\mathcal{G}$.

We will often refer to $HIST$ terms as trees, the canonical mapping to abstract syntax trees being trivial. We will write $ex \sqsubseteq ex'$ if ex is a subterm (subtree as abstract syntax tree) of ex'. A *HIST* term with no *init, term, suffix, sum* or *choice* terms will be called a *process tree*. For the management of variable instance numbers, when defining our semantics, we will in fact use $HIST^J$ terms built inductively as for *HIST* terms but from pairs ex^J where $ex \in HIST$ and j is a set of process instances, one for each process identification of the specification, giving the current set of local (i.e. on that parallel branch) instance numbers. A *HIST* term can be canonically derived from a $HIST^J$ term simply by forgetting the extra instances information.

2.3   LOTOS Execution States and Snapshots

We now show how we use the execution history terms introduced in the previous section to record how a LOTOS behaviour expression evolves over time. We define the execution history semantics, in a similar way to the usual operational semantics for LOTOS using transition axioms and derivation rules for transitions between states. Our states, instead of being behaviour expressions, are 4-tuples $< B, ex^J, I, J >$ where B is a relabelled behaviour expression, ex^J is a $HIST^J$ term, I is a set of instantiations, and J is the current set of global process instance numbers (c.f. j defined above). If $P_0 = B_0$ is the process equation of the specification, we define the initial state as the tuple $(P_0, init^{J_0}, \emptyset, J_0)$ where J_0 is the set $\{P.0 \mid P \text{ a process identifier of } P_0\}$.

The next possible states are then given by application of the execution history semantic rules a sample of which is given in appendix B. The semantics of a specification is the transition system constructed by the application of these rules. This transition system can be shown to be an unravelling, see for example [S], in fact a complete unravelling, of the transition system defining the usual LOTOS semantics[7]. For a given specification, we call any 4-tuple generated from the initial state of that specification by application of the execution history inference rules a *LOTOS execution state*. For all the following definitions we will use the *HIST* term canonically derived from the $HIST^J$ term of the LOTOS execution state. We will say that the pair $\langle B, ex \rangle$ where B is the first component of the LOTOS execution state and ex the *HIST* term canonically derived from ex^J, the second component of the LOTOS execution state, constitute the state *snapshot* of the execution of the whole specification modulo the third component I, the set of instantiations.

The above definitions enable us to represent the execution history of the whole specification. However, we also wish to consider the execution history of behaviour expressions which are subexpressions of our specification. It can be observed that if such a behaviour expression has been executed then there will be a subexpression (subtree) of the execution history which corresponds to it and represents its execution history. We need, therefore, to define, for a given LOTOS execution state, the notion of pairs (B, es) for which B is a relabelled behaviour subexpression and es is its execution history in that state. This notion is made precise using the $\xrightarrow{unrolling}$ relation between such pairs defined in appendix A: we define a *snapshot* modulo the set of variable instantiations I to be a relabelled behaviour expression, execution history pair, written $\langle B, ex \rangle_I$, generated by the transitive closure of the *unrolling*

---

[7] this can be done by application of the *Unroll* function, see below, to the terms in the inference rules to recover the usual inference rules

relation from the state snapshot. Though a snapshot, since it contains a relabelled behaviour expression, must be interpreted w.r.t the instantiation set, this set will be implicit so that the subscript I will usually be omitted. Of course, snapshots must be understood in the context of the specification they are derived from (e.g. all process names occur in declarations etc.). Notice that a snapshot $\langle B, es \rangle$ can be derived from a snapshot $\langle B', es' \rangle$ via the transitive closure of the *unrolling* relation (in which case we say that it is a sub-snapshot) iff $es \sqsubseteq es'$.

Given a snapshot, i.e. the current value of a subexpression together with its execution history, we wish to know what the current behaviour expression of that subexpression is. Evidently, the current execution history of this subexpression should enable us to derive its current behaviour expression. The function which accomplishes this is called the *Unroll* function. This function takes a snapshot and executes the steps recorded in its execution history component on its behaviour expression component to give its current behaviour expression. Its formal definition is given in appendix A.

The disadvantage of the semantics as defined by the execution history inference rules is that as we must always start at the level of the whole specification to calculate the next possible steps, after a large number of steps the calculations become rather heavy. One way to address this difficulty in an implementation would be to periodically unroll to obtain the current behaviour expression. However, this effectively resets the system so that we are no longer able to relate previous instances with future ones. Therefore an implementation should not calculate the next possible steps by directly mirroring the inference rules but should instead use a careful definition of the current state, see also Sect. 5.

2.4 Behaviour Expression and Process Instances

We will use the notation $\mathcal{E}$ for the state-dependent (or program) variable which, in each state, contains the value of the execution history of the behaviour expression of the whole specification (i.e. the value of the second argument of the LOTOS execution states generated from the initial state by application of the Plotkin rules). Recall that the execution history term derived from $\mathcal{E}$ by excising all *suffix*, *sum*, *choice*, *term* and *init* terms is called the *process tree* of the specification, see Sect. 2.2. We will denote by $\mathcal{I}$ the state-dependent variable which in each state contains the current set of instantiations (i.e. the value of the third argument of the LOTOS execution states). With the semantics outlined here, as we execute a LOTOS specification and change state, $\mathcal{E}$ grows from the leaves. Observe that the subtree at a particular position on the tree $\mathcal{E}$, which evidently then also grows from the leaves in the course of execution, represents the changing execution history of a subexpression of the whole behaviour expression. Therefore, to be able to dynamically treat the execution history of subexpressions of the whole behaviour expression we need a notation for subtrees of the execution history tree. This notation is provided by *dynamic references* which denote a position in a *HIST* tree defined using the functions n^{th}-*child* (written postfix as *.n*). For example, the dynamic reference $e.2.3$ represents the third child of the second child of e. If such a child does not exist in a state then we assume the value of the dynamic reference to be *init* in that state. Since $\mathcal{E}$ is a state-dependent variable then terms of the form $\mathcal{E}.n_1 \ldots n_m$ are also state dependent (or program) variables, which can be used to represent the changing execution histories of subexpressions of the whole behaviour expression.

Thus we will be interested in terms of the form $\langle B, \mathcal{E}.n_1 \ldots n_m \rangle_{\mathcal{I}}$ for B a relabelled behaviour expression. Such terms represent evolving behaviour expression instances - we will call them b.e. instances. In each state (for each value of $\mathcal{E}$), they denote a snapshot modulo the current value of $\mathcal{I}$. Therefore we will talk about the current snapshot of a b.e. instance. Of particular interest are b.e. instances whose behaviour expression component is a process instantiation. Such b.e. instances will be of the form $\langle P[[\bar{g}.p/\bar{g}]]([\bar{x}.p/\bar{x}]), \mathcal{E}.n_1 \ldots n_m \rangle_{\mathcal{I}}$ where $P[[\bar{g}.p/\bar{g}]]([\bar{x}.p/\bar{x}])$ is a process instantiation and where in each state for which it is not $init$, $\mathcal{E}.n_1 \ldots n_m$ has the value $apply(P.p, \bar{x}.p, \bar{g}.p, ex)$, for some value of ex. We will call such b.e. instances $process\ instances$ and will simply write them as $P.p$. Note that we use the term process instance and the same notation both for the pair (process name.instance number) and for the corresponding process instantiation behaviour expression together with the variable whose value in each state is its current execution history. Which of the two we are referring to will be clear from the context.

In any state, the $Unroll$ function applied to the value of a b.e. instance in that state gives the relabelled behaviour expression of that b.e. instance in that state.

3 Execution History in Simulation

The execution history is used to calculate state-oriented properties. Most of these properties are of snapshots modulo the current value of the variable instance set $\mathcal{I}$. The others count the number of process instances with a particular property. Since the properties of snapshots are calculated from the structure of their $HIST$ component, (a subterm of the current value of the execution history of the whole specification, $\mathcal{E}$) and the other properties directly from the current value of $\mathcal{E}$, we first define the relevent functions on $HIST$ terms.

3.1 Functions on Execution History Terms

We begin by defining the function $Next$ so as to reduce the size of the other definitions. This function returns the last argument of any well-formed execution history term except on: $par_\mu(ex, ex')$ and $init$, on which it is the identity, and $term$, on which it returns $init$. Next we inductively define some boolean-valued functions on execution history terms.

1. **Terminated**(ex): returns true on $HIST$ terms ex containing no $init$ subterms
2. **IsActive**(ex): returns true on $HIST$ terms ex for which there is at least one path between the uppermost node and an $init$ node which does not pass through an $apply$ node.
3. **LastFired**(ex_1, ex_2): returns true if ex_1 is a subtree of ex_2 and is on the same side of each par node between the two as the last action fired.
4. **Disabled**(ex_1, ex_2): returns true if ex_1 is disabled in ex_2.
5. **Component**(ex_1, ex_2): returns true if ex_1 is in parallel in ex_2.

6. **Living, Seqcomp and FiredSeqComp**: composite functions.

$Living(ex_1, ex_2)$
$\quad \Leftarrow \neg Terminated(ex_1) \land \neg Disabled(ex_1, ex_2)$
$SeqComp(ex_1, ex_2)$
$\quad \Leftarrow Component(ex_1, ex_2) \land \not\exists ex' : Component(ex', ex_1)$
$FiredSeqComp(ex_1, ex_2)$
$\quad \Leftarrow SeqComp(ex_1, ex_2) \land LastFired(ex_1, ex_2)$

Then we define some functions from *HIST* to the natural numbers.

1. **BexParNum**(ex): the number of behaviour expression instances in parallel in ex
2. **InstParNum**(P, ex_1, ex_2): returns the number of instances of the process P in parallel in ex_1 and living w.r.t. ex_2. By way of an example, we give the full definition:

$InstParNum(P, ex_1, ex_2)$
$\quad \Leftarrow \quad$ if $ex_1 = init \lor ex_1 = term$ then 0
$\qquad\qquad$ else if $ex_1 = par_\mu(ex', ex'')$ then
$\qquad\qquad\qquad InstParNum(P, ex', ex_2) + InstParNum(P, ex'', ex_2)$
$\qquad\qquad$ else if $ex_1 = apply(Q.p, \mathcal{L}_1, \mathcal{L}_2, ex')$ then
$\qquad\qquad\qquad$ if $P = Q$ then
$\qquad\qquad\qquad\qquad$ if $Living(ex_1, ex_2)$ then
$\qquad\qquad\qquad\qquad\qquad Max(1, InstParNum(P, ex', ex_2))$
$\qquad\qquad\qquad\qquad$ else 0
$\qquad\qquad$ else $InstParNum(P, Next(ex), ex_2)$

where *Max* is the function returning the maximum of two natural numbers.

3. **ActInstNum**(P, ex_1, ex_2): This function returns the number of instances of process P in parallel in ex_1, living w.r.t. ex_2 and which satisfy *IsActive*. It is obtained by replacing in the above definition of the function *InstParNum* the condition $Living(ex_1, ex_2)$ with the condition $Living(ex_1, ex_2) \land IsActive(ex_1)$.

3.2 Properties of B.E. Instance Snapshots

In this section we define the properties and features of the current state which the execution history semantics enables us to calculate and which enhance user understanding of the behaviour of the specification being simulated. Note that though the properties given in this paper are some of the most useful properties, others, such as how many times a certain process instance has made a certain non-deterministic choice, can also be calculated from the execution history. During simulation, we may, in each state, examine which of the state-oriented properties are satisfied by the current snapshot of a given b.e. instance.

Whether a particular process in the specification under study has been instantiated or not in the current state and if so, how many times, can be observed from the current value of $\mathcal{J}$. We define here some boolean valued properties of snapshots using the *HIST* functions of the previous section on the current value of the execution history $\mathcal{E}$. The first of these properties define the notion of the *status* of a process instance. Suppose the value of $\mathcal{E}$ resp. $\mathcal{I}$ in state s is E resp. I (written $s \models \mathcal{E} = E$ resp. $s \models \mathcal{I} = I$) then:

$$Terminated(\langle B, ex\rangle) \Leftarrow Terminated(ex)$$
$$Killed(\langle B, ex\rangle) \quad \Leftarrow Disabled(ex, E)$$
$$Alive(\langle B, ex\rangle) \quad \Leftarrow Living(ex, E)$$
$$Dead(\langle B, ex\rangle) \quad \Leftarrow \neg Living(ex, E)$$
$$Active(\langle B, ex\rangle) \quad \Leftarrow Living(ex, E) \ \wedge$$
$$(\ \text{if } ex = apply(P.p, \mathcal{L}_1, \mathcal{L}_2, ex')$$
$$\text{then } IsActive(ex') \text{ else } IsActive(ex) \ )$$
$$Idle(\langle B, ex\rangle) \quad \Leftarrow Alive(\langle B, ex\rangle) \wedge \neg Active(\langle B, ex\rangle)$$

We say that a b.e. instance satisfies a property $\mathcal{P}$ in a state if the snapshot of it in that state satisfies property $\mathcal{P}$. We will thus use the properties in state-dependent expressions such as $Terminated(P.3)$ in which the argument is a (state-dependent) process instance. This defines the notion of a process instance status which, in a given state, can be one of $Dead$ and $Terminated$, $Dead$ and $Killed$, $Alive$ and $Idle$ or $Alive$ and $Active$. A process instance is $Terminated$ if it has terminated successfully, that is to say, an $exit$ event has been offered. A process instance is $Killed$ if it has been disabled by another process instance. A process instance is $Alive$ if it has not been $Killed$ and has not yet successfully terminated. A process instance is $Active$ if it is $Alive$ and has at least one parallel branch on which it has not instantiated another process. The status of each process instance is easily calculated on each simulation step.

Other useful properties of b.e. instances are defined by the following snapshot predicates. In the same way as for those properties of snapshots used to define the process instance status, we say that a b.e. instance satisfies one of the next four properties in a certain state if the snapshot of it in that state satisfies the property. Thus we will also use the properties in state-dependent expressions such as $LastActor(P.2)$.

1. $LastActor$ tells us whether a snapshot involved participation in the last event offer:

$$LastActor(\langle B, es\rangle) \Leftarrow LastFired(es, E)$$

2. $Communicating$ tells us whether the last event offer involved a non-terminating synchronisation of the two snapshots given as arguments:

$$Communicating(\langle B_1, ex_1\rangle, \langle B_2, ex_2\rangle)$$
$$\Leftarrow Alive(ex_1) \wedge Alive(ex_2)$$
$$\wedge \ \exists par_{\mu|c}(ex'_1, ex'_2) \sqsubseteq E$$
$$(\ (LastFired(ex_1, ex'_1) \wedge LastFired(ex_2, ex'_2))$$
$$\vee (LastFired(ex_1, ex'_2) \wedge LastFired(ex_2, ex'_1)) \ )$$

There are two points which the user must bear in mind when using the last two properties. Firstly, if we wish to restrict our use to process instances, we may find that in the current state there is none other than that of the whole specification, which satisfies $LastActor$. Alternatively, we may find that though a synchronisation occurred in the last event offer there are no pairs of distinct process instances whose current snapshots satisfy $Communicating$. These complications arise when the instances involved are behaviour expression instances which are not process instances. Secondly, if a certain b.e. instance satisfies either of these properties in the current state then so do all its ancestors, a feature which could obscure the search for the real participators in an event offer. We thus define the following two properties:

1. *LastSeqActor*, which is satisfied by snapshots which are in parallel but which contain no further parallelism and also satisfy *LastActor*.

2. *Communicators*, which is satisfied by those pairs of snapshots involved in a communication (so they satisfy *Communicating*) which also both satisfy *LastSeqActor*.

The formal definitions are obtained by replacing *LastFired* by *FiredSeqComp* in the definitions of *LastActor* and *Commmunicating*.

3.3 Other Uses of Execution History in Simulation

Also of interest during simulation are the following properties. The number of behaviour expression instances in parallel in the state s is given by $BexParNum(E)$ (recall that $s \models \mathcal{E} = E$). The number of alive resp. active parallel instances of a process P in the state s, denoted $Inst(P)$ resp. $ActInst(P)$ (these expressions being, of course, state-dependent) is given by:

$$s \models Inst(P) = n \quad \Leftarrow \quad InstParNum(P, E, E) = n$$
$$s \models ActInst(P) = n \quad \Leftarrow \quad ActInstNum(P, E, E) = n$$

The number of alive resp. active parallel instances of a process P which are subinstances of $\langle B, \mathcal{E}.n_1 \ldots n_m \rangle$ in the state s is given by $InstParNum(P, E.n_1 \ldots n_m, E)$ resp. $ActInstNum(P, E.n_1 \ldots n_m, E)$.

The value of variable instances can be obtained from the current value of $\mathcal{I}$. This provides us, for example, with the value that any particular variable was instantiated to, for a particular instance of its containing process. Recall also that the treatment of formal gates means that, in the same way, we can find out the actual gates used for a particular instance of a process. As the instance number of a variable instance is that of the containing process instance, comparison with the process tree helps to locate the desired variable instance.

Of interest also are features which a simulator using the execution history semantics is able to calculate and present when computing the next possible event offers. The first of these, analogous to the property *LastActor* for the last event offer, is the ability to indicate which process instance is offering which event offer of the next possible event offers. Thus, in step by step simulation the user can choose between event offers knowing exactly who is offering what. In the case of synchronisations all the process instances participating in the event offer are indicated. Understanding of the place of these instances in the executing specification is gained by reference to the process tree. The second such feature is the property *Terminal* which is true of a process instance which is waiting to terminate, i.e. can only offer the *exit* action. This property is particularly useful because of the constraint that parallel LOTOS behaviour expressions must terminate together, i.e. synchronise on the *exit* action. Thus, we can add *Terminal* as an extra field in the process *status*. Of course, only *Alive* processes can be *Terminal*.

The process tree, see Sect. 2.3, is the means by which the user is able to visualise the place of each process instance in the executing specification. As can be seen in the example in the following section, it shows the current process creation hierarchy. Since the process tree is a representation of the current state, it is not from this tree that the user can observe the paths through the specification (event sequences) explored so far in a simulation session. For this, a trace tree is constructed: for each event offer chosen, an outgoing arc labelled with this event offer is added to this tree. It is this trace tree which enables the user to jump back to a previously traversed state in order to explore another path leaving this state. It is different from similar structures used in other LOTOS simulation methods in that the structured nature of this type of simulation enables us to indicate for each event offer in the trace tree, the process instance(s) offering it. Again, understanding of the place of these instances is gained by comparison with the process tree.

4 Example

In this section, we give a small example to illustrate how the properties and features that can be explored in each state during simulation can be used. We take a very simple network. The terminals are connected to the exchange through the gate net. The exchange can estabish or break off a connection. For the sake of simplicity, exchange of data is not considered. The allocation of an unique id for each terminal is also not dealt with. Assuming the data types are defined by some data description, the behaviour of the network is formulated as follows:

```
hide net in
    exchange[net]
    |[net]|
    terminals[user,net]

where

  process terminals [user,net] : noexit :=
  (choice nr : nat []
   terminal [user, net] (nr) )
    |||
   i; terminals   [user,net]
  endproc

  process terminal [user,net] (number:nat) : noexit :=
  setup [user,net] (number) >> accept other : nat in
  ( busy >>
    disconnect [user,net] (number,other) ) >>
  terminal [user,net] (number)
  endproc

  process setup [user,net] (number:nat) : exit (nat) :=
  (* connection request *)
  user ! number ? destination : nat ;
  net  ! number ! destination ;
  ( net ! number ! connect ; exit (destination)
    []
```

```
      ( net ! number ! disconnect ; exit
        >> setup [user,net] ( number ) ) )
  []
    (* connection requested by another *)
    net ! number ? calling_number : nat ! connect ;
    user ! number ! connect ; exit (calling_number)
  endproc

  process busy :exit := i; exit endproc

  process disconnect [user,net] (number,other:nat) : exit :=
   (* disconnect requst *)
   user ! number ! disconnect ;
   net ! number ! other ! disconnect ; exit
   []
   (* disconnect requested by the other side *)
   net ! number ! disconnect;
   user ! number ! disconnect ; exit
  endproc

  process exchange [net] : noexit :=
   (* establish a connection *)
   net ? calling : nat ? called : nat ;
   net ! called ! calling ! connect ;
   ( net ! calling ! connect ; exchange [net]
   []
      i; net ! calling ! disconnect; exchange [net] )
   []
   (* break off a connection *)
   net ? number1, number2 : nat ! disconnect ;
   net ! number2 ! disconnect; exchange [net]
  endproc
```

The process terminals is an artificial process creating terminals. A terminal is created by an internal event. Initially, a terminal is not in use. It can request a connection with another terminal or be connected by another terminal. After a connection has been established, it enters the busy phase in which, for example, data exchange may take place. A connection can be broken by either terminal. To improve the clarity of this illustration, we discuss the properties and features under consideration for a particular possible execution state of our example, i.e. a particular value of $\mathcal{E}$, which we will refer to as the reference state.

Instead of presenting the user with the whole execution history tree in a particular state, the simulator presents the most important information contained in it in the form of a process tree, as defined in Sect. 2.4. The process instances contained in the process tree will be written in the form *process name.instance number*. If one or both sides of a parallel operator, disable operator or enable operator is some other type of behaviour expression than a process instantiation, any instances of this behaviour expression will be displayed in the process tree using the word *Bexp* followed by a number identifying this behaviour expression statically, followed optionally by an instance number. The process tree of the reference state is depicted in Fig. 1.

[htb]

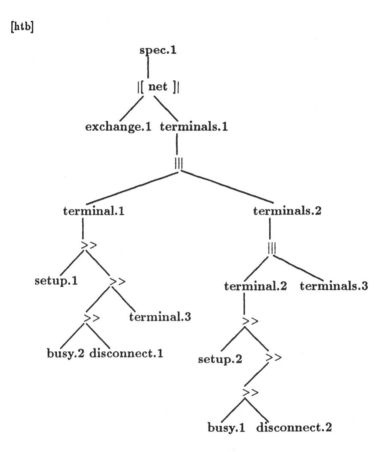

Fig. 1. The process tree of the reference state

The exact significance of process instances will depend on the specification under study. It is assumed that the specifier knows enough about his/her specification to be able to interpret them. In the specification used here, for example, each instance of the process terminal corresponds to a new communication attempt and not to a new physical terminal. Apart from that of the terminals with the exchange and that involving the creation of terminals, there is no parallelism in this system and the sequentially descendent instances of an instance of the process terminal all correspond to the same physical terminal. Thus to each physical terminal corresponds a sequential branch in the process tree. For a particular instance of the process terminal the identity of the physical terminal is easily checked by looking at the value to which the variable *nr* has been instantiated for that instance. For example, in the reference state, terminal.3 is the same physical terminal as terminal.1 and consequently $nr.3 = nr.1$

¿From the process tree, therefore, we see that there are two physical terminals in existence in the reference state. Let $nr.1$ (the value of the variable nr in instance terminal.1) be x and $nr.2$ be y. Without reference to the trace tree but simply from the instance numbers in the process tree we can see that the sequence of events was as follows: terminal with id x goes into setup phase and calls terminal with id y. Terminal y goes into setup phase followed by busy phase. Terminal x then enters busy phase and later disconnect phase. This then causes terminal y to enter disconnect phase. Finally, terminal x leaves disconnect phase.

In each state, the following properties are of interest:

1. How many terminals are in the network: $Inst$(terminal)
2. How many terminals are busy: $ActInst$(busy)
3. If terminal with id id is in setup phase: $Active$(setup.n) for any instance n of the process setup with $number.n = id$. Due to the sequential nature of the process terminal, all instances of setup on the same sequential branch have the variable $number$ instantiated to the same value. For this reason also, only one process is $Active$ on each physical terminal at any one time[8]. Thus, the $Active$ instance of setup with $number = id$ will be the most recent descendent on the sequential branch corresponding to the terminal with $nr = id$, so that this property can in fact be immediately observed from the process tree. For example, in the reference state we can observe that an instance of the process setup is not the most recent descendent on any sequential branch and therefore neither of the terminals in existence in this state is in the setup phase.
4. If terminal with id id is in the busy phase: $Active$(busy.n) is true for an instance n of the process busy which is a descendent of an instance of a terminal with $nr = id$. For our example specification this can be observed directly from the process tree as for the last property.
5. If terminal with id id is in disconnection phase: $Active$(disconnect.n) is true for an instance n of the process disconnect with $number.n = id$. For our example specification this can be observed directly from the process tree as for the last property.
6. If terminal with id id participated in the last event offer: $LastSeqActor$(terminal.n) where terminal.n is the first instance of the terminal with $nr = id$, this instance being the top of the sequential branch corresponding to that physical terminal. As only one process is $Active$ on each physical terminal at any one time it is a simple matter to see exactly which instance of the process terminal with $nr = id$ did in fact participate in the last event offer. In the reference state the last event offer was either a silent event, as terminal x left disconnect phase, or a user event at terminal y. In the former case, $LastSeqActor$(terminal.1), in which case it was in fact the instance terminal.3 which participated in the last event offer[9].

---

[8] in fact the same is true for the property $Alive$.

[9] Note that the property $LastSeqActor$ was deliberately designed to pick out the lowest level of parallelism and not the lowest level of sequentialism as this is the most convenient in most cases. It would have been a simple matter to define a property which is true

7. If terminal with id *id* has just been connected/disconnected: the last event offered was a connected/disconnected event at the gate net and *Communicators*(terminal.*n*, exchange.1) is true for some instance *n* of the process terminal for which *nr.n* = *id*. Since the property *Communicators* picks out the highest level sequential instance involved in the communication, in our example, any instance satisying it will always be the first instance of a physical terminal. The same considerations as for *LastSeqActor* then apply. Two states previous to the reference state, *Communicators*(terminal.2, exchange.1) was true as terminal *y* was disconnecting.

8. How many times a terminal has been used: From the process tree, one can count the number of times a terminal with the specified id has entered the setup phase. Here, this is the number of occurrences on one sequential branch. In the reference state, the terminal *x* has been used once.

9. With which terminal was the terminal with id *id* communicating in its first communication: This is found by asking the value of the variable *destination* in the first instance of the process setup for the sequential branch corresponding to that physical terminal, i.e with *nr* = *id*. In the reference state, to ask this question for terminal *x*, we ask the value of *destination*.1 which we will find is equal to *y*.

5   Implementation

5.1   Execution History as Annotations

A prototype simulator of the type described here has been successfully implemented for a language similar to LOTOS in the SPECS project, see [R]. The execution history semantics is implemented as annotations to the abstract syntax tree of the specification under study. For example, an annotation to indicate that the left branch of a choice construct has been chosen is attached to the choice expression node of the abstract syntax tree. In the case of a process definition being instantiated more than once, the annotations are accompanied by an instance number. The *apply* construct is the only one needing slightly different treatment in this scenario. The arguments of this annotation include a pointer attached to the node of a process instantiation and pointing to the process definition node, together with the number of this new instance. Note that this *apply* construct itself may also be accompanied by an instance number if the node it annotates is part of a process definition. The set of instantiations *I* is implemented by pointers from each abstract syntax node of a value identifer to a list of instantiated values. For efficiency reasons, by defining a suitable notion of current state we avoid mirroring the inference rules and recalculating at each step the route through the execution history tree leading to the next event offers. Such a notion is based on the current behaviour expression even though with the formal semantics, this is derivable from the execution history.

5.2   Implementation of the Unroll Function

There are in fact two different types of unroll possible, depending on whether

---

for the last sequential instance but this is unecessary as it can easily be deduced from *LastSeqActor* and study of the process tree.

or not we wish to keep the accumulated execution history information. A *remembering unroll* applied to any b.e. instance enables us to see what is the behaviour expression corresponding to its current snapshot and applied to the state snapshot it enables a complete retracing of steps. A *forgetting unroll* applied to the state snapshot enables a type of partial system reset, as explained in Sect. 2.3. However, in a more efficient implementation as described above, the need for the forgetting unroll is largely avoided as the current behaviour expression is already calculated at each step.

6   Possible Extensions

6.1   Symbolic Treatment of Data

An obvious extension of the ideas outlined in this paper, as mentioned in Sect. 1, is one which enables data to be treated symbolically. Here we briefly outline how this can be done. We use the argument I of the LOTOS execution states to store a list of accumulated conditions and assignments instead of just a list of assignments. The definition of the *unrolling* relation, the *Unroll* function and of b.e. instances does not change except that they are now relative to this condition set. There is also no difference in the management of local resp. global instance numbers using the sets j resp. J.

The variable instances which are used to relabel LOTOS variables are now treated as state-independent (mathematical) variables. A state together with its incoming transition then exists if there is a subsitution of values for the variable instances such that all the conditions in the condition list are satisfied, taking into account the assignments. To be of real use for simulation purposes, we need powerful proof facilities available to eliminate impossible branches by showing when such a substitution does not exist, as, for example, in the LOTOS simulator SMILE [EW].

Introducing symbolic treatment of data requires modification of the execution history inference rules. The transition labels now contain variable instances which are state-independent variables so that one transition in the symbolic case corresponds to a possibly infinite number of transitions of the non-symbolic case. This is reflected in the definition of the transition axioms. In those inference rules which involve a condition on the applicability of the rule, namely the axiom for action prefix expression and the derivation rules for the action prefix and guarded expressions, the condition is removed but is instead added to the condition list on the r.h.s. of the derived transition. For communication in the symbolic data case, value generation identifies variable instances and value matching or parameter passing generates assignments, i.e. equations between variable instances and terms (possibly involving other variable instances). This is reflected in the those parallel expression rules involving communication and for those enable expression rules involving the enabling of the behaviour expression to the right of the enable operator. When a rule involves unconstrained instantiation in the non-symbolic case, as may be the case for the action prefix expression and the sum over data expression, then in the symbolic case we add the variable instance to the condition list on the r.h.s. of the derived transition but not as part of any equation, to indicate that it has been instantiated but that its value is not constrained.

In the symbolic case, it is useful to use sets of local conditions i whose place in the inference rules is similar to that of the sets j of local instance numbers. This enables us to define the data constraints on a particular process instance (which of course may involve variable instances from other process instances). In the implementation, the use of these local condition sets helps to optimize the memory usage needed to permit jumps back to previously traversed states.

6.2 Evaluation of Temporal Properties

There are three possible facilities that the evaluation of temporal formulas may provide in a simulator of the kind discussed in this paper:

1. the ability to prove **true** liveness properties of the type "on some path eventually ϕ" - to signal during simulation if we arrive in a state where ϕ holds. Conversely, the ability to prove **false** safety properties of the type "on all paths always ϕ" - to signal during simulation if we arrive in a state where ϕ does not hold.
2. filtering of possible paths in random simulation, choosing only those paths whose next state (or next few states) satisfy ϕ
3. breakpoint conditions in random simulation, i.e. stopping the simulation run in any state where ϕ is true.

In all three cases, ϕ must be a "locally evaluable" property, i.e. its truth can be decided on by examination of properties in a small number of states local to the state in question or by examination of accumulated history information. The state-oriented properties defined in Sect. 3.2 could be used as a basis for such "locally evaluable" properties. For example, we may wish to check the property: it is always true that the instances of a certain process remain active until a certain event. As stated above we can only prove such a property to be false, we cannot prove it to be true. We can however give a degree of confidence in its truth.

7 Conclusions

We have presented a semantics for LOTOS specifications which enables us to define dynamic state-oriented properties of process instances. Simulation using this semantics allows a clear visualisation of the process instantiation hierarchy in each state. This visualisation, together with the possibility of checking various properties of the process instances, helps to increase confidence of a specification's correctness and to verify that it behaves as intended. Furthermore, first results have shown that as an event offer is presented together with the offering process instance, errors, if any, can be located efficiently, since the specifier generally knows what is the correct behaviour of that process in that state. This approach also aids the transformation of specification to implementation, as sequential composition is likely to be implemeted by one single object. Though in this paper we are concerned only with the LOTOS specification language, the approach described is applicable to any process algebra type language.

Acknowledgments. Thanks are due to Etienne Gallou for some presentation ideas and especially to Michel Dauphin, the originator of the execution history semantics ideas within the SPECS project.

References

[B]   Brinksma E. (ed.): LOTOS – A Formal Description Technique Based on the Temporal Ordering of Observational Behaviour. ISO 8807 (1988)

[BC]   Boudol G., Castellani I.: A Non-Interleaving Semantics for CCS based on Proved Transitions. INRIA Rapport de Recherche No. 919 (1988)

[BB]   Bolognesi T., Brinksma E.: Intoduction to the ISO Specification Language LOTOS. FORTE '88 tutorials (1988)

[EW]   Eertink H., Wolz D.: Symbolic Execution of LOTOS specifications. FORTE '92 conference proceedings (1992)

[EM]   Ehrig H., Mahr B.: Fundamentals of Algebraic Specification 1. Springer-Verlag EATCS Series (1985)

[H]   Hoare C. A. R.: Communicating Sequential Processes. Prentice-Hall International Series in Computer Science (1985)

[M]   Milner R.: Communication and Concurrency. Prentice-Hall International Series in Computer Science (1989)

[R]   Reed R. (ed.): Specification and Programming Environment for Communication Software – SPECS. To be published by Elsiever (1993)

[S]   Stirling C.: Modal and Temporal Logics. Univ. of Edin. report ECS-LFCS-91-157 (1991)

A Definition of Unrolling and Unroll

The $\stackrel{unrolling}{\longrightarrow}$ relation is defined between relabelled behaviour expression and execution history pairs, as follows (assuming the process definition $P[\bar{g}](\bar{x}) = B$ in clause 16):

$(exit(E_1, \ldots, En) , \; term)$ $\stackrel{unrolling}{\longrightarrow} (stop , \; init)$

$(g\,?\bar{x}\,!\bar{t}\,[\mathcal{P}]\,;B\,,\; suffix(\bar{x}.p, ex))$ $\stackrel{unrolling}{\longrightarrow} (B[\bar{x}.p/\bar{x}]\,,\; ex)$

$([\mathcal{P}] \to B\,,\; ex)$ $\stackrel{unrolling}{\longrightarrow} (B, ex)$

$(choice\,\bar{x}\,[]\,B\,,\; sum(\bar{x}.p, ex))$ $\stackrel{unrolling}{\longrightarrow} (B[\bar{x}.p/\bar{x}]\,,\; ex)$

$(B\,[]\,C\,,\; choice_l\,(ex))$ $\stackrel{unrolling}{\longrightarrow} (B, ex)$

$(B\,[]\,C\,,\; choice_r(ex))$ $\stackrel{unrolling}{\longrightarrow} (C, ex)$

$(B\,|[g_1, \ldots, g_n]|\,C\,,\; par_\mu(ex, ex'))$ $\stackrel{unrolling}{\longrightarrow} (B, ex)$

$(B\,|[g_1, \ldots, g_n]|\,C\,,\; par_\mu(ex, ex'))$ $\stackrel{unrolling}{\longrightarrow} (C, ex')$

$(B\,[>\,C\,,\; disable_l\,(ex))$ $\stackrel{unrolling}{\longrightarrow} (B, ex)$

$(B\,[>\,C\,,\; disable_t\,(ex))$ $\stackrel{unrolling}{\longrightarrow} (B, ex)$

$(B\,[>\,C\,,\; disable_r\,(ex, ex'))$ $\stackrel{unrolling}{\longrightarrow} (B, ex)$

$(B\,[>\,C\,,\; disable_r\,(ex, ex'))$ $\stackrel{unrolling}{\longrightarrow} (C, ex')$

$(B \gg accept\;\bar{x}\;in\;C\,,\; enable_l\,(ex))$ $\stackrel{unrolling}{\longrightarrow} (B, ex)$

$(B \gg accept\;\bar{x}\;in\;C\,,\; enable_r(\bar{x}.p, ex, ex'))$ $\stackrel{unrolling}{\longrightarrow} (B, ex)$

$(B \gg accept\;\bar{x}\;in\;C\,,\; enable_r(\bar{x}.p, ex, ex'))$ $\stackrel{unrolling}{\longrightarrow} (C[\bar{x}.p/\bar{x}]\,,\; ex')$

$(P[[\bar{g}.p/\bar{g}]]([\bar{x}.p/\bar{x}])\,,\; apply(P.p, \bar{x}.p, \bar{g}.p, ex))$ $\stackrel{unrolling}{\longrightarrow}$
$(B[\bar{g}.p/\bar{g}][\bar{x}.p/\bar{x}]\,,\; ex)$

and for any pairs not covered by the above clauses:

$(B, ex)\;\stackrel{unrolling}{\longrightarrow}\;(B, init)$

Notice that this relation is a function on all pairs except those whose execution history terms are of the form $par_\mu(ex_1, ex_2)$, $disable_r(ex_1, ex_2)$ and $enable_r(ex_1, ex_2)$. On pairs where the relation defined above is functional, we will denote its use as a function by $\overset{\text{unrolling}}{\longrightarrow}(\langle B, es \rangle)$. Recall the definition of snapshot, see Sect. 2.3, in terms of the unrolling relation. Notice that the first two components of all the 4-tuples occurring in the execution history inference rules are in fact snapshots modulo the third component.

We now define inductively the *Unroll* function on snapshots. This is the function which returns their current relabelled behaviour expression:

$$
\begin{aligned}
&Unroll(\langle A, ex \rangle) \Leftarrow \\
&\quad \text{if} \quad \langle A, ex \rangle = \langle B, init \rangle \quad \text{then} \quad B \\
&\quad \text{else if} \quad \langle A, ex \rangle = \langle B \,|[g_1, \ldots, g_n]|\, C, par_\mu(ex_1, ex_2) \rangle \\
&\qquad\qquad \text{then} \quad Unroll(\langle B, ex_1 \rangle) \,|[g_1, \ldots, g_n]|\, Unroll(\langle C, ex_2 \rangle) \\
&\quad \text{else if} \quad \langle A, ex \rangle = \langle B\, [> C,\ disable_l(ex') \rangle \\
&\qquad\qquad \text{then} \quad Unroll(\langle B, ex' \rangle)\, [> C \\
&\quad \text{else if} \quad \langle A, ex \rangle = \langle B\, [> C,\ disable_t(ex') \rangle \\
&\qquad\qquad \text{then} \quad \text{stop} \\
&\quad \text{else if} \quad \langle A, ex \rangle = \langle B\, [> C,\ disable_r(ex_1, ex_2) \rangle \\
&\qquad\qquad \text{then} \quad Unroll(\langle C, ex_2 \rangle) \\
&\quad \text{else if} \quad \langle A, ex \rangle = \langle B \gg accept\ \bar{x}\ in\ C,\ enable_l(ex') \rangle \\
&\qquad\qquad \text{then} \quad Unroll(\langle B, ex' \rangle) \gg accept\ \bar{x}\ in\ C \\
&\quad \text{else if} \quad \langle A, ex \rangle = \langle B \gg accept\ \bar{x}\ in\ C,\ enable_r(\bar{x}.p, ex_1, ex_2) \rangle \\
&\qquad\qquad \text{then} \quad Unroll(\langle C[\bar{x}.p/\bar{x}],\ ex_2 \rangle) \\
&\quad \text{else} \quad Unroll(\overset{\text{unrolling}}{\longrightarrow}(\langle A, ex \rangle))
\end{aligned}
$$

B Sample Execution History Inference Rules

Notation: note that each of these lists may be empty:
$\bar{x}$ is the list of variables $(x_1, \ldots, x_m)$,
$\bar{t}$ is the list of terms $(t_1, \ldots, t_m)$ which may contain variable instances,
$\bar{x}.p$ is the list of variable instances $(x_1.p, \ldots, x_m.p)$,
$\bar{y}.r$ is the list of variable instances $(y_1.r_1 \ldots y_q.r_q)$,
$[\bar{x}.p/\bar{x}]$ is the list of substitutions/relabellings $[x_1.p/x_1, \ldots, x_m.p/x_m]$,
$\bar{x}.p = \bar{v}$ is the list of instantiations $(x_1.p = v_1, \ldots, x_2.p = v_m)$,
$\mu|a$ for the concatenation of a to the list μ
proc for the syntactic function which on a value variable gives the process identifier
$Q(S)$ is the quotient term algebra defined in [B]
D is the derivation system defined in [B]
Action prefix expression: let $B' \equiv g\,?\bar{x}\,!\bar{c}[\mathcal{P}]; B$ then:

$$
< B',\ init^J,\ I,\ J > \overset{gv}{\longrightarrow} < B',\ suffix(\bar{x}.p, init^J)^J,\ I',\ J >
$$

where $proc(x_i) = P$ and $P.p \in j$
$\quad I' = I \cup \{\bar{x}.p = \bar{t}\}$, for $t_i \in v_i$, $1 \leq i \leq m$
iff $v_i \in Q(S_i)$, $1 \leq i \leq m$
$\quad v_i = [\![c_i]\!]$, $m + 1 \leq i \leq n$
$\quad D \vdash \mathcal{P}[\bar{t}/\bar{x}]$
$\qquad$ where each c_i like $\mathcal{P}$ may contain relabelled variables

$$\frac{< B[\bar{x}.p/\bar{x}],\ ex_1^j,\ I,\ J > \xrightarrow{a} < B[\bar{x}.p/\bar{x}],\ ex_2^{j'},\ I',\ J' >}{< B',\ suffix(\bar{x}.p, ex_1^j)^j,\ I,\ J > \xrightarrow{a} < B',\ suffix(\bar{x}.p, ex_2^{j'})^{j'},\ I',\ J' >}$$

Process instantiation: Let $P[\bar{g}](\bar{x}) = B$ be a process definition, that is, $< (P, [\bar{g}], (\bar{x}), func), B > \in CBS.P$, see [B].
Let $B' \equiv P[[\bar{h}.r/\bar{g}]]([\bar{y}.s/\bar{x}])$ and $B'' \equiv P[[\bar{g}.p/\bar{g}]]([\bar{x}.p/\bar{x}])$ then:

$$\frac{< B[\bar{h}.r/\bar{h}][\bar{y}.s/\bar{y}],\ init^j,\ I,\ J > \xrightarrow{a} < B[\bar{h}.r/\bar{h}][\bar{y}.s/\bar{y}],\ ex^{j'},\ I',\ J' >}{< B',\ init^j,\ I,\ J > \xrightarrow{a} < B'',\ apply(P.p, \bar{x}.p, \bar{g}.p, ex^{j''})^{j''},\ I'',\ J'' >}$$

where $P.(p-1) \in J$
$$J'' = J' \cup \{P.p\} \setminus \{P.(p-1)\}$$
$$j'' = j' \cup \{P.p\} \setminus \{P.n\} \text{ for } n \le p-1$$
$$I'' = I' \cup \{\bar{x}.p = \bar{y}.s\} \cup \{\bar{g}.p = \bar{h}.r\}$$

$$\frac{< B[\bar{h}.r/\bar{h}][\bar{y}.s/\bar{x}],\ ex_1^j,\ I,\ J > \xrightarrow{a} < B[\bar{h}.r/\bar{h}][\bar{y}.s/\bar{x}],\ ex_2^{j'},\ I',\ J' >}{< B',\ apply,\ I,\ J > \xrightarrow{a} < B'',\ apply',\ I',\ J' >}$$

where $apply = apply(P.p, \bar{x}.p, \bar{g}.p, ex_1^j)^j$
$$apply' = apply(P.p, \bar{x}.p, \bar{g}.p, ex_2^{j'})^{j'}$$

Parallel expression: let $B' \equiv B |[g_1, \ldots, g_n]| C$ then:

$$\frac{< B\ init^j\ I\ J > \xrightarrow{a} < B\ ex^{j'}\ I'\ J' >}{< B'\ init^j\ I\ J > \xrightarrow{a} < B'\ par_{\{l\}}(ex^{j'}, init^j)^{j'}\ I'\ J' >}$$

$name(a) \notin \{g_1, \ldots, g_n, \delta\}$

$$\frac{< B, init^j, I, J > \xrightarrow{a} < B, es_1^{j'}, I', J' > \quad < C, init^{j'}, I', J' > \xrightarrow{a} < C, es_2^{j''}, I'', J'' >}{< B'\ init^j\ I\ J > \xrightarrow{a} < B'\ par_{\{c\}}(es_1^{j'}, es_2^{j''})^{j''}\ I''\ J'' >}$$

$name(a) \in \{g_1, \ldots, g_n, \delta\}$

$$\frac{< B\ ex_1^{j1}\ I\ J > \xrightarrow{a} < B\ ex_2^{j2}\ I'\ J' >}{< B'\ par_\mu(ex_1^{j1}, ex_3^{j3})^{j1.3}\ I\ J > \xrightarrow{a} < B'\ par_{\mu|l}(es_2^{j2}, ex_3^{j3})^{j2.3}\ I'\ J' >}$$

$name(a) \notin \{g_1, \ldots, g_n, \delta\}$

$$\frac{< B, ex_1^{j1}, I, J > \xrightarrow{a} < B, ex_3^{j3}, I', J' > \quad < C, ex_2^{j2}, I', J' > \xrightarrow{a} < C, ex_4^{j4}, I'', J'' >}{< B'\ par_\mu(ex_1^{j1}, ex_2^{j2})^{j1.2}\ I\ J > \xrightarrow{a} < B'\ par_{\mu|c}(ex_3^{j3}, ex_4^{j4})^{j3.4}\ I''\ J'' >}$$

$name(a) \in \{g_1, \ldots, g_n, \delta\}$

Disable expression: let $B' \equiv B[> C$ then:

$$\frac{< B\ init^j\ I\ J > \xrightarrow{a} < B\ ex^{j'}\ I'\ J' >}{< B'\ init^j\ I\ J > \xrightarrow{a} < B'\ disable_l(ex^{j'})^{j'}\ I'\ J' >}$$

$name(a) \ne \delta$

$$\frac{< B\ init^j\ I\ J > \xrightarrow{\delta v} < B\ ex^{j'}\ I'\ J' >}{< B'\ init^j\ I\ J > \xrightarrow{\delta v} < B'\ disable_t(ex^{j'})^{j'}\ I'\ J' >}$$

$$\frac{< C\ init^j\ I\ J > \xrightarrow{a} < C\ ex^{j'}\ I'\ J' >}{< B'\ init^j\ I\ J > \xrightarrow{a} < B'\ disable_r(init^j, ex^{j'})^{j'}\ I'\ J' >}$$

$$\frac{< C\ init^j\ I\ J > \xrightarrow{a} < C\ ex^{j'}\ I'\ J' >}{< B'\ disable_l(ex_1^j)^j\ I\ J > \xrightarrow{a} < B'\ disable_r(ex_1^j, ex_2^{j'})^{j'}\ I'\ J' >}$$

$$\frac{< B\ ex_1^j\ I\ J > \xrightarrow{a} < B\ ex_2^{j'}\ I'\ J' >}{< B'\ disable_l(ex_1^j)^j\ I\ J > \xrightarrow{a} < B'\ disable_l(ex_2^{j'})^{j'}\ I'\ J' >}$$

$name(a) \neq \delta$

$$\frac{< B\ ex_1^j\ I\ J > \xrightarrow{\delta v} < B\ ex_2^{j'}\ I'\ J' >}{< B'\ disable_l(ex_1^j)^j\ I\ J > \xrightarrow{\delta v} < B'\ disable_l(ex_2^{j'})^{j'}\ I'\ J' >}$$

$$\frac{< C\ ex_1^j\ I\ J > \xrightarrow{a} < C\ ex_2^{j'}\ I'\ J' >}{< B'\ disable_r(ex_3^{j''}, ex_1^j)^j\ I\ J > \xrightarrow{a} < B'\ disable_r(ex_3^{j''}, ex_2^{j'})^{j'}\ I'\ J' >}$$

Enable expression: let $B' \equiv B \gg accept\ \bar{x}\ in\ C$ then:

$$\frac{< B\ init^j\ I\ J > \xrightarrow{a} < B\ ex^{j'}\ I'\ J' >}{< B'\ init^j\ I\ J > \xrightarrow{a} < B'\ enable_l(ex^{j'})^{j'}\ I'\ J' >}$$

$name(a) \neq \delta$

$$\frac{< B\ init^j\ I\ J > \xrightarrow{\delta v} < B\ ex^{j'}\ I'\ J' >}{< B'\ init^{j'}\ I\ J > \xrightarrow{i} < B'\ enable_r(\bar{x}.p, ex^{j'}, init^{j'})^{j'}\ I''\ J' >}$$

where $proc(x_i) = P$ and $P.p \in j$
$I'' = I' \cup \{\bar{x}.p = \bar{t}\}$ for $t_i \in v_i,\ 1 \le i \le m$

$$\frac{< B\ ex_1^j\ I\ J > \xrightarrow{\delta v} < B\ ex_2^{j'}\ I'\ J' >}{< B'\ enable_l(ex_1^j)^j\ I\ J > \xrightarrow{i} < B'\ enable_r(\bar{x}.p, ex_2^{j'}, init^{j'})^{j'}\ I''\ J >}$$

where $proc(x_i) = P$ and $P.p \in j$
$I'' = I \cup \{\bar{x}.p = \bar{t}\}$ for $t_i \in v_i,\ 1 \le i \le m$

$$\frac{< B\ ex_1^j\ I\ J > \xrightarrow{a} < B\ ex_2^{j'}\ I'\ J' >}{< B'\ enable_l(ex_1^j)^j\ I\ J > \xrightarrow{a} < B'\ enable_l(ex_2^{j'})^{j'}\ I'\ J' >}$$

$name(a) \neq \delta$

$$\frac{< C[\bar{x}.p/\bar{x}]\ ex_1^j\ I\ J > \xrightarrow{a} < C[\bar{x}.p/\bar{x}]\ ex_2^{j'}\ I'\ J' >}{< B'\ enable_r(\bar{x}.p, ex_3^{j''}, ex_1^j)^j\ I\ J > \xrightarrow{a} < B'\ enable_r(\bar{x}.p, ex_3^{j''}, ex_2^{j'})^{j'}\ I'\ J' >}$$

The SAZ Project: Integrating SSADM and Z.

Fiona Polack, Mark Whiston, and Keith Mander

Department of Computer Science, University of York, Heslington, York YO1 5DD, UK.

Abstract. This paper investigates the rationale for integrating a structured systems analysis method (SSADM version 4) and a formal notation (Z). It describes the integrated specification, and discusses the advantages and disadvantages of formal specification and development for information systems.

1 Introduction

The SAZ project is investigating the integration of structured and formal specification methods, specifically SSADM version 4[1] and Z. The first phase of the project resulted in preparation of draft guidelines for composing a Z specification from the products of SSADM version 4 Requirements Analysis and Requirements Specification modules [1].

Subsequently, work has concentrated on the specification of the state and of constraints. The latter are difficult to express in SSADM. The paper draws together this work, and shows the complementary nature of SSADM and Z.

2 SAZ Raison d'Etre

Software implementations are renowned for representing the wrong system. System users suggest that this is because implementations do not match their requirements, whilst system developers claim that their systems represent what the clients describe. In practice it is difficult for the developer to elicit user requirements reliably. Structured methods such as SSADM attempt to solve part of this problem by advocating significant user involvement in analysis, specification, and review. However, it is still common to find that requirements are not fully documented, or are misinterpreted by analysts or designers.

Formal notations reduce the possibility of misinterpretation, by recording precise mathematical statements of agreed systems requirements. They are recognised as powerful system specification tools, particularly in the area of safety critical systems. Information systems, however, are less clearly defined. They tend to be large, with complex data structures, whose specification is not immediately obvious. The specification of information system requirements requires more analytical power and structure than can be provided by formal notations alone.

In putting structured and formal methods together, SAZ addresses several problem areas.

---

[1] Structured Systems Analysis and Design Method, an open method sponsored by the CCTA (Central Computer and Telecommunications Agency) and mandated for information systems by the UK government.

1. The inclusion of formal specification facilities in a structured systems analysis method provides a precise record of functional system requirements. Such precision is not readily available in a structured specification method.
2. The precise thinking required to prepare the formal specification encourages analysts to address details of the requirements which otherwise may be addressed only when the system is implemented, tested or in use.
3. SSADM version 4 is a large method for use by a team of analysts. In common with other information systems design methods, it comprises a range of text and graphic formats which require cross-checking. Although CASE tools perform some checks, the varied formats make rigorous, complete checking difficult. The formal notation provides a common medium for recording functional aspects of the Requirements Specification. It is mechanically checkable, and provides a quality assurance mechanism for the SSADM products.
4. Formal notations may not be easily understood by mathematical novices. SSADM's graphical formats provide a comprehensible picture for the analysts who present the specification to clients. The combined method gives a communication medium underpinned by a precise formal interpretation. This reduces the chances of the system being misinterpreted or misrepresented.
5. Formal notations are perceived as difficult to learn. Z is founded on set theory, and is thus conceptually similar to information system data structures. The SAZ method should help the understanding of formal notations, as well as overcoming the problem of what to specify in Z.
6. The reuse of system specifications and designs is becoming increasingly attractive to the computer industry, as a way of reducing software development time and the risks associated with new software. Although both formal and structured specifications should be clear statements of the requirements of any system, formal notations give a more concise and less ambiguous definition of the system than the structured specification. In addition, the formal system may be represented at any level of abstraction, and permits more thorough examination of the effects of alterations.
7. Having prepared a Z specification, the Z methods of refinement and proof can be used in a formal system development, if required. SSADM version 4 uses Jackson design variants, which play a complementary role.

At an abstract level, SAZ does nothing that SSADM does not do. Both media provide specifications of the required state and processing. Both provide methods for refining the logical specification into a logical design, and guidance on moving from design to implementation.

However, there are areas in which Z has advantages over the SSADM, and vice versa. For instance, Z is very good at expressing data constraints and conditions. It is also a natural medium for recording the data manipulations required by more complex processing, since these are essentially mathematical set operations. In SSADM, these features may be recorded in documentation, but are not collected rigorously until logical design, by which time the specification has been approved and signed off. Thus the SSADM and the Z provide a more complete specification than either medium alone, and this specification can be used by analysts to guide design and implementation.

Conversely, SSADM provides graphical products which are easily understood by users. It is not particularly difficult to interpret a diagram to a user, or even to train user representatives in the graphical notations of SSADM. It is therefore a good medium for discussing requirements with users.

The benefit of the SAZ method is that it combines the useful features of Z and SSADM. The graphical notations are underpinned by precise formal interpretations, and the users and analysts still have the diagrammatic communications media.

In addition, Z allows all the functional features of the system to be specified in a common medium, facilitating checking and quality assurance activities. The specification of non-functional requirements, however, relies on the SSADM documentation. Furthermore, linking formal notations with a widely-used structured method is seen as a positive move towards the wider acceptance of formal development in industry. This improves the quality of Requirements Specification, and has the potential for stimulating better, low-cost software production.

The SAZ approach is therefore to use SSADM to specify the whole system. The state and those parts of the system processing which are particularly complex or critical can then be converted to the Z notation. This not only provides a structure to the specification, but also improves the scalability of formal notations.

3 Approaches to Using Z and SSADM Version 4

SAZ identifies two possible roles for Z. The positions of these approaches relative to SSADM and the project management which oversees it, are shown in Fig. 1, an adaptation of the diagram of the SSADM modules used in the version 4 manuals [2].

In the diagram, the top box represents the role of project management (the *project board*). The five lower boxes are the modules of SSADM, each of which is initiated, reviewed and signed off on the authority of the project board – that is, outside the SSADM method. The diagram has been modified to show the roles of Z identified in the SAZ project, and also to show the iterations with the project board which must occur in Logical Specification, when the technical options for the project are presented. The roles of the Z are now considered in detail.

> * NOTE Business System Options (BSO) is the stage of SSADM version 4 at which the project board decides among options for representing the required business system. Technical System Options (TSO) entails the equivalent technical decisions.

3.1 Z used for Quality Audits of SSADM Requirements

In the simpler case, the Z is written outside the core project team, and used solely for quality assurance. This exploits the precision and the mechanical type-checking facilities which are available for Z.

In this form, SAZ is used to prepare a formal data model for the chosen BSO after Requirements Analysis, and formal models of logical processing at the end of the Requirements Specification. The preparation of the Z specification entails a thorough review of the SSADM documentation, since features such as data constraints are not recorded in a uniform manner.

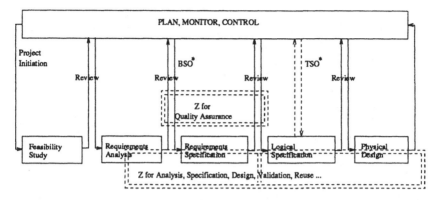

Fig. 1. Structure of SSADM from version 4 manual, with Z roles superimposed.

Some of the areas which benefit from the use of Z for quality audit (QA) are as follows.

- Data access. The Z processing and enquiry specifications navigate the data model. Mechanical type checking identifies any situations in which the Z state, and the LDM[2] from which it is derived, are unable to provide the required data access.
- Data integrity. The constraints and conditions on the data model are represented as Z predicates, which catalogue the correct operating conditions for the system. The formal specification can be proved, formally or informally, to ensure that these invariants are not broken by the processing, and that the specified processing maintains data integrity.
- Processing specifications. Z provides a medium for precisely specifying the effects of processing operations, without referring to the detailed implementation issues.
- SSADM documentation defines data item types in implementational terms, such as character strings, *ddmmyy* or integers. Z allows a more precise expression of the required qualities of attributes, in a concise and easily-read format.

When the Z preparation identifies problems or ambiguities in the structured analysis, alterations have to be referred back to the SSADM team. This is the same as any other review procedure, which may require modifications to the SSADM before signing off a module. Direct influence on the analysis is prevented because the Z team is distinct from the group responsible for the SSADM.

3.2 Z as an SSADM Technique

At a more sophisticated level, SAZ can be used as an integral SSADM technique. The Z is prepared by the project team, and the analysts exploit the power of the Z

---

[2] LDM stands for the SSADM Logical Data Model, that is, the required system entity relationship model with supporting text definitions. It is also used for the SSADM technique by which the model is produced, Logical Data Modelling.

notation directly. The technique is described in more detail in Sects. 4 and 5.

In this mode, as well as the QA benefits already considered, the Z approach encourages the analyst to ask more searching questions. It helps to address the details of the data structure and processing which require specification (and user involvement) at an early stage of the system development.

This form of use also encourages the analysts to adapt their use of SSADM. For example, a constraints catalogue may be used to record the predicates on state elements defined in Z. The LDM technique described in the version 4 manuals may be extended to deal more adequately with subtyping, type definitions, and data-related business rules. The SSADM method comprises a set of objectives and suggested techniques for achieving these. Not all techniques are appropriate in all projects, and some techniques require modification or extension to suit the form of project, or the working procedures used. If the SAZ method is used, the adaptation of SSADM should be seen as a positive feature. The combined method adds depth to the specification and provides another, complementary view of the system.

4 The SAZ Method for Deriving the State Specification

The SSADM method is laid out as a set of modules, comprising stages, steps and tasks, and a set of techniques appropriate to the fulfilment of objectives of each element. One of the features of project planning should be the identification of the path to be taken by a particular project, and, clearly, the decision to use Z will influence this.

If Z is used only for QA, the planning simply requires that the products of the SSADM Requirements Analysis and/or Specification modules be presented in such a way that the SAZ method can be followed by the QA review team, independently of the SSADM project team.

Where the Z is prepared in parallel with the SSADM, the SAZ method becomes an integral SSADM technique. This section looks at the detailed theoretical aspects of the SAZ method, as applied to the system state.

The aim of the SAZ state derivation technique is similar to that of the LDM. This SSADM technique is based on a variation of the typical entity relationship model, comprising a data structure or entity relationship diagram (the LDS[3]) and a dictionary of supporting information, collected on standard SSADM forms.

SAZ collects together all the functional information on the state, but does not consider the non-functional information recorded in LDM. For the functional aspects, SAZ actually does what the LDM technique claims to do. It provides a precise and unambiguous view of the system data requirements.

The SAZ method can be summarised as:

– challenging the analyst to define with mathematical precision the components of the LDM and data-related elements of the business;

---

[3] The LDS (Logical Data Structure) is the diagrammatic element of the LDM. In SSADM version 4, a finished LDS contains entities and relationships. Relationships are mandatory or optional at either end, but all are of the $1{:}m/m{:}1$ form.

- providing a concise record of the intended interpretation of the information conveyed in the LDM;
- identifying areas which need clarification (types, relationships etc) at an early stage in the development of the system;
- providing a record of the system data structure which is independent of any graphical notation or implementation, and can be abstracted to give a generic description of the system;
- feeding clarified concepts back into the SSADM, particularly the LDM, to improve the specification, design, implementation and user documentation

The relationship of the SAZ state specification technique to SSADM is defined by the inputs to the technique and the outputs from it.

Inputs

- The LDS provides an overview of the structure with names, degrees and optionality of relationships and names of entities.
- The SSADM Entity Description Form gives details of entity types.
- The Attribute/Data Item Descriptions and Grouped Domain Descriptions give details of attribute types. However, where types are defined in terms of a perceived implementation (*char string, ddmmyy* etc), the abstract features of the type may be represented in the Z.
- Relationship Descriptions support the information illustrated in the LDS, and provide information on conditional relationships.

Outputs

- Given sets introduce basic types, and free types define categorical types.
- Schema types specify grouped domain types and entities; predicates represent type constraints and related attributes.
- Standard format schemas define entity sets and relationships with predicates to represent data constraints and conditions.
- Schema calculus is used to specify entity subtyping.
- Predicates define entity subtyping and other global data features.
- Full documentation explaining features and changes, and cross-referencing the SSADM.
- A summary or catalogue of all the Z predicates.

The SAZ state specification uses normal Z concepts and notation as described in the many texts on the subject [3, 4, 5, 6]. For new users, two key papers describe the use of Z and the schema calculus [7, 8]. Using these notations, the Z specification can be prepared in several semantically-equivalent formats.

Similar techniques are available in other integrated methods, for instance the Yourdon or Telstar and Z QA methods developed for British Telecom [9], and the Yourdon/VDM method devised for safety critical software development at Rolls-Royce Associates [10].

The following illustration uses features from the LDM for a simple order processing system. The LDS is shown in Fig. 2. The description looks briefly at each state component in turn, giving some of the alternative formats.

In the diagram, entities are represented by soft boxes. Mandatory relationships are solid lines, and optional relationships are dashed lines. The detail or dependent end of the relationship has a crow's foot.

The relationships can be read off, for instance, "an instance of *Order Line* must *reference* one instance of the *Book* entity; an instance of the *Book* entity may *be referenced by* none, one or many instances of *Order Line*."

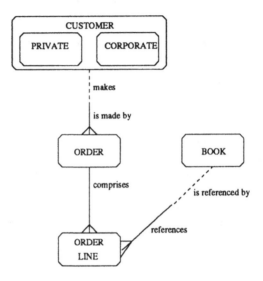

Fig. 2. LDS for the order processing system.

The diagram defines generalities. It shows the entity types which exist in the particular system of interest, and the relationships which may exist among them. It does not state the existence of instances of such entities, nor allow reasoning about them, but shows what the system data structure would be if they did exist. The Z can clarify this distinction.

The Z representations of the various features of the LDM is now described.

4.1 Attribute Type Definitions

The Z notation includes only one base type, integer. Given sets are used to introduce base types for a particular specification. The base types need not be the implementation types which SSADM uses. For instance, it is more meaningful to define a type, NAME than a restricted length sequence of CHAR.

In the illustration, the following given sets are defined. These may be refined into derivatives of implementation types if the Z is taken forward as a design and implementation technique.

[TITLE, ISBN, AUTHOR, NAME, TEXT, RATING, DATE]

Attributes of SSADM Grouped Domain types are defined by schemas. Elements of the type may be defined as given sets. For instance, ADDRESS might be defined as:

[HOUSE, NUMBER, STREET, TOWN, POSTCODE]

```
┌ ADDRESS ─────────────────┐
│ House_Name : HOUSE
│ House_Number : NUMBER
│ Street : STREET
│ Town : TOWN
│ Postcode : POSTCODE
└──────────────────────────┘
```

This specification also allows for the refinement of the elements.

A third form of type specification is the free type. This lists the values (text, symbols, bitmaps etc) which are acceptable for the attribute, as in,

PRINT_STATUS ::= in_print | out_of_print

The more sophisticated free type format allows the permitted values of a type to be themselves of different types. For instance, the house name and number attributes, above, might be replaced by a single attribute, the values of which are either names or positive integers:

$HOUSE ::= house\_name \langle\!\langle NAME \rangle\!\rangle \mid house\_number \langle\!\langle \mathbb{N}_1 \rangle\!\rangle$

4.2 Type Definitions for Entities and Subtypes

Entity types are defined in schemas, as for complex attribute types. An entity type is simply a collection of attributes. For instance, the BOOK entity comprises five attributes,

```
┌ BOOK ─────────────────────┐
│ ISBN_No : ISBN
│ Title : TITLE
│ Author : AUTHOR
│ Stock_Qty : N
│ Print_Status : PRINT_STATUS
└───────────────────────────┘
```

Other entities are declared in a similar way.

```
┌ ORDER ────────────────────┐
│ Order_Date : DATE
│ Delivery_Address : ADDRESS
└───────────────────────────┘
```

```
 ┌ ORDER_LINE ──────┐
 │ Ordered_Qty : $N_1$
 │ Amended_Qty : $N$
 │ Annotation : TEXT
 └──────────────────┘
```

In the case of subtyped entities, the supertype schema defines the attributes which are common to each subtype, whilst the subtype schemas list only the attributes relevant to the subtype. The types are then combined using schema calculus. For instance, the CUSTOMER entity in Fig. 2 is defined as

```
 ┌ CUSTOMER_SUPERTYPE ┐
 │ Name : NAME
 │ Address : ADDRESS
 └────────────────────┘
```

```
 ┌ PRIVATE_SUBTYPE ┐
 │ Credit_Rating : $N$
 └─────────────────┘
```

```
 ┌ CORPORATE_SUBTYPE ──────┐
 │ Company_Name : NAME
 │ Company_Address : ADDRESS
 └──────────────────────────┘
```

To obtain the full type definition for CUSTOMER, the elements are combined using schema calculus, as follows. In this form, the schema calculus describes inclusive or overlapping subtypes.

$$\text{CUSTOMER} \;\hat{=}$$
$$\text{CUSTOMER\_SUPERTYPE} \wedge$$
$$(\text{PRIVATE\_SUBTYPE} \vee \text{CORPORATE\_SUBTYPE})$$

The SSADM LDM technique describes simple exclusive subtypes, but the manuals state that,

A general description of super-types and sub-types is beyond the scope of this chapter [2]

In SAZ, the features of different categories and hierarchies of subtypes can be defined by extending or qualifying the schema calculus. To illustrate this, a more detailed subtype hierarchy is required, the theoretical COUNTRY type from [11]. The entity type, shown in Fig. 3, comprises a supertype and three partitions of subtypes – restrictiveness, coastal status, and farming status. The first two are exclusive subtypes, whilst the last is inclusive (it is possible for an instance to have the attributes of more than one of the farming status subtypes). The fishing subtype of the farming category is further subtyped into sea and fresh fishing. These are again inclusive subtypes.

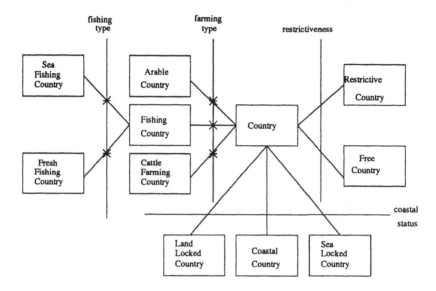

Fig. 3. Whittington's illustration of subtype categories.

Assuming that the sub- and super-types have been defined in schemas which declare the relevant attributes with types and predicates on these attributes, the diagram can be represented either in an extension of the form above, where each conjoined group represents a category, or in the following equivalent form, where each leaf is built up in turn:

RESTRICTIVE_COUNTRY ≅ COUNTRY ∧ RESTRICTIVE

FREE_COUNTRY ≅ COUNTRY ∧ FREE

LANDLOCKED_COUNTRY ≅ COUNTRY ∧ LANDLOCKED

COASTAL_COUNTRY ≅ COUNTRY ∧ COASTAL

SEALOCKED_COUNTRY ≅ COUNTRY ∧ SEALOCKED

ARABLE_COUNTRY ≅ COUNTRY ∧ ARABLE

CATTLE_COUNTRY ≅ COUNTRY ∧ CATTLE

FRESHFISHING_COUNTRY ≅ COUNTRY ∧ FISHING ∧ FRESH

SEAFISHING_COUNTRY ≅ COUNTRY ∧ FISHING ∧ SEA

The elements are again combined using schema disjunction, to give the full definition of the COUNTRY type.

FULL_COUNTRY_TYPE $\hat{=}$
 (RESTRICTIVE_COUNTRY ∨ FREE_COUNTRY) ∧
 (LANDLOCKED_COUNTRY ∨ COASTAL_COUNTRY
  ∨SEALOCKED_COUNTRY) ∧
 (ARABLE_COUNTRY ∨ CATTLE_COUNTRY ∨
  FRESHFISHING_COUNTRY ∨ SEAFISHING_COUNTRY)

The definition is extended to enforce the exclusive subtyping for the restrictive and coastal status categories. The semantics of exclusive subtyping are that any instance will have all the characteristics of the supertype plus the characteristics of exactly one of the subtypes. By implication, therefore, the supertype element of an instance with the characteristics of a particular subtype must be distinguishable from the supertype element of an instance with the characteristics of a different subtype. In implementation, this feature may be expressed by the addition to the supertype of an attribute whose value determines the appropriate subtype. In specification, it is sufficient to define the fact that there is a difference in the root or supertype elements. First, the root is defined as the part of the instance which is not characteristic of a subtype:

RESTRICTIVE_COUNTRY_ROOT $\hat{=}$
 RESTRICTIVE_COUNTRY \ RESTRICTIVE

FREE_COUNTRY_ROOT $\hat{=}$ FREE_COUNTRY \ FREE

Then, the uniqueness of values of the root type is asserted:

∀R : RESTRICTIVE_COUNTRY_ROOT; F : FREE_COUNTRY_ROOT •
 R ≠ F

Similarly, for the coastal status partition,

LANDLOCKED_ROOT $\hat{=}$ LANDLOCKED_COUNTRY \ LANDLOCKED

COASTAL_ROOT $\hat{=}$ COASTAL_COUNTRY \ COASTAL

SEALOCKED_ROOT $\hat{=}$ SEALOCKED_COUNTRY \ SEALOCKED

∀L : LANDLOCKED_ROOT; C : COASTAL_ROOT;
 S : SEALOCKED_ROOT • (L ≠ C) ∧ (L ≠ S) ∧ (S ≠ C)

Semantic information which is difficult to express diagrammatically can also be captured in the Z. For instance, in the above illustration, it is not possible for a landlocked country to have the characteristics of a seafishing country. Such additional exclusions may be partial, for instance related to attribute values, or total, as in this case. The exclusivity is expressed in the same way as above (using the definition of LANDLOCKED_ROOT from above):

SEAFISHING_ROOT $\widehat{=}$ SEAFISHING_COUNTRY \ SEA \ FISHING

∀S : SEAFISHING_ROOT; L : LANDLOCKED_ROOT • S ≠ L

4.3 Standard Schemas for Entity Sets

Sets of entities can now be defined. Structured analysis rarely makes clear the difference between types and sets, but the distinction is important in the formal specification. For instance, creation operations, generally referred to as *adding an entity*, add an instance of the relevant type to a set of entity instances but must not change the type.

The SAZ method defines the set of instances of each entity as a function mapping the type of the entity to the type of the unique identifier (the key) of the entity. This gives a set of pairs, of the form (IDENTIFIER, ENTITY). The use of surrogate identifiers is encouraged, to avoid the implementational issues of uniqueness, but where an attribute is a unique identifier, it may be used.

Where surrogate identifiers are used, the entity set specification is of the form,

[CUSTOMER_ID]

```
┌─ CUSTOMER_SET ─────────────────────
│ Key : CUSTOMER_ID ↦ CUSTOMER
└─────────────────────────────────────
```

The entity set schemas can be defined more generally by the generic schema,

```
┌─ ENTITY_SET[IDENTIFIER, ENTITY_TYPE] ─┐
│ Key : IDENTIFIER ↦ ENTITY_TYPE
└─────────────────────────────────────
```

This schema can be instantiated, as in,

BOOK_SET $\widehat{=}$ ENTITY_SET[ISBN, BOOK]

Where an attribute included in the entity type definition is a unique identifier, the predicate linking the identifier type in the function to the key can be defined thus.

∀b : BOOK_SET • ∀i : dom b.Key • (b.Key i).ISBN_No = i

Where an entity is subtyped, the entity set specification refers to the full entity (defined using schema calculus). A set of instances of a subtype may be declared as a subset of the full set:

```
┌─ PRIVATE_CUSTOMER_SET ──────────────────────────┐
│ CUSTOMER_SET                                     │
│ Private_Key : CUSTOMER_ID ⇸ PRIVATE_SUBTYPE      │
│ ─────────────────────────────────────           │
│ dom Private_Key ⊆ dom Key                        │
└──────────────────────────────────────────────────┘
```

4.4 Standard Schemas for Relationships

There are two elements to a relationship specification. The first is the specification of the types which are related. These can be introduced via instantiation of the generic schema,

```
┌─ RELATIONSHIP[MASTER, DETAIL] ─┐
│ Owns : MASTER ↔ DETAIL         │
│ Owned_By : DETAIL ⇸ MASTER     │
│ ───────────────────────        │
│ Owns~ = Owned_By               │
└─────────────────────────────────┘
```

The one-to-many end of a relationship is defined as a relation, and the many-to-one end as a partial function which is the inverse of the relation. The specification of the relation is implied by the specification of the partial function, and may be omitted from the generic (along with the predicate). However, the paired declarations and predicate is analogous to the SSADM relationships.

The second element of the relationship specification concerns the optionality of each end. The following pair of generic schemas defines a mandatory relationship, which is compulsory in both directions, and a contingent relationship which is optional at the master end.

Each of these generics represents a specialisation of the relationship schema, formed by the addition of a predicate. The predicate relates the sets of instances affected by the relationship to the entity sets defined for the system.

```
┌─ MANDATORY_REL[MASTER, MASTER_KEY, DETAIL, DETAIL_KEY] ─┐
│ RELATIONSHIP[MASTER, DETAIL]                            │
│ ─────────────────────────────                          │
│ ∀Mandatory_Rel : RELATIONSHIP[MASTER, DETAIL] •         │
│   ∃Master_Set : ENTITY_SET[MASTER_KEY, MASTER]          │
│     Detail_Set : ENTITY_SET[DETAIL_KEY, DETAIL] •       │
│       ran Mandatory_Rel.Owns = ran Detail_Set.Key ∧     │
│       dom Mandatory_Rel.Owns = ran Master_Set.Key       │
└──────────────────────────────────────────────────────────┘
```

```
┌─ CONTINGENT_REL[MASTER, MASTER_KEY, DETAIL, DETAIL_KEY] ─┐
│ RELATIONSHIP[MASTER, DETAIL]
├─────────────────────────────────────────────────────────
│ ∀Contingent_Rel : RELATIONSHIP[MASTER, DETAIL] •
│   ∃Master_Set : ENTITY_SET[MASTER_KEY, MASTER]
│     Detail_Set : ENTITY_SET[DETAIL_KEY, DETAIL] •
│       ran Contingent_Rel.Owns = ran Detail_Set.Key ∧
│       dom Contingent_Rel.Owns ⊆ ran Master_Set.Key
└─────────────────────────────────────────────────────────┘
```

All these generics are instantiated simply by naming the required relationship, and providing the master and detail entity and entity set key types:

[ORDER_ID, ORDER_LINE_ID]

References ≙
    CONTINGENT_REL
        [BOOK, ISBN, ORDER_LINE, ORDER_LINE_ID]
Comprises ≙
    MANDATORY_REL
        [ORDER, ORDER_ID, ORDER_LINE, ORDER_LINE_ID]

SAZ has not defined relationships which are optional at the detail end. Where these occur, a further two generic schemas are required, defining the other optionality combinations.

An equivalent of the Comprises instantiation, written without generics is:

```
┌─ ORDER_SET ─────────────────┐
│ Key : ORDER_ID ↠ ORDER      │
└─────────────────────────────┘
```

```
┌─ ORDER_LINE_SET ────────────────────┐
│ Key : ORDER_LINE_ID ↠ ORDER_LINE    │
└─────────────────────────────────────┘
```

```
│ Order_Comprises_Order_Line : ORDER ↔ ORDER_LINE
│ Order_Line_Makes_Up_Order : ORDER_LINE ↠ ORDER
├──────────────────────────────────────────────────
│ Order_Comprises_Order_Line~ = Order_Line_Makes_Up_Order
│ ∀Orders : ORDER_SET; Order_Lines : ORDER_LINE_SET •
│   ran Order_Comprises_Order_Line = ran Order_Lines.Key ∧
│   dom Order_Comprises_Order_Line ⊆ ran Orders.Key
```

5   Using Z Predicates to Add Detail to the SSADM

Having defined the basic state represented in the LDM, the Z can be extended to make precise statements about features of the business data represented. These are illustrated with reference to the relationship between BOOK and ORDER LINE. Fig. 4 shows the relationship, extracted from Fig. 2, above.

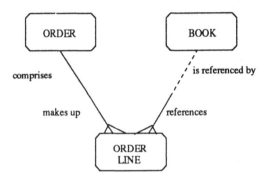

Fig. 4. Relationship between ORDER LINE and BOOK from Fig. 2

The *is referenced by* relationship is read as, "an instance of the *Book* entity may be *referenced by* none, one or many instances of *Order Line*".

This gives rise to two possible scenarios, which are indistinguishable in the LDM. In the obvious interpretation, an instance of the Book entity may be referenced on only one Order Line for a particular Order. However, the LDM does not preclude the interpretation that an instance of the Book entity may be referenced by more than one Order Line of a particular Order.

The Z representation of the required system state can be amended with the addition of predicates to make the situation clear. The state elements are defined above, namely,

- the entities ORDER, ORDER_LINE, BOOK;
- the entity Sets ORDER_SET, ORDER_LINE_SET, BOOK_SET;
- the relationships References (contingent), Comprises (mandatory).

These statements alone express the second scenario, in which a book may be referenced by more than one order line on a particular order. In order to represent the first scenario, which includes the restriction that a book is referenced by only one order line, a global predicate is added:

$$\forall o : ORDER;\ a,\ b : ORDER\_LINE;\ c : Comprises;\ r : References\ |$$
$$\{a, b\} \subseteq c.Owns(\!|\{o\}|\!) \land a \neq b \bullet$$
$$r.Owned\_By\ a \neq r.Owned\_By\ b$$

A variety of constraints on the state (or processing) can be expressed in this way. For instance, a maximum number of order lines on one order may be specified:

$$\forall o : \mathsf{ORDER}; \ c : \mathsf{Comprises} \bullet \#(c.\mathsf{Owns}(\!\{o\}\!)) < \mathsf{Max\_Lines}$$

Such predicates are an important feature of the SAZ method. While on the one hand, they are difficult for the untrained analyst to write (and perhaps read), on the other hand they can be used to give precise statements about those parts of the specification where precision is required. Several circumstances can be envisaged. First, they can be used in applications where the costs of making errors exceed the costs of developing the formal specifications: safety-critical applications are one example. Second, they can be used to define 'common knowledge'. Here we envisage a library of such specifications that can be re-used in different applications. This helps to solve the problem of supposedly common knowledge being interpreted in different ways by different people. (As a trivial example of supposedly common knowledge, ask several people to define the properties of the board on which the children's game of *snakes and ladders* is played, and see how many unexpected properties you get.) Formal specifications not only provide a precise specification of such things, they provide a focus for analysis and discussion from which accurate specifications of requirements can be elicited.

6 Conclusion

This paper describes the SAZ method for preparing a Z state specification from the products of an SSADM version 4 systems analysis. It suggests ways in which the Z specification can be used for quality checking), and describes the use of Z as a specification technique. This can form the basis of further refinement and proof in the logical design and system implementation phases.

Issues raised by the use of an integrated method have been discussed, in particular documentation and cross-referencing of the products of SSADM and the Z specification. (General solutions are not given, since it is necessary to tailor the documentation to a particular project in the project plan.)

The description of the SAZ method shows ways in which the state specification can be written, using the LDM as a source. The same technique could be applied to any other form of entity relationship model. It is assumed that the more rigorous Z specification will identify errors or inconsistencies in the data model. The Z also records data invariants, an under-emphasised aspect of data specification.

A key role of the Z specification produced by SAZ is to bring together the functional aspects of the system specification in a common, mechanically checkable notation. This may be used as an index or summary of the SSADM specification, or as unambiguous documentation of the system.

Acknowledgements

The SAZ project is supported by the Science and Engineering Research Council under grant GR/F98529. The CADiZ tool has been used to type-check the Z specifications. This was developed in the Department of Computer Science at the University of York by Dr Ian Toyn, who also offered advice on some of the more exotic features of Z. The advice and assistance of Brian Sharp, York Software Engineering Ltd, has been invaluable in preparing the LaTeX version of the document.

References

1. Polack F., Whiston, M., Hitchcock, P.: The SAZ Method - Version 0.1. University of York (May 1992)
2. CCTA: SSADM Version 4 Reference Manual. NCC Blackwell Ltd (1990)
3. Spivey, J. M.: The Z Notation: A Reference Manual. Prentice Hall London (1989)
4. Potter, B., Sinclair, J., Till, D.: An Introduction to Formal Specification and Z. Prentice Hall (1991)
5. Lightfoot, D.: Formal Specification using Z. MacMillan (1991)
6. Diller, A. Z.: An Introduction to Formal Methods. Wiley Chichester (1990)
7. Woodcock, J. C. P.: Structuring specifications in Z. Software Engineering Journal 4 (1), (1989) 51-65
8. Spivey, J. M.: An Introduction to Z and formal specifications. Software Engineering Journal 4 (1), (1989) 40-50
9. Semmens, L., Allen, P.: Using Yourdon and Z : an Approach to Formal Specification. Proceedings of Fifth Annual Z User Group Meeting Oxford, Springer Verlag (1991)
10. Hamilton, V.: Experiences of combining Yourdon and VDM. Workshop on Methods Integration Leeds, Sept 1991 (for Publication, 1993)
11. Whittington, R. P.: Database Systems Engineering. Oxford (1988)

Maintaining Consistency Under Changes to Formal Specifications

Kelvin J. Ross and Peter A. Lindsay

Software Verification Research Centre
Department of Computer Science
University of Queensland, St Lucia 4072, Australia

Abstract. Configuration Management is an integral requirement of the Software Engineering process. This paper outlines an approach to Configuration Management specifically tailored to support formal development of software. A model of VDM developments is defined in which each development is provided as a configuration of its low level components, such as operation definitions and formal proofs. Consistency checking is defined on this model to determine if verification criteria required by the methodology have been carried out. The basis of the consistency checking is determined from relationships between components of the configurations provided by the development tools and the developers themselves. A small VDM case study to which a change is applied is provided to illustrate the model and the support envisaged through the use of consistency checking.

Keywords: formal methods, VDM, configuration management, change control, verification.

1 Introduction

1.1 A Fictitious Scenario

Consider the following scenario: a railway signalling client's representative decides that the functionality of the system requires a slight change, and after discussion with the developer a small change is agreed upon within the formal specification. The developer modifies the formal specification and the remainder of the development is reviewed with a few minor changes occurring within further specifications and proofs. All changes are well recorded within an off-the-shelf Configuration Management (CM) package, with a reasonable review being applied to the software. After the extensive auditing process the certification of the software is approved, the software is placed into service.

After effective operation over a number of months, the system falls into non-termination while deciding to separate the paths of oncoming intercity trains. Fortunately disaster is averted by a backup mechanical signalling system. However the failure is noticed and an enquiry is called.

Upon review by the enquiry board, the development is found to be inconsistent. The change in functionality modified the system and caused a small change within an existing proof that was overlooked. This was not due to gross neglect by the developer: the sheer size of the development prevented the developer reapplying proof checking on every proof. The CM system did not support formal methods effectively to diagnose the items which would be altered by changes in the specification.

1.2 The Need for Configuration Management

Configuration Management in software engineering is concerned with recording and controlling the evolution of software systems. As the scenario above illustrates, CM has a vital role to play in the development and maintenance of formally developed software, including:

- maintaining adherence to a prescribed methodology,
- checking that the development is complete, and
- checking that all proof obligations have been correctly discharged.

When developments are very large, as typically happens with formal methods, it is difficult to manually maintain conformance to a method. Although tool support is becoming available for certain aspects of the problem, such as checking correctness of proofs, very little work has been done on the kind of integrated CM support that would be required for checking whole developments.

The problem is exacerbated by change. It is well known that specifications often change during development, for any of the following causes:

- changes in requirements initiated by the client;
- proposals made by the developer for modifications to the design which would improve the software or exploit new discoveries;
- repairs resulting from problems discovered during the development or in-service life-cycle.

Relatively small changes in requirements percolate through a whole formal development and may introduce inconsistencies and incompletenesses which are difficult to detect using normal review procedures. Yet such changes may affect the correctness of the resulting development. Consistency checking is thus an important aspect of CM for formal methods.

As specifications change we should not require all proofs to be redone from scratch. Ideally, one would like to automatically identify those parts of the development which may need to be modified and concentrate resources on these areas, without wasting effort on components unaffected by the change. Change management is thus an important practical consideration for formal developments.

1.3 CM Support for Formal Developments

In general, existing CM practices can be adopted in the process of developing software formally. Current practices are quite mature and well documented [BIIS79], and in some cases CM practices are standardized [Soc87, Soc90]. However the reliability aspect and cost of formal development require more specific support to be provided beyond that of conventional software development methodologies.

Formal developments have important structural properties which a CM system could usefully exploit to improve the practices of developing software, for example:

- The structure, semantics and methodology provided by a Formal Method produces formal links between various components within the development. For example, verification connects components of a specification with proofs which discharge some correctness criteria; axioms and proof obligations can be directly linked back to the part of the specification which gave rise to them. A useful CM system would identify and record links between components from which one can deduce information concerning the overall status of the development.
- Components within a formal development tend to be grouped into strands of functionality which are closely related within themselves but mutually independent. For example, an operation may be linked to other refined operations through a data reification, with proofs linking the operations in different specifications, whereas operations within the one specification may remain largely independent. Effects of modifications are often localized to the strand in which the changed component belongs.

Effective CM system support will provide the user a range of CM services [Dar91] which will assist the formal development of software. Standard practices such as version storage, change requests, configuration control boards are required at the project management level. At the development level procedures are required which actively support the formal methodology, including:

Repositories Whole developments would be stored in the CM system.

Traceability Travelling along links within the development provides traceability at various levels of granularity.

Partitioning Different repositories may be created for different areas of work, separate projects, etc.

Team Work Access control allows the CM user to coordinate and control team work.

Change Minimization A combination of traceability and consistency checking would allow heuristics to be developed for minimizing the changes required to restore consistency.

Change Impact Analysis Establishing change minimization allows prediction of change impact, before the change is made.

1.4 Overview of This Paper

This paper explores the requirements of change management for formal software development. We concentrate on static checking for consistency and completeness of formal verifications of VDM specifications [Jon90]: that is, given a VDM specification and a theory (a collection of axioms and derived rules), what are the conditions under which the theory is an adequate verification of the specification? VDM was chosen since it is a complete development methodology for which the relationship between specifications and proofs which verify them is well developed [JJLM91]. Although we have chosen to concentrate on verification of specifications, we expect that support for full development (linking specifications through reifications and support for operation decomposition, etc.) would adhere closely to the approach presented here.

In this paper we provide a CM system model for VDM specifications and their correctness theories, and define verification correctness criteria by means of a configuration consistency check. We illustrate our concepts by way of a small VDM case study: the CM model is applied to an example specification and the effects of a change to the example are explored, together with the type of support one might expect from a CM system.

Note that VDM notation will be used for two different purposes within this paper:

- to describe the CM system model; and
- to give an illustration specification which will be placed under change control.

To avoid possible confusion, the VDM case study specification will be presented within figures; VDM appearing in the body of the text is used to define the CM model.

2 A CM System Model

This section defines an approach to consistency checking of verifications of specifications such as might be used in conjunction with VDM tools such as the syntax and type checker SpecBox [FMB89] and the development support tool and proof assistant mural [JJLM91]. We begin by describing a CM system model of specifications and theories. Following this we define consistency checks which may be applied on instances within our model to determine if the specification has been verified according to the VDM methodology. In section 3 below we illustrate the CM system model on an example specification and in section 4 we show how the model supports change control by considering several changes to the specification and showing how corresponding changes would be made to the theory; consistency checking reveals where inconsistencies remain.

2.1 Specification Model

The first step in defining a CM system model is to decide upon which objects are to be *Configuration Items* (CIs): i.e., the objects within a development which are to be placed under configuration control.

For simplicity we shall assume a VDM specification consists of a state definition together with sets of type definitions, explicit function definitions and implicit operation definitions only. (Other specification constructs follow much the same patterns.) The state definition consists of a sequence of state components, an optional invariant and an optional initial state. For this particular CM model, the structure of VDM specifications will not be analyzed any further than this; in other words, the atomic CIs for specifications are type definitions, function definitions, operation definitions and state component definitions. We are not claiming that this is the most appropriate level of granularity for CM of VDM specifications, but have simply chosen this level for the purposes of illustration.

Our system model thus corresponds to the abstract syntax tree for the pruned VDM specification as follows:

Specification ::   *Types* : *TypeDef*-set
      State : *StateDef*
   Functions : *FunctionDef*-set
  Operations : *OperationDef*-set

TypeDef is not yet defined

StateDef :: *Comps* : *ComponentDef**
      Inv : [*FunctionDef*]
     Init : [*FunctionDef*]

ComponentDef is not yet defined

FunctionDef is not yet defined

OperationDef is not yet defined

2.2 Theory Model

The verification process involves discharging various proof obligations derived from the specification. To do this, theorems are established from axioms by means of formal proofs. Axioms are derived directly from the specification or from an appropriate axiomatization of VDM (cf. section 8.2 of [JJLM91]). Examples are given in the case study below (section 3).

For the purposes of illustration, we shall consider a CM model in which statements of rules and formal proofs are the atomic CIs, and rules and theories are the composite CIs built from these.

Theory :: *Rules* : *Rule*-set

Rule ::   *Stmt* : *Statement*
    Proof : *ProofBody* | AXIOM

Statement is not yet defined
ProofBody is not yet defined

A theory consists of a collection of (inference) rules. Rules are either theorems or axioms, and consist of a statement and, in the case of theorems, a proof which justifies the statement. The statement part of the rule consists of a mathematical assertion, such as a proof obligation, an axiom definition, a lemma, etc.

For a theory to completely verify a specification, according to the VDM methodology, it should include rules which establish the following proof obligations:

- initial state declarations are of the appropriate types;[1]
- preconditions and data type invariants are well-formed formulae (denote Boolean values);[2]
- postconditions are well-formed formulae, under the assumption that their corresponding preconditions hold;
- function definitions agree with their signatures; and
- operations are implementable in principle (i.e. a final state exists such that the postcondition holds, under the assumption of the precondition).

Examples are given in the case study below (section 3).

2.3 Consistency Checks

In this section we describe the consistency checks that our CM system model should be able to make, in order to ensure the correctness of the verification tasks outlined in section 2.2 above. In doing so we are essentially formalizing the VDM verification process.[3] Consistency checking can be broken down into four subtasks as follows:

- the specification has been statically checked by a tool or tools, such as syntax and type checkers;
- all axioms within the theory are consistent with the specification;
- all proof obligations of the specification are stated within the theory; and
- all rules within the theory have been formally discharged.

This translates to the following relation:

$Specification\_Verified : Specification \times Theory \rightarrow \mathbf{B}$

$Specification\_Verified(S, T) \triangleq$
$\quad Spec\_Checked(S) \wedge Substantiated\_Axioms(T, S) \wedge$
$\quad Obligations\_Stated(S, T) \wedge Theory\_Checked(T)$

In the subsections that follow we shall describe each of these tasks in more detail, and shall elucidate the kinds of links the CM system would be required to track.

---

[1] In mural the initial state is given by an explicit definition.

[2] Note that, in the logic which underlies VDM as presented in [JJLM91], "well-formed formulae" has a specific technical meaning which goes beyond syntactic well-formedness, and which must be established by proof.

[3] A similar formalization has been carried out in the DEVA notation in [Laf90]; here however our interest is in extracting requirements for CM.

Tool Checking. Tool checking determines whether automatic checking by tools has been applied to the specification. For the purposes of this paper we shall assume that a tool such as SpecBox [FMB89] has been used to perform syntax and type checking on the specification. The output(s) of the tool should be stored in the CM repository, together with endorsement by someone with the appropriate authority to say that the output is satisfactory.

$Spec\_Checked : Specification \rightarrow \mathbf{B}$

$Spec\_Checked(S) \;\triangleq\; Syntax\_Checked(S) \wedge Type\_Checked(S)$

Substantiated Axioms. In establishing the consistency of a specification with respect to a theory we must check that each axiom within the theory is either

- a recognized axiom of an appropriate axiomatization of VDM, or
- derived from the corresponding specification.

$Substantiated\_Axioms : Theory \times Specification \rightarrow \mathbf{B}$

$Substantiated\_Axioms(T, S) \;\triangleq\; \forall r \in T.Rules \cdot r.Proof = \text{AXIOM} \;\Rightarrow$
$\quad VDM\_Base\_Axiom(r.Stmt) \vee Axiom\_Generated\_From(r.Stmt, S)$

Here we have assumed there is a tool VDM_Base_Axiom which checks whether a given rule is one of the recognized axioms for VDM primitives. In mural all other axioms are derived from the state, type or function definitions of the specification:

$Axiom\_Generated\_From : Statement \times Specification \rightarrow \mathbf{B}$

$Axiom\_Generated\_From(Stmt, S) \;\triangleq\;$
$\quad \exists t \in S.Types \cdot Type\_Axiom\_Generated\_From(Stmt, t) \vee$
$\quad State\_Axiom\_Generated\_From(Stmt, S.State) \vee$
$\quad \exists f \in S.Functions \cdot Funct\_Axiom\_Generated\_From(Stmt, f)$

where for example

$Funct\_Axiom\_Generated\_From : Statement \times FunctionDef \rightarrow \mathbf{B}$

$Funct\_Axiom\_Generated\_From(Stmt, Funct) \;\triangleq\;$
$\quad generates\_defn\_axiom(Funct, Stmt)$

and $generates\_defn\_axiom$ is derived from results provided by an axiom generation tool (see Fig. 9 below for an example):

$generates\_defn\_axiom(Funct, Stmt) \;\triangleq\;$
$\quad Stmt = \text{axiom\_generator}(funct, defn, Funct)$

Type_Axiom_Generated_From and *State_Axiom_Generated_From* can be defined analogously.

Proof Obligations Stated. The definition of *Obligations_Stated* is analogous to the inverse of *Substantiated_Axioms*. If a component of the specification has a proof obligation then there must be a rule within the theory which has the given proof obligation as its statement. We begin with a function which checks each component of the specification to ascertain if the proof obligations for that component exist within the theory:

Obligations_Stated : *Specification* × *Theory* → **B**

$Obligations\_Stated(S, T) \quad \triangleq$
$\quad \forall t \in S.Types \cdot Type\_Obligations\_Stated(t, T) \wedge$
$\quad State\_Obligations\_Stated(S.State, T) \wedge$
$\quad \forall f \in S.Functions \cdot Funct\_Obligations\_Stated(f, T) \wedge$
$\quad \forall o \in S.Operations \cdot Oper\_Obligations\_Stated(o, S.State, T)$

Function definitions have two proof obligations:

- the signature must be correct (i.e., the body of the function must be a well-formed expression of the appropriate type);
- the precondition (if any) must be a well-formed formula.

This leads to the following definition:

Funct_Obligations_Stated : *FunctionDef* × *Theory* → **B**

$Funct\_Obligations\_Stated(Funct, T) \quad \triangleq$
$\quad \exists r \in T.Rules \cdot generates\_wff\_po(Funct, r.Stmt) \wedge$
$\quad \exists r \in T.Rules \cdot generates\_pre\_wff\_po(Funct, r.Stmt)$

As in the generation of axioms, we access an external proof obligation generator to deduce the *generates_wff_po* relation (see Fig. 10 below for an example) at the lowest level:

$generates\_wff\_po(Funct, Stmt) \quad \triangleq$
$\quad Stmt = \text{obligation\_generator}(\text{funct}, \text{wff}, Funct)$

The absence of a precondition is an implicit precondition of true. Our definition of *generates_pre_wff_po* must therefore incorporate some support to detect the absence of a precondition. In this case we have a definition requiring access to two tools, one to detect whether the precondition is absent, and the obligation generator:

$generates\_pre\_wff\_po(Funct, Stmt) \quad \triangleq$
$\quad \text{precondition\_absent}(Funct) \vee$
$\quad Stmt = \text{obligation\_generator}(\text{funct}, \text{pre\_wff}, Funct)$

Proof obligations for other components of the specification are generated in a similar manner (see e.g. Fig. 11 below).

Theory Checked. Finally we need to show that all the rules are formally discharged:

$Theory\_Checked : Theory \rightarrow \mathbf{B}$

$Theory\_Checked(T) \quad \triangleq \quad \forall r \in T.Rules \cdot Rule\_Discharged\_In(r, T)$

A rule is discharged within a theory if it is in that theory and either:

- the rule is an axiom; or
- the rule's proof discharges its statement and every statement that the proof uses is discharged within that theory.[4]

A check is also included to ensure there are no circularities in the reasoning: no rule should be used, directly or indirectly, to prove itself.

$Rule\_Discharged\_In : Rule \times Theory \rightarrow \mathbf{B}$

$Rule\_Discharged\_In(R, T) \quad \triangleq \quad R \in T.Rules \wedge$
$(R.Proof = \text{AXIOM} \vee$
$(proof\_checked(R.Proof, R.Stmt) \wedge$
$\neg\, proof\_uses\_trans(R.Proof, R.Stmt) \wedge$
$\forall s: Statement \cdot proof\_uses(R.Proof, s) \Rightarrow In\_Scope\_Of(s, T)))$

We have here assumed the existence of two forms of tool support:

- a proof checker *proof_checked* which checks that a given proof is a correct and complete proof of a given statement;[5] and
- a tool *proof_uses* which determines whether a given statement is used within a given proof.

The relation *proof_uses_trans* is simply the transitive closure of *proof_uses*:

$proof\_uses\_trans : ProofBody \times Statement \rightarrow \mathbf{B}$

$proof\_uses\_trans(P, S) \quad \triangleq \quad proof\_uses(P, S) \vee$
$\exists r: Rule \cdot proof\_uses(P, r.Stmt) \wedge proof\_uses\_trans(r.Proof, S)$

---

[4] An alternative, less draconian approach would be to allow the presence of rules which have been 'rigorously' proven, and checked and authorized by some responsible authority. Similarly, we might allow rules to be incomplete provided they do not form part of any proof obligations.

[5] We choose to make links between a proof and the statements of the rules used in the proof, rather than the rules themselves, since the statement contains all the information required by the proof checker.

Finally, a statement is within the scope of a theory if it is the statement of some rule in that theory:

$In\_Scope\_Of : Statement \times Theory \rightarrow \mathbf{B}$

$In\_Scope\_Of(S, T) \quad \triangleq \quad \exists r \in T.Rules \cdot r.Stmt = S$

3   A Verification Case Study

Within this section we provide a verification case study which is placed within the framework of the CM model defined in section 2. Our case study consists of a specification of a *Dependency Management System* and a partial theory used in the verification of the specification. We outline the formal links within the development which indicate the consistency of the verification.

3.1   The Specification

To illustrate the population of the specification system model we use an initial specification of a Dependency Management System (DMS). Intuitively, the purpose of the DMS is to track and manage dependencies between objects, represented as nodes in a graph. Let us assume the specification has been committed to the CM system, and the overall specification is recorded as a CI object labeled DMS_0 (see Fig. 1). The specification has all its components committed to the system as CIs, all having a similar version-labelling notation.

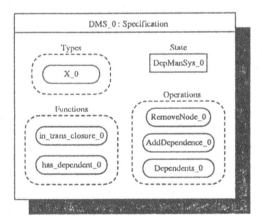

Fig. 1. Initial Dependency Management System specification composite object.

The DMS_0 specification describes a system which stores dependencies between objects, and allows the user of the system to add new information and query current information. The specification has a defined state (DepManSys_0: see Figs. 3–4) and provides a number of operations (RemoveNode_0, AddDependence_0 and Dependents_0: see Fig. 5). In providing the above we have declared a new type (X_0: see Fig. 2) and created a number of auxiliary functions (in_trans_closure_0 and has_dependent_0: see Fig. 6).

We shall assume that the specification is stored as a composite configuration item within the CM repository. All components of the specification may be accessed through the composite object, and are stored independently as CIs within the repository. This enables more efficient version storage: objects can be reused by other (composite) objects by simple referencing. Hence when a new item is created by modifying an existing composite object, duplicate objects need not be re-stored.

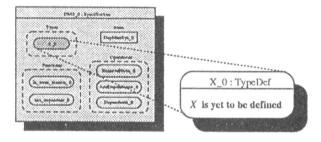

Fig. 2. Expansion of the X_0 component providing the type definition as an atomic object.

The DMS state has two state variables: *nodes*, which denotes a set of objects for which dependencies may be defined; and *ddo*, which records "direct dependency" information. The *ddo* component denotes a set of pairs (x, y) such that x directly depends on y (see Fig. 3).

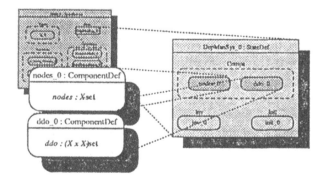

Fig. 3. The DMS state consists of two components, *nodes* and *ddo*.

The state invariant and the state initialization are optionally stored as function definitions with the state (see Fig. 4). The signature of these functions is generally implicitly defined from the state, however we explicitly provide the signature within the storage of the function definition in order to maintain completeness. In the DMS specification the invariant simply enforces both the domain and range of *ddo* pairs to be within the *nodes* set. Initially the specification state has empty sets for both *nodes* and *ddo*.

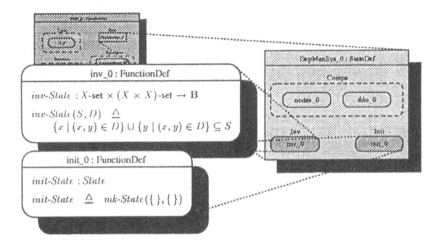

Fig. 4. The invariant and initialization are function definition objects.

In this example specification we include only three primary operations (see Fig. 5):

- *RemoveNode* allows the user to delete a node from the DMS system, together with all its dependencies; the operation has as a precondition that nothing should depend on the node being removed.
- *AddDependence* allows the user to add a dependency to the system; the dependency pair entered must have the domain and range values within *nodes*.
- *Dependents* provides a query operation for analyzing the dependencies created by the user; the operation returns a set of all nodes which depend (directly or indirectly, via the transitive closure of *ddo*) on the given node.

Other operations have been omitted from the specification to shorten the length: the operations chosen here are sufficient to provide a scenario for the CM requirements.

The DMS specification requires two auxiliary functions (see Fig. 6):

- *in_trans_closure_0*, representing the transitive closure of the *ddo* relation;
- *has-dependent*, which checks the *ddo* relation to determine if there is some element that depends on the given input node.

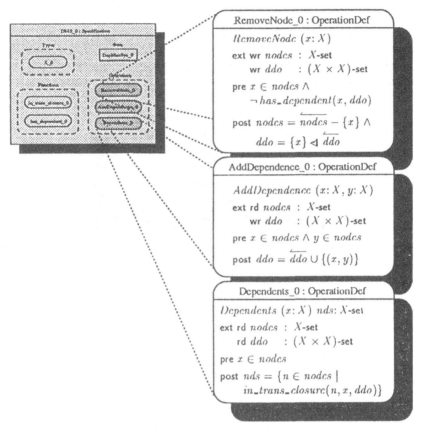

Fig. 5. The specification stores a collection of three atomic operation definition objects representing the operations that are applied on the state.

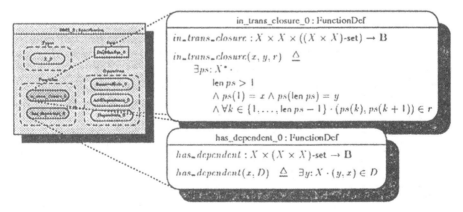

Fig. 6. The specification requires two auxiliary functions which are called within the definitions of the operations and the state.

3.2 The Theory

We illustrate our model with parts of the verification theory for the DMS_0 specification such as might be constructed using mural [JJLM91]. Space limitations mean we cannot provide the complete theory, so here we concentrate on those parts most directly to do with our specification.

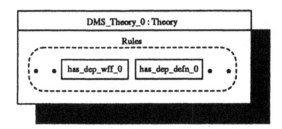

Fig. 7. A theory consists of a collection of parent theories and a collection of rules.

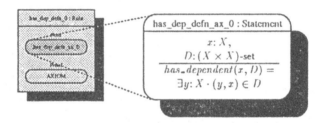

Fig. 8. An axiom is a rule which has a self-evident statement and a proof denoted as the constant object AXIOM.

The axiom corresponding to the definition of the *has_dependent* function is shown in Fig. 8. The link back to the component of the specification which gave rise to the axiom is shown in Fig. 9, together with the kind of link (required for consistency checking purposes). Fig. 10 shows the link between the definition of *has_dependent* and the statement of its well-formedness proof obligation. Fig. 12 shows a link between the statement of the proof obligation and its proof. (The proof has been partly elided to save space.) The fact that the proof uses the axiom corresponding to the definition of *has_dependent* is also shown in Fig. 12.

4 Changes to the Specification

In the following we explore a potential change to the example specification presented in section 2.1 above and indicate what manner of checking should be

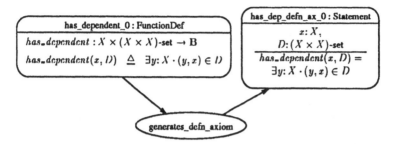

Fig. 9. The *generates_defn_axiom* predicate is derived by producing the definition axiom from a function definition using the axiom_generator tool.

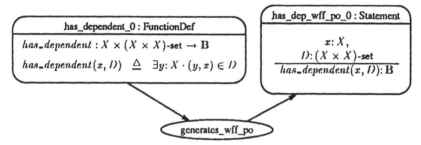

Fig. 10. The *generates_wff_po* predicate is derived by producing the well-formed formula proof obligation from a function definition using the obligation_generator tool.

provided by the CM system, as well as any inconsistencies we would expect to find.

4.1 Modifying the Specification

The modification we shall consider is to strengthen the invariant on the Dependency Management System so that dependencies are acyclic (no cycles in the transitive closure of the dependency relation). This involves also adding an auxiliary function *has_no_circs* to check acyclicity (see Fig. 13).

In order to illustrate the possible effects of change control we shall assume the CM model is implemented within an object-oriented database which provides the facility of immutable storage of components. Direct modifications of a pre-existing specification are not permitted within an immutable object base: we may only add new configuration items, we cannot modify or delete existing items. Links derived from deterministic tools between immutable components are only generated initially, and need not be regenerated if the components do not change.

Thus, to incorporate the changes to the specification we first create new configuration items inv_1 and has_no_circs_0 (see Fig. 13). To incorporate the change in the invariant within a specification, a new state definition is created, together with a new specification (see Fig. 14).

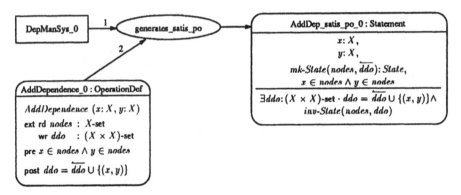

Fig. 11. The *generates_satis_po* predicate is derived by producing the satisfiability proof obligation from an operation definition using the obligation_generator tool. This predicate requires the state as a parameter to deduce the invariant call.

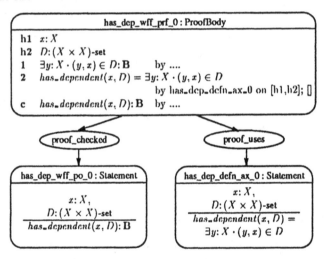

Fig. 12. The *proof_checked* relation is derived by a proof checker deducing the proof discharges the statement and the *proof_uses* relation is derived by a tool which analyses the proof to determine the statements which are used by the proof.

4.2 Updating the Theory

As a result of these changes there need to be corresponding changes to the theory:

- Add a definition axiom for the new function has_no_circs_0.
- Add a well-formedness proof obligation for has_no_circs_0.
- Replace the definition axiom for inv_0 by a definition axiom for inv_1.

But what should happen to the old axiom for inv_0? In general the most conservative option would be to create a new rule with the same statement as the initial definition axiom but which has a null proof, and to delete the old rule.

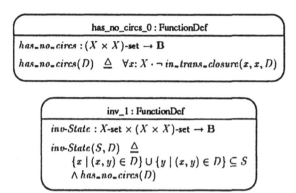

Fig. 13. A conjunct is added to the invariant to restrict states to those which do not contain circularities within the dependency component and a new function is created to complete the change.

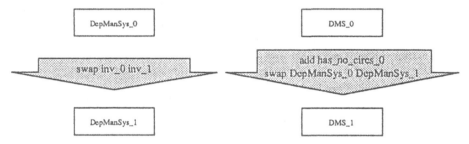

Fig. 14. The state is updated by incorporating the updated invariant and a new specification is created by incorporating the new state and the new function.

That way, any proofs which use the old axiom are still valid (since they only reference its statement) and so can be reused if the new rule can be proven. Unfortunately, in the current case the new axiom is inconsistent with the old axiom, so any proofs which use it will need to be redone.

The modifications described above could be performed automatically by a tool, to create a new theory **DMS_Theory_1** from the original theory **DMS_Theory_0**.

4.3 Checking Consistency

Let us assume the initial specification was fully verified, as defined in section 2.3: i.e. *Specification_Verified(* **DMS_0**, **DMS_Theory_0***)*.

When consistency checking is reapplied to the new pair (**DMS_1**, **DMS_Theory_1**) the following failures will be noted:

- *Spec_Checked* The specification has not yet been checked by the syntax or type checker. The restoration of this result may be made by executing the tools on the specification and having the output endorsed by the appropriate authority. As each specification is created through editing this step should be performed before modifications to the theory are made.

- *Theory_Checked* A number of rules do not have sufficient proofs. The well-formedness proof obligation for `has_no_circs_0` will require proof, and any proofs which used the `inv_0` definition axiom will need re-proving.

In keeping the theory in step with the specification as we have done above, however, both *Substantiated_Axioms* and *Obligations_Stated* are ensured by construction: the well-formedness proof obligation for the invariant is already within the theory, and the statement of the well-formedness proof obligation for the invariant has not changed (even though the definition has changed).

4.4 Managing Change

The proofs which may be affected by the change in the invariant's definition are proofs which reason about the state, including proofs such as operation satisfiability, etc. Proof obligations for auxiliary functions such as *has_dependent* go through unchanged, as do any proofs which do not actually use the definition axiom corresponding to `inv_0`. Thus for example, for an operation such as *Dependents* which has read-only access to the state, the original proof of satisfiability will probably go through unchanged.

We may expect within the new theory to need to reprove satisfiability for *RemoveNode* and *AddDependence* as well as well-formedness for *inv-State* and *init-State*.

A process of changing a formal development utilizing the CM system as outlined above is to: edit the specification; perform tool checking; update the basis for the theory by adding new axioms, changing invalid axioms to theorems and adding new proof obligations; prove any incomplete rules; and finally remove unproveable rules. Notice that most benefit of this system comes in the latter stages where the developer can diagnose which axioms of the theory are invalid and which proofs require reproving due to the theory being reorganized.

The technical report [RL93] extends this case study by considering further changes to the specification and how they would be managed.

5 Conclusions and Further Work

Even with tool support, formal development of verified software is highly labour-intensive, and in practice the work rarely proceeds in a systematic top-down fashion. Specifications change, either because of external forces such as customers, or because of improvements which suggest themselves as development proceeds. In the face of such variability, one does not wish to have to redo everything when something changes. Fortunately, the formal basis of formal development means that it is possible to analyze the structure of dependencies between different components of formal developments. The CM activity of *change control* is thus a feasible proposition (as we hope we have shown in the case study above) which promises to significantly enhance the practice of formal development of software, by tracking interdependencies between components of formal developments and localizing the impact of changes.

Just as importantly, all formal methods have methodological requirements that must be satisfied to ensure the method is being correctly applied — proof obligations, applicability conditions, completeness checks, and so on. Such requirements may be enforced or checked automatically by tools, while others may require user interaction with tools, or perhaps simply "eyeballing" by a person with the appropriate authority. The tools themselves may require consistency checks on their operation: for example, to ensure that all proofs have been fully discharged from axioms, or that there are no circularities present in the reasoning. Thus the CM activity of *consistency checking* takes on a vital role in support of formal development, since a single invalid step could contaminate a whole development.

In the case study above we identified some of the interdependencies between configuration items that are important for verification of VDM specifications. They include: the correspondence between axioms of the theory and components of the specification, the correctness of proofs of proof obligations, the use of rules in proofs, and the correspondence between proof obligations and components of the specification, to mention just a few. A CM system for formal developments would need to interface to tools which check such dependencies and more.

The case study applied to a particular CM system model for VDM specification for which definitions are the atomic configuration items. Finer levels of granularity are obviously possible, and would lead to finer-grained change control.[6] Had we chosen a different level of granularity, however, we would obviously have arrived at different types of interdependencies. The question becomes, to what extent can CM support be provided independent of a particular choice of granularity. We suspect it should be possible to build a system which would allow the user to move smoothly between different views of the system, and intend to investigate further the implications of such a requirement on the architecture of tool-sets for a given method. As a first step, we shall press further into the VDM abstract syntax, as well as studying support for data reification and operation decomposition.

We also plan to extend our analysis of CM for Formal Methods to cover other development methodologies, and in this regard we should mention the DEVA work (e.g. [Laf90]) which provides a notation tailored to expressing (apparently) all formal aspects of formal developments. Finally, we plan to also extend our analysis to other aspects of CM support for Formal Methods, and change-impact analysis in particular.

---

[6] For example, the structure of proofs could be further analyzed, so that changes are percolated through to individual lines in a proof, rather than having to redo whole proofs.

Acknowledgements

The initial ideas for this work were inspired by the *Jason* CM system [Wei90], which provides specification of classes of objects and configurations, families, versions, configuration consistency constraints and build plans. We would like to thank Susan Dart for her valuable discussions on the CM field, and also we acknowledge the feedback and contribution from Jim Welsh, Jun Han and Erik van Keulen.

References

[BHS79] E. H. Bersoff, V. D. Henderson, and S. G. Siegel. Software Configuration Management: A Tutorial. *IEEE Computer*, 12(1), Jan 1979.

[Dar91] S. Dart. Concepts in Configuration Management Systems. In *Proceedings of the Third International Software Configuration Management Workshop*, pages 1–18, Trondheim, Norway, June 1991. IEEE CS, ACM Press.

[FMB89] P. K. D. Froome, B. Q. Monahan, and R. E. Bloomfield. SpecBox - a checker for VDM Specifications. In *Proceedings of Second International Conference on Software Engineering for Real Time Systems*, Cirencester, UK, 1989. IEE 1989.

[JJLM91] C. B. Jones, K. D. Jones, P. A. Lindsay, and R. D. Moore. *Mural: A Formal Development Support System*. Springer-Verlag, London, 1991.

[Jon90] C. B. Jones. *Systematic Software Development using VDM*. Prentice Hall International, second edition, 1990.

[Laf90] C. Lafontaine. Formalization of the VDM reification in the DEVA meta-calculus. *Programming Concepts and Methods*, pages 333–368, 1990.

[RL93] K. Ross and P. Lindsay. Maintaining consistency under changes to formal specifications: an extended case study. Technical Report No. 93-3, Software Verification Research Centre, Dept. of Comp. Sci., University of Queensland, 1993.

[Soc87] IEEE Computer Society. IEEE Guide to Software Configuration Management. ANSI/IEEE Std 1042-1987, 1987.

[Soc90] IEEE Computer Society. IEEE Standard for Software Configuration Management Plans. IEEE Std 828-1990, 1990.

[Wei90] Douglas Weibe. *Generic Software Configuration Management: Theory and Design*. PhD thesis, Department of Computer Science, University of Washington, Seattle, WA 98195, 1990.

An EVES Data Abstraction Example*

Mark Saaltink, Sentot Kromodimoeljo, Bill Pase,
Dan Craigen and Irwin Meisels

ORA Canada
265 Carling Avenue, Suite 506
Ottawa, Ontario K1S 2E1
CANADA

Abstract. This paper provides an introduction to EVES. EVES is a formal methods tool consisting of a language based on set theory, called Verdi, and an automated deduction system, called NEVER. We provide a general introduction to EVES and demonstrate its capabilities using an example of data abstraction (table/list).

1   Introduction

The primary goal of the EVES project was to develop a "verification system" integrating techniques from automated deduction, mathematics, language design and formal methods, such that the resulting system is useful and sound. In our parlance, a verification system consists of a specification and implementation language (e.g., Verdi), a proof obligation generator, and automated deduction support (e.g., NEVER).

Verdi is a single language for mathematics (using a set theoretic framework), formal specification of procedures (using pre and post conditions), imperative programming (of the Algol-Pascal genre), and controlling EVES and NEVER. We made the explicit design choice to remain within a first-order set theoretic framework, as opposed to higher-order logic. We feel that set theory provides an adequate framework; that set theory is more widely disseminated through our likely client base; and that more is known about automated deduction in the first-order framework than in higher-order.

Currently, Verdi has a Lisp-like abstract syntax. (We expect to modify the syntax during 1993). Verdi consists of imperative statements (much as you would expect in Pascal-like programs), types (but only for executable constructs), set theoretic concepts (such as membership, comprehension, and intersection), first-order logic (including quantifiers), and declarations (e.g., mutually recursive procedures and functions, axioms, types).

As Verdi was being designed, we also developed the Verdi Logic and the proof obligations associated with the various declarations. The Verdi Logic is based on Predicate Calculus and includes named axioms, imperative features, and definitions. In general, the Verdi proof obligations guarantee the "semantic conservative extension" principle.

---

* The development of EVES was sponsored by the Canadian Department of National Defence through DSS contract W2207-8-AF78 and other contracts.

The general idea of a Verdi development is shown in Fig. 1. Essentially, development starts with an initial theory (which consists of all the built-in Verdi information) and each declaration extends the theory with new symbols and axioms. To demonstrate that the declaration maintains the conservative extension property, proof obligations must be shown to be true. Note that this guarantees that the new axioms do not introduce any inconsistencies. The library mechanism, described in Section 4, allows theories to be developed in parts, and allows useful theories to be re-used in different developments.

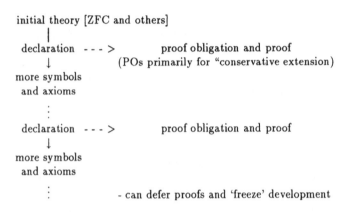

Fig. 1. Verdi development process.

The automated deduction component of EVES is NEVER. The development of NEVER was meant to be primarily and engineering exercise whereby we brought together a diverse set of automated deduction practices and, hopefully, produced a useful tool. We focused on developing a synergism between powerful automatic facilities with user commands. It is via the commands that the user can direct the prover. The main influences on the development of NEVER were Affirm [20] (interface and rewriting), the Bledsoe-Bruell prover [1] (interface), the Stanford Pascal Verifier [9] (simplification; semi-decision procedures) and the Boyer-Moore theorem prover [2] (heuristics). NEVER is further described in Section 5.

EVES is implemented in Common Lisp and has been successfully ported to Data General Aviions, Sun 3s, Sparcstations (our usual hardware base), VAXs, Symbolics and Apple MACs. Interaction with EVES may occur either through a command interface or through the EMACS editor. EVES also incorporates an interpreter for Verdi.

2 Verdi Logic

The Verdi Logic is based on the Predicate Calculus with the following differences: the syntax is based on Lisp S-expressions; there are no formulae, only terms; there are no constants (instead, functions of zero arguments are used); axioms are named; there are imperative features; and definitions are allowed.

The *initial theory* defines all the built-in functions. It includes functions and axioms pertaining to sets (all the ZFC axioms, excluding the schemas), Booleans (e.g., true, false, not, and, implies, or), Integers (e.g., the numerals, $+$, $-$, div, mod), ASCII Characters, elementary functions (e.g., $<$, $<=$) and Arrays.

Verdi makes a clear distinction between functions that may be used in code (the *executable* functions) and functions that can only be used in annotations and other non-executable contexts. In addition, certain constructs, such as quantification, are not executable. Certain declarations that introduce executable names: type declarations, typed function declarations, and procedure declarations. Executable declarations are restricted to use only executable names (except in annotations).

Executable constructs are strongly typed (to allow efficient implementation). The Verdi types include: Bool (Booleans), Char (Characters), Int (Integers), enumerated types, records, and arrays.

For each executable expression there is an associated *legality expression*. If the associated legality expression is true, then the expression can be executed without error. (The errors considered here include domain errors, such as division by zero and indexing errors, and arithmetic overflows.) Thus, while unbounded integers can be used in a specification, executable constructs are constrained to use only representable values. In a proven Verdi program, no arithmetic operation will overflow or underflow.

3 Procedures

Verdi procedures have bodies composed of statements. Verdi statements include **abort**, **return**, **exit**, assignment, block, procedure call, loops, and conditionals. Local variables are allowed in procedures, but local procedures or functions are not. In addition, Verdi does not provide global variables—only the variables passed as actual parameters are accessible to a procedure.

Procedures are specified in the usual pre/post style. Procedure specifications in Verdi consist of four parts:

- the *procedure header*, including the procedure name and formal parameter list;
- an *initial clause*, allowing the entry values of variables to be bound;
- a *precondition*, specifying the conditions that must be satisfied by the caller; and
- a *postcondition*, specifying the conditions guaranteed by the procedure when it returns. Postconditions can use variables bound in the initial clause to refer to values determined when the procedure was entered.

A proven procedure is guaranteed to terminate without run-time errors (other than storage exhaustion) provided the precondition is satisfied (and provided any assumptions used in the proof are valid).

4 Libraries

The main means for abstraction, information hiding and modularization in EVES is the Verdi library mechanism. The library mechanism is "institutional" in design in that the details of the mechanism are independent of the Verdi logic.

Figure 2 introduces some of the basic ideas of the library. A library is a repository for *specification units* and *model units*, together with a dependency relation between units. Specification units may introduce axiomatic descriptions of mathematical theories or Ada-like procedural specifications. Model units provide logical interpretations of mathematical theories and implementations of procedural specifications. Hence, as shown in the figure, one can present an axiomatic description of the Reals and then model the Reals using Dedikind Cuts. Or, one can develop an abstract data type package of stacks and then provide a model which implements the routines in terms of a concrete array type. Library units are also used to provide input, output, and other machine-specific features. Only specification units are provided for such "interface" modules; their implementations will be in terms of some other programming language.

Spec. units	Axiomatic theory	Procedural specification	Theory of Reals	Spec of Stacks
	⋮	⋮	⋮	⋮
	⋮	⋮	⋮	⋮
Model units	Model	Implementation	Dedikind cuts	Implementation (as array)

Fig. 2. Verdi Library Mechanism.

The Verdi Logic and EVES guarantee that there is no circular dependency between library units, and that a model is, in fact, a model of the corresponding specification unit. By this, we mean that (i) each declaration in the specification unit has a corresponding declaration in the model and (ii) all proof obligations for the declarations in the model are proved.

A library unit can only depend of other specification units, never on model units. Thus, an implementation of a module can be changed without invalidating the proof of any unit using that module. Furthermore, once a specification of a module is entered in the library, code using that module can be proved, even before the implementation exists. Thus, systems can be built in any order (with bottom-up and top-down as extreme cases).

EVES manages all operations on the library, to ensure the library remains consistent. For example, if a unit is deleted or modified, any units that depend on it are deleted.

Library units can be separately compiled.[2] A collection of useful library units is distributed with EVES; its contents are summarized in Appendix A.

---

[2] A compiler for Verdi is currently under development.

5 NEVER

NEVER is the automated deduction component of EVES. The basic philosophy of NEVER is to combine automatic strategies with user commands. Such a combination allows cooperation between the user and the system and, hopefully, makes proofs easier.

The NEVER database contains Verdi declarations, proof obligations and proofs. As described above, declarations extend the Verdi theory and, consequently, extend the NEVER database. NEVER allows for declarations and proofs to be undone.

A proof is performed on a "current formula." A declaration causes its proof obligation to become the current formula. However, the "try" command allows the user to change the current formula. The current formula and partial proofs may be saved and the user can move between different proof obligations. (NEVER determines the theory within which a proof obligation can be proved; hence, unsoundness arising from circularity between proof obligations is not possible.)

Each proof step transforms the formula into an equivalent formula; the goal of the transformations is to reach the formula (TRUE).

In the remainder of this section, we will discuss the main prover capabilities. Reduction is the main strategy used by the automatic theorem prover. It consists of a *traversal* of the current formula. The formula is scanned from left to right (the way it is written). NEVER keeps track of a *context* of assumptions pertaining to each part of the formula as it is considered. The particular processing applied to each subformula depends on the specific user command.

5.1 Simplification

The process of simplification attempts to reduce an expression to one that the system considers to be simpler. Propositional tautologies are always detected. In addition, the simplification process reasons about equalities, integers, and quantifiers. The theorem prover performs simplification by reducing subexpressions in context.

Frules and *grules* are applied during simplification. A *frule* is applied in a context when an instance of its condition is assumed. As an example, given the existence of the following *frule*:

```
(frule >=-same-type (x y)
    (implies (>= x y) (= (type-of x) (type-of y))))
```

if the formula (>= (f a) b) is assumed in some context, then the formula (= (type-of (f a)) (type-of b)) will also be assumed.

A *grule*, on the other hand, is applied when a subexpression being traversed by the simplifier matches the trigger expression of the *grule*. Thus, given the existence of the *grule* (grule f-non-neg (x) (>= (f x) 0)), when the simplifier encounters (f (g 1)) as a subexpression, then it will assume (>= (f (g 1)) 0). The simplify command performs simplification.

5.2 Rewriting

The rewriting process consists of the application of *rules*. While traversing a formula being rewritten, the theorem prover tries to apply rewrite rules that match the subexpression being traversed.

In the simpler case, the rule being applied is unconditional and so is applied immediately. The subexpression that has matched the pattern is replaced by the rule's right hand side, with the variables of the right hand side substituted by the expressions determined during the pattern match.

In general, the rule being applied can be conditional. The theorem prover must then prove the condition as a subgoal before the rule can be applied.

The **rewrite** command performs rewriting as well as simplification.

5.3 Invocation

The invocation process is similar to rewriting, except that function definitions are used instead of rewrite rules. Thus, function applications in the current formula may be "expanded," that is, replaced by the function definition with the actual parameters substituted for the formals. Non-recursive functions are always expanded (unless disabled). Heuristics developed by Boyer and Moore [2] are used in the case of recursive functions.

The **reduce** command performs invocation as well as rewriting and simplification.

5.4 Induction

The theorem prover performs induction using techniques based on those of Boyer and Moore [2]. Normally, induction schemes are heuristically chosen based on calls to recursive functions within the current formula. However, the **induct** command may be used with with an explicit term that determines the induction scheme. The following is an example of a user-directed induction.

```
> (try (implies (>= x 0) (= (double x) (two-times x))))
...
> (induct (double x))
Inducting using the following scheme ...
(AND (IMPLIES (AND (> X 0)  (*P* (- X 1))) (*P* X))
     (IMPLIES (NOT (> X 0)) (*P* X)))

produces ...
(AND (IMPLIES (AND (> X 0)
                   (IMPLIES (>= (- X 1) 0)
                            (= (DOUBLE (- X 1))
                               (TWO-TIMES (- X 1)))))
              (IMPLIES (>= X 0) (= (DOUBLE X) (TWO-TIMES X))))
     (IMPLIES (NOT (> X 0))
              (IMPLIES (>= X 0) (= (DOUBLE X) (TWO-TIMES X)))))
> (reduce)
    ...
(TRUE)
```

The above induction scheme consists of an inductive case and a base case, and follows directly from the definition of **double**. The induction case follows from the recursive call in the definition. Thus the conjecture, with X replaced by (- X 1), is assumed together with the condition governing the recursion. In the base case, the governing condition is the negation of the condition of the induction case.

Note that for the above example the heuristic would have chosen the same induction scheme, since there is only one call to a recursive function in the conjecture, and that call is exactly the term specified.

5.5 Miscellaneous Prover Capabilities

Most of the theorem prover commands described in previous sections automatically use axioms about declared symbols (the axioms may have been added using *frule*, *grule*, *rule*, and *function* declarations). Axioms may also be used manually with the **use**, **invoke**, and **apply** commands. The **use** command is used to add an axiom as a hypothesis to the current formula. Any kind of axiom can be used with the **use** command including those declared as **axiom**. An axiom declared using **axiom** can only be used in such a way. The **invoke** command is used to expand function definitions manually (i.e., it is used to apply axioms associated with **function** declarations in a special way). Similarly, the **apply** command is used to apply rewrite rules (including conditional ones) manually.

In addition to the commands described above, there are many more prover commands that can be used to manipulate the current formula. These include commands that perform quantifier manipulation (**instantiate, prenex, open,** and **close**), equality reasoning (**equality-substitute** and **label**), and formula rearranging (**rearrange, split, conjunctive,** and **disjunctive**).

There is also the case splitting mechanism which have commands that allow the user to focus on parts of the conjecture being proved by splitting those parts and allowing one to be the current formula. The relevant commands are **cases, next,** and **delete-hypotheses**.

6 Data Abstraction Example: Table/List

The "table/list" module was described informally in [10] as follows:

> One physical implementation of this module would be by means of a set of children's blocks where it is possible to write one "entry" on the upper surface. The blocks are arranged in a single row and covered with an opaque lid with a single window. Through this window one may read the entry on a single block, insert and remove blocks, or change the entry on the block that shows through the window. The entry on the block that shows through the current window is the *current entry.* Because the cover is opaque it is not possible to tell how many blocks are currently under it, but the cover is fitted with signals that tell whether or not there is a block to the right of the current entry, whether or not there is a block to the left of the current entry, and whether there are any blocks under the cover at all.

The operations that we want to perform include reading the value of the current entry, moving the lid one place to the right, moving the lid one place to the left, moving the lid and all blocks at the right hand side of the current block one place to the right so that a new current block may be inserted through the window, and removing the current block (moving the lid and all blocks to the right of the deleted block one place to the left).

Our specification was derived from a later corrected version [11] of the specification. The informal model changed slightly, allowing the window to move to the left of the first element, so that a new first element may be inserted.

Verdi specifications are "model-oriented" [4]. We describe the abstract data type by a mapping of concrete data values to some convenient set. Operations are specified in terms of this "abstract model" of the data. The specification omits the detailed definitions of the concrete data values and of the "abstraction function" that maps the concrete values to the abstract values; they are of no interest or relevance to the user of the ADT. These details appear as part of the implementation. The abstraction functions are usually not executable—usually they return values, such as sets, that have no executable representations.

There is no need to restrict oneself to the use of a single abstraction function. In the table/list example, we find it more convenient to use two abstraction functions than to use a single abstraction function returning a tuple.

We use two sequences in the model: one for the elements to the left of or in the window, and one for the elements to the right of the window. Each sequence is ordered with the elements closest to the window appearing first. The "current element" is then simply the first element of the left sequence (if the left sequence has any elements). This model suggests a change to the informal description: rather than describing the window, we describe the right edge of the window as a "cursor" that may be positioned before the elements, after the elements, or between any two elements.

The specification of table/list therefore makes use of a theory of sequences appearing in the EVES library. The functions of the theory, and their meanings, are as follows:

- (seq!emptyp x) — x is not a sequence or it is the empty sequence.
- (seq!seqp x) — x is a sequence.
- (seq!empty) — the empty sequence.
- (seq!tack x s) — the sequence with head x and tail s.
- (seq!head s) — head element of sequence s.
- (seq!tail s) — remaining (non-head) elements of sequence s.
- (seq!length s) — the number of elements in sequence s.

This theory is stored in a library unit called seq.

6.1 The specification

The specification begins by loading in the sequence theory that will be used in the annotations.

```
(load seq)
```

The type of element to be stored in the table and the capacity of the table are not further specified.

```
(type-stub entry)
(typed-function-stub capacity () (int) ())
```

A type **table** is declared. The definition of the type is omitted from the specification. The two functions **left** and **right** are abstraction functions that give the sequences of elements to the left and right of the cursor, respectively. Their definitions are also omitted from the specification.

```
(type-stub table)
(function-stub left (t))
(function-stub right (t))
```

Function **count** indicates the number of elements stored in a table. It can be explicitly defined in terms of the two abstraction functions.

```
(function count (t) ()
  (+ (seq!length (left t)) (seq!length (right t))))
```

Hoare's original method for data abstraction provided a mechanism for associating invariants with the implementation. Verdi does not have any such mechanism built in—indeed, the only mechanism provided by the library system is information hiding. Nevertheless, it is possible to associate an invariant with an implementation, by adopting a particular style of writing specifications. Function **ok** below is the invariant function. Like the abstraction functions, its definition is irrelevant to the user of the abstract data type (as its definition will involve the specific details of the implementation).

```
(function-stub ok (t))
```

While the definition of the concrete invariant is irrelevant, there are certain "abstract invariants" that may be relevant to the user of the table/list module. In particular, the left and right functions always return sequences, and the number of elements stored in the table is never more than the capacity. Axiom **ok-guarantees** expresses these facts.

```
(frule ok-guarantees (t)
  (implies (ok t)
           (and (= (type-of t) (table))
                (seq!seqp (left t))
                (seq!seqp (right t))
                (<= (count t) (capacity))))))
```

We are now in a position to specify the executable routines provided by the table/list module. Procedure **init** initializes a table by establishing the concrete invariant and setting the contents empty. (This is the only routine that does not require the incoming table to be "ok". Thus, users must always call **init** before calling any of the other routines.)

The specification of procedure **init** needs neither an initial clause nor a precondition; it always initializes the table.

```
(procedure-stub init ((pvar (t) (table)))
   ((post (and (ok t)
               (= (left t) (seq!empty))
               (= (right t) (seq!empty))))))
```

Function **exleft** indicates the existence of one or more elements to the left of the current element. Similarly, function **exright** indicates the existence of one or more elements to the right of the current element.

Executable functions in Verdi have preconditions that give a condition guaranteeing the function can be evaluated without causing a run-time error. However, there is no post-condition for a function. Instead, the effect of calling a function can be specified in one or more axioms.

```
(typed-function-stub exleft (((t) (table))) (bool)
   ((pre (ok t))))

(rule exleft-spec (t)
  (implies (ok t)
           (= (exleft t)
              (> (seq!length (left t)) 1))))

(typed-function-stub exright (((t) (table))) (bool)
   ((pre (ok t))))

(rule exright-spec (t)
  (implies (ok t)
           (= (exright t)
              (not (= (right t) (seq!empty))))))
```

Function **out** indicates that a current element does not exist (because the cursor is before the start of the list).

```
(typed-function-stub out (((t) (table))) (bool)
   ((pre (ok t))))

(rule out-spec (t)
  (implies (ok t)
           (= (out t)
              (= (left t) (seq!empty)))))
```

Function **current** returns the current element. It should only be called when a current element exists.

```
(typed-function-stub current (((t) (table))) (entry)
   ((pre (and (ok t)
              (not (out t))))))
```

```
(rule current-spec (t)
  (implies (and (ok t)
                (not (out t)))
           (= (current t) (seq!head (left t)))))
```

Procedure **delete** removes the current element from the list. It should only be called when a current element exists.

```
(procedure-stub delete ((pvar (t) (table)))
   ((initial (t0 t))
    (pre (and (ok t)
              (not (out t))))
    (post (and (ok t)
               (= (right t) (right t0))
               (= (left t) (seq!tail (left t0)))))))
```

Procedure **insert** adds an element to the right of the current element; or at the beginning of the list if there is no current element. This new element becomes current. This procedure should only be called when the count of the table is less than the capacity.

```
(procedure-stub insert ((pvar (t) (table)) (lvar (d) (entry)))
   ((initial (t0 t))
    (pre (and (ok t)
              (< (count t) (capacity))))
    (post (and (ok t)
               (= (right t) (right t0))
               (= (left t) (seq!tack d (left t0)))))))
```

Procedure **alter** changes the value of the current element. It should only be called when there is a current element.

```
(procedure-stub alter ((pvar (t) (table)) (lvar (d) (entry)))
   ((initial (t0 t))
    (pre (and (ok t)
              (not (out t))))
    (post (and (ok t)
               (= (right t) (right t0))
               (= (left t) (seq!tack d (seq!tail (left t))))))))
```

Procedures **goright** and **goleft** move the cursor by one position. They should only be called when such a move is possible.

```
(procedure-stub goright ((pvar (t) (table)))
   ((initial (t0 t))
    (pre (and (ok t)
              (exright t)))
    (post (and (ok t)
               (= (right t) (seq!tail (right t0)))
               (= (left t)
                  (seq!tack (seq!head (right t0)) (left t0)))))))

(procedure-stub goleft ((pvar (t) (table)))
   ((initial (t0 t))
    (pre (and (ok t)
              (not (out t))))
    (post (and (ok t)
               (= (right t)
                  (seq!tack (seq!head (left t0)) (right t0)))
               (= (left t) (seq!tail (left t0)))))))
```

6.2 Implementation

An implementation in Verdi includes all the information from the specification. In addition, it contains complete definitions of functions and procedures, and all the axioms of the specification must be proved.

A table is represented by a record with three fields: an array called **store**, and two indices called **lp** and **rp**. The contents of the table consists of all the elements of the array, in order, excluding the elements whose indices lie strictly between **lp** and **rp**. The excluded elements occupy the position of the cursor. Insertion of new elements is simple; **lp** is advanced one position and the new element inserted at that index. Deletion is similarly simple. Cursor motion is slightly more difficult: both **lp** and **rp** are moved by one position, and an element must be copied from one side of the gap to the other.

The listing of the implementation here includes all the user commands needed to complete the proofs. These commands are written in upper case to distinguish them from Verdi declarations. This is purely conventional; case is ignored in EVES.

The implementation begins with definitions of the element type and capacity, and loads sequence theory.

```
(type entry (int))

(typed-function capacity () (int) () 50)
(SIMPLIFY)

(load seq)
```

The following *grule* is used in legality proofs. (The value of (**int.last**) is the largest representable integer.)

```
(grule maxint-exceeds-capacity () (<= (capacity) (int.last)))
(SIMPLIFY)
```

As described above, tables are represented by records consisting of an array and two indices.

```
(type table (record ((store) (array 1 (capacity) (entry)))
                     ((lp rp) (int))))
```

The abstraction functions can be readily defined. The left sequence is composed of the elements of store, from lp down to the first element of the array. This is easily formalized by a recursive definition, using the auxiliary function left-aux. The recursive definition of left-aux has proof obligation to the effect that the measure (in this case i) decreases in each recursive call. A reduce command completes the proof.

```
(function left-aux (a i)
   ((measure i))
  (if (>= i 1)
      (seq!tack (aref a i) (left-aux a (- i 1)))
      (seq!empty)))
(REDUCE)

(function left (t) ()
  (left-aux (store t) (lp t)))
```

The right sequence is composed of the elements of store from rp up to capacity. The definition is similar to the definition of left.

```
(function right-aux (a i)
   ((measure (+ 1 (- (capacity) i))))
  (if (<= i (capacity))
      (seq!tack (aref a i) (right-aux a (+ i 1)))
      (seq!empty)))
(REDUCE)

(function right (t) ()
  (right-aux (store t) (rp t)))
```

We now prove some lemmas about the two auxiliary functions defined above. First, we show that each returns a sequence. Then we show that the value returned is unchanged when the array is modified outside the section of the array containing the elements. Finally, we show that the lengths of the sequences are determined from the parameter i. All these results will be needed in the main proofs later on. The lemmas are stated as *grules* or *rules* so that EVES can apply them automatically.

As the auxiliary functions are defined by recursion, the proofs proceed by induction.

```
(grule seqp-left (a i)
  (seq!seqp (left-aux a i)))
(PROVE-BY-INDUCTION)

(grule seqp-right (a i)
  (seq!seqp (right-aux a i)))
(PROVE-BY-INDUCTION)

(rule left-aset (a i j v)
  (implies (and (= (type-of a) (array 1 (capacity) (entry)))
                (<= 1 j)
                (< i j)
                (<= j (capacity))
                (= (type-of v) (entry)))
           (= (left-aux (aset a j v) i)
              (left-aux a i))))
(PROVE-BY-INDUCTION)

(rule right-aset (a i j v)
  (implies (and (= (type-of a) (array 1 (capacity) (entry)))
                (<= 1 j)
                (> i j)
                (<= j (capacity))
                (= (type-of v) (entry)))
           (= (right-aux (aset a j v) i)
              (right-aux a i))))
(PROVE-BY-INDUCTION)

(rule length-left (a i)
  (= (seq!length (left-aux a i))
     (if (<= 1 i)
         i
         0)))
(PROVE-BY-INDUCTION)

(rule length-right (a i)
  (= (seq!length (right-aux a i))
     (if (<= i (capacity))
         (+ 1 (- (capacity) i))
         0)))
(INDUCT)
(REDUCE)
(INVOKE RIGHT-AUX)
(REDUCE)
```

Function count is defined exactly as in the specification.

```
(function count (t) ()
  (+ (seq!length (left t)) (seq!length (right t))))
```

The concrete invariant function **ok** is given a full definition. The concrete invariant asserts that the left and right indices have reasonable values.

```
(function ok (t) ()
  (and (= (type-of t) (table))
       (<= 0 (lp t))
       (< (lp t) (rp t))
       (<= (rp t) (+ 1 (capacity)))))

(frule ok-guarantees (t)
  (implies (ok t)
           (and (= (type-of t) (table))
                (seq!seqp (left t))
                (seq!seqp (right t))
                (<= (count t) (capacity)))))
(REDUCE)
```

With the choice of representation for the table type, and the above bit of theory development in place, it is easy to implement and verify the executable procedures and functions of the modules. As can be seen from the Verdi text, the proofs are quite trivial, involving at most a few user steps.

```
(procedure init ((pvar (t) (table)))
    ((post (and (ok t)
                (= (left t) (seq!empty))
                (= (right t) (seq!empty)))))
  (:= (lp t) 0)
  (:= (rp t) (+ 1 (capacity))))
(REDUCE)

(typed-function exleft (((t) (table))) (bool)
    ((pre (ok t)))
  (> (lp t) 1))
(REDUCE)

(rule exleft-spec (t)
  (implies (ok t)
           (= (exleft t)
              (> (seq!length (left t)) 1))))
(REDUCE)

(typed-function exright (((t) (table))) (bool)
    ((pre (ok t)))
  (<= (rp t) (capacity)))
(REDUCE)
```

```
(rule exright-spec (t)
  (implies (ok t)
           (= (exright t)
              (not (= (right t) (seq!empty)))))))
(REDUCE)
(SPLIT (> (RP T) 50))
(REDUCE)
(INVOKE RIGHT-AUX)
(REDUCE)

(typed-function out (((t) (table))) (bool)
   ((pre (ok t)))
  (= (lp t) 0))
(REDUCE)

(rule out-spec (t)
  (implies (ok t)
           (= (out t)
              (= (left t) (seq!empty))))))
(REDUCE)
(SPLIT (= (LP T) 0))
(REDUCE)
(INVOKE LEFT-AUX)
(REDUCE)

(typed-function current (((t) (table))) (entry)
   ((pre (and (ok t)
              (not (out t))))))
  (aref (store t) (lp t)))
(REDUCE)
(INVOKE LEFT-AUX)
(REWRITE)

(rule current-spec (t)
  (implies (and (ok t)
                (not (out t)))
           (= (current t) (seq!head (left t))))))
(REDUCE)
(INVOKE LEFT-AUX)
(REDUCE)

(procedure delete ((pvar (t) (table)))
   ((initial (t0 t))
    (pre (and (ok t)
              (not (out t))))
    (post (and (ok t)
```

```
                    (= (right t) (right t0))
                    (= (left t) (seq!tail (left t0))))))
  (:= (lp t) (- (lp t) 1)))
(REDUCE)
(EQUALITY-SUBSTITUTE T0)
(INVOKE (LEFT-AUX (STORE T) (LP T)))
(REWRITE)

(procedure insert ((pvar (t) (table)) (lvar (d) (entry)))
    ((initial (t0 t))
     (pre (and (ok t)
                (< (count t) (capacity))))
     (post (and (ok t)
                (= (right t) (right t0))
                (= (left t) (seq!tack d (left t0))))))
  (:= (lp t) (+ (lp t) 1))
  (:= (aref (store t) (lp t)) d))
(REDUCE)

(procedure alter ((pvar (t) (table)) (lvar (d) (entry)))
    ((initial (t0 t))
     (pre (and (ok t)
                (not (out t))))
     (post (and (ok t)
                (= (right t) (right t0))
                (= (left t) (seq!tack d (seq!tail (left t)))))))
  (:= (aref (store t) (lp t)) d))
(REDUCE)
(INVOKE LEFT-AUX)
(REWRITE)

(procedure goright ((pvar (t) (table)))
    ((initial (t0 t))
     (pre (and (ok t)
                (exright t)))
     (post (and (ok t)
                (= (right t) (seq!tail (right t0)))
                (= (left t)
                   (seq!tack (seq!head (right t0)) (left t0))))))
  (:= (lp t) (+ (lp t) 1))
  (:= (aref (store t) (lp t)) (aref (store t) (rp t)))
  (:= (rp t) (+ (rp t) 1)))
(REDUCE)
(EQUALITY-SUBSTITUTE T0)
(REDUCE)

(procedure goleft ((pvar (t) (table)))
```

```
   ((initial (t0 t))
    (pre (and (ok t)
              (not (out t)))))
    (post (and (ok t)
               (= (right t)
                  (seq!tack (seq!head (left t0)) (right t0)))
               (= (left t) (seq!tail (left t0))))))
  (:= (rp t) (- (rp t) 1))
  (:= (aref (store t) (rp t)) (aref (store t) (lp t)))
  (:= (lp t) (- (lp t) 1)))
(REDUCE)
(EQUALITY-SUBSTITUTE TO)
(REDUCE)
```

7 Suggested Readings and Future Work

An article of this length cannot delve into all the technical aspects and applications of EVES. For further information on EVES see [3] (the Verdi Reference Manual), [13, 14] (the mathematical underpinnings for Verdi and EVES), [5] (the application of EVES to an interpreter for a small programming language), [18] (casting simple type theory in EVES), [8] (applying the Jackson System Design Methodology and EVES to the partial development of a boiler control program), [15, 16, 17] (for a general discussion of Z, the possible relationship of Z to EVES, and the incorporation of the Mathematical Toolkit [19] into the EVES library), [6] (for discussions of a series of enhancements to NEVER), and [7, 12] (for the development of an outline of CSP in EVES; along with a model-theoretic consistency proof of the relevant CSP axioms).

Current plans for future work on EVES include modifications to the syntax, the writing of a Users' Guide, and initial steps towards a proof checking tool. We expect that EVES will be used on applications both by us (the developers) and other interested parties. EVES is now available for distribution. We are currently developing a Verdi compiler. The compiler is being "rigorously" developed in that we are mathematically specifying the "machine independent" parts of the compiler (i.e., from scanning and parsing through to the generation of intermediate code).

A The EVES Library

This section summarizes the library units that are distributed with EVES. Many of these units are EVES versions of concepts derived from the Z Mathematical Toolkit.

cap: unary intersection
finite: finite sets and cardinality
fixpt: Tarski-Knaster Fixedpoint Theorem.
fn: a theory of first-class functions.
intfn: first-class functions on integers.
nat: the Natural numbers and induction.
pair: ordered pairs and cross products.

pairfn: first-class functions on pairs.
rel: a theory of binary relations.
setrules: axioms about on sets.
seq: a theory of sequences (algebraic).
zseq: a theory of sequences (model-oriented).

References

1. W.W. Bledsoe, P. Bruell: A man-machine theorem proving system. Artificial Intelligence 5(1):51–72, 1974.
2. R.S. Boyer, J.S. Moore: A Computational Logic. Academic Press, NY, 1979.
3. Dan Craigen: Reference Manual for the Language Verdi. ORA Canada Technical Report TR–91–5429–09a, September 1991.
4. C.A.R. Hoare: Proof of Correctness of Data Representations. Acta Informatica 1: 271–281, 1972.
5. Sentot Kromodimoeljo, Bill Pase: Using the EVES Library Facility: A PICO Interpreter. ORA Canada Technical Report TR–90–5444–02, February, 1990.
6. Sentot Kromodimoeljo, Bill Pase: Final Report for the Investigation of Proof Techniques Within the EVES Verification Technology. ORA Canada Technical Report FR–92-5451-02, May 1992.
7. Sentot Kromodimoeljo, Bill Pase: Development of a Skeletal CSP Theory in EVES. ORA Canada Technical Report TR-92-5469-02, July 1992.
8. Sentot Kromodimoeljo, Bill Pase: Investigating the Role of EVES in System Engineering and Security Evaluation. ORA Canada Technical Report TR-92-5464-02, September 1992.
9. D.C. Luckham, et al.: Stanford Pascal verifier user manual. Technical Report STAN-CS-79-731, Stanford U. Computer Science Dept., March 1979.
10. Dave Parnas and W. Bartussek: Using Traces to Write Abstract Specifications for Software Modules. Information Systems Methodology, Proceedings of ICS, Lecture Notes in Computer Science (65), Springer-Verlag, 1978.
11. Dave Parnas, David Smith, Trevor Pearce: Making Formal Software Documentation More Practical: A Progress Report. Technical Report 88-236, Department of Computing and Information Science, Queen's University at Kingston, November, 1988.
12. Bill Pase, Sentot Kromodimoeljo: A User's Guide to a Skeletal CSP Theory in EVES. ORA Canada Technical Report TR-92-5469-03, July 1992.
13. Mark Saaltink: A Formal Description of Verdi. ORA Canada Technical Report TR–89–5429–10, October, 1989.
14. Mark Saaltink: Alternative Semantics for Verdi. ORA Canada Technical Report TR–90–5446–02, November, 1990.
15. Mark Saaltink: Z and EVES. ORA Canada Technical Report TR-91-5449-02. (An abridged version is in the Proceedings of the 6th annual Z Users Meeting, Springer Verlag.)
16. Mark Saaltink: The EVES Library. ORA Canada Technical Report TR-91-5449-03.
17. Mark Saaltink: The EVES Library Models. ORA Canada Technical Report TR-91-5449-04.
18. Mark Saaltink and Dan Craigen: Simple Type Theory in EVES. Proceedings of the 4th Workshop on Higher Order Logic, G. Birtwistle, editor. Springer Verlag, 1991.
19. J.M. Spivey: The Z Notation: A Reference Manual. Prentice Hall, 1987.
20. D.H. Thompson, R.W. Erickson (eds.): AFFIRM Reference Manual, USC Information Sciences Institute. Marina Dey Ray, CA, 1981.

Putting Advanced Reachability Analysis Techniques Together: the "ARA" Tool

Antti Valmari[1,2], Jukka Kemppainen[1], Matthew Clegg[1,3] and Mikko Levanto[1]

[1] Technical Research Centre of Finland, Computer Technology Laboratory, PO Box 201, SF-90571, Oulu, FINLAND
[2] Currently at Tampere University of Technology, Tampere, FINLAND
[3] Currently at University of California San Diego, USA

Abstract. "ARA" is a verification tool which applies some recent improved speed verification techniques. ARA accepts as input systems described in Basic Lotos. With ARA, a system can be verified by showing that it is behaviourally equivalent with its specification. For comparing behaviours, ARA uses a novel CSP-like but catastrophe-free behavioural equivalence notion called "CFFD-equivalence". ARA can also reduce the behaviour of the system into a small "normal" form, and show the result graphically. ARA applies two techniques to cope with the state explosion problem: compositional LTS construction and the stubborn set method. The paper contains a detailed example of the validation of a communication protocol using ARA. The paper concentrates on the intuition behind the various novel ideas of ARA; formal details are mostly omitted.

1 Introduction

Automatic concurrent system verification tools are usually based on the technique called *exhaustive simulation* or *reachability analysis*. "Reachability analysis" means the detection of errors in a system by simulating it to all the states it can reach, and by investigating the reachable states and the reachability relation between them. The structure consisting of all the reachable states and the transitions between them is often called *state space* or *labelled transition system* (*LTS*, for brevity), the choice of the name depending on what aspects of the structure are considered most important. Many reachability analysis tools have been reported in the literature. Papers [2], [7] and [18] are surveys which list several tools each.

The construction of a state space or LTS is usually only one step in verification. There is a wide range of algorithms for verifying or analysing the behaviour of a system which work by investigating or comparing state spaces or LTSs. Examples are temporal logic model checking [5] [15] and the comparison of behavioural equivalence using algorithms such as in [8].

Reachability analysis together with a suitable postprocessing algorithm is in principle capable of detecting all violations against a specification, if the system has a finite number of states. Unfortunately its practical applicability is seriously limited by the *state explosion* problem: the number of states of other than the smallest systems is usually far too large for processing in a realistic computer. Recently several techniques have been suggested which facilitate verification without constructing all states. In this paper we discuss a new reachability analysis tool which applies two of them: *compositional LTS generation* [16] and the *stubborn set* method [20] [27].

The new tool is called "ARA". Its name is an abbreviation of "Advanced Reachability Analysis". ARA can read systems written in the language *Basic Lotos* [3]. Basic Lotos is a concurrency-oriented simplification of the ISO standard specification language Lotos [12]. ARA can verify that a system is equivalent to its specification, and it can construct a small "normal form" representation of the behaviour of a system and show it in a graphical form on a computer screen. ARA is a successor to the "PC-Rimst" tool developed at the Technical Research Centre of Finland [21]. ARA has also benefited from experience with the "TORAS" tool being developed at Telecom Australia Research Laboratories [28]. ARA has many ideas in common with other tools based on the use of behavioural equivalences, such as *Concurrency Workbench* [6], *Aldébaran* [9] and *Auto* [16].

For the comparison of behaviours of systems ARA uses a novel equivalence called *chaos-free failures divergences equivalence* or *CFFD-equivalence* [26]. CFFD-equivalence is a modification of *failures equivalence* originating from the theory of CSP [4] [11]. Its main benefit over failures equivalence is that it does not suffer from the so-called *catastrophic divergence* problem. Therefore it can be used for the verification of systems which may perform an infinite sequence of internal events. A communication protocol with unbounded retransmission (such as the one in Sect. 2) is an example of a system which can be verified using CFFD-equivalence but not with failures equivalence. Excluding the fact that CFFD-equivalence keeps track of the divergence traces of the system, it is significantly weaker than the *weak observation equivalence* from the CCS theory [17]. The weakness of an equivalence is an advantage, as will be discussed in Sect. 3.

The purpose of this paper is to give an overview of the basic ideas and new techniques behind the ARA tool. Details of the techniques can be found in the publications referred to in the text. The novelty of this paper is in that it shows that the techniques go together and can be beneficially applied in a computer tool.

Section 2 demonstrates verification using ARA with the aid of an example. Section 3 is devoted to an introduction to CFFD-equivalence and to a justification of its selection as the equivalence notion in a verification tool. The state reduction techniques utilized by ARA are discussed in Sect. 4. Section 5 contains a brief description of the current and planned features of the ARA tool.

2 Validation and Verification Using ARA

In this chapter we concentrate on an example which demonstrates verification using the ARA tool. The example has been designed to show the basic ideas clearly, and it is therefore fairly small. The example is a version of the classic alternating bit protocol with one way transmission, unlimited retransmission in the case of acknowledgement not arriving in time, and success indication to the customer in the sending end. The channels between the protocol entities can lose messages but they cannot do any other harm. The capacity of the channels is one. The alternating bit protocol has been named according to an alternating 0-1 value by which every data and acknowledgement message is augmented. With the aid of the alternating bit the protocol can avoid duplication of messages due to retransmission.

The protocol is shown in Fig. 1 together with its two clients *Source* and *Destination*. The protocol consists of *Sender, Receiver* and two noisy channels, via which *Sender* and *Receiver* communicate data and acknowledgement messages. *Source* communicates with *Sender* and *Destination* with *Receiver*.

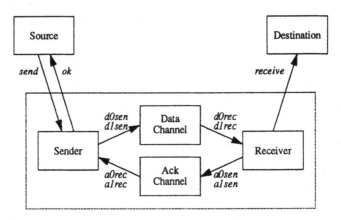

Fig. 1. Example Protocol

Source starts a session by executing the event *send*. The message to be sent should be thought of as a parameter to the event, but it is not shown in this model. The protocol transmits the message and delivers the arrived data to *Destination* via the event *receive*. Eventually *Sender* tells *Source* that the transmission has been completed by executing the event *ok*. The clients see no other events.

The Basic Lotos specification of the protocol is in Fig. 2. The structure of the specification resembles the way the protocol is intended to be built, that is, it specifies the protocol as a parallel composition of the four protocol and channel processes. However, the specification leaves visible only the events of interest to the client processes, i.e., *send, receive* and *ok*; the others are concealed using the **hide**-construction. That is, when the protocol processes perform *d0sen* etc. only an anonymous silent action denoted by *i* is seen at the specification level. Our eventual goal in this section is to investigate the behaviour of the protocol from the point of view of the clients. The hiding of the channel events is a step towards this goal.

Conforming to the usual practice with Lotos specifications, the client processes *Source* and *Destination* themselves are not included in the specification.

The behaviour of a process or a system specified in Lotos is often represented by a *labelled transition system* (*LTS* for short). Formally, a LTS is a four-tuple $(S, \Sigma', \Delta, s_0)$, where

- S is the set of *states* the system can reach.
- Σ' is a set of *events* containing the invisible event symbol *i*.
  We define $\Sigma = \Sigma' - \{i\}$.

600

```
process Alternating_bit_protocol[ send, receive, ok ] :=
(* Alternating Bit Protocol with unbounded retransmission
VTT Computer Technology Laboratory, ARA group Sept. 18, 1991 *)
    hide d0sen, d0rec, d1sen, d1rec, a0sen, a0rec, a1sen, a1rec in
            Sender[ send, ok, d0sen, d1sen, a0rec, a1rec ]
        |[ d0sen, d1sen, a0rec, a1rec ]|
            (
                Channel[ d0sen, d1sen, d0rec, d1rec ]
            |||
                Channel[ a0sen, a1sen, a0rec, a1rec ]
            )
        |[ d0rec, d1rec, a0sen, a1sen ]|
            Receiver[ receive, d0rec, d1rec, a0sen, a1sen ]
where
    process Sender[ send, ok, d0, d1, a0, a1 ] :=
        send; Try[ send, ok, d0, d1, a0, a1 ]
    where
        process Try[ send, ok, d0, d1, a0, a1 ] :=
                d0; Wait_ack[ send, ok, d0, d1, a0, a1 ]
        endproc
        process Wait_ack[ send, ok, d0, d1, a0, a1 ] :=
                (* unexpected acknowledgement *)
                a0; Wait_ack[ send, ok, d0, d1, a0, a1 ]
            []
                (* expected acknowledgement *)
                a1; ok; Sender[ send, ok, d1, d0, a1, a0]
            []
                (* timeout *)
                i; Try[ send, ok, d0, d1, a0, a1 ]
            endproc (* Wait_ack *)
        endproc (* Sender *)
    process Receiver[ receive, d0, d1, a0, a1 ] :=
            (* expected data *)
            d0; receive; a1; Receiver[ receive, d1, d0, a1, a0 ]
        []
            (* unexpected data *)
            d1; a0; Receiver[ receive, d0, d1, a0, a1 ]
    endproc (* Receiver *)
    process Channel[ in1, in2, out1, out2 ] :=
            in1; ( out1; Channel[ in1, in2, out1, out2 ]
                [] i; Channel[ in1, in2, out1, out2 ]
                )
        []
            in2; ( out2; Channel[ in1, in2, out1, out2 ]
                [] i; Channel[ in1, in2, out1, out2 ]
                )
    endproc (* Channel *)
endproc (* Alternating_bit_protocol *)
```

Fig. 2. Example Protocol in Basic Lotos

- $\Delta \subseteq S \times \Sigma' \times S$ is the *transition relation*, and
- $s_0 \in S$ is the *start state* of the system.

A LTS can be thought of as a directed graph whose edges correspond to the transitions of the system. Every edge is labelled by the name of the event of the corresponding transition. This leads to a natural graphical representation of (small) LTSs.

We can obtain understanding of the working of the individual protocol processes by investigating their LTSs. The LTSs can be constructed automatically by ARA LTS construction tool, and shown on a computer screen by ARA graphical layout tool. The LTS of *Sender* is given in Fig. 3[2]. After receiving the *send* command from *Source*, *Sender* transmits data to the channel by performing the event *d0sen* and starts to wait for the acknowledgement. The digit "0" in *d0sen* denotes the value of the alternating bit. The arrival of the acknowledgement is reported by the event *a1rec*. After participating *a1rec*, *Sender* sends *ok* to *Source* and is ready for the next transmission with the value of the alternating bit reversed. If the acknowledgement does not arrive in time *Sender* performs an invisible move (denoted by i) and transmits the data again. Acknowledgements with wrong alternating bit value are read and ignored by performing a local loop. Note that the digit in an acknowledgement always denotes the alternating bit value *Receiver* expects to see next.

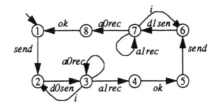

Fig. 3. LTS of Sender

The LTSs of *Receiver* and *Channel* are in Fig. 4. The latter LTS shows how transmission errors have been modelled: after receiving a message, i.e., after *in1* or *in2*, *Channel* may enter its initial state without performing *out1* or *out2*. This corresponds to the loss of a message in the channel. Furthermore, if the message is never received for some reason, the channel is not blocked but the message is eventually lost.

The protocol as a whole consists of *Sender, Receiver* and the two channels running in parallel. The LTS of the protocol as a whole can be constructed automatically using ARA LTS constructor tool. The result has 122 vertices and 296 edges. It is thus too large for manual inspection. However, most of the edges correspond to hidden events and are therefore more or less irrelevant regarding the client's view of the protocol. It is possible to represent the "essential" information in a much more compact form. ARA LTS condenser tool accepts a LTS as input (see Sect. 5 for

---

[2] ARA layout tool uses colours to denote event names. Since colours cannot be reproduced in this paper, we have redrawn all LTS figures with event names added.

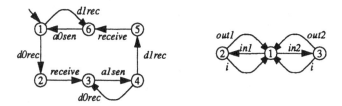

Fig. 4. LTS of Receiver and LTS of Channel

more information) and produces a condensed LTS which is CFFD-equivalent with the input LTS. The condensed LTS is typically much smaller than the original one. The condensed LTS of the example protocol has only four states and six edges. It is shown in Fig. 5.

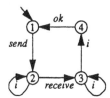

Fig. 5. Condensed LTS of the entire protocol

Figure 5 shows the clients' view to the protocol in a remarkably simple form. We see that after the sending request *send* the protocol executes an indefinite time (the *i*-loop), delivers the message via *receive* and executes again an indefinite time before issuing the *ok* event and returning to its initial state. Many properties of the protocol are obvious from Fig. 5. For instance, the protocol cannot duplicate messages (i.e., deliver twice a message sent only once), because there is no path where one *send*-edge is succeeded by two *receive*-edges. It is interesting to notice that the protocol as specified in Fig. 2 does not return to its initial state after *ok* but to a state where the alternating bits have been reversed. However, Fig. 5 does not show this because the two states are symmetric. The clients cannot see any difference in the future behaviour of the protocol in the two states. So the states are unified by the LTS condenser. This is appropriate from the clients' view and makes it more easily understandable.

The *i*-loops in Fig. 5 may need some explanation. They are due to the fact that there is no limit to the number of transmission attempts *Sender* may perform before receiving an acknowledgement. After the *receive* event, *Sender* still has some time to continue transmission attempts before the acknowledgement arrives. As a consequence, there is an *i*-loop also after *receive*. When the acknowledgement arrives the protocol ceases the transmission attempts and enters a state where it is no more able to continue internal computation. Instead, it is ready to give the *ok* indication. This explains the invisible move from state 3 to 4.

In general, the condensed form of a system may contain some invisible events in order to express accurately but user-friendly the deadlock and livelock behavior of the system. This is, however, only a representational aid. When condensing or comparing systems, the ARA tools pay attention only to the behavioural properties represented by the CFFD model described in Sect. 3.

The condensed LTSs are, of course, not always as small as in this example. Therefore ARA contains a LTS comparison tool. The user may write his idea of what the clients' view to the system is into a document which may be called the *black-box specification*. Fig. 5 is a reasonable black-box specification for our example protocol. The document in Fig. 2 is then called the *implementation specification*, because it specifies the way the system is intended to be implemented. The LTS comparator can be used to check whether the two specifications conform to each other. If they do not, the comparator reports differences in the form of a sample execution from which it is possible to trace whether the implementation specification is incorrect or the black-box view unrealistic.

To demonstrate the use of the LTS comparator tool we consider a protocol without the alternating bit. Such a protocol may duplicate messages and introduce other kind of transmission errors. Its externally observable behaviour is quite complicated, as can be seen from Fig. 6. We can use Fig. 5 as a black-box specification for the non-alternating protocol. ARA LTS comparator gives the following report when asked to compare the systems shown in Figs. 5 and 6:

> Protocol_ 5 and Protocol_ 6 are different:
> path:
> send receive
> Only Protocol_ 6 can go on with following labels:
> receive
> End of comparison

That is, the comparator detects that after the events *send* and *receive*, the protocol in Fig. 6 may execute another *receive*, which the protocol in Fig. 5 cannot do. So Protocol_ 6 is not a correct implementation of Protocol_ 5.

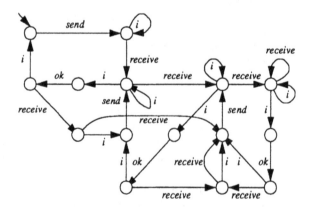

Fig. 6. Condensed LTS of a protocol without alternating bit

After the two specifications have been found equivalent it is possible to reason about the behaviour of the system by investigating the black-box specification only. The complicated implementation specification is no more needed for validation. This is a big advantage, since the black-box specification can be much smaller and much more understandable than the implementation specification, as is demonstrated by our example.

3 CFFD-Equivalence

In this section we introduce briefly to CFFD-equivalence, the equivalence notion used by ARA for the comparison of behaviours. We also justify the choice of a new equivalence instead of an established one. More information on CFFD-equivalence can be found in [26].

A behavioural equivalence used for verification should preferably have the following three properties:

1. It should be a *congruence* with respect to all operators used in building up the system. That is, if P is a component of a larger system $f(P)$ and Q is equivalent with P, then it should be the case that $f(Q)$ is equivalent with $f(P)$. This is to ensure that P and Q will not lead to different behaviour when put into their intended context. This also guarantees that the compositional LTS construction method discussed in Sect. 4.1 gives correct results. Although it may be surprising, the congruence requirement is very strong: equivalences picked at random are usually not congruences.
2. It should be strong enough to preserve the properties to be verified. For instance, if deadlocks are considered important, then the equivalence should not equate a deadlocking system with one which does not deadlock.
3. It should not be stronger than necessary. This is because a correct system cannot be shown equivalent to its specification, if the system and the specification differ in some irrelevant way which is nevertheless detected by the equivalence. Furthermore, the compositional method in Sect. 4.1 gives better results when the equivalence is weak, because then the LTSs can be condensed more.

Most of the research on behavioural equivalence -based verification has used *weak observation equivalence* and its variants [17]. Weak observation equivalence records plenty of information of the branching structure of the behaviour of a system, and is thus unnecessarily strong for many verification tasks. Regarding the strength of an equivalence, *failures equivalence* [4] is usually better because it is significantly weaker than weak observation equivalence. Yet it preserves sufficient information for many verification tasks.

However, failures equivalence suffers from what is sometimes called the *catastrophic divergence problem*: no information of the behaviour of a system is obtained after it has reached a state where it may start an infinite sequence of internal events. Consider the alternating bit protocol in Sect. 2, Fig. 5. After the *send* event it may execute the invisible loop $2 - i \rightarrow 2$ forever. Thus failures equivalence does not tell what it may do after reaching state 2. Therefore, failures equivalence cannot be used for the verification of systems such as the alternating bit protocol in Sect. 2.

Recently a modification of failures equivalence was introduced which does not suffer from the catastrophic divergence problem [26]. The new equivalence, called *chaos-free failures divergences (CFFD) equivalence*, is a congruence with respect to all operators of Basic Lotos. In [13] it was shown that it preserves all properties which can be specified in linear temporal logic without using the temporal operator "next state". It preserves also all traces, deadlocks and divergence traces. Thus it is suitable for many verification tasks. In the absence of divergences (and forgetting "*stable*"[3]) it coincides with failures equivalence. Therefore, excluding the handling of divergences and "*stable*", it is significantly weaker than weak observation equivalence. In [14] it was shown to be very close to the weakest possible congruence preserving "next"-less linear temporal properties. Due to these properties CFFD-equivalence is very well-suited for verification.

In the remainder of this section we give a formal definition of CFFD-equivalence and discuss the necessity of each of its components.

Let $(S, \Sigma', \Delta, s_0)$ be the LTS of process P, let s and $s' \in S$, and let $b, b_1, b_2, \ldots, b_n \in \Sigma'$. As usual, we write

- $s - b \to s'$ if $(s, b, s') \in \Delta$
- $s - b_1 b_2 \ldots b_n \to s'$ if there are $s_0, s_1, \ldots, s_n$ such that $s = s_0, s_n = s'$ and $s_0 - b_1 \to s_1 - b_2 \to \ldots - b_n \to s_n$
- $s - b_1 b_2 \ldots b_n \to$ if there is s' such that $s - b_1 b_2 \ldots b_n \to s'$.

As usual in process algebra literature, in order to abstract away from internal activity we define

- $s = a_1 a_2 \ldots a_n \Rightarrow s'$ if $s - i^* a_1 i^* a_2 i^* \cdots i^* a_n i^* \to s'$, where $a_1, a_2, \ldots, a_n \in \Sigma$, and i^* denotes a finite string consisting of zero or more i-symbols
- $s = a_1 a_2 \ldots a_n \Rightarrow$ if there is s' such that $s = a_1 a_2 \ldots a_n \Rightarrow s'$.

We say that $a_1 a_2 \ldots a_n$ is a *trace* of P, if $s_0 = a_1 a_2 \ldots a_n \Rightarrow$, where s_0 is the initial state of the LTS of P. The set of traces of P, denoted by $tr(P)$, is certainly an interesting aspect of the behaviour of P. Therefore we require that our equivalence preserves $tr(P)$.

Another interesting behavioural aspect of a system is its ability to deadlock. Therefore, we want the equivalence to indicate those traces σ of P such that σ may take P to a deadlock state. Now the congruence requirement (number 1 in the above list) forces us to preserve more. If $\sigma = c_1 c_2 \ldots c_m$ and $A = \{a_1, a_2, \ldots, a_n\}$, let $SfailTest(\sigma, A)$ denote the process in Fig. 7.

The process $P \parallel SfailTest(\sigma, A)$ (i.e., P in parallel with $SfailTest(\sigma, A)$ with all visible events synchronized) may deadlock after σ if and only if (σ, A) is a *stable failure* of P in the sense of the following definition:

$$sfail(P) = \left\{ (\sigma, A) \in \Sigma^* \times 2^\Sigma \mid \exists s : s_0 = \sigma \Rightarrow s \wedge \forall a \in A \cup \{i\} : \neg(s - a \to) \right\}$$

---

[3] Also the predicate "*stable*" (defined soon) distinguishes CFFD-equivalence from failures equivalence. "*stable*" was added to CFFD-equivalence in order to ensure congruence with respect to the Lotos choice operator "[]". Failures equivalence lacks "*stable*" because it was originally developed for a language without "[]"; when applied to Lotos, also failures equivalence would need "stable".

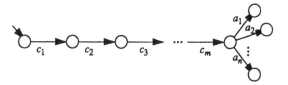

Fig. 7. SfailTest

In conclusion, in order to preserve all deadlocks of P and satisfy the congruence requirement, we have to preserve all stable failures of P.

The congruence property forces us to preserve also the so-called *stability* of P. The stability is a predicate defined as follows:

$$stable(P) \text{ holds iff } \neg(s_0 - i \rightarrow)$$

That $stable(P)$ has to be preserved can be verified by considering the stable failures of $P \, [] \, Div$, where Div is defined as "$Div := i; Div$" (that is, Div performs an infinite sequence of "i":s), and "$[]$" is the choice operator of Lotos (i.e., $P \, [] \, Q$ may behave like P or like Q). Let ϵ denote the empty string. If P is stable then $(\epsilon, \emptyset)$ is a stable failure of P but not of $P \, [] \, Div$; if P is not stable, then $P \, [] \, Div$ has the same stable failures as P.

We say that P and Q are *BKO-equivalent*, iff $tr(P) = tr(Q)$, $sfail(P) = sfail(Q)$, and $stable(P)$ holds iff $stable(Q)$ holds. The abbreviation "*BKO*" arises from the fact that Bergstra, Klop and Olderog proved that essentially the same equivalence is a congruence with respect to the language they used [1]. We have checked that BKO-equivalence is a congruence with respect to all operators of Basic Lotos.

Stable failures have one intuitively irritating feature: there are traces σ to which there are no corresponding stable failures (σ, A). This happens if P cannot reach a stable state after performing σ. Then it must be the case that after executing σ, P may execute an infinite sequence of i-events. We say that σ is a *divergence trace* of P, if there is s such that $s_0 = \sigma \Rightarrow s$ and $s - i^\infty \rightarrow$, where i^∞ denotes an infinite sequence of i-events. The set of the divergence traces of P is denoted by $div(P)$.

The divergence traces of P are interesting, because they contain information about the liveness properties of P. Therefore we have chosen to add $div(P)$ to our semantic model. In [26] it was proven that $tr(P) = div(P) \cup \{ \sigma \mid (\sigma, \emptyset) \in sfail(P) \}$. Therefore, $tr(P)$ is a redundant component in our semantic model and can be omitted. The behavioural equivalence used by ARA may now be defined as follows:

P and Q are *CFFD-equivalent*, iff $sfail(P) = sfail(Q)$, $div(P) = div(Q)$, and $stable(P)$ holds iff $stable(Q)$ holds.

CFFD-equivalence is a congruence with respect to all operators of Basic Lotos assuming that the systems considered are of finite state. The assumption of finite state is not a restriction in the context of ARA, because ARA cannot handle systems with an infinite number of states. In any case, the assumption can be eliminated by adding yet another component to the model: the set of infinite traces of P, and by requiring that it, too, is compared when checking behavioural equivalence. It can be proven that the set of infinite traces is a redundant component if the systems are of finite state, so the addition becomes significant only in the case of infinite state systems.

Towards the beginning of this section we justified that CFFD-equivalence is a good equivalence for verification. Now it is the time for some criticism. CFFD-equivalence does not distinguish invisible cycles which can be exited, from invisible cycles which cannot. For instance, it considers the following two systems equivalent:

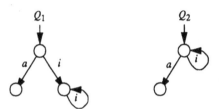

This problem is irritating if we suspect that the invisible cycle is due to some factor, such as repeated loss of messages in a channel, which does not cause endless repetition in practice. In such a situation the cycle would eventually be exited, if possible. However, we do not know whether exiting it is possible, because CFFD-equivalence does not preserve that piece of information.

The problem arises from the use of stable failures, and would be avoided by the use of the ordinary failures, defined below:

$$fail(P) = \left\{ (\sigma, A) \in \Sigma^* \times 2^\Sigma \mid \exists s : s_0 = \sigma \Rightarrow s \wedge \forall a \in A : \neg(s = a \Rightarrow) \right\}$$

Unfortunately ordinary failures have a deficiency of their own. It seems impossible to design an equivalence using ordinary failures which is a congruence with respect to the hiding operator. As we saw in Sect. 2, the hiding operator is essential for obtaining the clients' view of a system. The problem is demonstrated by the systems in Fig. 8. Processes P_1 and P_2 have the same ordinary failures, namely (a^n, B) and $(a^{n+1}b, AB)$ where $n \geq 0$, a^n denotes the string consisting of n "a"-symbols, and B and AB are any subsets of $\{b\}$ and $\{a, b\}$, respectively. Processes H_1 and H_2 are obtained from P_1 and P_2 by hiding the event a, so they can be thought of as systems containing P_1 and P_2 as subsystems. Process H_1 has $(\epsilon, \{b\})$ as an ordinary failure, whereas H_2 does not. With stable failures the difference between H_1 and H_2 disappears, because $(\epsilon, \{b\})$ is a stable failure of neither H_1 nor H_2.

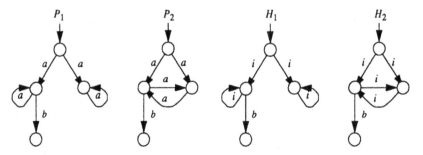

Fig. 8. Two systems, and the same systems after hiding of a

Also the designers of CSP and failures equivalence had to deal somehow with this problem. Their solution was to not store any information of the behaviour of a process after it has executed a divergence trace. For instance, failures equivalence sees H_1 and H_2 equivalent, because it pays no attention to their behaviours after their common divergence trace ϵ. Furhermore, because of the same reason, it sees H_1 and H_2 equivalent to Q_1 and Q_2, although Q_1 and Q_2 can execute a but not b, and H_1 and H_2 can execute b but not a. We consider CFFD-equivalence a better solution from the point of view of verification, because (excluding "*stable*") in the absence of divergence traces it coincides with failures equivalence, and it gives more information in the presence of divergence traces.

4 Reduction of the Number of States

The LTSs of systems are usually very big, often far too big to be processed by a computer. This problem is known as the *state explosion* problem. ARA applies two recent techniques to attack the state explosion problem: *compositional LTS generation* and *stubborn set method*. In this section we introduce them briefly.

4.1 Compositional LTS Generation

The basic idea of compositional LTS generation is to construct a LTS for the system under analysis stepwise, by constructing and combining LTSs for its subsystems. Before the combining, the LTSs of the subsystems are condensed. That is, they are made smaller, but in such a way that their externally observable behaviour does not change. Due to the condensation, also the combined LTS becomes smaller. We require that the equivalence notion used for comparing behaviours is a congruence with respect to the operators used for combining the subsystems. Therefore, and because the condensation preserves the externally observable behaviour of the subsystems, the externally observable behaviour of the system as a whole is not changed by the compositional method. As a consequence, the combined LTS is valid for verification. The compositional method may be applied hierarchically by constructing the subsystem LTSs compositionally.

The benefit of compositional LTS generation is in its ability to reduce the size of the resulting LTS. Sometimes this reduction is very significant. On the other hand, the generation of the subsystem LTSs introduces extra work. It is even possible that individual subsystem LTSs are larger than the ordinary LTS of the whole system, in which case effort is wasted instead of being saved (see [10] for an example). This is because the behaviour of a subsystem is often restricted by its environment, and an isolated subsystem may exhibit spurious behaviour leading to states which it will no more reach when it is put into its proper environment. For instance, an isolated fifo channel behaves as if it were generated inputs at random. Therefore it may store all possible message combinations, whereas the contents of the channel as a part of the protocol are restricted by the overall operation of the protocol. We call this the *spurious behaviour* problem. Due to it compositional LTS generation has to be used cautiously.

To guarantee that compositional LTS generation leads to correct results we required the following: the equivalence used for comparing the behaviour of processes has to be a congruence with respect to the operators used in composing the system. This requirement was one of our motivations in Sect. 3, where we developed the CFFD-equivalence used by ARA. Indeed, CFFD-equivalence is a congruence with respect to all operators in the Basic Lotos language. Therefore compositionality can be used freely in ARA.

Compositionality is applied in ARA by replacing a process definition by a reference to a LTS file. So, if one writes

$$\textbf{process test}[\ a,\ b,\ c\ ] :=$$
$$\textbf{external 'test.lts'}$$

instead of the definition of the process "test", ARA uses the (perhaps condensed) LTS found in the file 'test.lts'.

Experience with ARA has shown that compositional LTS generation tends to give good reduction when subsystems are fairly independent, but breaking a system between two closely coupled processes often leads to large subsystem LTSs. The so far most successful application of the method has been the compositional analysis of the well-known dining philosophers system. It turned out that the externally observable behaviour of the system does not change when more philosophers are added to it, provided that the number of philosophers is at least four. Therefore, the results obtained by analysing the four-philosopher system hold also for all larger philosopher systems. As a result, a limited analysis effort has produced results which are valid for arbitrarily large philosopher systems. For more detail see [26].

The idea of compositional LTS generation is built into process algebraic theories, but its explicit discussion in the literature seems to be rare. The oldest tool applying it we are aware of is described in [16]. The paper [10] develops a semi-automatic method for solving the spurious behaviour problem discussed above. Prerequisites of compositional LTS generation are analysed in [24]. Compositional LTS generation is applied in the context of the CFFD model in [26].

4.2 Stubborn Sets

Concurrency is a major contributor to state explosion. It introduces a large number of execution sequences which lead from a common start state to a common end state by the same events, but the events occur in different order causing the sequences to go through different states. Consider the system in Fig. 9 ("| [a] |" denotes parallel composition such that all a-events are executed synchronously by the component processes). Its ordinary LTS is in Fig. 10. The numbers of states in Fig. 10 are combinations of the numbers of the corresponding states in Fig. 9.

From Fig. 10 it is easy to see that the system has one terminal state, namely 33. The system may also fail to terminate e.g. by executing forever the loop $11 - b \rightarrow 21 - d \rightarrow 22 - c \rightarrow 32 - a \rightarrow 11 - b \rightarrow \ldots$. It seems, however, that Fig. 10 contains more information than necessary. It contains many sequences where same events lead from a common start state to a common end state but in different orders. Examples are $11 - d \rightarrow 12 - e \rightarrow 13 - b \rightarrow 23, 11 - d \rightarrow 12 - b \rightarrow 22 - e \rightarrow 23$ and $11 - b \rightarrow 21 - d \rightarrow 22 - e \rightarrow 23$.

The stubborn set method renders possible the construction of an LTS in such a way that the construction of redundant execution sequences is mostly avoided. This

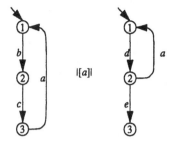

Fig. 9. Example system for illustrating the stubborn set method

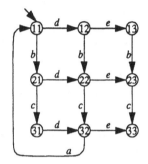

Fig. 10. Ordinary LTS of the system in Fig. 9

leads to a smaller LTS. To simplify the presentation of the basic idea of the stubborn set method, assume for the moment that the systems investigated are of the form

$$P = {}^1P \parallel {}^2P \parallel \cdots \parallel {}^mP$$

where the semantics of "$\parallel$" have been modified. For each $a \in \Sigma$, there is the set $uses(a) \subseteq \{1, 2, \ldots, m\}$, which specifies the component processes synchronizing via a. Formally,

$$
\begin{aligned}
{}^1P \parallel \cdots \parallel {}^mP - a \rightarrow {}^1Q \parallel \cdots \parallel {}^mQ, \text{ if and only if} \\
{}^jP - a \rightarrow {}^jQ \text{ when } j \in uses(a) \\
{}^jP = {}^jQ \text{ when } j \notin uses(a).
\end{aligned}
$$

The system in Fig. 9 can now be presented as $P = {}^1P_1 \parallel {}^2P_1$, where ${}^1P_i$ and ${}^2P_i$ denote the leftmost and rightmost process in their ith states, $uses(a) = \{1, 2\}$, $uses(b) = uses(c) = \{1\}$, and $uses(d) = uses(e) = \{2\}$. We define $next(X) = \{a \mid X - a \rightarrow \}$. For instance, $next({}^2P_2) = \{a, e\}$. To maintain the notation of Fig. 10, we denote ${}^1P_i \parallel {}^2P_j$ by ij.

Stubborn sets can now be defined as follows.

$A \subseteq \Sigma$ is stubborn at P, iff $next(P) \cap A \neq \emptyset$, and for each $a \in A$, the following hold:

1. $\neg(P - a \rightarrow)$ $\exists\, j \in uses(a) : \neg({}^jP - a \rightarrow) \wedge next({}^jP) \subseteq A$
2. $P - a \rightarrow$ $\forall\, j \in uses(a) : next({}^jP) \subseteq A$

Assume for a while that we are interested only in the termination-oriented properties of systems, that is, their sets of deadlocks and possibility of nontermination. There is a theorem saying that all deadlocks and at least one infinite execution (if exists) are present in a reduced LTS constructed using stubborn sets as follows [20] [27]:

> A *basic stubborn set reduced LTS* of a system is constructed otherwise like the ordinary LTS, but at each state, a stubborn set is constructed, and only the enabled events in it are used for constructing the transitions and immediate successors of the state.

The above technique is called the *basic stubborn set method*. We now illustrate it with the system in Fig. 9. There are several stubborn sets at its initial state. In particular, $\{d\}$ is stubborn, because $11-d\rightarrow$, $uses(d) = \{2\}$, and $next(^2P_1) = \{d\}$. So we construct the transition $11-d\rightarrow 12$, and forget about the transition $11-b\rightarrow 21$. (The reader is invited to try the stubborn set $\{b\}$ instead of $\{d\}$, if he wishes.)

There are two enabled events at state 12: b and e. Because $next(^2P_2) = \{a,e\}, 1 \in uses(a)$ and $next(^1P_1) = \{b\}$, any stubborn set at 12 containing e contains also a and b. On the other hand, $\{b\}$ is stubborn. $\{b\}$ is a smaller stubborn set than $\{a,b,e\}$, so we use $\{b\}$ and construct only the transition $12-b\rightarrow 22$.

Continuing this way we eventually construct the LTS in Fig. 11. It contains the same deadlock 33 as the LTS in Fig. 10, and it contains one loop demonstrating nontermination.

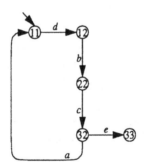

Fig. 11. A basic stubborn set reduced LTS of the system in Fig. 9

In ARA, the stubborn set method is used in such a way that the resulting reduced LTS of a system is CFFD-equivalent with the ordinary LTS of the same system. We can give only a very rough idea of the CFFD-preserving stubborn set method in the space available in this paper. Readers who are interested in more details are recommended [27].

We restrict the discussion to systems of the form

$$H = \textbf{hide } g_1, g_2, \ldots, g_n \textbf{ in} P,$$

where $P = {}^1P \parallel {}^2P \parallel \ldots \parallel {}^mP$, and "**hide**" is as in Lotos. To maintain the just adopted new semantics of "$\parallel$", we assume that none of ${}^jP$ may perform the invisible event i. If required, one may simulate $^jP -i\rightarrow {}^jQ$ by defining a new event ij such that $uses(ij) = \{j\}$, and adding ij to the list of hidden events. We say that a $\in \Sigma$ is invisible, if it appears in $\{g_1, g_2, \ldots, g_n\}$, and visible otherwise. The set of visible events is denoted by vis. There is a theorem saying that a reduced LTS of a finite state system is CFFD-equivalent with the corresponding ordinary LTS, if the following hold:

> For every state $H = \text{hide} \ldots \text{in} P$ in the reduced LTS and the stubborn set A_H used at H, the following hold:
>   1. If $\exists\, a \in vis \cap A_H : P -a\rightarrow$, then $vis \subseteq A_H$
>   2. If $\exists\, a \notin vis : P -a\rightarrow$, then $\exists\, a \in A_H - vis : P -a\rightarrow$
> Furthermore,
>   3. every cycle of the reduced LTS contains at least one state $H = \text{hide} \ldots \text{in } P$ such that $vis \subseteq A_H$.

Assumption (1) says that if the stubborn set contains an enabled visible event, then it should contain all visible events. This ensures that the CFFD-preserving stubborn set method preserves the relative ordering of visible events. Assumption (2) says that the stubborn set should contain an enabled invisible event, if there are any. Together with (1) this guarantees that the stable failures and the "minimal" divergence traces of the system are preserved. Assumption (2) also trivially guarantees the preservation of "*stable*". Finally, (3) guarantees that also the remaining divergence traces are preserved.

Efficient algorithms for constructing stubborn sets such that the above assumptions (1) and (2) are satisfied, and for controlling the reduced LTS construction such that also (3) is satisfied were first presented in [23]. The CFFD-preserving stubborn set method is developed in [27]. The stubborn set method was originally developed for Petri nets in [20], and [22] is a summary of the early versions of the stubborn set method. More references to stubborn set papers are found in [27].

The CFFD-preserving stubborn set method has given good reduction results in initial experiments. Graf and Steffen have described an n-customer token-ring system which cannot be efficiently analysed using the compositional approach because of the spurious behaviour problem mentioned in Sect. 4.1 [10]. The system has $9n \cdot 2^{n-2}$ states, which grows rapidly beyond the capacity of any computer when n becomes large. For instance, the number of states of the system is about $1.9 \cdot 10^9$ when $n = 25$. However, with the CFFD-preserving stubborn set method only $5n$ states need to be generated. Therefore, the ARA tool has been able to construct a 125-state LTS of the system for $n = 25$ in about 3 minutes of computer time. See [25] or [27] for more information.

5 ARA Tool

The ARA tool consists of three main components: *LTS constructor*, *LTS condenser* and *LTS comparator*. There is also a layout tool which can show small LTSs in fairly readable (although usually not very esthetic) graphical form.

The LTS constructor tool accepts specifications written in Basic Lotos and produces their LTSs. The tool can be run in normal mode to generate the ordinary

LTS, or the stubborn set method can be used to obtain reduction of states. The constructor can also be used for investigating the behaviour of the system step by step under manual control. This feature has proven useful for learning Lotos.

The language accepted by the constructor tool contains an extension: the **external** construct. With it the tool can be told to fetch the definition of one or more subprocesses from other files. An "external" file may contain a process definition written in Basic Lotos. As mentioned in Sect. 4.1, it may also contain a LTS which has perhaps been condensed by the LTS condenser tool. This facilitates the compositional analysis discussed in Sect. 4.1.

The LTS condenser takes a LTS generated by the constructor and produces a behaviourally equivalent condensed LTS. The condenser uses so-called *acceptance graphs (AG)* as an intermediate representation. Acceptance graphs are finite automata decorated with stability, failure and divergence information, and the condensation algorithm is based on determistization and minimization of finite automata. The condenser constructs a minimal acceptance graph from the input LTS. Then it constructs a LTS which is behaviourally equivalent with the minimal acceptance graph. See [26] for more information.

Because acceptance graphs are deterministic and LTSs may be nondeterministic, the LTS produced by the LTS condenser is not necessarily a minimal LTS for the system. As a matter of fact, it can even be larger than the input LTS. This phenomenon is related to the fact that the minimal deterministic automaton corresponding to a finite automaton may be larger than the original automaton, if the original automaton is nondeterministic. If this happens, then the condensation has obviously proven useless. However, most of the time the LTS produced by the condensation algorithm is much smaller than the input LTS. The condensation algorithm has proven very powerful in practice.

The minimal acceptance graph representation is unique up to isomorphism. Therefore it is possible to check whether two systems are behaviourally equivalent by comparing their minimal AGs. This can be done with the LTS comparator tool. If the systems are not equivalent, the tool provides a sample execution demonstrating a difference[4].

The ARA tools have been written in Turbo Pascal, and they run in PC under MS Windows. A MS DOS version also exists, but it has reduced functionality due to memory restrictions. The whole toolset has also been transported to Sun Sparc-Station using the public domain Pascal to C converter p2c. We intend to add more functionality to the tools, including the comparison of an asymmetric "implements" relation. We also plan to improve the speed of the stubborn set algorithm.

6 Conclusions

The goal of this paper was to describe the intuition behind the various novel techniques featured by the ARA tool. Formal details of the techniques can be found in

---

[4] This feature has not been fully implemented as yet. The sample execution produced by the current implementation extends only to the point where the comparator detects the existence of a difference. Due to the logic of the comparator this point may be different from the actual difference.

the publications referred to in the text.

The most important novel aspects of ARA are the semantic model it uses for comparing processes, and its techniques for attacking the state explosion problem. Because of the state explosion problem the performance of *any* currently existing verification tool leaves much to hope. In ARA the problem has been attacked by compositional LTS generation and the stubborn set method. Both methods avoid the construction of the big ordinary LTS of the system; instead, a smaller, but behaviourally equivalent reduced LTS is constructed more or less directly from a Basic Lotos description of the system.

As was mentioned in the paper, the compositional method has facilitated the analysis of a system of an arbitrary size by a fixed amount of effort, and the stubborn set method has reduced the size of the LTS of another system from exponential to linear in the size of the system. For instance, to verify a $1.9 \cdot 10^9$-state system, it was necessary to construct only 125 states with the stubborn set method. The stubborn set method is not redundant even if the compositional method is available, because the $1.9 \cdot 10^9$-state system is known not to be amenable to the compositional method. Similarly, the compositional method is sometimes very powerful while the stubborn set method fails. So the combination of the two methods is more beneficial than either of them alone.

One should remember, however, that these spectacular savings of states were obtained on "toy" examples. The true practicality of the stubborn set and compositional methods can be measured only by extensive tests with real systems. ARA is only a prototype and verification is very difficult. There is still a long way to go before computer-aided verification can be routinely applied in industrial scale software production.

7 Acknowledgements

ARA work has been funded by the Technology Development Centre of Finland (TEKES), the Technical Research Centre of Finland (VTT) and for a small part by Finnish industry. ARA research group has collaborated with the Computer Science department of the University of Helsinki and the Computer Science and Mathematics Departments of the University of Oulu. Professor Tienari of the University of Helsinki has given valuable comments on this paper.

References

1. Bergstra, J. A. & Klop, J. W. & Olderog, E.-R.: Failures without Chaos: A New Process Semantics for Fair Abstraction. Formal Description of Programming Concepts III, North-Holland 1987, pp. 77–103.
2. Bochmann, G. v.: Usage of Protocol Development Tools: The Results of a Survey. Proceedings of the 7th International IFIP WG 6.1 Symposium on Protocol Specification, Testing and Verification (1987), North-Holland 1988.
3. Bolognesi, T. & Brinksma, E.: Introduction to the ISO Specification Language LOTOS. Computer Networks and ISDN Systems 14 1987 pp. 25–59. Also: The Formal Description Technique LOTOS, North-Holland 1989, pp. 23–73.

4. Brookes, S. D. & Hoare, C. A. R. & Roscoe, A. W.: A Theory of Communicating Sequential Processes. Journal of the ACM 31 (3) 1984 pp. 560–599.

5. Clarke, E. M. & Emerson, E. A. & Sistla, A. P.: Automatic Verification of Finite State Concurrent Systems using Temporal Logic Specifications. ACM Transactions on Programming Languages and Systems, vol 8, 1986, pp. 244–263.

6. Cleaveland, R. & Parrow, J. & Steffen, B.: The Concurrency Workbench. Proceedings of the Workshop on Automatic Verification Methods for Finite-State Systems, Lecture Notes in Computer Science 407, Springer-Verlag 1990, pp. 24–37.

7. Feldbrugge, F. & Jensen, K.: Petri Net Tool Overview 1986. Advances in Petri Nets 1986, Part II, Lecture Notes in Computer Science 255, Springer-Verlag 1987, pp. 20–61.

8. Fernandez, J.-C.: An Implementation of an Efficient Algorithm for Bisimulation Equivalence. Science of Computer Programming 13 (1989/90) pp. 219–236.

9. Fernandez, J.-C. & Mounier, L.: A Tool Set for Deciding Behavioural Equivalences. Proceedings of CONCUR '91, Lecture Notes in Computer Science 527, Springer-Verlag 1991, pp. 23–42.

10. Graf, S. & Steffen, B.: Compositional Minimization of Finite-State Processes. In: Computer-Aided Verification '90 (Proceedings of a workshop), AMS DIMACS Series in Discrete Mathematics and Theoretical Computer Science, Vol 3, American Mathematical Society 1991, pp. 57–73.

11. Hoare, C. A. R.: Communicating Sequential Processes. Prentice-Hall 1985, 256 p.

12. ISO 8807 International Standard: Information processing systems – Open Systems Interconnection – LOTOS – A formal description technique based on the temporal ordering of observational behaviour. International Organization for Standardization, 1989, 142 p.

13. Kaivola, R. & Valmari, A.: Using Truth-Preserving Reductions to Improve the Clarity of Kripke Models. Proceedings of CONCUR '91, Lecture Notes in Computer Science 527, Springer-Verlag 1991, pp. 361–375.

14. Kaivola, R. & Valmari, A.: The Weakest Compositional Semantic Equivalence Preserving Nexttime-Less Linear Temporal Logic. Proceedings of CONCUR '92, Lecture Notes in Computer Science 630, Springer-Verlag 1992, pp. 207–221.

15. Lichtenstein, O. & Pnueli, A.: Checking that Finite State Concurrent Programs Satisfy their Linear Specification. Tenth ACM Symposium on Principles of Programming Languages, 1984, pp. 97–107.

16. Madelaine, E. & Vergamini, D.: AUTO: A Verification Tool for Distributed Systems Using Reduction of Finite Automata Networks. Formal Description Techniques II (Proceedings of FORTE '89), North-Holland 1990, pp. 61–66.

17. Milner, R.: Communication and Concurrency. Prentice-Hall 1989, 260 p.

18. Petri Net Newsletter 41, Special Volume: Petri Net Tools Overview 92. Gesellschaft für Informatik, Bonn, Germany, April 1992, 43 p.

19. Pnueli, A.: Applications of Temporal Logic to the Specification and Verification of Reactive Systems: A Survey of Current Trends. Current Trends in Concurrency, Lecture Notes in Computer Science 224, Springer-Verlag 1985, pp. 510–584.

20. Valmari, A.: Error Detection by Reduced Reachability Graph Generation. Proceedings of the Ninth European Workshop on Application and Theory of Petri Nets, Venice, Italy 1988, pp. 95–112.

21. Valmari, A.: PC-Rimst – A Tool for Validating Concurrent Program Designs. Microprocessing and Microprogramming 24 (1988) 1–5 (Proceedings of the Euromicro '88), pp. 809–818.

22. Valmari, A.: Stubborn Sets for Reduced State Space Generation. Advances in Petri Nets 1990, Lecture Notes in Computer Science 483, Springer-Verlag 1991, pp. 491–515.

(An earlier version appeared in Proceedings of the Tenth International Conference on Application and Theory of Petri Nets, Bonn, FRG 1989, Vol. II pp. 1–22.)

23. Valmari, A.: A Stubborn Attack on State Explosion. Formal Methods is System Design, 1: 297–322 (1992). (Earlier version appeared in Proceedings of the Workshop on Computer-Aided Verification 1990.)

24. Valmari, A.: Compositional State Space Generation. University of Helsinki, Department of Computer Science, Report A-1991-5, Helsinki, Finland 1991. 30 p. (An earlier version appeared in Proceedings of the 11th International Conference on Application and Theory of Petri Nets, Paris, France 1990, pp. 43–62.)

25. Valmari, A. et Clegg, M.: Reduced Labelled Transition Systems Save Verification Effort. Proceedings of CONCUR '91, Lecture Notes in Computer Science 527, Springer-Verlag 1991, pp. 526–540.

26. Valmari, A. & Tienari, M.: An Improved Failures Equivalence for Finite-State Systems with a Reduction Algorithm. Protocol Specification, Testing and Verification XI (Proceedings of the 11th International IFIP Symposium), North-Holland 1991, pp. 3–18.

27. Valmari, A.: Alleviating State Explosion during Verification of Behavioural Equivalence. University of Helsinki, Department of Computer Science, Report A-1992-4, Helsinki, Finland 1992. 57 p.

28. Wheeler, G. R. & Valmari, A. & Billington, J.: Baby TORAS Eats Philosophers but Thinks about Solitaire. Proceedings of the Fifth Australian Software Engineering Conference, Sydney, Australia 1990, pp. 283–288.

Integrating SA/RT with LOTOS [*]

Anthony W. van der Vloedt[1] and Kees Bogaards[1]

Information Technology Architecture b.v.,
Institutenweg 1, 7521 ZE Enschede, The Netherlands

Abstract. This paper presents a method for the derivation of a LOTOS specification starting from an SA/RT specification. We will show that LOTOS is able to capture information not described in an SA/RT specification. SA/RT, on the other hand provides an intuitive approach which is helpful in establishing a formal LOTOS specification. The resulting integrated method is therefore both intuitive appealing and rigorously precise.

1 Introduction

In the early stages of requirements analysis, and especially for large systems, it is difficult to apply a formal method. In this stage the ideas about what the system should do are vague. It is easier to express these ideas informally. Nowadays a natural language description is often used as the starting point for the production of a formal specification. CASE supported methods could improve this situation. A well-known method is Structured Analysis [10], SA for short. For the specification of real-time systems there exists variants with real-time extensions that are commonly referred to as SA/RT. SA/RT methods are widely used in industry. They are more formal than natural language. (It is sometimes called a semi-formal method.) For large systems SA/RT will be better suited as input to the production of a formal specification than natural language, due to its systematic nature of collection, analysis and description of the requirements. The benefit of our transformation method is, that it uses the SA/RT specification as a support for the formal specification in LOTOS. Thus we benefit from both worlds. We believe that a method for the transformation of an SA/RT specification to LOTOS will encourage the industrial acceptance of FDTs.

1.1 Structure of the paper

The remainder of this paper is structured as follows: sections 2 gives a short explanation of SA/RT and section 3 gives a short explanation of LOTOS. These sections are an introduction to section 4 that discusses the differences between the methods and the impact of these differences on the integration of the methods. In section 5 a transformation approach is presented. Section 6 contains the conclusions.

---

[*] The work described in this paper was carried out as part of the COMPLEMENT project. COMPLEMENT is partially funded by the Commission of the European Communities as an ESPRIT II project (project number 5409).

2 SA/RT

2.1 Structured Analysis

Structured Analysis (SA) is a method for the specification of the functional requirements of a system using a graphical notation. It visualises the system by a network
of data transforming units (processes) and data storage units (stores) linked by directed arcs (data flows). The arcs indicate how the output of one unit is used by
another. Such a diagrammatic description is called a data flow diagram. An overview
of the elements is given in figure 1. Each of the items in a data flow diagram can
be described in more detail. For the stores and data flows this is done textually in
a document called the data dictionary. The data dictionary describes how the data
on a data flow or on a data flow is composed of component data. In case data is
not composite this is also indicated. The processes can be described in more detail
either by a textual description (mini-spec) or by another data flow diagram. The
latter allows the specification to be hierarchically structured. A hierarchically lower
data flow diagram is always used, when the designer thinks that a textual description
would be too large to understand it directly. The method starts by producing a top
level data flow diagram, that consists of a single process—representing the system
that is being modeled—that is linked by data flows to the entities in its environment,
represented by so called terminators.

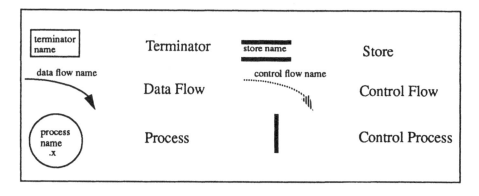

Fig. 1. Elements of SA/RT diagrams

2.2 Real-time extensions

The original SA method has been extended in several ways to improve its suitability
for the specification of real-time systems (SA/RT methods). The best known are
the methods of Ward and Mellor [9] and of Hatley and Pirbhai [4]. In our paper we
focus on the latter.

In the SA method the processes in a data flow diagram are constantly active,
whenever inputs are present it produces an output. In SA/RT a process may also

be inactive, in this case it will not produce an output. The conditions for activation and deactivation of a process are specified in a control process. The control processes get their data from control flows. The control processes and control flows have a representation distinct from the normal processes and data flows A control process is specified in a control specification. Apart from informal text and pseudo-code, this control specification can be expressed as a state machine. Another real-time extension is that in the descriptions of every process it is allowed to refer to a global time.

2.3   An example

In the remainder of this paper we will illustrate our method by means of an example: a control system for a station where cans are filled with paint (or any other liquid). In this system, tins entering the system are first weighed empty and then filled with paint. The filled tins are weighed again and a decision is taken to accept or reject the filled tins for further shipment. Rejection occurs if the percentage of filled tins which deviate too much from a preset content value threatens to excess a certain limit. The weights of the empty and filled cans are used in a feed-back control loop that controls the amount of paint that is put in the tins. The deviation signal is filtered by the system. When too much cans contain less paint than required a filter with a low bandwidth is used. Otherwise a filter with a high bandwidth is used. Understanding of the exact nature of the feed-back control loop is not necessary for the understanding of this paper. For this example an SA/RT specification is given in figure 2. For presentational reasons the data flow diagrams and the control flow diagrams have been merged into flow diagrams (FD). For every primitive process in the SA/RT specification a short textual description is provided. The example also contains a control specification (CS). This control specification is given by a graphical representation of a state machine. Whenever a transition is caused by **excess** the process **fast_filter** is activated. The semantics of the control process are such that when a transition occurs the processes that the state machine controls and are not activated are deactivated. In our example the state machine controls the processes **fast_filter** and **slow_filter**. Thus, the transition caused by **excess** will also deactivate the processes **slow_filter**. Transitions caused by **short** will activate **slow_filter** and deactivate **fast_filter**.

Normally, an SA/RT specification also contains a description of all data on data flows and in stores (the data dictionary). In this paper the data dictionary is omitted. An example of the content of the data dictionary is the data store **statistics**, that stores the number of filled cans and the number of cans that do not contain enough paint. It is described by two components **cans_filled** and **underfilled_cans**. In the data dictionary this is represented as:

`statistics = cans_filled + underfilled_cans.`

3   LOTOS

LOTOS is a Formal Description Technique (FDT) for the specification of data communication systems. Experience with LOTOS gained in several projects such as e.g.

described in [1] [7] have led to a method for the application of LOTOS in the requirements and design phase of the lifecycle of a system. In the requirements phase, the system is specified as a single black box entity that exchanges information with its environment by means of interactions. An interaction is defined as the joint establishment of a data value among two or more parties. It is simular to an ADA rendez-vous The specification of a system consist of an enumeration of the interactions in which the system is willing to participate, the possible order in time in which these interactions are executed (temporal relationships), and the data associated with the interactions. LOTOS uses the algebraic specification language ACT ONE to specify data as Abstract Data Types (ADTs).

To clarify the concepts of LOTOS, we will present two temporal relations. These temporal relations can be thought of as part of a specification of the can filling system in LOTOS. The aspects described here have not been described in the SA/RT specification. Thus we see that the LOTOS specification contains more information than the SA/RT specification.

We will only present those aspects of LOTOS that are of interest to paper.

3.1 Temporal relation: can handling sequence

A characteristic of the total system behaviour is that a can, when entered to the system must first be weighed when empty, then filled and finally weighed as a full can. Thus, the system can be modeled as the aggregated behaviour of the processing of single cans. In this relation the processing of single cans is considered not related. In LOTOS this is specified as the disjoint set of single can handling processes.

```
process can_handling_sequence[weigh_empty, fill, weigh_full]
: noexit :=
  single_can_handling [weigh_empty, fill, weigh_full]
  |||
  i ; can_handling_sequence [weigh_empty, fill, weigh_full]
```

In this specification weigh_empty, fill and weigh_full represent the abstract interfaces between the system and its environment.

The parallel operator (|||) is used to denote that single_can_handling is fully independent from the handling of other cans. Due to the recursion in the expression an arbitrarily large number of cans can be processed concurrently.

The explanation of the internal event operator i is out of the scope of this paper.

Modeling the processing of a single can is rather simple. It comprises the sequence of actions that are necessary to process a single can. This is done using the sequential operator (;).

```
where
  process single_can_handling [weigh_empty, fill, weigh_full]
  : exit :=
    weigh_empty ?tare_weight : Weight;
    fill ?flow : Flow;
    weigh_full ?gross_weight : Weight ?reject : SwitchSignal;
    exit
```

```
  endproc
endproc (* can_handling_sequence *)
```

The LOTOS specification of the handling of a single can can be explained as that first a weighing event will take place at abstract interface **weigh_empty** where a value **tare_weight** of type **Weight** will be established. (The input data items are preceded by a question mark.) Following this event, a filling event will take place, and the filling value is established. After the filling event has taken place, a weighing of the filled can event takes place in which the filled weight is established and at the same time the can is accepted or rejected. The event taking place at the **weigh_full** interface shows that simultaneous synchronisation on more than one value can take place.

After the last event the handling of the can is finished, denoted by (**exit**).

3.2   temporal relation: maximum can capacity

Although not mentioned in the SA/RT specification, the system will have an upper limit on the number of cans the system can handle simultaneously. This can be specified by counting the cans that enter the system at the empty can weighing interface and the cans leaving the system at the full can weighing interface. When the limit is reached, the system refuses to accept new cans by refusing to weigh new empty cans.

```
process max_can [weigh_empty, weigh_full] (n: Nat) : noexit:=
  [n <= upper_limit] ->
    weigh_empty ?tare_weight : Weight;
    max_can [weigh_empty, weigh_full] (n + 1)
  []
  weigh_full ?gross_weight : Weight ?reject : Bool;
  max_can [weigh_empty, weigh_full] (n - 1)
endproc (* max_can *)
```

The state variable n contains the number of cans in the system. The guard
```
  [n <= upper_limit]->
```
functions as a predicate for the interaction to take place, ensuring that a can may only enter the system when the maximum number is not yet reached. The choice operator ($\Box$) denotes a non-deterministic choice. In this case it means that the environment may either select a **weigh_empty** event,. if the guard allows it, or a **weigh_full** event.

3.3   The total temporal behaviour

The total temporal behaviour of the system can be specified as a combination of all temporal relations. All temporal relations must hold simultaneously during the life time of the system.

```
  max_can [weigh_empty, weigh_full] (0)
  |[weigh_empty, weigh_full]|
  can_handling_sequence[weigh_empty, fill, weigh_full]
```

The synchronisation operator (| [weigh_empty, weigh_full] |) is used to denote that both relations max_can and can_handling_sequence have to agree on the possibility of the interactions on weigh_empty and weigh_full. Thus, if one of the relations is not satisfied, the interaction will not take place. In this way it is possible to specify any of the conditions which must be satisfied simultaneously in order for the interaction to take place in an independent way.

The interaction fill is not present in the synchronisation operator, as max_can is not concerned with the filling of cans. Any additional relations can be formulated in isolation and added in a similar way.

4   Differences between SA/RT and LOTOS

Both SA/RT and LOTOS are part of a system development method. Each method produces (intermediate) system descriptions in a method specific notation. Associated with the production of the intermediate descriptions are heuristics and procedures. Within the scope of this paper we will concentrate on the notation. We do not look at the production process and therefore ignore the heuristics. The notation used for SA/RT consists of data flow diagrams and control flow diagrams. Clearly the LOTOS method uses the LOTOS language. Both notations are able to describe certain aspects of the system. The aspects handled by both notations give rise to transformation from one notation into the other. The aspects not covered by both notations give rise to addition or loss of information during transformation (see also figure 3). This includes:

- synchronous a-synchronous communication
- temporal relations
- I/O aspects
- environment structuring.

4.1   synchronous a-synchronous communication

SA/RT does not describe events; it describes continuous flows. Hence any interpretation about the nature of the communication of the system with its environment is allowed: synchronous in which both parties participate simultaneously in the interaction (the output of the one system coincides with the input of the other system, or a-synchronous in which the action of one party is independently described from the action of the other communicating party. LOTOS uses a synchronous communication model. LOTOS descriptions are mainly concerned with the transition that occurs when an interaction takes place.

4.2   Temporal relations

In SA/RT it is possible to omit at which moment an input is possible in relation to another input. In contrast, the main feature of LOTOS is the ability to specify the temporal relationships between the information exchanges of the system with other systems or the environment. The LOTOS model describes synchronous communication and the specification details the temporal ordering of the information exchanges of the system. Other types of communication are expressed using synchronous communication primitives. In the SA/RT specification of the can filling system it is for example not specified that a can is only to be filled after its predecessor has been weighed. In LOTOS this can easily be specified. It even is obligatory. Therefore, transformation of an SA/RT specification to a LOTOS specification may require the addition of the temporal relations between the information exchanges of the system and the environment.

4.3 I/O aspects

LOTOS does not differentiate between inputs and outputs, while SA/RT does. However, the meaning of this difference is not clearly defined due to the informal nature of SA/RT.

In LOTOS, we only consider the contribution of a process to the enabling of an interaction. Whether this is an input or an output is not so important at an abstract level. Only in the implementation phase, when interactions are mapped onto I/O operations, we consider the difference between inputs and outputs relevant.

For this reason the loss of this information during the transformation is considered not severe. A way to retain this information is to use a naming convention for events and gates. However, this is not a part of the standard architectural semantics for LOTOS.

4.4 Environment structuring

Another difference between SA/RT and LOTOS is that the semantic model of LOTOS does not support the concept of 'terminator'. In SA/RT this concept corresponds to an entity in the environment of the system. In LOTOS there is no architectural concept for environment.

5 Transforming SA/RT to LOTOS

Our approach to transformation consists of the following steps:

1. selection of interactions
2. specification of the temporal relationships between the interactions
3. formalisation of data and data transformations

As an illustration of our approach we will transform the earlier presented SA/RT specification of the can filling system to LOTOS.

5.1 Selection of interactions

In the comparison of SA/RT with LOTOS it was shown that the temporal relationships of the information exchanges between the system and the environment have to be added before an SA/RT specification can be transformed into a LOTOS specification. The addition of this information consists of the selection of interactions and the establishment of temporal relationships among them. Interactions do not necessarily correspond one-to-one with the terminators or the data- and control flows to or from the terminators. Only, every flow to or from the environment should be related to at least one interaction and every data item in an interaction should be related to at least one flow to or from the environment. For the can filling system we can define the following interactions:

- weighing an empty can (determination of the `tare_weight`),
- filling an empty can (with a quantity determined by flow) and determining its filled weight (determination of the `gross_weight`),
- an interaction that decides on the acceptance or rejection of a can (operating the `switch_signal`).

At an abstract level of specification we can group the filling of a can and the weighing of a filled can together. In a real system there will be a certain time delay between the weighing and the decision to accept or reject. This delay is only dependent on the CPU speed required to process the weight of the filled can, and not on any other event. Therefore we do not need to specify the event in relation to the other events.

5.2 specification of the temporal relationships between the interactions

After the interactions are selected the temporal relations among them are specified. This will lead to a more complete description of the temporal behaviour of the system. These temporal relations were not fully described in the SA/RT specification. The SA/RT specification may suggest some temporal behaviour, but, due to the informal nature of the SA/RT specification, it is not possible to extract this temporal information automatically. Even the control flow specification, that consists of state machine descriptions, does not allow straight-forward derivation of temporal relations, due to the interplay with the informal parts of the specification. The specifier has to take care that the formal specification of the temporal behaviour in LOTOS does not contradict the informal information present in the SA/RT specification. The specifier himself must define the interactions and their temporal relationship from the informal descriptions. The selection of interactions impacts the temporal relations that can be specified. Therefore, selection of interactions and specification of the temporal relations will be an iterative process. For the can filling system the following temporal relationships be defined:

1. empty cans will first be weighed, then filled and weighed full, and then accepted or rejected,
2. whenever more than a maximum number of cans are inside the system, weighing empty cans is stopped. (Refusing to weigh empty cans will prohibit new cans to enter the system.)

These relationships have already been specified in more detail in section 3; the first was specified by the LOTOS process `can_handling_sequence`, the second by `max_can`.

5.3 Formalisation of data and data transformations

In another step we derive the data and data transformations from the SA/RT specification. Some operations that are derived depend on the selected interactions. Therefore this step can not be performed completely independent from the other steps.

Structure. For every process in the SA/RT specification we produce one ACT ONE type. When SA/RT processes contains other SA/RT processes, the ADT definition for the process uses the ADT definitions for the other processes. This way, the derived ACT ONE specification will follow the structure of the SA/RT specification. For example, the type definition of the process `can_filling_system` that is described in more detail in flow diagram 0 (FD0) will use the type descriptions of the processes `mean_tare_weight` (FD1), `calculate_net_weight` (FD2), `calculate_deviation` (FD3), `evaluate_can` (FD4) and `determine_flow` (FD5).

```
type FD0 is DataDictionary, FD1, FD2, FD3, FD4, FD5
```

Additionally, these ADT definitions will use the type definitions that are derived from the data dictionary. Structuring the specification in this way will produce textual overhead. However, it brings the advantage, that the ACT ONE specification is structured in a comprehensive way. The SA/RT specification can be used as an index into the formal specification.

State. A SA/RT process may contain stores and state machines, either directly or indirectly by its subprocesses. Together they record the abstract state of the process (not to be confused with the states of the state machines in the control specifications of the SA/RT specification; this state encompasses more). For example: the state of the process `can_filling_system` consists of the store `statistics`, the state of process `mean_tare_weight` (process number 1 in figure 1) and the state of `determine_flow` (process number 5) (the other processes do not have a state). Part of the ACT ONE definition is presented below.

```
sorts
  State0
opns
  Statistics: State0 -> Statistics
  State1: State0 -> State1
  State5: State0 -> State5
```

For every component of the state an initial value can be specified. For example:

```
Statistics(InitialState0) = InitialValue_statistics
```

The states are numbered by the identification number of their process. It is also necessary to store the inputs in an abstract state. This abstract state is the state of the system. Sometimes outputs have to be queued. In the example of the can filling system a particular can is rejected or accepted depending on the status of the system after it has been filled and weighed. There could be a queue of cans between the tare scale and the separator gate. So, the actual rejection or acceptance can take place after other cans have been filled and weighed. Therefore, the values of the switch signal are put in a queue. A queue of outputs is part of the system state. The abstract state of the system will therefore also reflect decisions on the way the system communicates with the environment.

Outputs. An SA/RT process provides a mapping from its inputs and its state to its outputs. For every output of a process a function has to be provided. For the non-primitive functions these functions will be defined by the composition of functions defined in the types of its subprocesses. This composition will be done according to the input/output relations depicted in the SA/RT specification. The names of the functions consist of the name of the flow whose value they produce with the number of the process they belong to appended. For example: there will be a function `flow0` in type `FD0` that derives the flow from the state of the system `state0`. One of the components used in the definition of this function will be `mean_value1` that is defined in type `FD1`.

```
flow0: Weight, State0 -> Flow
flow0(gross_weight, state0) =
  flow5(deviation3(net_weight2(gross_weight,
                               mean_value1(state1(state0)))),
                   State5(state0));
```

The specification of functions of primitive processes has to be derived from the informal descriptions of the processes.

State changes. Whenever an interaction occurs, the state of the system can change. For every process we have to provide functions that specify what the state will be after an interaction has occurred. This new state depends on the inputs to the process, its old state and the interaction. The names of the state changing functions contain the name of the state they change appended with the interaction that causes the change. For example: the state of the system will change when an empty can is weighed and whenever a can is filled and weighed. In this case the following functions have to be incorporated in the ACT ONE specification of type FD0.

```
NewState0_weigh_empty: Weight, State0 -> State0
NewState0_fill_and_weigh: Weight, State0 -> State0
Statistics(NewState0_weigh_empty(tare_weight, state0)) =
  Statistics(state0);
Statistics(NewState0_weigh_full(gross_weight, State0)) =
  statistics4(
    deviation3(
      net_weight2(gross_weight, mean_value1(State1(state0)))),
    Statistics(state0));
```

We introduce here a relationships between interactions and state changes. This is also temporal information, that was previously not present in the SA/RT specification.

Integration of data and interactions. The data transformations are encapsulated in a LOTOS process:

```
process data_transformations[weigh_empty, fill_and_weigh, decide]
    (state : SystemState) : noexit :=
  weigh_empty ?tare_weight : Weight;
  data_transformations[weigh_empty, fill_and_weigh, decide]
    (NewSystemState_weigh_empty(tare_weight, state))
  []
  fill_and_weigh !flow(state) ?gross_weight : Weight;
  data_transformations[weigh_empty, fill, weigh_full]
    (NewSystemState_fill_and_weigh(gross_weight, state))
  []
  decide !switch_signal(state);
  data_transformations[weigh_empty, fill_and_weigh, decide]
    (NewSystemState_decide(state))
endproc (* data_transformations *)
```

This enables us, finally, to specify the complete system by the following LOTOS expression:

```
( max_can[weigh_empty, decide] (upper_limit)
  |[weigh_empty, decide]|
  can_handling_sequence[weigh_empty, fill_and_weigh, decide] )
||
data_transformations[weigh_empty, fill_and_weigh, decide]
(initial_systemstate)
```

6 Conclusion

Integration of SA/RT and LOTOS is more than just a formalisation of the information contained in the SA/RT specification; it requires the additional specification of the temporal behaviour of the system. The main benefit of integration is that SA/RT provides an informal, intuitive, yet CASE tool supported method to explore the problem. This helps the designer in constructing a full fledged formal LOTOS specification. Such a LOTOS specification can be validated by tools, for example by the simulator SMILE [2]. Although not further elaborated in this paper, it has been demonstrated that not the complete SA/RT has to be transformed to LOTOS, but only those aspects that relate to the temporal ordering of the system. Thus both methods may co-exist presenting different views of the same system: LOTOS by its description of the temporal behaviour specifying the real-time aspects, and SA/RT for the data processing behaviour. Provided that both views are consistent, the two aspect may give rise to two development methods which are best suited for the aspects concerned.

6.1 Comments on the transformation method

The constraint oriented style is the preferred style for a requirements specification. The transformation approach presented in section 5 of this paper enables the construction of a constraint-oriented specification. When the temporal relationships between the interactions that are added by the user are specified in the constraint oriented style, the resulting LOTOS specification will be in constraint-oriented style entirely.

Writing out the entire specification for the can filling example presented in section 2.3 folowing the presented approach will show that the mayor part of the system will be specified in ACT ONE. Although the SA/RT specification describes in fact the ADT part of the LOTOS specification, and thus the mapping of the SA/RT specification on ACT ONE is appropriate, we consider the large ACT ONE specification to be a disadvantage of the presented approach.

6.2 Future Research

Currently we are building a prototype tool for the transformation of SA/RT specifications to LOTOS. This tool will be based on the ProMod platform (produced by CAP debis GEI). The ProMod platform forms the basis of an industrial CASE tool set that includes tools for SA/RT specification and analysis. This prototype tool will support the user in the transformation of an SA/RT specification by helping him to specify his interactions and the relationships of these interactions with the flows and the changes of the abstract state. The tool will produce a skeleton for a LOTOS specification that the user has to complete. The tool will also perform checks on these user-specified interactions and relationships to ensure that the resulting LOTOS framework will be an appropriate basis for a LOTOS specification that is a valid implementation of the SA/RT specification.

References

1. Bogaards, K., Schot, J., Pras, A., Pires, L.F.: The Pangloss method. ESPRIT Conf. 88, 1988
2. Eertink, H., Woltz, D.: Symbolic execution of LOTOS specifications. Memoranda Informatica 91-47, University of Twente, 1991
3. Fraser, M.D., Kumar, K., Vaishnavi, V.K.: Informal and Formal Requirements Specification Languages: Bridging the Gap. IEEE Trans. Software Eng., vol. 17, pp. 454–466, May 1991
4. Hatley, D.J., Pirbhai, I.A.: Strategies for Real-Time System Specification. New York, Dorset House Publishing, 1987
5. ISO: Information processing systems - Open Systems Interconnection - LOTOS - A formal description technique based on the temporal ordering of observational behaviour. IS8807
6. Manas, J.A., de Miguel, T.: ¿From LOTOS to C. Proceedings Forte 88, 1988
7. Pires, L.F., Vissers, C.A.: Overview of the Lotosphere Design Methodology. ESPRIT Conf. 1990, pp. 371-387, Kluwer Academic Publishers, Dordrecht, 1990
8. Toetenel, H., van Katwijk, J., Plat, N.: Structured Analysis - Formal Design, using Stream & Object Oriented Formal Specification. Proc. ACM Sigsoft, International Workshop on Formal Methods in Software Development, Software Engineering Notes, Vol. 15, pp. 118-127, ACM Press, Napa, California, USA, 1990
9. Ward, P.T., Mellor, S.J.: Structured Development for Real-Time Systems. New York, Yourdon press, 1985

10. Yourdon, E.: Modern Structured Analysis. Prentice-Hall, 1989

FD Context

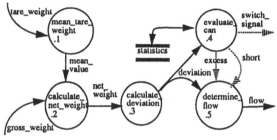

FD 0 Can_Filling_System

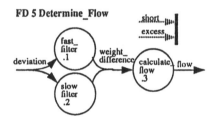

FD 5 Determine_Flow

CS 5 Determine_Flow

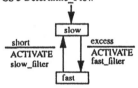

1 mean tare weight
Get tare_weight and calculate the mean_-
value of all tare_weights that have been
weighted since the system started.

2 calculate net weight
net_weight = gross_weight - mean_value

3 calculate deviation
deviation = net_weight - target_weight

4 evaluate can
Add 1 to cans_filled in statistics
IF deviation < minimum_deviation
THEN
   add 1 to underfilled_cans in statistics
IF 100 * underfilled_cans / cans_filled<
   allowed_percentage_underfilled_cans
THEN
   short = deviation < minimum_deviation
   excess = deviation > maximum_deviation
ELSE
   short = false
   excess = true
   ISSUE switch_signal

5.1 fast filter
Apply a high bandwidth filtering method to
deviation to obtain weight_difference.

5.2 slow filter
Apply a low bandwidth filtering algorithm to
deviation to obtain weight_difference.

5.3 calculate flow
Adapt flow according to weight_difference.

Fig. 2. SA/RT specification of a can filling system

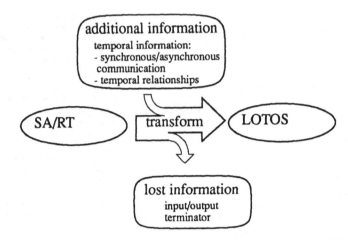

Fig. 3. Information lost and added

Symbolic Model Checking
for Distributed Real-Time Systems*

Farn Wang, Aloysius Mok, E. Allen Emerson

Department of Computer Sciences, University of Texas, Austin, U.S.A.

Abstract. In this paper, we examine the symbolic model checking problem for distributed real-time systems where time is represented by the real numbers and multiple clocks are allowed. A symbolic model checking algorithm is proposed. This algorithm handles timing constraints that are written in inequalities whose two sides refer to readings of the same local clock. The timing inequalities are used as triggers for transitions in Multiclock Continuously Timed Automaton (MCTA), a variation of the Timed Safety Automaton [11] which we propose as the specification language for distributed real-time systems. We also propose MTCTL, an extension of TCTL by the introduction of multiple local clocks, for specifying system behavior to be verified.

There are three major contributions of this paper. First, we give a symbolic model checking algorithm for Timed Safety Automata and TCTL which naturally makes use of the BDD approach of Bryant[4] and Burch et al[5], and avoids the complications in [11]. Second, we propose a unified approach for checking both real-time and state properties by treating inequalities as propositions that are governed by some axioms. This is not only a more elegant way to represent the finite structure of the state space, but is also more suitable for symbolic manipulation. Third, we introduce MTCTL and MCTA together as a new tool for specifying and reasoning about distributed real-time system behavior that allows for different granularities for local clocks and clock jitters.

1 Introduction

Many concurrent and distributed systems are finite-state in nature. For these systems, their qualitative behavioral properties, as specified by temporal logic are often amenable to verification by the technique of *model checking*[6, 7]. While model checking algorithms are typically PTIME in the size of the system state space, the state graph itself may be too big to be represented explicitly in computer memory.

To overcome this limitation, *symbolic* model checking[5] has been proposed, where the state space is not represented explicitly, but rather is succinctly described symbolically using Binary Decision Diagrams (BDDs)[4]. In [5], the formulas of temporal logic can also be represented using BDDs as the canonical representation through a unified intermediate representation, the μ-calculus. This makes it possible to give

* Supported in part by a research grant from the Office of Naval Research under ONR contract number N00014-89-J-1472. Farn Wang can be reached by email: farn@cs.utexas.edu or (512)471-9573

very efficient symbolic model checking algorithms in practice. Systems with more than 10^{20} states have been handled with this approach.

The success in [5] has prompted researchers to investigate whether the same success can be repeated for real-time logics[1, 2, 3, 9, 10, 17]. The first such attempt is [11]. In that paper, good results were obtained by using a clever *next* relation on real time (real numbers), as defined in the following way:

$$|\varphi_1 \rhd \varphi_2| \equiv \exists \delta \in \mathbb{R}^+.((\phi_\Box \wedge pre(|\varphi_2|)) + \delta \wedge \forall \delta' \in \mathbb{R}^+.(\delta' < \delta \rightarrow (|\varphi_1| \vee |\varphi_2|) + \delta'))$$

where $\phi_\Box$ is the invariant of the system, $|\varphi|$ is the canonical form (symbolic representation) of φ, *pre* is a relational term that calculates the precondition for another relational term, and $\mathbb{R}^+$ is the set of nonnegative real numbers. One thing that is unresolved (or at least unexplained) about this approach is how to incorporate the existential and universal quantification on real numbers in the calculation of $|\varphi_1 \rhd \varphi_2|$ from $|\varphi_1|$ and $|\varphi_2|$. A possibility is to employ traditional term rewriting techniques. But this seems to require us to deviate from the BDD approach of Bryant[4] and Burch, et al [5] in the calculation of the canonical form of the next relation. In practice, the combination of two dissimilar approaches may turn out to be a significant handicap since empirically, it is staying within the framework of BDDs that is responsible for the outstanding performance of symbolic model checking. In this paper, we provide a symbolic model checking algorithm that avoids this difficulty.

We consider real-time systems where time is represented by the real numbers and multiple clocks are allowed. Specifically, we propose Multiclock Continuously Timed Automaton (MCTA), a variation of the Timed Safety Automaton[11] as our model specification language. The formulas to be checked are written in Multiclock Timed CTL (MTCTL), an extension of TCTL that does not require the problematic next-operator ($\rhd$) introduced in Henzinger, et al[11], as mentioned above.

The timing constraints in MCTA as well as MTCTL are written using inequalities such that both sides of an inequality must refer to readings of the same local clock. We shall show that the (symbolic) model checking problem for real-time logics can be accomplished if we carry a finite amount of information about the timing inequalities in each state by an innovative way. This is achieved by using the idea of region graph from [1] and representing a region, which is a class of states that share the same future behavior, as a set of (μ-calculus relational term on) inequalities and propositions. Since in an asynchronous distributed system, the local clocks may advance at different speeds with different granularities and clock jitters are unavoidable, we also argue that MCTA and MTCTL actually provide a better alternative than Timed Safety Automata and TCTL for the formal specification and verification of distributed real-time systems.

There are three major contributions of this paper. First, we obtain a symbolic model checking algorithm for TCTL and Timed Safety Automata completely within the successful BDD framework proposed by Bryant[4] and Burch, et al[5], since Timed Safety Automaton and TCTL[11] can be considered as special cases of respectively MCTA and MTCTL when there is only one clock. Being able to stay within the BDD framework allows us to pursue the hope of an empirically fast model checking algorithm.

The second major contribution of this paper is that we provide a unified view on atomic propositions and timing inequalities. In previous research in real-time temporal logics, propositions and timing inequalities are treated as two different kinds of objects. In contrast, we treat the inequalities of a region as a set of propositions that are governed by a set of axioms. *This actually opens up the possibility for deriving straightforward reduction from many real-time automata and logics to untimed automata and logics.* Thus our main concern in this paper is how to express these axioms, describe the relation between adjacent regions, and rewrite the temporal logic formulas in the μ-calculus of [5].

In [1, 11], state regions are treated as a data structure that keeps track of the proposition values, the integral parts of clock readings, and the ordering among the fractional parts of clock readings. In this paper, we identify each state region with a set of propositions and inequalities. This is not only a more elegant way to exploit the notion of state regions, but is also more suitable for symbolic manipulation.

The third contribution of the paper is that we propose a system model (MCTA) and temporal logic MTCTL which together give us a new tool for the formal specification and verification of distributed real-time systems. Our approach allows for the possibility of clock jitters and different clock granularities.

In section 2, we review briefly the μ-calculus defined in [5]. Section 3 introduces the Multiclock Continuously Timed Automata. Section 4 defines Multiclock Timed CTL. The type of clock synchronization scheme that can be specified in MTCTL is also discussed. Section 5 deals with symbolic model checking of MTCTL formula for MCTA structures, within the framework of Bryant[4] and Burch, et al[5].

The techniques we shall propose may not work well by manual translation or with a prover like SMV[14]. This is because of the fact that naive enumeration of the state regions in our framework requires double exponential time complexity. In subsection 5.4, we shall go into some of the implementation issues and propose optimization techniques to reduce the time complexity for enumerating state regions to a single exponential. Techniques for better memory utilization will also be discussed.

Section 6 discusses the possibilities of extending the result to multiclock discrete-time systems with either traditional inequalities or asynchronous inequalities[17]. Section 7 is the conclusion.

In the following, we shall use c, d, e, h, k as nonnegative integer constants, i, j as positive integer constants, and r, t as nonnegative real numbers. For a given array Γ of m elements, $m \geq 1$, we refer to the i'th element of Γ as Γ_i for all $1 \leq i \leq m$. If the i'th element of Γ has value γ_i, we also use the notation $\langle \gamma_i \rangle_{1 \leq i \leq m}$ for the m-element array Γ.

2 μ-calculus

We adopt the μ-calculus defined in [5]. Suppose we are given a finite signature Σ in which each symbol is either an *individual variable* or a *predicate variable* with positive arity. There are two syntactic categories of interest: *formulas* and *relational terms*. Formulas have the following syntax.

$$z_1 = z_2 \mid \neg f \mid f_1 \vee f_2 \mid \exists z[f] \mid L(z_1, \ldots, z_n)$$

Here $z, z_1, z_2, \ldots, z_n$ are individual variables, f, f_1, f_2 are formulas, and L is an n-ary relational term.

n-ary relational terms have the following syntax.

$$Z \mid \lambda z[f] \mid \mu Z[L]$$

Here Z is an n-ary predicate variable in Σ. $\mu Z[L]$ is the *least fixed point* of an n-ary relation term L. A relational term L is *formally monotone* in the predicate variable Z if all free occurrences of Z in L fall under an even number of negations.

The truth value of a formula is determined with respect to a *structure* $\mathcal{M} = (D, I_L, I_D)$ where D is a non-empty set called the *domain* of the structure, I_L is the *relational variable interpretation* and I_D is the *individual variable interpretation*. We let $\mathcal{I}_D$ to be the set of possible individual variable interpretations. Let $\mathcal{I}_L$ be similarly defined.

The semantic function $\mathcal{D}$ maps formulas to elements of

$$(\mathcal{I}_L \rightarrow (\mathcal{I}_D \rightarrow \{true, false\}))$$

and n-ary relational terms to elements of

$$(\mathcal{I}_L \rightarrow (\mathcal{I}_D \rightarrow 2^{(D^n)}))$$

The semantic function $\mathcal{D}$ is defined inductively on the structure of formulas and relational terms.

$$\mathcal{D}([z_1 = z_2])(I_L)(I_D) \stackrel{\text{def}}{=} (I_D(z_1) = I_D(z_2))$$
$$\mathcal{D}(\neg f)(I_L)(I_D) \stackrel{\text{def}}{=} \neg(\mathcal{D}(f)(I_L)(I_D))$$
$$\mathcal{D}(f_1 \vee f_2)(I_L)(I_D) \stackrel{\text{def}}{=} \mathcal{D}(f_1)(I_L)(I_D) \vee \mathcal{D}(f_2)(I_L)(I_D)$$
$$\mathcal{D}(\exists z[f])(I_L)(I_D) \stackrel{\text{def}}{=} \exists e \in D.[\mathcal{D}(f)(I_L)(I_D \langle z \leftarrow e \rangle)]$$
$$\mathcal{D}(L(z_1, \ldots, z_n))(I_L)(I_D) \stackrel{\text{def}}{=} \langle I_D(z_1), \ldots, I_D(z_n) \rangle \in \mathcal{D}(L)(I_L)(I_D)$$
$$\mathcal{D}(Z)(I_L)(I_D) \stackrel{\text{def}}{=} I_L(Z)$$
$$\mathcal{D}(\lambda z[f])(I_L)(I_D) \stackrel{\text{def}}{=} \{\langle e_1, \ldots, e_n \rangle \mid \mathcal{D}(f)(I_L)(I_D \langle z_1 \leftarrow e_1, \ldots, z_n \leftarrow e_n \rangle)\}$$
$$\mathcal{D}(\mu Z[L]) \stackrel{\text{def}}{=} \text{lfp } \lambda Q \in 2^{(D^n)}.[\mathcal{D}(L)(I_L \langle Z \leftarrow Q \rangle)(I_D)]$$

where lfp denotes the least fixed point over the inclusion ordering. It is clear from elementary fixed-point theory that the requirement that L be formally monotone in Z is sufficient to ensure the existence of the fixed point in the last definition above.

Given a formula S in the μ-calculus, it has been shown in [5] that if we know the reduced BDD for the subformulas of S, then there is an efficient algorithm to produce the reduced BDD of S. So, the main concern in this paper is to show how to rewrite the formulas in MTCTL in the μ-calculus.

3 Multiclock Continuously Timed Automaton

We shall describe the behavior of distributed real-time systems by *Multiclock Continuously Timed Automata (MCTA)*. Unlike Timed Safety Automata[11], we allow an array Ω of m clocks $\Omega_1, \ldots, \Omega_m$ for an m-clock MCTA. The readings of the clocks in Ω increase continuously (in the domain of the real numbers) at independent speeds and the clocks cannot be reset. To specify timeouts etc., we have a set R of register arrays and each register array also has m elements. We allow the contents of all the elements in a register array to be set simultaneously to the corresponding readings of the clocks in Ω. This "set" operation is called *"freezing"* and is performed independently for each register array in R when the corresponding transition is taken.

Definition 1 *State predicate.* Given a set P of propositions and a register array set R for an m-clock system, the syntax of a *state predicate* H on P and R is defined in the following way.

$$H \quad ::= \quad p \mid \mathbf{x}_i + c \leq \mathbf{y}_i + d \mid \neg H_1 \mid H_1 \vee H_2$$

Here $p \in P$, $\mathbf{x}, \mathbf{y} \in R \cup \{\Omega\}$, $1 \leq i \leq m$, and c and d are natural numbers. Parentheses may be used for disambiguation. In particular, we call a state predicate of the form $\mathbf{x}_i + c \leq \mathbf{y}_i + d$ an *inequality predicate*. □

The following abbreviation is also used.

$$
\begin{aligned}
true &\equiv \Omega_1 \leq \Omega_1 \\
false &\equiv \neg false \\
\mathbf{x}_i + c \geq \mathbf{y}_i + d &\equiv \mathbf{y}_i + d \leq \mathbf{x}_i + c \\
\mathbf{x}_i + c < \mathbf{y}_i + d &\equiv \neg(\mathbf{x}_i + c \geq \mathbf{y}_i + d) \\
\mathbf{x}_i + c > \mathbf{y}_i + d &\equiv \neg(\mathbf{x}_i + c \leq \mathbf{y}_i + d) \\
\mathbf{x}_i + c = \mathbf{y}_i + d &\equiv \mathbf{x}_i + c \leq \mathbf{y}_i + d \wedge \mathbf{x}_i + c \geq \mathbf{y}_i + d \\
H_1 \wedge H_2 &\equiv \neg((\neg H_1) \vee (\neg H_2)) \\
H_1 \rightarrow H_2 &\equiv (\neg H_1) \vee H_2 \\
H_1 \leftrightarrow H_2 &\equiv (H_1 \rightarrow H_2) \wedge (H_2 \rightarrow H_1)
\end{aligned}
$$

Note that unlike in [17], here we disallow the comparison of readings between two different clocks in an inequality. This simplifies the verification algorithm, but is also compatible with a novel model for distributed real-time systems. We shall elaborate on this later in section 6.

Definition 2 *Multiclock Continuously Timed Automaton (MCTA).* An MCTA is an octuple $(Q, q_0, m, \Omega, R, P, \nu, \tau)$ where
- Q is the set of meta-states;
- q_0 is the initial meta-state;
- m is the number of local clocks used in the automaton;
- Ω is the single clock array of m local clocks;
- R is a register array set such that $\Omega \notin R$;
- P is the set of propositions;
- ν is a function labelling each meta-state with a state predicate on P and R such that $\nu(q_0)$ implies $\bigwedge_{\mathbf{x} \in R; 1 \leq i \leq m}(\mathbf{x}_i = \Omega_i)$;
- τ is a function such that for all $\hat{q}_1, \hat{q}_2 \in Q$, $\tau(\hat{q}_1, \hat{q}_2)$ is a finite subset of
$$\{(\hat{H}, \hat{R}) \mid \hat{H} \text{ is a state predicate on } P \text{ and } R, \hat{R} \subseteq R\}$$
and if $(\hat{H}, \hat{R}) \in \tau(\hat{q}_1, \hat{q}_2)$, then there is a transition from meta-state $\hat{q}_1$ to $\hat{q}_2$ such that
    - the enabling condition is $\hat{H}$, and
    - as a result of the transition, the content of Ω are frozen in the register arrays in $\hat{R}$.

Note that the proposition values change only as a result of transitions. However, in a particular meta-state, the corresponding state predicate determined by ν must be satisfied.

At the beginning of execution of an MCTA, we require that for all $\mathbf{x} \in R$ and $1 \leq i \leq m$, $\mathbf{x}_i$ has the same reading as Ω_i. This is enforced by the requirement on $\nu(q_0)$. □

Example 1. Fig.1 illustrates a 2-clock MCTA with $Q = \{q_0, q_1, q_2\}$, $P = \{a, b, c\}$, and $R = \{\mathbf{x}, \mathbf{y}\}$. At each transition, we label a set of pairs of enabling condition and the set of register arrays in which the content of Ω are frozen (updated in a transition). □

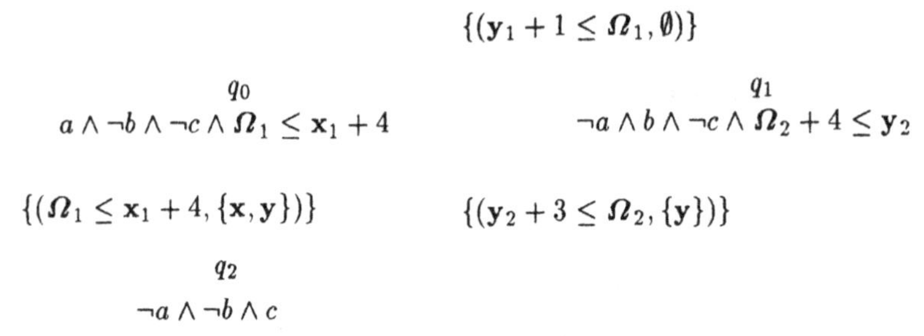

$$\{(\mathbf{y}_1 + 1 \leq \Omega_1, \emptyset)\}$$

q_0 $\qquad\qquad\qquad\qquad\qquad\qquad$ q_1

$a \wedge \neg b \wedge \neg c \wedge \Omega_1 \leq \mathbf{x}_1 + 4$ $\qquad\qquad$ $\neg a \wedge b \wedge \neg c \wedge \Omega_2 + 4 \leq \mathbf{y}_2$

$\{(\Omega_1 \leq \mathbf{x}_1 + 4, \{\mathbf{x}, \mathbf{y}\})\}$ $\qquad\qquad$ $\{(\mathbf{y}_2 + 3 \leq \Omega_2, \{\mathbf{y}\})\}$

q_2

$\neg a \wedge \neg b \wedge c$

Fig. 1. An MCTA example illustration

There are three main differences between MCTA and Timed Safety Automaton[11]. First, we use an array of clocks whose reading can be frozen in register arrays, while Timed Safety Automata uses a set of clocks that can be reset independently. The two approaches (freezing vs. reset) are equivalent and can simulate each other. We use the registers because they seem to be more concise for specification purposes and more convenient for formulating our algorithm.

Second, we get rid of the traditional tuple of automata which labels each $q \in Q$ with a set of propositions. However, we can incorporate this labelling function in ν which is a more general function than the traditional proposition-labelling function.

Third, we consider each transition as a set of pairs of enabling condition and the register array set to be updated during the transition. Thus the same transition triggered by different enabling conditions may set different register arrays.

Definition 3 *State.* Given an MCTA $A = (Q, q_0, m, \Omega, R, P, \nu, \tau)$, a *state* of A is a mapping from

$$P \cup \{\mathbf{x}_i \mid \mathbf{x} \in R \cup \{\Omega\}, 1 \leq i \leq m\}$$

such that

- for all $p \in P$, $\phi(p) \in \{true, false\}$; and

- for all $\mathbf{x} \in R \cup \{\Omega\}$ and $1 \leq i \leq m$, $\phi(\mathbf{x}_i)$ is a real number.

Given an array δ of m real numbers, we use $\phi + \delta$ to denote the state that

- for all $p \in P$, $(\phi + \delta)(p) = \phi(p)$;
- $(\phi + \delta)(\Omega_i) = \phi(\Omega_i) + \delta_i$ for all $1 \leq i \leq m$; and
- for all $\mathbf{x} \in R$ and $1 \leq i \leq m$, $(\phi + \delta)(\mathbf{x}_i) = \phi(\mathbf{x}_i)$.

We use $\phi R'$, where $R' \subseteq R$, to denote the state such that

- for all $p \in P$, $(\phi R')(p) = \phi(p)$;
- for all $1 \leq i \leq m$, $(\phi R')(\Omega_i) = \phi(\Omega_i)$; and
- for all $\mathbf{x} \in R$ and $1 \leq i \leq m$, if $\mathbf{x} \notin R'$, then $(\phi R')(\mathbf{x}_i) = \phi(\mathbf{x}_i)$, else $(\phi R')(\mathbf{x}_i) = \phi(\Omega_i)$.

□

Intuitively $\phi + \delta$ is the state that we get from ϕ through the advancement of the clocks $\Omega_1, \ldots, \Omega_m$ by, respectively, $\delta_1, \ldots, \delta_m$ time units, with no change to the proposition values and the contents of the register arrays. $\phi R'$ is the state that we get from ϕ by setting the register arrays in R' to the current readings of the clocks.

Given a state predicate H and a state ϕ of an MCTA $A = (Q, q_0, m, \Omega, R, P, \nu, \tau)$, we define $\phi \models H$, (i.e. ϕ *satisfies* H), in the following way.

- $\phi \models true$.
- $\phi \not\models false$.
- $\phi \models p$ iff $\phi(p) = true$.
- $\phi \models \mathbf{x}_i + c \leq \mathbf{y}_i + d$ iff $\mathbf{x}, \mathbf{y} \in R \cup \{\Omega\}$, $1 \leq i \leq m$, and $\phi(\mathbf{x}_i) + c \leq \phi(\mathbf{y}_i) + d$.
- $\phi \models \neg H_1$ iff it is not the case that $\phi \models H_1$.
- $\phi \models H_1 \vee H_2$ iff either $\phi \models H_1$ or $\phi \models H_2$.

Given an MCTA $A = (Q, q_0, m, \Omega, R, P, \nu, \tau)$, we say A is *well-defined* iff for every state ϕ of A, there is at most one meta-state $q \in Q$ such that $\phi \models \nu(q)$. An MCTA that is not well-defined can always be transformed into a well-defined one by including in the state predicate P the Boolean variables that encode the names of the meta-states. ¿From now on, we assume that all given MCTAs are well-defined.

Definition 4 *A Run for MCTA and its partitions.* Given an MCTA $A = (Q, q_0, m, \Omega, R, P, \nu, \tau)$, a *run* ρ for A is a mapping from nonnegative real numbers to states of A such that

1. for all integers $1 \leq i \leq m$ and real numbers $t' > t \geq 0$, $(\rho(t'))(\Omega_i) > (\rho(t))(\Omega_i)$;
2. for all real number $r \geq 0$ and integers $1 \leq i \leq m$, there is a real number t such that $(\rho(t))(\Omega_i) = (\rho(0))(\Omega_i) + r$; and
3. there exist
   - a nondecreasing divergent real number sequence $t_0 t_1 t_2 \ldots \ldots$, with $t_0 = 0$;
   - an infinite state sequence $\hat{\phi}_0 \hat{\phi}_1 \hat{\phi}_2 \ldots \ldots$; and
   - an infinite meta-state sequence $\hat{q}_0 \hat{q}_1 \hat{q}_2 \ldots \ldots$

   such that for all integers $k \geq 0$,

   a. for all $t_k \leq t \leq t_{k+1}$, $\hat{\phi}_k + \langle (\rho(t))(\Omega_i) - \hat{\phi}_k(\Omega_i) \rangle_{1 \leq i \leq m} \models \nu(q_k)$;

   b. for all $t_k \leq t < t_{k+1}$, $\rho(t) = \hat{\phi}_k + \langle (\rho(t))(\Omega_i) - \hat{\phi}_k(\Omega_i) \rangle_{1 \leq i \leq m}$; and

   c. if $\hat{\phi}_k + \langle \hat{\phi}_{k+1}(\Omega_i) - \hat{\phi}_k(\Omega_i) \rangle_{1 \leq i \leq m} \neq \hat{\phi}_{k+1}$, there is a $(\hat{H}, \hat{R}) \in \tau(\hat{q}_k, \hat{q}_{k+1})$ such that

       i. $\hat{\phi}_k + \langle \hat{\phi}_{k+1}(\Omega_i) - \hat{\phi}_k(\Omega_i) \rangle_{1 \leq i \leq m} \models \hat{H}$, and

ii. $\hat{\phi}_{k+1}(\mathbf{x}_i) = ((\hat{\phi}_k + \langle \hat{\phi}_{k+1}(\Omega_i) - \hat{\phi}_k(\Omega_i) \rangle_{1 \le i \le m}) \hat{R})(\mathbf{x}_i)$ for all $\mathbf{x} \in R$ and $1 \le i \le m$.

Given a run ρ and such three sequences $t_0 t_1 \ldots, \hat{\phi}_0 \hat{\phi}_1 \ldots$, and $\hat{q}_0 \hat{q}_1 \ldots$ for ρ as stipulated in condition 3 above, we call the triple $(t_0 t_1 \ldots, \hat{\phi}_0 \hat{\phi}_1 \ldots, \hat{q}_0 \hat{q}_1 \ldots)$ a *partition* for ρ. □

Intuitively, condition 1 of Definition 4 says that the readings of all clocks are strictly increasing as time progresses.

Condition 2 says that for $1 \le i \le m$, Ω_i must go through every real number $\ge (\rho(0))(\Omega_i)$. This implies two things; the readings of all clocks are *divergent* and the reading of each clock must take on every real number that is greater than its reading at system-start time. The divergence requirement means that for every real number r, there is a nonnegative real number t such that for all $1 \le i \le m$, $(\rho(0))(\Omega_i) + r \le (\rho(t))(\Omega_i)$. Due to the progressiveness of time, only divergent runs are of interest to us.

Condition 3 means that ρ can be divided into infinitely many intervals. For every integer $k \ge 0$, interval k is defined to be $[t_k, t_{k+1})$. Condition 3.a means that the states in the same interval are in the same meta-state. Condition 3.b says that the state changes in the same interval are due to the mere passage of time and not because of meta-state transitions. Condition 3.c says that if between intervals the state change is not caused by the mere passage of time, then it is caused by meta-state transitions. Note the relation between condition 3.a when $t = t_{k+1}$ and 3.c.i. In condition 3.a we allow $t = t_{k+1}$ because we do not want the meta-state transition to be fired when $\nu(\hat{q}_k)$ is violated.

The divergence requirement on $t_0 t_1 t_2 \ldots \ldots$ means that there are infinitely many intervals in each run and the intervals cover the entire future. The nondecreasing requirement, together with the divergence requirement on $t_0 t_1 t_2 \ldots \ldots$ means that we may have an unbound but finite number of transitions happening at the same time instant. For all $k > h \ge 0$, if $t_h = t_{h+1} = \cdots = t_k < t_{k+1}$, then it means that at time t_h, there is a sequence of instantaneous meta-state transitions through $\hat{q}_h, \hat{q}_{h+1}, \ldots, \hat{q}_k$, and we call $\hat{\phi}_h, \ldots \hat{\phi}_{k-1}$ the *instantaneous states* for the partition $(t_0 t_1 \ldots, \hat{\phi}_0 \hat{\phi}_1 \ldots, \hat{q}_0 \hat{q}_1 \ldots)$. Conceptually these meta-state transitions are temporally ordered but happen at the same instant and the automaton stablizes at meta-state $\hat{q}_k$ for the interval $[t_k, t_{k+1})$.

Note that a run by itself is an incomplete description of an MCTA execution because it does not record the instantaneous states. On the other hand, a run and a partition for it together constitute a complete description of an MCTA execution.

4 Multiclock Timed Computation Tree Logic

4.1 Syntax

The syntax of an MTCTL formula S for an MCTA $A = (Q, q_0, m, \Omega, R, P, \nu, \tau)$ is defined below.

$$S ::= H \mid \neg S_1 \mid S_1 \vee S_2 \mid \mathbf{x}.S_1 \mid \exists S_1 \mathcal{U} S_2 \mid \exists \Box S_1$$

where H is a state predicate and $\mathbf{x} \in R$. The notion of *free* and *bound* variables are as in first order logic. The symbols $\exists \mathcal{U}$ and $\exists \Box$ correspond respectively, to the *EU* and *EG* modal operators in [8]. That is, $\exists$ means "there exists a future", $\mathcal{U}$ means "until", and $\Box$ means "from now on forever". Parentheses may be used for disambiguation. The following shorthands are also used.

$$\exists \Diamond S_1 \equiv \exists \, true \, \mathcal{U} S_1$$
$$\forall \Box S_1 \equiv \neg \exists \Diamond \neg S_1$$
$$\forall \Diamond S_1 \equiv \neg \exists \Box \neg S_1$$
$$\forall S_1 \mathcal{U} S_2 \equiv \neg((\exists \neg S_2 \mathcal{U} \neg(S_1 \vee S_2)) \vee (\exists \Box \neg S_2))$$
$$S_1 \wedge S_2 \equiv \neg((\neg S_1) \vee (\neg S_2))$$
$$S_1 \rightarrow S_2 \equiv (\neg S_1) \vee S_2$$
$$S_1 \leftrightarrow S_2 \equiv (S_1 \rightarrow S_2) \wedge (S_2 \rightarrow S_1)$$

Note that in MTCTL, we do not have a *next* modal operator like the one introduced in [11].

Given an MTCTL formula S, the *subformulas* of S are defined in the following way.

- S and *true* are two trivial subformulas of S.
- If any one of $\neg S_1$, $\mathbf{x}.S_1$, and $\exists \Box S_1$ is a subformula of S, then S_1 is a subformula of S.
- If either $S_1 \vee S_2$ or $\exists S_1 \mathcal{U} S_2$ is a subformula of S, then both S_1 and S_2 are subformulas of S.

4.2 Semantics

Given an MTCTL formula S and a state ϕ of an MCTA $A = (Q, q_0, m, \Omega, R, P, \nu, \tau)$, we define the notion that $\phi \models S$, i.e. ϕ *satisfies* S, in the following way.

- If S is a state predicate, then $\phi \models S$ iff ϕ satisfies S as a state predicate.
- $\phi \models \neg S_1$ iff it is not the case that $\phi \models S_1$.
- $\phi \models S_1 \vee S_2$ iff either $\phi \models S_1$ or $\phi \models S_2$.
- $\phi \models \mathbf{x}.S_1$ iff $\phi\{\mathbf{x}\} \models S_1$.
- $\phi \models \exists S_1 \mathcal{U} S_2$ iff there is a run ρ of A and a partition $(t_0 t_1 \ldots, \hat{\phi}_0 \hat{\phi}_1 \ldots, \hat{q}_0 \hat{q}_1 \ldots)$ for ρ such that
  - $\hat{\phi}_0 = \phi$; and
  - there is an integer $k \geq 0$ such that
    * $\hat{\phi}_k \models S_2$;
    * for every integer $0 \leq h < k$, $\hat{\phi}_h \models S_1$; and
    * for every real number $0 \leq t < t_k$, $\rho(t) \models S_1$.
- $\phi \models \exists \Box S_1$ iff there is a run ρ of A and a partition $(t_0 t_1 \ldots, \hat{\phi}_0 \hat{\phi}_1 \ldots, \hat{q}_0 \hat{q}_1 \ldots)$ for ρ such that
  - $\hat{\phi}_0 = \phi$;
  - for every integer $k \geq 0$, $\hat{\phi}_k \models S_1$; and
  - for every real number $t \geq 0$, $\rho(t) \models S_1$.

Given an MTCTL formula S and an MCTA $A = (Q, q_0, m, \Omega, R, P, \nu, \tau)$, we say that A satisfies S, hence is a *model* for S, iff there is a state $\phi \models \nu(q_0)$ and for all states ϕ' such that $\phi' \models \nu(q_0)$, $\phi' \models S$. $\qquad\qquad\Box$

In defining the semantics of $\exists S_1 \mathcal{U} S_2$, we require that "for every integer $0 \leq h < k$, $\hat{\phi}_h \models S_1$" in addition to "for every real number $0 \leq t < t_k$, $\rho(t) \models S_1$", because ρ by itself does not record the instantaneous states. We take care of those instantaneous states by considering a particular partition for ρ. The same holds for $\exists \Box S_1$.

There is one difference between the semantics of $x.S_1$ in our MTCTL and the $x.S_1$ in TCTL[1]. In [1], "x." means a *"reset"* operator and x must be a clock name not used in the automaton. In our version, x can be a register array actually used in the automaton and we treat "x." as a *"freezing assumption"* operator with the intended meaning "if we set x_i to the current reading of Ω_i for all $1 \leq i \leq m$, S_1 must be true".

4.3 Clock jitters and synchronization in MTCTL

Clock jitter is a phenomenon resulting from unstable clock speeds. In a distributed system, clock jitter may be manifested by a time-varying but bounded ratio between the ticking rates of two clocks at different sites of the system. In [17], we proposed a modelling technique to formally specify this phenomenon and the corresponding synchronization specification. MTCTL also has the expressive power to describe the clock jitter phenomenon. For example, in a two-clock system, $\exists \Box x.\forall \Box y.(x_1 + 1 = y_1 \rightarrow x_2 + 3 \leq y_2)$ specifies that there is a run such that for every interval of one time unit according to the first clock, the second clock must have its reading incremented thrice.

5 Symbolic model checking for MTCTL against MCTA

Given an MCTA A and an MTCTL formula S, our goal is to translate S with respect to A into a μ-calculus formula f such that S is satisfied by A iff f is true.

In subsection 5.1, we shall show how to partition the infinite state space into a finite number of state regions. The finiteness of the number of state regions means that we can express the consistency requirement on a state region and state transitions among state regions in the μ-calculus. In subsection 5.2, we shall show how to describe the state transitions among state regions. In subsection 5.3, we express the MTCTL formulas in the μ-calculus. Subsection 5.4 discusses some implementation optimization techniques for the algorithm.

5.1 State regions

The key idea of our new symbolic model checking algorithm is also based on the concept of the region graph in [1]. Given a state ϕ in the Timed Safety Automata, the future behavior of the system will be affected only by the

- proposition values,
- the integral parts of the readings of the clocks, and
- the linear order among the fractional parts of the readings of the clocks,

as noted in [1], Also, if a clock reading is bigger than the biggest constant used in the Timed Automaton and the TCTL formula[1], then only the Boolean values of the corresponding inequalities are relevant. This observation is the key to the recognition of the finite representability of the state space.

Similarly for our MCTA and MTCTL formulas, each region corresponds to a class of states, and the state space is partitioned into a finite number of regions. The states in each region will exhibit the same behavior. The number of states is infinite for MTCTL structures, but the number of state regions is finite. We shall use a region as sort of a super-state and perform model checking on the region graph. This is accomplished by constructing the following finite representation of the states, i.e., *state regions*. A state region roughly corresponds to a region in [1].

Given an MCTA A and an MTCTL formula S, we define

$$C_A^S = \max(\{0\} \cup \left\{ c \left| \begin{array}{l} c \text{ is an integer constant in the} \\ \text{inequality predicates of } A \text{ and } S \end{array} \right. \right\}$$

and we call

$$P \cup \left\{ \mathbf{x}_i + c \leq \mathbf{y}_i + d \,\middle|\, \mathbf{x}, \mathbf{y} \in R; 1 \leq i \leq m; 0 \leq c, d \leq C_A^S \right\}$$

the *atom set* of A and S. Since c and d are integer constants (recall the notation at the end of section 1), so this set is of finite size. For convenience, we shall assume that $C_A^S \geq 1$.

Definition 5 *State region.* Given an MCTA $A = (Q, q_0, m, \Omega, R, P, \nu, \tau)$, a state ϕ of A, and an MTCTL formula S, the *state region* of ϕ for S, denoted as ϕ^S, is the following set.

$$\{p \,|\, p \in P; \phi \models p\} \cup \left\{ \mathbf{x}_i + c \leq \mathbf{y}_i + d \,\middle|\, \begin{array}{l} \mathbf{x}, \mathbf{y} \in R \cup \{\Omega\}; 0 \leq c, d \leq C_A^S; \\ 1 \leq i \leq m; \phi \models \mathbf{x}_i + c \leq \mathbf{y}_i + d \end{array} \right\}$$

□

We can show the following key lemma.

Lemma. *Given an MCTA $A = (Q, q_0, m, \Omega, R, P, \nu, \tau)$, an MTCTL formula S, and two states ϕ_1 and ϕ_2 such that $\phi_1^S = \phi_2^S$, then $\phi_1 \models S$ iff $\phi_2 \models S$.*

Proof. The proof is similar to the proof for the first lemma in section 5 of [1]. □

Given a state predicate H, we can similarly define the satisfaction of H by a state region ϕ^S for an MTCTL formula S and an MCTA A in the following way.
- $\phi^S \models p$ iff $p \in \phi^S$.
- $\phi^S \models \mathbf{x}_i + c \leq \mathbf{y}_i + d$ iff $\mathbf{x}_i + c \leq \mathbf{y}_i + d \in \phi^S$.
- $\phi^S \models \neg H_1$ iff it is not the case that $\phi^S \models H_1$.
- $\phi^S \models H_1 \vee H_2$ iff either $\phi^S \models H_1$ or $\phi^S \models H_2$.

Given an MCTA A and an MTCTL formula S, a state region is a subset of the atom set of A and S. Of course, not all subsets are legitimate state regions. The following rules are enough to check whether a subset ψ represents a legitimate state region.
- The state region must be in one of the meta-states, that is $\psi \models \bigvee_{q \in Q} \nu(q)$.
- Also the usual arithmetic axioms for real numbers must also hold.
  - In comparing a real number with another, at least one of the "$\leq$" and "$\geq$" relations must hold. That is, for all $1 \leq i \leq m$,

$$\psi \models \bigwedge_{\substack{x,y \in R \cup \{\Omega\} \\ 0 \le c,d \le C_A^S}} (x_i + c \le y_i + d \vee y_i + d \le x_i + c)$$

- The ordering of integers must hold. That is, for all $1 \le i \le m$,

$$\psi \models \bigwedge_{x \in R \cup \{\Omega\}} \left(\begin{array}{c} \bigwedge_{0 \le c \le d \le C_A^S} x_i + c \le x_i + d \\ \wedge \bigwedge_{0 \le c < d \le C_A^S} \neg(x_i + d \le x_i + c) \end{array} \right)$$

- The transitivity law must hold. That is, for all $1 \le i \le m$,

$$\psi \models \bigwedge_{\substack{x,y,z \in R \cup \{\Omega\} \\ 0 \le c,d,e \le C_A^S}} ((x_i + c \le y_i + d \wedge y_i + d \le z_i + e) \longrightarrow x_i + c \le z_i + e)$$

- Adding the same constant to two sides of an inequality does not change its truth value. That is, for all $1 \le i \le m$,

$$\psi \models \bigwedge_{\substack{x,y \in R \cup \{\Omega\} \\ 0 \le c \le C_A^S \\ 0 \le d \le C_A^S - c}} \left(\begin{array}{c} (x_i + c \le y_i \longleftrightarrow x_i + c + d \le y_i + d) \\ \wedge (x_i \le y_i + c \longleftrightarrow x_i + d \le y_i + c + d) \end{array} \right)$$

This can be expressed as the μ-calculus relational term *legit* shown in Table 1. Thus

$$legit \equiv \lambda s \left[\left[\left(\begin{array}{c} \left(\bigvee_{q \in Q} \nu(q) \right) \\ \\ \wedge \bigwedge_{\substack{x,y \in R \cup \{\Omega\} \\ 0 \le c,d \le C_A^S}} (x_i + c \le y_i + d \vee y_i + d \le x_i + c) \\ \\ \wedge \bigwedge_{x \in R \cup \{\Omega\}} \left(\begin{array}{c} \bigwedge_{0 \le c \le d \le C_A^S} x_i + c \le x_i + d \\ \wedge \bigwedge_{0 \le c < d \le C_A^S} \neg(x_i + d \le x_i + c) \end{array} \right) \\ \\ \wedge \bigwedge_{1 \le i \le m} \wedge \bigwedge_{\substack{x,y,z \in R \cup \{\Omega\} \\ 0 \le c,d,e \le C_A^S}} \left(\begin{array}{c} \left(\begin{array}{c} x_i + c \le y_i + d \\ \wedge y_i + d \le z_i + e \end{array} \right) \\ \rightarrow x_i + c \le z_i + e \end{array} \right) \\ \\ \wedge \bigwedge_{\substack{x,y \in R \cup \{\Omega\} \\ 0 \le c \le C_A^S \\ 0 \le d \le C_A^S - c}} \wedge \left(\begin{array}{c} x_i + c \le y_i \leftrightarrow \\ x_i + c + d \le y_i + d \\ x_i \le y_i + c \leftrightarrow \\ x_i + d \le y_i + c + d \end{array} \right) \end{array} \right) \right]\right] (s)$$

Table 1. The μ-calculus relational term for *legit*

given a subset ψ of the atom set of A and S, $legit(\psi)$ is true iff ψ is a legitimate state region of a state of A for S.

5.2 Characterization of the transitions among state regions

Given a state ϕ and a register set $R' \subseteq R$, it is possible to compute $(\phi R')^S$ symbolically from ϕ^S and R'. The idea can be illustrated as follows. If we are given an inequality $x_i + c \le y_i + d \in \phi^S$ with $x \in R'$ and $y \notin R'$, then $x_i + c \le y_i + d \in (\phi R')^S$ iff $\Omega_i + c \le y_i + d \in \phi^S$ since at the freezing operation, we set x to Ω. Accordingly, we define the μ-calculus relational term $freeze_{R'}$ in Table 2 for each $R' \subseteq R$ to embody this idea. It can be shown that given ϕ_1, ϕ_2, and $R' \subseteq R$, $\phi_2^S = (\phi_1 R')^S$ iff $freeze_{R'}(\phi_1^S, \phi_2^S)$ and $\forall p \in P(p \in \phi_1^S \leftrightarrow p \in \phi_2^S)$.

$$
\textit{freeze}_{R'} \equiv \lambda s_1 \left[\lambda s_2 \left[\bigwedge_{\substack{1 \le i \le m \\ 0 \le c,d \le C_A^S}} \left(\begin{array}{l} \bigwedge_{\mathbf{x},\mathbf{y} \in R'} \left(\begin{array}{l} (\Omega_i + c \le \Omega_i + d)(s_1) \\ \leftrightarrow (\mathbf{x}_i + c \le \mathbf{y}_i + d)(s_2) \end{array} \right) \\ \land \bigwedge_{\mathbf{x} \in R', \mathbf{y} \notin R'} \left(\begin{array}{l} (\Omega_i + c \le \mathbf{y}_i + d)(s_1) \\ \leftrightarrow (\mathbf{x}_i + c \le \mathbf{y}_i + d)(s_2) \end{array} \right) \\ \land \bigwedge_{\mathbf{x} \notin R', \mathbf{y} \in R'} \left(\begin{array}{l} (\mathbf{x}_i + c \le \Omega_i + d)(s_1) \\ \leftrightarrow (\mathbf{x}_i + c \le \mathbf{y}_i + d)(s_2) \end{array} \right) \\ \land \bigwedge_{\mathbf{x},\mathbf{y} \notin R'} \left(\begin{array}{l} (\mathbf{x}_i + c \le \mathbf{y}_i + d)(s_1) \\ \leftrightarrow (\mathbf{x}_i + c \le \mathbf{y}_i + d)(s_2) \end{array} \right) \end{array} \right) \right] \right]
$$

Table 2. The μ-calculus relational term for $\textit{freeze}_{R'}$

Given a state ϕ, it is also possible to compute $(\phi + \delta)^S$ symbolically from ϕ^S such that δ is either $\langle 0 \rangle_{1 \le i \le m}$ or a *minimal* nonnegative real number array with the property that $\phi^S \ne (\phi + \delta)^S$. δ is minimal in the sense that if there is a $\delta' \ne \delta$ such that $\phi^S \ne (\phi + \delta')^S$, then $\exists 1 \le i \le m(\delta_i < \delta'_i)$. This computation gives us back the new state region that could be entered simply by the passage of time without the firing of any meta-state transitions. We shall derive the μ-calculus relational term adv such that for any two given states ϕ_1 and ϕ_2, $(\phi_1 + \delta)^S = \phi_2^S$ with such a δ iff $adv(\phi_1^S, \phi_2^S)$. We construct adv as the conjunction $adv_1 \land adv_2 \land adv_3 \land \bigwedge_{p \in P}(p \in \phi_1^S \leftrightarrow p \in \phi_2^S)$. The conjunct $\bigwedge_{p \in P}(p \in \phi_1^S \leftrightarrow p \in \phi_2^S)$ is used to check that the proposition values remain unchanged since there is no meta-state transition. The conjuncts adv_1, adv_2, and adv_3 are used to check that the inequalities change their Boolean values consistently and are explained below.

The passage of time by itself can only change the values of those inequalities that compare register contents with clock readings. This is captured by adv_1 which is given in Table 3 in terms of the μ-calculus.

$$
adv_1 \equiv \lambda s_1 \left[\lambda s_2 \left[\bigwedge_{\substack{\mathbf{x},\mathbf{y} \in R \\ 1 \le i \le m \\ 0 \le c,d \le C_A^S}} ((\mathbf{x}_i + c \le \mathbf{y}_i + d)(s_1) \leftrightarrow (\mathbf{x}_i + c \le \mathbf{y}_i + d)(s_2)) \right] \right]
$$

Table 3. The μ-calculus relational term for adv_1

To make the constructions of adv_2 and adv_3 clear, we define that at every state ϕ, $\Delta_{\mathbf{x}_i} = \phi(\Omega_i) - \phi(\mathbf{x}_i)$, i.e., $\Delta_{\mathbf{x}_i}$ is the difference between the reading of Ω_i and the content of $\mathbf{x}_i$, for all $\mathbf{x} \in R$ and $1 \le i \le m$.

Since all timing constraints are specified by integer constants, this means that the system will remain in the same state region through the mere passage of time unless for some $\mathbf{x}_i$, $\Delta_{\mathbf{x}_i}$ either

(1) increases from an integer in $[0, C_A^S]$ to a non-integer; or

(2) increases from a non-integer to an integer in $[0, \mathcal{C}_A^S]$.

Notice that these two conditions are mutually exclusive. Condition (1) will occur due to the mere passage of time iff there is an $\mathbf{x}_i$ such that $\Delta_{\mathbf{x}_i}$ is an integer in $[0, \mathcal{C}_A^S]$. Condition (2) will occur due to the mere passage of time iff there is no such register. This follows from the density of the real numbers. Thus we can tell whether condition (1) will occur or not due to the mere passage of time by evaluating the Boolean value of the following state predicate.

$$int \equiv \lambda s \left[\bigvee_{z \in R; 1 \le i \le m; 0 \le e \le C_A^S} (z_i + e = \Omega_i)(s) \right]$$

Condition (1) is captured by adv_2 which is shown in Table 4 in terms of the μ-calculus.

$$adv_2 \equiv \lambda s_1 \left[\lambda s_2 \left[\begin{array}{l} int(s_1) \\ \rightarrow \bigwedge_{1 \le i \le m} \left(\begin{array}{l} \bigwedge_{\substack{\mathbf{x} \in R \\ 0 \le c \le C_A^S}} \left(\begin{array}{l} (\mathbf{x}_i + c \le \Omega_i)(s_1) \\ \leftrightarrow (\mathbf{x}_i + c < \Omega_i)(s_2) \end{array} \right) \\ \wedge \bigwedge_{\substack{\mathbf{y} \in R \\ 0 \le d \le C_A^S}} \left(\begin{array}{l} (\Omega_i < \mathbf{y}_i + d)(s_1) \\ \leftrightarrow (\Omega_i < \mathbf{y}_i + d)(s_2) \end{array} \right) \\ \wedge \bigwedge_{\substack{\mathbf{x} \in R \\ 0 \le c \le C_A^S}} \left(\begin{array}{l} (\mathbf{x}_i + c = \Omega_i)(s_1) \\ \rightarrow (\mathbf{x}_i + c < \Omega_i)(s_2) \end{array} \right) \end{array} \right) \right] \right]$$

Table 4. The μ-calculus relational term for adv_2

At a state ϕ, we say that a register $\mathbf{x}_i$ is *interesting* iff $\Delta_{\mathbf{x}_i} \in [0, \mathcal{C}_A^S]$. When the condition (2) above occurs, for each $1 \le i \le m$, only the interesting register (there may be more than one), say $\mathbf{x}_i$, whose $\Delta_{\mathbf{x}_i}$ has the biggest fractional part $(\Delta_{\mathbf{x}_i} - \lfloor \Delta_{\mathbf{x}_i} \rfloor)$ among all interesting registers with subscript i, is elegible to have its $\Delta_{\mathbf{x}_i}$ advanced to a new integer in $[0, \mathcal{C}_A^S]$. To detect this eligibility for all registers $\mathbf{x}_i$ and integers $c \in [0, C_A^S]$, we use the following relational term $\max_{\mathbf{x}_i}^c$.

$$\max_{\mathbf{x}_i}^c \equiv \lambda s \left[\left(\begin{array}{l} \Omega_i < \mathbf{x}_i + c \wedge \Omega_i + 1 > \mathbf{x}_i + c \\ \wedge \bigwedge_{\substack{\mathbf{y} \in R \\ 0 \le d \le C_A^S}} \left(\left(\begin{array}{l} \Omega_i < \mathbf{y}_i + d \\ \wedge \Omega_i + 1 > \mathbf{y}_i + d \end{array} \right) \rightarrow \mathbf{x}_i + c \le \mathbf{y}_i + d \right) \end{array} \right) (s) \right]$$

Thus, at a state ϕ where $int(\phi^S)$ is false but $\max_{\mathbf{x}_i}^c$ is true, we know condition (2) is going to hold at ϕ due to the mere passage of time, and inequalities that compare Ω_i with $\mathbf{x}_i + c$ may change their Boolean values. Condition (2) is captured by the μ-calculus relational term adv_3 in Table 5. Note that under condition (2), the eligibility of $\Delta_{\mathbf{x}_i}$ to change to a new integer in $[0, \mathcal{C}_A^S]$ does not mean that it must happen. The only requirement is that for all $1 \le i \le m$, the same decision must be made for all eligible registers with subscript i.

Under the assumption of the well-definedness of a MCTA, we identify the relational term *edge* with the μ-calculus relational term shown in Table 6 which captures

$$adv_3 \equiv \lambda s_1 \left[\lambda s_2 \left[\bigwedge_{1 \le i \le m} \left[\begin{array}{l} (\neg int(s_1)) \rightarrow \\ \left(\begin{array}{l} \bigwedge_{\substack{y \in R \\ 0 \le d \le C_A^S}} \left(\begin{array}{l} (\Omega_i < y_i + d)(s_1) \\ \leftrightarrow (\Omega_i \le y_i + d)(s_2) \end{array} \right) \\ \wedge \bigwedge_{\substack{x \in R \\ 0 \le c \le C_A^S}} \left(\begin{array}{l} (x_i + c < \Omega_i)(s_1) \\ \leftrightarrow (x_i + c < \Omega_i)(s_2) \end{array} \right) \\ \wedge \bigwedge_{\substack{x, y \in R \\ 0 \le c, d \le C_A^S}} \left(\begin{array}{l} (max_{x_i}^c \wedge max_{y_i}^d)(s_1) \\ \rightarrow \left(\begin{array}{l} \Omega_i = x_i + c \\ \leftrightarrow \Omega_i = y_i + d \end{array} \right)(s_2) \end{array} \right) \\ \wedge \bigwedge_{\substack{y \in R \\ 0 \le d \le C_A^S}} \left(\begin{array}{l} (\Omega_i < y_i + d \wedge \neg max_{y_i}^d)(s_1) \\ \rightarrow (\Omega_i < y_i + d)(s_2) \end{array} \right) \end{array} \right) \end{array} \right] \right] \right]$$

Table 5. The μ-calculus relational term for adv_3

$$edge \equiv \lambda s_1 \left[\lambda s_2 \left[\begin{array}{l} legit(s_1) \\ \wedge \; legit(s_2) \\ \wedge \left(\begin{array}{l} adv(s_1, s_2) \\ \vee \bigvee_{\hat{q}_1, \hat{q}_2 \in Q} \left(\begin{array}{l} (\nu(\hat{q}_1))(s_1) \wedge (\nu(\hat{q}_2))(s_2) \\ \wedge \bigvee_{(\hat{H}, \hat{R}) \in \tau(\hat{q}_1, \hat{q}_2)} \left(\begin{array}{l} \hat{H}(s_1) \\ \wedge \; freeze_{\hat{R}}(s_1, s_2) \end{array} \right) \end{array} \right) \end{array} \right) \end{array} \right] \right]$$

Table 6. The μ-calculus relational term for $edge$

the transitions between states in different state regions. Given two subsets ψ_1 and ψ_2 of the atom set, $edge(\psi_1, \psi_2)$ is true iff both ψ_1 and ψ_2 are legitimate state regions and the following disjuction holds:

- ψ_1 is identical to ψ_2; or
- there is a state ϕ_1, whose state region is ψ_1, such that $(\phi_1 + \delta)^S = \psi_2$ for some minimal δ; or
- there are states ϕ_1 and ϕ_2, whose state regions are respectively ψ_1 and ψ_2, such that ϕ_2 is obtained from ϕ_1 through a meta-state transition.

5.3 The symbolic model checking algorithm

With all the building blocks assembled in the last two subsections, we are now ready to propose our symbolic model checking algorithm. Given an MCTA A and an MTCTL formula S, we want to translate S with respect to A into a μ-calculus formula f asserting requirements on the state regions. The satisfaction of S by A is then equivalent to the truth value of f.

Definition 6 *State region path.* Given an MTCTL formula S and an MCTA $A = (Q, q_0, m, \Omega, R, P, \nu, \tau)$, an infinite (a finite) *state region path* for S and A is an infinite (a finite) sequence of state regions for S and A, $\phi_0^S \phi_1^S \ldots \ldots (\phi_n^S)$, such that for all integers $k \ge 0$ ($0 \le k \le n$), $edge(\phi_k^S, \phi_{k+1}^S)$ is true (if $k < n$). $\quad\square$

It may happen that for a given MCTA, the specification may not be stringent enough to enforce the progressiveness of time. Thus we assume that for every automaton, there is a particular register array Ω' such that at every state ϕ,

- $\phi \models \bigvee_{1 \leq i \leq m} \Omega_i \leq \Omega'_i + 1$; and
- if $\phi \models \bigwedge_{1 \leq i \leq m} \Omega_i \geq \Omega'_i + 1$, then there is a transition from ϕ to $\phi\{\Omega'\}$.
  (Remember the notation in Definition 3.)

Given an arbitrary MCTA $A = (Q, q_0, m, \Omega, R, P, \nu, \tau)$ without such an Ω', we can always convert A to an MCTA $A' = (Q, q_0, m, \Omega, R', P, \nu', \tau')$ such that

- $R' = R \cup \{\Omega'\}$;
- $\nu'(q) = \nu(q) \wedge \bigvee_{1 \leq i \leq m} \Omega_i \leq \Omega'_i + 1$ for every $q \in Q$ with $q \neq q_0$;
- $\nu'(q_0) = \nu(q_0) \wedge \bigwedge_{1 \leq i \leq m} \Omega_i = \Omega'_i$;
- for every $\hat{q}_1, \hat{q}_2 \in Q$ with $\hat{q}_1 \neq \hat{q}_2$, $\tau'(\hat{q}_1, \hat{q}_2) = \tau(\hat{q}_1, \hat{q}_2)$; and
- for every $\hat{q} \in Q$, $\tau'(\hat{q}, \hat{q}) = \tau(\hat{q}, \hat{q}) \cup \{(\bigwedge_{1 \leq i \leq m} \Omega_i \geq \Omega'_i + 1, \{\Omega'\})\}$.

Then for A', the divergence of a run means that along the run, Ω' gets set infinitely often which is a fairness condition. ¿From now on, we assume that the automata we are interested in are the ones obtained from this conversion. Based on the observation, we now define the satisfaction of an MTCTL formula by a state region. Given two MTCTL formulas S and S_1, an MCTA $A = (Q, q_0, m, \Omega, R, P, \nu, \tau)$, and a state ϕ of A, we define the assertion that state region ϕ^S satisfies S_1, (written as $\phi^S \models S_1$) in the following way.

- If S_1 is a state predicate, then $\phi^S \models S_1$ iff ϕ^S satisfies S_1 as a state predicate.
- $\phi^S \models \neg S_1$ iff it is not the case that $\phi^S \models S_1$.
- $\phi^S \models S_1 \vee S_2$ iff either $\phi^S \models S_1$ or $\phi^S \models S_2$.
- $\phi^S \models \mathbf{x}.S_1$ iff there is a ϕ_1^S such that $freeze_{\{\mathbf{x}\}}(\phi^S, \phi_1^S) \wedge \forall p \in P(p \in \phi^S \leftrightarrow p \in \phi_1^S)$ and $\phi_1^S \models S_1$.
- $\phi^S \models \exists S_1 \mathcal{U} S_2$ iff there is an infinite state region path $\phi_0^S \phi_1^S \ldots\ldots$, with $\phi^S = \phi_0^S$, such that
  - along the path, Ω' gets set infinitely often; and
  - there is an integer $k \geq 0$ such that $\phi_k^S \models S_2$ and for all $0 \leq h < k$, $\phi_h^S \models S_1$.
- $\phi^S \models \exists \Box S_1$ iff there is an infinite state region path $\phi_0^S \phi_1^S \ldots\ldots$, with $\phi^S = \phi_0^S$, such that
  - along the path, Ω' gets set infinitely often; and
  - for all nonnegative integers k, $\phi_k^S \models S_1$.

Theorem. *Given an MCTA $A = (Q, q_0, m, \Omega, R, P, \nu, \tau)$, an MTCTL formula S, a subformula S' of S, and a state ϕ, then $\phi \models S'$ iff $\phi^S \models S'$.*

Proof. The "only if" part is obvious by the definition of state regions. By induction on the length of S' and case analysis on the syntax of S', the "if" part can also be proven. In particularly, when S' is of either the form $\exists \Box S_1$ or $\exists S_1 \mathcal{U} S_2$, we know there is an infinite state region path that satisfies S', according to the definition of $\phi^S \models S'$. We can thus construct a run and its partition for S' such that the k'th interval along the run of the partition corresponds to the k'th state region along the state region path. By checking the construction of $freeze_{R'}$ and adv, we find that the run and its partition indeed satisfy S'. $\square$

In [5], a formula in CTL is treated as a μ-calculus relational term in BDD. We shall adopt this convention such that given two MTCTL formulas S and S_1 and a state region ϕ^S, we write $S_1(\phi^S)$ iff $\phi^S \models S_1$. The previous theorem gives a recipe for the model checking of an MTCTL formula against an MCTA by state regions. Disjunction, negation, and state predicate are handled as in [4]. The "freezing assumption" (**x.**) formulas can be rewritten in μ-calculus as

$$\mathbf{x}.S_1 \equiv \lambda s \left[legit(s) \wedge \exists s' \left(\begin{array}{l} legit(s') \\ \wedge\, freeze_{\{\mathbf{x}\}}(s,s') \\ \wedge \left(\bigwedge_{p \in P} p(s) \leftrightarrow p(s') \right) \\ \wedge\, S_1(s') \end{array} \right) \right]$$

We handle $\exists S_1 \mathcal{U} S_2$ and $\exists \Box S_1$ below.

For each subformula S_1 of S, we construct the following least fixed-point relational term $paths_{S_1}$ such that $paths_{S_1}(\phi_1^S, \phi_n^S)$ is true iff there is a finite state region path $\phi_1^S \ldots \phi_n^S$ and, for all $1 \leq k \leq n$, $\phi_k^S \models S_1$.

$$paths_{S_1} \equiv \mu Z \left[\lambda s_1 \left[\lambda s_2 \left[S_1(s_1) \wedge S_1(s_2) \wedge (edge(s_1, s_2) \vee \exists s_3 (Z(s_1, s_3) \wedge Z(s_3, s_2))) \right] \right] \right]$$

To monitor the progressiveness of the clock readings along runs, we construct the least fixed-point relational term $progress_{S_1}$ for each subformula S_1 of S, such that $progress_{S_1}(\phi_1^S, \phi_n^S)$ is true iff there is a finite state region path $\phi_1^S \ldots \phi_n^S$ such that along $\phi_1^S \ldots \phi_n^S$, Ω' gets set at least once, and for all $1 \leq k \leq n$, $\phi_k^S \models S_1$. In terms of the μ-calculus, $progress_{S_1}$ is given by

$$progress_{S_1} \equiv \mu Z \left[\lambda s_1 \left[\lambda s_2 \left[\begin{array}{l} \left(\begin{array}{l} edge(s_1, s_2) \\ \wedge \bigwedge_{1 \leq i \leq m} \left(\begin{array}{l} (\Omega_i \geq \Omega'_i + 1)(s_1) \\ \wedge (\Omega_i = \Omega'_i)(s_2) \end{array} \right) \\ \wedge\, S_1(s_1) \\ \wedge\, S_1(s_2) \end{array} \right) \\ \vee \exists s_3 \left(\begin{array}{l} (paths_{S_1}(s_1, s_3) \wedge Z(s_3, s_2)) \\ \vee (Z(s_1, s_3) \wedge paths_{S_1}(s_3, s_2)) \end{array} \right) \end{array} \right] \right] \right]$$

This means that we can write $\exists \Box S_1$ as

$$\exists \Box S_1 \equiv \lambda s \left[\exists s_1 (paths_{S_1}(s, s_1) \wedge progress_{S_1}(s_1, s_1)) \right]$$

Similarly, $\exists S_1 \mathcal{U} S_2$ can be expressed in the μ-calculus as

$$\exists S_1 \mathcal{U} S_2 \equiv \mu Z \left[\lambda s \left[\begin{array}{l} (S_2(s) \wedge \exists s_1 (path_{true}(s, s_1) \wedge progress_{true}(s_1, s_1))) \\ \vee (S_1(s) \wedge \exists s_2 (edge(s, s_2) \wedge Z(s_2))) \end{array} \right] \right]$$

Note the use of $\exists s_1 (path_{true}(s, s_1) \wedge progress_{true}(s_1, s_1))$ in the terminating condition. This means that there is a divergent run starting from the state that satisfies S_2.

5.4 Remarks on implementation optimization

The μ-calculus formulas we have generated employ rather large conjunctions and disjunctions such as

$$\bigwedge_{\mathbf{x}, \mathbf{y} \in R \cup \{\Omega\}; 1 \leq i \leq m; 0 \leq c, d \leq C_A^S} (\mathbf{x}_i + c \leq \mathbf{y}_i + d \vee \mathbf{y}_i + d \leq \mathbf{x}_i + c)$$

It may seem impractical to generate such a conjunction since a straightforward implementation may require an exponential number of literals. However, a further examination reveals the regularity of the literals. In particular, we need not generate the whole conjunction structure before generating the reduced BDD. We can enumerates these literals while we are generating the reduced BDD. This should significantly reduce the memory requirement of the algorithm.

We identify each state region with a subset of the atom set. Suppose we are given an MTCTL formula S with atom set $\mathcal{A}_S$, and $\mathcal{F}$ is a functional term with s as a predicate parameter in the μ-calculus. According to [5], the $\exists s(\mathcal{F}(s))$ structure is treated as

$$\bigvee_{s \in 2^{\mathcal{A}_S}} \mathcal{F}(s)$$

This construction may demand double-exponential time complexity in the worst case to enumerate all the possible state regions in a naive implementation. However, in the translation we provide from MTCTL to the μ-calculus, the s in such an $\mathcal{F}$ must also be an element in *legit*. So we can exploit the axioms governing inequalities to reduce the enumeration time.

At every state ϕ, for every $\mathbf{x}, \mathbf{y} \in R$ and $1 \leq i \leq m$, suppose we know in which of the following $4\mathcal{C}_A^S + 3$ intervals

$$(-\infty, -\mathcal{C}_A^S), [-\mathcal{C}_A^S, -\mathcal{C}_A^S], \ldots, (-1, 0), [0, 0], (0, 1), [1, 1], (1, 2), \ldots, [\mathcal{C}_A^S, \mathcal{C}_A^S], (\mathcal{C}_A^S, \infty)$$

the value $\phi(\mathbf{x}_i) - \phi(\mathbf{y}_i)$ falls. Then for every $0 \leq c, d \leq \mathcal{C}_A^S$, the Boolean values of the inequalities $\mathbf{x}_i + c \leq \mathbf{y}_i + d$ and $\mathbf{x}_i + c \geq \mathbf{y}_i + d$ are determined at ϕ. This observation implies that the number of legitimate state regions is about single exponential, instead of double exponential, in the number of bits of the input, and we can enumerate them in single exponential time by enumerating the interval $\phi(\mathbf{x}_i) - \phi(\mathbf{y}_i)$ falls, for every $x, y \in R$ and $1 \leq i \leq m$.

Thus we propose the following implementation for a formula like $\exists s(\mathcal{F}(s))$. We need to implement an enumerator to enumerate all state regions s such that $legit(s)$ is true in single exponential time. Suppose the enumerator generates $s_1 s_2 \ldots \ldots s_n$, then the formula $\exists s(\mathcal{F}(s))$ is equivalent to

$$\mathcal{F}(s_1) \vee \mathcal{F}(s_2) \vee \ldots \ldots \vee \mathcal{F}(s_n)$$

With the technique mentioned in the beginning of this subsection, the desired BDD can be computed in single exponential time with efficient memory usage.

6 Multiclock discrete time systems

6.1 With traditional inequalities

It is straightforward to modify our result in section 3, 4, and 5 to obtain a similar result for multiclock discrete-time systems. In this case, the clocks may advance their readings by any nonnegative integers independently. We still require that both sides of an inequality must refer to the readings of the same clock. Correspondingly, we call the automaton Multiclock Discretely Timed Automaton (MDTA) and the logic Multiclock Discrete Computation Tree Logic (MDCTL).

6.2 With asynchronous inequalities

We may also extend MDCTL and MDTA by incorporating the asynchronous inequalities introduced in [17] and get ACTL (Asynchronous Computation Tree Logic, corresponding to APTL[17] in linear time logic) and ATA (Asynchronous Timed Automaton). The main difference here is that asynchronous inequalities are defined on state sequences. This is different from the inequalities we have used here so far since their semantics is defined on states. Thus ATA may need a clairvoyant implementation if a transition is labelled with enabling conditions such as $x_i + 3 \trianglelefteq y_j + 2$, a timing assertion about the future.

ACTL is an interesting specification language in itself. The satisfiability of ACTL has an elementary decision procedure. The model checking problem for ACTL against ATA can also be solved, with a more complicated algorithm. However, its usage may be questionable because of the clairvoyant nature of ATA. Under prudent restrictions, however, we believe that it can still be useful because of the expressiveness of the asynchronous inequalities. In particular, the model checking problem for ACTL against MDTA seems to be very useful for discrete-time applications that are concerned with the temporal precedence among event occurrences at different sites.

7 Conclusion

There are three major contributions of this paper. First, we propose a symbolic model checking algorithm for Timed Safety Automata and TCTL, completely within the framework of BDDs[4, 5]. Unlike other work in this area, this allows us to naturally retain the implementation advantage of BDD for model checking of real-time logics.

The second major contribution of this paper is that we provide a unified view in treating propositions and inequalities, by identifying each state region with a set of propositions and inequalities. This is not only a more elegant way to exploit the notion of state regions, but is also more suitable for symbolic manipulation.

The third contribution of the paper is that we propose a system model/specification language, MCTA and a temporal logic MTCTL that together give us a new tool for the formal specification and verification of distributed real-time systems where local clocks may have different clock granularities and clock jitters are allowed.

References

1. R. Alur, C. Courcoubetis, D.L. Dill, Model Checking for Real-Time Systems, IEEE LICS, 1990.
2. R. Alur and T.A. Henzinger, A really temporal logic, in Pro. 30th IEEE Symp. Found. of Computer Sciences, pp. 164-169, 1989.
3. R. Alur and T.A. Henzinger, Real-time logics: Complexity and expressiveness, technique report, Stanford University, STAN-CS-90-1307.
4. R.E. Bryant, Graph-based Algorithms for Boolean Function Manipulation, IEEE Trans. Comput., C-35(8), 1986.
5. J.R. Burch, E.M. Clarke, K.L. McMillan, D.L.Dill, L.J. Hwang, Symbolic Model Checking: 10^{20} States and Beyond, IEEE LICS, 1990.

651

6. E. Clarke and E.A. Emerson, Design and Synthesis of Synchronization Skeletons using Branching-Time Temporal Logic, Proceedings of Workshop on Logic of Programs, Lecture Notes in Computer Science 131, Springer-Verlag, 1981.

7. E. Clarke, E.A. Emerson, and A.P. Sistla, Automatic Verification of Finite-State Concurrent Systems Using Temporal Logic Specifications, ACM Transactions on Programming Languages and Systems 8(2), 1986, pp. 244-263.

8. E.A. Emerson, Temporal and Modal Logic, Handbook of Theoretical Computer Science, editted by J.v. Leeuween, North Holland Pub. Co.

9. C. Ghezzi, D. Mandrioli, and A. Morzenti, TRIO: A Logic for Executable Specifications or Real-Time Systems, Journal of Systems and Software, May 1990, pp. 107-123.

10. E. Harel, O. Lichtenstein, and A. Pnueli, Explicit Clock Temporal Logic, The Weizmann Institute of Science.

11. T.A. Henzinger, X. Nicollin, J. Sifakis, S. Yovine, Symbolic Model Checking for Real-Time Systems, IEEE LICS 1992.

12. Farnam Jahanian and Douglas A. Stuart, A Method for Verifying Properties of Modechart Specifications, Proceedings of the Real-Time Systems Symposium, 1988, pp. 12-21.

13. L. Lamport, Sometimes is Sometimes "Not Never"-on the temporal logic of programs, 7th Annual ACM Symp. on Principles of Programming Languages, 1980, pp. 174-185.

14. Kenneth L. McMillan, Symbolic Model Checking : An approach to the state explosion problem, Ph.D. dissertation, School of Computer Science, Carnegie Mellon University, 1992.

15. G. Plotkin and V. Pratt, Teams Can See Pomsets, extended abstract, Aug. 1990.

16. A. Pnueli, The Temporal Logic of Programs, 18th annual IEEE-CS Symp. on Foundations of Computer Science, pp. 45-57, 1977.

17. F. Wang, A. Mok, E.A. Emerson, Asynchronous Propositional Temporal Logic, Proceedings of the 14th International Conference on Software Engineering, 1992.

Adding Specification Constructors to the Refinement Calculus

Nigel Ward

Computer Science Department, University of Queensland, Queensland 4072, Australia

Abstract. This paper examines how specification construction operators may be added to the refinement calculus. These operators are useful for the incremental construction of specifications of larger systems from component specifications. The overall aim is to provide a single coherent framework, in which one may both build specifications and refine these specifications to program code.

In particular, we add generalisations of Z schema conjunction and disjunction operators to the refinement calculus. These operators have been found effective for building Z specifications of substantial systems, and our aim is to provide similar facilities within the framework of the refinement calculus. The conjunction and disjunction operators are generalised so that they may be used to combine not just specification statements (the intuitive equivalent of the Z schema), but also arbitrary programs.

1 Introduction

The Z notation [4, 9] has been used successfully to construct specifications of substantial systems. One of the distinctive features of Z is that it allows a specification to be built up from basic components — Z schemas — using operators, such as schema conjunction and disjunction, that combine components. However, (unextended) Z is not suitable for the refinement of specifications to program code, primarily because it has little in the way of programming language constructs.

On the other hand, the refinement calculus [1, 7, 8] has been developed with the precise aim of facilitating the process of step-wise development of a program from a specification. However, the refinement calculus has little in the way of operators for constructing specifications, perhaps because these operators are not of use in the process of refining a specification to code.

The aim of this paper is to combine the strengths of these two approaches to give a framework within which one may both build specifications from components and refine these specifications to code. Specifically, we add specification constructors, similar to Z schema conjunction and disjunction, to the refinement calculus. Schema conjunction and disjunction give Z the ability to deal with large-scale specifications. It is hoped that the addition of similar constructors to the refinement calculus will enable it to work with substantial specifications.

While overviews of Z and the refinement calculus are given in Sects. 2 and 3 it is assumed that the reader has some familiarity with the two notations. We make use of the notation of [6] for the refinement calculus within this paper. Section 4 gives a detailed comparison of the two notations, explaining why each is better suited to a different part of the software development process. Sections 5 and 6 describe the extensions to the refinement calculus to overcome its specification shortfalls. Section 7 gives a formal semantics for these extensions. Section 8 describes techniques for refining specifications built using these constructors.

2 Overview of the Refinement Calculus

The refinement calculus is based on the extension of Dijkstra's guarded command language [2] with a *specification statement*:

$$w : [\, pre \,, \, post \,] \quad .$$

When executed in a state satisfying the predicate *pre* this statement terminates in a state satisfying the predicate *post* by only changing the values of the variables w. Zero subscripted variables in *post* refer to the values of those variables in the initial state.

Specifications are usually written in the refinement calculus as a mixture of executable statements and specification statements. Thus, the refinement calculus blurs the distinction between specification and program and the two terms can be used interchangeably.

As an example of a specification in the refinement calculus, consider a system which maintains a set which is limited to a maximum of N elements. Operations on the system allow the addition, selection and removal of elements. Initially the set is empty. This system could be specified as follows.

> **module** *BoundedSet*
>
> > **var** $S : \mathbf{P}\, X$ **and** $\#S \leqslant N$;
> >
> > **procedure** $RC\_Add(\textbf{value}\; x : X) \;\widehat{=}$
> >
> > $$S : \begin{bmatrix} x \notin S \\ \#S < N \end{bmatrix}, S = S \cup \{x\} \Big] ;$$
> >
> > **procedure** $RC\_Select(\textbf{result}\; x : X) \;\widehat{=}$
> >
> > $$x : [\, S \neq \varnothing, \, x \in S \,] ;$$
> >
> > **procedure** $RC\_Remove(\textbf{value}\; x : X) \;\widehat{=}$
> >
> > $$S : [\, x \in S, \, S = S_0 - \{x\} \,] ;$$
> >
> > **initially** $S = \varnothing$
>
> **end**

The **and** clause in the variable declaration introduces the module invariant that $\#S \leqslant N$. The RC_Add operation has $\#S < N$ as part of its precondition to ensure that this invariant can be maintained. The other operations trivially maintain it.

Once a specification has been obtained the refinement calculus gives the developer a collection of refinement laws which can be applied to the specification to transform it into (hopefully) executable code. These laws capture traditional design and implementation intuition and guarantee correctness. A program, P, is refined by another program, Q, (written $P \sqsubseteq Q$) when the second is "at least as good" as the first. For example, to introduce an assignment statement the following law could be used.

Law 1 Introduce Assignment. If $(w = w_0) \wedge pre \Rightarrow post[w \backslash E]$ then

$$w, x : [pre, post] \sqsubseteq w := E \ . \qquad \qquad \square$$

These laws often have side conditions (such as $pre \Rightarrow post[w \backslash E]$ above) which must be proven for the refinement to be correct.

3 Overview of Z

Z specifications are made up of collections of *schemas*. A schema consists of a named collection of typed variables and a predicate. The collection of variables is called the *signature* of the schema. The predicate ranges over the variables in the signature and gives the relationship between them. Schemas can be used to describe both states and operations which change states.

For instance, the state of the system described above could be specified in Z as:

$$
\begin{array}{l}
\underline{\ BoundedSet\ } \\
\quad S : \mathbf{P}\, X \\
\hline
\quad \#S \leqslant N
\end{array}
$$

The signature appears above the line, the predicate below.

Operations in Z are usually built from *delta schemas* which introduce the state before and after the operation. In our example we define

$$
\begin{array}{l}
\underline{\ \Delta BoundedSet\ } \\
\quad S, S' : \mathbf{P}\, X \\
\hline
\quad \#S \leqslant N \wedge \#S' \leqslant N
\end{array}
$$

It introduces the state before the operation, S, the state after the operation, S', and ensures that they both satisfy the invariant.

The operation which adds an element to the set, if it is not already present, could be defined with the following schema.

$$
\begin{array}{l}
\underline{\ Z\_Add\ } \\
\quad \Delta BoundedSet \\
\quad x : X \\
\hline
\quad x \notin S \\
\quad S' = S \cup \{x\}
\end{array}
$$

The appearance of $\Delta BoundedSet$ in the signature of this schema is called a *schema inclusion*. It adds the signature of $\Delta BoundedSet$ to the signature of Z_Add and conjoins the predicate of $\Delta BoundedSet$ with the predicate of Z_Add. Z_Add can be expanded to

$$\begin{array}{|l}
\hline
\_\,Z\_Add\,\_\!\!\!\!\!\rule{8cm}{0pt} \\
\quad S, S' : \mathbf{P}\,X \\
\quad x : X \\
\hline
\quad \#S \leqslant N \wedge \#S' \leqslant N \\
\quad x \notin S \\
\quad S' = S \cup \{x\} \\
\hline
\end{array}$$

Schema inclusion is an example of one of the operators in Z's schema calculus which allow the incremental development of specifications.

Refinements from specifications to designs in Z are typically less calculational than in the refinement calculus. They are often done by choosing a piece of specification to be refined, conjecturing a refinement for it and then proving this correct from first principles. This is sometimes called a "posit and prove" style of program refinement.

4 Comparison of the Two Notations

In this section we compare the two notations and explain how their differences make Z more useful for the specification of large systems and the refinement calculus better for refinement. Many of the points made in this section can also be found in [5] and [10].

4.1 Trivial Notational Difference

Z and the refinement calculus distinguish between variables in the initial and final states in different ways. In Z the final state variables are decorated with a dash ('). In the refinement calculus the initial variables in the postcondition of a specification statement are subscripted with a nought.

4.2 Implicit vs Explicit Preconditions

One of the most obvious differences between schemas and specification statements is that the former has only one predicate and the latter has two: a precondition and a postcondition.

The precondition of a specification statement characterises the initial states from which execution of the operation is guaranteed to terminate. The postcondition of a specification statement gives the relationship between the initial and final states of the operation assuming that the precondition holds. The predicate part of a Z operation schema is like the conjunction of the two predicates in a specification statement. It describes both the pre- and postconditions of the operation in one predicate.

The precondition of an operation specified by a schema can be calculated from the schema's predicate using the "pre" operator. The precondition is the condition that there exists a final state for the operation to terminate in. It is calculated by existentially quantifying the output variables in the schema's predicate. For example,

$$\text{pre } Z\_Add$$
$$\equiv (\exists S' \bullet \#S \leqslant N \wedge x \notin S \wedge \#S' \leqslant N \wedge S' = S \cup \{x\})$$
$$\equiv \#S < N \wedge x \notin S \ .$$

Given that Z experience shows that it is possible to specify systems using just one predicate over the initial and final states, why does the refinement calculus use more complicated specifications? There are two main advantages to having separate preconditions.

Firstly, they make formal verification of refinement steps simpler. Program Q is usually considered to be a refinement of program P iff

$$pre\_P \Rightarrow pre\_Q \wedge$$
$$pre\_P \wedge post\_Q \Rightarrow post\_P \ ,$$

where pre_P and $post\_P$ are the pre- and postconditions of P and pre_Q and $post\_Q$ are the pre- and postconditions of Q respectively. These conditions are obviously simpler to verify if the preconditions are explicit.

Secondly, having separate pre- and postconditions allows the specification of *infeasible* or *miraculous* operations. An operation is *feasible* if for any initial state satisfying the precondition there is a final state which satisfies the operation's postcondition. Since, by definition the precondition of a Z schema is the condition that there exists a final state satisfying the predicate of the schema, Z schemas are always feasible. Specification statements on the other hand are not. For instance, consider

$$S : \begin{bmatrix} \#S \leqslant N & \#S \leqslant N \\ x \notin S & S = S_0 \cup \{x\} \end{bmatrix} .$$

When S is initially of size N and does not contain x there is no final state satisfying the postcondition of the operation. However, by definition, the statement still terminates in a state satisfying the postcondition. A specification such as this is called *infeasible* or *miraculous*. Only feasible specifications can be implemented. This is why Z does not allow the specification of miracles.

During refinement, however, miracles can be useful. By allowing them, the side conditions on refinement rules can be simplified. Allowing them also introduces the possibility of refinement rules which combine a number of infeasible specifications into a feasible specification. See [7] for details.

4.3 The Schema Calculus

Another difference between Z and the refinement calculus lies in Z's ability to develop specifications incrementally using its *schema calculus*. As well as schema inclusion, which we have already seen, other commonly used operators of the schema calculus are extensions of propositional logic operators which work on schemas. For instance, if A and B are schemas, then their *schema conjunction*, $A \wedge B$, is formed by merging the signatures of A and B and conjoining their predicates. If A and B are both operations then $A \wedge B$ intuitively specifies an operation which has the effect of both

A and B. *Schema disjunction*, $A \vee B$, can be defined similarly. Intuitively it means do either A or B.

As an example of the use of the schema calculus we add error checking to the *Z_Add* operation defined earlier. We update the operation so that when the element being added to the set is already present the operation returns an error report, otherwise it returns a report signifying success. This functionality can be added to the original Z specification by defining schemas pertaining to success and error conditions:

```
┌─ Success ──────────────
│ rep : Report
├────────────────────────
│ rep = "ok"
└────────────────────────
```

```
┌─ AlreadyPresent ───────────────
│ ΔBoundedSet
│ x : X
│ rep : Report
├────────────────────────────────
│ x ∈ S
│ S' = S
│ rep = "already present"
└────────────────────────────────
```

and using schema conjunction and disjunction to build a new operation:

$$Z\_Add\_1 \mathrel{\widehat{=}} (Z\_Add \wedge Success) \vee AlreadyPresent \ .$$

This can be expanded to

```
┌─ Z_Add_1 ──────────────────────────────────────────
│ S, S' : P X
│ x : X
│ rep : Report
├────────────────────────────────────────────────────
│ #S ⩽ N
│ #S' ⩽ N
│ (x ∉ S ∧ S' = S ∪ {x} ∧ rep = "ok") ∨
│ (x ∈ S ∧ S' = S ∧ rep = "already present")
└────────────────────────────────────────────────────
```

The refinement calculus does not have operators like Z's '$\wedge$' and '$\vee$' to add detail to a specification incrementally. The only way to *develop* such a specification is to write it down in one hit:

$$S, rep : \begin{bmatrix} (x \notin S \wedge \#S < N) \vee \\ (x \in S \wedge \#S \leqslant N) \end{bmatrix}, \begin{pmatrix} \begin{pmatrix} x \notin S_0 \\ S = S_0 \cup \{x\} \\ rep = \text{"ok"} \end{pmatrix} \vee \\ \begin{pmatrix} x \in S_0 \\ S = S_0 \\ rep = \text{"already present"} \end{pmatrix} \end{pmatrix} \ .$$

4.4 Frames

Another difference between the two notations is that a specification statement has a frame which lists the variables that the specification may change, while a schema has a signature which lists the variables that the schema references (and possibly changes.)

One of the ramifications of this difference is the way the two notations specify change. In the signature of an operation schema, (undashed, dashed) variable pairs indicate which variables may be changed. If these pairs do not change then this is often specified by adding predicates like $x' = x$ to the schema. In contrast, a specification statement's frame specifies which variables can change. Any variables outside the frame have an implicit $x = x_0$ conjunct in the postcondition. This suggests the following identity (Law 6.9 in [6]).

Law 2 Expand Frame. If x is a variable in scope, then

$$w : [\, pre, post \,] = w, x : [\, pre, post \wedge x = x_0 \,] \quad . \qquad \qquad \Box$$

Thus the frame of a specification statement often simplifies the postcondition of an operation.

Given this fact it would seem sensible for Z schemas to have frames. It is possible to add frames to Z schemas [3], however, the schema calculus lessens the need for them. In Z, a system is often described in terms of a number of sub-states and the effect of operations on those sub-states. These partial specifications are then combined using the schema calculus to build a complete specification. If the division into sub-states is done intelligently then the number of predicates of the form $x' = x$ can be reduced.

4.5 Signatures

Z and the refinement calculus also declare the variables referenced in their specifications differently. Refinement calculus specifications give precise details about the point of declaration and scope of the variables used by declaring them as either module state variables, local block variables, or parameters to procedures.

In contrast, Z specifications don't give precise details about the point of declaration of variables. Z simply declares variables (and their associated types) in the signatures of schemas. This gives an implementation of the specification more flexibility with respect to how it declares its variables. However, it also means that the specification's interface to the environment is not precise.

4.6 World Views

The difference between schemas and specification statements that we are most concerned with is the way they treat variables they do not mention. A schema places no restrictions on the variables which it does not mention in its signature. This means that if a schema A does not mention variable x but a schema B changes x then their conjunction, $A \wedge B$, can still change x. Following the terminology of Utting [10] we call this an *open-world view* of specification.

Let the *implicit signature* of a specification statement be the set of variables that it references in its frame, precondition and postcondition. This implicit signature must be a subset of the variables currently in scope. Unlike a schema the variables in the implicit signature of a specification statement which do not also appear in its frame cannot be changed by the statement. Utting calls this a *closed-world view* of specification. This world view makes it difficult to design operators for specification statements which build up specification detail incrementally like Z's schema calculus operators: if a specification statement does not mention a variable in its frame then that variable can never be changed.

The refinement calculus foregoes the use of such specification constructors in favour of a closed-world view for the sake of brevity during refinement. As refinement progresses more variables are usually added to the state space. In a state space with a large number of variables it is often more convenient to describe what does change rather than what does not.

5 Getting the Best of Both Worlds

As mentioned in the introduction we would like a framework within which we may both build specifications from components and refine these specifications to code. One way of getting such a framework is to specify the system under development in Z, do some refinement steps in that notation, translate to the refinement calculus, and finish the development in that notation. This approach is the subject of a paper by King [5] which gives rules and heuristics for changing between the notations.

Another way to get such a method is to extend the refinement calculus with operators similar to those in Z's schema calculus. One advantage of this approach is that only one, rather than two notations is needed for the overall development of a large software system.

The rest of this section informally describes how two such operators, specification conjunction (λ) and specification disjunction ($\curlyvee$) can be used to combine specification statements. Section 7 gives a formal semantics for these extensions to the refinement calculus and shows how they can be used to combine arbitrary specifications.

5.1 Frame-complete Specification Statements

In Sect. 4.6 the implicit signature of a refinement calculus specification was defined to be the set of variables mentioned in the specification. If a specification statement has a frame made up of all of those variables in its implicit signature then it is *frame-complete*.

Frame-complete specification statements are used to make the definitions of λ and $\curlyvee$ below simpler. These definitions are made in terms of frame-complete specifications with the understanding that any specification statement can be made into an equivalent frame-complete specification statement using Law 2.

5.2 Mixed-world View

The closed-world view of specification statements means that any variable in the signature of a specification statement which is not also in its frame cannot be changed. As a result the combination of two specification statements cannot in general produce a new specification statement which can change all of the variables in both frames.

We overcome this problem by giving specifications an open-world view when they are composed with other specifications using $\curlywedge$ and $\curlyvee$. When specifications are considered in isolation of these operators they have the usual closed-world view. We call this combination of open and closed views a *mixed-world view* of specifications. The details of how we achieve this view are delayed until Sect. 7.

5.3 Specification Conjunction

Suppose we are composing two frame-complete specification statements

$$S \,\widehat{=}\, w : [\, pre_S \,,\, post_S \,] \qquad \text{and} \qquad T \,\widehat{=}\, x : [\, pre_T \,,\, post_T \,]$$

using specification conjunction.

In Z, the conjunction of two schemas A and B, specifies an operation which terminates in a state satisfying both A and B. This suggests that the postcondition of the conjunction of S and T should be $post_S \wedge post_T$. In Z, $A \wedge B$ terminates whenever A and B can terminate in the same state. That is, whenever there exists a final state satisfying the predicate of both A and B. This suggests that the precondition of the conjunction of S and T is $pre_S \wedge pre_T \wedge (\exists v \bullet post_S \wedge post_T)[v_0 \backslash v]$, where v is the set of variables in the combined signatures. The existential quantification is renamed since initial variables do not have zero subscripts in the precondition. It can be rewritten as $(\exists v' \bullet post_S[v \backslash v'] \wedge post_T[v \backslash v'])$.

Definition 3 Conjunction of Specification Statements. If $v = w \cup x$ and $S \,\widehat{=}\, w : [\, pre_S \,,\, post_S \,]$ and $T \,\widehat{=}\, x : [\, pre_T \,,\, post_T \,]$ are frame-complete specification statements then

$$S \curlywedge T \,\widehat{=}\, v : \begin{bmatrix} pre_S \wedge pre_T \\ (\exists v \bullet post_S \wedge post_T)[v_0 \backslash v] \end{bmatrix}, post_S \wedge post_T \end{bmatrix} .$$

$\square$

Specification conjunction can be used in a similar way to schema conjunction. For example, we can extend RC_Add with a success report:

$RC\_Add\_Success$

$\,\widehat{=}\, S : \begin{bmatrix} x \notin S \\ \#S < N \end{bmatrix}, S = S_0 \cup \{x\} \end{bmatrix} \curlywedge rep : [\, true \,,\, rep = \text{"ok"} \,]$

$= \text{"Law 2"}$

$\quad S, x : \begin{bmatrix} x \notin S & S = S_0 \cup \{x\} \\ \#S < N & x = x_0 \end{bmatrix} \curlywedge rep : [\, true \,,\, rep = \text{"ok"} \,]$

$= \text{"Definition 3"}$

$\quad S, x, rep : \begin{bmatrix} x \notin S & S = S_0 \cup \{x\} \\ \#S < N & rep = \text{"ok"} \\ & x = x_0 \end{bmatrix}$

$= \text{"Law 2"}$

$\quad S, rep : \begin{bmatrix} x \notin S & S = S_0 \cup \{x\} \\ \#S < N & rep = \text{"ok"} \end{bmatrix} .$

5.4 Specification Disjunction

In Z, the disjunction of two schemas, $A \vee B$, specifies an arbitrary choice between A and B. This choice terminates whenever pre A or pre B holds. It must achieve the effect of either A or B. Whenever pre A holds it may achieve A and whenever pre B holds it may achieve B. This suggests the following definition.

Definition 4 Disjunction of Specification Statements. If $v = w \cup x$ and $S \cong w : [pre_S, post_S]$ and $T \cong x : [pre_T, post_T]$ are frame-complete specification statements then

$$S \curlyvee T \cong v : \begin{bmatrix} pre_S \vee & (pre_S[v \backslash v_0] \wedge post_S) \vee \\ pre_T & , (pre_T[v \backslash v_0] \wedge post_T) \end{bmatrix}$$

□

Note that the preconditions pre_S and pre_T are renamed to range over initial variables in the postcondition.

This definition assumes that the two frame-complete specifications have the same frames. If this is not the case then the frames can be expanded until they are identical using Law 2.

As an example of the use of specification disjunction, we add the error case to $RC\_Add\_Success$

$RC\_Add\_Success$

$\curlyvee$

$rep : [\, x \in S \,, \, rep = \text{``already present''} \,]$

$= \text{``Definition of } RC\_Add\_Success \text{ and Law 2''}$

$$S, rep, x : \begin{bmatrix} x \notin S & S = S_0 \cup \{x\} \\ \#S < N & , rep = \text{``ok''} \wedge x = x_0 \end{bmatrix}$$

$\curlyvee$

$$S, rep, x : \begin{bmatrix} x \in S \,, & rep = \text{``already present''} \\ & S = S_0 \wedge x = x_0 \end{bmatrix}$$

$= \text{``Definition 4''}$

$$S, rep, x : \begin{bmatrix} x \in S \vee \\ \#S < N \end{bmatrix}, \begin{pmatrix} x_0 \notin S_0 \wedge \#S_0 < N \\ S = S_0 \cup \{x\} \\ rep = \text{``ok''} \wedge x = x_0 \end{pmatrix} \vee \\ \begin{pmatrix} x_0 \in S_0 \\ rep = \text{``already present''} \\ S = S_0 \wedge x = x_0 \end{pmatrix} \end{bmatrix}$$

$= \text{``Law 2''}$

$$S, rep : \begin{bmatrix} x \in S \vee \\ \#S < N \end{bmatrix}, \begin{pmatrix} x_0 \notin S_0 \wedge \#S_0 < N \\ S = S_0 \cup \{x\} \\ rep = \text{``ok''} \end{pmatrix} \vee \\ \begin{pmatrix} x_0 \in S_0 \\ S = S_0 \\ rep = \text{``already present''} \end{pmatrix} \end{bmatrix}.$$

6 Specification Statements with Signatures

Often when developing specifications we want to leave details about the point of declaration and scope of a variable undetermined until a later stage of the specification. Z allows this style of specification by declaring its variables in the signatures of the schemas. We adopt a similar approach and allow specification statements with *explicit signatures* called *contextual specification statements*. For example, assuming x and S have already been declared, we allow

$$\left(rep : Report \bullet S : \begin{bmatrix} x \notin S \\ \#S < N \end{bmatrix}, S = S_0 \cup \{x\} \right] \right) .$$

Here, the explicit signature of the specification statement is written before the dot and the frame, precondition and postcondition, are written in the usual syntax after the dot. As before, the implicit signature of the specification is all of the variables referenced within it.

As with Z schema inclusion we allow one specification statement, say S, to be included in the explicit signature of another contextual specification statement, say T. The result is a contextual specification statement with an explicit signature part consisting of the union of the explicit signatures of S and T and a specification statement part equivalent to $S \wedge T$.

6.1 Example

As an example of how contextual specification statements can be used to build specifications in a Z-like style we give an incremental exposition of the *BoundedSet* system.

Rather than declaring S as a state variable of the module we declare the state using a contextual specification statement:

$$\Delta BoundedSet \cong \left(S : \mathbf{P}\, X \bullet S : [\, \#S \leqslant N \,, \#S \leqslant N\,] \right) .$$

As with the Z specification the basic operations can then be defined by extending this definition. For example,

$$Add \cong \left(\begin{matrix} \Delta BoundedSet \\ x : X \end{matrix} \bullet S : [\, x \notin S, S = S_0 \cup \{x\}\,] \right) .$$

Expanding this definition gives

$$\left(\begin{matrix} S : \mathbf{P}\, X \\ x : X \end{matrix} \bullet S : \begin{bmatrix} \#S \leqslant N \\ x \notin S \\ \left(\begin{matrix} \exists S \bullet \\ S = S_0 \cup \{x\} \\ \#S \leqslant N \end{matrix} \right) [S_0 \backslash S] \end{bmatrix}, \begin{matrix} \#S \leqslant N \\ S = S_0 \cup \{x\} \end{matrix} \right] \right)$$

$$= \left(\begin{matrix} S : \mathbf{P}\, X \\ x : X \end{matrix} \bullet S : \begin{bmatrix} \#S < N & \#S \leqslant N \\ x \notin S & , S = S_0 \cup \{x\} \end{bmatrix} \right) .$$

6.2 Sealing the Specification

A variable in the explicit signature of a contextual specification statement can be removed by placing the statement within the scope of a declaration of that variable. For example,

$$
\textbf{procedure } RC\_Add(\textbf{value } x : X) \triangleq
\begin{pmatrix} S : \textbf{P} \, X \\ x : X \end{pmatrix} \bullet \ S : \begin{bmatrix} \#S < N & \#S \leqslant N \\ x \notin S & , & S = S_0 \cup \{x\} \end{bmatrix} ,
$$

is equal to

$$
\textbf{procedure } RC\_Add(\textbf{value } x : X) \triangleq
\left(S : \textbf{P} \, X \bullet \ S : \begin{bmatrix} \#S < N & \#S \leqslant N \\ x \notin S & , & S = S_0 \cup \{x\} \end{bmatrix} \right) .
$$

When all of the variables in a specification have been explicitly declared in this way we say that the specification is *sealed*. In general a specification containing contextual specification statements can be sealed in a number of ways. For instance, our example can be sealed as

$$
\begin{aligned}
&\textbf{module } BoundedSet \\
&\quad \textbf{var } S : \textbf{P} \, X \textbf{ and } \#S \leqslant N; \\
&\quad \textbf{procedure } RC\_Add(\textbf{value } x : X) \triangleq Add \\
&\quad \vdots \\
&\textbf{end } ,
\end{aligned}
$$

or as

$$
\textbf{procedure } RC\_Add(\textbf{value } x : X; \textbf{ value result } S : \textbf{P} \, X) \triangleq Add .
$$

This illustrates the points made in Sect. 4.5 that unsealed specifications are more flexible about the way their variables are declared, but don't give precise details of how a specification interfaces with its environment.

7 Semantics

The definitions given in Sect. 5 only describe specification disjunction and conjunction when their arguments are specification statements. This section gives more general definitions for these constructs so that they can be used to combine arbitrary programs and gives theorems relating these definitions to the original definitions. The proofs of these theorems can be found in [12].

7.1 Weakest Preconditions

The semantics of the refinement calculus is described in terms of weakest preconditions [2] We briefly outline a description of weakest preconditions similar to that given in [11].

Let $Pred_v$ be the set of predicates which range over the variables v. This set forms a complete boolean lattice under the $\Rightarrow$ ordering.

A total function from $Pred_v$ to $Pred_v$ is called a *predicate transformer on* v. We write the set of all such predicate transformers which are monotonic with respect to $\Rightarrow$ as $Mtran_v$.

Given these definitions, the weakest precondition style of defining program semantics classifies the outcomes of a computation under control of a program in one of the following mutually exclusive categories:

- "finally R" – the computation terminates in a state satisfying the predicate R,
- "finally $\neg R$" – the computation terminates in a state satisfying the predicate $\neg R$,
- "eternal" – the computation does not terminate.

The semantics of a program (specification) S with signature v are said to be known "sufficiently well" if for a given predicate $R \in Pred_v$ we can surmise the set of the above categories that computations of S can fall into by examining the state S was initiated in. We make this categorisation by identifying S with an element from $Mtran_v$ called the *weakest precondition* predicate transformer for S. Informally,

$wp.S.R$, the "weakest precondition of program S corresponding to postcondition R", holds in exactly those initial states from which every computation of S belongs to the class "finally R".

For example, the semantics of a specification statement $w : [pre, post]$ with signature v is

$$wp.(w : [pre, post]).R \mathrel{\widehat{=}} pre \wedge (\forall w \bullet post \Rightarrow R)[v_0 \backslash v] \ ,$$

for $R \in Pred_v$.

7.2 Reasoning About Specifications

Before we give a semantics to specification conjunction and disjunction we define some useful operators on specifications. The *precondition* operator, $Pre.S$, returns a predicate characterising the states from which S is guaranteed to terminate. The *guard* operator, $Grd.S$, characterises those states from which S can possibly terminate. That is, the states from which S is feasible.

Definition 5 Precondition and Guard Operators.

$Pre.S \mathrel{\widehat{=}} wp.S.true$
$Grd.S \mathrel{\widehat{=}} \neg wp.S.false$

□

Definition 6 Dual. The *dual* of a specification S is another specification $\overline{S}$ such that

$$wp.\overline{S}.R \,\widehat{=}\, \neg\, wp.S.(\neg\, R)$$

□

Using the intuition for weakest preconditions given above we can interpret the dual of a specification as follows.

$wp.S.(\neg\, R)$ characterises those initial states from which every computation of S belongs to the class "finally $\neg\, R$".

Thus,

$\neg\, wp.S.(\neg\, R)$ characterises those initial states from which some computation of S does not belong to the class "finally $\neg\, R$".

That is,

$\neg\, wp.S.(\neg\, R)$ characterises those initial states from which some computation of S belongs to the class "finally R" or the class "eternal".

But, by definition, $\neg\, wp.S.(\neg\, R)$, is the weakest precondition for $\overline{S}$ to achieve R, so when $\overline{S}$ is executed in such a state it is guaranteed to achieve R. That is, $\overline{S}$ is *guaranteed* to achieve any R that S can *possibly* achieve.

Definition 7 Generalisation. The *generalisation* of a specification S with respect to a set of variables z is another specification $(S \Uparrow z)$ such that

$$wp.(S \Uparrow z).R \,\widehat{=}\, wp.S.(\exists z \bullet R)\ .$$

□

If $S \in Mtran_w$ then $(S \Uparrow z) \in Mtran_{w \cup z}$. It changes the values of w so that they satisfy the specification S and allows the values of z to be influenced by the environment that S is placed in. Thus $S \Uparrow z$ is a specification which has an open-world view with respect to the variables z.

7.3 Miraculous Conjunction

We gradually build up an intuitive interpretation for the conjunction of two specifications, S and T. Firstly we define *miraculous specification conjunction*, $\bigotimes$, which behaves like $\wedge$ when its result is feasible, but which does not guarantee a feasible result. Let

$v = sig.S \cup sig.T$ – the set of variables referenced by S and T
$y = sig.S - sig.T$ – the set of variables referenced by S but not T
$z = sig.T - sig.S$ – the set of variables referenced by T but not S

For some list of values represented by the fresh variables v' consider the predicate

$$wp.(\overline{S} \Uparrow z).(v = v')\ .$$

This is the weakest precondition for $\overline{S}$ to achieve a state where $v = v'$, disregarding the values of z. That is, it characterises the states from which S can *possibly* achieve a state where $v = v'$ with an open-world view for z (the variables which S does not reference).

Next consider,

$$(\forall v' \bullet wp.(\overline{S} \Uparrow z).(v = v') \wedge wp.(\overline{T} \Uparrow y).(v = v') \Rightarrow R[v\backslash v']) \ .$$

This predicate holds exactly when all of the states $(v = v')$ which the open world views of S and T can both possibly achieve also satisfy R.

Finally consider,

Definition 8 Miraculous Specification Conjunction. Let S, T, v, y and z be defined as above, then,

$$
\begin{aligned}
wp.(S \ &\textcircled{A}\ T).R \ \widehat{=} \\
&Pre.S \wedge Pre.T \ \wedge \\
&(\forall v' \bullet wp.(\overline{S} \Uparrow z).(v = v') \wedge wp.(\overline{T} \Uparrow y).(v = v') \Rightarrow R[v\backslash v'])
\end{aligned}
$$

(1)

(2)

□

The predicate $wp.(S \ \textcircled{A}\ T).R$ holds exactly when

(1) both S and T are guaranteed to terminate,
(2) all final states which the open-world views of S and T can both possibly terminate in satisfy R.

Theorem 9 Miraculous Conjunction of Specification Statements. *If* $v = w \cup x$ *and* $S \ \widehat{=}\ w : [\,pre_S, post_S\,]$ *and* $T \ \widehat{=}\ x : [\,pre_T, post_T\,]$ *are frame-complete specification statements then*

$$S \ \textcircled{A}\ T = w, x : [\,pre_S \wedge pre_T, post_S \wedge post_T\,] \ .$$

□

We call $\textcircled{A}$ miraculous specification conjunction because combining two feasible conjuncts can give an infeasible result. For example,

$$S : [\,x \notin S, S = S_0 \cup \{x\}\,] \ \textcircled{A}\ S : [\,\#S \leqslant N, \#S \leqslant N\,]$$
$$=$$
$$S : \begin{bmatrix} x \notin S & S = S_0 \cup \{x\} \\ \#S \leqslant N & \#S \leqslant N \end{bmatrix} \ ,$$

which is infeasible.

7.4 Conjunction

The definition for specification conjunction extends the definition for miraculous specification conjunction with a feasibility check.

Definition 10 Specification Conjunction. For S, T, v, y and z as in Definition 8,

$$wp.(S \curlywedge T).R \mathrel{\widehat{=}} Grd.(S \circledA T) \wedge wp.(S \circledA\ T).R \ .$$

□

Theorem 11 shows that this definition agrees with Definition 3.

Theorem 11 Conjunction of Specification Statements. *If* $v = w \cup x$ *and* $S \mathrel{\widehat{=}}$ $w : [\,pre_S\,,\,post_S\,]$ *and* $T \mathrel{\widehat{=}} x : [\,pre_T\,,\,post_T\,]$ *are frame-complete specification statements then*

$$S \curlywedge T = w, x : \left[\begin{array}{c} pre_S \wedge pre_T \\ (\exists\, w, x \bullet post_S \wedge post_T)[v_0\backslash v] \end{array} , \ post_S \wedge post_T \right] \ .$$

□

7.5 Disjunction

The definition for the disjunction of two arbitrary specifications is simpler than that for specification conjunction.

Definition 12 Specification Disjunction. Let S and T be two arbitrary specifications. Let $v = sig.S \cup sig.T$, then for all $R \in Pred_v$,

$$wp.(S \curlyvee T).R \mathrel{\widehat{=}}$$
$$(Pre.S \vee Pre.T) \wedge (Pre.S \Rightarrow wp.S.R) \wedge (Pre.T \Rightarrow wp.T.R) \ .$$

□

The following theorem shows that specification disjunction can also be defined in terms of alternation. The result follows directly from the definition of alternation (see [8, page 293]).

Theorem 13 Disjunction in terms of Alternation.

$$S \curlyvee T = \textbf{if } Pre.S \longrightarrow S \mathbin{[\!]} Pre.T \longrightarrow T \textbf{ fi} \ .$$

□

The next theorem shows that Definition 4 for the disjunction of two specification statements agrees with the semantics given here.

Theorem 14 Disjunction of Specification Statements. *If* $v = w \cup x$ *and* $S \mathrel{\widehat{=}}$ $w : [\,pre_S\,,\,post_S\,]$ *and* $T \mathrel{\widehat{=}} x : [\,pre_T\,,\,post_T\,]$ *are frame-complete specification statements then*

$$S \curlyvee T = v : \left[\begin{array}{l} pre_S \vee \ (pre_S[v\backslash v_0] \wedge post_S) \vee \\ pre_T \end{array} , \ (pre_T[v\backslash v_0] \wedge post_T) \right] \ .$$

□

7.6 Novel Example

Definitions 10 and 12 are more general than Definitions 3 and 4 because they allow the combination of arbitrary programs, not just specification statements. For example, suppose we had refined the original specification of RC_Add as follows:

$$S : \begin{bmatrix} x \notin S \\ \#S < N \end{bmatrix}, S = S \cup \{x\} \end{bmatrix} \sqsubseteq S := S \cup \{x\} ,$$

and then decided to add the success report:

$$(S := S \cup \{x\}) \curlywedge rep : [\, true \, , rep = \text{``ok''} \,] \ .$$

Using Definition 10 it can be shown that this is equivalent to

$$S, rep : \begin{bmatrix} true \, , \dfrac{S = S \cup \{x\}}{rep = \text{``ok''}} \end{bmatrix} \ .$$

8 Refinement

The aim of our extensions to the refinement calculus was to give a notation which could be used easily for both incremental specification and refinement. This section discusses how specifications built with $\curlywedge$ and $\curlyvee$ can be refined toward code.

Neither $\curlywedge$ or $\curlyvee$ is monotonic with respect to the refinement relation. That is, if $S \sqsubseteq S'$ and $T \sqsubseteq T'$, then $S \curlywedge T$ is not necessarily refined by $S' \curlywedge T'$ (and similarly for specification disjunction). This means that, in general, to refine a specification built using these operators we must first remove them using Definitions 10 and 12. For arbitrary programs this can be a tedious business.

All is not lost though. In special cases some of the structure of a specification built using $\curlywedge$ and $\curlyvee$ can be maintained in subsequent refinements. For example, the structure of specifications built using specification disjunction can be maintained by appealing to Theorem 13. For instance,

$$S, rep : \begin{bmatrix} x \notin S & S = S_0 \cup \{x\} \\ \#S < N & rep = \text{``ok''} \end{bmatrix} \curlyvee rep : [\, x \in S \, , rep = \text{``already present''} \,]$$

$\equiv$ "Theorem 13"

$$\mathbf{if}\ x \notin S \wedge \#S < N \longrightarrow S, rep : \begin{bmatrix} x \notin S & S = S_0 \cup \{x\} \\ \#S < N & rep = \text{``ok''} \end{bmatrix}$$

$$[\![\, x \in S \longrightarrow rep : [\, x \in S \, , rep = \text{``already present''} \,]$$

$\mathbf{fi}$.

In [5] King gives similar rules for converting Z schema disjunctions to alternations in the refinement calculus.

Specification conjunctions can also be removed in special cases using a rule similar to one introduced in [5] for removing Z schema conjunctions.

Law 15 Disjoint Specification Conjunction. If w and x are disjoint and $S \ \widehat{=}\ w : [\, pre_S \, , post_S \,]$ and $T \ \widehat{=}\ x : [\, pre_T \, , post_T \,]$ then

$$S \curlywedge T \sqsubseteq S;\ T \qquad \text{and} \qquad S \curlywedge T \sqsubseteq T;\ S$$

□

For example,

$$S : \begin{bmatrix} x \notin S \\ \#S < N \end{bmatrix}, S = S_0 \cup \{x\} \Big] \, \lambda \, rep : [\, true \, , \, rep = \text{``ok''}\,]$$
$$\sqsubseteq S : \begin{bmatrix} x \notin S \\ \#S < N \end{bmatrix}, S = S_0 \cup \{x\} \Big] ; \, rep : [\, true \, , \, rep = \text{``ok''}\,] \quad .$$

9 Discussion

The aim of this paper was to develop a single framework in which one may both build specifications incrementally and refine those specifications to code. This was done by adding specification constructors similar to Z's schema conjunction and schema disjunction to the refinement calculus. These constructors are more general than their Z counterparts, allowing the combination of arbitrary programs as well as specification statements.

Schema conjunction and disjunction have been effectively used to build large specifications in Z. Our generalisations can be used to build specifications in the refinement calculus in a similar incremental style.

We also examined refinement from specifications built using the constructors. In special cases the structure of these specifications can be maintained in subsequent refinements. However, since the constructors are not monotonic with respect to the refinement relation, such structure cannot be maintained in general. Future research could include an investigation of constructors which do maintain structure during refinement.

Miraculous specification conjunction is such a specification constructor since it is monotonic with respect to the refinement relation. This means that each of its conjuncts can be refined before the operator is removed. However, miraculous specification conjunction does not allow the Z-like incremental style of specification shown in Section 6, where invariants which maintain feasibility of operations are added using inclusion (defined in terms of λ). For example, if we have

$$Add \stackrel{\frown}{=} S : [\, x \notin S, S = S_0 \cup \{x\}\,]$$
$$\Delta BoundedSet \stackrel{\frown}{=} S : [\, \#S \leqslant N, \#S \leqslant N\,] \quad ,$$

then $Add \, \lambda \, \Delta BoundedSet$ has a precondition which guarantees feasibility:

$$S : \begin{bmatrix} x \notin S & S = S_0 \cup \{x\} \\ \#S < N & \#S \leqslant N \end{bmatrix} \quad ,$$

but $Add \, \textcircled{\wedge} \, \Delta BoundedSet$ does not:

$$S : \begin{bmatrix} x \notin S & S = S_0 \cup \{x\} \\ \#S \leqslant N & \#S \leqslant N \end{bmatrix} \quad .$$

One technique often used to structure Z specifications is *promotion* [4, pages 102-104]. The addition of specification constructors which enable this technique to be used in refinement calculus specifications is another area for future investigation.

Acknowledgements

Thanks to Ian Hayes for many comments on earlier drafts of this paper and to the referees for a number of helpful suggestions.

References

1. R. J. R. Back. *On the Correctness of Refinement Steps in Program Development*. PhD thesis, Department of Computer Science, University of Helsinki, 1978.
2. E. W. Dijkstra. *A Discipline of Programming*. Prentice-Hall, 1976.
3. R. Duke, P. King, G. Rose, and G. Smith. The Object-Z specification language: Version 1. Technical report 91-1, Software Verification Research Centre, Department of Computer Science, University of Queensland, 1991.
4. I. J. Hayes, editor. *Specification Case Studies*. Series in Computer Science. Prentice-Hall, 1987.
5. S. King. Z and the refinement calculus. In *VDM and Z – Formal Methods in Software Development*, volume 428 of *Lecture Notes in Computer Science*, pages 164–188. Springer-Verlag, 1990.
6. C. Morgan. *Programming from Specifications*. Series in Computer Science. Prentice-Hall, 1990.
7. C. Morgan and K. Robinson. Specification statements and refinement. *IBM Journal of Research and Development*, 31(5), 1987.
8. J. M. Morris. A theoretical basis for stepwise refinement and the programming calculus. *Science of Computer Programming*, 9:287–306, 1987.
9. J. M Spivey. *The Z Notation: A Reference Manual*. Series in Computer Science. Prentice-Hall, 1989.
10. M. Utting. *An Object-Oriented Refinement Calculus*. Phd thesis, Department of Computer Science, University of New South Wales, Sydney, 1992.
11. J. von Wright. *A Lattice Theoretic Basis for Program Refinement*. Phd thesis, Department of Computer Science, Åbo Akademi, 1991.
12. N. Ward. Draft: Adding specification constructors to the refinement calculus. In *2nd Australian Refinement Workshop*. Department of Computer Science, University of Queensland, 1992.

Selling Formal Methods to Industry

Debora Weber-Wulff[1]

Technische Fachhochschule Berlin
Fachbereich Informatik
Luxemburger Str. 10
W-1000 Berlin 65 *
dww@informatik.tfh-berlin.dbp.de

Abstract. This paper addresses some of the questions involved in attempting to introduce formal methods into industry on a broader basis. Marketing aspects and the importance of teaching programmers how to use formal methods are stressed.

The very idea of selling formal methods is surely slightly distasteful to most developers of formal methods. After having invested so much time and effort in constructing an elegant and, in the eyes of the developers, clear formalism, many do not see the necessity of convincing others to use the method - they feel that it is imperative to just use it – any further argument is a waste of time. Many acquire an almost religious fervor to their support of a particular method. It seems to be the only way to "do it right", and developers or convertees will often speak with contempt about non-believers or users of a different methodology.

For example, on one of the Internet newsgroups someone who programs telephone systems for a living recently posted a note excitedly describing how he or she had used a formal method for the first time. The system to be implemented was formalized and run through a tool that tries to detect deadlocks. Some subtle problems in the model were found and corrected before coding began – one more success for the use of a formal method. The writer was almost immediately berated by another poster claiming that what the first person had done was just use a tool - that was not using real formal methods.

This is an unfortunate attitude that is perhaps the cause for the deep chasm that still seems to divide formal methodists from industrial programmers. The former feel that the latter must be so utterly stupid since they cannot comprehend their elegant formalisms; the latter find the former exceedingly arrogant and the formalisms incomprehensible and thus unusable. In a recent article in a German trade newspaper[2] Hartmut Skubsch discusses different software tools, and recommends flat out that industry avoid the use of methods that are overloaded with formalisms.

This paper attempts to bridge the gap by offering promoters of formal methods some aspects from the point of view of the industrial programmer on how their systems might be made more palatable to the plebian programmer. Even if we call

---

* This paper was written while the author was employed at the Freie Universität Berlin, ZI Fachdidaktiken, Didaktik der Informatik, Habelschwerdter Allee 45, W-1000 Berlin 33.

[2] *Computerwoche*, FOCUS 2 vom 28.8.92, p. 5

it by any other name, such as educating or discussing, we are concerned with a marketing problem: how to convince someone to invest time and money in learning and applying a particular formal method.

1 Definitions

What are formal methods exactly? The call for papers for this conference defines formal methods as the use of precise mathematical methods in program development. This seems to be a good, broad definition that encompasses many methods that can be used to reason about problems and proposed solutions before they are coded. It also restrains the rather religious zeal of some of the formal methods community – there is not one true formal method that will be all things to all projects. We consider a formal method to not only be a pencil-and-paper method of formalizing computations, but it should also include tools that implement or enforce formalities.

What is meant by the word industry? It conjures up connotations of long assembly lines in vast halls where objects are constructed by sweating workers and gently whirring robots. Actually, industrial software is software that is created and maintained under rather adverse conditions such as being subjected to ever-changing specifications, unreasonable constraints, short deadlines, and understaffed projects. Software must have some or all of such properties as adaptability, portability, fast response, secure operation. It is important that a program works, not that it be correct with respect to some criteria. This is an important distinction, because it can be possible to work with a program that is incorrect - people invent work-arounds or avoid problem corners of a program, as long as the program functions well enough for most of its other tasks. Despite all the errors in software such as Word for Windows, many people still use it. But since errors are not always obvious or known, they have a potential for causing harm and thus it is also important for a program to be correct. Formal methods would seem to be exactly what we need to move towards better software.

But why do people not use formal methods as much as we would expect? In a highly unrepresentative study, consisting of soul-searching and discussions with colleagues about the excuses we have for <u>not</u> using formal methods, combined with observations of student behavior in programming laboratories, a sizable list of complaints was collected. Inverting this list results is a collection of desiderata for formal methods. But this alone is not enough – selling formal methods to industry also means considering the qualities that a formal method must offer above and beyond the pure formalization, that will make a harried programmer <u>want</u> to use it. In the next section we will examine some aspects that are of concern to industrial programmers and analysts, and discuss some points that promoters of a formal method should consider while developing and marketing their product.

2 Ten Propositions for Industrial Strength Formal Methods

The desiderata concerning some of the characteristics a formal method should have in order that it might find widespread use in industry are given as a list of propositions. Each proposition states a property that a usable formal method should have, followed by some discussion of what exactly is meant by the proposition, and arguments as to why the author considers this particular proposition to be important.

Proposition 1 *An industrial formal method must be* confinable.

Confinable means that the use of a formal method can be restricted. It must be able to be used on just one aspect of a large computer project without disrupting the rest of the project. Should the formal method include a code generation tool, the process of embedding the generated code into the rest of the system must not invalidate the correctness of the proven code and must not disrupt the rest of the system.

This allows a formal method to be introduced gradually into the software construction process. It is not necessary to invest a lot of time and money before one can see some results. When the use of the formal method in confinement has been shown to be satisfactory, it can and will be used on a broader basis. From a psychological point of view, the success of the system in a confined, controllable portion of a project is a positive reinforcement, and will encourage users to repeatedly use it. It will also encourage those who do not yet use the method to give it a try.

An example of using a formal method to investigate and implement a small part of a larger system is given in [WW90].

Proposition 2 *The introduction of a formal method must be* reversible.

No matter what the reason for the decision to drop the use of a formal method - whether the method did not work, the programmers could not cope with it, or the method is no longer being supported - it should be possible to revert to the previous status in system development.

This can become impossible, for example, when an implementation must be coded in a non-standard dialect of a language in order for a mechanical verification to be attempted. Should the verification effort have to be abandoned, the code developed would have to be rewritten to the standard dialect, or completely reimplemented.

It is aggravating enough to have to write off an investment in education, software or special hardware. But if the systems developed with a formal method cannot migrate to new platforms as necessary, or are in some other manner unchangeable, they become dangerous.

A corollary of this proposition would be that if a formal tool makes any changes at all to human-generated texts, it must at least keep backup copies of the original text. It is highly improper for a tool to make code changes that it believes are semantics preserving without at least keeping a copy of the original source. If the changes inadvertently introduce an error, much irreversible damage can be done. If a formal method should fail, it must at least fail safe, in a non-destructive manner.

Proposition 3 *A formal methods system for industrial use should be* open.

"Openness" is not just a marketing buzzword. It covers ideas such as the interchangeability of components. Ideally, it should be possible to exchange parts of the system as needed. If a mechanical verifier is included in the system, it should be possible to replace it with another one that is perhaps better suited to checking the current type of proof. If the system generates compilable code, the code generation module should be adaptable to use other languages or dialects.

If the method covers different phases in the software life cycle, the output from one phase should be directly usable in the next - it should not be necessary to make changes by hand, or even to transform the results non-mechanically. Situations like these can introduce errors into an otherwise correct system. This also means that there should not be a large conceptual gap between the formalization and the actual implementation.

Proposition 4 *A tool based on a formal method should be* non-intrusive.

This is related to the reversability proposition. A non-intrusive tool does not scream for attention or interfere with the development process being used by demanding that many things be done differently. It should also be interruptible – one can leave off using it to continue in the old manner if that should become necessary, and resume after the interruption has been handled. This gives users a sense of security as well as the feeling of retaining control over the process. The method is user-driven – a genuine tool – instead of dictating the actions of the user.

A good example of a non-intrusive method would be one that hides specifications or control commands in comments, for example pre- and post-conditions. This allows a proof checker access to the specification statements so that appropriate verification conditions can be generated and proven, while the code can be compiled without any changes or special switches.

Proposition 5 *A formal method will more likely be accepted if it is* not coercive.

A formal method or tool should not be overly concerned with imposing and enforcing restrictions on trivial but emotional issues such as program syntax. Enforcing an indentation or capitalization scheme will alienate that portion of the potential user market which, no matter what illogical reasons they might have for doing so, insist on doing otherwise. It might seem a trivial requirement, but regulations on aspects that do not seem to have a connection with the goal at hand can be quite tiresome. Programmers who are not overly enthusiastic about using a formal method will gladly use an irritant like this to avoid the use of the method or the tool.

Proposition 6 *An ideal industrial formal method is* inexpensive

A good property for an industrial formal method to have is a low price – probably a property that is quite the opposite of what the producer of such a method or tool had hoped. But everyone is on a tight budget these days, in academia as well as in industry. If it does not cost too much to obtain a tool or to use a formal method, it has a chance of being evaluated and perhaps given a chance to be used. Introducing formal methods then moves from being an investment, which is also associated with the risk of losing the investment, to being chargeable under consumables.

If one examines any of a number of quite popular systems in different application areas, one often finds that the most widespread systems are very cheap or even free: In the programming language area, BASIC was given away free with many personal computers, the Turbo Pascal language was quite affordable; the editor emacs along with the entire GNU suite of languages, tools and systems are distributed without cost. Looking at the field of merchandise marketing, we can see that a good way of selling a product is to distribute free samples, so that people can try it without obligation. If the sample is good, they will tend to want more!

Proposition 7 *A formal method that is applicable to industrial problems must be* dynamic.

This means that a method or a tool must be adaptable to changes that will occur in an industrial setting, not only changes to specifications but also changes in target machines, in syntax, or in any area imaginable. It is a fact of industrial life that things change. Specifications turn out to be incomplete or unimplementable, customers desire extra functionality or are distressed by a particular feature, or the unforseeable happens.

It must be possible to make changes to the system being formalized and for the relevant consequences – replaying of the proofs, regeneration of code, retesting and such – able to adapt with minimal effort. If a compiling specification has been completely proven correct, and then a small change to the language must be incorporated and this invalidates the entire proof, the usefulness of such a proof is questionable. Just as software reuse is a major tenet of software engineering, so also must the reuse of formality as far as feasible be required.

Proposition 8 *A formal method which is not* teachable *will not be used.*

It is vital for the acceptance of a method for it to be easy to teach and to learn. It should not be necessary to spend one person-year to learn how to start using an industrial formal method. It can take longer to become fluent - one does not turn into a C expert in a year. But it should be possible to use the method and to see results as soon as possible.

In order to be teachable, those wishing to introduce a formal method must understand the level of sophistication of the intended users. It is a major tenet of didactics, formulated by the Swiss educator Pestalozzi[3], that one must begin teaching at the level the users currently understand. If it is necessary to have a doctorate in mathematics or computer science in order to understand the terminology and begin using a formal method, it cannot be expected to be widely used.

Since formal methods, as defined above, make use of mathematics, it will have to be accepted that many people, even or especially programmers, are afraid of mathematics. This malady, often termed math anxiety or mathophobia [Pap80], seems unfortunately to be encouraged by some of the methods by which mathematics are often taught in schools and universities. Only the very persistent or those with a special aptitude for mathematics often manage to make it through, to understand the beauty of the mathematical notations.

It is not acceptable to moan and berate the current standard of education. It does not help at all to demand that curricula be burdened with even more formal mathematics training. It is not a question of quantity, but of quality. Dijkstra [Dij89] sneers at the "infantilization" of computer science training. Of course it is easy for

---

[3] Johann Heinrich Pestalozzi (1746-1827)

him to understand mathematics and much seems trivial to him – he has been doing it most of his life! It is not a question of it being childish or mature mathematics. The goal is for people to learn how to use mathematics, and they surely will not want to learn if they are implied to be weak-minded at the outset. There is a dialectic of content and form here: the mathematics alone are not enough. We have to do research into methods of teaching mathematics and formal methodology, we have to find good mental models and effective training programs, we need to figure out why people find mathematics difficult and find ways to overcome this.

We need instructive textbooks with worked out examples - not just a finished proof of correctness of an implementation of a factorial function, but step-by-step explanations of the process of using formal methods on non-trivial examples. Hesselink and Jongejan have made a start with their technical note in CACM [HJ92]. They use a formalization for deriving a better program than Teuhola and Wegner had informally presented in [TW91] for removing duplicate entries from a bag in order to construct a set. The derivation is a bit terse, but a step in the right direction, especially as the proven correct implementation contains some minor errors, as pointed out by Teuhola and Wegner in their response. It is important to understand how the method can go wrong and to see how this can be detected and repaired and perhaps avoided in the future. If the formal method encourages and supports such double checking and repair, then it is easier to actually use.

This is a very painful demand. A scientist takes pride in demonstrating a neat, logical and concise development of a proof or a program. It is not easy to admit that one at first made errors, or followed a number of dead-ends until the proper path was found. But just as one never discovers a mathematical proof in the same order as it is presented to the public, a formal method is not used in the exact step-by-step manner in which it is presented. We must try and capture the process of actual use of our methods, and even encourage the publication of papers containing psychological, pedagogical, even sociological aspects of the use of formal methods[4]. When we understand this process, we can then more effectively teach it to others.

Proposition 9 *There must be adequate* documentation *available for a formal method to be useful.*

It seems that most methods suffer from one of two extremes of documentation level. Either there exist just a few terse notes on using the method or system, and thus it is only used by the people that developed it in the first place, or by persons dependent on them, i.e. graduate students, or there are many meters of documentation available that may or may not fit the system or method as it is currently used. Having too much is almost as bad as having too little documentation – one does not know where or how to begin.

A well-documented formal method or tool has a advertisement sheet (a one page description of what it does and how it works), an introduction booklet, a tutorial that guides beginners through some simple exercises, a more detailed and rigorous handbook for advanced use, and reference materials with proper indexing.

---

[4] An example of a description of the process of using a mechanical theorem prover to prove a non-trivial theorem about a very simple compiler is given in the author's forthcoming paper [WW93]

Proposition 10 *There must be a* migration path *for the introduction of a formal method.*

This proposition is based on the first proposition. It must be possible to introduce a formal methodology into a company without massive investments of time and money in purchase of software, special hardware and staff training. Just as the introduction of computers into an application area needs to be done gradually and with as much redundance as possible until the cut-over can be achieved, the introduction of formal methods must follow a similar path.

Each step in the integration of formal methods needs to be planned, and the users of the system need to understand what is happening and to feel that the step is not too big for them to take. It is also important that the users – the programmers – participate in the process of introducing the new methods. This gives them a feeling of ownership in the new methods, and will help reduce opposition and other barriers to the successful use of the methods.

3 Discussion

The selection of the ten propositions stated above is of course highly arbitrary and slightly prejudicial. It will also be argued that all of my arguments have absolutely nothing to do with mathematics. And that is exactly my point. Formal methods, just as mathematics, do not exist and function in a fully abstract space. They are to be used by people, who do not function as abstract, mathematical entities. We have to take the people and the institutions that will use our methods and systems into consideration, just as the programmers of application systems have to consider the human-computer interface. The challenge for the future is: Can we develop a confinable, reversible, open, non-intrusive, non-coercive, inexpensive, dynamic and teachable formal method for which good documentation is available and for which a clear migration path can be defined?

It is my hope that this paper might spark a discussion of these and further desiderata for industrial strength formal methods, and that we can come to consider the social aspects of their use. Many thanks to all who have debated this topic and these propositions with me, and to the anonymous referees for their valuable comments.

References

[Dij89] Edsger W. Dijkstra. On the cruelty of really teaching computing science. *CACM*, 32(12):1398–1404, Dec. 1989.

[HJ92] Wim Hesselink and Jan Jongejan. Duplicate deletion derived. *CACM*, 35(7):99–107, July 1992.

[Pap80] Seymour Papert. *Mindstorms. Children, Computer and Powerful Ideas.* Basic Books, New York, 1980.

[TW91] Jukka Teuhola and Lutz Wegner. Minimal space average linear time duplication deletion. *CACM*, 34(3):62–73, March 1991.

[WW90] Debora Weber-Wulff. A buffering system implementation using VDM. In D. Bjørner, C.A.R. Hoare, and H. Langmaack., editors, *LNCS 428 : VDM & Z! : Proceedings of the Third International Symposium of VDM Europe, Kiel*, pages 135–149, Heidelberg, 1990. Springer Verlag.

[WW93] Debora Weber-Wulff. Proof movie : A Proof with the Boyer-Moore prover. *Formal Aspects of Computing*, 5, 1993. To appear.

ProofPower

Description:

ProofPower supports document preparation, syntax checking, type checking and formal proof development using Higher Order Logic and/or the Z specification language. It follows the 'LCF paradigm' and the meta-language for proof development is an extension of standard ML.

Environment:

Sun SPARC, 50Mb disk

Contact:

Roger B. Jones
ICL Secure Systems
Eskdale Road
Winnersh
Wokingham Berkshire RG11 5TT
UK
Tel: +44 734 693131 ext. 6536
Fax: +44 734 697636
email: R.B.Jones%win0109.uucp@uknet.ac.uk

Availability:

Available under special conditions

Mural

Description:

The mural system supports formal reasoning about specifications. The main component of mural is the proof assistant. This is generic in that it can be instantiated to support reasoning about specifications in a wide range of specification languages. In addition to the proof assistant mural contains a VDM support tool.

Environment:

Sun SPARC, 16Mb memory, 32 Mb swap
Smalltalk-80 version 4.2

Contact:

Dr. Richard Moore
Department of Computer Science
University of Manchester
M13 9PL
England
Tel: +44 61 275 6273
Fax: +44 61 275 6236
email: richard@cs.man.ac.uk

Availability:

Available under special conditions

IPTES Toolset

Description:
The IPTES Toolset is a graphical specification, design and animation tool supporting the animation of multi abstraction level, structured analysis and design (SA/RT and SA/SD) notation for embedded software systems. The execution mechanism of the tool is based on high-level timed Petri nets and an executable subset of VDM-SL, hereby providing a very pragmatic approach to formal specifications.

Environment:
Sun SPARC, 16Mb memory, 10 Mb disk
X Windows

Contact:
René Elmstrøm
IFAD
Forskerparken 10
DK-5230 Odense M
Denmark
Tel: +45 65 93 23 00
Fax: +45 65 93 29 99
email: rene@ifad.dk

Availability:
Not available

The Centaur-VDM environment

Description:
The Centaur-VDM environment is an interactive and graphical tool for manipulating specifications written in BSI VDM-SL. Besides analyses for syntax and static semantics, it provides help for refinement and the generation of test cases.

Environment:
A Sun SPARC workstation running X11 version R4.

Contact:
Philippe Facon
CEDRIC-IIE
Institut d'Informatique d'Entreprise
18, allée Jean Rostand
F-91025 Evry Cedex
France
Tel: 16 1 60 77 97 40 number 165
Fax: 16 1 60 77 96 99
email: facon@cnam.cnam.fr

Availability:
Available under special conditions

IFAD VDM-SL Toolbox

Description:

The IFAD VDM-SL Toolbox supports the BSI (ISO) VDM-SL notation. The Toolbox includes syntax checker, static semantic checker, pretty printer generating LaTeX output. In addition to this it contains a debugger and an interpreter which can execute all executable constructs of VDM-SL. The debugger supports standard debugger functionalities like setting breakpoints, showing values of variables, examining the call stack etc. The debugger can be operated through a GNU Emacs interface.

Environment:

Sun SPARC, 8Mb memory, 8Mb disk
SunOS 4.1.1+, GNU Emacs

Contact:

Poul Bøgh Lassen
IFAD
Forskerparken 10, DK-5230 Odense M
Denmark
Tel: +45 65 93 23 00
Fax: +45 65 93 29 99
email: poul@ifad.dk

Availability:

Commercial available

DST-fuzz

Description:

DST-fuzz is a set of tool to support the formal development method Z. The product supports syntax checking and static semantics checking and LaTeX generation. Handling of errors detected by the typechecker is made easy by an integrated error browser. The tools are fully integrated into the Hewlett Packard CASE environment SoftBench.

Environment:

Sun SPARC, SunOS 4.1.x, 3Mb disk
HP 9000 /700 /400, HP-UX 8.0, 3Mb disk
HP-Softbench

Contact:

Hans-Martin Hörcher
Deutsche System Technik
Edisonstr. 3
D-2300 Kiel
Germany
Tel: +49 431 7109 478
Fax: +49 431 7109 503

Availability:

Commercial available

The LOTOS Toolbox

Description:

The LOTOS toolbox contains a number of tools supporting the specification and implementation of LOTOS specifications. The tools covers syntax checking and static semantic checking, symbolic execution of LOTOS specifications, a structure editor checking syntax and static semantics on the fly, a graphical browser and a c-code generator generating prototype implementations.

Environment:

Sun 3,Sun 4, SunOS 16Mb memory, 35 Mb disk

HP, HP Unix, 16Mb memory, 35Mb disk

Contact:

A.W. van der Vloedt

Information Technology Architecture B.V.

Institutenweg 1

7521 PH Enschede

The Netherlands

Tel: +31 53 309682

Fax: +31 53 309669

email: vdvloedt@ita.nl

Availability:

Commercial available

Centaur

Description:

The Centaur system is a set of tools that help in developing tools, or aids, for manipulating programs or objects. With the help of Centaur one can develop tools needed for a programming environment: structure editors, debuggers, interpreters and various translators. The tools are derived from a formal definition of a programming language.

Environment:

Sun SPARC, DEC Station, Silicon Graphics

UNIX, X11 (R4/R5), 32Mb memory, 30Mb disk

Contact:

Janet Bertot

INRIA

BP 93

2004 Route des Lucioles

06902 Sophia Autipolis CEDEX

France

Tel: +33 93 65 78 03

Fax: +33 93 65 77 66

email: jmi@sophia.inria.fr

Availability:

Available under special conditions

DisCo

Description:

DisCo is a method and a corresponding language for specification of reactive systems. The DisCo specifications are executable and a formal mathematical method - temporal logic of actions - can be used for correctness proofs. The DisCo tool is an experimental tool, which contains a compiler, and execution and animation capabilities. The user interface of the tool is highly graphical.

Environment:

Sun SPARC, SunOS 4.1 with OpenWindows 3.0, 16Mb memory, 12 Mb disk

Contact:

Kari Systa

Tampere University of Technology

Box 553

SF-33101 Tampere

Finland

Tel: +35 8 31 162585

Fax: +35 8 31 162913

email: ks@cs.tut.fi

Availability:

Avaliable under special conditions

The Boyer-Moore Theorem Prover

Description:

The Boyer-Moore theorem proving system (theorem prover) is a proof tool supporting specifications written in the Boyer-Moore logic. The tool provides a user with commands for extending the logic and to prove theorems. The theorem prover contains a simplifier and rewriter and decision procedures for propositional logic and linear arithmetic. It can also perform structural inductions automatically. The Boyer-Moore system contains an interpreter for the logic that allows the evaluation of terms in the logic.

Environment:

Sun SPARC

Contact:

William D. Young

Computational Logic, Inc.

1717 W. 6th Street, Suite 290

Austin, TX 78703

USA

Tel: 512 322 9951

Fax: 512 322 0656

email: young@cli.com

Availability:

Not Known

B-TOOLKIT

Description:
The B-TOOLKIT is designed primarily to assist the software engineer in the construction of formal proofs to mathematical theorems arising from formal software development and verification. The tools includes a proof assistant, specification and design assistant, coding assistant and environment tools.

Environment:
Sun SPARC, 32Mb memory, 32 Mb disk, Unix

Contact:
Ib Sorensen
B-Technologies SALR, Magdalen Centre
Robert Robinson Avenue, The Oxford Science Park
Oxford OX4 4GA
England
Tel: +44 865 784520
Fax: +44 865 784518
email: Ib.Sorensen@comlab.ox.ac.uk

Availability:
Commercial available

PET DINGO

Description:
The PET and DINGO tools support the formal notation Estelle. The Portable Estelle Translator (PET) syntactically validates an Estelle specification and the Distributed Implementation Generator (DINGO) produces a C++ code implementation of the specification. The tools encompasses the full semantics of Estelle. Run-Time libraries are provided to support aspects of Estelle statements and constructs, the synchronization protocol, interprocess communications, and a generated user interface.

Environment:
Sun SPARC, 4 Mb memory, 25Mb disk
SunOS 4.0.x, X11, GNU C++ 1.xx

Contact:
Brett W. Strausser
National Institute of Standards and Technology
Bldg. 225, Rm B141
270 & Quince Orchard Rd.
Gaithersburg
MD 20899 USA
Tel: 301 975 3620
Fax: 301 948 1784 or 301 590 0932
email: strauss@osi.ncsl.nist.gov

Availability:
Public Domain

SpecBox

Description:

SpecBox is a formal specification support tool for VDM. It contains a syntax checker (reflecting the latest BSI/ISO standard), static semantic checker, LaTeX generation facilities and an interface to the mural proof assistant

Environment:

Sun SPARC, 8Mb memory, 3Mb disk, SunOS 4.1

PC-AT 640K memory, 2Mb disk, MS-DOS 3.2

PC-386/486 4Mb memory, 2Mb disk, MS-DOS 3.2

VAX/VMS

Contact:

Peter Froome

Adelard

Coborn House

3 Coborn Road

London B3 2DA

UK

Tel: +44 81 983 0214

Fax: +44 81 983 1845

email: pkdf@dcs.ed.ac.uk

Availability:

Commercial available

RAISE

Description:

The RAISE tools are a fully integrated toolset which support rigorous and/or formal development of large software systems. The toolset includes a structure oriented editor supporting writing and continuous type checking of RAISE entities, a justification tool supporting formal and rigorous arguments for correctness of a specification, Pretty printers generating LaTeX output, and translators producing C++ and Ada.

Environment:

Sun 3/60 and SPARC,12Mb memory, 40Mb disk

X11, SunWindows and OpenLook supported

Contact:

RAISE

CRI

Bregnerødvej 144

3460 Birkeroed

Denmark

Tel: +45 45 822100

Fax: +45 45 821766

email: raise@csd.cri.dk

Availability:

Commercial available

ExSpect

Description:
Expect is an acronym for Executable Specification Tool. It is a software tool for designing, verifying and simulating hierarchical colored timed Petri nets. It contains a graphical editor, typechecker, an analysis tool to verify timing properties and to calculate S/T invariants and other structural properties, and a simulator.

Environment:
Sun SPARC, 12Mb memory, 20Mb disk, SunOS 4.1.1

Contact:
L.J.A.M. Somers
Fac. of mathematics and computer science
Technical University of Eindhoven
P.O. Box 513
5600 MB Eindhoven
The Netherlands
Tel: +31 40 472805 or +31 40 472733
Fax: +31 40 436685
email: wsinlou@win.tue.nl

Availability:
Commercial available

CADiZ

Description:
CADiZ is a suite of tools designed to check and typeset specifications produced in the Z specification language. CADiZ supports the standard Z core language and the mathematical toolkit. There are tools for checking a specification for syntactic, scope and types correctness. CADiZ also supports interactive browsing of specifications and typesetting integrated with both the troff and LaTeX document processing environments.

Environment:
Sun SPARC, 4Mb memory, 10Mb disk, SunOS 4.0.3+, X Windows R4

Contact:
David Jordan
York Software Engineering Ltd
University of York
York YO1 5DD
England
Tel: +44 904 433741
Fax: +44 904 433744
email: yse@minster.york.ac.uk

Availability:
Commercially available

Design/CPN

Description:

Design/CPN is based on Coloured Petri nets, and includes tools for simulation, animation and report generation. Design/CPN provides integrated life-cycle support including design, validation, performance evaluation and implementation.

Environment:

Macintosh, min 8Mb memory, 40Mb disk

Sun 3/Sun 4, HP9000, X Windows (X11 R4)

16Mb memory, 100Mb disk or connected to server with swap space.

Contact:

John Mølgaard

ElektronikCentralen

Venlighedsvej 4

2970 Hørsholm

Tel: +45 42 86 77 22

Fax: +45 42 86 58 98

email: jm@elctr.dk

Availability:

Commercial available

PVS

Description:

The PVS (Prototype Verification System) is an environment for writing specifications and developing proofs. PVS have an effective typechecker and proof checker serving as a productive medium for debugging specifications and for constructing readable proofs.

Environment:

Sun SPARC, 20Mb memory, 60Mb disk

Unix and GNU Emacs

Contact:

Dr. Natarajan Shankar

SRI Computer Science Lab

Menlo Park

CA 94025

USA

Tel: 415 859 5272

Fax: 415 859 2844

email: shankar@csl.sri.com

Availability:

Public Domain

TAV

Description:

The TAV system contains a number of tools for the specification, development and verification of parallel and non-deterministic processes expressed in the calculus of CCS. In particular TAV contains tools for deciding various notions of equivalence (or preorder) between processes specifications, and contains tools for model-checking with respect to a powerfull (recursive) modal logic. Analysis of real-timed processes is also supported in a prototype version.

Environment:

Sun SPARC, SunOS

Contact:

Kim G. Larsen & Arne Skou
Department of Computer Science
Aalborg University
Frederik Bajersvej 7E
9220 Aalborg
Denmark
Tel: +45 98 15 85 22
Fax: +45 98 15 81 29
email: {kgl,ask}@iesd.auc.dk

Availability:

Available for non-commercial usage

FDR

Description:

FDR (Failures-Divergence Refinement) is a software package which allows the automatic checking of many properties of finite state systems and the interactive investigation of processes which fail these checks. It is based on the mathematical theory of CSP.

Environment:

Sun SPARC,32Mb memory recommended, SunOS 4.1.1+
Support for other platforms is under development

Contact:

David Jackson
Formal Systems Ltd.
3 Alfred St. Oxford
OX 14EH
England
Tel: +44 865 728460
Fax: +44 865 201114
email: David.Jackson@prg.ox.ac.uk

Availability:

Commercial Available

ForMooZ

Description:

ForMooZ supports the construction of formal specifications written in MooZ (Modular Object-Oriented Z), an object-oriented extension of Z aimed at the specification of large software systems. The tool performs syntax, scope and type checking. Other facilities include a LaTeX pretty printer, help facilities, graphic hierarchic browsers, and schema expanders.

Environment:

Sun SPARC, 16Mb memory, 20Mb disk
SunOS 4.1 OpenWindows Version 2.0

Contact:

Silvio Lemos Meira
Departamento de Informática
Universidade Federal de Pernambuco
Caixa Postal 7851 CEP 50732-970 - Recife - PE
Brazil
Tel: +55 81 2713052
Fax: +55 81 2714925
email: srlm@di.ufpe.br

Availability:

Not commercially available

Lecture Notes in Computer Science

For information about Vols. 1–595
please contact your bookseller or Springer-Verlag

Vol. 632: H. Kirchner, G. Levi (Eds.), Algebraic and Logic Programming. Proceedings, 1992. IX, 457 pages. 1992.

Vol. 633: D. Pearce, G. Wagner (Eds.), Logics in AI. Proceedings. VIII, 410 pages. 1992. (Subseries LNAI).

Vol. 634: L. Bougé, M. Cosnard, Y. Robert, D. Trystram (Eds.), Parallel Processing: CONPAR 92 – VAPP V. Proceedings. XVII, 853 pages. 1992.

Vol. 635: J. C. Derniame (Ed.), Software Process Technology. Proceedings, 1992. VIII, 253 pages. 1992.

Vol. 636: G. Comyn, N. E. Fuchs, M. J. Ratcliffe (Eds.), Logic Programming in Action. Proceedings, 1992. X, 324 pages. 1992. (Subseries LNAI).

Vol. 637: Y. Bekkers, J. Cohen (Eds.), Memory Management. Proceedings, 1992. XI, 525 pages. 1992.

Vol. 639: A. U. Frank, I. Campari, U. Formentini (Eds.), Theories and Methods of Spatio-Temporal Reasoning in Geographic Space. Proceedings, 1992. XI, 431 pages. 1992.

Vol. 640: C. Sledge (Ed.), Software Engineering Education. Proceedings, 1992. X, 451 pages. 1992.

Vol. 641: U. Kastens, P. Pfahler (Eds.), Compiler Construction. Proceedings, 1992. VIII, 320 pages. 1992.

Vol. 642: K. P. Jantke (Ed.), Analogical and Inductive Inference. Proceedings, 1992. VIII, 319 pages. 1992. (Subseries LNAI).

Vol. 643: A. Habel, Hyperedge Replacement: Grammars and Languages. X, 214 pages. 1992.

Vol. 644: A. Apostolico, M. Crochemore, Z. Galil, U. Manber (Eds.), Combinatorial Pattern Matching. Proceedings, 1992. X, 287 pages. 1992.

Vol. 645: G. Pernul, A M. Tjoa (Eds.), Entity-Relationship Approach – ER '92. Proceedings, 1992. XI, 439 pages, 1992.

Vol. 646: J. Biskup, R. Hull (Eds.), Database Theory – ICDT '92. Proceedings, 1992. IX, 449 pages. 1992.

Vol. 647: A. Segall, S. Zaks (Eds.), Distributed Algorithms. X, 380 pages. 1992.

Vol. 648: Y. Deswarte, G. Eizenberg, J.-J. Quisquater (Eds.), Computer Security – ESORICS 92. Proceedings. XI, 451 pages. 1992.

Vol. 649: A. Pettorossi (Ed.), Meta-Programming in Logic. Proceedings, 1992. XII, 535 pages. 1992.

Vol. 650: T. Ibaraki, Y. Inagaki, K. Iwama, T. Nishizeki, M. Yamashita (Eds.), Algorithms and Computation. Proceedings, 1992. XI, 510 pages. 1992.

Vol. 651: R. Koymans, Specifying Message Passing and Time-Critical Systems with Temporal Logic. IX, 164 pages. 1992.

Vol. 652: R. Shyamasundar (Ed.), Foundations of Software Technology and Theoretical Computer Science. Proceedings, 1992. XIII, 405 pages. 1992.

Vol. 653: A. Bensoussan, J.-P. Verjus (Eds.), Future Tendencies in Computer Science, Control and Applied Mathematics. Proceedings, 1992. XV, 371 pages. 1992.

Vol. 654: A. Nakamura, M. Nivat, A. Saoudi, P. S. P. Wang, K. Inoue (Eds.), Prallel Image Analysis. Proceedings, 1992. VIII, 312 pages. 1992.

Vol. 655: M. Bidoit, C. Choppy (Eds.), Recent Trends in Data Type Specification. X, 344 pages. 1993.

Vol. 656: M. Rusinowitch, J. L. Rémy (Eds.), Conditional Term Rewriting Systems. Proceedings, 1992. XI, 501 pages. 1993.

Vol. 657: E. W. Mayr (Ed.), Graph-Theoretic Concepts in Computer Science. Proceedings, 1992. VIII, 350 pages. 1993.

Vol. 658: R. A. Rueppel (Ed.), Advances in Cryptology – EUROCRYPT '92. Proceedings, 1992. X, 493 pages. 1993.

Vol. 659: G. Brewka, K. P. Jantke, P. H. Schmitt (Eds.), Nonmonotonic and Inductive Logic. Proceedings, 1991. VIII, 332 pages. 1993. (Subseries LNAI).

Vol. 660: E. Lamma, P. Mello (Eds.), Extensions of Logic Programming. Proceedings, 1992. VIII, 417 pages. 1993. (Subseries LNAI).

Vol. 661: S. J. Hanson, W. Remmele, R. L. Rivest (Eds.), Machine Learning: From Theory to Applications. VIII, 271 pages. 1993.

Vol. 662: M. Nitzberg, D. Mumford, T. Shiota, Filtering, Segmentation and Depth. VIII, 143 pages. 1993.

Vol. 663: G. v. Bochmann, D. K. Probst (Eds.), Computer Aided Verification. Proceedings, 1992. IX, 422 pages. 1993.

Vol. 664: M. Bezem, J. F. Groote (Eds.), Typed Lambda Calculi and Applications. Proceedings, 1993. VIII, 433 pages. 1993.

Vol. 665: P. Enjalbert, A. Finkel, K. W. Wagner (Eds.), STACS 93. Proceedings, 1993. XIV, 724 pages. 1993.

Vol. 666: J. W. de Bakker, W.-P. de Roever, G. Rozenberg (Eds.), Semantics: Foundations and Applications. Proceedings, 1992. VIII, 659 pages. 1993.

Vol. 667: P. B. Brazdil (Ed.), Machine Learning: ECML – 93. Proceedings, 1993. XII, 471 pages. 1993. (Subseries LNAI).

Vol. 668: M.-C. Gaudel, J.-P. Jouannaud (Eds.), TAPSOFT '93: Theory and Practice of Software Development. Proceedings, 1993. XII, 762 pages. 1993.

Vol. 669: R. S. Bird, C. C. Morgan, J. C. P. Woodcock (Eds.), Mathematics of Program Construction. Proceedings, 1992. VIII, 378 pages. 1993.

Vol. 670: J. C. P. Woodcock, P. G. Larsen (Eds.), FME '93: Industrial-Strength Formal Methods. Proceedings, 1993. XI, 689 pages. 1993.